THE EARLY MORNING OF WAR

C&C

CAMPAIGNS & COMMANDERS

GREGORY J. W. URWIN, SERIES EDITOR

CAMPAIGNS AND COMMANDERS

THE EARLY MORNING OF WAR

Bull Run, 1861

EDWARD G. LONGACRE

UNIVERSITY OF OKLAHOMA PRESS | NORMAN

Also by Edward G. Longacre:

General Ulysses S. Grant, the Soldier and the Man (2006)
Worthy Opponents: Generals William T. Sherman, U.S.A., and Joseph E. Johnston, C.S.A. (2006)
Gentleman and Soldier: A Biography of Wade Hampton III (2004)
A Regiment of Slaves: The Fourth United States Colored Infantry, 1863–1866 (2003)
Lee's Cavalrymen: A History of the Mounted Forces of the Army of Northern Virginia, 1861–1865 (2002)
Lincoln's Cavalrymen: A History of the Mounted Forces of the Army of the Potomac, 1861–1865 (2000)
Joshua Chamberlain, the Soldier and the Man (1999)
Army of Amateurs: General Benjamin F. Butler and the Army of the James, 1863–1865 (1997)
General John Buford: A Military Biography (1995)
Pickett, Leader of the Charge: A Biography of General George E. Pickett, C.S.A. (1995)
The Cavalry at Gettysburg: A Tactical Study of Mounted Operations during the Civil War's Pivotal Campaign, 9 June–14 July 1863 (1986)
The Man Behind the Guns: A Biography of General Henry Jackson Hunt, Chief of Artillery, Army of the Potomac (1977)

Library of Congress Cataloging-in-Publication Data
Longacre, Edward G., 1946–
   The early morning of war : Bull Run, 1861 / Edward G. Longacre.
      pages cm. — (Campaigns and commanders ; volume 46)
   Includes bibliographical references and index.
   ISBN 978-0-8061-4498-6 (hardcover : alk. paper)
   1. Bull Run, 1st Battle of, Va., 1861. I. Title.
   E472.18.L66 2014
   973.7'31—dc23   2014012900

The Early Morning of War: Bull Run, 1861 is Volume 46 in the Campaigns and Commanders series.

The paper in this book meets the guidelines for permanence and durability of the Committee on Production Guidelines for Book Longevity of the Council on Library Resources, Inc. ∞

Interior layout and composition: Alcorn Publication Design

For my accountant, Mary Kelly,
who keeps a busy author from being overtaxed

Lots of people—honest folks, too,—see [First] Bull Run in the haze, see it in the air,—among the clouds,—see it upside down. . . . The legends concerning that battle, its causes, methods, situations, and battle incidents are almost as prolific as the names on the United States veteran pension roll,—and like that roll the faster the occupants die off the longer and fuller the list grows.

—*Horatio Staples, U.S. Volunteers, 1903*

Contents

Illustrations

Figures

Maps

Preface

Despite its undeniable importance as the first major battle of America's most critical war, for nearly a century First Bull Run (or First Manassas) received scant book-length attention. For several decades following the appearance of R. M. Johnston's seminal study, *Bull Run: Its Tactics and Strategy* (Boston, 1913), no scholarly analysis of the battle or the campaign of which it formed a part appeared in print. With some notable exceptions, including Joseph Mills Hanson's *Bull Run Remembers* (Manassas, Va., 1953) and Russel H. Beatie, Jr.'s *Road to Manassas* (New York, 1961), not until 1977, with the publication of *Battle at Bull Run* by William C. Davis, did battle and campaign again receive detailed coverage. Over the ensuing thirty-six years, however, the trickle of Bull Run studies became a gush (though not quite a flood) upon publication of John Hennessy's *The First Battle of Manassas: An End to Innocence, July 18–21, 1861* (Lynchburg, Va., 1989); JoAnna M. McDonald's *"We Shall Meet Again": The First Battle of Manassas (Bull Run), July 18–21, 1861* (Shippensburg, Pa., 1999); Ethan S. Rafuse's *A Single Grand Victory: The First Campaign and Battle of Manassas* (Wilmington, Del., 2002); and David Detzer's *Donnybrook: The Battle of Bull Run, 1861* (New York, 2004). The campaign has been examined to some extent in a few more-general studies, including Beatie's *The Army of the Potomac: Birth of Command, November 1860–September 1861* (New York, 2002) and Brent Nosworthy's *Roll Call to Destiny: The Soldier's Eye View of Civil War Battles* (New York, 2008). A more recent study of the early months of the conflict, Adam Goodheart's *1861: The Civil War Awakening* (New York, 2011), sets the stage for Bull Run but does not cover the fighting itself.

Each of these books strives to provide a fresh look at a previously neglected subject; each adds a facet to the mosaic that is First Bull Run. And yet three of them—Hennessy's, McDonald's, and Rafuse's—are relatively brief accounts, and the first two limit themselves to the fighting of July 18–21. Davis's older work, while a groundbreaking study, is in need of some revision, and Detzer's, although it offers some new perspectives on the campaign, is not the product of a military historian. Moreover, each author uncritically repeats venerable theories that may not be historically sound. The present work, which attempts to add greater tactical and strategic detail to its subject than any previous study, makes bold to question some of these long-accepted verities. For example, it reexamines the strategic planning of Brigadier General Gustave Toutant Beauregard and concludes that at least some of the Confederate commander's ideas were more viable, or less impractical, than legions of historians have contended. It refutes some of the criticism long directed at Beauregard's opponent, Brigadier General Irvin McDowell, including the supposedly unconscionable dawdling that permitted Beauregard and his superior, General Joseph E. Johnston, to combine against him on the eve of battle. It also questions the virtually sacrosanct notion that the Manassas Gap Railroad, by which Johnston linked with Beauregard, was essential to Confederate victory.

As for the campaign's culminating battle of July 21, 1861, *The Early Morning of War* offers support to the minority view that the immortal title "Stonewall" conferred at the height of the battle on Brigadier General Thomas J. Jackson and his Virginia brigade was not an expression of praise and admiration. It questions the circumstances surrounding a pivotal event, the capture on Henry Hill of the Union batteries commanded by Captains James B. Ricketts and Charles Griffin, and reassigns blame for the critical blunder.

This is the first study to devote extensive coverage to operations on the Union left flank throughout the battle, not merely late in the day when the forces in that sector were attacked by Confederates seeking to gain their enemy's rear and cut off the escape route to Washington. And while every previously published account has concentrated on the retreat of McDowell's beaten forces, this one follows instead the various units that attempted to overtake the Federals and deal them a crippling blow, turning rout into ruin.

In a very real sense, Bull Run was not one campaign but two simultaneous campaigns. This book details the strategy and tactics of Union major general Robert Patterson in the Shenandoah Valley, examining the weaknesses of his army and the supposed incapacity of its commander. It throws new light on why and how Patterson permitted his opponent, Johnston, to escape the Valley and join Beauregard in time to erase McDowell's numerical advantage. Though long pilloried for incompetence and timidity, the Union commander was abetted by subordinates and superiors alike who largely have escaped blame for their roles in the failed campaign.

Among the most culpable was commanding general Winfield Scott, whose mismanagement of the Valley operations equaled, if it did not exceed, Patterson's.

Finally, the book attempts to place First Bull Run in a broader context than heretofore. It investigates not only its effects on Union and Confederate strategy but also the impressions it made on the European powers, especially Great Britain and France, the Confederacy's most accessible sources of economic and diplomatic support and, in the case of England, a potential military ally. It is hoped that examination and reexamination of these and other aspects of the subject will facilitate a deeper appreciation of a clash of arms that, even considering its recent publishing history, has lacked the attention lavished on later, larger battles of the war it ushered in.

Acknowledgments

One unfortunate consequence of spending almost four decades researching a book is that a majority of those deserving of an acknowledgment are long retired from the positions in which they rendered assistance, and an unknown number are deceased. Foremost among those whose support was critical to this endeavor are the historians at Manassas National Battlefield Park, beginning with Mike Tennent and extending to the present-day staff, most especially Greg Wolf. It should go without saying that any factual errors or misinterpretations are solely those of the author.

Others deserving of thanks and gratitude include: Colonel James B. Agnew and Dr. Richard J. Sommers, U.S. Army Heritage and Education Center; Helen Ball, Miami (of Ohio) University Libraries; Marilyn Bell, Tennessee State Library and Archives; Pamille Berg and Gregory A. Johnson, Alderman Library, University of Virginia; Bernard A. Bernier, Jr., Serial Division, Library of Congress; Rev. Theodore F. Blantz, University of Notre Dame Archives; John C. Broderick, Manuscript Division, Library of Congress; David W. Brown, William R. Perkins Library, Duke University; Pamela F. Brown, Auburn University Archives; Marie T. Capps, U.S. Military Academy Library; Victor Des Rosiers, New York State Library; Susan Catlett, Special Collections, Old Dominion University Library; Gayle L. Chandler, Graham Duncan, and Allen H. Stokes, South Caroliniana Library, University of South Carolina; Margaret Cook, Mary Molineux, Amy Schindler, Elizabeth Tompkins, and Don Welsh, Earl Gregg Swem Library, College of William and Mary; Dr. Joseph K. Corson, Plymouth Meeting, Pennsylvania; William C. Davis, Blacksburg, Virginia; Anthony R. Dees, University of Georgia Libraries; Maria Gast, Cornell University Libraries; Carroll Hart, Georgia Department of Archives and History; Lucy L. Hrivnak, Historical Society of Pennsylvania; Karen L. Jackson, Southern Historical Collection, University of North Carolina; Mary M. Jenkins, West Virginia Department of Archives and History; Gaines Kincaid, Austin, Texas; Donald R. Lennon, East Carolina University Manuscript Collections; Susan B. Lyon, Franklin, Tennessee; David J. Martz, Jr., and Stuart C. Sherman, John Hay Library, Brown

University; Linda M. Matthews, Emory University Library Special Collections; Britt McCarley, Yorktown, Virginia; Tom Mullusky and Sandra Trenholm, Gilder Lehrman Collection; Suzette Ortiz, Field Artillery Association; Ruby J. Shields, Minnesota Historical Society; and George F. Tyler, Jr., Philadelphia, Pennsylvania.

Special thanks go to Chuck Rankin, editor in chief of the University of Oklahoma Press, whose patience, advice, and support sustained me though the last ten years of my research and writing; Dr. Greg Urwin, professor of history, Temple University, editor of the Campaigns and Commanders series, and another source of unflagging support; my able editor, Kevin Brock; Paul Dangel, my indispensable mapmaker; and my wife, Melody Ann Longacre, who, although not aboard during the formative years of this project, made up for lost time in a variety of research and clerical capacities.

THE EARLY MORNING OF WAR

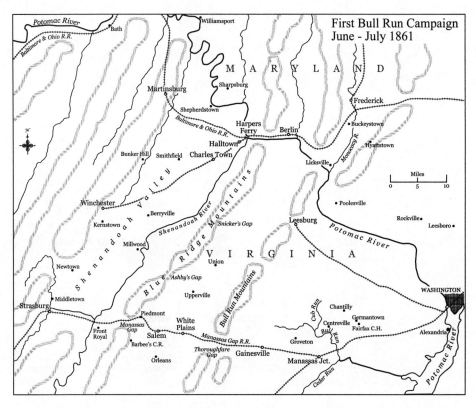

First Bull Run Campaign, June–July 1861. *Map by Paul Dangel.*

PROLOGUE

PORTENTS

The president of the United States awoke from a restless sleep and a troubling dream. In the murky dawn he sat on the counterpane of the bed that had been custom built to his six-foot, four-inch frame. While his wife, Mary, slumbered beside him, he recalled as much of the dream as his consciousness had captured. It was, like most dreams, a shadow play of dimly perceived objects and imperfectly realized sensations. He had felt himself being borne upon a vast body of water, a passenger aboard "some singular, indescribable vessel . . . moving with great rapidity towards an indefinite shore."[1]

Abraham Lincoln had experienced the same dream three months earlier, on the eve of South Carolina's bombardment of Fort Sumter, the opening act of a war that was now inundating the country. In retrospect, that dream had been a terrible omen. In the weeks since the violent confrontation in Charleston Harbor, ten Southern states had followed South Carolina out of the Union to form the Confederate States of America. Perceiving no other course, Lincoln had called for the enlistment of 75,000 militiamen to put down the nascent rebellion, an act that spawned the formation of armies in all quarters of the fractured nation. Recruits had flooded enlistment offices from Missouri to New Jersey, Florida to Maine. Washington, D.C., and its outlying areas had become an armed camp crammed with would-be warriors eager to haul their former countrymen back into the Union. Equally untried enlistees, determined to resist Federal coercion, had established defensive positions in diverse parts of Virginia, one of them along a stream called Bull Run a few miles north of a railroad depot, Manassas Junction, only twenty-two miles southwest of the U.S. capital.[2]

With a decisive confrontation taking shape almost outside his bedroom window, the president could only hope that his recurrent vision portended an acceptable outcome. The speed at which his dream vessel had moved suggested a quick resolution of the military situation in northern Virginia—perhaps a well-managed offensive, one that delivered a complete victory at minimal cost in Northern and Southern lives. Yet given the unhappy events that had followed the dream's first occurrence, Lincoln felt a nagging concern about the coming passage of arms. The forces fated to meet at Manassas were equally untutored and undisciplined—not even the presumed superior strength of the Union forces could be counted on to sway the result. Thus, the fate of the American Republic would be decided by ignorant armies clashing by day.

As he sat on the edge of his bed in the slowly dissipating darkness, Lincoln must have wondered if he would ever again enjoy a night of quiet, contented sleep.

Lesser mortals shared the president's fixation on omens. Among the would-be soldiers encamped along Bull Run was cavalryman Luther W. Hopkins. The seventeen-year-old was not ordinarily given to flights of fancy, but he could not say the same of some of his comrades. In later years he would recall that "as the hour for the battle drew near, those of a mystical turn of mind saw, or thought they saw, a strange combination of stars in the heavens. Some said, 'I never saw the moon look that way before.' Clouds assumed mysterious shapes. Some saw in them marching armies, and other fearful phenomena."

As the summer of 1861 wore on and rumors of an advance from Washington grew more numerous and intense, his buddies' metaphysical unease began to infect Hopkins: "I have always claimed that I am not superstitious, but I must admit that there is an atmosphere that hangs around the camp on the eve of an approaching battle that was well calculated to give one's imagination full play. . . . In fact, everything takes on a different attitude. The very air seems to be laden with an indescribable something that made sleep difficult and wakefulness an ordeal of tension and anxiety." The tension mounted as the temperature climbed. By mid-July, the young trooper doubted it would endure much longer.[3]

Not everyone who saw peculiar signs in the sky was indulging an overactive imagination. In the first days of July, the proper Bostonian

Charles Francis Adams, Jr., son of the U.S. minister to the Court of St. James, while drilling with his militia unit at the corner of Washington and Boyleston Streets, beheld a comet—remarkable for its brightness, its golden hue, and its fan-shaped tail, fully forty degrees long—as it streaked across the northern hemisphere in parabolic orbit. The heavenly body, whose nucleus equaled a star of magnitude two, had first been observed in the southern hemisphere in mid-May; it achieved perihelion on June 12 and passed closest to the Earth on the last day of that month. Although he was no astronomer, young Adams observed correctly that "its stay seems likely to be as short as it is brilliant." July 7 would be the last day of observation of the comet in Ursa Major, although it was still discernable, faintly, through high-refractor telescopes as late as the following spring.

The Great Comet of 1861 had a disquieting effect on many who tracked its luminous path. "Where did it come from, and how did it get here?" Adams wondered. "But here it is, brilliant beyond description as it streams across the sky. Already it is vanishing, and in a few nights will be invisible. What a curious coincidence! . . . It has come on our National Anniversary, bursting upon us unheralded and in the midst of our civil commotions. . . . Who can read us the riddle?"[4]

Adams was not ruled by superstition, but the sudden and unexpected appearance of the comet disturbed him in ways he could not explain. It was a sensation he shared with countless other observers across the length and breadth of the war-torn land.

CHAPTER I

THE GREAT CREOLE AND THE OBSCURE OHIOAN

G ustave Toutant Beauregard had a penchant for exactitude, one
befitting his carefully cultivated image as a military aristocrat.
On March 1, 1861, the day he accepted a commission in the newly
organized Provisional Army of the Confederate States of America,
Brevet Major Beauregard bade farewell to Colonel Joseph G. Totten,
his mentor and superior in the U.S. Army Corps of Engineers. In his
letter the Louisiana Creole made no attempt to explain what motivated him to leave the army in which he had served for twenty-three
years; he intended merely to square himself officially with his old
employer. The meticulous officer declared that he had closed out
his accounts with the corps and had come out ahead. Upon submitting his last voucher to the Paymaster's Department, Beauregard had
discovered that the army owed him one cent, presumably in reimbursement for professional expenses paid out of his own pocket.
Magnanimously, he foreswore any attempt to collect the debt.[1]

Beauregard could afford to be generous. A few days before he
wrote Totten, he had traded his rather lowly rank in the engineers
for a brigadier generalship in the Confederate forces. The salary that
came with his new position would be paid in currency printed by a
nation that had only begun to raise the revenue to support a war that
almost every Southerner considered imminent. Even so, Beauregard
was confident of his ability to meet his financial obligations, including the cost of outfitting his person in a well-tailored uniform: a
tunic of gray broadcloth, blue pantaloons, a gilt-spangled kepi, and
a pair of English riding boots. The ensemble went far toward making
him appear what he had long considered himself to be—a soldier of
presence and distinction.

Physically, he appeared to fit his idealized self-image. Though his physique and stature were less than impressive—he stood five feet, seven inches tall and weighed something less than 150 pounds—he had the mien and bearing of a patrician. Not quite forty-three, his darkly handsome features were highlighted by an olive complexion suggestive of his European ancestry. Pierre G. T. Beauregard (as a teenager he would drop his first name) had been born on a sugar plantation in the countryside south of New Orleans, the son of second-generation Americans who traced their French and Italian lineage to the thirteenth century. Dark eyes, high cheekbones, and a jutting chin were framed by a neatly cropped mustache and a jaunty tuft of beard. His physical appearance was complemented by a soft, lightly accented voice that helped relieve the formal and sometimes reserved manner he displayed to intimates and strangers alike.[2]

Beauregard was not lacking in those social graces that helped promote an officer's career. That he had risen no higher than captain in the U.S. Army he attributed to fossilized personnel policies rather than personal inadequacy. He was a stranger to self-doubt, to fears of failure and incapacity; once he made a decision, he knew instinctively that it was the correct one. Having devoured volumes of military history since early youth, he saw himself as a latter-day Napoleon, the soldier he admired above all others. He could not believe that the great captain ever doubted the efficacy of his strategy, even in the aftermath of Leipzig and Waterloo, where conditions beyond his control had denied him victory but not glory.

While still in his teens, Beauregard bent his intellect and energy toward preparing for a military career. His parents initially disapproved of his chosen profession, but the young man was a model of determination. When he failed to maneuver his son toward more genteel pursuits, in the spring of 1834 Jacques Toutant-Beauregard played his social and political connections to secure him an appointment to the U.S. Military Academy.[3]

Given his strong will and rigid self-discipline, it is not surprising that from the outset of his West Point career Cadet Beauregard excelled in the classroom and on the drill plain. Throughout his four years on the Hudson River, he indulged his long-held interest in the military campaigns of Napoleon. To some extent he did so through the writings of Baron Antoine Henri Jomini, the Corsican's most industrious chronicler and interpreter. Historians, including Beauregard's principal biographer, T. Harry Williams, believe that at West Point Beauregard immersed himself in those Jominian concepts of strategy and tactics advocated by Dennis Hart Mahan, the academy's professor of military and civil engineering.

Yet the extent of Beauregard's academic exposure to Jomini is difficult to gauge. Although West Point was the country's leading military institution, essentially it was an engineering school. In the realm of general military science, it emphasized small-unit tactics. During the Louisianan's cadetship, the curriculum did not offer courses in military history or strategy, and its library contained no English translations of Jomini's works. This deficiency would have posed no obstacle to Beauregard, who was so fluent in French that during his last two years at West Point, he served as a teaching assistant in that discipline. Thus, he could have committed to memory most of the maxims that Jomini articulated through repeated references to Napoleon's campaigns. Some historians contend, however, that the baron's influence on Beauregard was acquired not at West Point but during postgraduate professional study.[4]

The Creole's native intelligence, his aptitude for engineering and higher mathematics, and the avidity with which he devoured those texts unavailable to his classmates ensured academic achievement. His academy career was a triumph. At the close of his fourth-class (that is, his first) year of study, he ranked fourth among fifty-seven students. Not only did he perform well in the classroom, his deportment and behavior were exemplary. During his first two years, Beauregard was assessed, respectively, eleven and three demerits for infractions of the academy's many, arcane, and often arbitrarily applied rules of conduct, well short of the number (two hundred) that subjected a violator to immediate dismissal. During his second- and first-class years, he acquired not one black mark, a record of iron-willed conformity that nearly equaled that of a famous predecessor, Robert Edward Lee of Virginia, Class of 1829. Though not a single demerit had been lodged against his name during his cadetship, Lee, upon graduation, had ranked no higher than G. T. Beauregard nine years later.[5]

As his paucity of demerits suggests, Beauregard permitted himself little time for recreation and none for carousing at Benny Havens's Tavern, a celebrated den of cadet debauchery in nearby Highland Falls. Yet he excelled in the few physical exercises offered at the academy and was especially proficient at horsemanship. Although he made numerous acquaintances among the cadet corps,

he formed no intimate associations. He considered himself intel-
lectually and professionally superior to his peers and rarely sought
them out except when needing someone to quiz him on his text-
book knowledge. T. Harry Williams suggests that "probably nobody
at the Academy really knew him." This observation could apply to
the extent of Beauregard's military career.[6]

Irvin McDowell, of Scotch-Irish ancestry, was born on October
14, 1818, in Columbus, Ohio. In his youth his family emigrated to
France; there he attended the College of Troyes (a civilian institution, not a military school). Returning to the Buckeye State, where
his father, Selden McDowell, was elected mayor of Columbus, the
fifteen-year-old sought and obtained an appointment to the U.S.
Military Academy. There his early education, especially his grasp of
French and mathematics, served him well in the classroom while the
culture he had assimilated on the Continent helped him socially.[7]

Because McDowell later acquired a reserved disposition, he has
come down through history as cold and aloof. Yet at West Point he
was anything but pallid and dull. Some historians pronounce him a
mediocre student, but they fail to understand that his relatively low
class ranking upon graduating (23rd of 45 cadets in the Class of 1838)
was in large measure the product of a boisterous personality. One's
standing on the conduct roll had a direct bearing on one's academic
ranking, and McDowell received a substantial number of demerits,
including 177 in his third-class year and 190 in his graduation year.
Most of his transgressions were of a routine nature, but they were
various: late at dinner or roll call, failure to close ranks while on
the parade ground, absent from reveille, reading after lights out, loi-
tering in areas of the campus off limits to underclassmen. That he
earned many of those black marks for visiting in other cadets' rooms
after hours and for joining in such pranks as hurling snowballs at
the windows of his barracks suggests an outgoing nature and a frol-
icsome spirit. And the fact that in his first-class year he ranked 190
out of 218 cadets on the conduct roll hints at a propensity to take
risks that has gone undetected or overlooked by scholars.[8]

Upon leaving the academy, Second Lieutenant McDowell was
assigned to the 1st U.S. Artillery, the service arm to which most mid-
class graduates were posted (standout performers such as Lee and
Beauregard gained commissions in the army's most elite branches,
the topographical and construction engineers). McDowell's first

posting was to the Maine frontier during America's "disputed territory" standoff with Canadian authorities. After two years of desultory service on the northern border, he was returned to West Point
as an assistant instructor of artillery. The assignment indicates
that although his scholastic scores may have been low, his tactical
acumen was of a high order. In addition to his academic duties, in
November 1841 he was appointed adjutant of the academy. In this
role he not only kept the institution's administrative files but also
maintained a seat on its academic board, the body that set the curriculum, conducted semiannual examinations, and by ranking the
cadets' progress in every subject determined their class standing.[9]

Adjutant McDowell did not confine himself to the rather ster-
ile social scene of the academy. On several occasions he took leave
to visit friends and army colleagues who had settled in upstate New
York. He also made the acquaintance of a high-ranking officer who
was to have a major influence on both his career and his personal
life: Brigadier General John Ellis Wool, a distinguished veteran of
the War of 1812 and former inspector general of the army. From
their first meeting McDowell struck Wool as an officer of talent and
merit. Over time he won the general's trust, confidence, and it would
appear, his friendship. Through him McDowell was introduced to a
friend of the Wool family, Helen Burden of Troy, New York. Love
blossomed, and the couple married in November 1844. Over the
next several years, they reared two sons and two daughters. Most
of the children were healthy and led normal lives, but the fragile
constitution of the eldest son resulted in his early death, "a blow,"
McDowell wrote, "to which I never shall become reconciled."[10]

When Lieutenant Beauregard left his academic surroundings to begin
active duty, he immediately impressed his superiors. Thanks to the
patronage of Colonel Totten and other leading lights of his branch
of service, he gained choice assignments that took him from Fort
Adams in Newport, Rhode Island, the social capital of New England,
to the mouth of the Mississippi River, where he could work amid
familiar venues, visit his family, and enjoy the cosmopolitan attrac-
tions of New Orleans.

At first he enjoyed the life of an engineer officer, and he appreciated the prestige that his corps commanded within the army. His
pay was not munificent, but it permitted him to take a wife, Marie
Laure Villere, the sister of an old friend and the favorite daughter of

one of south Louisiana's most prominent Creole families. The couple enjoyed a happy marriage and started a family that would include two handsome sons. Despite or perhaps because of his now-settled existence, Beauregard soon discovered that peacetime soldiering had limited allure. Providentially, an opportunity for more-active service, and perhaps for battle laurels and promotion, came his way.[11]

In May 1846 diplomatic and military tensions between the United States and Mexico—simmering for years and recently raked into flame by the announced intent of the Republic of Texas, formerly a Mexican possession, to seek admission to the American Union—erupted into a shooting war. Even before the initial clash of arms, First Lieutenant Beauregard applied for a position with Brevet Brigadier General Zachary Taylor's Army of Occupation, then preparing to cross the Rio Grande to confront the larger but less capable forces of General Antonio Lopez de Santa Anna. Beauregard was furiously disappointed when his application was pigeonholed. Not until November did orders send him to Tampico, a supply base on the eastern coast of the invaded country. The port's defenses needed improving, providing the lieutenant with his first wartime duty. He entered upon it with characteristic energy, but almost incessant labor under a tropical sun took a physical toll that made him question for perhaps the first time whether he could endure the hardships his profession entailed.[12]

In March 1847 he was rescued from his undesirable situation when assigned to accompany an expeditionary force into the Mexican interior under Major General Winfield Scott. Though sixty years old, Scott, the Republic's *beau ideal* of a soldier, was at the height of his mental and physical powers. Beauregard's first stint of combat service began at Veracruz, a fortified stronghold on the Gulf coast 150 miles below Tampico, which Scott successfully besieged. Never one to slight his own accomplishments, Beauregard believed that he made a critical contribution to this victory by choosing positions for three of the five artillery batteries that pounded the garrison into submission on March 29. He also took pride in successfully arguing against an exposed position for a sixth battery recommended by a colleague. Characteristically, the lieutenant was chagrined when Colonel Totten, in his report of the siege, failed to single out his work. Instead the Creole was included in an omnibus commendation along with other members of the engineering staff, including Captain R. E. Lee. In the 1850s, when he penned a memoir of his war service, Beauregard's resentment had not subsided. "Without wishing to detract one iota from the reputation of my brother officers," he wrote, "have I not the right, if not to complain, at any rate to feel surprised and pained at his [Totten's] lack of memory in this instance? . . . For I had done more than my legitimate duty, not only in selecting the positions of those batteries, but especially in condemning one *which I had received orders to mark out!*"[13]

By April 2, when Scott's army departed Veracruz for the enemy interior via the so-called National Highway, Beauregard was attached to the staff of Major General Robert Patterson. An Irish-born resident of Philadelphia, Patterson had risen through the ranks of the Pennsylvania militia and the Regular infantry and now commanded a division of volunteers in Scott's vanguard. On April 12 Patterson's force reached Cerro Gordo, a mountain stronghold that concealed several batteries of heavy artillery. Beauregard conducted a reconnaissance of the position that convinced him of the desirability of an indirect attack. His opinion flew in the face of head-on assault tactics that another of Scott's division commanders, Brigadier General David E. Twiggs, strongly advocated. Beauregard's articulate and well-reasoned defense of his view persuaded Patterson, Twiggs's senior, to defer the direct assault, which would have inflicted heavy casualties, until Scott himself reached the scene, took charge, and approved the change of plan.[14]

Hoping to avoid a bloodbath, the commanding general devised a turning movement of the enemy's left flank. In advance of that operation, Beauregard conducted a second reconnaissance that carried him as far as Santa Anna's outer lines. He discovered a hill, Atalaya, that rose a quarter mile behind the enemy's position. He decided that its capture would turn the entire Mexican position, but he could not persuade General Twiggs, who had charge of the mission, to adopt his suggestion. One reason was that halfway through the mission, Beauregard was felled by the malaria-like condition he had contracted at Veracruz. Captain Lee stood in for him; his avid promotion of Beauregard's idea gained its acceptance and enabled Scott to strike Cerro Gordo from the rear and gain a major victory.[15]

From Cerro Gordo, Scott's little army followed the fleeing enemy toward the City of Mexico. One result was the August 20 battle of Contreras. There Beauregard distinguished himself by guiding a portion of Brigadier General Persifor F. Smith's brigade (including a volunteer regiment under one of Beauregard's former engineer colleagues, Lieutenant Colonel Joseph E. Johnston) in an attack that routed the Mexicans and drove them inside their fortified capital. Sent to Scott's field headquarters to report the triumph, Beauregard was warmly received by his commander, who exclaimed, "Young man, if I were not on horseback, I would embrace you!"[16]

Beauregard—now a brevet captain thanks to his heroics on the roads to Mexico City—did not see combat again until the end of the summer, following the lifting of a lengthy armistice during which negotiators from Washington had failed to "conquer a peace." During the second week in September, prior to renewing active operations, Scott several times sent Beauregard, Lee, and other engineers to scout the approaches to the heavily defended capital.

Prior to the climactic assault on Mexico City, Beauregard made a memorable showing at a war council called by Scott in the Convent and Church of Piedad to determine the most practicable path to the objective. Although six of the commanding general's subordinates endorsed the recommendations of Captain Lee and other engineer officers that the army move south via the San Antonio *Garita* (Gate), Beauregard boldly argued in favor of a different route. From personal observation he knew that the capital's southern defenses must be approached over terrain "entirely open to the enemy's view." Therefore, he called for a feint toward the south and an all-out attack from the west.

The ground in that sector was so broken and treacherous that Santa Anna would not expect an attack in that direction. One of Jomini's celebrated maxims—which Beauregard cited on this occasion as if delivering a West Point recitation—cautioned against acting in a manner that met the enemy's expectations. His audience was duly impressed. At least one member, Brigadier General Franklin Pierce, changed his opinion based on Beauregard's arguments. After further discussion, Scott himself announced that Beauregard's recommendation would be adopted, whereupon the council broke up.[17]

On September 12, when Scott's army attacked the fortified castle of Chapultepec outside the walls of Mexico City, Beauregard turned in another bravura performance, this time while accompanying the regiment of *voltiguers* (light infantry armed with rifled muskets) led by Lieutenant Colonel Johnston. When Johnston's troops halted after capturing an outwork, Beauregard borrowed a rifle and popped away at any Mexican who showed his head above the parapet. To emphasize his coolness under fire, each time he took aim he shouted to Johnston, "Colonel, what will you bet on this shot?" As Beauregard later recalled, Johnston promised "drinks in the City of Mexico." Taking careful aim, the captain hit his mark and shouted to his colleague: "You have lost; you will have to pay it!"[18]

Morning of the thirteenth revealed an evacuated city and a flag of truce flying from the captured citadel. Beauregard, who had been slightly wounded in the side and thigh, was sent to confer with the truce bearer, whom Santa Anna had designated to receive terms for the surrender of the city. To Beauregard's astonishment, the officer offered to turn over the entire city provided he was furnished with a receipt of possession. With theatrical panache, the captain replied that Americans "gave our receipts with the points of our swords! That if he did not give up the property under his charge willingly, we would *take it.*" The officer promptly handed over his sword—and his capital—and Beauregard joined Major General John A. Quitman's division in taking possession of the city. In his official report of the engagement, the captain noted that he "planted the star spangled banner on the walls of the palace at 7 o'clock A.M." The city's capture would end major combat operations; in time its loss would persuade the Mexican government to sue for peace.[19]

Lieutenant McDowell remained at West Point until October 1845, when released from his position to accept a berth on Wool's staff. Soon after hostilities with Mexico began in the spring of 1846, President James K. Polk assigned Wool command of a yet nonexistent column with which to occupy and pacify the Mexican province of Chihuahua. The general and his aide were sent to oversee its formation at recruitment depots in the Old Northwest and the Upper South. In those venues they were to enlist, organize, and arm thousands of eager but abysmally untutored volunteers "with the least possible delay."[20]

Through early summer, Wool and McDowell gathered more than 12,000 recruits from Illinois, Indiana, Ohio, Missouri, Kentucky, and Tennessee. Volunteers were a species of soldier with whom McDowell had little experience. He was wholly unprepared for the decidedly unmilitary appearance and behavior of those who flocked to Wool's standard, no doubt sharing the impression of another Regular who wrote the governor of Ohio, "Such a gathering of awkward boys you never saw." McDowell's opinion of citizen-soldiers, enlisted men and officers alike, would not improve much over the years.[21]

In mid-August Wool went on ahead to San Antonio, Texas, where he established his headquarters, McDowell having been left behind in Louisville, Kentucky, to recuperate from a fall from a fractious horse. Once recovered, he had to hasten to catch up with his commander. Because San Antonio was not populous enough to provide the supplies needed for an active campaign, Wool's "Center Division," 2,500 strong, was en route to the fort at Eagle Pass known as the Presidio del Rio Grande. From there Wool would press on to Chihuahua, a bustling commercial center two hundred miles south of El Paso, Texas.[22]

Although many of Wool's troops considered him a martinet— officious, egocentric, and "old-womanish"—McDowell admired the general's strategic gifts. So too did the theater commander, Zachary Taylor, who in November adopted Wool's advice to abort the Chihuahua mission and have the Center Division join his main body near Monterrey, closer to Santa Anna's forces. Wool's subsequent move to Saltillo, southwest of Monterrey, increased Taylor's available force to 4,600 men, mostly volunteers. With these, "Old Rough and Ready" believed that he could effectively oppose the much larger army that Santa Anna was forming almost three hundred miles to the south at San Luis Potosi.[23]

On the twenty-second Santa Anna attacked the American positions south of the ranchero of Buena Vista. The volunteers holding Taylor's left flank under Wool's command (Taylor had delegated to him "active duty of the field") initially gave way but executed a fighting withdrawal. Thanks principally to the inspired handling of Taylor's Regular artillery, the battle ended in a narrow victory. Especially given the disparity in numbers engaged, Taylor, Wool, and several subordinates, including Colonel Jefferson Davis of Mississippi, received deserved credit for breaking Santa Anna's lines and forcing him to retreat on the evening of the twenty-third. While the American forces had suffered heavily, Taylor had inflicted on his enemy more than twice as many casualties.[24]

The battle also burnished the reputation of Lieutenant McDowell, who had run a gamut of musketry and artillery fire to deliver orders to Wool's subordinates while also helping position infantry detachments. In his report of the day's action, Wool praised several members of his staff, but McDowell's name headed the list. He recommended his aide "to the especial notice of the commanding general for his activity and gallant bearing at all times . . . on the field of battle."[25]

McDowell downplayed his performance. In a letter to a correspondent in Troy, he rejected any suggestion that he had acted bravely, instead emphasizing the anxiety he felt before the battle began. It had been just as unsettling for the volunteers who had experienced combat for the first time. Employing a popular phrase to describe one's first battle, McDowell wrote that they had "seen the Elephant . . . and have found his feet heavy enough and his tusks long and sharp enough" to satisfy them.[26]

Buena Vista effectively ended major operations in northern Mexico. In mid-May 1847 McDowell, now a captain by brevet, accompanied his boss back to Saltillo, where Wool established his headquarters as commander of an occupation district. The assignment did not cause McDowell to revise his low opinion of the volunteer troops of the division, especially when in August he had to help quell a deadly mutiny by Virginia, Mississippi, and North Carolina troops anxious to be discharged and sent home. McDowell was relieved when in June 1848, a peace treaty having been signed, Wool and his staff left Monterrey for the States. The voyage home carried the party to Washington, where the general received the thanks and commendation of Polk and his secretary of war, William Marcy. Then it was on to Troy, where on August 23 Wool was feted by the people of his adopted hometown. McDowell shared in the festivities as well as in the honors bestowed. An even greater boon was the ability to join his wife and children in the house he had recently purchased in the city.[27]

Beauregard spent nine months on occupation duty in Mexico City. During this period he suffered unrelievedly from boredom and intermittently from ill health, recurrences of the condition that had laid him low en route to Cerro Gordo. He was both disappointed and angry when the postaction reports of Scott, Patterson, Quitman, and other commanders under whom he had served failed to accord him the special praise he knew he deserved. Obtaining the brevet rank of major failed to relieve his discontent.[28]

Not until mid-June 1848 did Beauregard accompany the first contingent of occupation troops to return to American soil. He was soon involved in improving the coastal defenses of Florida and Alabama as well as those guarding the mouth of the Mississippi at New Orleans. The work consumed much of the next decade, a seminal period in his life. In March 1850 he became a widower, Marie

Laure having died while giving birth to their third child, a daughter. Two years later he mixed love and politics by wedding another Creole beauty, Caroline Deslonde, sister-in-law of Louisiana senator John Slidell.[29]

Beauregard himself entered the political arena following the successful presidential bid of Franklin Pierce, a Northern Democrat who had been one of his superiors in Mexico and whose campaign the major had conspicuously supported. In 1858, three years after landing the plum position of superintending engineer of the customs house in New Orleans, Beauregard accepted the Democratic Party's nomination for mayor of the city. Without resigning his commission, he ran a vigorous campaign against a member of the American (or Know-Nothing) Party but lost the election due, at least in part, to political chicanery.[30]

He continued in charge of custom-house design for another two years, while the sectional divide that had long threatened the survival of his nation became a yawning abyss. Although a generally astute observer of the political scene, he often expressed doubts that a decisive conflict was inevitable. As late as January 1860, he dismissed the fears of a former colleague, Ohio-born William T. Sherman—now the president of a military academy at Alexandria, Louisiana, attended by Beauregard's sons—that a crisis was approaching. Ten months later, however, following the ascension of a "Black Republican," Abraham Lincoln, to the presidency, Beauregard beheld the approach of war.[31]

Even then he suspected the conflict was months away. In January 1861, shortly after South Carolina left the Union, Beauregard took a step that seemed to fly in the face of reality and logic, accepting an ill-advised offer to become superintendent of West Point. He must have appreciated the incongruity of his situation: a career officer fiercely loyal to his state and region assuming a major position at the nation's primary officer-training school. Even so, on January 23 he reported at West Point to take up his duties. Biographer Williams surmises that while Beauregard suspected his tenure would be brief, he realized that the posting would look good on his record, ensuring him of high station should he seek a commission in the defense forces of Louisiana.

The government quickly realized its mistake and sought to rectify it. Only one day after arriving at the academy, Beauregard received a directive from Colonel Totten in response to a demand from Secretary of War Joseph Holt that the Creole vacate the post. Although Louisiana declared for secession only two days after Holt acted, Beauregard assumed the role of an aggrieved party, as if his superiors had no basis for questioning his loyalty. He insisted that he had accepted the superintendency in good faith—had even counseled Southern-born cadets to stay in school until their states left the Union. The Louisianan himself would refrain from resigning his commission until war broke out.[32]

Beauregard waited until the twenty-eighth to leave West Point for his home state, an act that effectively severed his connection with the U.S. Army. Even then he appears not to have appreciated fully the consequences of his action. Soon after reporting to Baton Rouge for an interview with Louisiana governor Thomas O. Moore, he formally resigned his commission in the Corps of Engineers effective February 20. The following month, having rejected a colonelcy in his state's forces in hopes of gaining higher rank in Confederate service, Beauregard wrote to the assistant quartermaster general in Washington, seeking reimbursement for expenses incurred in traveling from West Point to New Orleans. When the government refused, he professed indignation.[33]

A war behind him, McDowell returned to the prosaic duty of military administration. He spent a month overseeing the muster out and discharge of the volunteers who had proven themselves poor soldiers but good fighters. Once that assignment ended, he departed General Wool's staff to accept a position in the Adjutant General's Department in Washington. He may well have regretted the decision, for the work assigned him in the capital proved neither challenging nor fulfilling. Less than a year after accepting the office, he secured a transfer to the headquarters of the army, then located in New York City, where he joined the staff of Commanding General Scott.

Scott and McDowell would forge a mutually beneficial relationship, but one that had its difficulties. Scott, though not himself a West Pointer, admired academy graduates, whom he considered largely responsible for the army's triumph south of the Rio Grande. He was duly impressed by McDowell's quiet professionalism, his administrative skill, and the air of suavity he exuded as personified by his fluency in French. In return, his subordinate was properly deferential to his patron, offering advice only when it was sought and providing it without assuming an air of superior knowledge. It was only natural, however, that on occasion McDowell would be put off by Scott's many defects of character: his domineering personality, his egotism and arrogance, and the pettiness and jealousy that led him to quarrel with subordinates and on occasion with his civilian superiors. To a soldier seeking his own path to career success, being constantly under the thumb of an autocratic septuagenarian could be a most unpleasant experience.[34]

Scott did attempt, however, to promote his aide's professional advancement. In an effort to broaden the younger officer's experience, between January 1851 and May 1857, he three times detached McDowell to other duty stations: the Second Military Department, headquartered at Detroit, Michigan; installations in the Old Northwest within the Sixth Military Department; and on two separate occasions, the headquarters of the Department of Texas.[35]

His career received a boost when in November 1858 Scott selected him to observe military maneuvers in Europe. The year McDowell spent on the Continent saw the climax of the French-Austrian War (also known as the Second Italian War for Independence). If McDowell composed a report of his views on the conflict, it is no longer extant. In September 1860, upon the expiration of a four-month leave of absence, he was assigned for the first time duties that bore directly on the ever-intensifying sectional crisis. An inspection tour he made of federal installations in Minnesota, Missouri, and the Kansas Territory enabled him to inform Scott of the state of readiness of such garrisons as Jefferson Barracks and Fort Leavenworth.[36]

By February 1861, two months after the disaffected states had begun to leave the Union, McDowell was in Washington, where army headquarters had relocated. He found the city (with a population of 62,000) in a state of incompleteness and disrepair, qualities symbolic of the condition of the nation. The Capitol dome remained under construction, complete only up to its second tier of columns. The Patent Office and Treasury Building were unfinished. The War and Navy Departments were housed in dilapidated three-story brick buildings, and the shaft of the Washington Monument, which one day would rise five hundred feet above the city, barely ascended two hundred feet after thirteen years of construction. The only paved streets were Pennsylvania Avenue and a portion of Seventh Street; even so, slime oozed from under their cobblestones. In spring and summer the spectacularly unsanitary city sank in pools of filth and piles of offal. For much of the year, it lay buried beneath a suffocating fog of dust.

Likewise incomplete were the capital's defenses, a scandalous deficiency in a time of crisis. The only standing fortification was antiquated Fort Washington, on the Maryland side of the Potomac twelve miles below the city. In a desperate effort to provide municipal security, sections of planking on the three bridges across the river—Aqueduct Bridge in the northwestern suburb of Georgetown; Chain Bridge, three miles above Georgetown; and Long Bridge, at the foot of Fourteenth Street—were taken up at night to prevent enemy incursion. Unlike most other national capitals, Washington lacked a sizable garrison. An inspection report around this time enumerated its only defenders as three hundred officers and men at the Marine Barracks and sixty ordnance specialists at the Washington Arsenal.[37]

At General Scott's order, McDowell returned to the business of inspecting troops, mainly local militiamen, whom he considered "nothing more than clubs, who wear a uniform and carry arms." He was also tasked with securing government facilities, including the Capitol, against an attack that, in the wake of South Carolina's mid-April bombardment of the U.S. Army garrison inside Fort Sumter, appeared imminent. When late that month militia regiments began to trickle into the capital, ensuring at least its short-term safety, McDowell furnished them with living quarters. (At the insistence of high officials, many troops were housed in public buildings, including the Capitol and even in one of the rooms in the president's mansion.) In this work McDowell conferred more or less closely with Colonel Charles P. Stone, inspector general for the District of Columbia; Adjutant General Lorenzo Thomas; and Major David Hunter, then serving as an ex-officio liaison between the War Department and the Frontier Guards, a body of volunteers formed by Kansas senator James Lane to safeguard the president and his residence.[38]

At this point in his career, Irvin McDowell looked the part of the veteran regular-army officer, though hardly the prototype of a great captain. At forty-two he had begun to display a paunch, one not relieved by his long torso and short legs. While capable of impressive feats at the table, when it came to stimulants he was an "ultra total abstainer," avoiding even tea and coffee. Nor did he engage in card playing or other games of chance—for him gambling was not only an unseemly vice but too often an addiction.

Despite his weight problem, he affected the ramrod-straight profile of the career officer, an image imposing enough to impress many observers. There was, wrote one admirer, "a look of solid strength about him." Another described him, perhaps with some slight exaggeration, as "in the full lush of mature manhood, fully six feet tall, deep-chested, strong-limbed, clear-eyed." More-critical acquaintances were apt to comment on McDowell's bullet-shaped head, which rested on an inconsiderable neck; his fleshy face and jowls; and the short, bushy beard and droopy mustache that gave him a French or Germanic appearance.[39]

Over the years, McDowell had cultivated a reputation as a military intellectual. Though short on operational experience, he struck one who knew him well as "one of the most thoroughly educated and accomplished theoretic soldiers I ever met." Others believed his personality and conduct needed improvement. He could be cold and formal even to close acquaintances, and his "too indifferent" manner gave offense to superiors and subordinates alike. At times he could be a clever conversationalist; just as often his mind wandered and his speech drifted off. He had trouble remembering the names and faces even of everyday associates. Nervous energy caused his face to flush and his speech to thicken, causing strangers to mistake the teatotaling Ohioan for an inebriate.[40]

These were behavioral issues, however, not flaws of character. Other qualities seemed more important: McDowell had a solid background in military affairs, was intensely loyal, and appeared to have the strong support of General Scott. The integrity and earnestness he habitually displayed could not fail to impress his civilian superiors, many of whom came to see him as a soldier of vitality and intellect with a vision for dealing with those who would destroy the Republic. In Washington in April 1861, such men were in short supply.[41]

Another officer was winning plaudits many miles to the south. By the spring of 1861, G. T. Beauregard had come to be regarded as one of the most accomplished military engineers in the country, his reputation exceeded only by a handful of colleagues, including Robert E. Lee. That reputation, and his identity as a stalwart of the Deep South, made the Creole a sought-after commodity in the eyes of the military and political leaders of the infant Confederacy. In late February, shortly after Beauregard entered the Confederate ranks, his newly inaugurated commander in chief, Jefferson Davis, called him to Montgomery, Alabama, where the fledgling government had set up quarters.

Davis and his military advisors, including Secretary of War Leroy Pope Walker, had decided to assign Beauregard to the post of immediate importance to the Confederate cause: Charleston, where U.S. troops under Major Robert Anderson continued to occupy Fort Sumter in defiance of demands to evacuate. The president believed that Beauregard's sterling career would impress the source of those demands, South Carolina governor Francis W. Pickens. He also suspected that the officer's old-world courtliness would charm Charlestonians. Above all, Davis hoped the Creole's engineering expertise and his lesser-known aptitude for artillery operations would enable him to gain Sumter's evacuation, preferably without having to force the issue by firing on the garrison.[42]

Davis's confidence appeared to be justified. Two days after informing Colonel Totten of his commissioning in the Confederate service, Beauregard reached Charleston and on March 6 took control of local military preparations. The officers and men assigned to him were impressed by the new brigadier's commanding presence and distinguished reputation, and the local citizenry were dazzled by his impeccable social grace. Over time, however, Governor Pickens perceived in Beauregard deficiencies, or at least limitations. He came to consider the Creole "too cautious, and his very science makes him hesitate to make a dash. His knowledge of Batteries and Cannon and engineering is great, but he relies nothing upon the spirit and the energy of [his] troops, and has not experience in the management of infantry. His Reputation is so high that he fears to risk it, and yet he wants the confidence of perfect genius." Yet Pickens had nothing but praise for the man's character: "I think Beauregard a finished and pure gentleman . . . of excellent temper, great activity—and a true patriot."[43]

Over the next several weeks, the forces at Beauregard's disposal grew to more than 4,000 state and Confederate troops. He worked diligently to supervise the positioning of the men and the placement of the cannon and mortar batteries on the lands that surrounded Sumter until they bore directly upon the occupied fort in the center of the harbor. During much of this period, Beauregard maintained cordial relations with Anderson, who had been one of his favorite instructors at West Point. He permitted the garrison to receive mail and secure provisions from Charleston's stores and shops. He even saw that Anderson's subordinates were supplied with cigars, liquor, and other luxuries that helped compensate for the nerve-wracking service required of them. By early April, however, negotiations aimed at a peaceful evacuation of Sumter, carried on by Southern emissaries and officials of Lincoln's administration, broke down, and Beauregard was ordered to cease all intercourse with the fort. Thus deprived of supplies, Anderson would have to evacuate unless reprovisioned by sea.[44]

On the eighth Washington informed Governor Pickens that a supply ship was being sent to the garrison. The turn of events resulted in an order from Secretary Walker that Beauregard prevent the provisioning by any and all means. Two days later, with a relief expedition from the North approaching Charleston, Walker ordered Beauregard to call for Sumter's surrender. The demand was duly issued; Anderson rejected it, although he expected that the garrison would be starved out in a matter of days. At first Beauregard seemed inclined to wait him out, but when Anderson intimated that he would not evacuate if resupplied, the Creole determined to force the issue. At four-thirty on the morning of the twelfth, barely an hour after the last of Beauregard's emissaries ended attempts to negotiate the fort's capitulation, Southern batteries began to rake Sumter with shot and shell.[45]

Hundreds of rounds hurtled toward the isolated fort before some of its forty-eight cannons began to return fire at about 7:00 A.M. on April 13. The distance was such that Sumter suffered few direct hits— one of which, however, set her wooden barracks afire. Conversely, Anderson could inflict little damage on the hostile shore batteries. By midday of the thirteenth, the fort was replying to Beauregard's salvos only intermittently. Surely by this time, and probably much earlier, Anderson had come to see the hopelessness of his position. Later that day, during a temporary cessation of fire, he met under a truce flag with parties sent by Beauregard to offer to help extinguish the fire inside the barracks. The visitors were surprised to learn that minutes earlier Anderson had informally surrendered the fort to Confederate senator Louis T. Wigfall of Texas, a volunteer aide to the general. Although at first outraged by Wigfall's unauthorized intervention, Beauregard eventually agreed to the terms Anderson and the senator had worked out. After thirty-four hours of near-constant bombardment, Sumter capitulated.

The evacuation took place the following morning. Bowing to Anderson's wishes, Beauregard permitted the departing garrison to fire a fifty-round salute to the flag of its now-fractured nation.

The ceremonious gesture, an example of time-honored civility destined to become a quaint anachronism, was marred by an explo-
sion inside the fort's powder magazine that killed one enlisted man,
mortally wounded a second, and injured four others. Though barely
under way, the war had claimed its first casualties.[46]

The firing on Sumter was the spark, the match, the taper (the incen-
diary device is an inescapable metaphor) that touched off a nation-
wide powder keg. It set ablaze North and South alike and generated
an outpouring of war fever and patriotism that swept thousands
of young and not-so-young men into uniform. On the fifteenth
Lincoln issued a call for 75,000 militia from the loyal states to meet
the insurrection that had been set in motion by Beauregard's hand.
Troop quotas would be apportioned by population, New York to
furnish 17,000 men, while sparsely settled states like Michigan,
Iowa, and Minnesota were to supply 1,000 men each. (Later the
president would be criticized for failing to call for thousands of volunteer troops, but his options were limited by existing statutes.)
In the same message Lincoln called Congress into session on July
4 to construct the legal apparatus that would place the Union on
a wartime footing. Meanwhile, the states that had echoed South
Carolina's declaration of secession welcomed the Confederate
Congress's March 6 authorization of a regular army to consist of
10,600 men and a provisional army of 100,000 one-year volunteers.
In subsequent weeks President Davis called for 7,700 men to gar-
rison the forts of the South and an additional 19,500 volunteers for
Confederate service.[47]

The early military situation in both North and South was uncertain, dynamic, and abounding in irregularities. Logic dictated, for
instance, that those chosen to command the warring forces should
combine operational experience, leadership skill, organizational talent, and an ability to inspire confidence and respect. Beauregard
may have possessed all or most of these qualifications, but the
man chosen to oppose him—to command the volunteers flooding
Washington and its environs—appeared to share none of them.

The responsibility for selecting a Union field leader rested
with Brevet Lieutenant General Scott, although President Lincoln
had approval authority. As commanding general of the army, Scott
might have been expected to assume the position himself, but the

hero of Lundy's Lane, Veracruz, and Mexico City was seventy-four and felt the weight of every one of those years. Though his once-erect frame still approached six feet, five inches in height, Scott's girth had ballooned to more than three hundred pounds. Stooped with gout, wracked by arthritis and edema, he could barely mount a horse. Accompanying an army on campaign was out of the question. All too aware of his infirmities, "Old Fuss and Feathers" had selected a subordinate to take his place in the field: Brevet Colonel Robert E. Lee, the most celebrated member of his staff in Mexico.[48]

Lee appeared an inspired choice. He had acquired significant operational experience, having left the Corps of Engineers in 1855 to become executive officer of the 2nd U.S. Cavalry, which he had helped shape into a highly efficient regiment. Lee's most recent assignment was command of the Department of Texas, where he had overseen a slow and difficult struggle against Comanches and Kiowas, one that wearied and frustrated him. In early February 1861—only days after Texas passed an ordinance of secession—the War Department rescued Lee by ordering him to Washington. Upon returning to his baronial estate, Arlington, in the first days of March, he crossed the Potomac to report to Scott.

The two had a serious and somber conversation. Although like his visitor a native Virginian, Scott owed his loyalty to the nation and its army, and for three hours he tried to persuade Lee to adopt the same sentiment. Scott informed the younger man that he was going to recommend him for command of the troops to be raised to suppress the rebellion (the offer was formally tendered a few days later by an emissary of Lincoln). During his first meeting with Scott, Lee did not commit himself to a certain course, but during a return visit on April 18, he declared his unwavering loyalty to Virginia. Regretfully but unequivocally, he refused the appointment and the major generalship that accompanied it.[49]

His decision did not surprise Scott: Lee had made "the greatest mistake of your life; but I feared it would be so." At Scott's suggestion, two days later Lee, having learned of Virginia's imminent secession, tendered his resignation from the army. He was not without a position for long. On April 23 Governor John Letcher appointed him commander of Virginia's military and naval forces and ordered him to begin building the state's war defenses. On May 10 Lee was also placed in charge of Confederate forces operating in the Old Dominion.[50]

With their first choice out of the picture, Scott and Lincoln were forced to plan anew. There should have been a sense of urgency to their search, for the troops to be entrusted with the defense of the capital were expected to begin arriving any day. Even so, a month passed before a decision was made on whom to appoint. During that time, potential candidates were discussed and successively dismissed. Scott appears to have been partial to some of his subordinates in the War Department, including Colonel Joseph K. F. Mansfield, the army's inspector general. Mansfield already filled a major office, command of the newly created Department of Washington, which embraced not only the District of Columbia but also Maryland as far north as Bladensburg. Another candidate was Major General Charles W. Sandford, a New Yorker whom Scott considered "an energetic and intelligent commander" of a "fine division of the state uniformed militia," an early and much-appreciated addition to the capital's defense forces.[51]

Instead of these likely choices, the position fell to Major McDowell of the Adjutant General's Office. To this day, the circumstances of his appointment to head what became the Department of Northeastern Virginia remain obscure. Some historians contend that he was handpicked by Scott, on whose staff he had served off and on for the previous twelve years. Other scholars claim that the sudden rise of the Ohioan was due primarily to the political clout of Salmon P. Chase, former senator from Ohio, former governor of the state, and Lincoln's newly confirmed Treasury secretary.

Scott's role in McDowell's promotion is not clear cut. It appears that he approved it only because his civilian superiors, Lincoln and Secretary of War Simon Cameron, considered Mansfield indispensable in his current position and deemed Sandford unqualified due to his lack of regular-army service. The old general not only seemed miffed when McDowell was chosen but also not-so-subtly suggested that his subordinate respectfully decline the promotion. The Chase factor appears more significant; it seems likely that the secretary, an artful dispenser of political influence, pulled strings in McDowell's behalf. Their association probably predated the war's outset (McDowell's father had been a political figure of some prominence in Chase's adopted hometown of Columbus), and the two had been conferring regularly since Chase's return to Washington from Ohio on March 1. Their relationship would have been strengthened by McDowell's assignment in the early spring of 1861 to oversee governmental security. In time Chase would size up the younger man as "a loyal, brave, truthful, capable officer. . . . He resorts to no arts for popularity. He is attended by no clacquers and puffers."[52]

But Chase was not the major's only patron. McDowell also gained the confidence of Secretary of War Cameron and Ohio governor William Dennison. The latter, in fact, had considered appointing McDowell commander of Ohio's volunteer forces. By some reports Dennison had offered him the post before changing his mind in favor of a more prominent figure, George B. McClellan.[53]

In all likelihood, Lincoln had a hand—perhaps the critical hand— in McDowell's appointment. The president may have considered the fifty-seven-year-old Mansfield too aged or deskbound to lead a field campaign against the enemies of the Republic. McDowell, fourteen years younger than the colonel, appeared capable of doing more than guarding government buildings. Although he had spent most of his career running errands for various superiors, he was a West Pointer who had made an impressive record in Mexico, winning a brevet promotion for gallantry under fire. As would become apparent to many officials, McDowell possessed the ability to develop campaign plans that were clearly crafted, suggestive of tactical ability, and based on hard reality, including limitations on available troops, weaponry, and supplies.[54]

His superior had a very different approach to grand strategy. General Scott's pet plan called for 25,000 regulars as well as thousands of volunteers to apply concentric pressure on the enemy's homeland, squeezing its defenders to death in the manner of a gigantic snake. To be sure, the plan had its merits—in the long run it would be substantially adopted by Scott's successors and civilian superiors. In the spring of 1861, however, its flaws—primarily those of a political nature—were all too obvious. For one thing, the so-called Anaconda Policy focused on occupying enemy territory and blockading Southern ports (the latter effort would be put into effect at an early date) instead of confronting the Rebels on the field of battle. Most Northern politicians and editors had no patience for a long, drawn-out conflict that would waste the nation's blood and treasure. They scorned Scott's reptile in favor of quick and bold action that would achieve the overthrow of those few secessionists who had erected breastworks and cannons almost within view of the capital. Once those barriers were razed, the victors would stream down the roads to Richmond and deconstruct the Confederate government.

Anyone who thought differently was an obstructionist. As the weeks passed and thousands of raw recruits made their way to the upper Potomac, it became increasingly clear that the man who would be called upon to achieve these objectives was not the nation's most celebrated soldier but an officer known to relatively few in the army and almost none outside it.[55]

The chronology of Irvin McDowell's ascension to star rank—a promotion he assuredly never dreamed of attaining—is somewhat muddled. Exact dates are lacking, but the chain of events apparently began within days of Lincoln's May 3 announcement that steps would be taken to create a formidable volunteer force as well as to enlarge the regular establishment. Through the efforts of the governors of the loyal states, more than 42,000 volunteers would be recruited to serve for three years unless sooner discharged. The regulars would be increased from their tiny prewar total of 16,367 to 22,714 officers and men. The expansion would amount to eight regiments of infantry and one each of cavalry and artillery.[56]

Several new brigadier and three major generals would be appointed to command the enlarged force. Around the second week in May, the president convened his cabinet to discuss the matter. Chase, prominent among the attendees, was determined that McDowell should receive one of the two-star billets. According to McDowell's future adjutant general, James Barnet Fry, Cameron was just as anxious to see that officer advanced. During the conference Chase, with Cameron's approval, called McDowell to the Executive Mansion and left the meeting to inform him of his pending promotion.

The news not only gratified but also alarmed McDowell. He feared that such a jump in rank would antagonize those officers senior to him; he probably suspected that Scott would not approve of it. His reticence also suggests that he was uncertain that he could handle the responsibilities accompanying high command. He would be more than satisfied, he told Chase, with a single star and suggested other candidates for the higher rank, including George McClellan. In due course Chase and Cameron saw that his preference was granted.[57]

Over Scott's subdued objections, McDowell's promotion to brigadier general came through on May 14. The commanding general saw to it that his old friend Mansfield received the same promotion as of the same date. Scott was aware that the latter's higher rank in the prewar army would grant him seniority over McDowell should the two wind up serving together in the field. That prospect, however, seemed unlikely given the need of Mansfield's services in his present position. An indication of Scott's mixed feelings toward appointing his former staff officer was that at about the time he called on McDowell for a preliminary plan of operations against the defenders of Manassas, he asked the new brigadier to refuse command of the force that would execute it. Considering himself unable to decline a position tendered him in good faith, McDowell rejected this suggestion.[58]

McDowell did respond positively to his superior's other initiative. In brief time the new general produced a plan to overawe the enemy not only in northeastern Virginia but on other fronts as well. He submitted it on the sixteenth—not to Scott, whose approval he may have doubted, but to Chase, who was known to favor an immediate advance on Richmond. The document addressed a wide range of strategic possibilities covering a war zone extending into western Virginia and as far south as Charleston. In scope it reminded one of Scott's Anaconda Policy but, based as it was on invasion and offensive action, was more politically acceptable.

Although McDowell's sphere of authority encompassed only northern Virginia, he suggested that the main line of Union operations should run not only along the Potomac River but also down Chesapeake Bay. He called for Rebel troops to be driven from selected points, including Harpers Ferry at the confluence of the Potomac and Shenandoah Rivers, home to a U.S. armory and arsenal that Virginia state forces had seized on April 18. An invading army should then take possession of "the most defensible line from the Blue Ridge to the Potomac—or as much of such a line as may be necessary." McDowell identified Richmond as the prize of greatest value to the enemy; thus it became his major objective along with the railroads that ran from the city south to the Carolinas and west to Lynchburg. Before targeting the enemy capital, however, Federal troops must gain a foothold south of the Potomac by occupying Alexandria, Arlington Heights, and other positions within artillery range of Washington. Larger forces would then advance south and west, attacking or outflanking the works at Manassas, recapturing Harpers Ferry, and blocking the roads to Leesburg on the upper Potomac.[59]

The speed of execution inherent in McDowell's plan suggested that its author believed the Bull Run defenses could be quickly overrun. Their capture would disrupt enemy access to Maryland, Washington's communications link to the North and the Old Northwest. Defeating the defenders of Manassas would also give the Federals control of the railroads that met at the junction: the Orange and Alexandria (O&A), which came down from the north, and the Manassas Gap Railroad, which led westward through the Blue Ridge to Winchester and Strasburg. But McDowell did not pretend to have everything figured out at so early a date. As he told Chase, he lacked the data to estimate the size of the force that would implement his strategy. He stressed, however, that it should include as much artillery as available.[60]

McDowell was aware that two operations subsidiary to his projected offensive, and which would serve to support it, were already underway. The first, designed to clear the enemy from the Shenandoah Valley, had been assigned to Robert Patterson, Scott's second in command in Mexico. On April 15 Patterson had been named a major general of Pennsylvania troops; two weeks later he was assigned command of a military department that encompassed not only the Keystone State but also Delaware and all of Maryland not embraced in the concurrently established Departments of Annapolis and Washington. Before the end of April, he had been ordered to send thousands of troops supplied by Pennsylvania governor Andrew Gregg Curtin to Maryland preparatory to a movement on Harpers Ferry in the lower (that is, northern reaches of the) Shenandoah, where defenders under Colonel Thomas Jonathan Jackson were gathering.[61]

The second supporting operation targeted Maryland, a state of divided loyalties. On April 21 Benjamin F. Butler of the Massachusetts militia, soon to become a major general of volunteers, had occupied the state capital at Annapolis. Three weeks later he took possession of Baltimore, where a prosecessionist mob had shot and stoned the first regiment sent from the North to defend Washington—the very troops who led Butler's advance into the city on May 13. This precipitate action angered General Scott, who feared antagonizing the populace of a border state in which Unionist sentiment appeared fragile. Still, Butler's move effectively removed pockets of potential resistance to the future movements of Patterson and McDowell.[62]

Secretary Chase and those officials with whom McDowell shared his plan for action were impressed by its prospects. All realized, however, that its execution would have to be deferred, if only

briefly. Although increasingly outmaneuvered by junior officers rising to prominence such as McDowell and McClellan (by late May
the latter was preparing to invade Virginia's western counties),
Winfield Scott was still influential, and he was determined to postpone an invasion of his native state as long as possible.

That time came on May 23, when Virginia's voters ratified the
state's secession ordinance by a three-to-one margin. Shortly after
midnight on the twenty-fourth, eleven regiments of militia and
volunteers, accompanied by some regular cavalry and artillery—
the whole under General Sanford, with Colonel Stone leading the
advance—crossed the river to seize Arlington and, six miles downstream, Alexandria. Few pickets remained in Arlington; caught
between two columns of recently disembarked Federals, most were
quickly captured. Alexandria, which had been abandoned by most
of its defenders weeks earlier, was taken by one of the columns out
of Arlington led by Colonel Orlando B. Willcox of the 1st Michigan
Infantry and Colonel Elmer E. Ellsworth of the 11th New York.
Thirty-six Rebels were snatched up without the shedding of blood.[63]

The only notable casualty of the twin operations was Ellsworth,
who had organized an infantry outfit recruited from Manhattan's
firehouses. The unit was widely known for its colorful uniform,
based on that worn by French colonial troops that Ellsworth, a drill-
team impresario, had made nationally popular in the years leading
to Fort Sumter. The impetuous colonel had drawn attention to himself by personally removing a Confederate banner from atop one
of Alexandria's hotels. Upon descending the stairs from the roof,
he had been ambushed by the establishment's shotgun-toting pro-
prietor. The latter was immediately shot and bayoneted by one of
Ellsworth's "Fire Zouaves." As befit his national prominence, the
colonel received a state funeral, his remains laying in repose in the
East Room of the Executive Mansion. Lincoln, Ellsworth's close personal friend, wept unashamedly over his bier. The first Union mar-
tyr of the conflict, he was mourned throughout the North, although
some criticized his rashness. A District of Columbia volunteer who
had accompanied Ellsworth into Alexandria opined that "the idea of
a Col. leaving his regiment before they were half formed and going
with some four or five men to pull down a flag shows that he was a
brave man but not a prudent one."[64]

Northern Virginia having been invaded, the troops within
General Mansfield's department began to extend their reach toward

Upton's and Munson's Hills, Bailey's Cross Roads, and Falls Church. Reconnaissance teams penetrated suspected enemy positions, while field works and artillery revetments went up. Within days Sandford's troops were joined by units newly arrived in the District of Columbia as well as by many that had relocated from the increasingly overcrowded encampments stretching north of the capital toward Rock Creek and Anacostia, Maryland, and westward beyond Chain Bridge.

In the wake of Alexandria's seizure, construction began in earnest on a defensive system for the capital. The structure later known as Fort Corcoran was erected above Arlington near the Virginia end of the city aqueduct. It was soon supported by smaller outworks such as Fort Haggerty on the Georgetown–Alexandria Road. Fort Runyon rose half a mile from the end of Long Bridge at the junction of the Alexandria and Fairfax Roads. Fort Albany on Arlington Heights was built to cover the approach to Long Bridge by way of the Columbia Turnpike. And the recently christened Fort Ellsworth went up on Shuter's Hill, just west of Alexandria. These hastily created works gave a false sense of security to the capital's Unionists. But Scott, Mansfield, and McDowell knew they would not withstand a determined attack on the city.[65]

Equally vulnerable were the spans that gave access to the capital, some of which were in need of repair as well as security. While the Aqueduct Bridge and Chain Bridge (the latter formerly a cable-suspension span now supported by piers and abutments) were in fairly good condition, Long Bridge—half of which was actually a causeway built upon the mud flats of the Potomac—was considered too rickety to support the passage of troops. It would have to be strengthened to accommodate soldiers, horses, wagons, ambulances, cannons, caissons, and limbers passing to the Virginia side.[66]

Though far from complete, work to increase the capital's security at least was under way. The time now seemed ripe for the government to examine McDowell's plan. Secretary Chase, whose influence in the government's most critical workings was at its height, promoted the general's ideas to Lincoln, his cabinet, and General Scott. Although still unhappy over McDowell's rise to star rank and concerned that his own counsel was being ignored while his subordinate's strategic advice was being sought on a daily basis, Scott agreed to give the plan his full attention, with a view to fleshing and smoothing it out.

Increasingly resigned to McDowell's prominence, the commanding general consented to his appointment to field command. On May 27 General Orders No. 26 created an as-yet-unnamed department consisting of that portion of Virginia east of the Alleghenies and north of the James River except for Fort Monroe and its dependencies. That same day this fiefdom—officially a part of the vast Department of the East—was assigned to Brigadier General McDowell, "headquarters in the field."[67]

Those quarters were physically imposing. Within hours of his appointment, McDowell crossed the river and took possession of the manor house at Arlington, only recently evacuated by R. E. Lee's invalid wife. An officer and gentleman, the general wrote to Mrs. Lee, who had relocated to a relative's plantation, assuring her that he would do all in his power to secure the home and grounds against the looting that had followed her departure. He also declared that, rather than take up residence in the majestic Greek Revival mansion, he would establish living quarters in a grouping of tents discreetly erected in a corner of the 1,100-acre estate. McDowell would soon find this arrangement inadequate to his needs, forcing him to relocate to Arlington itself. Helen joined him there; most days she could be seen on the portico reading or knitting. She and her husband strove to cause as little wear and tear as possible to the premises.[68]

On the twenty-eighth McDowell officially superseded General Sandford in command of the forces on the south side of the Potomac. Only then, it appears, did he gain a realistic appreciation of the enormity of his situation, especially the panoply of responsibilities that had devolved on him. Observing the mass of volunteers inundating the area, he realized that he had no exact count of the men and boys who answered to him, but he knew one thing: they were far from being soldiers. They were eager, enthusiastic youngsters who knew nothing of war and little of army life, having enlisted as much to join their friends in a great adventure as to avenge the loss of Fort Sumter and save the Union. They were strangers to discipline and order, as were the majority of their political-appointee officers. The Mexican War veterans and regulars who leavened this gaggle of rookies were too few to instill a knowledge of what it took to become an effective soldier. Yet from his first day at Arlington, McDowell felt the tug of public pressure to strike a blow with this unready force. That pressure, he knew, would only increase in the days and weeks ahead.

He did not know where to turn for help in managing his predicament. For some time he would lack a full-size staff. Nor could he
count on the unwavering support of a superior who seemed increasingly cool toward him. Civilian friends were of no assistance except
as sounding boards for his growing unease. When one visited army
headquarters, he found McDowell deeply concerned about the future,
quoting the general as saying repeatedly: "This is not an army. . . . It
will take a long time to make an army." The visitor understood the
implication: time was a luxury McDowell would never enjoy.[69]

Across the war-obsessed South, the commander of the guns that
had forced Sumter's surrender was hailed as a paladin on par with
Washington, Scott, and Andrew Jackson. Politicians, editors, and
common folk showered G. T. Beauregard with praise and gifts.
Expressions of thanks came from the Congress, still sitting in
Montgomery, as well as from the South Carolina legislature. Davis
and members of his cabinet echoed the feelings of the general public. Outwardly, the object of their appreciation accepted these plaudits with becoming modesty, but Beauregard believed himself fully
deserving of every honor as well as worthy of dispensing military
advice to the fledgling government. Three days after Sumter fell,
he was warning Secretary Walker of the need to defend against a
Yankee incursion via the Mississippi River.[70]

Beauregard was savvy enough to perceive that the focal point of
the war lay east of the Mississippi. As a student of Jomini, he understood the political and military significance of operating against an
enemy's capital. To subjugate the South, the Federals would have to
invade the Confederacy with the intent of overthrowing its nascent
government. This task appeared to become easier, the objective less
distant, after April 17, when a long-sitting convention in Richmond
voted for Virginia's secession. The decision was to be ratified by public referendum the following month, but there was little doubt that
it would pass. Accordingly, efforts were soon underway to transfer the Confederacy's capital to Richmond, whose well-developed
infrastructure, especially its transportation system, would put the
Confederacy on a surer footing. Virginia was where the fighting
undoubtedly would begin, and Beauregard probably sensed it even
before the ruling officials in Alabama did.

Once his work in Charleston was complete—the strengthening of the local defenses, which he considered vulnerable to attack

from land or sea, consumed the rest of April—Beauregard headed for Montgomery, his rail route lined by well-wishers, including a growing number of men already in some semblance of uniform. On May 5 he conferred with President Davis and Secretary Walker. Details of the meeting remain obscure, although after the war Beauregard claimed his superiors asked him to assist Brigadier General Braxton Bragg, then erecting coastal defenses at Pensacola, Florida, and planning an attack on Union-held Fort Pickens. According to Beauregard, he talked his way out of the project, apparently to the disappointment of the president. The incident may have been the first of many disagreements the two were fated to have over the next four years.[71]

Until a mutually acceptable assignment could be decided upon, Beauregard returned to Charleston to complete his buildup. Subsequent events suggested that he would not remain there long. Before month's end, Walker informed the South's first public hero that he would be sent to Mississippi to command the works under construction along the Confederacy's western exterior. Though Beauregard preferred to serve in Virginia, he accepted the assignment and delivered a long and dramatic farewell to the troops he had led to victory at Charleston. Apparently believing that morale would sag as soon as he departed, he exhorted Charlestonians of all walks of life—especially those engaged in agricultural pursuits—to actively oppose the expected Yankee invader, making "every bush and haystack . . . an ambush and every barn a fortress." He reminded his audience that "a gallant and free people, fighting for their independence and firesides, are invincible against even disciplined mercenaries."[72]

Reports of Federal forces swamping training camps from Boston to Chicago and especially around Washington, D.C., were now rampant. With a melodramatic flourish that would come to define his public persona, Beauregard referred to them as "an armed rabble, gathered together hastily on a false pretense, and for an unholy purpose." Incensed that the Union's response to Fort Sumter was being directed by a Southern-born officer under whom he had faithfully served in Mexico, Beauregard scorned Winfield Scott as a decrepit, befuddled figurehead who could not be depended on for competent leadership. The traitorous Virginian would meet the same ignominious fate as the unmilitary recruits he would lead to defeat.

His local duties at an end, Beauregard prepared to depart for distant climes. At the last minute, however, he learned that he would not be heading west after all. On May 28 new orders called him to Richmond. That city of 38,000—hardly more sanitary than Washington, although it stank not of raw sewerage but of tobacco—had been functioning as the capital of the Southern nation for barely a week. There Beauregard was to confer again with Davis as well as with the recently assigned commander of Virginia's defense forces, Major General Robert E. Lee.

He arrived in the capital on the thirtieth. His route had again been lined with hero-worshipping countrymen, and upon alighting from the train he was greeted by a throng whose exuberance stirred his spirits as never before. He spent that night in the city's foremost hotel and the following morning met with his civilian and military superiors. Beauregard had had relatively little contact with Davis since leaving Montgomery, and he had been in Lee's company infrequently since their Mexican War days. His reacquaintance with his engineering colleague was cordial enough, no doubt more so than his already growing uneasiness in Davis's company.[73]

Following the obligatory round of small talk, Davis explained that since Federal forces had invaded Virginia, Beauregard was needed there more than on the Mississippi. Along with forces from the other seceded states, hundreds of Virginians—soon to be transferred to Confederate service for the duration of the existing emergency—had taken up defensive positions along, above, and below Bull Run. At present they were commanded by Brigadier General Milledge L. Bonham of South Carolina. A lawyer and former U.S. congressman, Bonham was not a West Pointer although he boasted military experience dating to the Seminole Wars in Florida and the fighting in Mexico. Davis, however, intended that the position go to a career officer with impressive credentials and public visibility, attributes that would draw additional recruits to northern Virginia and bolster their morale; thus, he offered Beauregard the command. Perceiving the importance of the assignment, one that would only enhance his standing in his new army, the Creole accepted it. The next day, the first of June, he was again on a northbound train, headed for what he firmly believed to be an appointment with destiny.[74]

CHAPTER 2

THE FRETFUL VIRGINIAN AND THE HESITANT IRISHMAN

Joseph Eggleston Johnston hailed from the backwoods of south-western Virginia, but his youth was not spent in poverty. Born on February 3, 1807, near Farmville, at age four he moved with his parents and six brothers from central Virginia to the mountain village of Abingdon. Less than sixty miles from the Kentucky border, he grew to adolescence in a comfortable two-story home grandly styled Panecillo, which his father, a jurist of the Virginia General Court and a veteran of the Continental Army, had built for his still-growing family. An oasis of culture amid the wilderness and a magnet for the social elite of that small community—lawyers, physicians, and other professionals—Panecillo provided Peter Johnston's seventh son with a relatively privileged upbringing. As his most recent biographer has observed, Johnston "grew up amidst the contradictory influences of the Appalachian frontier and Abingdon society." Contradictory influences would define the man throughout his life and military career.[1]

Impressed by the pride his father and the other local veterans took in their Revolutionary War service, Joseph developed an early interest in things military. Like other boys in his neighborhood, as a youth he learned to ride, shoot, and hunt, and he gained a reputation as a leader among his fellows. Another biographer, Johnston's great-nephew Robert Morton Hughes, notes that in his preteens the young-ster organized his brothers and a group of friends, each "hardly less zealous than himself," into an army that he commanded. Described by all who knew him as mature and self-reliant, he easily won "that obedience which is the foundation of discipline."[2]

Joseph's readiness to join in the rough-and-tumble life brought him more than his share of scrapes and bruises. Permanent facial scars resulted from a fall out of a cherry tree. At age ten he suffered a more serious injury that could have crippled him for life. During a hunting trip with his father and brothers several miles from home, he attempted to demonstrate to a family slave how a cavalry charge should be mounted. Thrown from his uncooperative horse, Joseph suffered a compound fracture of his leg. Unable to receive immediate medical attention, he endured not only the pain of his injury but also the suffering caused by two operations without benefit of anesthesia, the second made necessary by the doctor who had improperly set the broken bones.[3]

The high-spirited boy seemed equally comfortable in the subdued atmosphere of the classroom. At the Abingdon Academy, a classical school for the scions of the area's more prominent families, he developed a love of literature that would impel him to read and learn amid military operations. His equally avid interest in things military spawned an early desire to continue his studies at the U.S. Military Academy. His father's professional prominence and social connections made this ambition a reality: in March 1825 the local congressman offered eighteen-year-old Joseph a West Point appointment. That June, although heartsick at having to leave his terminally ill mother, he began the long, tortuous journey to the Hudson River highlands.[4]

From the outset the academy tested Johnston's physical and mental capacities to the fullest. His first summer encampment, especially the long, weary hours spent on the drill field, made strenuous demands on his compact but "hardy constitution." He weathered the physical exertions, although he had a more difficult time surmounting the new set of challenges when his class moved into barracks. Johnston excelled in neither of the subjects that monopolized the academy's fourth-class year, mathematics and French. One factor may have been a form of night blindness that prevented him from staying up late to study. Eventually, however, persistent and determined application paid dividends. At the close of his first year at West Point, he ranked twenty-seventh academically out of the 105 cadets who comprised the Class of 1829.[5]

His class standing was not lowered by the acquisition of numerous demerits. Although like many cadets he grudgingly tolerated the academy's archaic honor system, Johnston was penalized only seven times during his plebe year for such prosaic crimes as failing to police his quarters to an inspector's standards and going too long without a haircut. During the remainder of his academic career, the Virginian accumulated only twenty-seven demerits, testimony to a commendable restraint and a determined conformity to regulations.

Like Cadet Beauregard, he was never known to patronize Benny Havens's Tavern. He quenched his thirst with water or buttermilk, not with Benny's signature drink, the rum-based "hot flip."[6]

Although Johnston's classmates considered him a model soldier and nicknamed him "The Colonel," he was no self-abnegating stoic. Approachable and companionable, during his plebe year he made his share of friends, including both Northern- and Southern-born cadets. He forged complex and often difficult relationships with two Southerners with or under whom he was fated to serve during long periods of his military career: Jefferson Davis of Kentucky (Class of 1828) and Robert E. Lee, a fellow Virginian in his own class. The former drew Johnston's dislike for the prominent role he took in hazing lowerclassmen and for his frequent carousing at Benny Havens's. On one occasion, when caught off bounds after a night of drink, Davis was court-martialed and threatened with dismissal. When he escaped punishment by dazzling the court with legal footwork, Johnston was outraged.[7]

Davis also incurred Johnston's displeasure when he became involved in another round of cadet debauchery, the "Egg Nog Riot" of Christmas Eve 1826, when several cadets openly shared alcoholic beverages in two rooms of the academy's North Barracks and physically assaulted staff officers who tried to curtail the merriment. Though not involved in the ruckus, Johnston was called as a witness at the subsequent court of inquiry. Davis was not one of the seventeen rioters who were punished with temporary or permanent dismissal, but Johnston seems to have made some unflattering references to him, for the two reportedly clashed in the court's aftermath. According to rumor, the two later engaged in a fistfight over their shared affection for a pretty girl whose home adjoined academy grounds. Even if this account is apocryphal, the men's association at West Point foreshadowed their friction-laden relationship of later years, which had serious repercussions for Johnston's career in arms.[8]

Contradictory emotions—admiration and jealousy—characterized Johnston's relations with Lee. Thrown into close contact with the scion of Virginia's Northern Neck, Johnston could not help but measure himself against the handsome and gifted classmate. The comparison almost always left him wanting. While Johnston struggled to remain in the top quarter of his class, Lee appeared to master every subject and conquer every classroom problem no matter

how weighty or arcane. On the drill field Lee was the envy of everyone who failed to match his soldierly bearing and tactical prowess.
While Johnston would glory in his hard-won rank of cadet lieutenant, a position he held briefly during his second-class year before losing it for reasons unknown, Lee captured the most prestigious berth
to which a cadet could aspire, that of class adjutant, with the rank of
captain. In deportment too, Lee had no peer. While Johnston would
graduate with few demerits on his record, Lee would leave the academy without acquiring a single black mark. "The Colonel" may
have won the respect of his peers, but Lee, who graduated eleven
places above his classmate from Abingdon, had acquired a more
impressive moniker, one perfectly descriptive of his character and
gifts: "The Marble Soldier."[9]

For all that, Johnston was no slouch in the lecture hall and, being
a natural equestrian, excelled at the academy's riding exercises, suggesting that his proper sphere was the mounted arm. At this time,
however, the army included no units of dragoons, mounted riflemen, or cavalry—Congress would not fund their creation until 1833,
1845, and 1855, respectively. The cadet had also shown talent at
mapmaking, but his class standing was too low to gain him a berth
in his branch of preference, the Corps of Topographical Engineers.
Upon graduating on July 1, 1829, Johnston had to settle for a commission in a less elite arm but one that appeared to offer a satisfying
career, a chance to master military technology, and an opportunity
for regular advancement: the artillery.[10]

Irish-born and Pennsylvania-bred Robert Patterson was, like Winfield Scott, an early exception to the rule that the Civil War would
be fought by young men. At seventy-five, Scott would oversee
Union operations in every theater but would do so from behind a
desk. Upon war's outbreak, Patterson—only five and a half years
younger, though reportedly possessed of a much hardier constitution—was handed field command of an army that numbered some
20,000 officers and men and that had been assigned a major, indeed
a critical, mission.

Patterson was a child of revolution and war. In 1798 his father,
known to his County Tyrone neighbors as a "man of hot temper
and rash impulse," became "seriously involved" in supporting those
forces dedicated to overthrowing British control of their homeland,
an uprising inspired by the American and French Revolutions.

Indiscreet, injudicious, and unlucky, Francis Patterson was promptly arrested, tried, found guilty of treason, and sentenced to be hanged. He avoided the gallows only because his wife's relations were loyalists of stature and influence—via their intercession, Francis's sentence was commuted and his punishment reduced to banishment. At age six Robert accompanied his parents on a sea voyage to America. For the rest of his life, he displayed a marked hostility toward anyone and anything British. Anglophobia became a legacy in the Patterson family, bequeathed from generation to generation.[11]

Upon arriving in the New World, the family settled in Ridley Township, a Philadelphia suburb, and tilled the soil. Francis, his martial and political aspirations thwarted, never recovered from his forced separation from his birthplace. He sank into despondency and drink, whereupon his wife became de-facto head of the family. Ann Patterson, "a woman of strong intellectuality," encouraged her son to absorb as much education as the county schools offered. This appears to have been the extent of the boy's formal schooling, although some sources mention a term or two at an unidentified college.

Largely through his mother's influence, at sixteen Robert ventured into the business world. In Philadelphia he took a position in the countinghouse of Edward Thompson. Later he went to work for James Engle & Company, silk, indigo, and tea merchants in the East India trade. Intelligent and ambitious, he worked his way up to chief clerk, junior partner, and eventually, head of Engle's firm. By the age of twenty he had become, in the words of one anonymous biographer, a "merchant prince." Although shrewd enough to marry his employer's only daughter, he had earned success through hard work, a carefully controlled ambition, and persistent attention to the bottom line.

Military service would become another Patterson legacy. In October 1812, four months after the United States declared war on his hated enemy, England, the young man left his firm in the hands of a senior employee and enlisted in the 2nd Regiment, Pennsylvania State Militia. His leadership ability quickly became evident; in rapid succession—as he had in the mercantile world—he rose through the enlisted ranks, gained a commission, and ascended all the way to colonel. In April 1813 he traded his militia eagles for a first lieutenancy in the 22nd U.S. Infantry, then posted to upper Canada. After participating in the expedition that captured Forts Toronto and York, he sought transfer to a staff position in another unit. His business acumen helped him become assistant quartermaster of the 32nd Infantry Regiment, stationed at Woodstock, Vermont.[12]

Two years later, following congressional approval of the Treaty of Ghent, which ended hostilities with Britain, Patterson resigned his commission and returned to his family and business interests. In his absence his firm had failed, perhaps the result of English restrictions on American overseas trade, one of the grievances that had brought on the war. He started anew, founding a grocery concern that after a slow start attracted customers as far west as Independence, Missouri, and as far south as New Orleans. An admirer notes that "his business methods were aggressive, his style fearless. . . . He possessed foresight [combined] with recklessness, cautiousness with nerve."[13]

By 1844 Patterson & Company, Wholesale Grocers, occupied the better part of a city block in midtown Philadelphia. Its growth was largely due to emerging markets in the South, whose plantation world he fed, both literally and figuratively. The wealthy entrepreneur purchased a three-story stone residence on the southwest corner of Thirteenth and Locust Streets. (Years later the modified Greek Revival mansion would become the home of the Historical Society of Pennsylvania.) Patterson's wife, Sarah, made a comfortable home of the stately residence, where the couple's surviving children—three daughters and two sons—grew to young adulthood; five siblings died in infancy.

Although he had married into Quaker stock, Patterson never shed his interest in military affairs. Two years after resigning his regular commission, he organized and took command of a militia company, the Washington Blues. Once again he rose through the ranks until commissioned colonel of Pennsylvania's 1st Militia Regiment. Six years later he was a brigadier general heading the state's First Brigade, First Division. By 1833 he was commanding the division with the rank of major general.

Patterson was proud that both of his sons, Francis Engle Patterson and Robert Emmet Patterson, shared his interest in things military. At twenty-six Frank would enlist in the regular artillery, later transferring to an infantry outfit before resigning to accept a commission in his father's division. Bob would gain an appointment to West Point, from which he would graduate in 1851 prior to joining the 6th U.S. Infantry. Their eldest sister, Mary, would extend the family tradition by marrying Brevet Major John J. Abercrombie of the 5th U.S.

Infantry, who two decades hence, by then a colonel, would serve under her father during the early months of the war for the Union.[14]

In the winter of 1838–39, Patterson, by now Pennsylvania's senior major general, gained another taste of field command during the so-called Buckshot War. The battleground encompassed the streets of the state capital, Harrisburg, where political opponents rioted over efforts to reorganize the Pennsylvania house of representatives. Arming his militiamen with shotguns, Patterson cowed the mob and restored order throughout the city. Six years later he led units of his division in suppressing a series of riots in his home city, where anti-immigrant groups ransacked and burned Catholic churches, rectories, and seminaries. Although having displayed a prudent restraint during the Harrisburg crisis, Patterson met the Philadelphia rioters with a firm hand; clashes between nativists and militiamen resulted in numerous deaths and injuries before the violence was quelled. Though most of the victims were Irish, Patterson did not allow his heritage to influence his judicious application of force, which won him favorable publicity. Yet he remained fiercely proud of his ethnic origins; in 1856 he happily accepted the presidency of the Hibernian Society of Philadelphia.[15]

After bidding farewell to his classmates, instructors, and (presumably) the unattainable girl next door, Joseph E. Johnston entered upon his duties as the junior second lieutenant of the 4th U.S. Artillery. His first active-duty station was Fort Columbus on Governors Island in upper New York Bay. Built in 1783 to guard the entrance to New York Harbor, the rather seedy installation was a relic of outmoded warfare. Even so, the seventy-acre fort was sufficiently commodious to accommodate a garrison, and as the closest major installation to West Point, it enabled Johnston to keep in touch with instructors and lowerclassmen he had known at the academy.

The fort also served as a convenient posting for recent graduates prior to their transfer to more-permanent stations. In October 1831 Johnston's unit, Company C, 4th Artillery, was shipped to Fort Monroe at the tip of the Virginia Peninsula. There military life became somewhat more demanding, though also more satisfying. While he had no bad memories of Governors Island, the native Virginian felt more comfortable at this historic post, home of the army's Artillery School of Practice. He enjoyed interacting with the local populace, who seemed much more respectful of professional soldiers than the aloof big-city Yankees among whom he had lived for two years.[16]

While at Fort Monroe, the young soldier became aware, perhaps for the first time, of the sectional rift that would bring on civil war. By 1831 the South had begun to resist the power of a national government that imposed cripplingly high tariffs on imported goods needed by Southern farmers. Virginia politicians were joining Deep South colleagues in talking openly of secession. Then too, a few months before Johnston reached Virginia, Nat Turner's Rebellion, a brief but bloody slave uprising just across Hampton Roads from Fort Monroe, struck fear in the heart of every slaveholder. As an army officer Johnston owned no slaves and probably had no thought of acquiring any. But as the scion of a family whose livelihood was based to some extent on slave labor, he would have defended the peculiar institution as an economic necessity to his region.[17]

By the spring of 1832, Johnston had grown weary of seacoast-garrison routine and longed for more active service. The opportunity came in June, when his company was added to an expedition against hostile Indians of the Northwest that would precipitate the Black Hawk War (1832). The venture got off to a promising start but was waylaid by an outbreak of cholera aboard Scott's transports as they crossed Lake Erie. Johnston was not stricken, but his unit got only as far as Fort Dearborn, Michigan Territory, where it was quarantined for several weeks.[18]

That December Johnston's company, finally having been declared free of the dreaded plague, was sent to man the forts in the harbor of Charleston, South Carolina, there to monitor local demonstrations against congressional passage of an especially draconian tariff. When the crisis calmed, Johnston and his comrades were returned to Fort Monroe, but Indian troubles in the Southwest sent them to Alabama to overawe troublesome Creeks, then to the swamps of southern Florida during the Second Seminole War (1835–42). In March 1836 the "foot artillerymen" joined a column, commanded by General Scott, that fought an indecisive battle against the warriors of Chief Osceola along the Withlacoochee River.[19]

In the aftermath of the failed campaign, Johnston's company suffered through a round of garrison duty at Fort Brooke, which guarded the settlement of Tampa, Florida. Here the lieutenant grew increasingly restive and frustrated with his career, which he saw as static and unfulfilling. Having been offered a position more in line with his native talents—a civilian appointment in the Topographical Bureau in Washington—he resigned his commission on May 31, 1837.

He spent only a few months in the nation's capital before returning to Florida as a member of a coastal-survey expedition. If he dared hope that his new assignment would provide action, adventure, and career advancement, he was not disappointed. By mid-January 1838, the one-hundred-man expedition, a mixed force of soldiers and seamen, had penetrated to the mouth of Jupiter Inlet, two hundred miles south of Saint Augustine. There the expedition's aggressive leader, Lieutenant L. M. Powell, USN, laid aside his surveying tools and launched an attack on a Seminole village on the upper edge of the Everglades.[20]

Powell may have been a man of action, but he was not one of stealth. His clumsy advance on the village alerted Osceola's people to his approach. The Seminoles struck first, inflicting casualties on soldiers, sailors, and civilians. Early in the battle a round from an Indian rifle struck Johnston on the top of his skull, stunning but not seriously injuring him. Forced into retreat, Powell's party might have been overtaken and annihilated had not Johnston stepped into a leadership void, cobbling together a rear guard that held back the pursuers until the expedition could paddle upriver to the safety of Fort Pierce. There Johnston discovered that word of his exploits had preceded him. He had gained a reputation for "coolness, courage, and judgment," one inapplicable to Lieutenant Powell.[21]

Johnston's heroics at Jupiter Inlet opened a door that returned him to active duty in his desired service branch. On July 7, 1838, he was recommissioned in the army with the rank of first lieutenant of topographical engineers. The position brought him back to Washington, though only briefly, before sending him on an eight-year tour of navigational improvement projects in such diverse venues as upstate New York and the Texas Republic. Career-enhancing assignments included plotting the border between the United States and the British provinces (1843–44) and taking part in the Atlantic Coast Survey of 1844–46. During this period Johnston was introduced to Lydia McLane, daughter of a former congressman and U.S. minister to Great Britain. It was love at first sight, and on July 10, 1845, the two were wed in a lavish ceremony in Baltimore. Although the marriage produced no children, it was a happy one throughout. A family friend would remark, "I never knew two people more devoted to each other."[22]

When the Rio Grande beckoned for U.S. military action, Robert Patterson, who had made a solid record in both the militia and the regular army, was a likely candidate for a major command. In this conflict, in which a commander's political orientation appeared to count more than his soldierly abilities, Patterson's credentials as an active Democrat recommended him to President James K. Polk's solicitude. On July 7, 1846, Polk appointed him one of two major generals to lead the volunteer forces then organizing for active service. Patterson was dispatched to upper Mexico, where he was assigned to the army of Zachary Taylor.[23]

Already, the combative Taylor had won notable victories at Palo Alto and Resaca de la Palma, feats that had earned him promotion to major general, though his Whig tendencies had led Polk to regard him as a prospective political opponent. In turn, Taylor had become distrustful of his civilian superiors, especially Secretary of War William L. Marcy. He doubted that Washington would grant him the necessary latitude to prosecute the war as he thought best. Thus he determined to thwart the administration by relegating Patterson to the command of the supply depot at Camargo, which Taylor considered a "cesspool" of rowdy volunteers, stragglers, malingerers, camp followers, and war profiteers.[24]

By early September, four months since his latest major victory, Taylor was feeling pressure from the president, the press, and the American public to descend deeper into the enemy's country. Polk had proposed negotiations toward ending the fighting through "a peace, just and honorable to both parties," but the Mexican government had deferred consideration of the offer until it received advice from a new congress, to assemble three months hence. Marcy reminded Taylor that "the progress of our arms, and the positions we may occupy" farther south would influence that body's actions: "Should the campaign be successful, and our troops be in possession of important departments of the enemy's country, the inducements for a speedy peace will be greatly strengthened."[25]

Sensitive to political currents, Taylor had already begun a march on Monterrey, 125 miles southwest of Camargo, a position he mistakenly doubted the enemy would defend. On September 11 he resumed his advance at the head of approximately 6,000 troops, half of them regulars. He left Patterson behind to hold a line of outposts between Camargo and the mouth of the Rio Grande, including the coastal city of Matamoros. On paper Patterson's command comprised more than 7,000 officers and men, mostly volunteers, but his effective strength was much less—several hundred sick and wounded crowded the hospitals at each post within his realm.

Soon after Taylor departed, Patterson was shaken by a report that 10,000 Mexicans were heading for Camargo. He sought to improve the local defenses by mounting 6-pounder cannons in the ditches surrounding the city's central plaza. Their hasty, faulty placement was a source of amusement for the few regular officers Taylor had left behind. Fortunately for the as-yet-untried commander, the enemy advance never materialized.[26]

As September ended, so did Polk's halfhearted efforts to broker a peace with Mexican strongman Mariano Parades. The War Department determined the logical next step to be a land invasion across the province of Tamaulipas, which included Tampico, Mexico's second-most-important port. Polk and Marcy decided to appoint Patterson, despite his operational inexperience, to head the invasion by way of Victoria. They ordered the commander of naval forces in the Gulf of Mexico to prepare an amphibious assault on Tampico and General Scott to draft a plan for an offensive against the coastal stronghold of Veracruz.

To support these operations, the War Department called on Taylor, who having won a dramatic but costly victory at Monterrey, was considering a southwestward movement on strategic Saltillo. Taylor believed that he would need as many men as he could muster for the expedition, but now he was ordered to reinforce Patterson with 4,000 of those already on hand. Convinced that Polk intended to deny him further successes that would support his settled resolve to run for president in 1848, Old Rough and Ready exploded. Without informing his superiors, he decided that after taking Saltillo he would join the Tampico invasion via Victoria, thus preserving Patterson's subordination to him.[27]

Taylor reached Saltillo on November 16, then turned southeast, expecting to meet Patterson at Victoria. Patterson, however, had yet to arrive; moreover, he upset the general's plans by ordering a several-hundred-man column from Matamoros to reinforce the naval forces that had occupied Tampico on November 14. In doing so he was following War Department guidance, but Taylor had not been notified of the change in plans. On November 28 he sent a courier at a "breakneck gallop" to Patterson's headquarters, conveying his strong disapproval of the Tampico mission. He also dashed off a letter to Washington, protesting his subordinate's "direct and unwarrantable interference with plans . . . for a combined movement against Victoria" and decrying Patterson's "position of quasi-independence . . . against which I have protested, and again protest." He followed his verbal assault with precipitate action born of pique. When Patterson finally reached Victoria at the head of his own division and that of "Old Davey" Twiggs, he found the city in Taylor's hands. Once Patterson continued on to Tampico, Old Rough and Ready—satisfied that he had injected himself into the operation—returned to Monterrey.[28]

Although he must have been stung by the slights Taylor had dealt him—which Polk later described as both unwarranted and "bad tempered"—Patterson showed sympathy for his superior's difficulties with Washington. He would claim that he neither sought nor desired command of the Tampico operation, one reason being that "no proper outfit[ting] could be made on the Rio Grande for such an expedition." Another reason was his reluctance to hurt Taylor's sensitive pride. Though of a different political faith, Patterson respected his old War of 1812 comrade, and he considered his instructions to reinforce Tampico without the general's prior knowledge or approval an unfair slight. Even so, the sometimes shabby treatment Taylor received from the War Department would not prevent him from going on to win the greatest victory of his career at Buena Vista.[29]

When he was sent to New Orleans late in 1846 preparatory to service in Mexico, Captain Joseph E. Johnston eagerly embraced the opportunity to join in a fight against a European-style enemy. Thus he was disappointed to have taken no part in Taylor's victories at Palo Alto, Resaca de la Palma, and Monterrey, concerned for the effect this might have on his career prospects. But the war had waited for him; when the operations in northern Mexico failed to bring about a peace conference, a second front was opened along the Gulf coast under Winfield Scott. Beginning in March 1847, Johnston accompanied this expedition, aimed at capturing Veracruz.

On the seventh of that month, he was aboard a reconnaissance ship almost sunk by shore batteries. Better gunnery would have claimed a host of high-ranking passengers, including Scott; Generals Patterson, Twiggs, and William J. Worth; and staff officers such as Johnston's fellow engineers Lee and Beauregard. The risky mission suggested to Scott the benefits of besieging Veracruz

rather than mounting the costly assault that several of his subordinates favored. Although thousands of regular and volunteer infantry conducted the siege, it succeeded largely through the efforts of
artillerymen, who pounded the city's defenses, and engineer officers such as Johnston, who located critical avenues of approach to
the garrison.[30]

In the first days of April, having occupied Veracruz, Scott led
his 12,000-man army inland to capture the seat of Santa Anna's
government. On the eighteenth his troops broke through the gorge
at Cerro Gordo, their path paved by information about the enemy's
position gathered by Johnston, Lee, Beauregard, and other engineers. On one such mission Johnston was wounded by an artillery
fragment; he spent two weeks in the hospital recuperating from the
nearly fatal injury.[31]

Not until early August, following the unsuccessful effort to
end the conflict short of further bloodshed, did Scott's offensive
resume. A recuperated Johnston accompanied the movement in an
unfamiliar capacity but one he embraced: second in command of a
regiment of *voltigeurs*—soldiers armed with rifles rather than muskets—with the temporary rank of lieutenant colonel of volunteers.
He saw action almost immediately. On the twentieth his regiment
penetrated Santa Anna's fortifications at Churubusco, which commanded the road to Mexico City. The following day Johnston led a
large detachment in driving the Mexicans inside the outer works of
the capital. Impressed by the energy, courage, and determination of
his troops, the Virginian formed a much higher opinion of volunteer
forces than most of his regular-army brethren ever displayed.[32]

When a second, briefer armistice failed to produce a capitulation, Scott on September 8 attacked and carried a series of fortifications southwest of the capital, then deployed his men to confront the
walled city itself. On the morning of the thirteenth, Johnston, leading
the left wing of his rifle outfit, braved a variety of defenses, natural and
manmade, to gain possession of the fortified castle of Chapultepec. As
he noted in his after-action report, his detachment dashed through a
breach in the works at the foot of the castle. Once on the other side, it
crossed largely open terrain "in a run, each company firing as soon as
deployed; drove the enemy from the parapet . . . into the works; and
attacked and quickly carried the two outworks on our right."[33]

From the advanced position thus secured, the castle appeared
accessible, but its approaches were commanded by infantry and

cannons on the ramparts. Johnston's men were not assigned a direct role in the subsequent storming operation; they would support other troops supplied with scaling ladders. But when those units went forward, Johnston's detachment received "a warm fire from the parapets of the east terrace and the battery at its base." Unwilling to remain immobile, the riflemen abandoned their position and followed the assaulting troops to the castle's escarpments. As they ran forward, they were showered with shells and musket balls and sustained heavy casualties. Johnston himself collected three wounds, but none severe enough to knock him out of action. It was during this operation that he supposedly placed a bet on Captain Beauregard's marksmanship. Beauregard would claim to recall the incident with absolute clarity, but Johnston remembered nothing about it.

Before ten o'clock, the Stars and Stripes waved from Chapultepec's heights. "The action being now over," Johnston reported, "the regiment was [re]united." He added, with pardonable pride, "The success of this little party in performing the service assigned to it . . . is sufficient evidence that both officers and soldiers did their duty bravely and well."[34]

Johnston's conduct did not go unrecognized. Several superiors praised his leadership of troops previously unfamiliar to him, suggesting that he had a bright future as a field officer should he wish to quit his staff position. As a result of their commendation and the praise he had received for his service at Cerro Gordo, he would win three brevets for gallantry in action. The first two made him a major and a colonel. A third brevet, for lieutenant colonel, was awarded him for leading the voltigeurs at Chapultepec. Two anomalies resulted from these honors: the second and third brevets were out of sequence, and the third was bestowed even though Johnston had been acting as a full-rank lieutenant colonel on the day he won it. Over time the confusion would have a negative effect on his standing on the army's seniority roll.[35]

On November 26 Secretary Marcy informed Zachary Taylor of a revised strategy that dealt additional blows to his self-esteem while redounding to the benefit of General Patterson. With Tampico occupied, the War Department had turned its attention to taking Veracruz, a mission that Winfield Scott would command. Although Scott, like Taylor, was a Whig, the commanding general had made himself acceptable to Polk by crafting an impressive plan for taking the strategic port, and the president was pleased that Scott had been reduced to virtually begging for the assignment.[36]

Polk had never seriously considered Taylor for the command—he regarded the general's run-ins with Marcy as proof of his "great weakness and folly"—but he had toyed with the notion of appointing Patterson. In the end he discarded the idea strictly for political reasons. Polk was actively grooming high-ranking Democrats to succeed him, but Patterson's foreign birth would disqualify him for the presidency even if he gained success and celebrity on a par with Taylor. In later years Patterson would claim that Polk had offered him command of the Veracruz expedition "and ultimately against the city of Mexico; and had even directed the different Departments of Supply to honor my requisitions, to which no limit was set." This claim is dubious because more than a few administration and War Department officials whom Polk trusted considered Patterson unequal to so important an assignment. Passing over him in favor of an officer the president neither liked nor trusted appeared to confirm these opinions. Patterson himself seems to have had doubts about his qualifications for the position. When he learned of Scott's selection ("this I did not regret"), he sounded sincerely relieved.[37]

Many of Patterson's soldiers shared the perception that he was unqualified for high command; some considered him lacking not only in military ability but also in stature and style. Observing him riding through the streets of Matamoros prior to the advance on Tampico, Lieutenant George McClellan of the engineers found him "looking for all the world like an old farmer going to market." Beneath the unimpressive aspect was a man McClellan described as easily excitable, ruled by "mingled emotions of fear, anxiety, impatience, and disgust." Volunteer officers were no kinder in their assessments of the division leader. A Mississippi captain characterized Patterson as an obsessive disciplinarian and "a great stickler for courtesy and etiquette—ready to insult and blaze out against any one who does not pursue the strict military rule." He even disparaged the merchant prince's civilian accomplishments, calling him "a salesman of pack thread and quick lime converted into a Major General of the U.S. Army in actual service."[38]

Perceived flaws notwithstanding, when the Veracruz mission got under way, Patterson accompanied Scott's expedition in the role of second in command. His original force, later augmented, comprised nine infantry regiments and a small force of cavalry from New York,

Pennsylvania, Illinois, Tennessee, Kentucky, and South Carolina. On March 9, 1847, the vanguard of Scott's 12,000-man army hit the beach below the fortified city and began siege operations. Patterson's command, which held the center of Scott's lines, made a major contribution to the investment by chasing Mexican horsemen from the heights of Malibran, which gave Scott control of the city's water supply. After the garrison capitulated on the twenty-ninth, Patterson's men fired the "national salute" during the surrender ceremony.[39]

When Scott moved on Mexico City, Patterson personally contributed to the army's fortunes. On April 11 his three brigades reached Cerro Gordo. Two days later, influenced by the arguments of Lieutenant Beauregard and other officers, Patterson left a sickbed to quash General Twiggs's plan for an assault on the position pending Scott's arrival on the scene. Instead of receiving favorable publicity for canceling a potentially suicidal charge, Patterson was criticized for failing to take part in the subsequent operations. Although prevented from doing so by a "most violent attack of fever" that laid him low on the thirteenth, he was condemned as a coward by some of his own men. A Pennsylvania volunteer asked: "Where was [sic] Gens. Patterson and [Gideon] Pillow during this heavy firing? They were not where they promised to be, nor could the three messengers sent by Col. Wyncoop [George C. Wynkoop] . . . find them."[40]

Patterson's health was slow to return, and it cost him his command; on April 9 Scott relieved him from field duty. Officially the removal was temporary, but when Patterson remained ill and fatigued a month later, Scott designated him as supernumerary with the army and assigned him to accompany to the coast and then homeward some 3,000 volunteers whose one-year enlistments were about to expire. Once back in the States, the general was to report in person to the War Department, where as soon as his health permitted, he would receive further orders.

The assignment may have suggested that Patterson was expendable, but Scott was sincerely appreciative of his services, especially for the cool head and good sense he had displayed at Cerro Gordo. Moreover, in contrast to such obstreperous subordinates as Taylor and Pillow, Patterson had always extended to his commander not only his best efforts but also his goodwill. When Patterson went to the rear he bore "the thanks of the general-in-chief, for the gallant, able, and efficient support uniformly received from the second in rank of this army." Scott's regard for his subordinate would not diminish over the next fourteen years.[41]

The volunteers' departure would leave Scott with no more than 7,000 troops of all arms with which to oppose a numerically superior enemy. He did not disparage them as quitters or cowards, noting that they had rendered "long, arduous, faithful, and gallant services" up to that point. But when leading them back to Veracruz in the first week of May, Patterson must have felt a sense of unease, for it appeared that the volunteers were quitting the war in droves at the outset of a critical operation. How could a commander plan a campaign if unable to rely on the willingness of his troops to serve? As it turned out, the defections would not fatally weaken Scott's army and prevent it from gaining a final victory, but no one could have predicted this with confidence. All Patterson knew was that volunteer soldiers would insist on their rights as civilians even when their services seemed absolutely critical to victory.

Patterson did not return to the war zone until two months after the fighting around Mexico City had ceased. On November 1 he departed Veracruz at the head of 3,400 recruits, reinforcements for Scott's army, 2,600 of whom he delivered to the rear echelon at Jalapa one week later. Although Scott at one point fretted over Patterson's apparent tardiness, he welcomed these additions who, along with others, increased his numbers to almost 16,000 men. Assigned to occupation duty, Scott's senior lieutenant closed out his wartime service behind a desk. In mid-1848 Patterson again returned to the States with the remnants of his division. On July 20, four months after the U.S. Senate ratified the treaty that terminated the conflict, he was honorably discharged.[42]

With Mexico City occupied, the war was also over for J. E. Johnston in most respects, although semi-active operations dragged on for several months while a peace was hammered out and approved by the warring governments. Dull routine was the result, the only major change in Johnston's status being his return to the topographical engineers at the full rank of captain upon the disbanding of the voltigeur regiment in August 1848. A few months later, after a round of desultory service including the escort of supplies and reinforcements from northern Mexico to Scott's headquarters, the brevet colonel received long-awaited orders to decamp for Texas.

His homecoming marked the start of a series of rewarding events, the first and foremost being his reunion with Lydia. Late in 1848 Johnston was named chief topographical engineer of the Department of Texas, in which capacity he explored military roads and proposed railroad routes. The duty proved so interesting that he briefly considered resigning his commission to accept a management position in a railroad company. In 1853 he returned to supervising river- and harbor-navigation projects on stretches of the Mississippi. The arduous nature of this work and his near-constant exposure to harsh weather caused health problems that induced Johnston to lay aside his engineering duties and make himself available for a position in a line regiment. In March 1855 his demonstrated ability as a combat leader in Florida and Mexico gained him a plum position: second in command of the recently organized 1st U.S. Cavalry.[43]

Johnston's initial assignment with his new outfit was at regimental headquarters on the Kansas prairie. Lydia joined him at Fort Leavenworth; her comforting presence helped him endure the long duty hours, which involved not only mounted service—in the main, keeping Free State and Slave State settlers from killing each other as well as innocent bystanders—but also the surveying of Kansas's southern boundary in anticipation of the territory's application for statehood. Repressing his native sympathies, he maintained a strict neutrality throughout the border wars as well as a studied aloofness from local politics that helped his regiment avoid being caught in a sectional crossfire.[44]

Under the weight of operational command, Johnston's once-lighthearted personality underwent a noticeable change. He began to display a penchant for severe discipline that gained him a reputation as a martinet. He developed an almost avuncular attitude toward his enlisted men, especially the younger recruits, but his relations with subordinates and colleagues were sometimes less cordial. Especially when interacting with officers he found lacking for one reason or another, he could be impatient, dismissive, and even condescending. Conversely, he displayed a lofty regard for his own abilities as an engineer and a tactical officer. He considered few others, no matter how high their rank, his equals, and almost none his superior.

Johnston's persona was multifaceted; most of his associates glimpsed a single side of it. One described him as possessing not only "intellectual power and cultivation" but also "a flashing, sunny smile, which betrayed . . . a genial nature & a ready appreciation of humor." Others perceived a darker side; they spoke of his inherent moodiness and hair-trigger temper. A future subordinate would write that although capable of charm and courtesy, Johnston was also "critical, controversial, and sometimes irritable by nature." Major John Cheves Haskell, who served on Johnston's staff early in the Civil War, described this volatile temperament: "His handsome face . . . could light up as brilliantly and look as kindly as it seemed possible for a face to look, yet it could change as suddenly to as stern and menacing [an] expression as any face ever could."[45]

Johnston's frontier service ended temporarily in the fall of 1857 when he was called east to serve on a panel to systematize cavalry equipment and ordnance. Lydia went with him and stayed in the capital after the study group was dissolved. The following spring her husband returned to Fort Leavenworth to inspect a column bound for the Utah Territory, where Colonel Albert Sidney Johnston (no kin to Joseph) was attempting to suppress rebellious Mormons. The disagreeable shuttling resumed in September 1858 when Johnston was returned to the nation's capital on detached service. The assignment provided a much-anticipated reunion with Lydia and other relations, including a prominent in-law, John B. Floyd, President James Buchanan's secretary of war.[46]

Weary of long-distance postings and increasingly conscious of the war clouds hovering over the nation, Johnston desired a permanent position, preferably a high-ranking staff assignment in the War Department. In such a post he could make careful decisions about what to do and when to do it should a shooting war commence. In June 1860 he spoke to Floyd of his desire to succeed the recently deceased Thomas B. Jesup as quartermaster general of the army, a promotion that would help quench Johnston's burning desire for career advancement. This was not the first time he had sought his relative's support; three years earlier Floyd had overturned the decision of two predecessors, one of them Jefferson Davis, that Johnston was not entitled to his post-Chapultepec brevet of colonel. Now he again went to bat for Johnston, ramming through the appointment despite the high qualifications of other candidates such as R. E. Lee and in defiance of widespread charges of nepotism from more-senior applicants. All protests proved unavailing; for the next ten months, Johnston would serve as the army's procurement, supply, and transportation chief.[47]

As he had in 1815, once back in postwar America, Patterson reimmersed himself in his business affairs, which had suffered during his long absence. With profits from local operations in sharp decline, he reestablished connections with the Southern plantation market that had made him a handsome profit years earlier. He purchased interests in cotton plantations in the Deep South and gained a firm foothold in the sugar-refining industry. His investments soared even during the Panic of 1857, when several partners were forced to sell him their shares, giving him control of thirty cotton mills in the Philadelphia suburbs. By the early 1860s Patterson owned factories and warehouses throughout the city, which he managed from an imposing office building at Second and Chestnut Streets. Snatching time from his business commitments, he promoted railroad and steamship commerce throughout the middle Atlantic states, served a term as Pennsylvania's commissioner of internal improvements, was a trustee of Lafayette College in Easton, and was twice a Democratic presidential elector.[48]

As always, he devoted time to military affairs. The militia unit he had founded in 1817 continued to hold regular musters; over time it expanded to two companies of infantry. He oversaw its administration as often as the demands of business permitted. One of his subordinates was his eldest son, who shared his father's military aspirations. During the fighting in Mexico, Frank Patterson had served as a subaltern in the 1st U.S. Artillery, and he had remained in the regular service until 1857. At the outbreak of the Civil War, he would organize and lead a ninety-day militia outfit of his own.[49]

When war loomed in the spring of 1861, Robert Patterson, though white-haired and a bit more rotund than he had been in Mexico, considered himself vigorous enough to shoulder a field command in active campaigning. Even before the Fort Sumter crisis reached its climax, he sought from Governor Curtin a position of rank and authority commensurate with his record of service in two wars. Like many another state official, Curtin was then embroiled in the myriad tasks of reorganizing, enlarging, and strengthening a militia system that had been allowed to wither and nearly die. An energetic, get-things-done executive, he anticipated a call for volunteers well in advance of Lincoln's May 3 proclamation that fixed Pennsylvania's quota at sixteen regiments of infantry. Curtin speedily drafted "An Act for the Better Organization of the Militia of This

Commonwealth" and guided the resulting bill through the legislature, which passed it on the day Beauregard began to pound Sumter.[50]

The measure not only rejuvenated the existing organization but also provided for the appointment of six general officers of Pennsylvania volunteers: two would be major generals, the others brigadiers. On April 19 Curtin, after careful consideration of the material at his disposal, selected four civilians with Mexican War experience for promotion. He conferred two-star rank on Patterson as well as on William High Keim, a native of Reading, a former student at the Mount Airy Military Academy, and a prominent figure in the state militia. Patterson was named senior general, Keim his ranking subordinate. Brigadier generalships went to four militia officers, the senior member of this group being fifty-five-year-old George Cadwalader, a Philadelphia lawyer who had been Patterson's right-hand man during the nativist riots of 1844 before leading a brigade of volunteers in Mexico. The other brigadiers were James Scott Negley of Pittsburgh, who had risen from private in the 1st Pennsylvania Volunteers to division commander of the organized militia; George C. Wynkoop, former commander of Negley's outfit (the officer who supposedly failed to locate Patterson during the fighting at Cerro Gordo); and Edward C. Williams of Dauphin County, who had served capably at Veracruz and with great gallantry in the assault on Chapultepec.[51]

Over the next three months—until the Federal government withdrew from state officials the power to appoint general officers of volunteers—these six men would outrank officers of many years' service in the regular establishment. Another early war anomaly granted Patterson additional seniority. Three days after being commissioned by Curtin, Patterson—evidently at the behest of his old superior Scott—had his rank transferred to the Federal service for a period of three months. This unusual arrangement reflected Scott's regard for Patterson's abilities and his confidence that now, as in Mexico, the Pennsylvanian would salute and obey orders without question or quibble, behavior the commanding general considered indispensable in a senior subordinate.[52]

Although he enjoyed the status of his new position almost as much as the promotion to star rank, Quartermaster General Johnston found staff work less satisfying than he had anticipated. He did not welcome the paperwork piled daily on his desk, the archaic and complex bureaucracy he had to contend with, or the constant need to placate his military and civilian superiors. He stayed on the job mainly for the financial security it brought him and Lydia and because it provided a sense of stability in uncertain times.[53]

Once Lincoln won the presidential contest of 1860, civil war was no longer a dire prospect but a tragic inevitability. Over the next five months, as the states of the Deep South prepared to leave the Union and arm themselves for conflict, Johnston may have regretted his inability to supply them with the resources they would need to oppose the forces of the Federal government. But while he had too much integrity to misdirect arms and supplies bound for Northern arsenals, his in-law succumbed to the temptation. Within weeks of resigning his cabinet post to accept a Confederate military appointment, John Floyd would be widely accused of stocking Southern depots in anticipation of an outbreak of hostilities, a treasonable act and a capital offense.[54]

To the end, Johnston clung to the hope that war could be avoided, as it had for decades, through conciliation and accommodation. He had expressed regret and also a certain amount of bemusement when South Carolina left the Union, but when early in the new year six other states opted to secede, he decided that the addition of Virginia to the Confederacy was a matter of time. He resolved that as soon as his state seceded, he would go with it. Like many another Southern-born officer, Johnston felt cruelly torn by his allegiance to the army that had molded and nurtured him and by his inherent, reflexive loyalty to the state and region from which he had sprung. He had no illusions about the problems his native region faced in the fighting ahead. He fully appreciated the Herculean task involved in creating a nation virtually overnight and in recruiting, organizing, clothing, equipping, arming, and training a force for self-defense, one that would confront a strong, modern army with an established infrastructure and sustained by a region abounding in material resources.

He feared that the Confederacy's obstacles would mount due to the limited capacity of those entrusted with managing its government. Johnston did not trust the ability of many Confederate officials, especially Jefferson Davis. Nor could he believe that Davis, when conferring position, rank, and authority, would treat him fairly. He feared that the chief executive harbored ill will toward him dating from their West Point encounters. Then too, while secretary of war, Davis had blocked Johnston's brevet promotion, and as a U.S. senator he had opposed Johnston's selection as quartermaster general. Lydia, an astute observer of the political scene in Montgomery, warned, "he will ruin you."[55]

Lydia Johnston served as unofficial spokesperson for her husband's ambitions and inclinations. When it became clear what direction Virginia's secession convention would take, General Scott began to fear that the army was going to lose the services of one of its few general officers. At a social gathering in Washington, he begged Lydia to advise her husband to stand by the Union. According to one observer, Scott pledged that he would not assign Johnston a command that would pit him against his Virginia friends and relations. Her reply was succinct and firm: "My husband cannot stay in an army which is about to invade his native country."[56]

She knew whereof she spoke. On April 22, five days after Virginia voted to leave the Union pending public ratification, Johnston resigned his commission in the army of the United States. His action came two days after Colonel Lee had done the same. The time difference, while slight, proved to be a foreshadowing of later events, for Johnston would never quite catch up to the head start Lee had on him in terms of gaining seniority, fame, and the affection of the Southern public.[57]

Its first effect was that Lee beat Johnston to Richmond. The Marble Soldier reached the city, not yet the seat of the Confederate government, on April 24 to accept Governor Letcher's offer to command Virginia's military forces with the rank of major general. The following day, upon Johnston's arrival at the Richmond, Fredericksburg & Potomac depot, Lee warmly greeted his West Point classmate and Mexican War colleague. His goodwill was genuine. When, after settling Lydia in rented quarters, Johnston had a face-to-face with the governor, he learned that Lee had recommended him for a position of authority. Secretary of War Walker had already offered him a brigadier general's appointment in the army of the Southern nation, but Johnston, perhaps wary of casting his lot with an embryonic command, had withheld acceptance. He felt more comfortable taking a position in the defense forces of his state; thus, when Letcher proposed making him a major general to command those units assembling in and around Richmond, Johnston readily accepted. The assignment would place him under Lee, but it promised high rank and visibility, and he was gratified that the governor was offering him higher rank than Walker had. His elation must have taken a hit a few days later when every major general in the state except Lee was reduced to brigadier by act of the secession convention, which was now charged with putting Virginia on a war footing. Johnston may have suspected, however, that the increasing influx of troops assigned to him would result in the restoration of the rank he had accepted.[58]

In mid-May—having barely begun his duties in Richmond and lacking a full staff or a working knowledge of his subordinates—Johnston was called to Montgomery for an interview with Davis. Although the president was known for his imperious disposition, prickly temper, and willingness to go to great lengths to settle old scores, the meeting proved to be as cordial as Johnston's talk with Letcher, and more rewarding. While Davis did not immediately offer him a command, the president and his war secretary hinted that Johnston would be tendered high rank as soon as the military-affairs committee of the Confederate Congress cleared certain administrative hurdles. He was especially pleased to learn that one pending measure would provide for the appointment of full-rank general officers (four-star generals of a later era). Another legislative proposal called for an equitable transfer of rank in the case of officers who had resigned from the U.S. Army to join the Confederate forces. A draft of the legislation read: "The commissions issued shall bear one and the same date, so that the relative rank of officers of each grade shall be determined by their former commissions in the U.S. Army." Under these circumstances, Johnston fully expected to be named the senior officer in Confederate service.[59]

Field command came soon after Johnston's return to Richmond. On May 15 Confederate adjutant and inspector general Samuel Cooper ordered him to vacate his desk job and travel to Harpers Ferry. The assignment both gratified and concerned Johnston. It adhered to the preference he had made known to Davis, that he serve within the boundaries of his native state but not in its northern reaches. Even so, he seems to have accepted the posting with reluctance. Perhaps he was disappointed at being relegated to a comparatively remote sector defended by a relatively small garrison. Or perhaps he foresaw the difficulties and handicaps he would have to deal with in the Valley. Reports had a large Union force, with designs on Harpers Ferry, gathering in neighboring Pennsylvania and Maryland. Other reports suggested that the troops he would command were decidedly raw and inadequate to the task of guarding the gateway to what would become known as the "Breadbasket of the Confederacy." If the Valley could not be defended by the resources at Johnston's disposal, his first command in this new war might also be his last.

Patterson barely had time to disengage from his business interests when he learned that Scott had appointed him commander of the Department of Washington, an administrative domain that included not only the District of Columbia but also the entire states of Pennsylvania, Delaware, and Maryland, with headquarters, conveniently enough, in Philadelphia. The position promised its share of headaches. The Keystone State was so vast that Patterson would have to direct affairs at a multitude of installations, depots, and recruiting rendezvous. Delaware effectively was a border state; though generally supportive of the Union cause, its population included enough Southern sympathizers to keep provost marshals on their toes. And Maryland, especially riot-plagued Baltimore, was home to so many avowed secessionists that it would have to be ruled with an iron hand.[60]

On the day he received his appointment from Curtin, Patterson established his headquarters at Fifteenth and Chestnut in Philadelphia's Colonnade Row. Patterson and his principal aides occupied the ground floor of the spacious three-story building. His personal staff would remain small and makeshift for some time, but on the twenty-eighth it added a highly capable administrator when Brevet Major Fitz John Porter reported for duty as Patterson's adjutant general. The thirty-eight-year-old New Englander, a leading light of the West Point class of 1845, had just completed a stint in the War Department, where his intellect and capacity for hard work had caught the attention of Winfield Scott. Believing that Porter's abilities were more suited to field duty, the commanding general had sent him to Harrisburg to muster in and instruct volunteers before expressly directing his attachment to Patterson's staff. Porter would become one of the most influential and controversial members of Patterson's military family—on the one hand an indispensable source of support and advice, and on the other an agenda-driven manipulator whose ability to bend his superior to his own point of view would do great harm to Patterson's reputation.[61]

Every branch of departmental headquarters was kept furiously busy from the outset, but its supply bureau, which occupied the floor above Patterson's office, experienced by far the greatest difficulties.

The quartermasters issued multiple requisitions for resources housed at various Federal arsenals and supply depots, including the Frankford Arsenal outside Philadelphia, only to have their requests pigeonholed or superseded by competing demands from the War Department. During the first weeks of Patterson's tenure, almost every unit under his command wanted for adequate clothing, equipment, and weapons. A veteran of fifty years in the mercantile trade, he knew the importance of shipping without delay, conforming precisely to the bill of lading, and keeping the customer happy. Thus he was appalled as well as angered and frustrated by the inefficiencies in the Federal supply system.[62]

Even as he strove to surmount these obstacles, Patterson struggled to execute his orders from Scott. One of his earliest missions was to reestablish road, rail, and telegraph connection between Washington and points north. Many of these links had been broken by saboteurs who destroyed foot and rail bridges and railroad track outside Baltimore. At this stage of the conflict, the most reliable northern route to Washington was via the Potomac and then up the coast or by steamboat from the Susquehanna River near Harrisburg to Annapolis, Maryland. The only practical rail line ran from Harrisburg to the Relay House, eight miles below Baltimore and twenty-five above Washington, where the Baltimore & Ohio Railroad (B&O) branched, one line running down to the capital via Annapolis Junction, the other leading west to Frederick and Harpers Ferry.

None of these routes seemed capable of transporting efficiently the number of soldiers that Scott considered necessary to secure the seat of government. The commanding general estimated that 6,000 to 8,000 troops were required to open and hold the land lines between Harrisburg and Washington. He assured Patterson that if not enough Pennsylvania troops were available for this task, "the deficiency shall be supplied from the New Jersey and New York quotas."[63]

After conferring by telegraph with Governor Curtin, Patterson devised what appeared to be a viable solution. The plan was delivered to Washington by a civilian member of his staff, Ohio senator John Sherman, brother of future colonel William Tecumseh Sherman of the 13th U.S. Infantry. Patterson's plan called for troops coming to Washington from the north and west to proceed to Philadelphia and thence south by train to Havre de Grace, Maryland, at the head of Chesapeake Bay. From here the men could be ferried down the bay to Annapolis, bypassing Baltimore, prior to marching overland to the capital. This route Patterson believed could be secured "without great difficulty, as there are no bridges, and a few small war steamers can keep the Susquehanna and Chesapeake clear, and, if need be, aid Fort McHenry and threaten Baltimore."[64]

This idea appeared so promising that Scott approved it almost at once. Within days, Patterson began sending to Washington the volunteer units that had reached Philadelphia from points north. It was Patterson who dispatched Benjamin F. Butler, with a single regiment of Massachusetts infantry and six artillery pieces, to secure Annapolis and the rail junction at Relay House, missions accomplished on April 20 and May 5. The route thus opened to Washington, although a roundabout one, ensured the capital's security. On April 25 the celebrated 7th New York Militia trooped into Washington from Annapolis Junction, dispelling the fears of government officials and unionist citizens that a foreign flag would soon wave over the city. Two days later the Frontier Guards, the capital's first defense force, disbanded, its mission accomplished.[65]

With a "well-protected line of communication with Washington" in place, Patterson turned to securing Baltimore "and compelling the turbulent spirits of that city to submit to lawful authority." In his postwar memoirs he gives the impression that he quickly moved on Baltimore and personally overawed its secession sympathizers. In fact, although importuned by Scott to advance as soon as possible, Patterson delayed his march for three weeks, frustrating not only the War Department but also commanders already in Maryland, including Butler. One result was that he never received credit for removing the main obstacle to the efficient transportation of troops from the loyal states to Washington.[66]

One possible reason for Patterson's delay in taking the field was that before April was over, his department was reorganized. On the twenty-seventh, command of the Department of Washington was transferred to General Mansfield, with headquarters in the capital. On that date Patterson's post became known as the Department of Pennsylvania. His sphere of authority now embraced his home state, all of Delaware, and that part of Maryland not included in Mansfield's domain or Butler's newly constituted Department of Annapolis. But an administrative shakeup was not the principal factor in Patterson's immobility. Although by May 1 he reported no fewer than twenty-five regiments of Pennsylvania volunteers at his disposal (Governor Curtin having accepted thousands of enlistees above his assigned quota), the troops were spread across the eastern half of the state, encamped at Philadelphia and the suburb of West Chester as well as at Harrisburg, York, Chambersburg, and Lancaster. Before month's end three of the regiments would be ordered to Maryland for service at Woodbury, Havre de Grace, and Elkton-Perryville, and a Delaware outfit that had been attached to the department would still be in camp at Wilmington. The raw recruits, Patterson informed Washington, had enlisted for ninety days, barely long enough to absorb basic training. Moreover, they lacked essential supplies: "The troops are not fully armed, and are very incompletely equipped, having but few cartridge boxes, no canteens, tents, or cooking utensils."[67]

Patterson hoped to move without further delay to Baltimore "with an effective force of six thousand men via York and six thousand via Havre de Grace, and have sufficient [numbers] to guard the road as they advance." Yet by early May he was still at Fifteenth and Chestnut, complaining that recent deliveries of rifles and ammunition were insufficient to ready his command for the field. He described both officers and men as "anxious to move, but the former see and feel the responsibility, and know they should not move in their present condition." His growing belief that he had been assigned a nigh-impossible task was echoed by Major Porter, who early in May informed his West Point comrade George McClellan that Patterson's burdens were many and onerous, especially the task of "getting volunteers ready for duty under the most annoying circumstances. Equipping & fitting them out with nothing in store or likely to be, and pushed by the government to send on regiments quickly—but not till fully equipped."[68]

By now Patterson, with Porter's support, had succeeded in forming two columns supposedly ready to make the movement south. One, under General Cadwalader, would embark from Philadelphia; the other would proceed from York under General Keim. But those vexing supply deficiencies, added to a scarcity of transportation, kept both forces on hold. Patterson promised Washington that he would move no later than the second week in May, but that period passed with no outward sign of forward progress.[69]

Although he had not been substantially reinforced, Patterson's fellow departmental commander Butler experienced no such restrictions on mobility. At sundown, May 13, the Massachusetts general, having been assured by Scott that Baltimore lay within his sphere, led a detachment into the city by rail. His movements masked by a heavy rain, Butler occupied portions of the city and placed guns on its higher elevations. Proclaiming martial law throughout Baltimore, he used every measure at his disposal to quell the resulting outrage of the secessionist element. The invasion would seriously hamper the enemy's ability not only to isolate Washington but also to facilitate passage of recruits from Maryland and Delaware to Confederate positions in Virginia. In coming months Union troops would establish garrisons, camps, and picket posts throughout the Old Line State, whose legislature would never declare for secession.[70]

Repressing his misgivings, Johnston bade Lydia farewell and entrained for the Valley. In the early afternoon of May 23, he reached the small garrison at the confluence of the Potomac and Shenandoah Rivers and assumed command. In so doing he relieved Colonel Thomas J. Jackson, who had been trying since the first of the month to turn a gaggle of armed citizens into something resembling a military organization. Jackson had worked long and hard at this thankless duty, but from the moment he alighted from the cars, Johnston the perfectionist and faultfinder perceived his predecessor's efforts to be inadequate. Given the importance of the post, which was not only a corridor to western Virginia but also a likely avenue of enemy invasion, he was appalled to find only 5,200 troops on hand, few of whom displayed soldierly attributes. A small number had received some training in the militia, but it was obvious that their transition to wartime service had been imperfect. Even so, they appeared a cut above the majority of the volunteers, who lacked the slightest knowledge of military regulations and customs as well as, in many cases, serviceable weapons and equipment. When an officer of the 2nd Virginia introduced himself to the new commander and made bold to suggest that his motley looking outfit was ready for war, Johnston sniffed: "I would not give a company of regulars for the whole regiment."[71]

Although Jackson had been on the job for only two weeks and was not a miracle worker, Johnston may have blamed him for the unpreparedness of the troops as well as the condition of the local defensive works, which he considered poorly located and imperfectly constructed. If so, the prideful Jackson may have taken offense, especially if the general conveyed his opinions in the condescending tones of which he was capable. Because the local troops had yet to be sworn into Confederate service, Jackson refused to relinquish command of the garrison until ordered to do so by Richmond. The standoff ended quickly enough when the colonel was shown correspondence from Lee addressing Johnston as the local commander, but the confrontation may have ruffled feathers needlessly.[72]

Jackson, since his days as an instructor at the Virginia Military Institute in nearby Lexington, was used to being underrated, but he knew his value and understood his business. Born in western Virginia in January 1824, a graduate of the West Point class of 1846, and the recipient of two brevets for gallantry in Mexico, he had left the army in 1852 to teach on the state level. Even those students who had derided his many eccentricities and christened him "Tom Fool" respected his scholarly acumen and deep religious faith.

Jackson had carried his idiosyncrasies into Confederate service. Strange mannerisms and behavioral quirks would prompt at least one subordinate to declare him as crazy as a March hare. Beset by intestinal ailments, he avoided pepper because he believed it caused his leg to ache. He craved milk, cornbread, raspberries, and other fruits; he was rarely without a stash of lemons on his person and sucked on them perpetually. He ate standing up, believing that only when upright were his organs in peak working order. He would not read at night—artificial light could lead to blindness. He dosed himself with medicines to relieve recurrent inflammation of the ears and nose, and he fought dyspepsia through hydropathy, wrapping himself in wet sheets before going to sleep. A fervent Presbyterian, he led the choir at every church service, never missed morning and evening prayers, attributed military success to divine providence, and agonized over having to fight on Sunday.

Habitually clad in the sun-bleached blue coat and yellowish cap he had worn at VMI, outwardly Jackson was anything but a model soldier. To some he was awkwardness personified. His future staff officer Henry Kyd Douglas claimed that "from riding a horse to handling a pen, [he was] the most ungraceful man in the army." Only in battle would he rise above physical and emotional peculiarities to achieve greatness through a dazzling display of valor, tenacity, tactical ability, and an unwavering commitment to victory. Seemingly composed of equal parts stolidity and excitability, he was described by Richmond editor John W. Daniel as "Bessemer steel and electricity combined."[73]

From his experience with the voltigeurs, Johnston understood that volunteers, if properly instructed and disciplined, could make good soldiers and capable fighters. As soon as officially in command, he instituted an intensive program of drill and a concerted effort to standardize the troops' uniforms, equipment, and weaponry. In these efforts he was assisted by a number of highly capable subordinates, not only Jackson but also Colonels Edmund Kirby Smith and Ambrose P. Hill of the infantry, Lieutenant Colonel James E. B. Stuart and Captain Turner Ashby of the cavalry, and Colonel William N. Pendleton, the former Episcopal rector of Grace Church in Lexington, who commanded the garrison's most formidable gunnery unit, the Rockbridge Artillery.[74]

In the weeks following his arrival, even as his command grew (it neared 8,000 men by late June) and assimilated the basics of soldiering, Johnston became increasingly uneasy about his situation. Harpers Ferry was dwarfed by mountains on almost every side—Maryland Heights on the northeast, Loudoun Heights on the south and east, and Bolivar Heights to the west—requiring him to post substantial numbers of defenders on both the Virginia and Maryland sides of the Potomac. It was common knowledge that enemy troops with designs on the position were assembling not far to the north and east. Johnston could visualize foot soldiers and cannons topping the hills that surrounded him and compelling the garrison's surrender before it could mobilize.

He lost no time communicating his fears to his superiors. Two days after assuming command, he was telegraphing Richmond that his position was "untenable by us at present against a strong enemy." By early June his fears had heightened; he was sure that Harpers Ferry was a deathtrap. The town should be abandoned and the troops transferred thirty miles southwest to Winchester, which Johnston considered a more strategic position—the focal point of nine major highways, several of them macadamized—and much more defensible.[75]

His concerns, however forcefully expressed, failed to find a sympathetic audience. Neither Davis nor Lee wished to hand over to the enemy a major outpost as if on a platter. They agreed that unless Johnston was opposed by unassailable forces, he should hold his ground, if only to avoid revealing a strategic weakness. Their view mirrored that of Colonel Jackson, who urged that the town be held "with the spirit which actuated the defenders of

Thermopylae." He was convinced that abandoning Harpers Ferry would "result in the loss of the northwestern part of the state, and who can estimate the moral power thus gained to the enemy and lost to ourselves?"[76]

For some time Johnston wrestled with the dilemma posed by the risks inherent in remaining at Harpers Ferry and his fear that its evacuation would cause him to lose face. Indecisiveness had become one of his most conspicuous traits. Observers faulted his reluctance to make fateful decisions and accept responsibility for actions that might have undesirable consequences. As an old friend of Johnston's put it, "never in his life could he make up his mind that everything was exactly right, that the time to act had come. There was always something to fit that did not fit." The man illustrated his point by recounting a prewar hunting expedition with Johnston and Wade Hampton III, a wealthy planter from South Carolina who would become a Confederate officer of renown. During the outing Johnston, although a "capital shot, better than Wade or I," proved himself an abject failure as a sportsman. "The bird flew too high or too low—the dogs were too far or too near—things never did suit [him] exactly. He was too fussy, too hard to please, too cautious, too much afraid to miss and risk his fine reputation for a crack shot. . . . [He] did not shoot at all. The exactly right time and place never came."[77]

For Joe Johnston, Harpers Ferry in June 1861 was neither the place nor the time to begin a war for the defense of the Old Dominion. His challenge was to convince his superiors of the fact without making himself look frantic or fainthearted. His career in Confederate service had only begun, and he wished to do nothing to damage it. At the same time, everywhere he looked he saw those towering mountains, and he felt naked and vulnerable.

With Baltimore apparently pacified, Patterson focused on the next mission on his plate, the capture of Johnston's enclave in the lower Shenandoah. On May 24 Scott ordered his old subordinate to stop sending troops to Baltimore and Washington and push into Maryland, occupying Frederick, Hagerstown, and Cumberland in order "to threaten Harper's Ferry and support the Union sentiment in Western Virginia." To that end Patterson ordered the occupants of his elongated cordon of training camps to converge on Chambersburg, forty to fifty miles from Harpers Ferry. By late May the troops congregating in that South Mountain village under General Keim comprised ten infantry regiments (four of them "not accoutered") and five companies of cavalry.

Patterson doubted these would be sufficient to overawe Johnston's garrison, and so he petitioned the War Department for more troops, preferably not short timers. Governor Curtin, with his surfeit of volunteers, appeared willing to help, but on May 30 John Sherman, whom Patterson had sent to Washington, informed the general that Secretary Cameron had declined to accept for Federal service troops over and above the number that met the state's initial quota. Cameron admitted that three-year volunteers would be needed to suppress the rebellion, but "the question of their acceptance for the war cannot be decided until near the expiration of their present enlistment"—that is, until late July or the first days of August. Patterson would have to make do with his present force, still the largest at the disposal of any Union commander in this early stage of the conflict.[78]

On June 2 the commander of the Army of Pennsylvania finally bowed to the growing pressure to act. That day he left Philadelphia on a westbound train. At Chambersburg he superseded General Keim; greeted his son Frank, now the proud colonel of the 17th Pennsylvania Volunteers; and began to acquaint himself with regimental officers whom he knew very little if at all. Finding most of the regiments ready for the march, he prepared to "carry out a plan previously submitted to and approved by General Scott, to attack and capture or disperse the enemy at Harper's Ferry." That operation would entail a crossing of the Potomac at Williamsport, Maryland, followed by a two-column advance downriver to seize Shepherdstown, Virginia, and cut the railroad between Harpers Ferry and Winchester. These moves would isolate Johnston's garrison and force the town's evacuation. Patterson then planned to move against equally strategic Winchester, to which Johnston would probably retire once gouged out of his present position.[79]

After fretting and fuming over Patterson's many delays in taking the field, Scott on June 4 ordered him to postpone leaving Chambersburg until he could add to his force several units of regular infantry and artillery being sent from Washington. One of the batteries, F of the 4th Artillery, was only then being mounted, a process to be completed at Carlisle Barracks, thirty miles north of Chambersburg. This task would consume a few days, but Scott considered this addition to Patterson's force "indispensable." He also intimated that two regiments of Ohio volunteers would be added to the command.[80]

Patterson was still at Chambersburg, awaiting the promised additions, on June 8 when Scott sent him a long letter of instructions, a follow up to his approval of the plan of action against Harpers Ferry. Scott considered Patterson's strategy, to which Major Porter and other members of the staff had contributed, "an important step in the war." He warned, however, that "there must be no reverse" lest Union morale, still fragile at this period, be irreparably damaged. To ensure success, he also announced the imminent transfer to Patterson of yet another volunteer infantry regiment, the 1st Rhode Island of Colonel Ambrose E. Burnside, "about 1,200 strong," and an attached battery of light artillery.

Patterson, of course, welcomed the additions, especially the regulars, though the infantry component comprised a single battalion of the 3rd Infantry. He was made wary, however, by Scott's admonition that "we must sustain no reverse; but this is not enough: a check or drawn battle would be a victory for the enemy, filling his heart with joy, his ranks with men, and his magazines with voluntary contributions." Here was the first of a series of War Department arrests on the movements of a field commander who had already demonstrated a reluctance to act boldly and decisively.[81]

When Patterson, his reinforcements having arrived, began his march toward the Potomac on the morning of June 10 pursuant to specific orders from Scott, he did so with extreme caution, fearful of making a misstep, determined to err on the side of caution. The upshot was a most tentative start to the first Union offensive of the war—but at least that movement was under way.

CHAPTER 3

AWAITING THE INVADER

Bull Run, a tributary of the Potomac River, courses for almost forty miles through Virginia's Loudoun, Fairfax, and Prince William Counties. Rising from a spring in the foothills of the Blue Ridge about fourteen miles northwest of Manassas Junction, the stream flows generally southeastward through deeps and shallows to meet the Broad and Cedar Rivers. Joining with them to form the Occoquan River, it empties into the Potomac some forty miles south of Alexandria. Narrow and crooked for most of its length but at places wide and deep enough to resemble a river, its banks are steep, alternately rocky and marshy, and for long stretches it is flanked by heavy forest. The combination of sharply cut, brushy banks and the several shallow points at which it could be easily crossed made Bull Run, in the spring of 1861, a natural point of concentration for the defenders of northern Virginia.[1]

In 1861 the stream was a key feature of the local geography. The major roads leading south from Washington and Alexandria converged at the village of Centreville, then ran directly south, part of the way along a rather steep ridgeline, to Bull Run, a distance of about four miles. The intervening country was thinly populated, the poor soil of the area hampering productive farming. The principal road from Centreville crossed the run at Mitchell's Ford, on the south flank of the nearly eight-mile stretch of ground over which the first major land battle of the Civil War would be fought. On either side of Mitchell's Ford, other shallow stretches, most of them named for the owners of adjoining property, facilitated a crossing of the run. From southeast to northwest, the principal sites were Union Mills Ford (near where the Orange & Alexandria Railroad crossed the stream on a high trestle), McLean's Ford, Blackburn's Ford, Mitchell's Ford, Ball's Ford, and Lewis Ford. The distances between them averaged from nearly a mile to a mile and a half, though Ball's and Lewis Fords were less than half a mile apart.[2]

Still other crossings dotted the stream—Island Ford, Gates's Ford, Woodyard's Ford, and, well to the north, Sudley Ford and Poplar (or Red House) Ford—but their remote locations ensured that of these, only Sudley Ford would factor heavily in the fighting to come. Of the various shallows, only Blackburn's Ford was flanked by slippery, blufflike banks. The other fords, especially Union Mills, featured low, flat bottomland on both banks that would facilitate both attack and defense. Bull Run pursues a meandering course among these crossings. From Sudley Ford to Poplar Ford, it runs predominantly west to east. At the latter point it turns sharply south to Island Ford, then generally east to Blackburn's Ford. There it again veers south and east to McLean's and Union Mills Fords.[3]

Numerous roads crisscrossed the landscape, but only two were wide enough to accommodate heavy traffic. About 1,000 yards north-west of Lewis Ford, the major thoroughfare in this area, the Warrenton Turnpike—a macadamized toll road (its surface made of crushed and layered stones)—crossed Bull Run on a thirty-six-year-old stone-arch bridge. Descending from Sudley Ford was the major north–south road, which led travelers toward Manassas Junction. The Sudley Road (also known as the Manassas–Sudley Road and the Sudley–New Market Road) crossed both the Warrenton Pike and Young's Branch, a Bull Run tributary, adjacent to a two-and-a-half-story habitation known as the Stone House. Both the turnpike and the road from Sudley Springs would funnel thousands of troops into the future battle area, while the house would serve as both a forward-command post and a hospital.[4]

Especially given its many shallows, Bull Run may not have appeared the most formidable natural obstacle to a Federal advance from Washington. But its length, suitable to accommodating a defensive force of considerable size; its thick vegetation, which afforded cover for troops dug in along its banks; and its strategic position, twenty miles from the nearest Union camps and well in advance of the new Confederate capital at Richmond, had caught the eye of General Lee, who in the first week in May had designated it as the main line of resistance in northern Virginia.[5]

Aware that one of the enemy's principal objectives was control of Virginia's railroads, Lee deemed it imperative to guard the two lines that intersected at Manassas, the southwest-running O&A and the westward-leading Manassas Gap Railroad. While the former gave access to lower Virginia and, via connections, to the Deep South, the latter was of equal, and perhaps greater, importance to the Confederacy. Shorter, newer, and less prosperous than the venerable and well-maintained O&A, the Manassas Gap line passed through the Bull Run Mountains at Thoroughfare Gap and the Blue Ridge via its namesake defile, continuing to Strasburg, some fifty miles southwest of Harpers Ferry. Thus it constituted a link between the Virginia forces in the Shenandoah and the growing number of Confederate installations in the Virginia Tidewater, including Yorktown, Portsmouth, and Norfolk, where on April 20, Virginia militia had taken possession of the Gosport Naval Yard. The resources given up by that installation—numerous warships, an immense dry dock, and large supplies of ordnance, gunpowder, and coal—would support the creation of a Confederate naval force.[6]

While valuable to the Federals for closing off enemy access to points south and west, the railroads that met at Manassas were critical to the Confederacy's ability to exploit its interior lines of communication. Lee was especially concerned with the operating condition of the Manassas Gap line, which was poorly equipped, had little rolling stock, and whose right-of-way lacked for regular maintenance. He made it a point to discuss with company officials means of putting their resources into the best possible shape in order to accommodate the influx of defenders expected to journey to Manassas from the west in the weeks ahead.[7]

On May 8, two days after Lee ordered Manassas Junction held by "a force sufficient to defend that point against an attack likely to be made against it by troops from Washington," the first armed units arrived at the local depot (loftily styled "Tudor Hall," as was the meager community that enclosed it). Comprising four companies of infantry and horsemen, they would soon be joined by two full-size regiments and a two-gun section of artillery. They would come under the authority of the commander of the so-called Potomac Department, Brigadier General (of Virginia Troops) Philip St. George Cocke, a fifty-two-year-old native of Powhatan County. A country squire and scientific farmer in the mold of the more famous Edmund Ruffin, Cocke managed extensive plantation interests in Mississippi as well as in his native state. He also had a military background. An 1832 graduate of West Point, he had spent two years in the regular army before retiring to farm and was a member of the board of visitors of the Virginia Military Institute. These credentials, plus his reputation as an avowed secessionist, proved sufficient to gain Cocke not only a general's rank in his state's defense forces but also command of the so-called Alexandria Line, headquartered at Culpeper Court House.[8]

While it had been Lee's decision to fortify Bull Run, Cocke was the first officer of any rank to publicize the position's defensive potential. Sent to Manassas in the second week of May, he informed Lee's adjutant general that broken terrain north of the stream would impede an advancing enemy while making "a fortress . . . in which to carry on the destructive guerrilla warfare upon any marching column." On May 28 Lee left Richmond to look into this proposal. The visit validated Cocke's recommendations while confirming Lee's original thinking along the same lines.[9]

Cocke would never receive adequate credit for his logistical contributions. One reason was that he soon lost the rank and authority that might have bolstered his claim to making a battlefield of the hilly, wooded landscape between Bull Run and Manassas Junction. After June 8, when Virginia's forces were officially transferred to the Confederacy, Cocke found himself reduced to colonel in the Provisional Army of the Confederacy. Fiercely protective of his prerogatives, he felt humiliated by the demotion.[10]

Cocke suffered a further indignity on May 21, when he was superseded as head of the Potomac Department by a younger man, a non-Virginian, and an officer with a lesser military pedigree but who held a commission as a brigadier general in the Provisional Army. This was Milledge Luke Bonham of South Carolina, a close friend and political appointee of Governor Pickens. In civil life a lawyer, Bonham, like Cocke, had a quasi-military background, having fought in the Seminole War of 1836 and eleven years later in Mexico. Yet he was known more for his patrician mien, dignified appearance, and political gifts (at war's advent he was serving a term in the U.S. House of Representatives) than fitness for command. Indeed, these qualities appeared to be his primary qualification for the position he assumed at Bull Run.[11]

Bonham did not remain in command long enough to leave an imprint on Confederate operations in that sector. Though he supervised the erecting of additional works, he largely followed Cocke's planning rather than create a defensive program all his own. Bonham did, however, make a lasting impression on those officers who knew him best, one that was not uniformly positive. He was burdened with a volatile temper that he would regularly unleash on those closest to him, the members of his staff. "His manner is too excitable and dictatorial," wrote Lieutenant Colonel A. P. Aldrich. "Frequently he speaks very bluntly & abruptly to the gentlemen of the staff, & hurts their feelings. . . . [T]his generally happens when something has gone wrong, but it is no excuse, for a man capable to command others should be able to command himself, & this, he does not do." Because Bonham could not or would not moderate his behavior, at the close of the coming campaign, every member of his staff would transfer to another position.[12]

Upon his arrival, Bonham commanded little more than 1,000 soldiers, but he was soon joined by the brigade of South Carolina troops that Pickens had assigned to him, consisting of the 1st, 2nd, 7th, and 8th Infantry. Early in July the 1st, having been in service since April, would return home, its enlistment term up; it would be replaced by the 3rd South Carolina and 11th North Carolina Regiments. The Tar Heels' addition violated the Confederate army's preference for stocking brigades with regiments from the same state, a reflection of the nation's states' rights credo. And yet homogenous commands would be the norm in only one of the components of the army that originally defended Bull Run, the all-Virginia brigade assigned to Cocke upon his loss of overall command.

Although Cocke's troops had dug a few trenches in the vicinity of Lewis Ford, Bonham oversaw the first major effort to fortify the Bull Run line. One day after arriving, he was ordered by his superiors in Richmond to erect permanent defenses on both sides of the run. Naturally enough, most of these works went up on the south side, but a few arose around the village of Centreville, the most prominent of which was "Artillery Hill," an earthwork that included five embrasures for cannons. This work sat atop a four-hundred-foot-high knob south of the town and west of the road that led to Mitchell's Ford. It commanded the countryside for miles around, including the Warrenton Turnpike–Sudley Road junction.[13]

Despite having served in two wars, Bonham lacked the stature and reputation required of a commander for so important a position as the Bull Run defenses were likely to become. Cocke had been in charge there for less than two weeks; Bonham's tenure was even briefer. On May 31 the South Carolinian, who liked to refer to himself as the first general officer to take the field in Virginia, gave way to the newly arrived G. T. Beauregard. Although his rank was the same as Bonham's, the Creole's almost quarter-century of distinguished service in the regular army, not to mention the celebrity he had won at Charleston Harbor, made him the senior officer on the ground. Bonham would play a relatively prominent role in the fighting to come, but within six months his military shortcomings would persuade him to return to political life as a Confederate congressman and later as Governor Pickens's successor. When his term expired, only two months before war's end, Bonham would return to uniform. Thus he was in the field at the outset of Confederate operations and at the very end, distinguishing himself neither time.[14]

Beauregard found that the work of fortifying Bull Run and Manassas Junction had produced uneven results. What success had been achieved owed much to slave labor furnished by local planters—the more patriotic ones provided work crews for gratis, more materialistic ones for a fee. In many cases, however, the soldiers themselves—including many unfamiliar with picks and shovels—toiled beside the chattels. One enlisted man from a wealthy Maryland family recalled that "it was a novel treat for one who had never before handled either implement—although in that respect, it is almost needless to say, I had lots of company."[15]

By early June the men these works would protect were arriving in groups large and small. They joined the earliest comers, including some Virginia units under Colonel George H. Terrett. A former marine who appears to have had some engineering training, Terrett had already laid out a tent city and drill field just north of the depot that would become Beauregard's primary personnel rendezvous and supply base. Bonham had christened the installation Camp Pickens, a gesture his political patron would surely appreciate. According to Beauregard's adjutant general, Colonel Thomas Jordan, by the time of the Creole's arrival at Manassas, the inmates of Camp Pickens were already "daily gaining in experience and the general qualities of efficient troops."[16]

Terrett had begun to supervise the erection of earthworks and artillery revetments around Tudor Hall, some five miles below Mitchell's Ford. Given the enemy's assumed objective of seizing the railroads, these works quickly became the heaviest defenses on the Bull Run line. They consisted of a dozen earthen batteries, protected by gorges, about half a mile east of the rail junction as well as a trio of redoubts (enclosed square-shaped forts), which occupied higher ground north, east, and northeast of the depot. Almost three miles to the east was an oblong-shaped work capable of mounting sixteen pieces of heavy artillery. This work sat on an eminence later known as Signal Hill for the communications post established at its four-hundred-foot summit. To a great extent, the fortifying of Tudor Hall represented wasted labor. Though painstakingly erected and formidable by any measurement, none of the works that protected the depot would play a part in the fighting to come.[17]

Running counter to his penchant for dramatic entrances, Beauregard's arrival at Manassas at 2:00 P.M. on June 1 to lead what he would designate as the Army of the Potomac was a low-key affair. For several days, until word got around that a new commander was on hand, he attracted little notice. Because he wore a U.S. Army overcoat over his gray tunic, some soldiers mistook him for an intruder, or perhaps a prisoner. At this early stage of the conflict, uniform colors had not been standardized—for months to come, some Federal regiments would be clothed in cadet gray and Confederate units in a heterogeneous mix of styles and colors, including the gaudy uniforms favored by militia units. During their early weeks in the field, many Confederates would continue to wear the civilian clothes in which they had enlisted. Still, an officer who strutted about in Union blue raised eyebrows. Not until Beauregard began to make inspection tours on horseback, trailed by a large staff headed by Colonel Jordan, did the soldiers recognize him and snap to with salutes.

Even then, Beauregard made little display of rank, moving about, as one officer wrote, "almost undecorated . . . mounted on an unimposing animal not at all resembling a 'war horse.'" Although his outerwear may have drawn curious glances, the general's compact figure and sallow complexion failed to make him a conspicuous figure among men who had not seen his face except perhaps in some poorly wrought engravings. Recalling their first meeting, Beauregard's chief signal officer described him as "of medium size or a very trifle short, but compactly built, quick & alert, of fine carriage & aspect, & of unusual strength & activity." Beauregard's mane attracted the officer's notice: "His hair was black, but a few months afterward when some sorts of chemicals & such things became scarce it began to come out quite gray."[18]

William H. Russell, the celebrated military correspondent of the *Times* of London, had scrutinized Beauregard in South Carolina. He described the general as "a squarely built, lean man of about 40 years of age, with broad shoulders . . . [and] a true Gallic air. . . . The face is very thin, with very high cheek bones, a well-shaped nose, slightly aquiline, and a large, rigid, shapely-cut mouth, set above a full fighting chin."[19]

Enlisted men's views of their new leader were mixed. Most were suitably impressed by his dignified air, his ever-somber expression (one who served for months under him "never saw a smile upon his face"), and his Continental mannerisms. As one soldier observed, "with the left hand in his trousers pocket, a cigar in his mouth, a buttoned-up coat, and small cap, he is the exact type of a French engineer, and could not anywhere be mistaken for a civilian. He is jaunty in his gait, dashing in manner, and evidently takes delight in the circumstance of war." Another observer was less taken with the appearance of the Creole, "a monkeyish looking man to my notion of thinking, and looks the real Frenchman."[20]

In turn, Beauregard was not impressed by the quality of the troops he had inherited or the strength of the fortifications they and the borrowed slaves had erected. Examining the countryside with an engineer's eye, he decided that the overall layout of the defenses was generally sound. Yet its elongated extent, its half-finished condition, and the abundance of low, open ground north of Bull Run were sources of concern. His opinion of the defenses—many of them scarcely more than piles of upturned dirt to which trees and brush had been added haphazardly—matches the observations of an English-born visitor of slightly later date, who "could scarcely believe that this was a great military depot, there being nothing within my range of vision to indicate that such was the fact." Recognizing the strategic importance of Tudor Hall, he was shocked to find it

> a low, one-storied building, about seventy-five feet in length, with bales and boxes scattered about; a house of refreshment close by was uninviting, and except for one or two small cottages scattered here and there, naught was to be seen. Two or three tents were standing close to the depot, with lights in them, a guard here and there walked his post noiselessly, and in the distance, on neighboring hills, a few smouldering camp-fires were discernible. Only a mound of newly turned earth, here and there, indicated that the spade and shovel had been at work in fortifying, while the muzzles of a few guns in the embrasures pointed up the track towards Washington. A trooper or two would occasionally go jingling past in the direction of a cottage a few hundred yards in advance; and from the lights in windows, and groups seated round the camp-fires in the orchard, I learned that the dwelling was General Beauregard's head-quarters.[21]

Having come from a duty station, Charleston, where ample resources guaranteed success, Beauregard disapproved of the state of flux and incompleteness he found everywhere he looked. He was also dismayed by the disorganization, general unpreparedness, and lack of discipline he observed in the units under Bonham, Cocke, and Terrett. Not even the comfortable habitation he chose for his headquarters—the two-and-a-half-story brick manor house known as Liberia—eased his displeasure over the situation he had inherited. His attitude was only worsened by widespread rumors of an impending Union advance.

Two days after superseding Bonham, the general wrote President Davis that although "the plans of the works are good," the ground they covered was so extensive and so many fords had to be guarded that it would take upward of three weeks to complete them and would require at least 10,000 troops to hold them—perhaps as many as 15,000. Beauregard's principal concern was that the ground around Camp Pickens lacked "any strong natural features for the purpose of defense." He concluded, "I must therefore either be reinforced at once . . . or I must be prepared to retire (upon the approach of the enemy) in the direction of Richmond, with the intention of arresting him whenever and wherever the opportunity presents itself; or I must march to meet him at one of said fords, to sell our lives as dearly as practicable."[22]

While the condition of his defenses was a constant concern, Beauregard had confidence in his ability to move troops to threatened points—a benefit that any student of Jomini would have prized. As he recalled after the war, "I was anxiously aware that the sole military advantage at the moment to the Confederates was that of holding the *interior lines*." He trusted that the advance posts he had established at Centreville and Fairfax Court House, six and nine miles, respectively, from Bull Run, as well as at Sangster's Cross Roads, a mile and a half southeast of Sangster's Station on the O&A, would provide timely warning of the enemy's approach. Some of those troops would absorb the first shock of contact before falling back upon Beauregard's main line.[23]

He considered his flanks to be well covered, albeit remotely in the case of Johnston's little army at Harpers Ferry. On Beauregard's other (right) flank, some 2,500 men under Brigadier General Theophilus H. Holmes and Colonel Daniel Ruggles guarded Aquia Creek near Fredericksburg. These troops would prohibit or at least hinder a Union advance via the lower Potomac, and Bonham and later Beauregard devoted much attention to keeping open the lines of communications with the Fredericksburg area. Small outposts in the vicinity of Leesburg (under Colonel Eppa Hunton of the 8th Virginia), which Beauregard would augment, increased the efficiency of the upper Potomac early warning system. Another potential route of invasion, via the James River to Richmond, was guarded by troops stationed on both sides of Hampton Roads—at Norfolk under Brigadier General Benjamin Huger and on the Peninsula between Yorktown and Hampton under Brigadier General John B. Magruder.[24]

Soon after arriving, the general surely noticed the high incidence of sickness among the troops at Bull Run, especially diarrhea, dysentery, intermittent fever, measles, and mumps. Several victims succumbed to these and other camp diseases within weeks of his coming. The losses were made good, however, by a steady stream of incoming troops throughout June. One of these recruits recalled that "regiments poured in on every train, while others arrived on foot, and still others on horseback."[25]

They hailed not only from Virginia, which contributed the largest number of arrivals, but also from the Carolinas, Tennessee, and farther west—Arkansas, Mississippi, and Louisiana. The farther from Virginia, the longer, more roundabout, and more tedious the journey to war. Like their comrades to the north, the Cotton State volunteers had been cheered off to war by throngs of well-wishers, symbolizing the war frenzy that had stirred the South. A member of the 3rd South Carolina recalled the excitement of those who applauded them all the way from Columbia to Manassas Junction: "As the cars sped through the fields, the little hamlets and towns, people of every kind, size, and complexion rushed to the railroad and gave us welcome and Godspeed. Hats went into the air as we passed, handkerchiefs fluttered, flags waved in the gentle summer breeze from almost every housetop. The ladies and old men pressed to the side of the cars when we halted, to shake the hands of the brave soldier boys, and gave them blessings, hope, and encouragement. The ladies vied with the men in doing homage to the soldiers of the Palmetto State." A fellow South Carolinian agreed: "our journey here [Manassas] was almost a triumphal procession[, we] being saluted by every person whom we met whether white or black."[26]

An enlisted man from Mississippi observed that "as fast as regiments arrived they were assigned to brigades, and the brigades were combined into divisions." Via General Orders No. 20, issued on June 20, Beauregard announced the formation of six brigades, each comprised of three or four regiments of infantry. The heart of the command that would meet McDowell's Federals in battle (which Beauregard hopefully styled the "First Corps, Army of the Potomac"), these organizations later would be augmented by a seventh of smaller size, christened the Provisional (that is, temporary) Brigade. A couple of late-arriving additions from Louisiana and South Carolina would remain unattached but would see significant action in the fighting ahead. Subsequently, Beauregard would group his available cavalry—portions of four regiment- or battalion-size units from Virginia—into what amounted to another brigade. At a later date he would also consolidate his available artillery into a brigade-size force consisting of five Virginia batteries and a single battalion of the Washington Artillery of New Orleans, one of the South's most elite militia units.[27]

The Mississippian erred, however, when claiming that Beauregard created divisions. Although the orders of June 20 described the named regiments, battalions, and batteries as components of "the First Corps" of his army, he formed no organizations above the brigade level. He may have erred in not doing so. On the one hand, nine brigades under as many commanders saddled the fledgling army with an unwieldy decentralization of authority. On the other hand, there was wisdom in keeping things simple and avoiding extra layers of command. Then too "Old Bory" was not sufficiently acquainted with his subordinates to pronounce them deserving of leading more than a brigade.[28]

Not to say that these subordinates were unworthy of his trust. Even at the outset, Beauregard saw that a number of them were experienced soldiers of high reputation capable of making a name for themselves in this war. Others would reveal deficiencies only in later weeks or months. Per Bonham's seniority, Beauregard assigned his command the title of First Brigade, Army of the Potomac. The army's Second Brigade, comprising three Alabama and Louisiana regiments, was entrusted to a newly minted brigadier not from either of those states but from Virginia. This was Richard Stoddart Ewell, a balding, bewhiskered West Pointer who had made an exemplary record during the Mexican War and later on the Indian frontier as a dragoon officer.

Though highly regarded by his peers, the popeyed, beak-nosed Ewell was known for an assortment of quirks and peculiarities, some of them rather charming. An artillery officer described him as "a queer character, very eccentric, but upright, brave, and devoted" to the cause of Southern independence. Other qualities could be exasperating, including a susceptibility to nervous excitement; when in its grasp, a subordinate wrote, "no man could comprehend [him]. At such times his eyes would flash with a peculiar brilliancy, and his brain far outran his tongue. His thoughts would leap across great gaps which his words never touched, but which he expected his listener to fill up by intuition, and woe to the dull subordinate who failed to understand him."[29]

Command of the army's Third Brigade—three regiments from Mississippi and South Carolina—went to Brigadier General David Rumph "Neighbor" Jones, a soldier of modest ability who had served as Beauregard's chief of staff at Charleston and credited with hauling down the flag of the surrendered Fort Sumter. Beauregard's Fourth Brigade—originally made up of the 1st, 11th, and 17th Virginia, to which the 5th North Carolina would later be added— was headed by Colonel Terrett until the first week of July when assigned to Brigadier General James Longstreet, another native of South Carolina. A graduate of the U.S. Military Academy class of 1842, Longstreet had forged a distinguished career in the old army that included two brevets for gallantry in Mexico.[30]

Because he had been on staff duty for much of the intervening period, Longstreet expected to be offered a desk job in Richmond. He asked to be assigned "for service in the pay department, in which I had recently served for . . . I had given up all aspirations of military honor, and thought to settle down into more peaceful pursuits." Two days after arriving in the capital, Longstreet, to his astonishment, was notified of his appointment to brigadier general and his assignment to Beauregard at Manassas. The man would quickly justify the Confederacy's faith in his military capacity.[31]

The Fifth Brigade, Army of the Potomac, was assigned to now-colonel Cocke. Nicknamed the Game Cock Brigade (a feeble play on its commander's name), the command comprised some of the units the general had led on the Potomac Line—the 18th, 19th, and 28th Virginia—subsequently joined by the eight-company 8th Virginia, the three-company 49th Virginia, and the three companies of District of Columbia and Maryland volunteers under Captain Francis B. Schaeffer. Though the fifty-two-year-old Cocke appeared a sturdy physical specimen, there were grounds for questioning his mental stability. One of his regimental commanders described him as "too often abstracted and evidently oblivious of his surroundings; the expression of his eye was not normal." Such behavior may offer clues to Cocke's suicide six months later.[32]

Colonel Jubal Anderson Early of Franklin County, Virginia, was tendered command of the army's Sixth Brigade, composed of Virginians and Louisianans. West Pointer, Mexican War veteran, and militia officer, Early was a dogged campaigner, although a mordant spirit and a volatile temper would earn him a reputation as one of the most cantankerous officers in the Confederate service.

Beauregard tendered a seventh brigade, an understrength one, to Major Nathan G. Evans, whom Lee had sent to Manassas on June 20. Evans was a capable officer—when sober. Too often, however, he gave in to a weakness for strong drink. Some reports had him accompanied, even into battle, by a human Saint Bernard: a Prussian orderly carrying a cask of whiskey on his back. A staff officer described Evans as "difficult to manage" and a constant source of concern to his superiors.[33]

Evans's little command consisted of Colonel John B. E. Sloan's 4th South Carolina and an attached unit referred to in official correspondence as the 1st Special Battalion Louisiana Volunteers, otherwise known as the "Tiger Rifles." The latter, five companies strong, was led by Major Chatham Roberdeau "Bob" Wheat, a resourceful officer with a colorful past as a Southern patriot and soldier of fortune. Captain E. Porter Alexander, Beauregard's signal chief, referred to Wheat's unit as "a battalion of wharf rats" whose roughhouse ways only the genteel but iron-fisted Wheat could control.[34]

General Orders No. 20 failed to address Beauregard's cavalry arm, which as of early July consisted mainly of a single regiment, ten companies strong, officially designated the 30th Regiment of Virginia Mounted Volunteers and commanded by Colonel R. C. W. Radford. On the basis of seniority, Radford, a West Pointer, Mexican War veteran, and leading light of his state's militia, was also given authority over additional mounted units designated "Independent Virginia Cavalry," a total of thirteen companies. Beauregard would relegate the relatively small command to guarding the flanks of his main body and picketing the Bull Run line, though many horsemen would play a more active role in the fighting ahead.[35]

Likewise undermanned given the size of Beauregard's command was his artillery. Yet its four Virginia batteries and Major J. B.

Walton's battalion of the Washington Artillery of New Orleans were efficient organizations. Their officers, many of whom were graduates of West Point or the Virginia Military Institute, had a sharp eye for terrain and a knack for placing fire on target, and their gun crews were well drilled and highly motivated. A majority of their field pieces were 6-pounders, in contrast to the 10- and 13-pounders that predominated in McDowell's artillery. Command of Beauregard's cannons originally rested with the senior unit commander, Walton, but before the campaign ended, he would be superseded as chief of artillery and ordnance by Colonel Samuel Jones, a Virginian, member of the West Point class of 1838, and former captain in the 1st U.S. Artillery.[36]

By mid-June Beauregard had nearly 20,000 soldiers with whom to defend his vulnerable position. Some were short-term militia, but most had come to him under provisions of a bill, passed by the Confederate Congress early the previous month, authorizing the acceptance into the Provisional Army of as many volunteers as considered needed for the duration of the conflict. While some of these men understood what they were getting into by enlisting, many others—country lads eager to prove their manhood and uphold family honor—viewed the war as a combination militia muster and country frolic, with just enough danger and hardship to make the experience memorable. Three verities sustained them: the coming struggle would be brief, the battle to be fought along Bull Run would be decisive, and the cause of Southern nationhood would prevail.

At first Beauregard seemed not to appreciate the temperament of the troops assigned to him. As though concerned that their commitment to the struggle might need bolstering, four days after assuming command he issued an address ostensibly aimed at enlisting the material support of the neighboring citizenry. To attain this goal, Beauregard set out to demonize an enemy who in occupying Virginia had violated every rule of civilized warfare. It began: "A reckless and unprincipled tyrant has invaded your soil. Abraham Lincoln, regardless of all moral, legal, and constitutional restraints, has thrown his abolition hosts among you, who are murdering and imprisoning your citizens, confiscating and destroying your property, and committing other acts of violence and outrage too shocking and revolting to humanity to be enumerated. All rules of civilized warfare are abandoned, and they proclaim by their acts, if not on their banners, that their war-cry is 'Beauty and booty.'"[37]

When Beauregard addressed an audience he desired to impress, he could rarely resist pulling out all the stops. As T. Harry Williams has observed, this was "the kind of rhetorical document which he would compose several times in the war and which would always endear him to the populace if not to the government." If aimed at his men as well as their civilian hosts, the Creole's discourse on "Beauty and Booty" was a misguided effort. The great majority of the troops at Manassas did not need grandiloquent exhortations to motivate them to do their duty. Devotion to cause and region ran high in the Army of the Potomac.[38]

The sentiment sprang from many sources, including a strict reading of constitutional law, which they believed preserved to the various states the remedy of secession when their individual rights were infringed upon by the central government. Another incentive to serve was a desire to preserve social and economic institutions under threat by said government, including the ownership of slaves, a privilege that many nonslaveholders aspired to, one they wished to remain available. For most Southerners in arms, however, the main incentive to fight, one easily understood and keenly felt, was the desire to protect their homes, their families, and their communities against invasion.

The better-educated soldiers were articulate, if perhaps overly dramatic, in explaining why they had gone to war. As Lieutenant Charles C. Jones of Georgia observed, well before his state seceded "did I endorse and earnestly advocate our secession movement, and now when it is evident that our national independence can be secured only at the point of the bayonet and at the cannon's mouth, I shall not shrink from testifying even with my blood." The common soldiers were just as earnest in explaining their willingness to serve. An enlisted man in the 4th South Carolina wrote home: "It is an accepted fact here now that we will have some hard fighting to do before a great while. If so I say let it come, that is what we came here for, and the sooner we go at it perhaps the sooner it will end, and I mean to do what fighting I have to do as soon as possible and get back home to Dixie." Another South Carolinian had no doubts about his comrades' eagerness for the fray: "I do believe they would go into the fight as cheerfully as they would to dinner."[39]

Another Georgian, who would not reach Manassas till the eve of battle, spoke for many comrades when he wrote, "Animated by the sparks of patriotism and upheld by brave hearts we have nothing to fear of our foe, when we feel as we do, conscious of the justice of our cause." A Mississippi soldier asserted that "with God and right on our side, we can defy the angels of the infernal regions, let alone the legions of Abraham Lincoln." Some would-be combatants saw historical parallels in the effort to turn back enemy invasion. Virginia matron Judith McGuire heard a young cavalry lieutenant declare, "we have entered upon a more important revolution than our ancestors did in 1775."[40]

Highly motivated as the men appeared to be, all but the relative few who had regular-army or Mexican War experience were as untutored in the ways of soldiering as a toddler and as raw as uncured leather. A Virginian commenting years later on the rookies at Bull Run marveled that "they were able to fight at all. They were certainly not soldiers. They were as ignorant of the alphabet of obedience as their officers were of the art of commanding [them]."[41]

Many Southerners were nevertheless convinced that they were made of stronger fiber than their enemy, whom they regarded as extremely poor soldier material—unmotivated, unpatriotic, and unmanly. Editors, politicians, and even some clergymen spread the gospel that men of the South enjoyed inherent advantages in the area of soldiering. Governor Pickens, for one, frequently cited "the spirit and superior experience in shooting that the South has."[42]

But military potential would not ensure victory; the young Confederates needed to be trained at length in the manual of arms and taught how to maneuver on a battlefield, how to concentrate firepower against a common target, how to sustain unit cohesion under fire, and many other tactical lessons. With a Yankee army in Washington prepared to march south, time in which to absorb the basics of soldiering, let alone the nuances, was at a premium. Drillmasters did their best to ensure that these lessons were absorbed and retained, but not surprisingly, results were uneven. Some recruits received what they considered a surfeit of training, far more than impatient country lads could tolerate. A member of the 6th Alabama of Ewell's brigade who got his fill of the repetitive instruction in tactics bristled at the unreasonable degree of discipline demanded of him. In a letter home he complained that the typical defender of Bull Run was "under worse task-masters than any negro. He is not treated with any respect whatever."[43]

An Arkansan stationed at Fredericksburg, one who would join Beauregard's army before the fighting began, recalled that his regiment was introduced to drill as soon as it went into camp, "and I should say they did drill us! Eight hours a day, with a big gun, knapsack, and accoutrements weighing us down, the hot sun blazing over us." A Virginian at Manassas agreed that his life pivoted around "drill, drill, drill, three times a day."[44]

On the other end of the spectrum, many recruits received only a smattering of instruction. A young Georgian actually complained of the lack of it in his regiment, the result of a nearly constant shifting of its camp: "We have not drilled the first time since we left Atlanta and to keep us going all the time we never will get drilled enough to fight to any advantage." Slack attention to instruction left the men of some outfits with much time for nonmilitary affairs, including camp amusements and socializing. A South Carolinian admitted that his camp at Manassas was "a great thoroughfare for the young ladies of this place—coming in large numbers every morning to see us, remaining all evening, and sometimes of a morning." Other regiments in which discipline was lacking seemed to spend as much time lounging around, playing cards, and passing around the jug as they did lurching about on the drill plain.[45]

At the outset, tactical instruction was compromised by a general scarcity of weapons. Many volunteers arrived on the ground toting antiquated firearms brought from home: flintlock rifles, fowling pieces, "pepperbox" derringers, other handguns so petite they looked like toys, and knives so sharp as to be hazardous to those who wielded them. A Virginia girl who visited Camp Pickens in early June expressed concern that "our troops are fewer and more indifferently armed than I expected to see." She took comfort in the conviction that "with such indomitable spirits . . . they can never be beaten."[46]

As spring merged into summer, deficiencies in the resources at Manassas steadily lessened. Shipments of rifles, pistols, bayonets, and swords from the ordnance bureau in Richmond and the various state arsenals were frequent enough that by mid-July Beauregard's soldiers were sufficiently, if not amply, armed. Newly arrived weaponry included hundreds of .577-caliber Model 1853 Enfield rifles, a prized shoulder arm imported in large quantities from England. By this point too, enough cannon were on hand to stock the masked batteries being erected at several points on Bull Run and around Manassas Junction, while large quantities of gunpowder sent up from the naval yard at Norfolk helped ease a once-acute shortage of ammunition.

Beauregard's army did suffer from supply deficiencies. In June and July the Creole waged a battle of invective with Lieutenant Colonel Abraham C. Myers, the acting Confederate quartermaster general, who too often failed to honor the commander's requisitions. One famous example was a request for rope to use in the wells around Manassas, which Myers rejected on the ground that every coil had been earmarked for the Confederate navy. Upon reading Myers's reply, Beauregard began shouting, "If they would only send us less law and more rope!" A cheeky member of his staff asked, "To hang ourselves with, General?" "It would be better," Beauregard retorted, "than strangulation with red tape."[47]

As much as Myers bedeviled him, Beauregard vented most of his wrath on Commissary General Lucius B. Northrop. The initial dispute involved Beauregard's preference for purchasing foodstuffs from the local area; the obstinate and peevish Northrop demanded they be requisitioned from Richmond. Beauregard also found the transportation of rations from the capital to the front unacceptably slow. His belief was shared by Joe Johnston, who later in the campaign joined him in castigating Northrop's managerial deficiencies. Another critic was John D. Imboden, in 1861 commander of a Virginia artillery battery and later a Confederate brigadier general. Imboden was the source of a much-publicized claim that on the day fighting began at Manassas, not one full day's ration was available to the army. He also charged that even if enough food had been on hand, it could not have been properly distributed for Richmond had failed to provide enough wagons and teams to transport them to where they were needed.[48]

In a stream of letters to Jefferson Davis and other civilian superiors, Northrop answered his critics by denying that he had blocked efforts to feed the Army of the Potomac. Though always on the defensive, the commissary general managed to score debating points and refute some of the most serious charges against him. He stressed the fact that Beauregard was a poor steward of his army's physical resources. The general frequently requisitioned rations and material from Richmond and after they arrived forgot about them, with the result that the former spoiled and the latter were returned, unused, to the capital. Beauregard's neglect extended to ordnance supplies; according to multiple reports, eighteen cannons were never unloaded from the cars at Manassas in time to be fired at the Yankees.

Northrop also charged the army leader with taking more than one hundred unloaded boxcars off the tracks and refusing to return them. Supposedly, Beauregard turned them into storage houses not only for provisions but also for officers' personal baggage. This claim was supported by the president of the railroad that shipped most of the war goods to Manassas, suggesting that the army's supply problems were not wholly Northrop's fault. The commissary general has come down through history as a cold and callous administrator more interested in complaining about the bureaucratic hurdles he faced than in finding ways to surmount them. A dispassionate evaluation of the evidence, however, must conclude that while he made mistakes, they were mainly due to inexperience rather than obstinacy and that too many of the problems that beset him and, to a lesser degree, Lieutenant Colonel Myers—especially the slow and erratic shipment of rations and equipment by overburdened railroads—were beyond their ability to solve.[49]

In addition to better-trained, better-armed, and well-led defenders, by the second week in June critical portions of the Bull Run line were protected by an array of earthworks, ditches, abatis (rows of felled trees, sharpened for defense), and artillery emplacements. A newspaper correspondent who visited the works less than ten days after Beauregard assumed command offered his impression of their strength and complexity. He described the position as "a line of forts some two miles in extent, zigzag in form, with angles, salients, bastions, casemates, and every thing that properly belongs to works of this kind." The entire line "has [been] fortified so strongly, that . . . 5,000 men could there hold 20,000 at bay," and "there is scarcely a possibility of its being turned."[50]

The influx of men and arms and the apparent perfection of the Bull Run–Manassas line suggested that no matter how many Yankees advanced against it, the Army of the Potomac would not be at a marked disadvantage in battle. This growing realization paid dividends in nonmaterial ways. An increase in morale was palpable throughout the command as well as at army headquarters. Whether or not completely satisfied with the strength of his position, G. T. Beauregard had grown so confident of its defensive potential that he had begun to develop a grand scheme for cooperating with Johnston in defeating McDowell's and Patterson's armies through judicious application of Jominian principles. The plan that evolved from his fecund brain was typical of the Creole's strategic thinking—bold, energetic, complex, but in his mind absolutely viable. All that was needed for it to succeed with marvelous effect was the endorsement of Davis, Walker, Lee, and Johnston. Beauregard was sure that once these men were privy to his plan, they would endorse it quickly and wholeheartedly.[51]

CHAPTER 4

GREEN AND GREEN ALIKE

O n the day Irvin McDowell assumed command of the Army of
Northeastern Virginia, the call for an early advance was heard
for the first time—a faint, discordant, but compelling beat soon to
echo throughout the North. On May 27 Fitz-Henry Warren, the
recently hired Washington correspondent of Horace Greeley's *New
York Tribune,* issued a challenge that would resonate not only with
Greeley's subscribers but also with newspaper readers far and wide:
"TO RICHMOND! TO RICHMOND ONWARD!" Warren, soon to be commissioned colonel of the 1st Iowa Cavalry and a year hence to wear
the star of a brigadier general of volunteers, would claim that his
catchphrase was "the voice of the people. . . . Let her [Richmond's]
sowing of the wind, have a generous harvest of the whirlwind, and
let it be *now.*"[1]

In subsequent dispatches—up to the time he entered the service—Warren repeated his call to action, demanding that Union
forces occupy the new enemy capital before its government was
fully functioning. Treason should be nipped in the bud; Lincoln
must "pierce the vitals of Virginia, and scourge the serpent seed of
her rebellion on the crowning heights of Richmond!" By June 22,
no advance on Richmond having begun, the correspondent began
to castigate the president for his foot dragging, which he considered indicative not merely of sloth but of faintheartedness. "Shall
I tell you frankly and honestly," he asked his readers, "what I hear
all around and abroad? It is, that there is no intention to press the
suppression of the rebellion—that the patience of the people is to be
worn out by delay."[2]

Horace Greeley, always quick to recognize a popular issue, had
come to embrace Warren's fiery rhetoric. On June 26 he ran a mast-
head awash in boldface and bombast:

THE NATION'S WAR-CRY.
Forward to Richmond! Forward to Richmond!
The Rebel Congress must not be allowed to meet
there on the 20th of July! BY THAT DATE THE
PLACE MUST BE HELD BY THE NATIONAL ARMY!

At the suggestion of Greeley's managing editor, Charles A. Dana, the banner "Forward to Richmond" ran every day for three weeks.[3]

The clamor for an early offensive soon was taken up by other journals, whose editors tried to appropriate the sentiment for their own. By the close of June, Warren's mantra seemed to be on the mind, if not the lips, of every Northerner. Of necessity, the government took heed and, to a certain extent, embraced the call for action. To quell a growing criticism of the White House and the War Department, on the morning of the twenty-eighth, President Lincoln called Warren to his office. The president, who appreciated the need for a quick and decisive resolution of the national crisis, shared with the correspondent the substance of recent conferences with military officials, including Generals Scott and McDowell. In a late edition that same day, Warren was able to inform his readers that the long-awaited offensive was forthcoming.[4]

The "On to Richmond" incantation had served Greeley's purposes, goading Lincoln and Scott into action while increasing the *Tribune*'s readership. But it only complicated matters for the man who would direct the forward movement. By late June Irvin McDowell had spent weeks struggling with the daunting task of readying his eager but untutored troops for the field. That task involved problems that ran the gamut of organization, administration, leadership, training, engineering, and supply. As was the case with the Rebels gathering along Bull Run and in the Shenandoah, the troops in camp on the Potomac lacked the basic resources—arms, equipment, ammunition, and transportation—to support such a campaign as the *Tribune* and other newspapers were urging on the army.

A principal concern was the continuing vulnerability not only of Washington proper but also of the ground to be held on the Virginia side of the Potomac. If the district's defenses were few and unimpressive, strategically located Alexandria and its environs were almost completely devoid of them. The tools needed to build a suitable number of works, including the most basic implements—shovels, pickaxes, and wheelbarrows—were greatly lacking, as were wagons to transport them to work sites.[5]

Alexandria was especially lightly held; its garrison consisted of only a few of the troops who had taken possession of the city. Many soldiers were unruly, given to looting and vandalism. Part of the problem was that the historic city held no charms for the occupants. A private in a Maine regiment called Alexandria "the most forsaken sunken decayed looking place that ever I was in. The places of business are most all closed [and] a great many of the enhabitants are gone."[6]

The lawless defenders posed an additional problem for McDowell, who felt himself bound by General Scott's policy of restraint toward Virginians, at least until blood had to be spilled. Two days after assuming command, the army leader informed Lieutenant Colonel E. D. Townsend, the assistant adjutant general, that the local populace had been alarmed and outraged by numerous acts of "trespass, depredations, and attempts at burglary." Because many of Virginia's courts had ceased to function, the general recommended that the perpetrators be tried by military commission. His strict notions of discipline and his desire to avoid antagonizing noncombatants, even those with Southern sympathies, would remain one of his most consistent attitudes.[7]

Inadequate communications and logistical facilities south of the river was a constant concern to the high command. McDowell had access to no wagons of any kind, including those designed to carry rations and forage from Washington. One of his earliest efforts was to construct a depot in Alexandria to hold foodstuffs and forage. Telegraph lines having been downed during the evacuation of the city, McDowell's widely dispersed units could not readily keep in touch with one another. Repair work was slow to get underway, and for some days progress was virtually imperceptible.

Then there was the problem of training the soldiers crossing to Alexandria and surrounding areas. The near-constant influx of troops from the capital demanded a large and well-coordinated instructional system, but this too was lacking. McDowell was reduced to asking West Point's superintendent to detail recent academy graduates as drillmasters for those crabapple-green volunteers who were expected to do the marching on Richmond.[8]

McDowell's troubles were immeasurably worsened by a lack of cooperation from superiors and colleagues alike. One was General

Scott, whom McDowell later described to the congressional watchdog panel known as the Joint Committee on the Conduct of the War as "piqued and irritated" that his subordinate should have been given command south of the Potomac. McDowell believed he knew one source of his superior's animosity: that an officer so recently on staff duty should lead the largest fighting force in American history, one that dwarfed the army Scott had led in Mexico. At the same time, McDowell incurred the hostility of General Mansfield by refusing to request the backdating of his own appointment in order to award his fellow brigadier seniority.[9]

Giving vent to wounded pride, Scott and Mansfield, who had the final say over which regiments would cross the Potomac and when, obstructed McDowell's efforts to build his army. As McDowell told the congressional inquisitors, "I was on the other side [of the Potomac] a long while without anything" in the way of military supplies and the technical assistance urgently required from drillmasters, engineers, and mapmakers. Cavalry and artillery came to him in driblets, and even the bedrock of his army—volunteer infantry— was withheld. When he called on Mansfield for additional troops to hold Alexandria, the head of the Department of Washington plead an insufficiency of transportation. When he afterward directed his request to Quartermaster General Montgomery C. Meigs, he learned that vehicles were in fact available but that Mansfield had forbade their release until the army was ready to march on Manassas. Overlooking this duplicity, McDowell agreed with his colleague's reasoning but bemoaned its effect: "I get nothing." One consequence was that "some of my regiments came over very late; some of them not till the very day I was to move the army."[10]

McDowell was obliged to toil without the assistance of a fullfledged staff, perhaps because, given his well-publicized rift with Scott, to join his inner circle was to commit professional suicide. Fortunately, he secured the services of one man who had no qualms about attaching himself to Scott's least favorite subordinate and whose intelligence and work ethic would prove indispensable to the Army of Northeastern Virginia. This was Brevet Captain James Barnet Fry, an Illinois-born West Pointer who became McDowell's adjutant general. Fry boasted an exemplary record: fourteen years in the regular artillery broken only by a stint as adjutant of his alma mater, the same post McDowell had filled twelve years earlier. He would serve the general faithfully and well, though his postwar recollections of the First Bull Run Campaign occasionally gave his boss more credit for strategic and tactical achievements than he deserved.[11]

Fry's commitment to McDowell seems to have encouraged others to follow his lead. Those who would join him on staff duty included officers who would forge distinguished careers in the eastern theater, including Major John G. Barnard (later a brigadier general), the army's chief engineer; Captain Henry F. Clarke, commissary of subsistence; and Major William S. King, chief surgeon. Two other additions—Lieutenant Haldimand S. Putnam of the topographical engineers and Major James S. Wadsworth, volunteer aide-de-camp—would gain high rank, the former a colonelcy, the latter a brigadier generalship, and would be killed in action in 1863 and 1864, respectively.[12]

One of the most vexing problems McDowell encountered in his dealings with Scott and Mansfield concerned the organization and staffing of his field forces. "With difficulty," he complained, "could I get any officers." Several men of high rank, however, had preceded him to Alexandria and Arlington, appointed to the army by Mansfield in his role as departmental commander, presumably with the approval of Scott and Cameron and perhaps Lincoln as well (whether McDowell's input was sought is unknown). Some of these appointees, to whom McDowell felt compelled to assign command of brigades and divisions, would make their mark as combat leaders in the months and years ahead. Others would fail, see their reputations wither and die, and be cast aside as the war increasingly demanded that only highly capable professionals be awarded high command.[13]

McDowell's first brigade-level appointees, two of whom he was well acquainted with, were soldiers of modest talent. On May 28, the day he formally assumed command at Alexandria, he created three brigades comprising a total of nine regiments of volunteer infantry. The first was assigned to Colonel Stone, McDowell's coadjutor in the effort to secure the capital. Stone, who would soon be detached from his new command to lead an expeditionary force along the upper Potomac, was a capable regular with an impeccable prewar record but whose conservative political orientation and continuing friendships with old-army comrades who were now Confederate officers would land him in hot water with the Republicans who oversaw the war effort. Over time these views and connections would cost Stone both his commission and his liberty. In February 1862 the man who had diligently safeguarded Lincoln before and during his inauguration would be imprisoned on trumped-up charges of treasonous behavior. When finally released six months later, both his health and his reputation would be in sharp decline.[14]

Another colleague of McDowell's from the war's early days, David Hunter, took command of the army's second brigade. The scion of an old Virginia family who had become a fierce abolitionist, the fifty-eight-year-old Hunter was a West Pointer (class of 1822) who had resigned from the army in 1836 to dabble in Chicago real estate, only to reenter the ranks five years later as a paymaster. His Republican sympathies, close acquaintance with Lincoln, and affiliation with the Frontier Guard had recommended him for high rank (he had been appointed brigadier general three days after McDowell), even if his undistinguished prewar career did not.

With his rotund figure, jowly face, and bald head (which he covered with an ill-fitting wig), Hunter seemed an odd choice as the fourth-highest-ranking officer in the volunteer army, but McDowell had worked well with him in the capital and believed they could mesh in Virginia. Although Hunter had been named colonel of the 3rd U.S. Cavalry (formerly the army's Regiment of Mounted Riflemen) on May 14, he had not experienced field service in more than a quarter century. McDowell, who had been confined to staff duty almost as long, was in no position to denigrate Hunter's fitness for active campaigning, although other officers would.[15]

Command of McDowell's third brigade went to another officer judged elderly by the standards of the day, fifty-five-year-old Samuel P. Heintzelman. An 1826 graduate of the military academy, the Pennsylvania Dutchman was a veteran of the Mexican War and operations against the Indians of the Southwest and the Pacific Coast, winning two brevets for gallantry. A colleague described the bewhiskered, perpetually scowling Heintzelman as an excellent officer, too candid and critical for the good of his career but honest and forthright: "Diogenes would have ended his quest with him."[16]

He was also prideful and thin-skinned. Outraged that junior officers were outstripping him in gaining rank, since the firing on Fort Sumter, Major Heintzelman had been actively campaigning for a colonelcy. Upon learning that McDowell had ascended to an even higher station, he had importuned his frontier comrade Mansfield for a promotion. His efforts were more or less successful: between May 8 and 14, he was appointed, successively, acting inspector general of Mansfield's department and colonel in command of the newly formed 17th U.S. Infantry.

Ever conscious of his place in history, at 2:00 P.M. on May 23, mounted on his coal-black charger, Heintzelman led his new regiment across Long Bridge to Alexandria. That night he added an entry to his voluminous diary, proudly if inaccurately declaring the movement "the first operation against the rebels in front of Washington." Yet he remained unhappy over his rank and position, bluntly complaining to McDowell that numerous volunteer colonels had already gained seniority over him. The general tried to placate him by promising that he, as a regular officer, would receive preference in the assignment of brigades. The gesture failed to mollify Heintzelman, but McDowell later won his goodwill by naming him to head one of the army's five divisions, a command normally given an officer two levels above Heintzelman's grade.[17]

McDowell's army grew in fits and starts from its modest origins to a mighty host, though one that lacked the knowhow and polish to take the field with any hope of sustained success. Most of the enthusiastic youngsters who composed it, however, would not have agreed with this gloomy assessment; they were convinced that victory was a foregone conclusion. In early June an enlisted man in the District of Columbia infantry predicted that "two weeks from this time the U.S. troops will be in the Sacred City of Richmond with very little fighting." A recruit of the 3rd Maine agreed that Richmond would soon be in Union hands: "We are going to visit Jefferson Davis at his residence." A fellow Down Easterner spoke of descending on the Rebel capital "& cleaning the d—n rebels out." This would happen only if the enemy would stand and fight, something a great many recruits doubted. A Jerseyman wrote his family from Alexandria that "as we advance they retreat. And we are bound to make them run wherever we go."[18]

Unlike Southerners, who had overriding personal reasons to take up arms, McDowell's recruits had a variety of reasons for joining up. Not all enlisted with the goal of whipping the scoundrels down south. Elnathan Tyler of the 3rd Connecticut was typical of those who regarded war as an adventure, a release from the humdrum of life in a small town. "I never fully made up my mind," he later confessed, "whether I enlisted out of simon pure patriotism or not. . . . Many of my mates were going, business was dull, I was young and ready to go in for anything new or exciting." Thrilling stories of warfare, digested in boyhood, had. induced thousands of youngsters to join McDowell's ranks. "We were all young then," a member of the 2nd Michigan wrote after the war, "and the imagination was more active, the ambitions were greater. . . . Every man carried a baton in his knapsack and Hope, the enchantress, was clad in the most roseate hues."[19]

Most of these young men, however, had not enlisted out of ambition or boredom. Although at this early stage of the conflict, few were fighting to abolish slavery, hundreds affirmed their commitment to saving the Union, if necessary at the cost of their lives. A Pennsylvanian wrote: "I would not like to have it sayed we was Holladay Soldiers, for I am bound to see this out or fall" on the battlefield. A Maine man was certain that "the cause is just, and if my humble life can help drive out those traitors from the soil it may freely go." A Rhode Island officer declared, "I am too thoroughly convinced of the justice of this war—know too well the peril of our free institutions and the value to the world of our American civilization, even to hesitate to cast in my life if it is called for."[20]

McDowell did his best to see that these young men—the excessively confident, the seekers of adventure, and the highly committed—received enough training to give his army at least a modicum of professionalism. In later months he would be criticized for failing to drill his soldiers properly and adequately, but this does not seem to be the case. When not distracted by other responsibilities, he conscientiously oversaw his army's instruction. His troops—all but those who failed to reach him until the eve of battle—received enough training to achieve adequate mobility on the field of battle.

Overall, however, the instructional program proved deficient in a number of respects. This is not surprising given the complexity of mid-nineteenth-century infantry tactics and the inability of many volunteers to assimilate and execute them. Especially in these early days of the war—before the conflict became extended enough to compel the government to induce older, married men to join the ranks—most recruits were quite young (the average age being somewhere between the late teens and early twenties) and without much in the way of a formal education. Yet as soon as they signed up, these youths were expected to digest instruction such as the following, taken directly from the War Department–published *Infantry Tactics* of 1861. The passage describes one the most basic tactical evolutions, the shift of a single company (on paper, approximately one hundred officers and men) from a marching column to a line of battle:

> At the command *march*, the two files on the left (or right) of the company will mark time, the others will continue to march straight forward; the two rear rank men of these files will, as soon as the rear rank of the company shall clear them, move to the right by advancing the outer shoulder; the odd number will place himself behind the third file from that flank, the even number behind the fourth, passing for this purpose behind the odd number; the two front rank men will, in like manner, move to the right when the rear rank of the company shall clear them, the odd number will place himself behind the first file, passing for this purpose behind the even number. If the files are broken from the right, the men will move to the left advancing the outer shoulder, the even number of the rear rank will place himself behind the third file, the odd number of the same rank behind the fourth.[21]

This lesson, fairly stupefying in its complexity, represented a small sample of what the infantry recruit was told to learn before going into combat. If and when he absorbed these company-level lessons, he was also expected to learn the so-called School of the Battalion as well as skirmisher tactics, flanking maneuvers, deployments in column, and advances in line of battle. These evolutions he would have to perform under combat conditions—on unfamiliar terrain and under fire. It may be surmised that a recruit fresh from the farm (perhaps one of many who did not know his right foot from his left) would have trouble remembering such basic facts as which file he was in and whether he was the odd or the even man, let alone how to conform his movements as precisely as possible to the other men in his unit.

Even in outfits with an unusually high number of semi-experienced soldiers, the various levels of instruction, especially those covering the larger formations, were frustratingly difficult to assimilate. One recruit in a regiment mustered into service much later in the war recalled that in contrast to most outfits, "only a small minority of the thousand men and officers were absolutely ignorant of military drill; moreover, the mass of them were intelligent Americans, who learned quickly and easily. When we left the home camp a few weeks after enrollment, we could march deceptively well, and the regiment actually received praise for its fine appearance from spectators." Even so, he added, "the battalion, not the company, is the tactical unit, and until a regiment has mastered the battalion drill and has learned skirmish work it is unfit for modern warfare. In these essential things we were utterly unpracticed."[22]

In addition to battle evolutions, the recruits had to master the care and handling of their weapons. The primary infantry shoulder arm of the day was the U.S. Rifle-Musket (Models 1855 and 1861), known as the Springfield for the Massachusetts armory where first manufactured. The Springfield was a muzzle-loading, single-shot percussion rifle. It fired a minie ball, a cylindro-conoidal .577-caliber bullet made of soft lead with a hollow base that, upon discharge, expanded to grip the grooves of the rifling inside the barrel. The rifling imparted a spin that helped steady and direct the missile while greatly increasing its effective range.[23]

Another weapon widely distributed to Federal recruits was the Model 1851 Harpers Ferry Rifle, a product of the armory that Virginia forces had seized five days after Fort Sumter's surrender. Enfield rifles were also made available to several regiments, for the North as well as the South imported large quantities of this highly effective shoulder arm. With these weapons, an infantryman could deliver an accurate fire up to six hundred yards from his target and could kill at nearly twice that distance. This was three times the range of a smoothbore weapon such as the Model 1842 Musket with which some volunteer regiments were armed due to the relative scarcity of rifles in the early weeks of the war. According to the instructional manuals of the day, a veteran rifleman firing the minie ball should have been able to reload, aim, and fire in something under three minutes. How long it would take a rookie to complete the reloading process, especially under fire, was anyone's guess.[24]

The minie ball, which had been adopted for general use by the U.S. Army only six years earlier, would revolutionize the employment of infantry arms in battle. Infantry tactics, however, had not changed appreciably in twenty years or more. Based largely on lessons learned during the Napoleonic Wars, they promoted close-order formations in which two lines of riflemen formed for an attack beyond the range of an opposing force, began shooting, absorbed a largely ineffective return fire, and then before the enemy could reload, dashed across a relatively short stretch of ground to engage in hand-to-hand fighting.

Though the manuals of 1861 continued to advocate such formations, infantry units had become vulnerable to a destructive fire at much longer range. This fact effectively made frontal assaults, unless directed at an incoherent or demoralized enemy, exercises in futility and suicide. Nor would artillery (many cannons were also rifled) find it safe to maneuver as close to the opponent's infantry as in the past. As one tactical historian has noted, "artillerymen would thus have to operate at greater distances from the enemy, where problems of range estimation, primitive fusing, and poor fragmentation of ammunition made them much less effective. Cavalrymen, who presented still larger targets, were even less useful than artillery on the battlefield itself and would soon be relegated to its fringes."[25]

Given technological advances and complex, outmoded tactics, McDowell's drillmasters had their work cut out for them. From the start the training program was deficient. A major shortcoming was its heavy concentration on small-unit tactics. When the continuing flow of recruits from Washington forced the general to add to the original three brigades and group the expanded force into divisions, McDowell found his enlarged command difficult to maneuver. As he later testified, "I had no opportunity to test my machinery; to move it around and see whether it would work smoothly or not." When he finally managed to collect a body of eight regiments for his personal inspection, General Scott scolded him for "trying to make some show." Later criticisms by Scott in this same vein appear to have curbed McDowell's enthusiasm for having multiple units drill together as interlocking elements of a cohesive formation. Because his troops did not train as brigades and divisions, McDowell would not employ them as brigades and divisions, a defect certain to have consequences.[26]

To be sure, McDowell's was not the only fighting force in Virginia to limit its tactical training to small formations. At this early stage of the conflict, this was the norm; there is no evidence that Beauregard's troops—or for that matter Johnston's or Patterson's—trained any differently. But because the Lincoln administration had begun to cave in to the public pressure for an advance on Richmond, McDowell's troops would be compelled to take the offensive, attacking the works between Fairfax Court House and Manassas. For an army like Beauregard's, holding a position and fighting on the defensive, maneuvering by large formations was not an imperative as it would be for an army launching a broad-front assault.

The training the Army of Northeastern Virginia received was deficient in still other ways. Little time was devoted to such basic necessities as target practice and skirmisher drill. More than any other defect, however, a lack of full-pack maneuvering would hamstring McDowell's command. Virtually up to the day it started for Bull Run, none of his men would have hit the road for any length of time to build up stamina and strengthen those parts of the anatomy that would absorb the wear and tear of extended marching. By contrast, Patterson's and Johnston's forces gained marching experience, though mostly in retreat. Beauregard's soldiers, if they adhered to the defensive, would not need to develop leg strength and lung capacity.

If McDowell did not train his troops fully or properly, neither did he manage to instill in them an acceptable degree of discipline. One of his army's greatest inadequacies was a shortage of provost marshals to keep in line men habitually given to disorderly and destructive behavior aimed at the property of avowed or suspected secessionists. The brigadier was especially concerned by lawless acts perpetrated against former neighbors by those District of Columbia militiamen who, having resided "so near their present station . . . , have stronger personal feelings in this matter and are more liable to be influenced by them than troops coming from a distance."[27]

The army leader's efforts to protect the homes and possessions of enemy civilians did not sit well with the majority of his troops, who perceived the rules he laid down as wrongheaded and faintly treasonous and strove to subvert them. An officer of the 2nd Ohio Infantry who conversed with McDowell during the latter's visit to his regiment's camp at Upton's Hill, six miles northwest of Alexandria, recalled "the rather pompous way in which he said that it was his policy to cultivate the good will of the natives and allow no foraging; that I was to instruct my successors to that effect, etc." This prompted the officer to remonstrate: "General, you need have no concern as to the Second Ohio. The men are gentlemen, not thieves." As he spoke, his visitor's attention was drawn to a garden on a nearby hill where a group of soldiers appeared hard at work. McDowell inquired: "What men are those?" With "shame and humiliation" the officer recognized them as "gentlemen of the Second Ohio" appropriating foodstuffs for the regimental commissary: "The air was dark with cabbages and garden truck that was being plucked and with frantic zeal thrown over the fence to willing coadjutors on the outside."

Some historians have ascribed McDowell's concern for protecting the property of Southern sympathizers to a straight-laced mentality inherited from his Puritan forebears. Yet his attitude mirrored that of General Scott, and McDowell had already antagonized his superior more than was professionally prudent. In this instance he was glad to oblige the senior general by endorsing a policy of moderation toward the enemy, even one that smacked of accommodation and provoked indignation and resentment among his own troops.[28]

By June 3 enough troops had reached the south side of the Potomac to necessitate a further expansion of army organization. That day McDowell created a fourth brigade, originally composed of two New York regiments—future additions would include three Connecticut regiments then en route to Washington. A few days later he stationed this force at Falls Church on the turnpike that ran northwest from Alexandria, at the time the most advanced point of the army's lines.[29]

McDowell assigned the command to Brigadier General Daniel Tyler, a sixty-two-year-old New Englander who had graduated from West Point in 1819, making him the oldest academy alumnus in McDowell's army. The white-haired, patrician-looking Tyler—before the war the president of two railroads—had left his native Connecticut at the head of the state's 1st Volunteer Infantry, a ninety-day regiment. Less than three weeks later, he was named a brigadier general of state troops by Governor William A. Buckingham.

Because he was neither a regular nor an officer of U.S. volunteers, and considering that he had reentered service after almost thirty years in civilian life, Tyler's advancement was another oddity. And yet in this spring of 1861, some subordinates were high on his abilities as a fighting man. William T. Sherman, for one, declared that Tyler "has a fair reputation" and believed he would comport himself well in high command. To enlisted men who knew him, however, the general "did not impress us favorably. He was a man of slight build, well advanced in years, and whose only claim to military command was that he had commanded a Connecticut regiment in the Mexican War." A disgruntled volunteer who served under him throughout the campaign wrote that as a soldier Tyler was "of no more significance or importance . . . than an old speckled hen."[30]

Nine days after forming Tyler's command, McDowell welcomed to his army Brigadier General Robert Cumming Schenck, whom

Washington had appointed to head another of the army's brigades, this one consisting of the raw recruits of the 1st Ohio Infantry and the assiduous foragers of the 2nd Ohio. Schenck's qualifications for a command assignment were dubious at best, his achievements all civilian oriented. A graduate not of West Point but of Ohio's Miami University, the fifty-two-year-old was a four-time Whig congressman, a former minister to Brazil, and a tireless backer of Abraham Lincoln. In his time away from political and diplomatic duties, the social animal had gained a reputation as an authority on draw poker. As a *New York Times* correspondent observed, the Ohioan was "a determined and brave man, but apart from these characteristics, his Brigadier-Generalship seems to be the only qualification which entitles him to lead troops to battle."[31]

Over the next three weeks, McDowell created three more brigades while shuffling an existing brigade and providing it with a new commander. The new organizations were assigned to Colonels William B. Franklin (consisting of the 5th Massachusetts and 4th Pennsylvania, the command "to be hereafter increased"), Orlando B. Willcox (his own 1st Michigan and the 11th New York Zouaves, both of which had taken Arlington and Alexandria on May 24), and Andrew Porter (originally the 8th and 14th New York Militia, the latter better known as the 14th Brooklyn).[32]

Two of the newcomers, Franklin and Porter, had old-army backgrounds and recently had been assigned command of U.S. infantry regiments. Franklin had spent seventeen years in the topographical engineers before being named in mid-May colonel of the 12th Infantry. Considered a military intellectual, the Pennsylvanian had graduated at the head of the West Point class in which U. S. Grant ranked twenty-first, hence his posting to the army's elite corps. Another native of Pennsylvania, Porter had left West Point after a single term but, on the eve of the war with Mexico, secured a commission in the Regiment of Mounted Rifles. One of his subordinates, 1st Lieutenant William Woods Averell, lauded his superior as "an ideal officer . . . a gentleman of unfailing courtesy and of unwavering loyalty to his country and to his friends." The command McDowell had assigned him was composed of both reliable troops and those who could not be counted on in battle. Porter's original brigade was later augmented by an eight-company battalion of regular infantry led by Major George Sykes as well as by seven companies of regular cavalry and dragoons under Major Innis N. Palmer—the only mounted force assigned to the Army of Northeastern Virginia. Both organizations were made of stalwart material, but Porter would also acquire a small battalion of U.S. Marines, most of them raw recruits barely conversant with the basic duties of their branch.[33]

The third newcomer, Willcox, had not served in the army since 1857, a decade after graduating from West Point, having resigned his commission in the 4th U.S. Artillery to practice law in Detroit. Even so, he had performed ably when his 1st Michigan Volunteers led the invasion of Virginia. Although this is all McDowell knew about him, it appears to have been sufficient to recommend Willcox for brigade command.[34]

The fourth newcomer, "Cump" Sherman, was assigned to lead David Hunter's brigade due to the latter's pending promotion to divisional command. Sherman had graduated in 1840 from West Point, where he had briefly known U. S. Grant, his future superior and patron. His rise through the ranks had been slow partly due to his relegation to staff duty in California during the fighting in Mexico. Although he was the ward of the powerful Senator Thomas Ewing of Ohio; the husband of Ewing's older daughter, Ellen, and the brother of Congressman (and newly elected senator) John Sherman, Sherman's pre–Civil War career proved so unfulfilling that he had left the army in 1853. The next eight years had been no more rewarding, prompting him to consider himself a "dead cock in the pit."[35]

The outbreak of civil war found Sherman unwilling to take part. From long residence in the South as both a soldier and a civilian, he understood that the region was prepared for war but that the Federal government was not. In May 1861 he finally consented to return to uniform as commander of another newly organized regular regiment, the 13th Infantry. Perhaps he should have aimed higher. One account has him, upon reporting to Washington, conversing with McDowell. When the latter learned that Sherman had accepted a colonelcy, he replied: "You should have asked for a brigadier general's rank. You're just as fit for it as I am." This may well have been true. Sherman's first weeks in command of his brigade—the 13th and 79th New York Volunteers, the 69th New York Militia, and the 2nd Wisconsin—would be filled with setbacks and difficulties, but they would showcase the talents and abilities that had been underutilized during decades of professional disappointment.[36]

While the Army of Northeastern Virginia was taking shape, other Federal forces were busy taking the offensive in their areas—not always successfully but in every case with a degree of mobility and initiative to which McDowell's command could only aspire. The first movement was made by the volunteers in George McClellan's Department of the Ohio, who late in May invaded western Virginia and chased an enemy force out of strategic Grafton. On June 3 McClellan caught up with the fleeing Rebels near Philippi, attacked, and drove them from the field.[37]

At about the same time, the war on the Virginia Peninsula and in the Fredericksburg area came alive. On May 27 a detachment of Ben Butler's command, now stationed on the Peninsula, gained a foothold on the James River at Newport News Landing, securing a degree of operational flexibility for his troops at Fort Monroe. On June 10, however, one of Butler's subordinates botched an attack on Confederate positions near Big Bethel Church, costing the Federals seventy-six casualties as against eight for the local enemy. On May 31–June 1, fighting also flared up along the Potomac and in Chesapeake Bay when Union warships shelled the batteries Colonel Ruggles had planted along Aquia Creek. Despite two days of pounding, however, the vessels inflicted minimal material damage.[38]

A more successful operation got underway on June 10, when Colonel Stone, now detached from McDowell's command, led a 2,500-man force of all arms—three regiments and four battalions of infantry, including Frank Patterson's 17th Pennsylvania; two cavalry companies; and two artillery pieces—from the outskirts of Washington toward enemy-held Leesburg via Rockville and Tennallytown, Maryland. The objectives of the Rockville Expedition, as it became known, were to thwart Rebel activity on the upper Potomac, secure such important positions as Edwards's and Conrad's Ferries, stanch the flow of supplies from Baltimore to forces in Virginia, and open the obstructed Chesapeake & Ohio Canal near Leesburg. Another purpose was to relieve pressure from General Patterson's imminent movement on Harpers Ferry.

The expedition, which consumed four weeks and featured intermittent contact with the foe, not only safeguarded the critical canal and ferries but also sent waves of alarm through Confederate forces as far west as the Shenandoah Valley. Stone's success, which eased General Scott's concerns for the safety of Washington's remote northern flank, left the commanding general "highly pleased with the whole conduct" of the operation. On July 7, his mission accomplished, Stone was ordered to march to Patterson's headquarters at Martinsburg, Virginia. There his troops were assimilated into the Army of Pennsylvania and formed into a brigade under the also recently arrived Charles Sandford.[39]

In early June the Army of Northeastern Virginia finally joined in the general activity with some tentative advances inside enemy territory. Four days after McDowell assumed command of the army, Hunter, from his brigade's camp outside Alexandria, suggested to a subordinate, Lieutenant Charles H. Tompkins of the 2nd U.S. Cavalry, that he probe to and if possible beyond the Rebel lines outside Fairfax Court House. Late that night Tompkins, who did not need a direct order to take action, led seventy-five troopers down the highway from Falls Church to the courthouse. Arriving in the dark of morning on June 1, the lieutenant moved to occupy the village from which, by interrogating residents, he hoped to gain information on Confederate outposts on the roads toward Bull Run.

Tompkins did not realize the town was occupied in some force. Therefore, he was surprised when upon entering, his party attracted a hail of rifle balls from two rudely awakened companies of Confederate cavalry and one of infantry, the whole under Richard Ewell (then a lieutenant colonel). The invaders were forced to run a gauntlet of fire as they dashed through the village and then beat a hasty retreat by the way they had come. But Tompkins was not defeated—yet. Uttering "oaths loud and deep," the young subaltern, who had been slightly injured by a fall from his horse, halted his men, turned them about, and led most of them back through the streets of town, which were now filled with newly arrived reinforcements under William "Extra Billy" Smith, a former governor of Virginia who, though without rank, had assumed command of a leaderless unit.

Thanks to Ewell's and Smith's ability to rally the almost unnerved defenders, the Federal horsemen were again halted by massed musketry. Hemmed in by roadside fences, his horses on the verge of bolting, and facing what he believed to be a thousand Rebels, Tompkins led his unit—which had suffered one officer wounded and nine horses killed—out of town by a circuitous route, this time heading for Falls Church. Though roughly handled, the attackers had given better than they got, having killed Captain John Quincy Marr of the Warrenton Rifles, a VMI graduate who thereby gained unenviable distinction as the first Confederate fatality of the war.[40]

Tompkins's dash on the courthouse had a beneficial effect on many careers. Acclaimed in the Northern press as an overdue sign of boldness and initiative, it would gain its leader a colonelcy in the volunteer cavalry as well as a Medal of Honor (one awarded thirty years later). For their staunch defense of the place, which played well in the Southern papers, Dick Ewell, who had been slightly wounded during the affair, was soon promoted to brigadier general and Smith to colonel of the 49th Virginia Infantry.[41]

McDowell's reaction to the raid was decidedly mixed. He could not deny that Tompkins had "most gallantly" fulfilled his intelligence-gathering mission at least as it pertained to Fairfax Court House, and the five prisoners he had taken there presumably imparted additional information. The general decided that the exploit "has given considerable prestige to our regular cavalry in the eyes of our people and of the volunteer regiments." At the same time, though, he criticized the lieutenant for undertaking the mission without orders and for unwittingly interfering with "a more important movement," one that McDowell never identified.[42]

The general did not perceive another drawback to Tompkins's operation. His wildly inflated estimate of the troops at the courthouse (in actuality, only about two hundred altogether) inhibited McDowell from making further reconnaissances of the disputed territory between the armies. Some historians claim that the lieutenant's overestimate postponed the Federal advance against Bull Run, giving Beauregard additional time to strengthen his defenses.[43]

The next advance toward enemy territory, sixteen days after Tompkins's foray, could not have been the "more important movement" McDowell had alluded to, for it lacked thorough planning and a coherent objective and quickly came to naught. On June 3, perhaps in response to Greeley's ubiquitous call for action, Scott directed his newly appointed field commander to estimate the number of troops he would need to make an advance on the Bull Run line and also perhaps against Manassas Gap in the Blue Ridge, the movement to occur more or less simultaneously with Patterson's approach to Harpers Ferry. His telegram implied that the operations would be mutually supporting, but even a casual reading made it clear that Patterson's was to be the main offensive.[44]

McDowell may have been surprised by his apparent relegation to a supporting role, but he wasted no time submitting a proposal to carry the Bull Run line and seize the roads to Culpeper Court House and Manassas Gap. The alacrity of his response indicates that he had put a lot of thought into what would be required to accomplish the various missions he was facing. To attain the objectives Scott enumerated, he would need 12,000 troops of all arms, including several hundred cavalry, plus a reserve force of 5,000 to be left at Alexandria until needed. Perhaps, the general suggested to his superior, a force this large would persuade Beauregard to abandon his position and fall back on Richmond, thus obviating the need for a pitched battle. Like many another Northerner, McDowell clung to the belief that the defenders of Virginia were playing a game of bluff, one they would quit if suitably threatened.[45]

McDowell's estimates were sound, but they rested on the supposition that Beauregard had fewer than half the troops now in position between Bull Run and Fairfax Court House. When a credible report reached Washington a few days later that the Creole commanded 20,000 men inclusive of a large detachment at Fairfax, the plan suddenly appeared impracticable. McDowell, however, proposed to make it work. As he informed Scott, he would bypass Fairfax by moving out the Loudoun & Hampshire Railroad to the hamlet of Vienna, some fifteen miles northwest of Alexandria. From this advanced position, he would turn southwestward and march on Centreville, which was thought to be lightly occupied. By the fifteenth Scott, having learned that Patterson was not ready to cross the Potomac and attack Harpers Ferry, called off the proposed movement.[46]

McDowell continued to believe that the plan to bypass Fairfax Court House had merit, and on the sixteenth he decided to test it. That morning he dispatched General Tyler, with a four-hundred-man detachment of the 1st Connecticut, by train to Vienna to learn if the area was in enemy hands. If not, several points were to be occupied and guarded, with campsites selected for the transfer there of Schenck's brigade.

Tyler's train proceeded three or four miles beyond the village without encountering any enemy beyond a single roadside sniper who wounded a Connecticut soldier. The general reported the track and bridges in good shape, but all local rolling stock had been burned by the Rebels to prevent their use by the Federals. The way appeared open to occupy the area in force, but apparently Tyler had loose lips. According to one involved in the operation, he and his subordinates discussed within hearing distance of several local people

McDowell's intention to send a larger force to the same area the next day and establish a presence there. Tyler departed Vienna and returned to home base only minutes before a body of Confederate cavalry and artillery passed through the area and learned from the natives what the Yankees were up to.[47]

The following morning McDowell ordered Schenck, with part of his brigade, out along the Loudoun & Hampshire to the point where, just east of Falls Church, the road from Fort Corcoran crossed the railroad. After establishing a base at that point, Schenck, "by suitable patrols[, was] to feel the way" up the tracks toward Vienna, "moving, however, with caution, and making it a special duty to guard effectually the railroad bridges" and inspect the condition of the track. The general complied by placing aboard a train of passenger and flat cars Colonel Alexander M. McCook's 1st Ohio, seven hundred strong. One participant considered the operation "an original move—a reconnaissance on a locomotive into the enemy's country."[48]

The train carrying Schenck and McCook started out in good order. It halted at several points to drop off six companies of Ohioans, two at the junction McDowell had indicated, two others near Falls Church, and two to guard the track toward Vienna. With the remaining four companies, fewer than three hundred men, Schenck pushed on to Vienna. The next stop, early that evening, was unplanned: at a bend in the track about a quarter mile short of the village, the train was shelled by a couple of cannons concealed on a tree-and-brush-fringed hilltop.

The ambush was the work of Colonel Maxcy Gregg of the 1st South Carolina Infantry, leading a reconnaissance force of more than seven hundred infantry and cavalry and a two-gun section of Captain Delaware Kemper's Alexandria Artillery. Acting upon the reports of those who had overheard Tyler's discussion, that morning Gregg had marched to Vienna from neighboring Dranesville. He found no Yankees but decided to remain in the area. When at about 6:00 P.M. he heard the whistle of Schenck's approaching train, the colonel improvised a reception with Kemper's guns, supported by infantrymen hidden in trackside foliage. Gregg's hasty but inspired dispositions ensured that his assault would come as a complete and destructive surprise.[49]

The blasts from Kemper's 6-pounder guns spread chaos and consternation among Schenck's troops, who were riding on the flat cars and in at least one passenger car pushed from the rear by the engine.

The first shells struck the lead car, throwing it into the air and spilling its riders onto the right of way. "It was a complete surprise," wrote one Buckeye, "and cost us a dozen lives, much mortification, and great loss of prestige." No passenger on the lead car was killed or badly wounded, but subsequent rounds made casualties of several men on the two following flats. Another shell struck and temporarily disabled the engine, preventing it from backing around the bend to safety.[50]

Frightened soldiers scrambled from the upright cars and took shelter in woods opposite Gregg's position. When Kemper and his supporting infantry raked their hiding place, a befuddled Schenck called retreat. Hastily collecting the survivors, he led them down the tracks toward home at the double quick. More resolute soldiers remained behind to gather up the wounded and carry them off on blankets and makeshift litters. By now the locomotive had regained mobility, but the engineer ran it back toward Alexandria, abandoning his passengers. Though pursued for a few miles by Gregg's cavalry, the Yankees made their escape in gathering darkness, finally rallying five miles from the scene of the ambush. A quick count revealed that eight of their comrades had been killed and four wounded; one man had been captured. Once the Ohioans were gone, their assailants gathered up the rifles many had tossed aside in their haste to escape. Gregg ordered the captured cars to be burned to their metal trucks.[51]

The debacle outside Vienna had repercussions for those involved and many who had not been. It cast a shadow over the budding career of General Schenck, who had failed to reconnoiter the area he had been tasked to occupy and had made no effort to engage his assailants. In his defense, because no Rebels had been found in the vicinity the day before, Schenck had no reason to suspect any would be there on the seventeenth. Some historians have accused him of plowing ahead on a high-risk operation in order to establish his bona fides as a field commander, but there is no evidence of this. Quite simply it was Schenck's misfortune to fall into a neatly sprung trap. Even so, he had looked feeble, inattentive, and complacent. One damning report had the general—admittedly a devotee of the good life—riding in a plush railcar, sipping champagne and puffing on a cigar, at the moment Gregg opened fire on his men.[52]

The waylaying of the 1st Ohio would make McDowell more cautious in ordering future incursions into the land between the armies.

In fact, it seems to have infected his men with a deep-seated fear of "masked batteries," one that politicians and newspaper editors would play up. In the short term Schenck's misadventure prompted General Scott to order the army to draw in its lines. Against the protests of both McDowell and Tyler, the latter's troops evacuated the Falls Church area, which they had only recently occupied, and withdrew closer to Fort Corcoran.[53]

Paradoxically, almost as soon as he contracted his area of operations, Scott again proposed to take the offensive. Four days after Schenck's botched reconnaissance, he ordered McDowell to plan an advance against Leesburg in cooperation with Patterson's ongoing operations in the lower Shenandoah. In responding, McDowell for the first time raised objections to his superior's strategy. A movement so far west, he argued, would overextend and overexpose his command. Despite reports of a major buildup along Beauregard's line, McDowell continued to regard Manassas–Bull Run as his primary objective. Though as of June 24 he had in his department fewer than 14,000 infantry, enough troops were crossing over from Washington every day (in a matter of weeks, his field force would more than double) to make him confident that if properly trained, organized, and motivated, they could beat Beauregard's Rebels—if they needed to fight them at all. He continued to believe that a well-mounted advance might persuade the Creole to quit Bull Run for a better defensive position along the Rappahannock River.[54]

In a sense, Scott decided to call McDowell's bluff. He was fully aware that his subordinate considered his army unready for the full-scale advance he appeared to be proposing. Yet public opinion was fast eroding the government's will to resist the temptation to strike a decisive blow regardless of the army's unfinished state. McDowell plead for more time, but what time there was seemed to be fast running out. As he later told congressional investigators, he had never maneuvered 30,000 troops: "I had seen them handled abroad in reviews and marches, but I had never handled that number, and no one [else] here had. I wanted very much a little time; all of us wanted it. We did not have a bit of it."[55]

It was bad enough that, even after weeks of drilling, the enlisted force remained largely ignorant of what to expect in battle. As McDowell had intimated, the high command was almost as unschooled as the lowliest member of the "awkward squad" (that portion of every regiment that required extra tutoring in the manual of arms). If the volunteers remained "utterly raw," a larger problem, as Major Barnard of McDowell's staff expressed it, was that they were led by "officers who, though generally of ability, were for the first time exercising these extensive commands, and who had hardly seen the troops they commanded." A New York officer agreed, doubting that any army the size of McDowell's had included "so small a number of officers educated in the science and art of war." Then too, many of those who knew their business were rendered unfit by personal weaknesses, especially alcoholism. Complaints of "drunken and unskilled officers" filled the letters that Union enlisted men sent home as the army's too-brief training period neared an end.[56]

In addition to inadequate training and unreliable leadership, McDowell's army was weakened by sickness. Diarrhea, dysentery, typhoid fever, pneumonia, and childhood ills such as measles and chicken pox ran rampant through camps filled with country boys who had gained no immunity to diseases bred of close confinement. Before the summer was over, fully one-third of McDowell's troops encamped around Arlington were sick with malaria or typhoid. Intestinal infections took an especially grievous toll. A Connecticut recruit, writing to his sister from Falls Church, claimed that more than half of his comrades had been laid low by dysentery: "200 good men could have wiped us out, we were in such bad condition." Given the local weather and the lack of municipal sanitation, Washington and its environs were sickly venues in any season, but that summer, according to a local physician, the city was "poisoned by the soldiers and everybody is ill."[57]

McDowell's problems were many and onerous, but by late June they were drawing little sympathy in high places. Whether addressed to Lincoln, Scott, or other superiors, his concerns met with the same response: "You are green, it is true; but they are green, also; you are all green alike." The government's growing lack of patience meant that the time McDowell desperately needed had almost run out. Evidence of this came on June 21, when Scott directed him to present, explain, and defend a finished plan "to sweep the enemy from Leesburg towards Alexandria" in cooperation with a column from Patterson's army. The stage had been set for an attack on those miserable wretches striving to dismantle the greatest government on the face of the earth.[58]

CHAPTER 5

ESCAPING THE DEATHTRAP

Joe Johnston never occupied a position he was not prepared to abandon. Ground was not worth holding if it left the defender vulnerable to attack, especially when the attackers had the advantage of numbers. By early June Johnston had convinced himself that Harpers Ferry could not be secured against capture. He knew that McDowell was forming a large army sixty-plus miles to the east, little more than a day's journey from Harpers Ferry via the Manassas Gap Railroad. A more likely opponent was Patterson, who appeared on the verge of departing Chambersburg, a two or three days' march away, at the head of another force that dwarfed Johnston's.

Either command, if it forced a confrontation, would make short work of the Army of the Shenandoah. There was also the possibility—remote, perhaps, given the growing concentration at Manassas but realistic under certain conditions—that McDowell and Patterson would combine against Harpers Ferry via too many routes of approach to be effectively blocked. Then too, the recent advance of McClellan's Federals into western Virginia suggested that Johnston might be caught in an even larger vise. For a soldier with his inherent caution and vivid imagination, a major reassessment of the situation seemed in order.[1]

Another factor in his growing desire to evacuate Harpers Ferry was his belief that it lacked strategic value and was thus not worth holding even by a force stronger than his. In Johnston's mind the town lay more than twenty miles east of the most accessible route to the Shenandoah from Maryland and Pennsylvania and thus was anything but an important position. When he explained his reasoning to his superiors, however, neither Jefferson Davis, Robert E. Lee, nor Samuel Cooper saw the wisdom in it. They wished to secure Harpers Ferry, which they considered the main entrance to the Valley, if only to make possible the disassembling and removal of the weapons-making machinery—planing and rifling machines, boring-banks, lathes, water turbines, and the rest—to a safer location.

Johnston considered this an insufficient reason to remain in a vulnerable spot. As he argued in a postwar article, even if it fell back to Winchester, his army would have been "within a day's march of the position, [which] would have protected that removal." Nor was he reassured by Richmond's assertions that the "corps of observation" that held the various outposts between Fairfax Court House and Leesburg would give him timely warning of the enemy's approach from Washington or Maryland. The crux of Johnston's predicament was that Davis and Lee put great stock in occupying and securing territory. The president, who had the final say in strategic matters, considered every acre of Confederate terrain holy ground, to be relinquished only in case of dire emergency; Lee felt just as protective of the sacred soil of Virginia.[2]

Even so, Lee at least raised the possibility that Johnston might have to abandon not only Harpers Ferry but also the Valley itself. On May 30, only days after Johnston had arrived at his post, the commander of Virginia's forces suggested how he should react if the observation forces on the upper Potomac failed to prevent an enemy incursion from the Leesburg area: "In the event of such a movement, should you deem it advisable, and should you be unable to hold your position, I would suggest a joint attack by you and General Bonham, commanding at Manassas, for the purpose of cutting them off." Here was one of the first references in official correspondence to a linkage between the forces in the Valley and those at Bull Run, the genesis of a plan of action adopted seven weeks later.[3]

Although beset by numerous threats, by mid-June Johnston could at least take comfort from the improving quality of the troops at his disposal, now 8,000 strong. Almost every man was more-or-less properly attired, in many cases in a uniform sewn by hand by family members or their slaves. Many still carried the antiquated arms they had toted from home, but the local arsenal had remedied most of the army's weapons shortage. Like Beauregard, Johnston too often lacked adequate supplies of horseflesh, ammunition, and equipment, though in the verdant Valley, his men did not want for subsistence. In some situations the supply problem would prove a boon to mobility. Johnston viewed his army as lightweight and fast moving; if given permission to evacuate his station, he would not be bogged down by excess impedimenta.

When informing Richmond of the vulnerability of his post, Johnston passed along a memorandum by his chief engineer, Major

William H. C. Whiting, that between 12,000 and 15,000 troops, including at least two regiments of cavalry, were necessary to hold Harpers Ferry under normal circumstances. Johnston would never have that many, but during June he received enough reinforcements to support the hope that if challenged by Patterson, he could at least make a fight of it. Still, he doubted that such a stand would be long or successful. On the sixth he wrote Lee regarding the latter's expressed concern that the abandonment of the post "would be depressing to the cause of the South." Johnston then asked what he believed to be a logical question: "Would not the loss of five or six thousand men be more so? . . . Might it not be better (after the troops here have delayed the enemy as long by their presence as they prudently can) to transfer them to some point where they may still be useful?"[4]

This time Lee laid these concerns before Davis, but the president's reply eased none of his field commander's fears. Lee informed Johnston, "he places great value upon our retention of the command of the Shenandoah Valley and the position at Harper's Ferry." Davis had added an argument to buttress his position: "The evacuation of [Harpers Ferry] would interrupt our communication with Maryland, and injure our cause in that State."[5]

The issue of secure communications bore heavily on Johnston's desire to evacuate. As Major Whiting had observed in his memorandum, giving up Harpers Ferry was necessary to secure the link between the Valley and either Manassas or Richmond as well as to prevent any chance of Patterson's turning the army's flank via the passes of the Blue Ridge, including Manassas Gap. Whiting speculated that Patterson and Richmond shared the same misperception: that Harpers Ferry was of greater strategic value than it really was.[6]

Brigadier General Edmund Kirby Smith, formerly of Johnston's staff, fully agreed with his superior's opinions of Harpers Ferry's vulnerability and Richmond's obtuseness. Smith, a native Floridian of New England parentage, a West Pointer who later taught mathematics at the academy, and a Mexican War stalwart who had risen to field-grade rank in the 2nd Cavalry, considered the Valley garrison "untenable and unimportant in a military point of view . . . only held in compliance with instructions from an Adj. General in Richmond, whose faults & blunders had nearly involved us in irreparable losses."[7]

The only reassurance Davis could give Johnston was his strong doubt that an advance against him from western Virginia was an "immediate" concern. A small army under Brigadier General Robert Selden Garnett had been sent to that part of the state to resist further incursions by McClellan and to restrict his access to the Baltimore & Ohio, the principal throughway to the Valley. "It is hoped by these means," Lee wrote Johnston in his most soothing tone, "that you will be relieved from an attack in that direction, and will have merely to resist an attack in front from Pennsylvania."[8]

Johnston, of course, saw nothing "mere" in the threat posed by Patterson, who as of the date of Lee's response was ready to move to Hagerstown, Maryland, six miles from the Potomac. That same day Patterson, cautious as always, was informing Winfield Scott of reports that the Confederates were guarding the approaches to Harpers Ferry so closely that he could not ascertain the strength of Johnston's force. Unaware of the Virginian's intentions to avoid a confrontation, Patterson suspected that his enemy proposed to "make a desperate struggle" to hold the town. Even so, he claimed to be determined to attack and capture the position with the force available to him—nearly three times as many troops as his opponent had for its defense.[9]

Johnston perceived at least a glimmer of hope that he had made Richmond appreciate the extent of his difficulties. In his June 7 reply to Johnston's latest request for authority to abandon Harpers Ferry, Lee had agreed that "you must exercise your discretion and judgment in this respect, to insure, if possible, your safety." He added that "precise instructions cannot be given you, but, being informed of the object of the campaign, you will be able to regulate its conduct to the best advantage." Here was an intimation that Johnston could evacuate if he thought it absolutely necessary but that it would run counter to Richmond's wishes.[10]

His superiors' concerns notwithstanding, Johnston believed his hand had been forced when, early on June 13, a reliable informant from Winchester brought word that the previous evening a large detachment from McClellan's army, supposed to be about 2,000 strong, had seized Romney, Virginia, one of the most valuable road centers west of the Valley. Situated little more than forty miles from Winchester, its seizure threatened the point Johnston considered his best fallback option. He had learned from Northern newspapers of the approximate size of Patterson's army boring down on him from another direction, and once again he imagined himself soon to be crushed between mighty forces.[11]

By fearing that McClellan could somehow cut his line of retreat, Johnston was overreacting to a remote possibility. Even so, within hours of hearing of the Romney raid, he dispatched the 10th and 13th Virginia by train to the threatened area with orders to retard McClellan should he be nearing the western reaches of the Valley. The move proved unnecessary, for the Yankees who had taken Romney, a small, far-flung force under Colonel Lew Wallace answerable not to McClellan but to Patterson, quickly withdrew up the north branch of the Potomac to Cumberland, Maryland.[12]

Johnston had selected wisely in naming A. P. Hill as commander of this force. The thirty-five-year-old Hill, a native of Culpeper, Virginia; a West Pointer; and a veteran of the Seminole and Mexican Wars, would make a distinguished reputation successively in brigade, division, and corps command. Once the Yankees released their hold on Romney, Hill rejoined Johnston.[13]

Unaware of Wallace's intentions, Johnston believed that he had to leave Harpers Ferry to avoid being taken simultaneously in front and rear. During the remainder of the thirteenth and throughout the following day, he supervised his subordinates in removing quartermaster's and commissary supplies as well as what remained of the armory's machinery, most of it already disassembled and hauled off. To prevent the enemy from gaining easy access to what remained, he took steps to destroy the railroad bridges across the Potomac and all other bridges between nearby Point of Rocks and Shepherdstown, a distance of eighteen miles. By the morning of the fifteenth, Johnston's vanguard would be leaving the ferry via the southwest-running road to Charles Town and from there by the Valley Pike to Winchester.[14]

The evacuation gained Richmond's tacit approval. On the thirteenth Adjutant General Cooper had reminded Johnston, in a letter that did not reach him for two days, that "you had been heretofore instructed to exercise your discretion as to retiring from your position." He added, however, that from Johnston's most recent dispatches, the War Department had received the impression that the general "considered the authority given as not equal to the necessity of the case"—that is, insufficient to absolve him of the responsibility for evacuating a post and abandoning materiel that could not be carried off.[15]

Johnston did in fact feel this way, for he believed that the government, not he, was seeking to avoid accountability in the matter.

After the war he contended that prior to Cooper's letter of the thirteenth, he had never been specifically authorized to use his judgment as to whether Harpers Ferry should be given up or held. Lee's
letter of the seventh appeared to extend this authority, and Johnston
was prepared to act upon it, but he wanted an unambiguous statement to this effect from Cooper or, preferably, Davis. He realized
his decision to withdraw might have serious consequences for his
career in the Confederate service, and he wanted to protect his reputation. Here was the Johnston of old—the crack shot and hesitant
hunter, reluctant to pull the trigger, to exercise judgment and take
action, for fear it might harm him professionally if something went
awry or looked blameworthy. Only if higher authority accepted the
responsibility would he act.

Johnston must have sensed that the abandonment of his post
would not be well received by his army or the Southern public.
Members of the garrison opposed the idea of turning their backs
to the foe even if critical to their well-being. Colonel Jackson told
his wife of the dejection of the troops as they marched out: "Their
reluctance was manifested by their snail-like pace." Private John
Singleton Mosby, a young lawyer from Bristol, Virginia, who had
joined Stuart's 1st Virginia Cavalry, declared that there was "no
necessity" for giving up the town, which dealt the garrison "a shock
for which we were not prepared, and it chilled our enthusiasm."[16]

A clerk in the war office at Richmond, John Beauchamp Jones,
made a note in his diary of early reports of the evacuation. From
what he could gather, the news produced much public dismay, "and,
for the first time, I heard murmurs against the government." Yet
Jones understood Johnston's motivation and even wrote a propa-
ganda piece for the local newspapers defending the move. Secretary
of War Walker was quite pleased by the effort and asked its author
to deliver it personally to Davis. It is doubtful that a single editorial
had a major effect on public opinion, but the following day Jones
observed that "the city is content at the evacuation. The people
have unbounded confidence in the wisdom of the administration
and the ability of our generals." He added, however, that Beauregard,
not Johnston, "is the especial favorite."[17]

By June 14, as Johnston made preparations to leave Harpers Ferry
and blow up the trestlework supporting that 1,300-foot-long railroad
bridge over the Potomac east of the town, Robert Patterson was still

in Pennsylvania. That day he informed his superiors in Washington of his inability to move his headquarters south "for want of transportation, which comes in slowly." The bulk of his army, however, had crossed into Maryland and was advancing on Hagerstown, where Patterson planned to join it the following day. Although the cautious warrior feared that "a determined stand will be made at Harpers' Ferry—a desperate struggle for supremacy," his command was formidable enough to overawe any force Johnston could throw in its path. For this he had to thank Governor Curtin, who had provided him with nineteen of the twenty-five three-months' volunteer regiments Pennsylvania had raised to date. He also owed General Scott for augmenting his command with a few units of regular infantry, artillery, and cavalry as well as with three volunteer regiments organized outside Pennsylvania: one that had been sworn in for six months' service (19th New York), one for nine-months' (4th Connecticut), and one for two years' (28th New York).[18]

Patterson appeared less beholden to his fellow Pennsylvanian Simon Cameron. On the tenth he had inquired of the secretary of war why a body of New Jersey troops supposedly earmarked for his army had instead been sent to McDowell. Patterson could have used those additions for the coming confrontation with Johnston: "The importance of victory at Harper's Ferry cannot be estimated. I cannot sleep for thinking about it." He asked Cameron to keep in mind "that my reputation and the reputation of our dear old State is at stake in this issue. I beseech you, therefore, by our ancient friendship, give me the means of success. You have the means; place them at my disposal, and shoot me if I do not use them to advantage."[19]

In truth, Patterson already had the means of victory at his disposal—almost 18,000 troops. He had organized his army into five brigades, divided between the divisions of Cadwalader and Keim. Three of the brigades continued to be led by officers who had assumed their posts while in training camp: Brigadier Generals Wynkoop, Williams, and Negley. These organizations were composed entirely of Pennsylvania ninety-day regiments, five in Wynkoop's brigade, four in Williams's, and two in Negley's.

The remaining brigades were led by regular-army colonels, one with an artillery and cavalry background, the other with long experience in the infantry. The leader of Patterson's variegated First Brigade—three regiments of volunteer infantry, three companies of the 2nd U.S. Cavalry, a detachment of the 14th U.S. Infantry, and a section of Company F, 4th U.S. Artillery (at this stage of the war, regular batteries were generally known as companies)—was forty-four-year-old George H. Thomas. Destined to become one of the war's great captains, Thomas at this early stage of the conflict was finding it difficult to establish a foothold in command circles. His slow-moving career was mainly due to his Virginia roots, which caused some War Department officials to question his allegiance to the Union. An 1840 graduate of West Point, where fellow cadet William T. Sherman described him as "never brilliant but always cool, reliable and steady," he had spent fifteen years in the artillery before transferring to the newly created 2nd Cavalry, to the command of which he had succeeded in early 1861.[20]

Two supposedly elite volunteer units rounded out Thomas's brigade. The 1st Rhode Island Infantry, a much-ballyhooed three-month outfit, was led by Colonel Ambrose E. Burnside, a West Pointer from Indiana who had resigned from the army in 1853 to manufacture firearms in Rhode Island and to command state troops. Then there was the First Troop, Philadelphia City Cavalry, a militia unit that had been in continuous service since the Revolutionary War.[21]

The officer of regulars who gained command of Patterson's Fourth Brigade boasted a long and varied career that appeared to qualify him for high station. This was Maryland-born Dixon S. Miles, West Point class of 1823, a veteran of both staff and line service and for the previous two and a half years a colonel of regular infantry. Career progression notwithstanding, Miles was unimaginative, erratic, and a martinet of the deepest stripe; he appears to have risen to regimental command solely on the basis of seniority. The same qualification had placed him in command of three volunteer outfits and detachments of two regular regiments, including Miles's own 2nd Infantry.[22]

On June 12 Patterson, still at Chambersburg, had issued detailed directions for the movement on Harpers Ferry. These were well thought out, although their execution would be both wanting and slow. Thomas's brigade, followed closely by Miles's, would march beyond Hagerstown to the Potomac at Williamsport. Thomas was to protect the ford at that location with his two artillery pieces; in turn, Miles would cover Thomas's open right flank. Williams's brigade was to take the turnpike from Hagerstown to Sharpsburg and camp there, thirteen miles downriver from Williamsport. The brigade under Wynkoop, after reaching Hagerstown by rail, would take position at Funkstown, two and a half miles to the southeast, covering the army's rear. Negley's command, also assigned to the rear echelon, would assume an intermediate position on the turnpike between Hagerstown and Williamsport.[23]

Patterson stressed that his subordinates were to establish a continuous line of sentinels, each brigade positioned so as to "protect the adjoining one, and in case of attack go to its assistance." The tone of Patterson's orders implied a need for great caution, perhaps stemming from Scott's warning (as most recently expressed in a communiqué to McClellan) that Patterson's campaign must not fail for fear of damaging the morale of Northerners and the unionists of Maryland and Virginia. On June 13 Scott did Patterson no favor by agreeing that Johnston would make "a desperate stand." The commanding general worsened the situation by relaying an erroneous report that Brigadier General Ben McCulloch, the well-known former commander of Texas state troops, was lying in wait for Patterson in advance of Harpers Ferry, accompanied by two regiments of sharpshooters.[24]

On the fourteenth Patterson ordered his ranking subordinate, General Cadwalader, to proceed cautiously toward the army's main objective. The division commander was instructed to feign an attack on Maryland Heights, then turn the Rebel left flank "through or near Martinsburg, with a strong column of mixed arms," supported from the rear by a force hefty enough to parry any effort to cut off the flanking column. The supporting force should be strong enough also to maintain the army's line of communication—a thinly veiled reference to keeping open a retreat route should Johnston counterattack.[25]

Early on the sixteenth, Cadwalader's advance echelon finally began to wade the Potomac at Williamsport. Although the local ferry had been destroyed, by day's end, as Patterson later claimed, two-thirds of the army had sloshed across the high-running but passable river. The forward movement suddenly appeared to require less caution, for the previous day a reconnaissance by one of Cadwalader's engineer officers, Captain John Newton, had observed the detonation of the B&O bridge, which suggested that Johnston was evacuating. Newton reported that Harpers Ferry was wreathed in smoke from burning facilities and that only a rear guard remained, apparently to monitor the progress of the destruction.

At first Patterson gave no credence to these findings, suspecting a Rebel ploy to lure him into a trap. To play it safe, he ordered

Cadwalader to advance a detachment up the railroad toward Martinsburg "to secure against surprise." Even now, with other observers insisting that Harpers Ferry was his for the taking, Patterson felt it necessary to remind his subordinates of "the momentous interests at stake, which would suffer even from a check, which would be construed into a [Confederate] victory." This initiative-sapping mantra would be intoned time and again in coming weeks: *For God's sake, advance slowly and with utmost care, scanning every rock and tree for the enemy lurking behind, lest you be ambushed and suffer a defeat that will crush the spirit and confidence of the army.*[26]

For those close enough to Harpers Ferry to observe it, Johnston's withdrawal produced memorable sights. Captain Newton was struck by the vastness of the destruction that accompanied the Confederates' departure. Not only were the B&O and Winchester & Potomac Railroad bridges in flames, but it also appeared that the rolling stock of both railroads—dozens of locomotives and cars of every description—had been run off the spans before their detonation. Virtually every building composing the armory was burning out of control; repeated explosions indicated that not all of the stored ammunition had been carried off.

The destruction appeared total, although ironically, perhaps fittingly, the engine house in which John Brown and his followers had holed up on that momentous day in October 1859 still stood. Newton then led his party along the B&O tracks toward Martinsburg to make sure that the Rebels were abandoning the Potomac line. They found the defenses of Martinsburg deserted and the local rail- and iron-manufacturing facilities demolished. It was evident that the Confederates were in full-scale retreat. Soon even Patterson was certain that Johnston was heading for Winchester via the Berryville Road.[27]

When Cadwalader's division crossed the Potomac, its commander was mulling over the cautionary advice his superior had given him even in the face of the Rebels' evident departure. Patterson was concerned that a pursuit of the Confederates would be hazardous; thus he continued to warn his subordinate to guard against a surprise assault and to "annoy their retreat" only "if it can safely be done." Cadwalader needed no call to wariness, for like his superior, he suspected that Johnston had hatched "a deep-laid plot to deceive us." Still, by early afternoon of the sixteenth, his five-hundred-man advance guard had entered the town and taken full possession. The troops observed no signs that a trap had been laid; Johnston's troops were heading southwestward at a rapid gait. They signaled for comrades to cross the river and join them amid the smoldering ruins of Harpers Ferry.[28]

Late that day a visibly relieved Patterson telegraphed Washington that the town—what remained of it—was in Federal hands. General Scott immediately inquired about "what movement, if any, in pursuit of the enemy" his subordinate proposed to make. Patterson replied, "cannot make it." Johnston had been "routed by fear," the implication being that he was withdrawing too fast to be overtaken short of Winchester. Instead, the Pennsylvanian proposed making Harpers Ferry his base for further operations, including an advance on Johnston's new position and perhaps from there to Strasburg.[29]

But while Patterson predicted bold future movements, he remained fixated on the present. "Harpers' Ferry has been retaken without firing a gun," he crowed. "The moral force of a just cause, sustained by a strong and equable Government, has conquered." Patterson claimed to see far-reaching political benefits in taking this town that had been delivered over to him by his enemy: "With Harper's Ferry in [our] possession, Baltimore falls. Maryland will be a quiet spectator, awaiting the result of the campaign, with her interests developing a feeling in favor of a permanent Federal Government." But all that could wait; for now, he wished to savor his triumph.[30]

No doubt Patterson expected a nicely phrased expression of praise and gratitude from Scott. He must have been shocked to receive a telegram that would precipitate a turning point of the campaign: "Send to me at once all the regular troops, horse and foot, with you, and also the Rhode Island regiment." Patterson was stunned by the demand that, if complied with, would leave him with an army composed almost entirely of three-months' volunteers, half of whose service terms had already expired or were about to.[31]

To be sure, some of the regulars, notably the troopers of the 2nd Cavalry who, while at Chambersburg, had gone on drunken sprees, had given the general headaches, but he feared losing their polish and poise in camp and in the field. He responded by asking that he be allowed to hold on to the regulars "for the present"—a few days at least. Patterson credited them with imparting to his army the rudiments of professionalism that had enabled it to take Harpers

Ferry. Until the town could be fully occupied and fortified, "I should fear the return of the rebels." Beyond this, the loss of so many troops would impede his ability to move against Johnston's presumed destination, Winchester.[32]

But there was no help for it. Scott replied later that same day that he saw no necessity for Patterson to confront Johnston in his new position, a move that might cause him to withdraw farther into the Valley or, worse, shift eastward to Richmond or Manassas Junction. The regulars, Scott insisted, were needed in Washington without further delay. He repeated the order on the seventeenth, claiming "we are pressed here."[33]

Scott never explained to Patterson what he meant by "pressed," and he has left students of the campaign guessing as well. There seemed to be nothing to suggest that the capital was under a new or heightened threat. Yet even at this late date, evidently Scott was concerned that much of McDowell's army, even after the recent efforts to contract its lines, was encamped too far from the capital to provide quick support in a crisis—whatever the nature of that crisis. The array of fortifications that one day would enclose Washington was still under construction and far from providing needed protection. Scott worried too that Alexandria and Arlington were vulnerable to attack from the troops at Bull Run. John Sherman believed that the old general anticipated a strike prior to the July 4 convening of the special session of Congress, called by Lincoln to pass a raft of war-related measures.[34]

Although historians have called Scott's fears farfetched, his concerns may have been valid: a plan aimed at attacking both Alexandria and Arlington was just then taking shape in the head of G. T. Beauregard. Another reason for the decision to transfer troops from the Valley to Washington was a belated realization that the present campaign would be won or lost in McDowell's theater. Scott had finally come to see Patterson's operations as supportive of McDowell's, valuable primarily as a means of preventing Johnston from reinforcing Beauregard.

Although undoubtedly shaken by Scott's peremptory demand, Patterson moved to comply as quickly as possible. He grouped his regular infantry and artillery under Colonel Miles and the cavalry under Colonel Thomas and prepared to send them off by eastbound trains. At the same time he rescinded orders recently given to Burnside and his Rhode Islanders (whom Patterson praised as "a gallant soldier and a gallant command"} to proceed west, along with some horseman and cannons, and reinforce Colonel Wallace, who was reported to be under siege at his latest station, Cumberland, Maryland. In the end Patterson would be able to retain some cavalry and artillery originally earmarked for Washington, along with Thomas himself, a critical asset to his or any other army. Yet he never quite recovered from having to divest himself of the only true professionals in his ranks. The loss of their expertise and élan would only make him more hesitant to confront Johnston and less confident of his ability to prevail against him.[35]

It took a day and a half to complete the evacuation of Harpers Ferry. This delay Johnston charged to having to haul off not only rations and materiel but also the heavy baggage of the troops; as he later wrote, "almost every private soldier had a trunk" full of personal items. After the war one of his veterans confirmed this observation. Early in the conflict resources were so abundant that "each man had his own trunk packed full of every thing that loved ones at home thought their soldier boy might, could, would, or should ever need. Each company had baggage enough (mess-chests, camp-equipage, cooking utensils, trunks, etc.) to load a wagon-train larger than . . . used afterward to allow to a brigade, or even a division."[36]

Seven miles from Harpers Ferry, the heavily laden Confederates tramped sullenly but defiantly through Charles Town, a village of divided sympathies though the secessionist element predominated. One who observed their passage on June 15 was a local unionist, author and graphic artist David Hunter Strother. Currently a correspondent for *Harper's Weekly* but soon to gain a commission as a topographical engineer on Patterson's staff, Strother had a rare opportunity to study the face of his sworn enemy without attracting undue attention to his loyalties. By careful count he noted that fourteen regiments of infantry, six hundred cavalrymen, twenty-three cannons, and 240 supply wagons made up the day-long procession that wended its way through the town—this in addition to an advanced guard, perhaps of brigade strength, that had passed through the previous day.

Strother was impressed by the determined expressions of the soldiers, if not by their raiment: "The infantry, despite its rags and dust, had a dangerous look. The regiments from the Gulf States were apparently of picked men. . . . Looking along the line you were struck with the uniformity of size and height, all healthy, athletic men, between the ages of twenty-five and thirty-five." He marveled that each regiment was accompanied by a gang of black servants, "all bearing arms of some kind, and apparently as much interested in the cause as the whites." He wondered that if the war ended short of emancipation, "will the hand that has acquired the usage of pistol and sabre quietly take up the shovel and the hoe again at the bidding of a master?"

Not every unit Strother observed merited his approbation. While some of the foot units were well armed and kept up a well-aligned marching pace, others appeared full of poorly clothed, indifferently equipped, and undisciplined troops. The correspondent thought the artillery units, with the exception of Pendleton's battery ("reputed the best drilled in the command"), were made of inferior material, "both in guns and equipment; and it was manned chiefly by raw volunteers, who had had so far very little experience in handling the pieces." He was quite taken with the horsemen of J. E. B. Stuart, whom he considered "admirably mounted, and better equipped according to its needs than any other arm." He described Stuart's men, each of whom had furnished his own horse for the war, as "bold and dashing riders, good shots, full of spirit and enthusiasm, and promised, with experience and iron discipline, to constitute a formidable body of cavalry."

Strother had to have the commander of this rather motley but formidable force pointed out to him. "General Johnston himself appeared in plain citizen's dress, with common round hat, his deportment and manner altogether as unostentatious as his dress. His person seemed to be rather under the medium size, erect, vigorous, with a military whisker and a handsome face. It required no imagination, however, to see through this unimposing exterior the leading attributes which the world characterizes as soldierly." Strother's judgments were well considered; most would be validated in the weeks ahead.[37]

Even after reaching Charles Town, Johnston expected to be pursued, pressed, and brought to battle. Early on the sixteenth Stuart, covering the army's rear, reported that Patterson's forces had begun crossing the river below Williamsport and were marching on Martinsburg, from there, perhaps, to turn south and cut the Confederates' retreat. As though suddenly confident of making a stand against a larger opponent, Johnston determined to place his command across Patterson's path down the Valley Pike at Bunker Hill, midway between Martinsburg and Winchester. Upon the defensible ground around that town, he would challenge Patterson, preventing him from descending further into the Shenandoah and thwarting any intention he might have to link with McClellan.[38]

One possible reason for Johnston's new combativeness was that his mind had been relieved of a nagging concern. While en route to Bunker Hill, he received General Cooper's letter of the thirteenth, reporting that Jefferson Davis had finally sanctioned the evacuation of Harpers Ferry. The president's approval came, however, with an implied rebuke, Cooper chiding Johnston for requiring that "the responsibility of your retirement should be assumed here." This the government was willing to do inasmuch as it felt no reluctance "to bear any burden which the public interests require."[39]

The same letter may have motivated Johnston to stand and fight, for Cooper urged him to strike a blow at any pursuers and make "an effective stand, even against a very superior force." Apparently, Richmond had learned that Johnston, perhaps in response to Lee's letter of May 30, was considering a junction with Beauregard at Manassas. According to Johnston's nephew and biographer, Robert M. Hughes, Beauregard, soon after assuming command at Manassas, had opened a correspondence with Johnston. The two had discussed at length matters of mutual interest and had "agreed in their views of the importance of mutual support." Although Hughes concedes that the proposition to join forces did not necessarily originate with Johnston, "its importance was so obvious that it had occurred to all concerned (the enemy included)." Johnston did seize the initiative to the extent of suggesting that Beauregard and he establish a line of communication via "relays of expresses" through Snicker's and Ashby's Gaps in the Blue Ridge Mountains. Before June was out, Johnston dispatched some of Stuart's riders to Snicker's, the upper of the two passes, for that purpose as well as to scout eastward into the Loudoun Valley.[40]

As of June 13, Davis and Cooper thought the timing wrong to take such a drastic step as uniting the two armies. The adjutant general duly warned Johnston not to uncover Winchester for fear of denying the Confederates access to the fertile Shenandoah, thus severing communications with the western counties of Virginia and provoking political consequences that would stir "the most painful emotions." Of course, the immediate consequence of giving up the Valley would be to allow Patterson to move in any direction he chose, including eastward to take the Bull Run defenses in rear. On the eighteenth Cooper enjoined Johnston to confine himself to keeping tabs on Patterson and striking his detachments when the opportunity arose: "Should we not be able to assume the offensive with prospects of success the war must for a time remain one of positions, and active operations be carried on against small detachments and lines of communication."[41]

Johnston accepted Richmond's rationale for not uncovering the Valley, but he was stung by the implication that he lacked the courage to make difficult decisions. Thus he retorted to Cooper, "I am confident that nothing in my correspondence with my military superiors makes me obnoxious to the charge of desiring that the responsibility of my official acts should be borne by any other person than myself." By lodging such a claim, he was being disingenuous; his repeated requests for official approval speak for themselves. Still, the critical tone of Cooper's letter had struck a nerve, and he was determined to answer what he considered an undeserved aspersion.[42]

As it turned out, Johnston did not have to cleanse his record by accepting combat. On the afternoon of the sixteenth, his vanguard reached the banks of the stream that waters the high ground around Bunker Hill. The army leader formed his troops in successive lines of battle and settled down to await the enemy—who never appeared. Major Bradley T. Johnson of the 1st Maryland recalled that "fences were levelled; troops massed or deployed; batteries held together to be put in position; cavalry galloped to and fro, and all the usual preliminaries to battle gone through with. But it was an unfounded anticipation." The next morning Stuart reported that instead of advancing from Martinsburg, Patterson was crossing to the north side of the Potomac. Robbed of the opportunity to demonstrate resolve and tenacity, Johnston pulled up stakes and continued on to Winchester, bivouacking three miles east of the town. By the morning of the eighteenth, his lines were secure; most of the infantry faced northward toward Martinsburg, while Stuart's horsemen fanned out toward the Potomac fords in close observation of the timid, regressive Federals.[43]

With access to Harpers Ferry restored, Johnston dispatched troops to gather up machinery and tools that had not been carted off and somehow had escaped the flames. The operation left behind "nothing worth removing" from the armory and arsenal. At the same time, Johnston planned another demolition effort, this at Martinsburg, a point to which Patterson might advance should he summon up the gumption to retake the offensive. On the nineteenth, ostensibly reacting to a recent order from General Cooper to deny railroad resources to the enemy by destroying tracks, bridges, and tunnels, Johnston directed T. J. Jackson, soon to be a brigadier general, to join Stuart's troopers in Martinsburg and destroy the B&O trains there before they fell into enemy hands.[44]

Jackson went there the next day at the head of a wrecking crew that ripped up rails, burned ties, and put to the torch forty-two locomotives and almost four hundred flatcars and boxcars, a loss of some fifty thousand dollars to the B&O. Johnston himself was on hand to witness the final conflagration. A few days later he wrote General Cooper that Jackson had "destroyed all the rolling stock of the road within his reach."[45]

If Johnston believed Jackson's work would find favor in Richmond, improving his relations with the government, he was mistaken. Maryland politicians and their constituents, especially B&O stockholders, loudly decried the destruction the generals had wrought. One angry citizen described it as "an act of diabolism . . . effected by means worthy of the spirits of the nether world." Unionists in the state made much of the issue, which gained them the support of many secessionist-leaning citizens. Historian Jeffrey N. Lash asserts that the destruction of the resources at Martinsburg "demonstrated Johnston's gross undervaluing of the rolling stock to the Confederate war effort." The misguided effort to carry out Cooper's instructions of June 19 only served to devalue his already underperforming stock with his military and civilian superiors.[46]

As soon as his army reached Winchester, Johnston devoted his attention to building up its strength and morale. The evacuation of Harpers Ferry, at first perceived as a demoralizing retreat, had become a strategic withdrawal in the minds of most of his troops, and the fact that the Yankees had declined to pursue stimulated not only esprit de corps but also recruiting. Regiments came in from Georgia and the Carolinas, augmented by some 2,500 militia under Brigadier Generals James H. Carson and G. S. Meem from Frederick, Shenandoah, and other Virginia counties.

Envisioning the newcomers as a semipermanent garrison, Major Whiting supervised the erecting of some light earthworks on high ground northeast of the town and the mounting of a few heavy guns on naval carriages. Johnston admitted that these weapons would prove "very ineffective," but they gave some comfort to the militia, which was what counted. The army also grew upon the return of A. P. Hill's expeditionary force from Romney and New Creek, where it had chased away a few Yankees guarding a B&O bridge before torching the structure. Hill's recall had stemmed from the discovery that no considerable enemy force was moving toward the rear of Johnston's army.[47]

The additions swelled the Army of the Shenandoah to nearly 10,000 effectives. The new arrivals included a trio of officers who would assume brigade command: Brigadier General Barnard Elliott Bee and Colonels Arnold Elzey and Francis S. Bartow. The first two were professional soldiers of some note.

Bee was South Carolina born but had spent part of his life in Texas, to which his family had moved (his father had served as secretary of state of the Texas Republic). An 1845 graduate of the U.S. Military Academy, Bee had campaigned in Minnesota and the Utah and Nebraska Territories before fighting in Mexico, where he was wounded and won two brevets for gallantry. In March 1861 the father of three had resigned his commission in the 10th U.S. Infantry to accept Governor Pickens's offer of a lieutenant colonelcy in South Carolina's forces. A man of many interests, Bee wrote poetry in his spare time, although he never claimed to have a gift for the form. As a military man he was much admired. One colleague described him as being "as gallant a soldier as ever drew a sword, and a splendid man in every respect." An enlisted man wrote that "no officer ever gained the affection of his men in such a short time as General Bee."[48]

Elzey (born Arnold Elzey Jones in Maryland in December 1816) had made a somewhat less distinguished record than Bee in the old army. He had spent the years following his 1837 graduation from West Point as a subaltern in the 2nd Artillery, fighting the Seminoles in Florida and gaining a brevet for distinguished service in Mexico. Afterward Elzey was relegated to a desk job; the outbreak of war found him commanding the U.S. arsenal at Augusta, Georgia. Prideful and ambitious, he coveted a field command and was much gratified when Johnston granted his wish.[49]

The third newcomer, Bartow, was one of the few politically connected civilians to gain high rank in the Confederate field forces at this early period. A Georgia planter and businessman and a graduate

of Yale Law School, he had served in both houses of his state's legislature as well as in the U.S. House of Representatives. In February
1861 he had won election to the Confederate Provisional Congress.
Preferring a military berth, Bartow parlayed his leadership of a local
militia unit into brigade command, but he had no illusions about
the firestorm to come, fearing that he himself would be consumed
by it.[50]

With his army now as large as it was likely to get, Johnston
reorganized it into five brigades. The first, assigned to Jackson, consisted of the 2nd, 4th, 5th, and 27th Virginia Regiments, later to be
joined by the 33rd Virginia and the four guns of Captain Pendleton's
Rockbridge Artillery. Violating accepted standards of seniority,
Johnston's Second Brigade was entrusted to Bartow, who led three
regiments from his native state, two battalions of Kentucky infantry, and the Wise Artillery under Captain Ephraim G. Alburtis and
Lieutenant John Pelham. Bee's Third Brigade was made up of the 4th
Alabama, two Mississippi outfits, and Captain John D. Imboden's
Staunton Artillery. Shortly before the command went into battle,
the 6th North Carolina Infantry would be added. Elzey took charge
of the Fourth Brigade: the eight-company 1st Maryland (erroneously
referred to in many accounts as a mere battalion), the 3rd Tennessee,
the 10th and 13th Virginia, and Lieutenant Robert F. Beckham's
Culpeper Artillery. Had Johnston had his druthers, he probably
would have named A. P. Hill of the 13th Virginia to lead the brigade,
but army politics tied his hands. Hill was a Virginian in an army top
heavy with Virginians, while Elzey, a border-state loyalist, was considered a drawing card for his fellow Marylanders, too few of whom,
in Richmond's opinion, had flocked to the Stars and Bars.[51]

The Army of the Shenandoah's cavalry remained in the capable
hands of Lieutenant Colonel Stuart. By mid-June Johnston affirmed
that the executive officer of the 1st Virginia had proven himself
"matchless as commander of outposts." The twenty-eight-year-old
native of Patrick County, Virginia, had made an exemplary antebel-
lum record on the Indian frontier, while during John Brown's raid
he had ably served R. E. Lee, commander of the U.S. forces that captured "Old Osawatomie" and his band. One of Stuart's Virginians,
Private Mosby, would laud his commander's "distinguishing traits
. . . dash, great strength of will, and indomitable energy." A genial,
amicable sort who reveled in the trappings of military life and the
glory and excitement of war, Stuart would become known as much

for his flamboyant affectations—ostrich-plumed hat, golden spurs, crimson-lined cape, and headquarters musicians—as for his hard-edged leadership.[52]

Prior to Stuart's arrival at Harpers Ferry, the local horsemen had been led by Captain Turner Ashby, a born horseman with the singular ability to slip inside enemy lines, gather intelligence, and place it while still warm in the hands of a superior. But his lack of a military education coupled with his inability or unwillingness to discipline his troopers had prompted Johnston to place the local horsemen, and Ashby himself, under Stuart.[53]

Johnston's artillery at Harpers Ferry was commanded by William Pendleton, who exercised a somewhat loose authority over the four-gun batteries attached to the Army of the Shenandoah. A West Pointer in the class that graduated one year after Johnston's, Pendleton had spent only three years in the army before resigning to teach, then to preach. At war's outbreak he vacated the pulpit in Lexington, Virginia, that he had occupied for eight years to lead the celebrated Rockbridge Artillery, which counted among its ranks at least twenty-five theological students.

A talented administrator rather than a gifted tactician, Pendleton owed his position as much as anything to his close association with Johnston. Because of his long estrangement from military service, he was the least experienced battery commander in the Shenandoah forces. John Imboden, who considered himself Pendleton's senior, would claim that Johnston had no true chief of artillery. Even so, in early July Pendleton was awarded the titular position with the rank of colonel. The appointment bruised the pride of other qualified candidates, whose resentment, felt in Richmond, prompted a shift of the power to make field-grade appointments in the artillery from the War Department to Congress.[54]

Despite Scott's peremptory order, Patterson did not give up his regulars at once. On the evening of the seventeenth, General Cadwalader relayed to army headquarters "extraordinary rumors" that Johnston had occupied Martinsburg with 15,000 troops and was preparing to advance against the seven regiments of Federal infantry that held the south side of the Potomac opposite Williamsport. Alluding to the transfer of regular units already begun, Cadwalader added that "the best troops have left here, and I have no artillery to defend the ford."[55]

The report of Johnston's advance to Martinsburg in force was empty of fact, but Patterson leapt to the conclusion that the enemy, "who knows all our movements," had learned of the regulars' departure and intended to exploit their absence. Stirred into action, he hustled Keim's division into position to support Cadwalader and ordered that the units that had left for Washington be halted at Hagerstown and returned to his field headquarters. He may have feared Scott's reaction to this spasm of resistance, but the commanding general, having heard the rumor about Martinsburg, had expected him to recall the regulars. But the next morning, when no enemy troops were discovered to be heading for Williamsport, Patterson ordered the resumption of the transfer of the units under Miles and Thomas.[56]

The requirement to give up his career soldiers continued to unnerve Patterson. His state of mind was conveyed to Washington by volunteer aide John Sherman. Writing on June 18 from Hagerstown, to which he had accompanied the departing regulars, the congressman informed Secretary Cameron that "we are all here deeply disappointed. This entire command on Sunday [the sixteenth] was in admirable condition. It had dragoons, artillery, a good body of volunteer infantry, good spirits, plenty of provisions, and needing nothing but transportation, and this was being rapidly supplied." But what a difference two days had made. Scott's order, Sherman reported, had left the army without a single piece of artillery, "dragoons, or any regular infantry to give confidence to volunteers." By now Patterson had withdrawn Cadwalader's division to Williamsport, thus placing the entire army on the north side of the Potomac. The troop losses would compel his forces to remain there indefinitely, although the general desired to recross the stream and confront Johnston. Sherman lamented: "See what a position this will leave these volunteers in! They are now keen for [a] fight. They must now stand on the defensive. Their time of enlistment will melt away, and they go home having done nothing, and little likely to enlist again. The demoralization of this column, of which so much was expected, will be generally injurious."[57]

Presumably, Cameron brought Sherman's concerns to Scott's attention, for the commanding general appeared to relent. He grudgingly authorized Patterson to hang on to one battery of regular artillery—F, 4th Artillery, Lieutenant D. D. Perkins commanding—and a battery of 30-pounder Parrott rifles under Major Abner Doubleday,

which had joined Patterson on the eighteenth from the camp of organization at Chambersburg. On the nineteenth Scott also permitted
him to retain half the cavalry ordered to Washington but specified
that Colonel Thomas accompany the remainder. This would leave
Patterson with four companies of horsemen, including the Philadelphia City Troop and McMullin's Independent Rangers, the latter
a company of scouts composed of Philadelphia police and firemen
who also served as the army commander's bodyguard. Patterson
may not have considered Scott's reconsideration much of a reprieve,
but it was more than he had expected. It got even better when Scott
agreed he could retain Thomas, his most talented subordinate.[58]

In his exculpatory memoir of the First Bull Run Campaign,
Patterson wrote that following the regulars' departure, "I was mortified and humiliated at having to recross the river without striking a
blow." He was determined, he claimed, to have another opportunity.
Even in this weakened condition, the army numbered almost 14,000
troops of all arms, although only one infantry regiment had signed
on for three years. Thus Patterson proposed to return to the south
side of the Potomac, to occupy Harpers Ferry as a base from which
to threaten Johnston at Winchester, and to rebuild the B&O bridge.
"I recommend this course," he wrote Scott, "if for no other reason
than to keep the volunteers employed and out of settlements"—that
is, from running roughshod over the local populace. He planned to
occupy Maryland Heights by the morning of June 20 but changed
his mind when officials of the B&O decided it would do no good to
restore the bridges unless the railroad could be guarded as far west as
Cumberland, something Patterson felt unable to do.[59]

The next day, the twentieth, Scott ordered his subordinate to
submit a new plan. It must cover, among other things, a movement
eastward to support Colonel Stone's planned attack on the outposts between Leesburg and Washington. This objective appealed
to Patterson because it would enable him to absorb Stone's brigade
while abandoning the "false" position he now occupied, preventing
him from keeping Johnston and Beauregard apart. By sidestepping to
Leesburg, he would trade an exterior line of operations for one that
more effectively threatened Johnston's communications. It would
also bring the Army of Pennsylvania and the Army of Northeastern
Virginia into supporting distance of one another.[60]

Patterson responded with a plan that called for him to abandon his present line, cross the Potomac north of Leesburg, and unite

with Stone. "From that point," he informed Scott, "I can operate as circumstances shall demand and your order require." The proposed movement would "keep alive the ardor of our men," but its greatest advantage, as Patterson saw it, would be to relieve him of the requirement to confront Johnston's army, the size of which kept climbing in the reports of his scouts and informants. It appears that he had accepted as fact General Cadwalader's recent estimate of 15,000 Rebels between Martinsburg and Winchester—almost 5,000 more than Johnston had gathered even after slightly reinforced.[61]

Patterson would later claim that had his plan been adopted, the entire course of the campaign would have been changed for the better. Most historians disagree. As Robert M. Johnston, the first twentieth-century historian to scrutinize McDowell's and Patterson's operations, has pointed out, to reach Leesburg the Army of Pennsylvania, which was anything but highly mobile, would have had to cross the Blue Ridge as well as the Potomac and then march some thirty miles to link with Stone. In the meantime Johnston, no longer held in the Valley, could quickly join with Beauregard. The historian Johnston is undoubtedly correct, although his suggestion that the general Johnston, while en route east, could have attacked Patterson in flank, keeping him from uniting with McDowell, seems farfetched.[62]

None of this mattered, for Patterson's plan was shelved almost as quickly as he developed it. On the twenty-fifth Scott, as if suddenly aware that Johnston remained in force between Winchester and the Potomac, directed Patterson to stay where he was. The Leesburg operation was abandoned on June 30, when Scott directed Stone to join the Army of Pennsylvania.[63]

If Patterson was disappointed at his plan's demise, he tried not to show it. The results of recent reconnaissances of Maryland Heights and adjacent positions made him believe that he could safely cross the Potomac at Williamsport as well as fifteen miles downriver at Shepherdstown. Both columns would converge at Hainesville, where Jackson's brigade, Johnston's advance guard, was encamped. Patterson's pioneers cut the tow path of the local canal to give the artillery a more open route to Shepherdstown. But later reports by Captain Newton, who had found the fords in that area heavily picketed and the riverbank too steep to cross without difficulty, persuaded Patterson to cross his entire force at Williamsport, covered by Doubleday's heavy artillery, and drive down the Valley Pike.[64]

Scott had approved Patterson's intent to cross and engage Johnston "if you are in superior or equal force." He counseled, however, that if the Rebels withdrew, it would not do to pursue them as far as Winchester. The warning was hardly necessary; the hesitant Irishman needed no reminder to proceed with caution.[65]

CHAPTER 6

FREEZING FOR A FIGHT

On June 12 General Beauregard gave his attention to a task dear to his heart and critical to his perception of himself as a great captain: strategic planning. That morning he addressed to President Davis a detailed plan based on what his literary collaborator, Colonel Alfred Roman, later described as "the leading ideas of concentration and aggression." The plan, which was carried to Richmond by Lieutenant Colonel Samuel Jones of Beauregard's staff, called for a union of the Armies of the Potomac and the Shenandoah.[1]

At this point Patterson had yet to advance on Harpers Ferry, but by June 12 his intentions seemed clear. In a matter of days, Beauregard feared, Johnston's garrison would be surrounded and pummeled into submission. Thus the Creole recommended that his colleague abandon the Valley altogether and march east through the Blue Ridge passes, which would be blocked afterward to prevent Patterson from pursuing. Johnston should link with Beauregard somewhere in advance of Bull Run and, "by a bold and rapid movement forward," cooperate with him in retaking Alexandria and Arlington Heights, "if not too strongly fortified and garrisoned." The offensive, he believed, would force every Federal in the Valley and on the upper Potomac to abandon his present position and rush to Washington's defense.

Being the thorough strategist he was, Beauregard had planned for contingencies. If unable to link with the army at Manassas, Johnston should retreat to Richmond, to which Beauregard would hasten as well as other Confederate units along the Potomac, on the Peninsula, and at Norfolk. At Richmond this concentrated force would be in a position to "crush, in rapid succession and in detail, the several columns of the enemy, which I have supposed would move on three or four different lines." If 35,000 or more troops could unite at this place, "I have not the least doubt that we could annihilate fifty thousand of the enemy."[2]

Beauregard's proposal was sweeping in scope, careless of details, and unsound in some of its conclusions. For these and other reasons, it has been universally condemned by historians and military analysts as a flight of self-indulgent folly, the unripe fruit of a mind bedazzled by Napoleonic-era glory and blind to the limited resources available to the Confederacy at this early stage of the war. And yet the plan had enough merit to prevent it from being dismissed out of hand as unworkable and impractical. By evacuating the Valley before Patterson forced him to give battle, Johnston would gain a critical degree of mobility. It seems likely that he could have used it to join Beauregard, perhaps via the Manassas Gap Railroad, for a concerted advance on Washington. That move would certainly have caught Scott and McDowell by surprise, forcing them into a hasty defense of the south side of the Potomac. There is no reason to suppose that Patterson could have prevented the linkup, and as the future would demonstrate, he had no stomach for pursuing Johnston to Manassas. That meant that the Confederates could have challenged McDowell for Washington on relatively equal terms or, if forces were called in from points such as Leesburg and Aquia Creek, at an advantage in numbers.

In the event that Beauregard and Johnston failed or found it impractical to seize Alexandria and Arlington, they could have gone over to the defensive on Washington's doorstep, forcing McDowell to attack them across a river, a difficult undertaking for a highly professional army let alone a gaggle of amateurs. Given the political significance assumed by any national capital, a truly "bold and rapid movement" on Washington, even if eventually deflected, would have created severe morale problems throughout the North and perhaps have produced an ill-advised reshuffling of the Union high command.

Finally, if they chose not to make a direct assault on the city, the Confederate leaders might have laid siege to it, prolonging the morale problem and perhaps fomenting disaffection among the Northern public. A siege of the capital was something that Lincoln, who fully appreciated its repercussions, had feared since the war's earliest days. Another advantage of Beauregard's plan, if it proved workable, would be to obviate his decidedly risky contingency plan of falling back to defend Richmond against Union attack, although the Creole was probably correct to imagine that under such a scenario the enemy would stage a multicolumn, multidirectional offensive that would prove difficult to coordinate.

Perhaps the only glaring defect in Beauregard's grandiose scheme was its blithe reliance on the support that the inadequate and inefficient Confederate logistical system was incapable of giving him. A wide array of supply and transportation deficiencies would have hamstrung and possibly crippled the sweeping offensive at one point or another. Another vexing drawback was the unsolved question of overall command. As senior officer, Johnston would have been faced with directing the effort, and he would have found it wanting, as he would any plan not devised by himself. Indeed, Johnston's postwar criticism of Beauregard's strategy is aimed less at its deficiencies than at the idea that someone of inferior rank had devised it and expected him to execute it (although assuredly Beauregard would have assumed that responsibility should Johnston be willing to waive seniority).[3]

Whatever the merits of Beauregard's brainchild, it stood no chance of finding favor in Richmond. One day after receiving it, having consulted with General Lee and Adjutant General Cooper, Davis rejected the scheme as impracticable. For one thing, the president questioned some of the assumptions on which it was based. He did not agree that Johnston was on the verge of being forced out of Harpers Ferry and in fact believed the man stood a good chance— even if forced to relinquish the position—of preventing the Yankees from occupying critical sections of the Valley.

As for attacking Alexandria and Arlington, Davis agreed that the effect on Northern military strategy and political opinion would be sensational, but Beauregard could not guarantee that Patterson would not move to take the combined Confederate forces in rear. Should he do so, the benefits of the offensive would be few and short lived. At bottom Davis found it impractical to develop such a comprehensive plan of cooperation as Beauregard had in mind while Richmond remained ignorant of the enemy's intentions. Until Scott and McDowell tipped their hand, Confederate strategy must remain flexible and military resources disposed so as to respond to any contingency.

Davis buttressed his courteous but firm rejection by alluding to the deficiencies and weaknesses of the army's transportation system, which would make a union of forces difficult in the first place. If Beauregard were correct that Johnston would have to evacuate the Valley, the latter's forces should join those at Manassas "before yours retired; but I have not anticipated the necessity of your retreat."

In closing, Davis held out the hope that Beauregard would be able to take the offensive at some point but not on the grand scale the Creole envisioned.[4]

To be sure, Davis and his military advisors had legitimate reasons for rejecting Beauregard's proposal. Under the conditions then prevailing, it had little chance of succeeding, at least in its present form. Yet there were also reasons to believe that such bold, aggressive action would have yielded some measure of success. No one in Washington would have expected the Rebels to launch an offensive on such a scale at this time. Especially given the unfinished state of McDowell's army and Washington's defenses and Patterson's evident lack of will to engage Johnston, there is reason to question the Federals' ability to join forces in the manner Beauregard envisioned for his army and Johnston's. On his own McDowell might have deflected an attack or raised a siege, but it would have taken time, and the very fact that he had to take measures to do so might have caused a crisis that the War Department did not need. Beauregard's call for a wide-ranging concentration of forces—an idea with which Johnston, Holmes, and Hunton eventually agreed—would have stolen the initiative from Washington and placed its defenders at a disadvantage. Much good might have come of such a bold stroke whether or not it resulted in the majestic coup he envisioned.

While Davis's rejection of Beauregard's blueprint of operations came wrapped in courteous language, it created a fissure in their already fragile relationship. The rift would widen in later weeks and, combined with other factors, would compel the Creole to accept a transfer out of the Virginia theater. Beauregard considered the unwillingness to adopt his strategy evidence of a small mind, a fitting complement to Davis's towering ego. The president's military advisors were no smarter, if perhaps less haughty. Unable to accept defeat gracefully, the general communicated his feelings to his staff, who began openly to denigrate their commander's military and civilian overlords. Davis they described as "a stupid fool," while Secretary of War Walker was "beneath criticism & contempt." The carping would only grow louder, for this was not the last plan for a wide-ranging offensive that Beauregard would put forth, nor the last that Richmond would disapprove.[5]

The rejection of his strategy shocked Beauregard for a time into adopting a defensive mindset. Less than a week after Davis issued his veto, the general inspected his works and decided to improve them by setting up a network of outposts to provide advance word of any forward movement by the enemy. He was especially concerned with covering the countryside between Manassas and the Fairfax Court House–Centreville–Germantown area, through which McDowell would almost certainly march when beginning his advance on Bull Run. The Creole's scouts and spies, many of whom resided in Washington, believed such a move to be imminent.

Beauregard's idea involved shifting the main bodies of two brigades—Bonham's and Ewell's—into a strategic triangle that would facilitate mutual support north of Bull Run. Sometime before June 23, he stationed all but one of Bonham's regiments, augmented by Cocke's 18th Virginia and a light battery, at Fairfax Court House and Germantown, at the time the army's most distant posts. This was strategically important territory, for in those areas the main roads from Washington and Alexandria converged.

Once in place, Bonham set his men to blocking hundred-yard stretches of those roads with fallen trees. The brigadier did not erect works in the area, for his mission was to delay the enemy, not engage him except at long distance. As soon as McDowell's larger numbers turned the position, Bonham was to fall back to Bull Run, drawing them after him. Of course, none of his soldiers looked forward to retreating under any circumstances. One of McDowell's civilian informants, who had passed unmolested through Fairfax County, reported that every South Carolinian was "in high spirits, 'freezing for a fight.'" They intended to make a stand, Alamo-fashion if necessary, rather than relinquish one square foot of the ground they now occupied.[6]

Although the informant failed to mention it, the occupants' enthusiasm was bolstered by the presence of one of the most rabid secessionists in all the South, sixty-seven-year-old Edmund Ruffin of Prince George County, Virginia. In prewar years a celebrated agriculturist, the steely-eyed, white-haired Ruffin had become alternately famous and infamous for his malignant antipathy toward the Yankee race. In 1860 he had traveled to Charleston to personally harangue South Carolina into leaving the Union. After that state's secession, he had stayed on to observe the bombardment of Sumter, during which he was given the honor of firing one of the first guns trained on the fort. Returning to Virginia, Ruffin had joined a militia outfit, despite being well over the enlistment age, until quitting it to head for Manassas to serve beside some of the same troops he had associated with in Charleston.[7]

Continuing his precautionary efforts, Beauregard placed detachments of Ewell's brigade at Centreville as well as halfway between that village and Germantown at Sangster's Station, covering the Braddock Road and the roads from Fairfax Court House and Fairfax Station. Ewell too was directed not to challenge any advancing Yankees; when confronted by superior numbers, he was to withdraw to an assigned position on the right flank of the Bull Run line. Ewell realized that his withdrawal, especially since it might be conducted under fire, entailed risks given the "rather rough and difficult country road" that was his only escape route. Lacking other options, the eccentric Virginian vowed to have his brigade intact and in position behind the creek within hours of quitting his advanced station.[8]

Two more of Cocke's regiments were posted on the high ground outside Centreville where the road from Fairfax Court House and neighboring Germantown met the Warrenton Turnpike. Those byways too were obstructed with downed trees, fence rails, and timber stripped from deserted houses and outbuildings. Once pressed, Cocke would head south to prepared positions of his own along the Confederate left. At about this same time, Beauregard strengthened the outposts previously established at Sangster's Cross Roads, Germantown, and other points within the Mitchell's Ford–Centreville–Fairfax Court House triangle.

The army commander distributed the main body of his troops so that it covered a suitably wide stretch of Bull Run and the country between it and the depot at Manassas. Three brigades would protect his far right flank. Longstreet's men were placed below Blackburn's Ford. Less than a mile to the south, Jones's brigade took position to cover McLean's Ford. Ewell's main body gathered around Union Mills Ford, a mile and a half farther south, where it could guard not only the Confederate right but also the Orange & Alexandria bridge over Bull Run. Augmenting these forces was Early's brigade, which Beauregard split up and placed in a series of positions northeast and northwest of the depot so that it could quickly reinforce the other brigades if or when attacked.

The rest of the Bull Run line was held by the main body of Bonham's brigade at and near Mitchell's Ford and, farther upstream, by Cocke's Virginians, covering Lewis, Ball's, and Island Fords. The far left of Beauregard's army would be defended by Nathan Evans, whose demibrigade was charged with holding Stone Bridge and opposing any Federals coming down the Warrenton Turnpike from Centreville. Theoretically, units on the left of Cocke's position, including some artillery, would be available to lend Evans assistance. Even so, enough open ground separated the two commands that should they be attacked simultaneously, Evans's little force would find itself fighting on its own.[9]

The troops holding the Fairfax Court House–Centreville line were in an exposed position, but one critical to the safety of their entire army. A member of the Nottoway Grays, a company in the 18th Virginia, recalled that for days after taking station at Fairfax, "war rumors from towards Washington were more plentiful than good bread—or even good water, and a man who could live on excitement had a chance here to grow fat."[10]

On the edge of the disputed territory between the armies, trigger fingers were itchy. Late on July 4 General Bonham dispatched a six-hundred-man expeditionary force under Colonel Joseph B. Kershaw of the 2nd South Carolina, augmented by six companies of Virginia cavalry and a battery, to reconnoiter Union positions near Falls Church. At daybreak the next morning, the leader of the mounted contingent, who had taken position on a road apart from the main body, sent some of his troopers forward to scout an enemy picket post. Their infantry comrades had not been informed of the mission; when the horsemen galloped past their position, several Carolinians fired into what they supposed were Yankees. Two members of the famed Black Horse Cavalry were killed, several others were wounded, and five horses were downed. Survivors speedily retired to their starting point.[11]

Other efforts to gather intelligence in the same area proved more fruitful. The same day Bonham launched his botched reconnaissance, a clerk at McDowell's headquarters with knowledge of his army's strength wandered drunkenly inside the lines at Fairfax Court House and was captured. Under interrogation he gave Beauregard a clear idea of the numbers opposing him, more than 30,000 officers and men. As the general later noted, "the increasing forces of McDowell, the clamor of the Northern press for an advance, and the private reports from Washington, all now indicated an early attack by an army more than twice the strength of ours in numbers."[12]

The news not only helped curb Beauregard's lingering hopes of taking the offensive but also added to his concerns. On July 8 he wrote Senator Wigfall, his aide at Charleston, asking "how can it be expected that I shall be able to maintain my ground unless reinforced immediately? I am determined to give the enemy battle no matter at what odds against us; but is it right and proper to sacrifice so many valuable lives (and perhaps our cause) without the least prospect of success? But I hope it may have the effect, at least, of delaying the advance of the enemy, and give our friends time to come to the rescue." This last was a reference to Johnston, with whom he still expected to link. And yet, even if the union proved unworkable, Beauregard saw a ray of hope: "If I could only get the enemy to attack me, as I am trying to have him do, I would stake my reputation on the handsomest victory that could be hoped for."[13]

Beauregard continued to impress anyone within range of his words with the difficulties he faced in his present condition. After writing Wigfall, he informed Davis that the enemy "will soon attack with very superior numbers. No time should be lost in reinforcing me here with at least ten thousand men." This was an unrealistic hope, for Richmond had nothing close to that number available to send him. Two days later he wired the president that if he were forced to receive the enemy's strike, he hoped it came sooner rather than later. He expected the blow to land heaviest on his right at Mitchell's Ford—after all, the road from Centreville to Manassas crossed the run there—but he also feared an attempt to outflank him via Stone Bridge, where he believed the terrain less suited to defense. His concern begged the question why he had stationed at the bridge the smallest component of his army, commanded by a known inebriate.[14]

In communicating with Davis, Beauregard passed on the information that McDowell commanded as many as 35,000 men. He enumerated his own strength as 16,500 effectives, not including the troops at Leesburg and Fredericksburg or the guard at Camp Pickens. He also informed Davis of the possibility that McDowell would attack his left flank. To get into position to do so, the Union commander would have to expose much of his army to a preemptive strike, but Beauregard feared that he had not enough troops to launch one safely. "If I had sufficient force," he declared, "one less unequal to that of the enemy, I would not permit him, with impunity, to attempt so dangerous a movement on his part; but in view of the odds against me, and of the vital importance at this juncture of avoiding the hazard of a defeat, which would open to the enemy the way to Richmond, I shall act with extreme caution."[15]

The substance of Beauregard's defensive strategy was spelled out in Special Orders No. 100, disseminated to his brigade commanders on July 8. The document, which his literary coadjutor Roman described as "one of the most remarkable . . . in military history," outlined a range of movements to be made if the army were attacked by superior numbers. It not only finalized the positions to be occupied by the brigades of Jones, Longstreet, and Early but also called on the three advance brigades to absorb the first shock of battle, then, before being overwhelmed, to fall back in good order to specific points on Bull Run. Bonham was to evacuate Fairfax Court House via Centreville and dig in at Mitchell's Ford. Cocke was not only to withdraw to the fords below Stone Bridge but, if possible, to make a stand at the suspension bridge one and a half miles up the Warrenton Pike, where the road crossed a branch of Bull Run known as Cub Run. Only three of the regiments assigned to Ewell were to retire to the railroad bridge at Union Mills Ford; the fourth, Sloan's 4th South Carolina (soon to be transferred to Evans's command), would fall back by a parallel road and then side roads to McLean's Ford or Union Mills Ford "as most practicable." Beauregard expected the burden of the fighting would be mainly borne by Bonham's, Cocke's, and Ewell's men: "These brigades, thus in position, will make a desperate stand at the several points hereinbefore designated on the line of Bull Run." They would be supported closely by the rest of the army, which would assume an offensive-defensive posture, assailing the enemy's flanks as opportunities arose.[16]

Beauregard's strategy for the fighting to come appeared to be set, if not in stone, then in quick-drying cement. But it failed to harden. On the afternoon of July 10, the army leader received an encrypted message that caused his thinking to shift 180 degrees. The message had come through Bonham's lines at Fairfax, delivered by a "beautiful young lady." She was Bettie Duval, a courier employed by a Confederate espionage ring based in Washington. Established by Colonel Jordan, the group sent to army headquarters intelligence from the capital two or three times a week, which after being copied, was relayed to the Confederate War Department.[17]

As the North's southernmost city, Washington was home to hundreds of Confederate sympathizers, one being Rose Greenhow, society matron, widow of a State Department official, and fervent secessionist. Through social and romantic attachments to government officials including Henry Wilson of Massachusetts, chairman of the Senate Committee on Military Affairs, Greenhow was privy to some of the most secretive doings of the Union high command. Her most recent acquisition, the one smuggled out of Washington by the brown haired, black-eyed Duval, was of utmost interest to the commander at Bull Run: definitive word that McDowell's army was to advance on Beauregard's lines beginning on the sixteenth. Once the Federals actually began their march, other informants, including the daughter of a Fairfax Court House merchant who walked the six miles to Beauregard's headquarters, reported the invaders' progress, heading, and apparent destination.[18]

When placed in his hands, the information prompted Beauregard to revisit the plan he had laid aside a month ago. On July 13 he dispatched to Richmond a private letter outlining ways to preempt the coming attack. The letter, which was carried by Colonel John S. Preston of his staff, called again for the unification of Beauregard's and Johnston's forces. That same day the general communicated its substance to Johnston, claiming that if adopted, "I think this whole campaign could be completed brilliantly in from fifteen to twenty-five days. Oh, that we had but one good head to conduct all our operations!" The melodramatic plea may have been intended as a swipe at Davis, Lee, Cooper, and Walker, but it seems likely that Beauregard considered himself the "one good head" to direct a combined operation. Apparently, Johnston failed to reply to his suggestions. This was a good thing, for it is unlikely that Beauregard would have appreciated his opinion.[19]

Not long after Colonel Preston galloped off, Beauregard decided to refine and amplify his proposal. On the fourteenth he forwarded to Richmond a memorandum of these revisions via Colonel James Chesnut, Jr., a member of the Provisional Confederate Congress who like Wigfall had been an aide to Beauregard in Charleston. In both communiqués the general pulled out all the stops, for he had hit upon a way to defeat all three Union armies in Virginia via a few crushing strokes. As Colonel Chesnut explained to Davis, Lee, and Cooper, Beauregard's new plan called for Johnston, with 22,000 troops (more than twice as many as he actually had), to depart the Valley for Manassas. Together Beauregard and he would march on Washington, place themselves between two wings of McDowell's army, attack each wing with a larger force than McDowell enjoyed, and "exterminate them or drive them into the Potomac." This accomplished, Johnston would return to the Valley with his own troops plus 10,000 of Beauregard's to finish off Patterson, a task the Creole now estimated to take no more than a week. While Johnston thrashed Patterson, he and the remainder of his army would seize and occupy the capital's defenses, which the defeated, demoralized Yankees would have abandoned. If this last operation proved unworkable, Beauregard would simply withdraw in triumph to Bull Run.

The Creole's strategic energy had not exhausted itself. Having crushed Patterson, Johnston would send a portion of his command to western Virginia to assist in halting McClellan's advance. Once McClellan had been neutralized, the western Virginia troops would accompany Johnston in crossing into Maryland, from there to attack Washington from the rear in conjunction with a renewed strike from the opposite direction by Beauregard.[20]

Chesnut's audience was floored by the exotic proposal. From the outset they considered it wholly unmanageable. The assumptions that underlay it—especially the overestimation of Johnston's numbers and the supposition that McDowell would oppose heavier numbers rather than withdraw inside Washington's defenses—coupled with the unrealistic timetable for achieving success, made it impossible for the ruling triumvirate to consider the plan seriously. And yet, as they had when reacting to Beauregard's June 12 proposal, they managed to create the impression that they had given it careful study even as they rejected it out of hand. As Douglas Southall Freeman observes, the revised plan "was considered merely a broad suggestion. As such, it was held to be hopelessly impractical for a multitude of reasons."[21]

There are no grounds on which to defend Beauregard's half-baked idea, which ranged far beyond the comparatively modest objectives and plausible claims of his early June strategy. By the middle of July, with McDowell poised to march on Manassas, no time remained to coordinate movements on two fronts, let alone three. Nor was it possible, given Johnston's numerical weakness, to turn his transfer to Bull Run (which would require an unrealistic degree of precision) into an offensive. R. M. Johnston describes Beauregard's strategic concept, unkindly but not inaccurately, as "almost down to the level of newspaper strategy . . . an unthinkable proposition that requires no serious consideration."[22]

For his part, Chesnut accepted Richmond's verdict with good grace, conceding that Beauregard's superiors had advanced some well-reasoned objections. Not surprisingly, the reaction of the colonel's boss was more pronounced. Beauregard found this latest rejection of his grand strategy almost too much to bear. A gilt-edged opportunity to achieve critical objectives had foundered on the stubbornness and timidity of paper shufflers, the chief obstructionist being Davis. Years after the war Beauregard continued to rail against the president's obtuseness. Added to his refusal to supply the Army of the Potomac with adequate transportation and his dismissal of the plan of June 12, Davis's disapproval of this latest and most promising proposal, "the certain result of which would have been the taking of Washington . . . *lost the South her independence.*" Too often insensible to hard reality, Beauregard clung to this belief until the day he died.[23]

Three days after Winfield Scott ordered him to draft a plan of cooperation with Patterson to defeat enemy forces between the upper Potomac and Washington, McDowell presented—in contrast to Beauregard's illogical design—a well-reasoned and carefully crafted blueprint for an offensive, one that did not, however, conform to Scott's strategic preferences. For one thing, the plan called for separate lines of operations, not a single unified movement. "The distance between General Patterson's force and this one," McDowell noted on June 24, "is so great and the line of march each has to take is such (a flank exposed), that, in my view, the force to move from each position should be constituted without reference to material support from the other."

To buttress his arguments, McDowell pointed out that a joint movement toward Leesburg, as Scott proposed, would be compromised by inadequate transportation—the same deficiency that vitiated Beauregard's plan to launch an offensive in concert with Johnston. Even if it could be undertaken, McDowell noted, the movement would expose the flanks of the armies, both of which would be making a movement so long and so wide as to exhaust troops not used to marching. That would be a grave mistake: "Any reverse happening to this raw force, pushed farther along, with the enemy on the flank and rear and an impassable river [the Potomac] on the right, would be fatal."[24]

Furthermore, a move to the upper Potomac might double McDowell's opposition. Feeling "tender on the subject," he feared that if he struck for Leesburg, "Johns[t]on might escape and join Beauregard, and I was not in a position to meet all their forces combined." McDowell would quote Scott as replying that if Johnston headed for Manassas, "he shall have Patterson on his heels." This bit of assurance, however, failed to assuage the brigadier's concerns. He might have added, but apparently did not, that any move against Beauregard via Leesburg and surrounding localities would jeopardize the line of communication with Washington.[25]

As McDowell saw it, his proper objective was not the four hundred Rebels at Leesburg but the thousands of soldiers along Bull Run. He proposed to take them on, even though he now estimated their strength as 25,000 infantry and cavalry (and an artillery force of unknown size), while his own army, which he described as smaller by almost 10,000 men, consisted primarily of "good, bad, and indifferent" infantry and barely a dozen artillery pieces, only half of them rifled and thus capable of long-range accuracy. McDowell anticipated the receipt of additional regiments and batteries before compelled to leave Washington for Manassas, but he also expected that by then thousands of reinforcements would have joined Beauregard.[26]

Having explained his objections to Scott's broad-front strategy, either that same day or the next, McDowell presented his superior with a second plan, one focused on striking at Beauregard. He proposed not to make the movement until he had a force at least 30,000 strong. He outlined four possible routes of approach to his objective, all converging in the vicinity of Fairfax Court House: one via Falls Church and Vienna; another from Alexandria over the Little River Turnpike; the third along the tracks of the O&A to a position south of the courthouse, thus cutting off the retreat of the local defenders; and the fourth via an unnamed road south of the railroad. The plan called for a large reserve force to guard the rail line and repair those sections that the enemy had already torn up.

McDowell included in his plan a fifth route to Manassas, one more roundabout and burdensome than the others, though viable. It called for shipping troops aboard transports down the Potomac to Dumfries and Evansport, then advancing on Manassas by overland march. McDowell recommended against the water route due to the long distance involved and the complex logistics it would require. He then delved into the nature and variety of the terrain to be covered by troops making any of these approaches. He identified various natural and manmade obstacles but concluded they could be overcome "with plenty of force and an adequate supply of proper materials."

Concentrating now on his primary objective, McDowell proposed to outflank rather than attack head-on the many batteries Beauregard was reported to have erected along Bull Run and at Manassas Junction. As for the stream, McDowell believed it to be "fordable at almost every place. After uniting the columns this side of it, I propose to attack the main position by turning it, if possible, so as to cut off communications by rail with the South, or threaten to do so sufficiently to force the enemy to leave his intrenchments to guard them; if necessary, and I find it can be done with safety, to move a force as far as Bristoe [a station on the O&A fifteen miles below Manassas], to destroy the bridge at that place." This span Beauregard must cross if forced into retreat.

Turning to logistical considerations, McDowell recommended a general reduction of baggage to limit the drag that the supply wagons would exert on the marching pace ("no tents; provisions only in the haversack; the only wagons being those necessary for carrying axes, spades, and picks, and ammunition for the infantry, and ambulances for the sick and wounded"). He called for the augmentation of his artillery, not only because firepower was essential to combat success but also "on account of the confidence it gives new troops." He mentioned the dearth of cavalry, although he believed that a larger body of horsemen would find its movements limited by the heavily wooded and watered country north of Bull Run. Finally, he hoped to place in command of his volunteer regiments as many regulars as became available in the days and weeks ahead. In closing, McDowell stressed his awareness of the critical importance of the coming battle "as establishing the prestige in this contest on the one side or the other—the more so as the two sections will be fairly represented by regiments from almost every State."[27]

Virtually everyone familiar with McDowell's plan believed it well thought out and eminently workable. It suffered from some deficiencies, however, that because they were never addressed, undercut its viability. Despite Scott's assurances that Johnston would not interfere with his operations, McDowell ought to have taken into account the possibility that the Confederate forces would unite against him. He was too trustful of his superior's ability to compel Patterson to occupy the Army of the Shenandoah. In fact, Scott paid little or no attention to this matter, casually assuming that his Mexican War subordinate would accomplish a complex and difficult mission without sufficient oversight and unambiguous orders from Washington.

One ambiguity in McDowell's strategy concerned the number of columns to advance against Beauregard and their routes of march. The plan he presented to Scott on or about the twenty-fourth called for three columns, but the one later submitted to President Lincoln and his cabinet for their approval called for four columns moving in as many directions. Their common objective was the area around Fairfax Court House, where McDowell expected to fight a pitched battle with Beauregard's advanced forces. He could not imagine—but perhaps ought to have been alert to the possibility—that these forces would be withdrawn before an encounter of any consequence could take place. If this were to happen, the axis of McDowell's advance would be exposed as too narrow, forcing him to realign in order to make a broader approach to Bull Run. This reorientation would take time, which would give the enemy an opportunity to strengthen his lines to meet the assault.[28]

McDowell's intention (only implied in his written plan but spelled out in the one he briefed to Lincoln) to move against the enemy by the left flank and strike his right entailed risk. Due to his lack of a good map of the area below Bull Run, the general was unfamiliar with the lay of the land in that area. He would have done better to maintain tactical flexibility until able to make a close-up inspection of the extent of the Confederate lines. McDowell should have considered sending a column well to the west of Beauregard's position with the intention of cutting the Manassas Gap Railroad. This would have prevented, with equal effectiveness, Johnston advancing to the attack at Bull Run and Beauregard linking with him in retreat.

Yet another potential shortcoming was the provision for leaving a large force on the O&A. The railroad could not have been repaired quickly enough to serve as a line of communications. Those to be detailed as guards and repair crews would be better employed on the battlefield. McDowell would need every man at the front when the shooting started, and he should have had enough foresight to anticipate this.

These and other potential holes in McDowell's planning were not readily apparent to Scott. The Ohioan's arguments, suggestions, and conclusions were deemed potent enough to persuade the commanding general to table the Leesburg-Alexandria plan and focus on

Bull Run–Manassas. Without further delay, he scheduled a presentation of the latter at the Executive Mansion.

According to Lincoln's personal secretary, John G. Nicolay, the plan was to have been presented to the president and select political and military officials on the twenty-fourth, but for unspecified reasons, its author was not on hand. Scott used the occasion to outline the positions and conditions not only of McDowell's army but of those of Beauregard, Patterson, and Stone. He explained his recall of Patterson's regular troops, believing them of no more need once Johnston abandoned Harpers Ferry. He then mentioned his previous intention to combine McDowell's and Patterson's forces for a move to Leesburg, an operation he had abandoned, at least for the time being. The commanding general also discussed, with input from subordinates including General Meigs, the number of troops needed to defeat Beauregard. An optimum figure was not arrived at, but Scott and Meigs agreed that the Army of Northeastern Virginia should include at least fifty artillery pieces. Other strategic considerations would await McDowell's personal presentation of his plan.[29]

On the afternoon of June 29, the army leader was present in the library of the presidential mansion to detail his strategy, with occasional commentary from Scott and Mansfield. McDowell's audience consisted of Lincoln; every cabinet officer; the members of Scott's staff; Generals Meigs, Tyler, and Sandford; and the visiting John C. Frémont, Mexican War hero and future commander of the Department of the West. Pointing to a wall map of Virginia— one he ought to have appropriated for his topographically challenged staff—the general explained that his right-flank column, the one to head south from Vienna, would be led by his senior subordinate, Tyler. The left (southernmost) column, which would march below and parallel to the railroad from Alexandria to Sangster's Station, had been assigned to Heintzelman. In between them would be a single column consisting of the divisions of Hunter and Miles (the latter had recently reached Washington along with the regular infantry units stripped from Patterson's army). Both divisions would take the Little River Turnpike to Annandale. From there Hunter's column would continue west to Fairfax Court House while Miles branched off to the south until striking the Braddock Road; thereafter, his route would parallel Hunter's.

After describing his multipronged advance, McDowell announced the relative strength of the columns (Tyler's would be the largest,

Miles's the smallest) and reiterated his intention to move by his left to outflank Beauregard's defenses rather than strike from the front. Heintzelman, to whom the general had briefed the substance of his plan earlier that day, recorded in his diary that his superior intended to break the Rebel line at its thinnest and most vulnerable point (that is, if he truly had an accurate picture of Beauregard's dispositions). McDowell still clung to the belief that if pressed, his opponent would abandon his position to protect his communications and avoid annihilation. If he decided to fight, McDowell would either continue his indirect offensive or shift to the defensive as conditions warranted.[30]

McDowell believed that carefully executed tactics would carry the day even if Beauregard had more troops than army headquarters estimated. In fact, a few days before he presented his plan to the president and the cabinet, he had informed Scott that even should Patterson hold Johnston in the Valley and Ben Butler keep the Confederates on the Peninsula busy, there was a real possibility that as many as 10,000 reinforcements would reach Beauregard before the Federals could attack. This would give the Creole some 35,000 men, roughly equal to the number McDowell would lead against him. Even so, the Union commander felt confident of defeating an enemy of that size, and his plans had been based on that ability.[31]

McDowell later recalled that his June 29 plan was "approved of, without any alteration," with only one attendee offering a suggestion. He identified that person as Mansfield, but it appears that Sandford was actually the one who spoke up; in fact, the New Yorker claimed to have raised a number of objections. The crux of his disapproval was that no march should be made on Manassas until it was certain that Patterson was in position to prevent a junction between Johnston and Beauregard. McDowell may well have remained "tender" on that subject as well, but Scott called Sandford's concern unfounded, just as he had on those occasions when McDowell made the same point.[32]

Scott may have seen in Sandford's comments an ulterior motive. The New Yorker was about to head for the Valley to join the Army of Pennsylvania. Scott, who had requested his transfer, suspected that the ambitious Sandford hoped to supersede Patterson—hence his implication that the Irishman would fail to curtail Johnston. Coincidentally, the next day the question of whether to retain Patterson in command was discussed at a meeting of the cabinet. It was decided that the man should retain his position for the present with the unspoken understanding that Sandford, as Patterson's senior lieutenant, would strengthen his resolve and combativeness through timely support and good advice.[33]

McDowell's memory of the June 29 presentation was obviously faulty, for it was Scott, not Sandford, who voiced the strongest objection to the plan by endorsing another approach altogether. Still partial to his anaconda concept, the commanding general made a final pitch for its acceptance in some form. As he told Lincoln and the rest of the audience, a campaign along the vital arteries of the Confederacy, especially down the Mississippi to New Orleans, was preferable to a modest offensive aimed at a relatively small defensive position. He argued passionately for his view's acceptance, but he might have saved his breath; once again his design failed to win over those whose approval was required.

The death knell for Scott's herpetological policy was sounded when McDowell, who "did not think well of that plan," felt obliged to speak against it. No doubt to his superior's displeasure and embarrassment, the brigadier detailed the immense difficulties involved in implementing the deceptively simple strategy. In his testimony before the Joint Committee on the Conduct of the War, McDowell elaborated on the arguments he advanced this day. He noted that the Confederates had erected batteries on the lower Potomac that had clamped a partial shipping blockade on Washington, one that months later had yet to be seriously challenged: "We do not venture to land and attack the batteries here, though this is a wide river with a broad channel, one well known and which does not change. We attempt nothing of the sort here, and yet we were expected to go down the Mississippi a thousand miles, supply our force all the way down, attack the batteries, and be diminishing our force all the while by leaving garrisons in all the places we should deem of sufficient importance to retain." Referring to the British attack on New Orleans in 1815, McDowell pungently observed, "I would rather go to New Orleans the way that Packenham attempted to go there."[34]

These arguments against the Anaconda Plan were deemed conclusive by every listener except its architect, and henceforth it was a dead letter. McDowell's strategy, which promised quick action and a decisive victory on the doorstep of Richmond, was more politically acceptable, more saleable to the Northern public. Its triumph owed much to the quality of its presentation. According to Lieutenant

Colonel Townsend, McDowell had explained the plan "with a clearness and precision that would have done credit to any West Pointer at his last annual examination."[35]

Even the heavens appeared to applaud McDowell's plans. The very day he gave the most important presentation of his military career, the Great Comet passed to within 11.5 degrees of the sun. On the thirtieth its brilliant fan-shaped tail was visible in the skies over North America. While many observers considered the phenomenon ominous of what lay ahead, hopeful Northerners, soldiers and civilians alike, viewed the celestial body as lighting the path to victory not just in Virginia but wherever armed secessionists lurked.

When giving their approval to the plan, Lincoln and his subordinates recommended its implementation at the earliest possible date—initially, Monday, July 8. This would give McDowell time to assimilate the incoming regiments that would boost his strength to well above 30,000 men, and it would arrive at least two weeks before the termination of the enlistment periods of his ninety-day troops. Thanks to the inadequacies of Meigs's department, however, the persisting shortage of supply wagons made the timetable unworkable, as did Mansfield's continuing failure to dispatch the newly arrived troops to McDowell's headquarters in a timely fashion. For these reasons, a later date was chosen, one that, thanks to Senator Wilson's infatuation with Mrs. Greenhow, would be known to the enemy well in advance.[36]

While preparing for the march, McDowell reorganized his newly expanded army, adding brigades and creating divisions to increase the centralization of operational control. On July 8, General Orders No. 13 announced the creation of five divisions to be commanded, respectively, by Tyler, Hunter, Heintzelman, Theodore Runyon (brigadier general of New Jersey volunteers), and Miles. Runyon's command, half of which consisted of three-months' militia, the other half of three-year volunteers, was not expected to see action in the pending confrontation. It would guard the outposts and supply depots McDowell left behind and protect his line of communications with Washington.[37]

The four brigades under Daniel Tyler were assigned to Colonel Erasmus Darwin Keyes, General Schenck, Colonel Sherman, and Colonel Israel Bush Richardson. The two newcomers, Keyes and Richardson, were West Point graduates of whom much was expected. Keyes (rhymes with "eyes"), a fifty-one-year-old native of Massachusetts, was experienced in both infantry and artillery operations, but he had not fought in Mexico and for the past year and a half had been General Scott's military secretary. Erudite, politically astute, and a man of strong, sometimes outspoken, convictions, he had clashed more than once with his boss on matters military, political, and diplomatic, yet he retained Scott's confidence.[38]

The forty-five-year-old Richardson, like Keyes a native New Englander (descendant of a Revolutionary War general), was homespun and unpretentious, a latter-day Zachary Taylor. His plainspokenness and charming eccentricities had made him a favorite with his men, one of whom recalled that "off duty he would be seen in linen pants, shirt sleeves and straw hat, and he had many most comical ways." He was also a staunch combat commander; in Mexico, where twice brevetted, he won an enduring nickname, "Fighting Dick."[39]

The other new divisions contained fewer brigades than Tyler's. The Second, assigned to David Hunter, a brigadier general of volunteers as of May 17, had only two, commanded by Colonels Porter and Burnside. The Third Division, Samuel Heintzelman's, consisted of three brigades led by Franklin, Willcox, and Oliver Otis Howard. The last named, at thirty the youngest brigade commander in the army, was unusually well educated, having graduated from Bowdoin College in his native Maine in 1850 and from West Point four years later. Howard had spent much of his prewar career at his second alma mater as an instructor of mathematics, but he had declined a professorship of natural philosophy because he believed he had a calling to the ministry. As he informed his superiors in February 1861, he intended to leave the army and "go to a theological seminary and so prepare as soon as possible for the work of my Blessed Master."[40]

Miles's Fifth Division, composed almost entirely of New York regiments (the single exception being the 27th Pennsylvania), comprised two brigades, both assigned to officers of limited capacity. Colonel Louis Blenker, the army's highest-ranking foreigner, was a native of Hesse-Darmstadt and a veteran of the Bavarian army. While beloved by the many German Americans in his command, he seems to have lacked the confidence of both Miles and McDowell. The other brigade leader, Colonel Thomas A. Davies of New York, was a graduate of the same West Point class as Lee and Johnston. A civilian since 1831, at war's outbreak he had assumed command of the 16th New York, a regiment he had not helped recruit or organize. Thus he was a stranger to its officers, to whom he appeared aloof and "rather mysterious." A strict disciplinarian, he was given to screaming and cursing at offenders, which hardly endeared him to the rank and file. During the march to Bull Run, Davies's tendency to come down hard on stragglers and looters would backfire, dealing him a stinging blow.[41]

July 8 came and went, but McDowell knew that the starting date of his advance could be pushed back only so long. He devoted the next week to completing his army's organization, tweaking his already much-tinkered-with strategy and familiarizing his ranking subordinates with his needs, hopes, and intentions. Within hours of his campaign plan's acceptance, the general began conferring closely with the likes of Hunter, Heintzelman, Sherman, and Franklin as well as with his engineer officers. All appeared to endorse the soundness of McDowell's general concept, although Captain Daniel P. Woodbury of the engineers made bold to question the merits of marching on Bull Run by the left flank. In a few words McDowell persuaded him that this approach was conclusively preferable. Beauregard's right was his most vulnerable point, and he would not strengthen it greatly because he would not expect an attack on it. The road network between Centreville and Manassas was such that a strike against the Rebel center was McDowell's logical move. But the Union commander did not intend to meet his opponent's expectations.[42]

The high-level discussions continued until the night before the march got underway. McDowell had told his commanders that they would move on the fifteenth, but throughout that day, regiments continued to stream across the bridges from Washington to the army's encampments on and beyond Arlington Heights. The newcomers barely had time to locate the headquarters of the brigades to which they had been assigned before being told to pack up and move out. The advance would have to wait another day.

Last-minute conferences took place not only at McDowell's headquarters but also in General Scott's office. On the thirteenth Scott entertained General Tyler, to whom he gave parting instructions, advice, and encouragement. The meeting was cordial, but it closed on a sour note when Tyler brought up the possibility of Johnston's interference with the offensive. Tired of trying to kill this bogey man, Scott loudly repeated his faith in Patterson's ability to hold the Virginian at bay. Tyler was not persuaded—he claimed to know both Valley generals well enough to put his faith in only one. He would be surprised, he told Scott, if "we did not have to contend with Jo. Johns[t]on's army in the approaching battle." The old general gave him a withering look and refused to discuss the matter further.[43]

The last of the strategy sessions took place on the fifteenth, less than twenty-four hours before the army left Washington. During this conference, attended by the division leaders and possibly by some brigade commanders as well, McDowell once again went over details of the converging advance on Fairfax Court House. The movements of Tyler, Hunter, Heintzelman, and Miles were spelled out so clearly and thoroughly that none of those officers would have any excuse for confusion, delay, or error. A glance at McDowell's map, even a poorly detailed one, displayed the simple genius of his strategy: Hunter's advance from the east would hold the attention of Beauregard's forces at Fairfax Court House; Miles and Heintzelman, moving farther south, would, by threatening their rear, force the Rebels' retreat; and Tyler's descent to Centreville via Germantown would neatly intercept the fugitives before they reached Bull Run. The hour of advance was clearly fixed. Three divisions were to move out at 2:00 P.M. on the sixteenth, while Heintzelman's troops would break camp a half hour later. The principal agenda items disposed of, following a final question-and-answer session, the gathering broke up. A few attendees lingered to discuss their respective tasks, but most of the generals and colonels quickly left McDowell's tent. Under a star-filled sky, they returned to their headquarters to oversee the pulling up of stakes.[44]

It may be supposed that Irvin McDowell slept poorly that night, the eve of his maiden effort in field command of an army, something he could not have anticipated at any point during his twenty-three years of military service. If worries assailed him as he lay on his army cot, he may have tried to deflect them by dwelling on the size of his command, which had grown to nearly 36,000 officers and men, 6,000 more than the number he had once considered adequate to the task he faced. But numbers alone would not guarantee victory. McDowell was fully aware of the inexperience and poor discipline that defined his short-term troops, wild cards in the fast-approaching game of battle. And yet he probably remained ignorant of the extent of his army's limitations and inadequacies.

Outside observers had a clearer view of its shortcomings. Two days earlier William H. Russell had visited the camps south of the Potomac. The venerable military correspondent was appalled by the condition of the army. In subsequent dispatches to the *Times*, he derided Northern newspaper accounts of McDowell's "magnificent force, complete in all respects," calling their authors "grossly and utterly ignorant of what an army is or should be." He described the infantry as unready for combat and the artillery as "miserably deficient; they have not, I should think, more than five complete batteries . . . , including scratch guns and these are of different calibres, badly horsed, miserably equipped, and provided with the worst set of gunners and drivers which I . . . ever beheld." As for cavalry, McDowell had "only a few scarecrow men, who would dissolve partnership with their steeds at the first serious combined movement." These were just the enlisted men; as a whole their officers were "unsoldierly-looking men" who appeared wholly ignorant of their responsibilities on campaign.

There was more. The army's transportation system was grossly inadequate, and its subsistence department was understaffed. Then too, "the camps are dirty to excess; the men are dressed in all sorts of uniforms; and from what I hear, I doubt if any of these regiments have ever performed a brigade evolution together, or if any of the officers know what it is to deploy a brigade from column into line." Lacking maps, McDowell "knows little or nothing of the country before him . . . , and he has not a cavalry officer capable of conducting a reconnaissance." Russell suspected that a few thousand British or French regulars properly supplied with cavalry and guns would make short work of McDowell's rookies and "march into Washington, over them or with them, whenever they please."[45]

Even taking into consideration Russell's admitted bias toward the professional armies of Europe, his analysis of the organizational, administrative, and operational deficiencies of McDowell's army appears all too accurate. How much trouble these flaws would cause when battle was joined was unforeseeable. This was fortunate; otherwise the Union commander might not have slept at all this night.

Ready for combat or not, the Army of Northeastern Virginia would taste it very soon. During the last nights before the march began, many officers and men must have looked back over their lives and reflected on their mortality. A certain number, including some of high rank, composed what they feared were their last letters to loved ones at home. William T. Sherman waited until hours before he came under fire to write to his wife. He tried to be humorous, assuring Ellen that the greatest danger he faced was being shot by his own awkward troops. This prospect aside, he had no worries; nor did he doubt that he would comport himself honorably. If anything should happen to him, he knew that Ellen would see to it that the children grew up straight and true. That was consolation enough to go into the fight with an unburdened mind.[46]

Sherman's fellow brigade commander William Franklin entertained similar thoughts and concerns. In a letter to his wife, Anna, written from Washington on the thirteenth, the colonel thanked God "that we have been so happy and that he gave me you as a wife." Reflecting on the vicissitudes of military life, he professed that "our happiness has not been alloyed even if we have not spent many wedding days together." Franklin's primary regret concerned the sacrifices Anna had made to support and advance his career: "In this I am afraid I have been selfish, but I know that you forgave me at the time. I find I can write these things better than I can say them, but I think I can say that I love you more significantly than I can write it."[47]

The remorse that Sherman and Franklin cited was bearable because neither man truly believed he would fall in battle. Time remained to undo past wrongs, to make amends for sins of omission and commission. It was different for thirty-two-year-old Major Sullivan Ballou of the 2nd Rhode Island Volunteers, a man of accomplishment and notability in his community and his state. A prominent lawyer, former college professor, stalwart of his state's Republican Party, and since 1857 speaker of the Rhode Island House of Representatives, Ballou had helped Governor William Sprague organize the 2nd Regiment and had been rewarded with high rank and authority. By all accounts, despite his military inexperience, he deserved his position. A conscientious officer who looked after his men, he strove to give them the leadership they needed. Late at night he could be found pouring over the manuals that helped him learn and retain the intricate tactics of his arm. The men appreciated his obvious concern for their well-being, and they gave him their trust and respect.[48]

When he went to war, Ballou left behind his wife, Sarah, and their two young sons. All three were very much on his mind on the evening of July 14 as he composed a letter in his tent inside the Washington-area camps that housed his regiment and the adjoining 1st Rhode Island. With the heaviest of hearts, he informed his wife that his regiment was about to break camp and that it appeared unlikely he could write again before it entered battle.

Like Sherman and Franklin, Ballou regretted the many slights and wrongs he accused himself of having dealt his wife. "Forgive my many faults," he begged Sarah, "and the many pains I have caused you. How thoughtless & foolish I have often times been! How gladly would I wash out with my tears every little spot upon your happiness, and struggle with all the misfortunes of this world to shield you, and our children from harm. But I cannot." He could not because he feared he lacked the weeks, the months, the years to make amends. "I can not describe to you my feelings on this calm Summer Sabbath night, when two thousand men are sleeping around me, many of them enjoying, perhaps, the last sleep before that of death, while I am suspicious that death is creeping around me with his fatal dart as I sit communicating with God, my country, and thee."

Though willing to make the ultimate sacrifice, he understood too well that it would be a shared gesture. "I have sought most closely and diligently, and often in my breast for a wrong motive in thus hazarding the happiness of those I love, and I could find none. A pure love of my country, and of the principles I have so often advocated before the people—another name of honor that I love more than I fear death, has called upon me and I have obeyed." Even so, "the memories of all the blissful moments I have spent with you come creeping over me, and I feel most grateful to God and to you that I have enjoyed them so long. And hard it is for me to give them up and burn to ashes the hopes of future years, when, God willing we might still have lived and loved together, and seen our sons grown up to honorable manhood around us."

Ballou's presentiment of approaching death was unshakable, but he clung desperately to one hope: "If the dead can come back to this earth and flit unseen around those they loved, I shall always be near you; in the gladdest days and in the darkest nights; advised to your happiest scenes, and gloomiest hours, *always, always*; and if there be a soft breeze upon your cheek, it shall [be] my breath, as the cool air fans your throbbing temple, it shall be my spirit passing by. Sarah do not mourn me dead; think I have gone and [will] wait for thee, for we shall meet again."

Having added a few lines of farewell to his mother and other family members, he closed with a fervent plea: "Oh Sarah, I wait for you there; come to me, and lead thither my children." Then he put down his pen, sealed the letter, and placed it in a trunk beside his cot. He left instructions that it be delivered to Sarah Ballou once word was received of her husband's death in battle.[49]

CHAPTER 7

A VICTORY UNEXPLOITED

Patterson had vowed to cross the Potomac within ten days of receiving permission from Scott—by then he expected all of his troops and resources to be on hand and ready to move. Inasmuch as he habitually underestimated the time he needed to get moving, he made himself look good on this occasion. On the morning of July 2, only seven days after Scott approved a crossing, Patterson executed it. But he had informed the commanding general that he would move on the first, only to issue an order postponing the march. He spent that day making final preparations, issuing necessary orders, and, one supposes, nerving himself for the contest. Bettering his usual timetable, however, did not impress his superior; Scott had expected him to cross on the twenty-seventh.[1]

The movement brought on the first sustained fighting of the campaign, though it was of relatively short duration and exerted little effect on either army's plans or future movements. Combat began soon after 7:30 A.M. on the second, when the first unit to cross, McMullin's Rangers, made contact with Stuart's cavalry about a mile in advance of Falling Waters. One of Patterson's men later described the locale, which lay four miles from Williamsport and eight from Martinsburg, as "a small and pretty mill-pond, which loses itself over the dam of a solitary grist-mill, within a stone's throw of the Potomac." The Rebel horsemen, who quickly withdrew, had been stationed near a turnpike tollhouse above Watkin's Ferry. Upon the Federals' approach, Stuart's men, as previously ordered, fell back on the main body of Jackson's brigade in and around Hainesville.[2]

Behind McMullin's gray-clad horsemen came the advance of Keim's division, the brigade formerly led by Colonel Miles and now by Patterson's son-in-law, John Abercrombie. Toward the rear, George Thomas's brigade of Cadwalader's division waited to cross the high, swift-moving river. To extend his line of advance, Patterson directed Negley's brigade to cross farther downstream, forming a parallel column in support of Abercrombie and Thomas.[3]

Abercrombie moved south, virtually unopposed, for about a quarter of a mile. As his troops advanced, they uprooted successive detachments of pickets, who fell back with alacrity. Not until ten o'clock did the Federals encounter a fixed defensive position, fallen-log and fence-rail breastworks below an unimpressive stream known as Hoke's Run.

The position, which crossed the farm of one William R. Porterfield, was defended "with much determination" by 380 members of Colonel Kenton Harper's 5th Virginia Infantry. The rookie soldiers under Harper were highly impressed by their approaching enemy. "On they came in battle array," wrote Private John Opie, "the first army we had ever beheld; and a grand sight it was—infantry, artillery, and mounted men; their arms and accoutrements glittering in the sunlight, their colors unfurled to the breeze, their bands playing and drums beating, the officers shouting the commands, as regiments, battalions, and companies marched up and wheeled into position."[4]

Opie's attention, and also that of his colonel, was initially directed at a body of Union skirmishers advancing on the Porterfield farm road. Wishing to strike the first blow, Harper asked his superior if he should advance on the enemy, but Jackson refused. He ordered the native Pennsylvanian and Mexican War veteran to detach a company and have it explore the woods along the Confederate left, where many of the skirmishers appeared to be assembling. As soon as the unit went forward, it drew a "brisk fire" from the Yankees concealed in a field of rye and grass. Harper then rushed five more companies to the threatened sector, and the action expanded rapidly.[5]

The first of Patterson's units to enter the fight was Colonel John C. Starkweather's 1st Wisconsin Volunteers, two companies in advance of the rest, the entire regiment backed by two sections of Perkins's battery. The latter's three 6-pounder guns and one 12-pounder howitzer unlimbered astride and to the right of the road from Falling Waters. There, supported by the First City Troop of Philadelphia, the artillerymen secured the rear of Starkweather's outfit; its right flank was quickly covered by Colonel Phaon Jarrett's 11th Pennsylvania. While Starkweather's men opened a fusillade against Harper's men on both sides of the road, three of Jarrett's companies swung about to rake some of Stuart's horsemen who appeared prepared to assault the right of Abercrombie's line.

As the fighting heated up, the opposing infantries exchanging sharp fusillades at close range and Perkins's shells whistling just

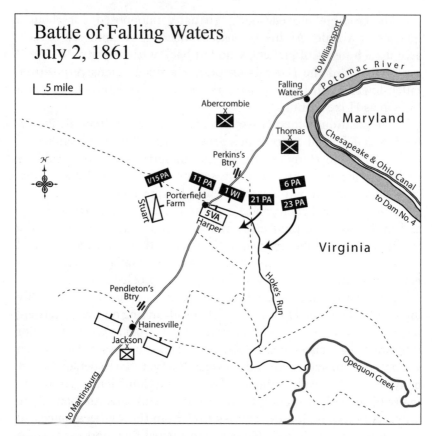

Battle of Falling Waters, July 2, 1861. *Map by Paul Dangel.*

above the heads of Harper's men, Abercrombie sought a way to cir-
cumvent the enemy's flank and, by crossing the run, strike his rear.
Recognizing that the 1st Wisconsin could not extend far enough to
do the job, the white-bearded Abercrombie dispatched a courier
to request help from the next brigade in line, Colonel Thomas's. Its
commander readily assented. Although known in the regular service as "Old Slow Trot" for his deliberate movements—the result of
a train accident of years past that still produced back and leg pain—
Thomas rushed the 21st and 23rd Pennsylvania, followed by the 6th
Pennsylvania, across Hoke's Run and into a position that overlapped
Harper's right.[6]

   The timely, well-executed movement turned the tide. Harper
would insist that his Virginians "stood well to their ranks and by

the severity of their fire held the enemy for some time in check, and when they attempted to advance, caused them to waver considerably—particularly on the right of their line." But Harper's problem was the pressure being exerted on the other end; he knew too that when one regiment is assailed by four or five, the outcome is usually preordained. Jackson had been ordered to hold back the enemy as long as possible and then withdraw without taking heavy casualties. Entirely content to fight a defensive battle, as soon as it became obvious that Harper was on the verge of being overwhelmed, he ordered the 5th Virginia to retire. Two outfits that Jackson had placed in supporting distance of Colonel Harper's men, the 2nd and 4th Virginia, fell back in turn.[7]

The Confederates moved to the rear slowly and in good order, something not expected of troops under fire for the first time. Within minutes they were beyond range of Abercrombie's and Thomas's riflemen, who did not appear anxious to pursue. One reason was the covering fire suddenly unleashed by a newcomer at the front, Captain Pendleton's battery. The guns of the clergyman-soldier shelled any Yankee unit that ventured across Hoke's Run. Seconds before each one fired, Pendleton raised his hands as if appealing to heaven and exclaimed: "May the Lord have mercy on their wicked souls! *Fire!*" The cannonade, although too steeply pitched to do maximum damage, enabled Jackson to evacuate Camp Stephens, his field headquarters. Critical to the success of the operation was the escape of the brigade's supply wagons, conveyed to Martinsburg by the 27th Virginia.[8]

Shortly before four o'clock, Thomas and Abercrombie finally advanced but, taking their cue from Patterson, halted at the abandoned camp near Hainesville. Two companies of the 2nd U.S. Cavalry staged a brief pursuit but were soon recalled. Technically, Patterson had emerged from the fight as the victor, but his failure to follow up his minor success meant that his only accomplishment was driving Jackson's brigade upon the main body of its army.

Casualties on both sides had been light. According to Johnston, the 5th Virginia lost two men killed and six or eight wounded. Abercrombie reported eighteen killed and fifteen wounded. Thomas's brigade, despite its aggressive handling, had sustained no casualties. Dozens of Federals had been taken prisoner, including—by Union count—thirty-five members of a Pennsylvania regiment. Jackson's number, probably a more accurate one, was forty-six.[9]

The Pennsylvanians had been duped into surrendering to J. E. B. Stuart. While threatening Starkweather's right flank early in the battle, the cavalry leader had become separated from his command. Riding alone through an opening in a fence that bordered Stumpy's Hollow, he was suddenly accosted by Company I, 15th Pennsylvania of Negley's brigade. Stuart may have surmised that the unit was detached from its regiment and thus exposed, but he realized that his only hope of avoiding capture was a bold-faced bluff. According to his future adjutant and biographer Henry Brainerd McClellan, the cavalryman "ordered the whole party to lay down their arms on the peril of their lives."[10]

The confused and irresolute Yankees obeyed—all but three, who were shot down by Stuart's belatedly arriving troopers. The captives were prodded through the gap in the fence and to the rear, bound for a Southern prison. For this feat, Johnston advocated Stuart's elevation to colonel, even as he sought a brigadier generalship for Jackson. Both promotions would come through in a matter of weeks.[11]

As Jackson withdrew, Johnston advanced. The following morning the Army of the Shenandoah was united at Darkesville, six miles from Falling Waters. In response to reports that Patterson was moving against him, Johnston drew up his command in lines of battle, but the enemy failed to appear. He kept the men under arms for four days, but when his challenge was not accepted, he returned to Winchester. By now he had taken the measure of his opponent and had found him wanting. If Patterson could not be enticed to offer battle when, as Johnston believed, he outnumbered the Valley Confederates three-to-one, he must lack the nerve and determination needed in a field commander. The Virginian would use that knowledge to good advantage in the weeks ahead.[12]

Although the strategic benefits of the engagement at Falling Waters were negligible, the Federals held the field when the shooting ceased and considered themselves victors. The impression that they had prevailed against a highly regarded Rebel army—even though only a fraction of it had been engaged—raised the spirits of Patterson's men, including those who had seen none of the fighting. Reporters accompanying the army were similarly elated. In bold type a newspaper in Patterson's hometown described the glorified skirmish as a "Brilliant Advance." The New York Times reported that when the first reports of the fight reached Washington, a jubilant

Winfield Scott personally awakened President Lincoln to relay the glad tidings. Patterson himself, in his after-action report, admitted that it was merely a "brush" but described it as "highly creditable to our arms, winning, as we did, the day against a foe superior in numbers to those engaged on our side."[13]

As he wrote, Patterson surely knew his claim to being outnumbered was a falsehood. Later, when addressing one of his regiments, he repeated the statement and received loud cheers from soldiers who wanted to believe it too. Years later one of those believers wrote of the thrill of victory that animated his comrades in the aftermath of the fight and their disappointment at not running the vanquished to earth. The engagement might have been a trifling affair in its scope and strategic results, but "it was the central feature and the only successful stroke in a campaign the opening of which promised great results, but which proved to be, on the whole, abortive."[14]

Not until July 3 did Patterson move his advance echelon into Martinsburg, which had been empty of Confederate forces for hours. Ruination greeted the invaders at every turn, the fruit of Johnston's misguided war against the Baltimore & Ohio system. There was no compelling reason for the army to remain in this still-smoldering wasteland. Patterson's primary mission was to keep tabs on Johnston, not to let him slip far from sight. Thus he should have pressed on to Winchester, where even if he did not engage his opponent he could at least remain in close touch with him. But he failed to exert himself; instead, he plunked his army down in the countryside outside Martinsburg and contented himself with sending a few cavalrymen to sniff at Johnston's indifferently fortified enclave.

One reason he gave for his inertia was the need to "send back for supplies," a hoary excuse indeed. He also wished to await the arrival from Maryland and Washington, respectively, of the troops under Stone (three regiments and some miscellaneous companies of infantry and a light battery) and Sandford (four regiments of New York foot soldiers, one of them a three-years' outfit). Apparently, the numerical advantage that had forced Johnston out of Harpers Ferry was no longer sufficient to ensure success.[15]

Stone's column reached Martinsburg on July 8, the advance echelon of Sandford's command two days later. Their arrival gave Patterson another excuse for inaction. On the tenth he organized the newcomers into a third division commanded by Sandford. Stone received command of half of this force, christened the Seventh

Brigade. The largest such organization in Patterson's command, it consisted of five infantry regiments—three from Pennsylvania, including the 17th under Colonel Francis E. Patterson; one from New York; one from New Hampshire; a company of District of Columbia volunteers that had been affiliated with Stone since the early weeks of the war; and one battery and an additional section of light artillery. The remainder of Sandford's command, the army's Eighth Brigade, comprised four New York regiments, three of them manned by ninety-day volunteers.[16]

Ultimately, the Eighth Brigade was assigned to Colonel Daniel Butterfield of the 12th New York Militia. Butterfield, a colorful character without professional military training or experience, would nevertheless leave his mark on the conflict. Born in Utica, New York, in 1831, son of the founder of two famous transportation agencies, American Express and Wells Fargo, Butterfield parlayed a stint as a sergeant in a Washington-area company into regimental command while somehow also gaining a lieutenant colonelcy in the regular service. A devotee of wine, women, and song, the flamboyant New Yorker would become notorious in some circles, but his lifestyle would not impede his meteoric rise to command or his career as a military musician, composer of a bugle call whose fame would long outlive that of its creator: "Taps."[17]

Additional troops reached Patterson during succeeding weeks; other reinforcements were diverted by War Department reconsideration. On the sixth the 3rd Wisconsin joined the army's rear echelon at Harpers Ferry, though without sufficient shoulder arms. The 4th Wisconsin was ordered to Patterson at the same time as the 3rd, but at the last minute it was assigned to the defenses of Baltimore. Lew Wallace's 11th Indiana reported to Patterson on July 12 and was placed in camp at Bunker Hill but was almost immediately recalled to Romney, Virginia, and assigned to McClellan. Also on the twelfth the 2nd Massachusetts Volunteers reported to army headquarters, having marched from Hagerstown via Williamsport, the only three-year regiment Patterson would ever command.[18]

The recent additions—especially the larger organizations under Stone and Sandford—should have given Patterson enough confidence of having a manpower advantage to take on Johnston without hesitation. The sticking point was that he had come to accept warped estimates of his adversary's numbers, derived from the reports of amateur spies, local secessionists masquerading as unionists, and poorly conducted cavalry patrols. He now believed that Johnston's army embraced 26,000 infantry and cavalry and at least two dozen guns, "many rifled," meaning that Patterson was outnumbered by at least 8,000 men. Thus he had good reason to wait and carefully consider his situation.[19]

While sitting idle in Martinsburg, Patterson began to dwell on another supposed impediment to forward action, the same shortage of rations, materiel, and wheeled transport that had postponed his departure from Chambersburg. But with the exception of ammunition for those few regiments armed with muskets, his supply inadequacies were few. His problem was not a lack of resources but the deteriorating condition of those on hand. Several hundred of the troops were clad in shoddy uniforms and brogans that, after two and a half months of wear, were literally falling apart. Patterson was well aware of the damage done to his army's physical health and morale by unscrupulous contractors in Philadelphia and Harrisburg, but he failed to alert his superiors to the trouble until too late to remedy it. Then he appropriated the problem for another excuse for his lethargy. On the nineteenth he finally warned the War Department that most of his ninety-day troops were "without shoes and without pants," making them anticipate even more the approaching close of their enlistment periods. The more they looked forward to going home, the less Patterson looked forward to reengaging Johnston.[20]

Taking a cue from their commander, the men of the Army of Pennsylvania spent a lot of time at Martinsburg lounging about—some actually complained of the enforced leisure. Orchestrated events, such as reviews and inspections, took up some of the down time. A few soldiers busied themselves by ministering to the needs of local unionists who had been forced by their neighbors to go into hiding without access to the basics of life. One enlisted man described the oppressed element as "poor, half-starved" victims who "crept out to the roadside from their hiding-places, and told the Union troops that they now first saw daylight for several weeks."[21]

The troops shared their abundant rations with these unfortunates, some of whom celebrated their salvation by displaying for the first time in months the U.S. flags they had hidden from the secessionists. Those who had not gone underground expressed an equal amount of joy at being liberated. General Sandford wrote that upon arriving in Martinsburg, he was met with an outpouring of unionist sentiment: "I had invitations from all the leading people to come and dine and sup with them. They were well disposed towards us, and indignant at the immense injury done by the enemy to their property throughout all that part of the country."[22]

Patterson's army celebrated Independence Day with parades, patriotic speeches, and in many of its camps, religious services. The "secesh" element did not approve of these activities, which they considered provocative, but few had the nerve to complain. Not so seventeen-year-old Isabella "Belle" Boyd. According to her own account, holiday revelers invaded her family's home to confiscate Confederate banners and attach a U.S. flag to her roof. The high-spirited teenager resented the intrusion because although an avid Rebel, she had socialized with some of the Yankees, which she believed entitled her to special consideration. Her vehement protests led to a physical confrontation; when the teenager's mother tried to intervene, a soldier cursed at her and may have manhandled her. An enraged Belle drew a concealed pistol and shot the offender dead. She was duly arrested and hauled before a board of inquiry, which surprisingly exonerated her on the grounds of justifiable homicide.

Though Belle was released from captivity, sentries were posted outside her home and her movements were closely monitored. These measures apparently failed to deter her from a career in espionage a la Rose Greenhow. In her postwar memoirs she claims to have pried military intelligence out of an infatuated Yankee officer, smuggling the information to Johnston's headquarters. Later in the war she supposedly spied for other leaders, including Ashby and Jackson. Corroborating evidence is elusive, and her activities are shrouded in myth and mystery, but Belle Boyd's escapades remain the stuff of Civil War lore.[23]

A week after Falling Waters, even an imperceptive commander such as Patterson understood that the troops of the Army of Pennsylvania had become restless and irritable, some of them perhaps verging on mutiny and not merely because their clothing was unraveling. The army was perched hardly more than twenty miles from the enemy's defenses, and no effort had been made to shorten that distance except temporarily. There had been desultory skirmishing on July 6, when forty Rebels drove in Patterson's pickets south of Martinsburg. It seemed obvious to many officers and men, if not to their commander, that the Rebels were goading them, daring them to advance and fight and sneering at their refusal to do so. The skirmish on the sixth seemed to presage a major encounter, but when Patterson refused to advance, as a member of the 4th Alabama of Bee's brigade recalled, "our boys were sadly disappointed and stacked their arms reluctantly, heaping on the heads of the Yankees innumerable curses, for being such infamous cowards."[24]

Belatedly deciding that he was not doing enough to keep Johnston occupied, and aware that he now commanded as many troops as he was likely to get, on the eighth Patterson drew up a circular order committing his army to a march on Winchester. He appears to have been prodded into action by a couple of considerations. July 8 was the day originally set for McDowell's departure for Bull Run, and even though Patterson had been advised that the timetable had been shelved, the date was a reminder that the Army of Northeastern Virginia would be in motion quite soon; Patterson had better get a closer hold on Johnston's attention.[25]

Three days earlier Scott had instructed his subordinate on the steps he should take after defeating Johnston and occupying Winchester: "If you can continue the pursuit without too great hazard, advance via Leesburg (or Strasburg) towards Alexandria." Either movement would confuse the now-beaten Johnston as to whether Patterson planned to stalk him or to turn east for a possible union with McDowell. Scott's advice was sound enough, but by stressing that Patterson should pursue the Strasburg option only "with great caution," the commanding general delivered yet another check to initiative and aggressiveness.[26]

Patterson's order for July 9 called for Thomas's brigade, including its artillery and cavalry, to advance on Winchester by the Valley Pike. The remainder of Cadwalader's division, augmented by Doubleday's heavy cannons, would follow at a distance. Meanwhile, Stone's brigade and Perkins's battery, preceded by a company of horsemen, would move down a road parallel to and east of the turnpike. Keim's division (temporarily augmented by the 19th and 28th New York) would proceed along both roads, Negley's brigade behind Stone's, and the brigades of Abercrombie and Wynkoop following Cadwalader. Keim would be responsible for furnishing a rear guard for the entire force and for safeguarding its supply train.[27]

The movement order, which indicated careful planning, suggested that Patterson was serious about engaging his adversary, an impression he gave to some members of his staff. Major Craig Biddle, his aide-de-camp, believed that Patterson was "very full" of the notion to advance on Johnston and "was bound to go ahead" to Winchester. But appearances deceived. That night tents were struck across the Martinsburg countryside, and the men received marching rations. But the next morning, after some regiments had been shaken out of their camps and formed into columns, the movement was called off, and tents were ordered back up. Many who obeyed the order were at a loss for reasons; less confused comrades supposed their commander had suffered a loss of nerve.[28]

This time the decision to stand down had been more or less thrust upon Patterson. At the urging of some of his staff officers, he had called his ranking subordinates to a council of war at his headquarters in the Queen Street home of unionist Henry C. Small. Patterson, whose determination to advance on Johnston was a fragile thing at best and whose tendency to rely heavily on the advice of his subordinates was never more evident than on this occasion, allowed himself to be talked out of executing his order of the previous day.

There were many reasons, or excuses, to delay. As his staff reminded him, Johnston appeared to outnumber them, while Stone's and Sandford's reinforcements had yet to be fully assimilated into the ranks. The lack of transportation remained acute, as Patterson's chief quartermaster affirmed. His commissary of subsistence testified that the insufficiency of supply wagons would force the troops to forage off the countryside within a few days of leaving Martinsburg. Then there were expiring enlistments. Eighteen of the army's twenty-six regiments were nearing the end of their enlistment terms; some were scheduled to be sent home for discharge within two weeks.[29]

The army's growing dissatisfaction with affairs in general remained an unvoiced but potent cause of concern—esprit de corps was not a strongpoint of the Army of Pennsylvania. Although a few regiments had seen combat, the rawness of the troops was an indisputable fact. Regiments continued to perform poorly on the drill field, ill-arranged and unsanitary camps suggested a general lack of discipline, and because the enemy lurked nearby, trigger fingers remained itchy. As the chaplain of the 13th Pennsylvania noted, even after weeks of field service, the troops were "excitable, and inexperienced. At night, the horse, cow, dog, or even shaking bush, that will not respond to the challenge of the sentinel, is sure to get a Minnie bullet whizzed at it."[30]

Hanging over every decision Patterson must make was the warning Scott had sounded a month ago: "We must sustain no reverse;
but this is not enough: a check or a drawn battle would be a victory to the enemy." During the council, Patterson submitted to the
attendees copies of his original instructions as well as the orders
issued to him since leaving Pennsylvania. Then he read a lengthy
statement that clearly conveyed his state of mind. The army's mission, it said, was to remain in the Valley as long as Johnston did, to
offer him battle, defeat him, and return to Washington.

Patterson then posed some rhetorical questions. Should Johnston
refuse battle and retreat, would that indicate a weakness on his part
or portend a ruse to lure his opponent into a trap? If he fled, should
the army pursue, and if so, how far? How would the soldiers react
if Johnston could not be overtaken? Patterson feared that "if our
men go home without a regular battle, a good field fight, they will
go home discontented, will not re-enlist, and will sour the minds
of others." But he also stressed the danger to the nation if the army
fought a battle and lost. A defeat would shatter what remained of
the army's morale, and it might not prevent Johnston from going to
Manassas. "What," he asked plaintively, "shall be done?"[31]

The general's audience made itself heard. A majority seemed
to favor delaying or even canceling the advance. Captain James H.
Simpson of the topographical engineers described the army's current
position as precarious because of the ease with which Johnston and
Beauregard could combine against it. He recommended an immediate withdrawal to Washington. Captain Newton of the construction
engineers feared that a movement on Winchester would seriously
expose Patterson's communications. He did not need to remind his
superior that the military telegraph ran only as far as Harpers Ferry
(a critic of Patterson's campaign later wrote that "it was a sad mistake that the telegraph was not advanced with the army"). Every
mile the army covered further isolated it, breaking its contact with
higher headquarters and subordinate commands. Newton recommended that Patterson advance no deeper into the Valley; he favored
a pullback to Harpers Ferry, a move to Charles Town, or a return to
the Potomac at Shepherdstown. From any of these positions, the
army could interpose between Johnston and the Blue Ridge, or at
least threaten to do so.

Major Porter, whose influence on Patterson was as strong as
anyone's, argued strenuously for delay. He reinforced his boss's fear

that to lurch forward was to fall into a well-laid trap. The adjutant's recommendation that the march be postponed until they could gain a clearer idea of Johnston's intentions was endorsed by nearly everyone in attendance, including Cadwalader, Keim, Abercrombie, and even the sagacious Thomas. Some believed that the army should remain in place. Others agreed with Newton's suggestion about sidling toward Charles Town. None counseled a bold, unambiguous move in any direction.[32]

The preponderance of opinion being opposed to an offensive, Patterson felt obliged to heed it. In doing so he was giving in to his deepest insecurities, which could not be stilled even by the knowledge that his primary mission was to engage Johnston, not stare him down. Acceding to the arguments of those whose judgment he trusted as much as his own, he called off the advance to Winchester.[33]

Though the order to return to camp stoked the army's discontent, Patterson believed that he had made the right decision. He considered his wisdom confirmed by a telegram from Scott on the eleventh. It conveyed a claim by a trusted informant that Johnston intended to lure his adversary so far up the Valley that should Patterson follow, fight, and be defeated, he could not retreat to the Potomac quickly enough to save his army from ruin. Then Johnston would head west to join the forces opposing McClellan and after beating them turn east, uniting with Beauregard and helping him defeat McDowell—a slightly modified version of the three-part offensive Beauregard was about to propose to his superiors.

In so many words Scott was warning Patterson that Beauregard's overly imaginative strategy was entirely feasible. Its successful execution, he feared, "will give the Confederate cause such prestige, and inspire in it such faith, as will insure the recognition of the Government abroad, and at the same time so impair confidence in the Federal Government as to render it impossible for it to procure loans abroad, and very difficult for it to raise means at home."[34]

Since it played on his fears of confronting Johnston, Patterson accepted this dire assessment of the military, political, diplomatic, and economic damage that would occur should he grope blindly at the enemy. His preferred course seemingly endorsed not only by his subordinates but also by the general in chief of U.S. forces, he had no alternative to deferring his confrontation with that wily, devious adversary to the south. From any point of view, Patterson's decision appeared entirely sustainable. It would prove, however, to be one of the worst he ever made as a soldier. The absolute worst was soon to follow.

Joe Johnston was a careful observer of his enemy's activities and a gifted predictor of his intentions, but he could not comprehend Robert Patterson. Throughout the week following his fallback from Darkesville, the Confederate commander believed on more than one occasion that his opponent was on the verge of attacking his lines outside Winchester. If the movement succeeded, Patterson would then shift eastward to strike Beauregard in flank. Each time that Stuart's scouts reported an enemy advance to be imminent, however, something appeared to have changed Patterson's mind. Given the man's clear numerical superiority (which Johnston knew to have grown in recent days) and the aggressiveness the Union commander had shown when crossing the Potomac and giving battle, Johnston could not fathom what it was that kept staying his hand.

The Virginian realized that his own troops were getting restive. The retreat from Falling Waters, like the evacuation of Harpers Ferry, had dealt a blow, albeit temporarily, to the corporate morale. The men desired to reaffirm their faith in Southern male superiority by coming to grips with the Yankees. Like their commander, they could not understand why Patterson denied them this opportunity. On July 4 Edmund Kirby Smith, who had recently been assigned command of the Fifth Brigade, Army of the Shenandoah, wrote his mother in Florida, "our men are eager for the contest but from appearances there is no prospect for engaging the enemy except on his terms." Smith described "being drawn up in position within hearing of Patterson's army, the booming of whose guns has been ringing the national salute into our ears. Powder is too scarce a commodity to waste in such festivities, but our bands have played 'Dixie' from one end of the line to the other."[35]

By July 8 Johnston had come to suspect that Patterson had lost the strength of will he had shown the week before. Undoubtedly, he had learned of Washington's growing dissatisfaction with Patterson's inactivity. Thus he must have suspected that the old general was on the verge of being relieved of command—perhaps he was already gone. Johnston knew that General Mansfield had moved Stone's brigade from lower Maryland to Martinsburg, and he deduced that Mansfield would replace Patterson. On the eighth he wrote to

Beauregard: "As Patterson has been too timid & slow it is reasonable to suppose that his superseder will endeavor to avoid those faults & advance immediately."[36]

The next day Stuart reported new indications of an impending advance. Johnston had learned to take any warning from Stuart seriously, and Martinsburg's civilians had slipped inside Confederate lines with word that Patterson (or his successor) had ordered the issuance of marching rations. Accordingly, Johnston had his infantry stand ready for action and set fatigue parties to erecting new earthworks; 24-pounder guns were placed on the parapets. The augmentation of his defenses eased the general's mind only to a degree. As he wrote Adjutant General Cooper that evening, "we are not prepared beyond the readiness of our men to fight." Once again, the reports of a Federal movement proved groundless—at least premature—and Johnston cancelled the high alert. In subsequent days nothing that portended an advance was observed at Martinsburg, and Patterson's status remained unknown.[37]

Johnston used the time given him not only to keep in close contact with Beauregard but also to firm up army organization in anticipation of either a confrontation with Patterson or, as seemed more likely, a transfer to Manassas. For weeks Davis had been promising him reinforcements. They began to trickle in just before the army withdrew from Darkesville. After July 10, they became a veritable flood. The recent arrivals included Colonel Arthur Campbell Cummings's 33rd Virginia, which Johnston assigned to Jackson's brigade, and the 9th and 11th Georgia, which, not surprisingly, joined Bartow. At about the same time, Davis sent to Winchester Colonel John H. Forney's 10th Alabama, earmarked for Smith's Fifth Brigade. Among the newcomers, only Cummings's regiment would serve Johnston in battle, but its performance would more than compensate for the absence of the other outfits. It was at this time too that Johnston, concerned about Patterson's known superiority in artillery, reorganized and resupplied his own. On July 13 he installed Colonel Pendleton as the titular commander of the army's artillery.[38]

His own army seemingly inactive at Winchester, Johnston began to hear rumblings not only from his troops but also from the Southern public. In barrooms and drawing rooms alike, Virginians were voicing doubts about their armies' ability to do anything but react reflexively to the movements, or threats of movements, of the enemy. A most influential observer of the Richmond social scene,

Mary Boykin Chesnut, wife of Colonel Chesnut of Beauregard's staff, would spend the next three years criticizing Johnston's Fabian policies in contrast to the aggressive warfare of Robert E. Lee and Beauregard. Late in the war she was still incensed at Johnston's willingness to trade territory for the safety of his army. He was happy, she wrote, to give up one position after another "when one must think he could fight."[39]

Yet not every observer condemned Johnston's strategy of defensive maneuver, especially considering the opportunities he had given to Patterson to fight him. In a letter to General Bonham at Manassas early in July, Governor Pickens opined that Johnston "has boldly marched in the face of an enemy far his superior in numbers. And his maneuvres have shown real talent. I like his game."[40]

Secure in the belief that he was acting properly under the circumstances, Johnston continued to watch and wait. His patience appeared to be rewarded when in mid-July, Patterson showed signs of a forward movement. As always, however, the indications were ambiguous and confounding. On the fifteenth, as Johnston's pickets duly reported, the Yankees advanced fifteen miles to Bunker Hill, less than ten miles from Winchester by direct road. A brisk skirmish broke out at that "dirty hamlet" with the historic name, resulting in Stuart's scouts being driven from their camps behind Mill Creek, one trooper having been killed and several others captured.[41]

Patterson's sudden aggressiveness continued into the next day. Although his main body remained stationary, a large detachment advanced another four or five miles, evicting Stuart from a secure-looking position. That night several thousand bluecoats pushed southeastward along a forgotten trail to a bridge over Opequon Creek, less than five miles northeast of Winchester. Johnston realized this force could interpose between his army and the Shenandoah River— all of Stuart's cavalry could not have prevented it.

At this point a series of strange events began. On the morning of the sixteenth, with the defenders of Winchester holding their collective breath, a combined-arms force moved down the pike toward them. It came up to an imperfect line of defense: fallen-tree and fence-rail barricades strewn across the road. These were easily removable, but instead of taking them apart, the Federals halted and dug in behind them. One of their cannons spewed canister at a knot of Stuart's men on the other side of the works, scattering the cavalry in all directions. But then the gun fell silent, and after a brief interval, the entire force faced to the rear and returned to Bunker Hill.[42]

Johnston, observing the proceedings, must have asked himself what was going on. As if content to take one step forward and two steps back, Patterson seemed to be simultaneously offering and rejecting battle. The mystery deepened the next morning, but it must have produced a sense of relief at Confederate headquarters. An hour or so before daylight, the Yankees moved again, this time in army strength—but east, not south. Johnston must have suspected another flanking movement, but instead of curving toward Winchester, the bluecoats kept marching. In a matter of hours they had disappeared from Johnston's view, their passage marked by columns of dust rising translucently toward the sun. The entire Army of Pennsylvania—lock, stock, and baggage wagons—had moved cross-country in the direction of Smithfield and Charles Town.[43]

If this was some kind of Yankee trick, Johnston could not fathom its purpose. Neither could Stuart, the army's intelligence-gathering chieftain. The only possible explanation was that Patterson was trying to reach the road beyond Smithfield that led south to Berryville, which might enable him to threaten Winchester from the east. But by thus breaking contact, he was abandoning his well-publicized commitment to keep his enemy in view and well occupied. Until now Patterson had been fulfilling at least the first half of that mission, but he could attain neither objective by taking his army completely off the board.

Stuart was immediately dispatched to monitor Union movements and, by striking the army's rear and taking prisoners, to attempt to determine what was happening. The cavalryman failed to do so, but just after midnight on the eighteenth, it no longer mattered. At that hour Johnston received a telegram from Richmond that required his complete and immediate attention. Patterson's gyrations continued to confound him, but suddenly he had more important business to attend to.[44]

Patterson's move to Bunker Hill on July 15 suggested that he had regained the momentum he had surrendered following Falling Waters. To one staff officer, who believed the general "had got his Irish blood up," Patterson suddenly appeared committed to holding Johnston in place and attacking him. He had finally found some reasons for doing so. His colleague George McClellan had been making headlines with a series of small but well-received victories in his theater—at Rich Mountain, near Beverly, Virginia, on July 11, and two days later at Corrick's Ford in the Cheat River valley. These successes appeared to secure the western portion of the state for the Union. In relaying the news, which would make McClellan a house-hold name throughout the North, General Scott urged Patterson to achieve on a par with Little Mac. Another reason for Patterson to engage Johnston without further delay was the intelligence, relayed to him by a predetermined signal from Washington, that McDowell would start for Bull Run on the sixteenth. The time had come for Patterson to make his move against Winchester.[45]

Early on the fifteenth Patterson ended his nearly two-week stay in Martinsburg, a hiatus he attributed to "the want of artillery and transportation." He started south toward Bunker Hill under a full head of steam, but his motive power dissipated quickly. By the time he reached the supposedly grimy village, it was almost gone. On its outskirts his vanguard confronted what he described as "all manner of impediments thrown in the way." The sight of these obstructions began to weaken Patterson's newfound resolve, and his army shud-dered to a virtual halt.[46]

During the delay, Patterson's officers interrogated prisoners and deserters who volunteered information about the formidable condition of Winchester's defenses and the tens of thousands of Confederates who manned them—self-proclaimed unionists among the local citizenry corroborated these fanciful tales. But other resi-dents, some of whom knew the informants personally, doubted their truthfulness and questioned their motives.

They were not the only ones. The newsman David Strother, now one of Patterson's engineers, insisted that Johnston had far fewer men than previously reported and that his ranks had been depleted by desertion and illness. Strother was speaking from firsthand obser-vation, but for reasons of their own, more influential members of the general's staff dismissed his estimates. Their commander chose to believe that Johnston's army now approached 42,000 men and dozens of cannons. In reality, even with his recent additions, the Confederate leader had fewer than 10,000 effectives.[47]

On the fifteenth General Sandford asked Patterson when the final movement on Winchester would get underway. He received a curious reply: "I don't know yet when we shall move. And if I did I would not tell my own father." Patterson continued to act strangely

the next day, when some of Sandford's men advanced via that lit-
tle-used path toward the Opequon. Although the move brought a
portion of the army to within five miles of Winchester, Patterson
seemed not to take notice. Later that day, however, the New Yorker
was told that those five miles would be covered beginning at four
o'clock the next morning, the seventeenth.

Sandford was anxious to get moving at the head of his 8,000-man
division, which included a small body of cavalry and two batteries.
But about three hours before the army was to march, he received
an "order of three pages from General Patterson, instructing me to
move on to Charlestown." As Sandford later informed a congressional investigating committee, his new destination was "nearly at
right angles to the road I was going to move on, and 22 miles from
Winchester."[48]

What had happened to cripple Patterson's determination to
fight? Only hours before giving the word to advance, he had convened another war council, more lightly attended than the last
but every bit as consequential. He had been urged to call it by
Major Porter, who all along had accepted the inflated estimates of
Johnston's strength and feared that their opponent was luring them
into a trap. At first Patterson resisted his adjutant's advice, but he
was finally persuaded to talk things over with Colonels Thomas and
Abercrombie.

Patterson suspected that both subordinates would counsel
against an advance, and he was correct. When the colonels reported,
the general posed a new round of questions for their consideration.
Should the army remain at Bunker Hill? Should it fall back to Martinsburg? Should it attack Winchester? Or should it keep Johnston in place by merely demonstrating against the town? Patterson
brought up the fact that General Scott had warned against risking a
defeat against an enemy that outnumbered him substantially. Since
this appeared to be the case, if the army attacked and was repulsed,
could it survive? Might not an attack have the opposite effect, driving Johnston from the Valley and toward Manassas? Finally, since
McDowell was reported to have left Washington yesterday, with
Johnston known to remain in the Valley, was an assault on Winchester necessary?[49]

Patterson may have advanced from Bunker Hill with the best of
intentions, but the questions he put to his audience and his framing of them gave the clear impression that he would be amenable

to being talked out of attacking. Porter, Thomas, and Abercrombie did not have to say much to convince him that the decision he was mulling over was the right one. Their motives are unclear, although one may assume that Porter, who thought of himself as the brains behind Patterson's decisions, truly believed the army unready to tackle Johnston. Thomas, who had already argued for a move to Charles Town, may have considered the village a base from which to slip between Johnston and the mountains. Abercrombie probably voted the way he believed his father-in-law wanted him to. In any case, Patterson was gratified and relieved by their unanimous opposition to bold action, and he suspected, no doubt correctly, that Cadwalader and Keim would have endorsed their view. The only subordinate who might have argued against it was Sandford, and his advice had not been sought, probably for good reason.[50]

Within a half hour of conferring with Thomas and Abercrombie, the general cancelled the order that would have sent the army south and issued one for a sidestep to Charles Town. The movement began at 3:00 A.M. on the seventeenth. Patterson's advance reached the village at about noon. Rear elements, forced to deploy several times en route to meet a phantom attack by Stuart's horsemen, did not arrive until late that evening.[51]

Later, when pressed to explain why he gave up a foothold in striking distance of the Valley Confederates, Patterson advanced a number of reasons. He claimed to see Bunker Hill as, in General Cadwalader's words, a "false" position from which the army could not seriously threaten Johnston and pin him down. Patterson was certain that his senior subordinate, Cadwalader, shared this opinion, but when questioned by government interrogators, the division leader denied this. Rather than advocate shying away from Johnston, Cadwalader claimed urging his superior, after leaving Bunker Hill, to attack without further delay. Patterson, in turn, denied having received any such advice. It appears that he never did, that Cadwalader's testimony was a shabby attempt to shield himself from the charge of having endorsed a shameful retreat.[52]

Patterson offered other reasons for departing Bunker Hill. The army had only two days' worth of supplies, and more could not be had from the surrounding countryside. At that village his communications were vulnerable to being severed by an enemy with enormous reserves of manpower and weaponry: "I should have considered it an act of utter insanity to have remained there with so long a line behind me, my force not nearly half the number, not more than one third the number of the enemy." Moving to Charles Town solved these problems. There Patterson could gather supplies and protect them while also keeping tabs on Johnston. In fact, as he had assured Scott when seeking permission to move to Charles Town, from that place, "I can move easily, [and] strike at Winchester."[53]

Patterson came up with still another reason—a patently false one—for leaving Johnston's front on July 17: Scott had told him to do so. He informed the joint committee, "I was ordered to go to Charles-town, and I obeyed my orders." In fact, Scott had approved his sub-ordinate's desire to move there as a prelude to an immediate attack on Johnston. It seems likely that the general in chief, then preoccu-pied with McDowell's operations, had failed to consult his maps—if he had he would have seen the fallacy in Patterson's contention that Charles Town was a better jumping-off point for striking Winchester. Even so, Scott did not *order* him to go there, and Patterson knew it.[54]

At least one of the reasons he gave for not advancing against Johnston was absurd. Unreconciled to the move, once his division reached Charles Town, General Sandford began to rail against it. To calm him down—and hush him up—Patterson had his son-in-law inform him that the detour had been made necessary by "reliable information that Johnston was re-enforced with 20,000 men from Manassas, and was going to attack and destroy Patterson's army." Sandford suspected that Abercrombie's tale was so much nonsense, and he resented the implication that he was gullible enough to swal-low it.[55]

Patterson's explanations for passing up one final chance to fight Johnston—approximately equal parts deception, evasion, and spe-cial pleading—would fail to salvage what remained of a military rep-utation in tatters. And yet one of the excuses he offered, which he failed to emphasize in his congressional testimony, provides a legiti-mate motive for shying away from contact; in some measure, it even serves to justify his apparent cowardice. This was his inability to rely on the will of his soldiers to serve beyond the imminent termi-nation of their enlistment periods.

As of mid-July the army's fighting spirit was a subject of much debate among those who tried to gauge its overall morale. Some of Patterson's subordinates believed that the troops, having been held so long on the sidelines, were eager for the fray. Colonel Butterfield, for one, described his troops as "spoiling for a fight" (although he added the significant caveat "some of them"). Patterson was not convinced this was the case, and with each passing day he became less sure. On the day the army entered Charles Town, eighteen of its regiments were within a week of being sent home, and he doubted the majority would vote to extend their terms. Already the commanders of nine of the ten companies in the 6th Pennsylvania Volunteers had sent their colonel a petition reminding Patterson that their enlistment term expired on the twenty-second and declaring that they "decline continuing in the service after that day." Patterson had discussed the problem with some of his colonels and on a few occasions with bodies of enlisted men, but despite his efforts to persuade, in the end only three regiments announced their intention to stay and fight for as long as their commander deemed necessary.[56]

Patterson would testify that even before leaving Martinsburg, he had heard "the mutterings of many of the volunteer regiments, and their expressed determination not to serve one hour after their term of service should expire. I anticipated a better expression of opinion as we approached the enemy, and hoped to hear of a willingness to remain a[n extra] week or ten days. I was disappointed." He claimed that on July 16, after issuing the order to advance on Winchester, "I was assailed by earnest remonstrance against being detained over their term of service, complaints by officers of want of shoes and other clothing, all throwing obstacles in the way of active operations."[57]

A correspondent for the New York Times traveling with the army was not surprised that Patterson's troops displayed "lukewarmness" about staying beyond their terms. "They have been hardly used, poorly clothed, poorly fed, compelled to endure day after day the monotonous hardships of camp life." The men also suffered from their commander's "unconcealed want of confidence" in them. The reporter's findings suggest a self-fulfilling prophecy: by hesitating to depend on his soldiers, Patterson had rendered them undependable.[58]

As their enlistment terms neared an end, the members of some regiments, fearing they would be kept in service illegally, began to talk mutiny. These men shouted their unwillingness to fight under any circumstances and demanded to be sent home to Pennsylvania. Patterson realized that even in those few outfits that had responded well to his entreaties, the prevailing sentiment had not been unanimous. A vocal minority could compromise their outfit's reliability, especially if they acted out their disapproval. From a worst-case per-spective, the general could count on only the few regular units in his command plus the three-year 2nd Massachusetts, the two-year 28th New York, the nine-month 4th Connecticut, and the six-month 19th New York, a total of perhaps 3,500 effectives.

Patterson cannot be blamed for his reluctance to lead unwilling warriors into battle. He must have recalled the dismay and alarm he had felt fourteen years earlier when forced to conduct out of the war zone in Mexico thousands of volunteers who refused to extend their enlistment periods. But in a real sense, Patterson had brought this crisis on himself by failing to reengage Johnston after Falling Waters. Had he moved against Winchester at any time between July 3 and 16, his short-termers would have been obliged to stay and fight. But regardless of where the blame lay, the army commander was now facing a situation beyond his control.

Historians have long debated whether most of Patterson's men were resolved to quit the army rather than take on the enemies of their nation. Not only have we been unable to measure soldiers' opinions on the subject, but we also have gained little insight into the conditions that influenced the many who demanded to go home. A rarely perused and never-before cited collection of letters from the Pennsylvania home front, sent to the men of Patterson's command during a critical period in their service, helps place these influences in a compelling perspective. Nearly one hundred pieces of correspon-dence written by soldiers' wives, sweethearts, parents, siblings, rela-tives, and friends, sent from Philadelphia and numerous towns and hamlets throughout southeastern and south-central Pennsylvania between late June and mid-July 1861, can be found in the George Cadwalader Papers at the Historical Society of Pennsylvania. None of these letters reached its intended recipient—all were returned to Philadelphia unopened. Not until 1939, when the collection came into the possession of the society, were the letters opened and read. The collection is truly unique; no other large body of letters sent by civilians at home to soldiers in the same army has been unearthed.[59]

Beyond its unparalleled scope, the collection is important for the corrective it deals to the long-held belief that in these early weeks of the conflict, the Northern public was fully supportive of the war effort. After all, they had sent their young men into the army with parades, picnics, and patriotic rallies, the huzzahs of proud towns-people ringing in their ears. But very few of these letters offer words of appreciation and encouragement. Those that do were written within a few weeks of war's outbreak. "You are a soldier now and bully for you," a friend wrote to Private G. W. Baskins on June 3. He hoped "to . . . hear your name on the list of Heroes. I hope to hear of Major Col. or something added to Baskins."[60]

The great majority convey darker emotions—gloom, doubt, fear, depression—suggesting that only three months into the conflict, home-front morale, at least in this particular section of the Union, was in steep decline. This is not surprising, for the war's effects were still being felt principally on the local level. It would not become a national experience, in which civilians and soldiers fully shared the hardships, privations, and anxieties that war promotes, for weeks or months to come.

One who reads these letters a century and a half after their composition, especially given that no soldiers received them, feels something uncomfortably akin to eavesdropping, to violating family privacy. This sensation is only enhanced by the personal items attached to many of the letters—newspaper clippings, pressed flowers, locks of babies' hair—carefully preserved decades after caring hands inserted them into envelopes adorned with patriotic slogans and the images of heroes of past wars.

Any discomfort the present-day reader feels is greatly increased by the contents of these missives. Numerous wives and sweethearts pour out their loneliness, insecurity, heartbreak, and despair. Sallie from Philadelphia wished to tell her lover, Charley, that she could not sleep for fear that he would not return: "I *feel* so *bad* to *night*. I think my heart will break. I worry so much about you. . . . I awaken up at night and lay for hours wondering if I ever shall see my dear Pet again. . . . *You are my all in* this world and without you now my Pet I *feel* as though I could *not live*." Adding to her plight is the fact that she is virtually destitute; apparently, Charley has failed to send her part of his pay as promised. Lacking an alternative, Sallie lives off the grudging charity of his family, primarily a brother whom she fears has sexual designs on her: "I wonder how he thinks I am to live. . . . Oh I cannot tell you what a three months this will be to me. I shall never want to see a three months like it, if it be God's will, for I have suffered more in *mind* and *body* than aney *Wife* and the *best one* in Phila. could have done."[61]

Another Philadelphian, Mely, could no longer stand being separated from her lover: "Oh henry dear I am nearly heartbroke about you. I am troubled so much that I am not able to work. Oh henry dear you are in my mind all the time. O I cant sleep at night fore think[ing] about you my dearest henry. O I am so afraid something will happen, oh henry dear if eney thing would happen [to] you it would kill me fore this trouble has sat so hard on me that I don't think that I will ever get over it. . . . I hear bad news every day. I heard that the southern men were killing all of our men but I can hardly believe [this]. Oh henry dear I hope the lord will save you[r] life and bring you back safe to me." Fearing that her soldier has not received her every letter, during a period of ten days, Mely had written him five times. Her fears were well founded—none of the letters ever reached Henry.[62]

For some who wrote, pangs of loneliness and trepidation had fostered malignant thoughts. Josephine "Josie" Copeland, wife of 1st Lieutenant R. Morris Copeland, regimental quartermaster of the 2nd Massachusetts, was at the end of her tether. Writing on July 8 from their summer home at Roxbury, she hints at taking her own life: "Oh Kittie, I cannot try any longer, my heart aches, aches, aches. I am so dreary. I stretch forward to see the future you speak of as a fainting man would struggle for breath. Morris tell me some time that no matter what I do, or what happens to me, that you shall work for the little ones. Thank God that you have the strength of a man, & use it faithfully. Thank you for the burning words of love, thank you for the promises to take care of yourself. . . . God grant that you may be left to us, if only to come back sick or wounded." One year later Morris Copeland would return home safely, having resigned his commission to resume his prewar career as one of the country's foremost landscape architects. Of Josie, we know no more.[63]

A Pennsylvania father reached out to his hospitalized son, "not knowing whether I am Wrighting to the Living or to the Dead. . . . It has made me feel verry sorrowful to hear of yower week and helpless Condition and Bad health without Being Able to Render you Aney help." The father's only consolation was that if Private William Bartley left the hospital, he would be immediately discharged from the service. So anxious to have his son home, he proposed to travel from their Lancaster County farm to meet the hospital boat at Havre de Grace and by so doing "shorten yower Rout 100 miles." Should William pull through, and should his regiment reenlist as a body, "I know that you Will not."[64]

Hopes for an early homecoming by sons, brothers, fathers, and nephews is the theme of virtually every letter in this collection, especially those composed after reports of the fighting at Falling Waters made the newspapers. Garret Pittenger prayed that his brother Henry, last heard of at Martinsburg, was in "a safe place . . . and we hope you will be till your term is out." The family longed for his return; their father "says you must not minde what any one says, you must not [en]list any longer, you must come home."[65]

Melvina Buckman, writing from Philadelphia on July 12, heard that her husband's regiment had "gon[e and reenlisted] for three years but I hope you have not done the same. If you have you may expect never to see me and saly for she does nothing but talk about you coming home and cry when eneybody says you are not. I hope I will soon see you again and in a bout too weeks. if I do not I shall go wild." Her closing words were a desperate plea: "come home soon and don't delay." Sarah Bowman urged the same on her son: "I don't want you to enlist for 3 years. If you do think of [reenlisting] do not until you come home for it you would enlist for 3 years and then come home you might not want to go back again." A family friend made this mistake; almost at once he regretted his decision but could not undo it.[66]

The effect of missives such as these can only be imagined. Although these particular letters could not influence anyone, it must be assumed that others similar in content worked their will upon the short-timers of the Army of Pennsylvania. It is therefore not surprising that their commander failed to secure a commitment to stay and fight from so many impressionable youngsters who, hungry for news from home, were being fed heaping portions of misery and suffering.

CHAPTER 8

"CIVILIZED WHITE MEN"
ON THE MARCH

Warm, sunny weather greeted the Federal capital when it awoke
on the morning of Tuesday, July 16, 1861. The first military
units to break camp hit the road at about 2:00 P.M., a starting time
that reflected poorly on the readiness of McDowell's army. Another
troubling sign was McDowell's inability to accompany any of the columns during the first several hours of the march. William H. Russell,
just then returning to Washington from Annapolis, found the general
sometime after five o'clock at the local B&O station awaiting two
artillery batteries supposedly en route from Maryland. One was being
accompanied by Major William F. Barry, whom McDowell would
assign, on the basis of seniority, to command the army's artillery.
The general asked if Russell knew anything of the overdue units; the
great war correspondent did not.

Russell expressed surprise that an army commander should personally attend to such rather mundane business as locating a couple of units that had "gone astray." Rather sheepishly, McDowell
explained that every member of his small staff was running another
errand. This, however, was no excuse. Russell knew that he had
had ample time to form a staff capable of handling such matters.
He wondered how an army that appeared so unprofessional could
operate successfully in the field. The information must have shaken
his relatively favorable impression of McDowell, as did the signs of
worry and uncertainty that the general conveyed on this occasion.

As he informed the newsman, rumors had reached Washington
that Beauregard had transferred a large portion of his army to Fairfax
County. The prospect of a major battle at and around the local courthouse, probably to occur on the second day of the march, appeared
to unsettle him—he openly questioned how well the army would
react to such an early encounter. Russell, however, wrote this off as
an attempt at humor because even as McDowell expressed concern

about the trial to come, he made a playful jab at the Englishman and his American counterparts, inviting the tweedy correspondent to accompany him on the road. He had made the same offer to a number of domestic reporters, asking only that they observed certain restrictions, including a ban on divulging the army's strength, destination, and route. McDowell now suggested that if Russell wished to avail himself of the opportunity, he should don a white suit and hat, attire befitting the gentlemen of the press. The costume, he remarked, would signify the "purity of their character."[1]

Russell accepted the invitation, though he would not overtake the army until the morning of the twenty-first. By then reporters from New York, Chicago, Philadelphia, Boston, Cincinnati, and other major population centers as well as those employed by the Associated Press would have formed themselves into a group that accompanied the moving columns, sending back dispatches to their employers at various and sundry points. Their accounts would be firsthand; in fact, several reporters would find themselves closer to the action than they could have anticipated.[2]

While McDowell searched in vain for his cannons, the rear element of his army moved slowly through the streets of Washington and over the Potomac via the various bridges. It passed the fortified heights of Arlington, where many of the 25,000 troops manning the capital's defenses remained on duty but off limits to McDowell. This force included four recently arrived regiments from New York: the 17th, stationed at Fort Ellsworth; the 21st, at Fort Runyon; the 25th, at Fort Albany; and the 28th (a ninety-day outfit, not to be confused with the two-year 28th New York of Patterson's army), at Fort Corcoran. General Mansfield had decreed that none of these units was to be moved from its present duty station "except in an emergency."[3]

To the hundreds of onlookers who thronged the streets of the capital as the troops marched out, the mighty Army of Northeastern Virginia made what Captain Fry of McDowell's staff called "a glorious spectacle." A more eloquent observer described the departure from an even better vantage point, Arlington Heights. Twenty-eight-year-old first lieutenant William Woods Averell of the Regiment of Mounted Riflemen, a member of Andrew Porter's staff, was highly impressed by the sight of an army "going forth to the first great battle between civilized white men in our country since the War of 1812." Years later he recalled sitting his horse along a road crowded with marching men, drinking in the pageantry of warfare: "The balmy air wafted the music of numerous fine bands and gently unfolded and toyed with bright banners from Arlington down to Alexandria. The gleaming bayonets of columns wending from camps to highways, the glint of field guns and the rumble of their carriage wheels, the loud commands of voice and louder of trumpet, trampling squadrons and galloping aides, wise-looking general officers with imposing staffs—all the concomitants of a freshly panoplied army." The glittering spectacle, evocative of a mighty nation determined to preserve American democracy and thwart those who would destroy it, "excited and fascinated the radiant throngs of lovely women, attired in summer costumes, whose carriages crowded the roads and fields and occupied every point of vantage from which smiles and flowers and precious souvenirs could be bestowed on the departing soldiers."[4]

The army's routes of advance had been spelled out in General Orders No. 17, issued that morning. Tyler's division would leave its camps between Washington and Falls Church and proceed by what Colonel Sherman called "the gravel road" to Vienna. Hunter's division, Burnside's crack Rhode Island brigade in advance, would descend the Columbia Turnpike to its intersection with the Little River Turnpike, where it was to halt until the morning of the seventeenth, when, the road being clear, it was to move west on the turnpike toward Fairfax Court House. Meanwhile, Heintzelman's division would follow the old Fairfax Court House road south of the Orange & Alexandria Railroad as far as Accotink Creek or Pohick Creek, whichever its commander found more "convenient" to cross. The Fifth Division (Miles's new command) would proceed out the Little River Turnpike to Annandale. There it would turn left onto the Braddock Road, which ran north of and roughly parallel to the line of the O&A. Well to the rear of the moving columns, General Runyon (who also had charge of all troops not on the march, including those in the forts along the Potomac) was to guard the line of the Loudoun & Hampshire Railroad as well as aid in the rebuilding of the enemy-damaged portion of the O&A.[5]

The panoply of war was inspiring and memorable both to those marching to battle and the civilians who cheered them onward. One observer, seventeen-year-old Thomas L. Livermore, described the passing units as clothed in a "queer medley of costumes." He singled out the Highlanders of the largely Scottish 79th New York, a

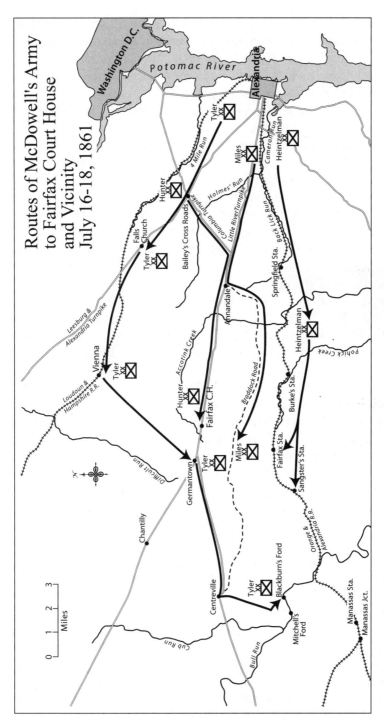

Routes of McDowell's Army to Fairfax Court House and Vicinity, July 16–18, 1861. *Map by Paul Dangel.*

unit in Sherman's brigade commanded by Colonel James Cameron, younger brother of the secretary of war. For weeks the outfit had strutted about "in tartans and bare legs," though for the march all but a few officers had traded their ceremonial kilts for the long pants of the regulation uniform.

Other units were just as colorful and interesting. Livermore observed that the Garibaldi Guards—named for the general who had fought for the unification of Italy, otherwise known as the 39th New York Volunteers—was largely composed of European immigrants who spoke "in a Babylonian confusion of tongues, [and wore] red shirts, linen trousers, and straw hats." Also unorthodox was the uniform of the 1st Minnesota of Franklin's brigade, each of whose enlisted men sported a red or blue shirt rather than a tunic or jacket, along with blue woolen pants, a blanket to take the place of an overcoat, and a black slouch hat.[6]

Most of McDowell's troops were clothed in traditional attire—blue coats and caps and light blue kersey pants—but some militia units were notable for their "fancy-trimmed blue uniforms," others for their gray pants and blouses, a color that would place them in hot danger once the shooting started. New Englanders especially appeared to favor cadet or militia gray; those units wearing this hue included the 1st and 11th Massachusetts; the 2nd, 3rd, and 5th Maine; and the 2nd New Hampshire. Other regiments garbed entirely or mostly in that color included the 8th New York and 2nd Wisconsin. Still others wore gray pants and blue coats. Lieutenant Averell spied a few units, who fancied themselves sharpshooters, wearing green. The young officer also observed that "the gaudiest of all were the red baggy trousers, sashes, and turbans of the irrepressible Zouaves," most of whom also sported brightly colored fezzes or kepis and white gaiters. Such organizations included the Fire Zouaves of the 11th New York and various companies in regiments that were not otherwise garbed in Zouave attire, including the Irish Zouaves, Company K of the 69th New York Militia.

The 11th New York, once a notable fashion plate, was now a pale imitation of its original self. Except for their tasseled fezzes, its men no longer wore Zouave garb. With consummate style, Colonel Ellsworth had dressed his men in light gray "chasseur" jackets trimmed in red and blue, baggy gray trousers, and tan leggings. Made of shoddy material foisted on the government by unscrupulous contractors, the uniforms had fallen apart during moderate field use and were replaced by army-issue blue uniforms. These the men detested, though many of them spiced up the ensemble with red shirts. The chasseur model also found expression in the uniform of the 14th Infantry, New York National Guard, better known as the 14th Brooklyn. These sartorially splendid militiamen wore kepis of navy blue and red, red and dark blue tunics with false red vests, and bright red flannel trousers of the Zouave type, though not quite as baggy.[7]

The officers of some regiments had supplied their men with havelocks, white strips of cloth worn under the cap to prevent a soldier's neck from sunburn, a fashion statement popularized by British troops. In keeping with this profusion of European styles, Irvin McDowell this day wore a white helmet such as an officer of French or Austrian troops might favor, complete with a "bright lance-head on top." Presumably, the distinctive headgear would make it easier for his subordinates to locate him on the field of battle.[8]

As per McDowell's preference for limiting transportation to baggage wagons, the marching men carried their own fare—three days' cooked rations, mainly salted pork and beef and the cracker-like hardtack, and only as much drinking water as their canteens would hold. The infantry generally had the right of way, although on the more commodious thoroughfares such as the Columbia and Little River Turnpikes, foot soldiers shared the road with horses, guns, caissons, and limbers.

The few vehicles were held to the rear to keep them out of harm's way and to prevent the dust they raised from engulfing the marchers. The small contingent of horsemen at McDowell's disposal—seven companies of regulars under Major Palmer of the 2nd Cavalry—should have been in the forefront of the army, guiding it through unknown territory. Instead, the brigade to which the horsemen had been attached, Porter's, was bringing up the rear of Hunter's column. The absence of experienced cavalry forced the cautious foot soldiers in the vanguard to slowly and carefully scout the roads ahead and the country to either side, causing much stop-and-start aggravation.[9]

At intervals throughout the column rumbled the fifty pieces of artillery that McDowell had managed to secure for his army, almost equally divided between rifles and smoothbores. Even without the errant batteries under Major Barry (they and their commander would catch up with the army before battle loomed), the number gave McDowell a significant edge in firepower. He commanded a total of twelve batteries, five composed of six guns, the rest of no more than four pieces each. All but two batteries and a separate two-gun section were regular units.

The army's advantage in artillery had been diminished by unimaginative organization. For one thing, the arm lacked a reserve force, depriving McDowell of a mass of guns (something he had declared a dire need of) for use in a pinch. Distribution of artillery resources was uneven throughout the army: some brigades were assigned two batteries, others none at all. Lax planning meant that any changes of organization and command would have to be made on the fly—even on the battlefield. Because the arm lacked a divisional organization, there was no clear channel of command for the new chief of artillery.[10]

McDowell appeared to have chosen wisely, however, when filling that position. William Farquhar Barry (West Point, 1838) was a distinguished veteran of the Mexican War, the campaigns against the Seminoles, and the Kansas border wars of the late 1850s. Later it would become apparent that his talents as an administrator were his greatest asset, but in the fighting to come he would prove himself a capable field leader even though lacking familiarity with his new subordinates.[11]

The majority of the men who made up McDowell's fifty infantry regiments, inexperienced as they were at marching, made indifferent progress on their first day out of Washington. Throughout the afternoon, each of the four columns was slowed not only by overly cautious scouts but also by natural obstacles—steep hills, deep ravines, wide and fast-moving streams that lacked easily accessible fords, and the narrow, winding roads that in places accommodated no more than two or three men marching abreast. These hurdles could not have been foreseen given the army's lack of detailed maps.

One of the most vexing was the Accotink, which crossed the path of Heintzelman's column as it passed below the O&A. No bridge connected the steep banks of the stream, forcing the men to improvise a way to get across. When Colonel Howard, whose troops marched in rear of the division, reached the creek, he learned that each preceding brigade had crossed, single file, over a couple of fallen logs. He was astounded that his predecessors "had taken full two hours to pass a stream not more than twenty yards wide and the water nowhere above their knees." Unwilling to put up with such foolishness, he ordered his men into and through the water regardless of wet feet and soggy brogans.[12]

The army was also slowed by impediments that should have been anticipated. Many of the forest trails that various detachments followed had been blocked by felled trees, fence rails, and piles of lumber stripped from neighboring outbuildings by the same enemy who had ripped up long stretches of the O&A. Teams of pioneers armed with pickaxes, spades, and crowbars slowly cleared the obstructions and rebuilt the many destroyed or damaged bridges the columns encountered. "Frequently we had to leave the main road," wrote Edwin S. Barrett, a civilian physician accompanying the 5th Massachusetts Militia, "and pass our whole column through a corn or wheat field, leaving behind a swath of destruction."[13]

Virtually every regiment made periodic stops to attend to men who had fallen out of the ranks from exhaustion or illness. The marching pace was not grueling; most of the army covered no more than a half-dozen miles on either of the first two days out. According to a member of the 5th Massachusetts, however, the first day's march, which led his regiment "over hills and through valleys, across creeks and every other thing . . . was about 13 miles as near as we can calculate." The vegetation of northeastern Virginia took an especially memorable toll. A member of Tyler's division recalled that before July 17 ended, "the pretty white stripes on our broadcloth pants were in shreds and our hands and faces scratched with the blackberry bushes we had pushed through."[14]

Recruits unused to roadwork in summer weather suffered greatly. On the first day out, fourteen members of a single company of the 1st Minnesota were felled by sunstroke. Hundreds of soldiers who had been issued new, ill-fitting shoes were disabled by raw and blistered feet and had to be carried forward aboard wagons. Dozens of others were brought almost to their knees by the weight of their impedimenta. After a few miles of travel, the normal baggage of the soldier—knapsack, haversack, bedroll, ammunition pouch, and canteen—felt immeasurably heavier than when worn in camp or on the parade ground.[15]

Manmade obstructions also delayed the marchers. A member of the 2nd New Hampshire of Burnside's brigade recalled that his regiment "invaded two or three rebel camps, which were hurriedly abandoned at our approach." But not every Confederate had cleared the area north of Fairfax; each column endured a smattering of rifle fire that inflicted few casualties but increased the wariness of those in advance. As Dr. Barrett observed, "the mounted rebel scouts were always prancing in our front, occasionally exchanging shots with our advance skirmishers, and as our regiment was at the front [of Franklin's column] it made our onward march quite exciting." It also made it dangerous for trigger-happy recruits, more than a few of whom, when returning fire, shot themselves instead.[16]

Other delays owed to unauthorized halts. Throughout the sixteenth, soldiers would fall out by twos and tens to forage among enemy property or, more often, find a creek or brook. The day was hot enough and the marching pace strenuous enough that canteens ran dry quickly. Sources of potable water were scarce on the army's route, and what was available was, as one New Yorker wrote, "of an indifferent quality, however it was drunk with a hearty relish." McDowell would later complain that the men "stopped every moment to pick blackberries or to get water. They would not keep in the ranks. . . . [T]hey were not used to denying themselves much." Other men broke ranks to scare up additional food. As correspondent Russell learned, numerous soldiers, having consumed their allotment of rations on the first day, faced the prospect of going hungry on the rest of the journey unless they took matters into their own hands.[17]

One other reason for the deliberate pace was especially galling to McDowell, who blamed it on Generals Scott, Schenck, and Butler. In published orders the army commander had made a point to warn everyone to exercise extreme caution when moving through the enemy's country. Largely as a result, a general sense of fretful wariness ran through the entire army, one spawned by Schenck's ambush at Vienna and Butler's debacle at Big Bethel. A soldier from Maine observed that his outfit endured "hardly a musket shot" during the march to Fairfax Court House, "but our commanders were fearful of masked batteries, and proceeded as timidly as old maids. . . . I doubt there was a soldier in our regiment who hadn't already written home tall tales of concealed rifle-pits, mined roads and bridges, and masked batteries, which had nonexistence except in the ink pots of penny-a-line journalists. All the advancing columns were now searching for hidden perils and finding none."[18]

McDowell himself bore some responsibility for this. General Orders No. 17 instructed officers and men in how to conduct themselves in enemy territory. In it he emphasized three "things [that] will not be pardonable in any commander: 1st. To come upon a battery or breastwork without a knowledge of its position, 2d. To be surprised,

3d. To fall back. Advance guards, with vedettes well in front and flankers and vigilance, will guard against the first and second."[19]

The spectrum of hurdles and hindrances made for one long, hot, dusty day. In his memoirs E. P. Alexander of Beauregard's staff declared that of every Union advance in the eastern theater of the war, McDowell's "holds the record for slowness." When McDowell and his division leaders, especially Heintzelman, attempted to accelerate the pace, they met with resistance from their own subordinates. None wished to be the officer who led his men into a trap. The troops in the rear, kept immobile without explanation for hours at a stretch, became fatigued, frustrated, and demoralized.[20]

Enforced idleness gave rise to unauthorized foraging. Weeks earlier, General Scott had attempted to dampen the growing enthusiasm for a march on Richmond by predicting that unseasoned troops would starve for want of sustenance—they "would find every house deserted; not a cow, or a chicken, or an accidental pig on the entire route." This turned out not to be the case. Although most property owners on the roads to Fairfax Court House and Sangster's Station had evacuated, many avowed unionists remained, and those who fled had left behind enough poultry and livestock to tempt the soldiers who had already consumed their rations. The result in many cases was wholesale vandalism, even when the victims asserted their loyalty to the Federal government.[21]

Officers who had yet to win their men's respect and obedience were powerless to halt the plundering. Some who tried to intervene paid for their imprudence. Colonel Davies came down hard on some members of his brigade whom he found looting a farmstead, cursing and threatening them from the saddle. Fearing Davies would run him down, one pillager tossed aside a beehive from which he had been filching honey. A swarm of angry bees engulfed the colonel and his horse, both of whom were stung many times over. Upon rejoining his command, Davies, who had "one eye practically closed, with swollen lips," was in "a state of general demoralization."[22]

McDowell's strict notions of conduct would not permit him to ignore the bad behavior of his troops. On the eighteenth, "with the deepest mortification," he issued an order calling the army's attention to the widespread looting and threatening to arrest any man who engaged in it. A perpetrator would be conducted under guard to Alexandria and imprisoned there. The penalty sounded severe, but there is no indication that the prohibition had the slightest effect.

In fact, the problem worsened with every mile the army covered. By the time the columns converged on Fairfax Court House, private dwellings were being ransacked on an hourly basis, and some— the abodes of suspected secessionists—were being torched. Reports reached the general of soldiers carting off an amazing variety of plunder. Men's fashion items—hats, coats, pantaloons, gloves, canes, and umbrellas—appeared to be the targets of choice, perhaps signifying the looters' longing to reassume the trappings of civilian life.[23]

McDowell could only hope that his men's desire to wage war would not be exhausted in this way. Somewhere up ahead more formidable enemies waited; they would protest the invasion of their homeland not with curses but with bullets.

Mrs. Greenhow's warning of McDowell's impending march, relayed to Bonham's headquarters on July 10, was confirmed via a second coded message from the Washington socialite, smuggled out of the capital six days later. By 9:00 P.M. on the sixteenth, the information was in Beauregard's hands. According to the general, the message sharpened his awareness that McDowell was coming but told him little that was new. From what he had already learned of the movement, he probably estimated that the Federal vanguard would be within striking distance of Fairfax Court House the following afternoon.[24]

Beauregard reacted quickly, predictably, and multidimensionally. To General Bonham he reiterated his order of July 8 to fall back on Mitchell's Ford before he could be outmaneuvered and engulfed. To oversee the evacuation of Bonham's substantial supply train, Beauregard dispatched to the courthouse Colonel James Lawson Kemper of the 7th Virginia, an officer of "energy and efficiency" experienced in logistics. The same instructions were sent to General Ewell and Colonel Cocke at and near Centreville. Ewell was reminded particularly to alert Colonel Robert E. Rodes's 5th Alabama, which was encamped at Farr's Cross Roads, where the Braddock Road crossed Ox Road; the latter led to both Fairfax Court House and Fairfax Station.[25]

Beauregard could not abide a plan wholly defensive in nature. Once his subordinates withdrew to Bull Run, he would transform the army's retrograde into an advance. Still believing that McDowell would march on Manassas Junction via Mitchell's Ford, he plotted how to deflect the movement and turn it back upon itself. Under terms of Special Orders No. 120, he ordered Bonham, once fully in place at Mitchell's, to assume a defensive-offensive position, ready to attack as soon as the initial enemy thrust was repulsed. When the Federals struck, Longstreet was to move his entire command to the north side of Blackburn's Ford and lash the Union left flank and rear. D. R. Jones's brigade was to move from its present position, Camp Walker, to cross the run at McLean's Ford and attack the enemy's flank in concert with Longstreet. To top off the offensive, Ewell was to cross at Union Mills Ford and take a more northerly road to Centreville, striking the village after McDowell's advance had passed it to engage Bonham. Lesser responsibilities were assigned to the brigades of Early and Cocke, which would stand ready to support Ewell's move on Centreville.[26]

While putting this complex and ambitious plan on paper, Beauregard addressed the critical need of securing reinforcements. On the evening of the sixteenth, he sent an urgent telegram to Richmond requesting that Johnston be ordered to join him as soon as possible. He followed up with a message to Johnston himself, reminding him that he had promised to help in an emergency and making clear that one was now at hand. His first communiqué triggered a hurried conference at the Confederate war office and resulted in a telegram sent to Johnston by General Cooper. The wire reached Johnston's headquarters at 1:00 A.M. on the eighteenth. Thirty minutes later the cable from Beauregard, which had been "unaccountably delayed" in transit, was received at Winchester.[27]

These measures did not exhaust Beauregard's efforts at reinforcement. His message to Richmond included an insistent plea that Holmes's brigade near Fredericksburg be sent to him at once as well as Hunton's Virginians at Leesburg. When orders to this effect reached these commands, they responded with alacrity. Despite the possibility that McDowell's forces, scattered from Vienna to Fairfax Station, would intervene, Hunton reached Beauregard's side at noon on the nineteenth. Holmes, coming up from the south with his 1st Arkansas and 2nd Tennessee and the six guns of the Purcell Artillery, arrived later that same day. Beauregard attached Hunton to Cocke's brigade, while the troops of the fifty-six-year-old Holmes—who as a major in the 8th U.S. Infantry had been one of fifteen field-grade officers to resign from the U.S. Army and enter Confederate service— were designated a reserve force. Though not destined to be engaged in the fighting ahead, Holmes would support Ewell's brigade and the right flank in general.[28]

Without waiting for additional prompting, Beauregard's superiors ordered to Manassas some units that had been earmarked for Johnston or had yet to be assigned to either army. These included the 5th, 6th, and 11th North Carolina and the 13th Mississippi. Another unit belatedly earmarked for Beauregard was the Hampton Legion, a regimental-size force of all arms that had been organized, armed, and equipped out of pocket by Wade Hampton III of South Carolina, one of the South's largest landowners and slaveholders. Upon their arrival, Beauregard would assign the 5th North Carolina to Longstreet and the 11th North Carolina to a reserve position in rear of the main army and later to Bonham's brigade. The 13th Mississippi would be assigned to Early, while the 6th North Carolina, which would reach Beauregard barely in time for the battle, would be thrown into the action initially without brigade affiliation.[29]

Insufficient transportation would prevent the cavalry and artillery of the Hampton Legion from reaching Manassas in time to see action. Its infantry component, though, six companies strong, boarded the train from Richmond just before midnight on July 16–17 and would chug into Manassas Junction scant hours before the main fighting began. Its late arrival, with Hampton at its head, would prevent it too from being attached to a specific brigade; instead, it became part of an ad-hoc reserve command. Even so, the South Carolinians would see extensive action on many parts of the battlefield and suffer heavily.[30]

Late on July 17, one day after issuing the special orders and before any reinforcements had reached him, Beauregard hastily revised his strategy. With McDowell now almost within sight of Bull Run, he contacted Ewell: "The enemy being in such force we may not be able to attack Centreville with safety. You will confine yourself to protecting the right flank and rear of Jones' brigade, and be careful to protect your own flank from any attack in the direction of Fairfax Station." Then, perhaps regretting the passive tone of his orders, he added, "but should you in the course of events find it practicable to make a sudden and successful attack on Centreville you are at liberty to do so." This was much more in tune with Beauregard's natural inclinations. Under the current circumstances, however, any effort to salvage an offensive was unlikely to work. As William C. Davis points out, "that the idea was as hasty and impractical as anything Beauregard ever proposed is borne out by the lack of evidence that he ever informed any of his other brigade commanders of the discretion given to Ewell. Should the Virginian decide to move on Centreville, no one else would be ready to move to his aid."[31]

Beauregard not only had to inform his troops of the shift to a fall-back-and-fight strategy but also had to make it palatable to them. The order he issued fairly oozed with the sort of rhetoric that never failed to inspire the typical Southerner: "At length the enemy have advanced to subjugate a sovereign [nation], and impose upon a free people an odious Government. Notwithstanding their numerical superiority, they can be repelled, and the general commanding relies confidently on his command to do it and to drive the invader back beyond his intrenched lines; but to achieve this the highest order of coolness, individual intelligence, and obedience on the part of each officer and man are essential." The underlying message was clear: do not question the seemingly timid nature of the battle plan, which involves a wholesale withdrawal from the army's most advanced positions. A temporary retreat is necessary to lure the enemy into a well-designed and carefully laid trap. Above all, trust in the wisdom of your commander—he knows what he is doing.[32]

While the order was being distributed, Beauregard told Bonham to begin withdrawing to Mitchell's Ford that evening "if necessary"; he was given discretion as to "when and how" to march to Bull Run. Once at Mitchell's, Beauregard added, the First Brigade would be augmented by the 11th North Carolina and the six-company 8th Louisiana, which would "support you as a reserve or to extend on your left for the defense of Bull Run in that direction."[33]

It appeared that over the past twenty-four hours, the Creole's plans for dealing with McDowell had shifted markedly. Yet his orders to his brigade commanders contained subtle hints that their leader retained a preference for the offensive. This was not surprising, for try as he might, G. T. Beauregard could never stifle the urge to strike hard even when his opponent packed a heavier punch.

Despite the frustrating delays, the start-stop pace, and the lawless defections from the ranks, the first day's march of the Army of Northeastern Virginia was a success in that each column reached its designated position, albeit belatedly. While Hunter's column reached its assigned destination at about 10:00 P.M., some of Heintzelman's regiments did not make bivouac along Pohick Creek until half past three in the morning. Even though it made better time after splashing across that vexing Accotink, Howard's brigade, the last in the marching column, reached its designated position so late that its men got barely an hour of sleep before being routed out of their bedrolls and returned to the road.[34]

When the march resumed at sunup on the seventeenth, McDowell's men realized they would probably close with the enemy before they got another night's sleep. Consequently, the columns moved even more warily than on the first day. Tyler's troops, who only now left their staging area at Vienna, moved more slowly than anyone else. McDowell would blame their leader for the unconscionably slow pace of the entire army, but Tyler's lack of progress was to some degree understandable. For one thing, the road to the farming village of Germantown was positively infested with felled trees and other improvised barriers, which especially retarded the heavy vehicles in the column. A Connecticut enlisted man wrote that the roadblocks "delayed the artillery and we had to stay with it and furnish details to chop the obstructions away."[35]

Another check to Tyler's progress was a menacing-looking artillery position—one of those hidden batteries that the army was forbidden to stumble upon. A party of intrepid scouts inched their way through woods and underbrush until they outflanked the position. Springing forward, rifles at the ready, they found it abandoned. Just as the men at the head of the column began to relax, riflemen opened fire on them from a roadside cabin. Fearing a major ambush, Tyler called a halt, threw out skirmishers, and sent back for his artillery, which included a "monster" 30-pounder Parrott rifle, the largest field piece in the army. A battery was brought up, laboriously unlimbered, and began shelling the house, but by then, as Tyler ought to have foreseen, its occupants had departed. The march resumed, even more deliberately than before.[36]

Later in the day some men toward the rear of Tyler's column joined in the unauthorized but widespread foraging. A member of the 69th New York Militia of Sherman's brigade described the activities of his hungry comrades when they finally reached the all-but-vacant Germantown. "Pigs were shot down and cut to pieces," he wrote, "the dripping fragments being pounced upon and carried off in triumph by the butchers. Turkeys and chickens shared the same fate. Everything left behind them in the village by the retreating inhabitants, whether useful or otherwise, was seized and swept away." When the gray-clad soldiers of the 2nd Wisconsin came up in the 69th's rear, the New Yorker saw a private "stumbling along with a feather bed across his shoulders. I saw another with a sledge hammer taken from the vacant forge. A third had a large looking-glass under his arm. A fourth had a patched quilt or counterpane wrapped about him—a curious piece of needle-work, gaily enough to please a Carib prince, and sufficiently heavy for a winter's night in Nova Scotia."[37]

Sherman was absolutely appalled. In a letter to Ellen, he opined that "no Goths, no Vandals ever had less respect for the lives & property of friend and foe." The red-haired Ohioan yelled and cursed and ordered back into line every looter he encountered, perhaps adding a swat with the flat edge of his saber. Indignant at this treatment, many of his troops came to believe Sherman harbored "the sourest malignity" toward the entire brigade. His were not the only men to run amuck. By the time Richardson's brigade, farther to the rear, reached Germantown, a man in the 2nd Michigan found "several houses in flames & the men of our brigade burned nearly all the rest before they left." Unsurprisingly, the enemy was incensed at such behavior. Dick Ewell, for one, likened McDowell's troops to "a swarm of locusts—burning and destroying."[38]

While Tyler's men dawdled, Miles and Hunter made decent progress along the separate routes they had taken after converging on Annandale, the former on the Braddock Road, the latter on the Little River Turnpike, two miles farther north. Even so, both divisions had gotten a late start. Miles, in the advance, had not left the Annandale vicinity until 8:00 A.M., while thanks to the slowness of Burnside's brigade to take the road ahead of Porter's, Hunter's column lost two hours getting started. Thus the progress of both divisions appeared nearly as meager as Tyler's.[39]

The fourth column, Heintzelman's, fared little better. Willcox's brigade was expected to reach Fairfax Station by eight o'clock, but the lead brigade, Franklin's, which was heading farther up the railroad to Sangster's Station, moved so slowly that Willcox did not arrive until early afternoon. The extreme caution that Heintzelman's wing was displaying would seem uncalled for if only because the army had made frequent reconnaissances of this vicinity over the past several weeks—Schenck's brigade had scouted the area as recently as the thirteenth—and McDowell ought to have had a good idea of what awaited his army there.

When almost to Fairfax Station, Willcox's advance guard heard intermittent firing from the vicinity of the depot. Their commander hastened his troops forward, supposing that the former occupants—Rodes's men—remained in place. It took a while to get there; the troops had to haul the trunks of heavy trees out of the road. Finally arriving, Willcox discovered that he had been preceded by members of Blenker's brigade, Miles's advance echelon, which had hastened there from the north without orders. The shooting had been done by Italian and French immigrants of the Garibaldi Guard, foraging for wild turkeys, abundant in that area. Colonel Rodes was long gone, but Willcox's lead regiment, the celebrated Fire Zouaves, mistook their fellow New Yorkers for Rebels. The comrades exchanged several shots before the error could be rectified.[40]

Understandably upset at the mix up, Willcox was also aggravated by the delays caused by Franklin's brigade in advance of him. He would complain that had Fairfax Station and other enemy positions along the railroad been reached three hours earlier, as many as 3,000 Rebels would been cut off and captured. Meanwhile, when the First Brigade reached Sangster's, it caused a stir at army headquarters. Heintzelman, who had accompanied Franklin, failed to report his arrival at the depot as he had been instructed (his biographer charitably ascribes the lapse to physical exhaustion). Not until the next morning, and only after a personal visit from McDowell, did the division leader realize his oversight. The root of the problem was that no means of communication had been established between the columns, nor between the sometimes widely separated components of each column.[41]

Although they had arrived late, Heintzelman's men had gained a position from which to cut off the enemy's retreat from Fairfax Court House. Yet during the balance of the seventeenth, they seized only a few stragglers. The captives reported that the recent occupants—primarily Bonham's South Carolinians—had evacuated as a body several hours earlier. To Heintzelman this was, of course, worrisome news. For some unknown reason, the carefully laid plan to cut off and capture Beauregard's forward position had miscarried.

Thomas J. Goree of Houston, Texas, one of those stationed at Fairfax Court House, had an opportunity to observe at close range the local commander, General Bonham. The young Baylor University graduate, a volunteer aide-de-camp to James Longstreet, did not think much of his superior's fellow brigadier. Bonham, he believed, was "*totally* unfit for a military leader."

The general's shortcomings were never better displayed than on the morning of July 17, when Hunter's division, moving in from the east, and Tyler's, coming down from the north and west, converged on him. Although bound to withdraw to Centreville as soon as he drew the enemy's fire and gained some appreciation of his size, Bonham had told Beauregard that he preferred to fight it out for as long as possible. Lieutenant Goree, however, believed the avowedly combative South Carolinian "all the time appeared very much flurried. After moving his troops around and making some demonstrations as if for a fight, he ordered a retreat, which ought to have been done before the enemy was so close." As a consequence, "everything was done very hurriedly, and a considerable amount of property was left behind—consisting of provisions, forage, tents, some guns, and ammunition. . . . From the number of canteens, knapsacks, blankets, &c. which our men threw away on the road, our retreat no doubt appeared more like a rout."[42]

For weeks many of Bonham's troops had supposed they would have to fight a full-scale battle, perhaps until they were overwhelmed. The thought was unnerving to raw recruits, who feared that they were to be sacrificed in the name of gaining time for comrades farther south to prepare to engage the Yankees. Their officers attempted to assure them that Bonham would not permit his command to be annihilated, but they too were understandably nervous about their exposed position.

One who appreciated the danger the defenders faced was twenty-seven-year-old Lieutenant Thomas Henry Pitts of Company I, 3rd South Carolina Infantry. On July 11 the planter's son from Clinton District wrote his fiancée: "We have slept on our arms nearly every night for the last week, supposing Abraham's forces would pay us a visit, and being desirous that we might give him a warm reception we have been impatiently awaiting his approach. . . . I know not when we will have a fight, perhaps in a few days or it may be a long time. I think however that something must and will be done soon, for two armies to be so close together as we are now can not be inactive." Pitts believed that his army's defensive policy was the right one, "that we will not march upon them. . . . I contend that we should never risk anything. We should be certain of victory at all times, and I would ten fold rather retreat back to Manassas Junction, although it would have a bad influence upon our cause, than be defeated at this point."

Thus the lieutenant was both stressed and relieved when early on the seventeenth, he was awakened by "the bustle and tumult made by fifteen or twenty wagons" moving to the rear. When no alarm was sounded, he tried to go back to sleep, but then the bugles began sounding reveille, so he washed and dressed, buckled on his saber, and joined the men of his company on picket duty. For some hours all was quiet, but before the morning was done, sustained firing in the near distance announced the arrival of the enemy. Some of Pitts's men had heard that the Yankees were "encamped by the tens of thousands only a few miles away, and will pour down upon us like an earthquake in a few hours."[43]

Within minutes the courthouse was a scene of frenetic activity. By noon Pitts's company, in common with the rest of the 3rd South Carolina and other outfits assigned to Bonham, including the 18th Virginia of Cocke's brigade, were double-quicking down the road to Centreville, seven miles away. Pitts believed, as did many another fugitive, that the enemy was on their heels, "and they rushed on sure of victory." But he overestimated the enthusiasm and determination of the troops under Hunter and Tyler. Hoping to buy time for the other units to escape, Colonel Kershaw sent two companies of his 2nd South Carolina to confront the Yankees in advance of the village. When the Confederates blocked its path, the head of Burnside's brigade, leading Hunter's column, recoiled as if facing ten times as many adversaries. Burnside's vanguard withdrew in some disorder; slowly it regrouped and resumed its advance.[44]

Eventually, the Rhode Islanders drew within rifle range of the South Carolinians, who had taken up a dubious defensive position in front of a fence line. At least one of Kershaw's officers predicted aloud that both companies would be surrounded and cut to pieces. Yet no one withdrew from the fence until the colonel ordered the entire regiment to fall back through the town. Many officers and men obeyed grudgingly, concerned that, as Lieutenant Pitts feared, such a retreat would give the Yankees "great confidence. . . . The men were all in the breastworks, hot for a fight, which they all expected," and they had to be prodded into giving up the idea.[45]

At first the retrograde went smoothly. This was at least partly due to the support offered the infantry by four companies of Independent Virginia Cavalry that six months hence would become part of Stuart's 4th Virginia. Then came word that the Federals were shifting around their flanks to cut them all off from Centreville.

A frantic cry went up: "Hurry up, men, they are firing on our rear!" Panic ensued; the result was a mad dash toward a place of safety. A member of the 18th Virginia recalled his regiment moving "at double quick for about a quarter of a mile in order to make room along the road for the two South Carolina regiments that had been camped a little in advance of us." Other Confederates could not move so quickly, being forced to negotiate the intricate series of earthworks and ditches they and their comrades had fashioned over the past several weeks.[46]

Despite the reports of Yankees on their heels, Bonham's troops were not closely pursued. For the most part, the enemy seemed content to have captured Fairfax Court House. Some of Bonham's cavalry, which remained well to the rear of their infantry comrades, got a good view of the Federals as they flooded into the town. "They seemed to overflow [it] in a minute," a Virginia officer recalled, "and we could hear their yells as they entered—thinking the whole Rebel army had fled before them." Most of the yelling was done by the first regiment to arrive, the 2nd Rhode Island, which came charging in on the Little River Turnpike (later the 71st New York Militia would claim the honor of "taking" the town, having forged ahead of the Rhode Islanders).[47]

Upon reaching Germantown, where the road turned southwest, the fugitives believed that they were beyond likelihood of being overtaken. Suddenly, the retreat slowed to a normal marching pace. This was a blessing for men who had been toting rifles, knapsacks, and bedrolls at a dead run for miles. Many had nearly reached the end of their endurance—so too had their civilian cohort Edmund Ruffin. The legs of the venerable Virginian had given out, his back was "aching for want of any support to lean against," and he was wheezing from shortness of breath. But his fighting spirit remained strong, and he would be heard from again before this campaign ended.[48]

Bonham's retreat ended shortly before sundown, with his men filing into the works that had been erected on the outskirts of Centreville, including the enclosed earthwork on Artillery Hill. The defenses, formidable at first look, had been imperfectly laid out (inspecting them three days later, General Heintzelman pronounced them "very indifferent"). Electing not to rely on them, Bonham drew up his men in line of battle as if anticipating the fight he claimed to have wanted all along. But his mettle went untested, for Hunter decided to rest his men in the town they had so easily, and so vocally, occupied.[49]

The weather having changed in advance of a storm system that would arrive the next day, Bonham's soldiers spent several "dark & chilly" hours at Centreville, which its former occupants, Ewell's infantry and a battalion of Virginia cavalry under Lieutenant Colonel Walter H. Jenifer, had recently vacated. Ewell's men had dragged off the cannons that had provided the only real security for the position. According to the Virginian himself, the evacuation had been a near thing, both of his flanks having come perilously close to being turned by the enemy, which had failed to press the advantage.[50]

The lack of viable defenses may have discouraged Bonham's alleged inclination to stay and fight. As soon as he received a positive order from Beauregard to fall back on the main army, the South Carolinian decamped with impressive speed. Lieutenant Samuel West of Thomas Pitts's regiment recalled that Bonham, who gave commands to his subordinates "not above that of a whisper[,] had his brigade formed with a death like stillness and set out in the same way to Bull Run."[51]

The withdrawal proceeded simultaneously on two roads. Many South Carolinians as well as the men of the 18th Virginia took the Warrenton Turnpike toward Stone Bridge. The majority of Bonham's men followed the more southerly road to Mitchell's Ford. Most of Ewell's troops settled back into position at Union Mills Ford though some of Rodes's men (who, according to a company officer, "ran and walked 20 miles that day") at first were halted near McLean's Ford where they temporarily augmented Jones's brigade.[52]

Almost dead on their feet after hours of fighting and fleeing, the last of the escapees passed inside Beauregard's lines shortly before daylight of the eighteenth. The greater part of the day had been intensely warm, and the heat and humidity, added to the frantic pace of the retreat, had broken down more than a few soldiers. A member of the 18th Virginia recalled that several of his comrades "never recovered from the extreme fatigue and heat" during their flight from Fairfax. At least one South Carolinian dropped dead before reaching Bull Run.[53]

The retreat elicited mixed reviews from those caught up in it. Bonham and his staff officers, wishing to put the best face on it, acclaimed the movement as a logistical marvel. It had begun only after escape routes had been nearly cut off, and by then the

Confederates had gained important information on the size and composition of the forces arrayed against them. Moreover, it had been conducted in orderly fashion with minimal loss of life, a credit to all involved. Governor Pickens would assure his friend Bonham that "in fact it was a triumph, and showed that your men were drilled and knew when to retreat and when to fight."[54]

Many unwilling participants did not see it that way. Privately they described the flight from the front as dishonorable and even cowardly, a stain on the Confederate escutcheon. Lieutenant West feared that "we Carolinians whose name was synonimous with that of the Brave would be forever disgraced and all the bright hopes of Laurels which were expected to be won" had been dashed. The men strove to keep this impression from taking hold either in the army or among the civilian population. A private in the 7th South Carolina wrote his family, "Do not think that we retreated through fear for every man was begging to give them [the Yankees] a trial but it was gen. Beauregard['s] orders."[55]

One positive result ascribed to the retreat was the skill with which Bonham had brought off his supply and baggage wagons. Upon entering Fairfax Court House, however, Hunter's troops discovered that the Rebels had left behind enough rations, weapons, and other materiel to feed, arm, and equip whole regiments. Reportedly, the evacuees abandoned wagons filled with provisions, including two hundred barrels of flour. According to a soldier from Maine, "they also left some of their tents [standing] & even their kettles were on the fire boiling." Boston reporter Charles Carleton Coffin, who accompanied some of the first units to enter the town, appropriated an abandoned carpetbag filled with the personal belongings of a South Carolina officer.[56]

Well conducted or not, the evacuation of Centreville may not have been sound strategy. Given the limitations of Bull Run as a line of defense, Beauregard would have done well to consider making a stand on the heights of Centreville instead of using it as an outpost to be given up upon the enemy's approach. It took no great fund of foresight to predict that McDowell would launch his offensive from the area. A strong defense of the high ground by major elements of Beauregard's army would have denied him that opportunity. Even should the Southerners be forced to relinquish the position, the enemy would have received a significant check. In that event, the several roads that connected Centreville with all sectors of

Beauregard's main line would have facilitated an orderly withdrawal to Bull Run. It would seem, however, that the idea of entrenching at Centreville and fighting to hold it never occurred to the eminent Confederate strategist.

The capture of such an important objective as Fairfax Court House appeared to call for a celebration. The bands of Burnside's 1st Rhode Island and 2nd New Hampshire formed on the tree-shaded grounds of the courthouse and played patriotic tunes, including "The Star Spangled Banner." Some listeners described the experience as "inspiring beyond description." An appreciative audience was not found, however, among the citizenry. As the musicians serenaded, one of Burnside's staff officers encountered a "lovely, but indignant *high-toned* Va. lady [who] made faces at me." Edwin Barrett received the same treatment: "Women scowled at us from the doors and windows of their houses, children fled in terror, but the slaves could not conceal their delight, and were always ready to do us service." The mood of the local whites did not improve when some New England soldiers noticed "a want of correctness in the flag which floated from the Court House." A member of the 2nd Rhode Island pulled down the banner "and ran up one which had more stars and stripes on it."[57]

A frustrated Irvin McDowell was not soothed by the martial music, for he was vastly disappointed at not having fought and won a battle at Fairfax Court House. Apparently, he never suspected that Beauregard would refuse to fight in advance of Bull Run. It seemed out of character for McDowell's West Point classmate to abandon positions he had spent weeks building and strengthening without mounting at least a large-scale delaying action.

Only Colonel Rodes's men had made an effort to contest the Union advance, not only along the railroad against Heintzelman but also on the Braddock Road against Miles's advance. Rodes and other regimental leaders in Ewell's brigade had erected stout defenses on both sides of the O&A, and those manning them were confident the works could be held against all comers. A private in Colonel John J. Seibels's 6th Alabama believed "we can repel a force of ten-thousand, with the aid of our intrenchments." Formidable or not, the works were quickly abandoned when Ewell ordered the withdrawal to Bull Run. By then, however, some of his troops had given better than they had received. Rodes reported only two of his men slightly wounded and claimed the killing or wounding of at least twenty of the enemy. These casualties appear to have been the first since the Union advance to Bull Run began.[58]

Bonham's withdrawal left McDowell in a quandary of his own making, for he had no contingency plan. His only course was to push on to Centreville and build a staging area and a jumping-off point for an assault on Beauregard's right flank. McDowell soon learned that there too he would find no Rebels to bring to battle, the town having been completely evacuated. It appeared that there would be no preliminary clash of arms, no tune-up to the major bout to come. Only along Bull Run would McDowell be able to take the measure of his opponent.

Given General Tyler's current position near Germantown—which thanks to his late start from Vienna and his glacial marching pace, he had reached too late to interpose between Bonham and Centreville—his column was the logical choice to follow up the Rebel withdrawal the next morning. Whether the First Division would be in peak shape, however, was an unanswerable question. Most of Tyler's regiments got only a few hours of sleep, and that sleep was not undisturbed. About 1:00 A.M. on the eighteenth, a battery horse broke free of its restraints and rampaged through the camp of the 69th New York. Believing the regiment under attack, guards fired wildly into the night, buglers sounded "To Arms," and even the soundest sleepers were suddenly awake. Things finally settled down, but many soldiers—not only those of the 69th—did not.[59]

Around 7:00 A.M. Tyler placed his lead brigade, Richardson's, in column on the road to Centreville. Although he knew the town had been evacuated, Richardson—as was the norm with this army—moved out slowly, gingerly, and covered by a 160-man force of "light infantry" skirmishers. When at about nine o'clock this force reached the outskirts of Centreville and carefully entered, no one had anything good to say about the surroundings. A Maine man described the place as "about 40 miles from nowhere," while a later arriving soldier found it "dingy, aged, [and] miserable . . . the coldest picture conceivable of municipal smallness and decrepitude." As for its defenses, most observers concurred with Heintzelman's opinion of their less-than-formidable appearance. The first occupiers decided to give Centreville a more inviting look. By the time the rest of the division reached town, the Stars and Stripes were flying from the abandoned rifle pits as well as from the roof of the town's only tavern.[60]

Peering south, Tyler's men found the rutted, washed-out highway to Manassas littered with the same hastily discarded baggage Heintzelman's men had found at the courthouse. While his troops appropriated the spoils, Tyler conferred with General Richardson, perhaps with a view to overtaking the Rebels' slow-moving supply vehicles. At seven that morning McDowell, who was traveling somewhere in the rear, had ordered his senior subordinate to "observe well the roads to Bull Run and to Warrenton. Do not bring on an engagement, but keep up the impression that we are moving on Manassas" via Beauregard's right flank. McDowell did not know how far that flank extended, but he believed it stretched at least as far as the O&A trestle. He hoped Tyler would confirm this information while selecting a convenient place to cross the run—if not at Union Mills then somewhere in the general vicinity.[61]

About 10:30, after fruitlessly waiting for McDowell to join him and provide additional details of his mission, Tyler dispatched toward Mitchell's Ford Richardson's brigade, accompanied by two 20-pounder rifled cannons from Captain Romeyn B. Ayres's Company E, 3rd U.S. Artillery and a squadron of horsemen under Captain Albert G. Brackett, 2nd U.S. Cavalry. Although unable to provide the particulars Tyler apparently desired, McDowell believed that he had clearly conveyed his wants and needs. It appears, however, that he failed to impress upon the division commander the damage that would be caused by stirring up the enemy. If Tyler intended to demonstrate caution and restraint, he should not have entrusted the mission to a subordinate whose nickname was Fighting Dick.[62]

Once Bonham reached his assigned positions on Bull Run, where he set his already exhausted men to work improving the existing defenses, Beauregard saw that the hour of battle was at hand. He also knew that unless Johnston managed to join him in time to meet McDowell's attack, the Army of the Potomac was doomed. As of daybreak on the eighteenth, Beauregard was ignorant of Johnston's preparations to leave Winchester for Manassas—he was not even certain Johnston had been ordered to make the movement. Throughout the eighteenth, he would remain in the dark as to what his colleague was planning.

Richmond had been of no help on this point. The day before, General Cooper had advised Beauregard, "if possible, [to] send to General Johnston to say he has been informed, via Staunton, that you

were attacked, and that he will join you if practicable with his effective force." The communiqué was so ambiguous that Beauregard
could not have determined if the Virginian had been informed of the
attack on Fairfax Court House or, if he had, whether he had agreed
to hasten to Manassas. Even if Johnston was en route, Beauregard
feared that the Army of the Shenandoah might not reach him in
time to parry the blow he was certain McDowell would land this
day, the eighteenth.[63]

His nerves frayed from sleepless nights and mounting anxiety, the Creole threw Cooper's telegram to the floor of his tent and
shouted to ashen-faced members of his staff: "It is too late!" Within
minutes, however, he had recovered his composure and began to
plan anew. As they always seemed to in a moment of crisis, strategic possibilities opened up to him, creating opportunities not only
for his army but also for the forces under Johnston—assuming that
by some miracle they reached Manassas before the Army of the
Potomac was a bloody ruin.[64]

Brig. Gen. G. T. Beauregard,
CSA (National Archives,
Washington, D.C.)

Brig. Gen. Irvin McDowell,
USA (U.S. Army Heritage
and Education Center,
Carlisle Barracks, Pa.)

Gen. Joseph E. Johnston, CSA (Library of Congress, Washington, D.C.)

Maj. Gen. Robert Patterson, USA (U.S. Army Heritage and Education Center, Carlisle Barracks, Pa.)

Brig. Gen. Milledge L. Bonham, CSA (U.S. Army Heritage and Education Center, Carlisle Barracks, Pa.)

Bvt. Lt. Gen. Winfield Scott, USA (U.S. Army Heritage and Education Center, Carlisle Barracks, Pa.)

Brig. Gen. James Longstreet,
CSA (National Archives,
Washington, D.C.)

Brig. Gen. Daniel Tyler,
USA (U.S. Army Heritage
and Education Center,
Carlisle Barracks, Pa.)

Brig. Gen. Richard S. Ewell, CSA (U.S. Army Heritage and Education Center, Carlisle Barracks, Pa.)

Col. Samuel Heintzelman, USA (U.S. Army Heritage and Education Center, Carlisle Barracks, Pa.)

Brig. Gen. Barnard E. Bee, CSA (U.S. Army Heritage and Education Center, Carlisle Barracks, Pa.)

Col. Dixon S. Miles, USA (U.S. Army Heritage and Education Center, Carlisle Barracks, Pa.)

Col. Francis S. Bartow,
CSA (U.S. Army Heritage and
Education Center, Carlisle
Barracks, Pa.)

Col. William T. Sherman,
USA (Library of Congress,
Washington, D.C.)

Maj. Nathan G. Evans,
CSA (U.S. Army Heritage and
Education Center, Carlisle
Barracks, Pa.)

Col. Ambrose E. Burnside,
USA (U.S. Army Heritage
and Education Center,
Carlisle Barracks, Pa.)

Col. Wade Hampton,
CSA (From *The Photographic
History of the Civil War* [New
York, 1911])

Col. Israel B. Richardson,
USA (U.S. Army Heritage
and Education Center,
Carlisle Barracks, Pa.)

Col. Oliver O. Howard, USA (From *Sherman and His Campaigns* [New York, 1865])

Capt. James B. Ricketts, USA (U.S. Army Heritage and Education Center, Carlisle Barracks, Pa.)

Capt. Charles Griffin,
USA (U.S. Army Heritage
and Education Center,
Carlisle Barracks, Pa.)

Lt. William W. Averell,
USA (Library of Congress,
Washington, D.C.)

William H. Russell in later life
(From *Harper's Monthly*,
November 1881)

Fairfax Court House in Union hands (National Archives, Washington, D.C.)

Blackburn's Ford in Union hands, 1862 (Library of Congress,
Washington, D.C.)

Brig. Gen. Thomas J. Jackson, CSA, and his brigade on Henry Hill
(Library of Congress, Washington, D.C.)

McDowell's army advancing at the outset of the battle (note the civilian spectators depicted in right foreground) (From *The Soldier in Our Civil War* [New York, 1884])

The 30-pounder Parrott rifle firing the battle's opening shots (From *Harper's Weekly*, August 3, 1861)

The Contest for the Henry Hill (From *Battles and Leaders of the Civil War*, vol. 1 [New York, 1887])

Stuart's cavalry attacks the New York Fire Zouaves (From *Harper's Weekly*, August 10, 1861)

CHAPTER 9

A BUNGLED SKIRMISH

Around one o'clock on the morning of the eighteenth, Joe Johnston received a telegram from Adjutant General Cooper alerting him that "General Beauregard is attacked; to strike the enemy a decisive blow, a junction of all your effective force will be needed. If practicable, make the movement, sending your sick and baggage to Culpeper Court House by railroad or by Warrenton." A half hour later came Beauregard's telegram, declaring the time had come to provide the aid Johnston had pledged in such an emergency.[1]

Beauregard had reminded his colleague of this arrangement as recently as the thirteenth, when broaching his plan to combine against not only McDowell but also Patterson and McClellan prior to assaulting Washington via Maryland. Beauregard believed that by uniting, at least 40,000 troops would be available to defend the Bull Run line. This number, he confidently predicted, "would enable us to destroy the forces of Gels Scott and McDowell in my front." The wonder was that Beauregard did not call for Johnston's entire force, recommending that he leave 4,000–5,000 men behind to guard the Blue Ridge passes.[2]

Considering the gravity of the crisis at Manassas and the critical timing of the activities necessary to ameliorate it, why Richmond had seen fit to instruct Johnston to join Beauregard "if practicable" defies understanding. To any man chronically reluctant to pull the trigger, to commit himself to a course fraught with uncertainty and dire repercussions, Cooper's words offered an excuse for avoiding precipitate action. But Johnston had strong incentives to act on what amounted to a mere recommendation by his superiors. Because a junction of forces had long been a major element of Confederate strategy, one that Johnston himself had endorsed, were he to fail to offer aid and Beauregard be overwhelmed, the Virginian's reputation would not withstand the blame and censure he would receive. Yet if he marched but joined Beauregard too late, or if he arrived in time to fight and both armies were defeated, the responsibility could be laid at the War Department's doorstep. There was another equally self-serving reason for marching to Manassas: it would spare Johnston's army from harm should Patterson attack from his new position or—as seemed more likely—should a more pugnacious successor such as Mansfield or Sandford mount the kind of offensive Patterson appeared incapable of.

Tempted to leave Winchester as soon as Cooper's telegram arrived, Johnston decided he must first ensure that Patterson would not interfere with his departure. Even as he briefed his brigade leaders on his decision to march on Manassas, Stuart, with a picked force, rode forth to scrutinize Patterson's most recent movements. The cavalry chieftain got close enough to exchange shots with some advanced outposts. He detected no signs that the Federals were going anywhere in particular, though on the eighteenth some detachments had taken up positions between Smithfield and Charles Town. These units could menace Johnston's eastern flank and block any movement through the Blue Ridge.[3]

The stationary posture of every Yankee Stuart saw through his field glasses, however, persuaded him that Patterson had no intention of threatening anyone. Shortly after 9:00 A.M. he reported his findings to army headquarters. In his memoirs Johnston claims that he had considered offering battle to Patterson and attempting to defeat him, but Stuart's report indicated that the Yankees were "too far from our road" to interfere with a march to the mountains. Thus the information "left no doubt of the expediency of moving as soon as possible."

This day Johnston proved that, once he made up his mind, he could act quickly and decisively. His first decision was to refrain from transferring his sick to Culpeper as Cooper had recommended. There were upward of 1,700 ill and disabled men in his camps, and to move them such a distance would have consumed "several days, when hours were precious." He would leave them in Winchester to be ministered by a few army surgeons, assisted by local physicians. The two brigades of militia under Generals Carson and Meem that had augmented the regular garrison would remain in town. Johnston had Stuart beef up his scouting detachments and picket posts to cover the imminent evacuation. Then he ordered the bulk of his command—perhaps 8,500 officers and men—to stand ready to move out.[4]

Accustomed to give up one position for another, by noon Johnston's advance echelon, Jackson's brigade, was in column on the

road to Ashby's Gap. At first the march proceeded slowly and halt-
ingly, not only because the men were still unused to hard travel but
also because, as when they evacuated Harpers Ferry, their hearts were
not in this movement. At first the men were in high spirits, believing
that after so many weeks of avoiding contact they were going to confront Patterson and destroy him in battle. The mood changed drasti-
cally when, as one marcher recalled, "the head of the column turned
in the opposite direction from the enemy. The street, as the regiment
passed down it at a long swinging gait, was thronged with ladies, old
men, and children wringing their hands and crying out in distress:
'Oh, you will certainly not leave us to the mercy of the Yankees.'"[5]

Believing that they were being forced into another disgraceful
retreat, dozens of men cursed and swore when the long roll called
their unit into marching formation. One of Jackson's battalions at
first threatened not to move at all. Only after the rest of the brigade
confronted the recalcitrants, enclosing them inside a square formed
by aimed riflemen, did the would-be mutineers fall in line.[6]

When the march got underway in earnest, the men were sullen and quiet. "It was a silent march indeed," recalled a member of
Elzey's 1st Maryland, which along with the rest of the Fourth Brigade
left Winchester well behind Jackson. "There were no bright smiles,
no waving of handkerchiefs, no expression of joy, for all believed
that the Confederate army was retreating." This impression was not
dispelled until each brigade's rear guard cleared the town, whereupon staff officers and couriers briefly halted the marching men so
that the object of the march could be explained to them. As one
soldier recalled, each regiment was "drawn up in line as on dress
parade" to hear a message from Johnston. It affirmed "the necessity
of a forced march, and exhorted [all] to strive to reach the field in
time to take part in the great battle then imminent."[7]

Some commanders personally addressed their men, informing them of what lay ahead and adding words of inspiration and
encouragement. In doing so for benefit of his old regiment, Colonel
Elzey added a stern warning: "You are on the march to meet the
enemy, and, in the hour of battle, you will remember that you are
Marylanders. He had better never been born who proves himself
a craven when we grapple with the foe." The words were greeted
with "a cheer that might have been heard for miles." An enlisted
man observed that "all discontent was forgotten, fatigue and hardship, past and to be undergone unheeded, and exclamations of 'Lead

us on,' 'We are on the road to Maryland and will march forever,' were heard all down the line."[8]

Once anxiety and anger were dispelled, the pace of withdrawal picked up. Still the columns moved slowly enough along the Millwood Pike to worry Johnston that he would reach Manassas too late to influence the fighting there. Not until 9:00 P.M. did Jackson's vanguard reach the west bank of the Shenandoah, which the men were ordered to ford in a state of complete undress, their way made visible by bonfires glowing on the far bank. An Alabamian who crossed the river at a later hour reported that "as a brigade would reach the bank of the river they would halt, pull off boots, socks, and breeches, and fastening them in a bundle on their guns [held above their heads], 'fall in' again and cross the river, when the putting on process would begin." Although one enlisted man complained of being "wet up to our knees," most of his comrades plunged through cold, waist-deep water; shorter men such as George Baylor of Jackson's 2nd Virginia reported water up to his shoulders. An officer recalled that "many were the jokes and laughs we had crossing that river. Some tall fellows, being waggishly inclined, and seeing short ones behind, would walk in a stooping position, making the water appear very deep, and then enjoy immensely the disconsolate looks of the little fellows, who were manfully stemming the tide."[9]

Although some of the later arriving units, notably Bee's brigade, took as long as five hours to cross the river, Jackson's men made better time, as they also did when hitting the open road. Once on the east bank, they dressed; slung their rifles, canteens, and bed-rolls over their shoulders; and began to hike toward the mountains, five miles distant. John Esten Cooke, one of Jackson's earliest biographers, described the men as "toiling up the rough pathway at Ashby's Gap . . . without rations, ignorant of their destination, but knowing one thing only, that the moment for *action* had arrived."[10]

The lack of rations, rather than the march itself, appeared the principal impediment to a faster pace. Some regiments had nothing to eat on the first day's march, and only two hardtack per man on the second day out. At critical times, however, civilians succored the hungry soldiers. Having passed Ashby's Gap and turned south toward the Manassas Gap Railroad depot of Piedmont Station, Jackson's troops entered a village whose residents lined the streets to offer up baskets of provisions. These were seized, one man remembered, "as if by a pack of wolves and in a few minutes emptied."[11]

Johnston continued to worry about the marching pace. On the evening of the eighteenth, he made an effort to expedite progress. Major Whiting of his staff was sent on ahead to Piedmont Station to secure rail service for the balance of the journey. Upon reaching the depot, the engineer officer gathered information about the local rail resources and headed back to the column. Rejoining Johnston in the village of Paris, just east of Ashby's Gap and six miles north of Piedmont, Whiting delivered a report that his superior considered "so favorable as to give me reason to expect that the transportation of the infantry over the thirty-four miles between Piedmont and Manassas Junction could be accomplished easily in twenty-four hours."[12]

It appears that Whiting relayed a pledge by the railroad's president, whom he met at Piedmont, that his line would convey the Army of the Shenandoah in its entirety to Manassas by sunrise on July 20. If he said this, he was promising more than he could deliver. The Manassas Gap Railroad, a much smaller and poorer enterprise than the Orange & Alexandria and other roads of the Virginia Tidewater, lacked sufficient infrastructure to transport an army the size of Johnston's anywhere quickly. At this time the railroad owned fewer than twenty engines, many of them aged and unreliable, only two of which were available on short notice. These were enough to carry a portion of the command to Manassas by the twentieth, but certainly not all of it. Furthermore, the line had only enough personnel to operate one or two trains at a time. The lack of relay crews would surely complicate the journey to Manassas. Even so, Johnston believed that the railroad could carry to the prospective battlefield more men than would have gotten there by any other means.

The question of who conceived the idea of using the railroad for a troop transfer remains difficult to answer even at this late date. Various sources credit Beauregard, Johnston, Jefferson Davis, and War Department officials. After the war Beauregard claimed credit for stockpiling cars at Piedmont and alerting Johnston to their availability. But before he was able to inform his colleague, the latter reached the station and began to entrain for Manassas. This suggests that Johnston did not need to be told. Then too, the concentration of rolling stock at Piedmont appears to have been accomplished locally, without Beauregard's assistance. The logical inference is that no one had to have his attention turned to the railroad, an expedient whose supposed value was evident to all concerned.[13]

Ignorant of the obstacles that awaited them at Piedmont, Jackson's troops kept moving but more slowly than hitherto—in the words of historian David Detzer, like "a snake with a badly broken spine." Even so, some of the brigades in its rear made worse time. Logistical shortcomings and some understandable confusion delayed the departure from Winchester of Bee's command, which did not get on the road until almost sundown, almost five hours after Bartow's troops had started out. Compared to Bee's tortoise-like pace, Bartow was moving with the speed of a hare. Elzey's brigade, the next to leave Winchester, would move almost as slowly as Bee, while General Smith's command, the last to depart, would make even less progress on the first and second days of the march, limiting its chances of reaching Manassas in time to fight.[14]

At least one of Bartow's regiments, however, was long delayed. As the brigade prepared to hit the road, a false report reached Winchester that Patterson's army was advancing on the town. To counter the movement, the 8th Georgia was sent two miles out the road to Berryville, where for some hours it awaited a confrontation. A private in the 8th reported, "we pulled down about 2 miles of fences so as to have a good battle ground but no enemy appeared . . . as if they were going to Alexandria." The Yankees' refusal to give battle further confirmed the view that their general was a craven scoundrel. A private in the 4th Alabama, addicted to sarcasm, wrote his family, "The best Genls of the age say it requires more tact and military learning to conduct a good retreat than to fight and win a battle, therefore I assert that Patterson is the best Genl they have."[15]

By 2:00 A.M. on the nineteenth, Jackson's brigade was enjoying a brief rest outside Paris, having marched sixteen miles in fourteen hours. The general could not have been pleased—even green troops ought to have covered almost two miles per hour—but the river crossing had taken time, as had the uphill and downhill climb through Ashby's Gap. Although Jackson, the one-time professional soldier, would become renowned for the hard marching of his "foot cavalry," this day he was bested by the civilian Bartow, whose men had reached the Shenandoah, only three and a half miles from Paris, by 11:00 P.M.

Here Jackson allowed his weary but well-fed marchers a few hours of sleep. Over the years a story arose that Old Jack—still clad in the dark blue double-breasted frock coat he had worn in the classroom at VMI— stayed awake the entire time, keeping night watch over his flock like the good shepherd his men took him to be. The general's most distinguished biographer, James I. Robertson, Jr., refutes this fable, noting that Jackson himself slept but only after a vigilant circuit or two of his brigade's camp.[16]

The march from Paris (which one soldier, who was probably fed there, called "the most beautiful place that I ever beheld") resumed in the darkness of early morning. Just before eight o'clock on the nineteenth, Jackson's advance reached Piedmont Station. The men received more edibles there, provided by citizens who had flocked to the depot from miles around. "We had a regular picnic," reported John O. Casler of the 33rd Virginia, "plenty to eat, lemonade to drink, and beautiful young ladies to chat with."[17]

Also on hand was General Johnston, who had ridden on ahead from Paris, and a train of cars that the director of the Manassas Gap Railroad had pieced together in record time. Jackson's men clambered aboard the cars and by ten o'clock began the long run to Manassas. For the most part, accommodations were something less than first class. While some officers lounged aboard passenger cars, the majority of the enlisted men traveled inside (and in some cases atop) boxcars that had recently conveyed cattle to market or squatted aboard flatcars used for hauling freight. One of Jackson's surgeons recalled that "we packed ourselves like so many pins and needles" and "slowly jolted the entire day." In actuality the train chugged along at an acceptable rate, almost six miles per hour. Thus the trip took a little more than six hours, although given the cramped conditions it must have seemed at least twice as long.[18]

Not until just before sundown did the train, now empty of passengers, return to Piedmont to take on the 7th and 8th Georgia of Bartow's recently arrived brigade as well as, apparently, the 33rd Virginia of Jackson's brigade. But by the time these outfits started for Manassas (years later Johnston recalled the hour as 3:00 P.M., though a member of the 8th, writing one day afterward, gave it as 7:00 P.M.), the men had been idling at Piedmont Station for at least eight hours. For lack of accommodations, Bartow was forced to leave at Piedmont his 9th Georgia and the 1st and 2nd Kentucky Battalions. One Georgian recalled that "many were the curses long loud and deep that were given to Gen Johns[t]on by our troops for detaining us."[19]

Barnard Bee's command was the next to reach Piedmont. Its men trooped in about an hour after sundown on the nineteenth "broken down and starved," in the words of one Alabamian. Although they were ready to board at once, no train was available. Johnston would recall that although enough cars were ready for the run to Manassas by midnight, "the conductors and engineers disappeared immediately, to pass the night probably in sleep, instead of on the road." His surmise was undoubtedly correct, but some of his officers suspected that at least a couple of crewmen were covert unionists and were deliberately obstructing the troop transfer. One conductor was accused of staging a collision on the evening of the twentieth that stalled the passage of the 11th Mississippi. The man was arrested, pronounced a Yankee saboteur, and summarily executed. Whatever the real reason, Bee's men did not entrain until sunrise on the twentieth, almost twelve hours after reaching Piedmont. The engine, which was now feeling the wear and tear of heavy travel, made slower progress than it had when hauling Jackson's men—no more than four to five miles per hour.[20]

Johnston could see that transporting even one brigade and portions of two others was overtaxing the railroad. He therefore gave directions to Colonels Stuart and Pendleton, who reached Piedmont late in the evening of the nineteenth, that their units should proceed to Manassas over country roads. Neither cavalry nor artillery was well in hand. Stuart had departed Winchester with only four of his companies—a fifth would join him en route to Manassas from its camp of instruction. The remainder of the still-embryonic regiment would remain in the Valley on scouting duty along with Turner Ashby's horsemen. By seniority Pendleton should have overseen the massing and transporting of the artillery available to the Valley army. After the war, however, Captain Imboden of the Staunton Artillery claimed that General Bee, his brigade commander, ordered him to collect all five of Johnston's batteries and conduct them to Manassas. Imboden claimed that he did so, although Pendleton took credit for the operation.

Stuart and Pendleton attempted to carry out Johnston's orders but found it impossible to make progress on roads clogged with regiments awaiting transportation at Piedmont. As William Blackford of the 1st Virginia Cavalry recalled, the infantry could not help getting in the cavalry's way, "and we had constantly to be on the lookout to keep from riding over them in the dark." Ultimately, both artillerists and troopers adopted the expedient of moving through open fields until able to clear the roadblocks. Stuart would proudly declare that despite every obstacle, he got his horsemen to Manassas by the evening of the twentieth. Johnston's artillery made almost as good progress, passing inside Beauregard's lines by one o'clock the next morning.[21]

Thus Johnston did his part to ensure that the Manassas Gap Railroad would not be so overburdened as to be put out of commission. If Beauregard had had his way, the line would have been taxed to an even lesser extent. Just after midnight on July 19, Johnston was met at Piedmont by a high-ranking messenger from Manassas, Colonel Alexander R. Chisolm of Beauregard's staff. The South Carolinian, who had ridden the thirty-four miles from Manassas at breakneck speed, carried a suggestion from his superior that Johnston head for Manassas in two columns, only one by railroad. While the latter passed through Thoroughfare Gap in the Bull Run Mountains, the rest of the army should hoof it through Aldie Gap, a dozen miles farther north, and take the Little River Turnpike to Centreville, the assumed location of McDowell's far right flank. In this way the Army of the Shenandoah could strike the enemy's right and rear while the Army of the Potomac attacked his front.[22]

Unlike some of the Creole's earlier plans that had a core of logic, his latest proposal was wholly impractical, primarily because of the difficulty Johnston would experience trying to coordinate an offensive with a distant colleague. Sensibly, he rejected the proposal: "It would have been impossible, in my opinion, to calculate when our undisciplined volunteers would reach any distant point that might be indicated. I preferred the junction of the two armies at the earliest time possible, as the first measure to secure success."[23]

Yet it appears that for a time, Johnston considered implementing Beauregard's plan. Soon after Bee's brigade reached Paris late on the nineteenth, Johnston ordered it to take the Little River Turnpike to Manassas while the rest of the army rode the rails. According to one of Bee's aides, his superior liked the idea and, relaying the order to his subordinates, started for Manassas. After marching a few miles, however, he was overtaken by one of Johnston's staff officers with a message countermanding the order and recalling the brigade to Piedmont Station. Bee's men were forced to wait their turn to board the train. Later the general told his aide that he wished Johnston had allowed him to make the road march, believing that only in this way would he get his entire command to Manassas in time to be of help to Beauregard. As it was, the insufficiency of railroad transportation would prevent almost half of his brigade from taking part in the impending battle.[24]

Beauregard appears to have accepted the rejection of his suggestion with reasonably good grace, although when he learned of it and gave credence to it is a matter of dispute. Immediately upon his return to Manassas, Colonel Chisolm should have informed his boss of Johnston's decision. But Jubal Early, who was privy to the goings-on at Beauregard's headquarters, would state that the army leader did not get word of it until Jackson reached Manassas late that same afternoon, met with Beauregard, and announced that the entire Army of the Shenandoah was coming by rail. According to Early, Beauregard did not believe the stolid, eccentric Virginian, whom he considered something of a dolt. Only when Johnston joined him the following day did the Creole realize that Jackson had been right. Until that moment, it would appear, he had supposed that Johnston had accepted his suggestion.[25]

The problems inherent in relying on the limited resources of the Manassas Gap Railroad became evident as soon as the train that had conducted Jackson and then Bartow to Manassas returned to Piedmont Station shortly before midnight and the crewmen promptly disappeared to grab some sleep. "It was not until seven or eight o'clock Saturday morning," Johnston wrote, "that the trains could be put in motion." The first train carried two regiments from the Third Brigade, the 4th Alabama and 2nd Mississippi, plus two companies of the 11th Mississippi; Bee accompanied this force. Wishing to delay no longer his union with Beauregard, Johnston climbed aboard the slow-moving train, leaving his ranking subordinate, General Smith, to oversee the shipment of the majority of the army: the rest of Bee's and Bartow's brigades, Elzey's brigade, and Smith's own command.[26]

By the time this train got going, its passengers had been lounging on the right of way for nearly twelve hours. The troops scheduled to follow Bee's half brigade would wait even longer, apparently the result of a breakdown of the locomotive carrying the 6th North Carolina or, as another report has it, due to a collision between the train carrying the 6th and an unloaded train returning from Manassas. According to some sources, the 6th was put to work repairing a break in the track near Piedmont Station, a project supervised by its colonel, Charles F. Fisher, former president of the North Carolina Railroad. As a reward for this service, Fisher's Tar Heels boarded a train late in the evening of July 20, taking the place in line originally assigned to Smith's brigade.[27]

For most of the remaining units of the Second and Third Brigades, the lost time could not be made up. Fisher's North Carolinians would reach Manassas early on the twenty-first, Elzey's brigade several hours later—thus the latter's participation in the fighting could not be assured. Smith's Fifth Brigade, like the remnants of Bee's and Bartow's, would be stranded at Piedmont Station, looking in vain for a ride. Only the four guns attached to Smith's command—the Thomas Artillery of Captain Philip B. Stanard, a Virginia unit formed in Richmond—and the brigadier himself would reach Beauregard in time to fight. Stanard's would be the only unbrigaded Confederate field-artillery unit to see action on the twenty-first.[28]

Those soldiers who experienced a long wait at Piedmont but would still reach Manassas in time to fight probably used the respite to prepare themselves physically and mentally for what lay ahead. Yet it may be argued that they had too much time on their hands, time in which to dwell deeply on the critical confrontation to come and to consider their chances of surviving it, thoughts detrimental to the corporate morale. Perhaps more to the point, instead of idling at the depot, they could have been marching alongside the tracks or, a few miles farther south, on the roughly parallel road to Haymarket, which met the smooth-surfaced Warrenton Turnpike at Gainesville. These routes would have decreased the distance to the army's destination while keeping both the bodies and minds of its men occupied. Perhaps Beauregard's idea of having at least a portion of Johnston's army hoof it to Manassas was not so illogical after all.

According to Colonel George H. Gordon of the 2nd Massachusetts Volunteers, upon reaching Charles Town around noon on July 17 following a fatiguing march in "the hottest kind of weather," Patterson's vanguard entered "as conquerors receiving an ovation." This may have been the attitude of the town's many unionists, but since most of the local population were Southern sympathizers, the army's reception was not uniformly cordial. For one thing, the home guard, although hopelessly outnumbered, put up a stiff, if brief, fight, desisting when charged simultaneously from east and west by members of the 2nd U.S. Cavalry and the Philadelphia City Troop.[29]

When the ruckus ceased and they went into bivouac around the town, the newcomers continued to draw an icy response from the locals, many of whom were quietly pleased by the evident fact that the Yankees were on the run. Even the loyalists of the town wondered why so many blue uniforms were in their midst since it was common knowledge that Johnston's army remained at Winchester. The female secessionists, whom the occupiers described as "more outspoken" than their counterparts at Martinsburg, "scowled and spat" at the soldiers while taunting them with frequent questions about why they had backtracked so far from the enemy's lair.[30]

Patterson's men had no answers. They too could see no reason for the sideways movement that had put an additional seven or eight miles between them and Winchester. At the outset of the march—Cadwalader's division in advance, followed by Keim's, then the supply wagons—many men had supposed they were taking up a more advantageous position from which to attack Johnston. They were quickly disabused of this notion. The column halted several times between Smithfield and Charles Town, and flanking forces were thrown out as if to oppose attackers, though none were discovered.

As the march progressed, rumors ran the length of the column that the Confederates were on the verge of evacuating the Valley. The news appeared to be confirmed when the troops spied pillars of smoke rising in the direction of Winchester, suggesting that supplies were being burned to deny them to captors. The relatively few members of the Army of Pennsylvania who strongly desired a fight feared that the Rebels were slipping through their fingers. Later rumors, however, had Johnston being reinforced by rail from Strasburg, which suggested he would remain in the Valley after all. Others, including Colonel Lew Wallace of the 11th Indiana, feared that the clatter of trains to the south meant that Johnston was beginning to transfer his army to Manassas. When Wallace suggested as much to higher headquarters, his idea was met only "with a smile."[31]

The men's perplexity over the recent move was shared by the newspaper reporters traveling with them. A *New York Times* correspondent, who got no answers from anyone on the headquarters staff, confessed that what the movement to Charles Town meant, "Heaven only knows. I think it would puzzle the spirits of Caesar, Saxe, Napoleon, Wellington, and all the departed heroes, to make it out." The most recent explanation referenced reports that Johnston had been reinforced to a strength of 20,000 men or more and at least twenty-two guns, "but," the newsman wrote, "I don't believe it."

He was right to be skeptical, even though the army's commander appeared to cling to the belief that Johnston outnumbered him handily in terms of both manpower and ordnance. If these numbers were even close to accurate, the newsman wondered, why did the enemy show no inclination to fight? The road to Charles Town was strewn with fence rails and fallen logs, Johnston's only visible effort to contest his enemy's movements. Few Confederates showed themselves at any point on the seventeenth, suggesting they had "no desire to meet us." The previous day, however, Patterson had reconnoitered toward Winchester to ascertain if Johnston remained there in force. At least three combined-arms forces, under Lieutenant Colonel David Bell Birney of the 23rd Pennsylvania Infantry and Captain Richard W. Johnson and Lieutenant Thomas M. Anderson of the 2nd U.S. Cavalry, penetrated to within a few miles of the enemy-held town. Johnson reported finding it held in "heavy force," but neither Birney, who ran into some of Stuart's troopers, nor Anderson, who apparently encountered no Confederates, believed Winchester to be strongly garrisoned. While Patterson reported the dissenting findings to Washington, he probably placed greater confidence in Captain Johnson's report, which confirmed his belief that he must exercise continued caution in moving against Johnston.[32]

When it finally became clear that their commander was avoiding contact with the enemy, "enthusiasm died out" in Patterson's army. The word "retreat," which had been whispered from rank to rank, was soon being shouted to the skies. Some officers had uttered the term while on the march, especially after the army passed through Smithfield instead of turning south onto the last direct road to Winchester. When Colonel Butterfield inquired why one of his regiments had marched with colors encased, its commander replied that he "would never show his flag in a retreat." Upon reaching Charles Town, many soldiers repaired to the site where John Brown had been hanged a year and a half earlier. Some remarked of the contrast between the unswerving commitment of the militant abolitionist and the vacillation and timidity of their commander.[33]

With the prospect of combat apparently behind them, even those who desired to go home rather than fight—and they were very much in the majority—claimed they had wanted to engage the Rebels all along and now cursed the lost opportunity. A few days later, when Patterson's ignominious flight became evident beyond all doubt, these self-professed warriors turned their anger on their leader. Whenever the general rode past at the head of his staff, an angry chorus went up, "Go home, you old coward!" Some voices shouted, "Hang him!" "Throw him in the river!" "He's an old secessionist—shoot him!" Instead of halting and facing his accusers, a red-faced Patterson, quivering and spluttering, galloped off.[34]

Patterson believed himself unfairly condemned; he was convinced that he had ample authority to make his latest shift of position. In his telegram of July 12, General Scott appeared to endorse his subordinate's intention, first expressed three days earlier, to move to Charles Town even if it meant driving Johnston from Winchester to Manassas. In fact, wrote Scott, Charles Town was a good point to begin a pursuit of the Valley Confederates via Leesburg and Alexandria. But this wording did not accurately convey his intent: he had supposed that the move from Bunker Hill was a prelude to an attack on Winchester. His poor choice of words gave Patterson the happy impression that he might move as he saw fit, whether or not it put him in contact with Johnston.[35]

The following day, the thirteenth, Scott tried to clarify his wants but succeeded only in muddying the waters even further. Now, he authorized Patterson, "if not strong enough to beat the enemy early next week [when McDowell was expected to attack at Manassas], make demonstrations so as to detain him [Johnston] in the valley of Winchester; but if he retreats in force towards Manassas, and it be too hazardous to follow him, then consider the route via Key's Ferry, Leesburg, &c." This latest communiqué reiterated Scott's emphasis on keeping Johnston pinned down but should he escape, Patterson was authorized to pursue him by the roundabout route to Alexandria. This told the Pennsylvanian that he no longer needed to engage the enemy, merely feign an attack as a means of persuading him to stay in the Valley.[36]

Although weeks earlier Scott had considered Patterson's operations of paramount importance, he was now focusing on McDowell's offensive. By failing to keep close tabs on what was happening in the Shenandoah, he was giving Patterson too much leeway. Based on his memory of Patterson's service in the Mexican War, Scott believed that he could trust him to follow orders and discern the meaning, overt and hidden, in those orders. In fact, Patterson had never shown that degree of perceptivity.

Nor had he demonstrated an aptitude for independent command; even in Mexico he had been dependent on superiors to tell him what to do, how to do it, and when. Lacking confidence in his own decision making, he relied on articulate and professionally educated subordinates to do his thinking for him. He was only too willing to accept their arguments against taking action and to overestimate his enemy's strength as an excuse for not behaving at odds with his cautious, conservative nature—nothing ventured, nothing lost. Perhaps his greatest flaw was his knack for misconstruing orders, either unintentionally or deliberately. Misreading Scott's underlying intentions protected him from the uncertainties inherent in assuming and maintaining the offensive.

For weeks Scott and Patterson had been working at cross-purposes. This finally became evident to Washington within hours of Patterson's occupation of Charles Town—a movement he failed to report to his superiors. Scott reminded the general of this on the evening of the seventeenth, when he tried to reach the Pennsylvanian at his assumed location, Harpers Ferry: "I have nothing official from you since Sunday [July 14], but am glad to learn, through Philadelphia papers, that you have advanced. Do not let the enemy amuse and delay you with a small force in front whilst he reinforces the [Manassas] Junction with his main body. McDowell's first day's work has driven the enemy beyond Fairfax Court-House. The Junction will probably be carried tomorrow."[37]

This communication, relayed to Patterson's headquarters by a "special messenger" from Harpers Ferry and handed to the general by one of the newest members of his staff, Major William W. Russell, told him some things he did not want to hear. Evidently, Scott had been under the impression that he had advanced not to Charles Town but to Winchester. This invalidated Patterson's belief that he need not engage Johnston directly. Because McDowell had yet to attack, time remained for Johnston to "amuse and delay" Patterson while slipping away to Manassas—something that may have occurred already.

All of this was, of course, Patterson's fault. Had he put himself in contact with Scott while at Bunker Hill, he could have kept abreast of McDowell's progress or lack thereof and acted accordingly. Upon learning that the attack on Bull Run had been delayed, Patterson might have canceled the move to Charles Town and either confronted Johnston at Winchester or, failing to stop him from leaving the Valley, tailed him to Manassas.

Patterson was shocked by his gross misunderstanding of Scott's expectations, and he was greatly concerned when, in reply to his request for an unbiased opinion, Major Russell declared that the general in chief's dispatch was a positive order to attack and that "in the event of a misfortune in front of Washington, the whole blame will be laid to your charge." Fearing professional ruin, early on the nineteenth Patterson convened a conference of his ranking subordinates, to whom he disseminated hastily drawn-up marching orders. He then assembled several regiments and made an impassioned plea for the short-timers to remain under arms long enough to engage the foe.[38]

The results were most discouraging. A few men in each regiment agreed to stay, but the majority promised nothing or refused outright. In a typical regiment, the 1st Pennsylvania, only a single company expressed a willingness to extend its service time. Many units could not have gone into battle had they desired to, for they lacked complete uniforms, especially serviceable shoes, and sufficient ammunition. Conveniently overlooking Charles Sandford and many lesser-ranking officers whose resolve had not failed, Patterson later told his congressional inquisitors that "no regiment, or colonel, or general, or officer, under my command, ever asked to be led to the front—not one."[39]

A deeply discouraged Patterson dismissed the troops and wired the unhappy results to Washington. Already he had sent a plaintive message to his superior, asking "shall I attack?" He would claim that Scott never responded to this needless inquiry. In fact, the commanding general shot back a reply that conveyed anger and reproof, sentiments that had not characterized their earlier correspondence. "I have certainly been expecting you to beat the enemy," Scott wrote. "If not, to hear that you had felt him strongly, or, at least, had occupied him by threats and demonstrations. You have been at least his equal, and, I suppose, superior, in numbers. Has he not stolen a march and sent reenforcements toward Manassas Junction?"[40]

In reply Patterson, his feelings hurt, insisted that "the enemy has stolen no march upon me." But even as he wrote, his scouts were reporting signs that Johnston was evacuating Winchester for points east. In later telegrams Patterson attempted to defend his course, asserting that, despite reports to the contrary, "I have succeeded, in accordance with the wishes of the General-in-Chief, in keeping General Johnston's force at Winchester." Through the nineteenth he continued to claim that Johnston remained in situ, but the following day—one day before McDowell launched his assault on Beauregard—he was forced to admit that "with a portion of his force Johnston left Winchester by the road to Millwood on the afternoon of the 18th."[41]

Unknown to Patterson, by the time he sent this wire, the Adjutant General's Office in Washington had issued an order discharging him from service effective July 27. He was to be replaced by Major General Nathaniel P. Banks, formerly in charge of the Department of Annapolis. Banks's new command would be known as the Department of the Shenandoah, "headquarters in the field." His initial duty station would be at Harpers Ferry, to which Patterson returned his tattered, angry soldiers on the twenty-first.[42]

As Patterson left the military, his reputation in shreds as his aide had predicted, he continued to believe that despite daunting obstacles, he had fully and faithfully obeyed the orders he had received from Washington. Winfield Scott did not agree. Although some of his orders had led Patterson astray, the commanding general refused to hold his subordinate blameless. On the twenty-first Major Russell called at Scott's office to try to explain what had gone wrong in the Shenandoah. When Scott demanded to know why his subordinate withheld an attack critical to Union success, the aide replied that Patterson had been led to believe he was not to strike for fear of driving Johnston's army to Manassas. The old general was dumbfounded, then enraged, thundering at his visitor, "I will sacrifice my commission if my dispatches will bear any such interpretation!"[43]

This charge—that Patterson had failed to obey orders throughout his weeks in the Shenandoah—became a club in the hands of his many critics. Even before he returned to Philadelphia following his discharge, editors and politicians were calling him a blunderer, an incompetent, an idiot; a few even echoed the absurd charge that he was a traitor to his nation. Newspapers, including some in his home city, gave coverage to the officers and men of his army who condemned Patterson for failing to lead them into battle—even as they silently thanked him for keeping them out of harm's way.

The outcry against the old general reached a crescendo in January 1862, when he spent three days being beaten about the head and shoulders by the Joint Committee on the Conduct of the War. The panel's Republican majority fired a continuous barrage of accusations and aspersions that the harried and flustered defendant was unable to effectively counter. By the time enough blood had been drawn to satisfy his inquisitors, Patterson's name had become a byword not only for incompetence but also for arrant cowardice. Many months of war, replete with campaigns that dwarfed his in terms of size, scope, and ineptitude, would pass before his failures of commission and omission faded from the public consciousness and the old soldier allowed, mercifully, to slip into obscurity.[44]

Patterson had been suitably chastised and properly barred from taking further part in the conflict, but his superior, who had done as much as he to bungle the Valley campaign, retained his preeminence as head of the army. This was a manifest injustice, for while General Scott could not have been attuned to every limitation and flaw in Patterson's constitution, he should have been skeptical that the man could be trusted to execute given orders promptly and properly. Instead of minimizing Patterson's weaknesses, Scott had aggravated them through fear-mongering, constantly warning against precipitate action and risk taking that might harm the morale not only of his army but also of the Northern public. For the most part the commanding general failed to keep Patterson informed of McDowell's movements and progress even though close coordination between the two armies was critical to the success of the campaign. His greatest failing, however, was his inability or unwillingness to monitor Patterson's unsteady progress and yank him back on the road when he veered off course. By allowing his subordinate to fatally mishandle a critical mission, Scott bore as much responsibility for the outcome as the officer who would absorb the lion's share of the blame.

Before departing Centreville sometime after nine o'clock on the morning of July 18, General Tyler entertained a group of local civilians at his field headquarters. From them he learned that the former occupants of Fairfax Court House had split up during their flight to Bull Run, one column taking the Warrenton Turnpike, the other the road to Mitchell's Ford. Armed with this information, Tyler rode off to overtake Richardson's men. He discovered that they had turned off the Mitchell's Ford road onto a farm track leading to Blackburn's Ford, where the creek made a horseshoe-shaped bend toward the north. The upper bank of the ford was a ridge about twenty yards long that rose at least fifty feet above water level. An extension of the high ground descending from Centreville, the ridge abounded in trees and tangled underbrush. The southern bank fronted a flat, open plain that sloped gradually toward Manassas, covered by only a few trees and little plant growth. The ford was not, as it first appeared, an easy place to cross; R. M. Johnston describes it as "difficult and boggy" and notes that for that reason it "had almost fallen into disuse."[45]

Richardson had left the road to reach a small cluster of springs a mile southwest of the village where his men might refill their canteens. Meeting his subordinate there just shy of noon, Tyler, accompanied by Major Barnard, the army's chief engineer, and escorted by two companies of foot soldiers as well as Brackett's squadron of horsemen, rode out to a road fork below Butler's farm. The right-hand road led to Mitchell's Ford, the other, more easterly road, to Blackburn's Ford. Up ahead on the left-hand road could be seen a Rebel force, size indeterminate; the obviously less-traveled road to Mitchell's appeared unobstructed.[46]

Hoping to get some idea of how strongly each ford was held, Tyler ordered up Richardson's main body as well as a section of 10-pounder Parrott rifles of Captain Ayres's Company E, 3rd U.S. (which also comprised two 12-pounder howitzers and two 6-pounder guns). The guns had been borrowed from Sherman's brigade; also on loan was its commander, Ayres having been posted to the 5th U.S. Artillery. Coincidentally, the battery was known throughout the army as "Sherman's Battery"—not for the Ohio general but for its former commander, Mexican War stalwart Thomas West Sherman, no relation to Cump.

When brought into battery shortly after noon, Ayres, at Tyler's order, sent a few shells from his rifles down the road to Mitchell's Ford. The target comprised the four 6-pounders of Captain Kemper's Alexandria Light Artillery, attached to Bonham's brigade. Upon his retreat from Fairfax and Centreville, Bonham had placed Kemper's guns on a hill just below the junction of the roads to the two fords. The battery protected the South Carolinians' position, which due to the course of the stream formed a salient protruding toward the enemy. Bonham supported Kemper's small guns with two companies of Kershaw's 2nd South Carolina, thrown out six hundred yards north of the stream.

Ayres's shelling did not dislodge Kemper or his support, but when Richardson's brigade came up and began to form, another company of Kershaw's regiment, which had been picketing the road to Centreville, hastily retired across the run. Ayres's Parrotts increased their rate of fire, but Kemper held his position until the enemy appeared to find his range, whereupon he loosed a half dozen shots—"apparently most effective" ones—and returned, along with his support, to the trenches Bonham had erected on the south bank. Kershaw noted that "after a few shots at this retreating party the enemy turned their attention almost exclusively to the troops posted to the right of our brigade."[47]

While Ayres's section had been blasting away at Mitchell's Ford, Tyler and his escort, "feeling our way carefully," pressed to within sight of Blackburn's. Though the ford was well defended by James Longstreet's brigade, Tyler's presence attracted no response. Peering through the foliage on the north side, the general thought he spied an artillery unit on the opposite bank. Eventually, his party drew a smattering of rifle fire, but he could discern "no great body of troops" across the stream.[48]

Frustrated that he had provoked no reaction from the enemy, whom he suspected were in force opposite him, Tyler decided to flush them out. Captain Fry, McDowell's adjutant general, had reached the scene just as Ayres was committed; he sent another officer from the army-headquarters staff to remind Tyler that he had been ordered to bring on no engagement. Major Barnard had already told him as much, but the brigadier ignored both officers. He ordered forward Richardson's brigade, covered in front by the 160-man battalion that had led the march to Centreville under Captain Robert Brethschneider of Richardson's old regiment, the 2nd Michigan.

Hoping to scour the thick woods along the creek, Brethschneider's men deployed some five hundred yards in advance of Richardson's vanguard. The skirmishers passed through a woodlot into the road that led to the ford, but not even this advance stirred up the Rebels. Tyler, his fighting blood up, refused to withdraw without locating the enemy's position and estimating his strength. "I thought it my duty, under the circumstances," he wrote later, "to ascertain the truth positively."[49]

The general had already exceeded his orders from McDowell, but he intended to go further. To augment Richardson and Ayres, he ordered up a section of hefty 20-pounders from Company G, 1st Artillery—the only guns serving with the battery this day—under Lieutenant S. N. Benjamin. Meanwhile, he emplaced Ayres's pieces on a crest overlooking Blackburn's Ford. At a distance of about a mile, they opened on the artillery positions spotted earlier. Ten or

twelve rounds went screeching over the run. Although Tyler considered the elevation of Ayres's guns to be "favorable," the projectiles
flew too high. They did no discernable damage to their intended
targets, but the New Englander would report that they took effect
"on a large body of cavalry, who evidently thought themselves
out of range." This was probably a detachment of Radford's 30th
Virginia, positioned between Mitchell's Ford and Blackburn's. The
shelling also displaced the section of the Washington Artillery,
under Lieutenant J. J. Garnett, attached to Longstreet's command.
Longstreet had ordered Garnett to withdraw as soon as the heavier
guns of the enemy fixed his range. According to one of Longstreet's
infantryman, as soon as it was targeted, the artillery "at once moved
back toward Manassas and the old McLean House."[50]

The shelling had other effects as well. The first few overfly-
ing rounds came crashing down on the farm of Wilmer McLean, for
whom the ford just below Blackburn's was named. McLean's house,
christened Yorkshire, had been appropriated by General Beauregard
that morning for his command post. Inadvertently, it would appear,
it became a target of the Union gunners, with baleful results for
the headquarters mess. One round struck the chimney of McLean's
summer kitchen, scattering the stew that servants had been preparing for the high-ranking occupant and causing the Creole to go
without his midday meal. Of greater concern, the continued shelling endangered the field hospital that the surgeon of the 1st Virginia
had established in the McLean barn, forcing the rapid evacuation
of wounded men. Beauregard noted that a yellow hospital flag had
flown from the roof of the building. "I hope for the sake of past associations," he wrote, referring to his West Point classmate McDowell,
that it "was ignorantly mistaken for a Confederate flag."[51]

The previous afternoon, having received word of McDowell's advance
through Fairfax County, Longstreet had stationed elements of his
three infantry regiments, perhaps 2,400 men all told, on both sides
of Blackburn's Ford. When the enemy drew near, he moved up six
companies of Colonel Patrick T. Moore's 1st Virginia and put them
in line of battle covering the farm lane to the ford. On the left these
units abutted the 17th Virginia under Colonel Montgomery D. Corse;
Colonel Samuel Garland's 11th Virginia was deployed still farther to
the southwest, close to the bank of the meandering stream. The entire
line was covered by the remaining four companies of the 1st Virginia.

Longstreet had deployed perhaps a hundred men on the north side of the run to send back word of the enemy's approach. The maneuver was essential to the security of his entire position, which through poor planning on his part as well as Beauregard's boasted only rudimentary defenses instead of the earthworks and rifle pits that protected Bonham's men farther west. Those defenses worked wonders. A South Carolinian who hunkered down behind them wrote that his outfit "had to stand and endure a fire of shot and shell from the enemy all the time without the privilege of returning the compliment [but] . . . none of us were touched."[52]

After failing to flush out the Rebels, shortly after noon Tyler ordered Colonel Richardson to advance a substantial portion of his 3,900-man brigade to the ford. This movement had some effect, though not much. Preceded by Brethschneider and his skirmishers, two companies from Colonel Robert Cowdin's 1st Massachusetts moved down to the marshy creek bottom. While the skirmishers filed off into a woods a short distance from Bull Run, the gray-clad New Englanders, led by Lieutenant Colonel George Wells, pressed to within rifle range of the stream. They succeeded in drawing only intermittent small-arms fire. The response tantalized Tyler, who began to believe that the opposite bank was so weakly held he might be able to rush across the ford and gain the road to Manassas Junction. Reportedly, he informed one of his staff officers that the first Federal to cross Bull Run would be the "greatest man of the war"; the general left little doubt that he intended to be that man. Ironically, he would later charge that the entire campaign "was gotten up by General McDowell and his friends, and was intended to make him the hero of a short war." Now Tyler planned to outfox his superior by snaring the hero's mantle for himself and, in the words of a contemporary historian, winning "cheap glory."[53]

At least one historian, David Detzer, has questioned the long-accepted view that Tyler was glory hunting, arguing that he was merely reconnoitering as he had been ordered. If so, one must ask why Tyler elected not to advance on Mitchell's Ford, where there was a large enemy force to probe, and instead chose the path of least resistance, which led to an apparently lightly guarded crossing within striking range of his army's principal objective. Detzer cites the fact that the general moved toward Blackburn's with a single brigade as proof that he had no intention of attacking. In his after-action report, however, Tyler admitted that he ordered the next brigade in line, Sherman's, to stand "ready for any contingency," including, presumably, a march on Manassas.[54]

Years later, when he wrote a memoir of his campaign under McDowell, Tyler clung to the belief that his men alone could have whipped Beauregard's army "before sundown"—the latter could not have placed enough defenders across his path to prevent it. He also claimed that he had told this to McDowell and that had his advice been acted upon, the campaign would have ended quickly, victoriously, and with minimal effusion of blood.[55]

When Tyler through his field glasses spied "an opening low down on the bottom of the stream where a couple of howitzers could be put into battery," he believed his golden opportunity was at hand. He had Ayres advance his howitzer section, supported closely by Brackett's horsemen, and occupy the clearing. As soon as the section unlimbered, however, Longstreet's troops finally unleashed a series of volleys in which Kemper's guns joined. The combined fire downed several cannoneers and every horse assigned to one of the pieces. Ayres hauled the other tube to the rear and sent for a fresh team to bring off the one he had temporarily abandoned. In his report of the engagement, Captain Kemper took pleasure in claiming responsibility for forcing the withdrawal of Sherman's famous battery.[56]

Apparently without consulting Tyler but believing he was anticipating his superior's intentions, Richardson formed Colonel Ezra L. Walrath's 12th New York in line of battle on the left of Ayres's guns and instructed the regiment to move forward and sweep the woods of the enemy. The order—which some historians claim to have originated with Tyler, although he later denied it—exceeded the restrictions under which the division commander was operating. This was bad enough, but Richardson exacerbated the situation by immediately riding to the other end of his line to tend to the just-arriving 2nd and 3rd Michigan. Instead of remaining behind to shape and guide the first attack by any regiment, Union or Confederate, in the Virginia theater, he left Walrath and his men to their own devices.[57]

In their brigade leader's absence, the New Yorkers advanced unsteadily and in loose order. When they came within range, the Confederates scorched them with a "murderous fire" that seemed to come from every angle. One of Bonham's officers, looking on from Mitchell's Ford, described the musketry as "continual thunder upon thunder until the Earth seemed to shake to its very foundations."

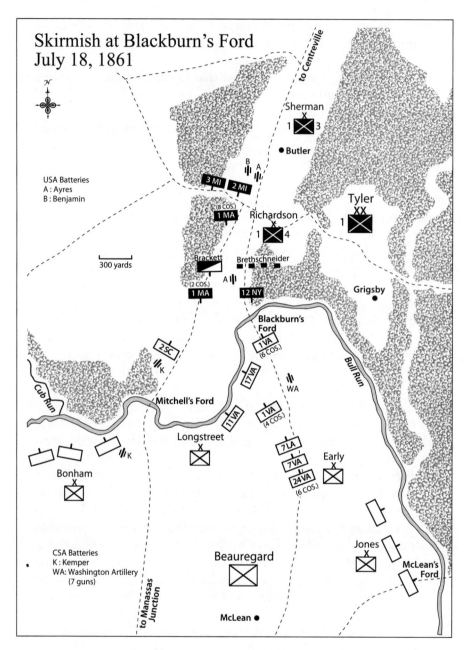

Skirmish at Blackburn's Ford, July 18, 1861. *Map by Paul Dangel.*

A correspondent for the *Charleston Mercury* wrote that "never until now have I dreamed of such a spectacle; for one long mile the whole valley is a boiling crater of dust and smoke."[58]

The effect of the fire was immediate and devastating. Several of Walrath's men fell dead or wounded along the length of the stream; the fatalities included a color bearer decapitated by a solid shot, apparently delivered by Kemper's battery. The sight of such carnage, for which no participant could have prepared himself, caused panic in the ranks. Men began to falter and fall out, looking for safer climes. Due to inexperience, ineptitude, or survival instincts of his own, their colonel failed to stem the mounting rush to the rear.

One of the New Yorkers' problems was an inability to tell friend from foe. At one point a detachment nearly opened fire on the two companies of the 1st Massachusetts, whom they found advancing along a ravine on their right flank. When Colonel Wells later wrote of "balls humming like a bee-hive" around his men's heads, he was referring not just to Confederate bullets. One of Wells's subordinates was shot dead by a Confederate whom the officer mistook for one of his own gray-clad soldiers. The error would be repeated again and again on other parts of the field, especially on July 21.[59]

Those enlisted men unable to advance but too close to the enemy to withdraw were told by their sergeants to lay flat on their stomachs. Some thereby escaped the rain of Rebel missiles, but it was virtually impossible to load and fire from that position, especially when, after a few rounds, rifles began to overheat and foul. One unfortunate rifleman had a round discharge prematurely as he stared down the barrel. Despite the support provided by Ayres, Benjamin, and Wells, those men of the 12th who were not pinned down turned to the rear almost as a body and rushed wildly up the road to the Butler farm.[60]

When he saw what was happening to Walrath, Richardson left his Michiganders and galloped back to the scene. Arriving at the 12th's initial position, he was aghast to find only two companies in some semblance of order. Their less steadfast comrades had left behind—strewn on the ground, as one Confederate reported—"guns, hats, coats, canteens, blankets, anything that would lighten them at all." Richardson hastened to the rear until he overtook a gaggle of fugitives, still running though well beyond range of Longstreet's muskets. "What are you running for?" he shouted. "There is no enemy here!"[61]

Yelling and swearing, Richardson tried his best to whip the frightened men into line and renew the attack. The brigade leader seemed to be "everywhere at once," one man recalled, but his efforts were only temporarily successful. After much exertion—and without assistance from Walrath—he managed to re-form a portion of the regiment. But when a new round of rifle fire lashed them, the New Yorkers fled once again. Eventually, they ran out of breath, milling about indecisively too far from Blackburn's Ford to be of further use to their brigade. The two companies that had stood the initial fire joined them there, having disengaged from the fight in tolerable order. Meanwhile, Brethschneider's skirmishers continued to hold their position in the woods, while the remaining regiments on the right, as Richardson reported, "remained firm and determined." But it would not be enough to salvage a bad day for the advance forces of the Army of Northeastern Virginia.[62]

Longstreet's ability to keep his men hidden until they could rise up and deliver a destructive fire at point-blank range enabled him to repulse what he later described as four successive assaults. But victory did not come effortlessly or without making his men fear for their lives. Tyler's opening cannonade was difficult enough to withstand; by the time his infantry approached the ford, one Virginian wrote, "all nerves were strung to a high tension." Some quickly came unstrung. When the 12th New York began shooting, another Virginian recalled, "it seemed as if 10,000 had opened [up], so terrible was the fire." Thoroughly demoralized, several defenders left their assigned posts and ran for the rear. Most were prodded back into line by their officers, including a saber-wielding Longstreet, who was "determined to give them all that was in the sword and my horse's heels, or stop the break." For the most part, however, drastic measures were not needed; the majority held their ground and delivered a fire accurate and destructive enough to send their attackers reeling backward in wholesale disorder.[63]

Their success in repulsing a host of attackers not only gave the Virginians confidence and a sense of pride but also inspired them to vocalize their feelings in a unique way—a wavering, spine-tingling falsetto raised by one soldier after another. As a member of the 11th Virginia later described it, "each man just opened his mouth as wide as he could, strained his voice to the highest pitch and yelled as long as his breath lasted, then refilling the lungs, repeated it again and again." A Boston newsman who heard the chant likened it to "the war-whoop of the painted warrior or the Western plains." Thus was born the Rebel yell, destined to become the battle cry of Confederate troops in every theater of the conflict.[64]

Even after the Yankees retreated, their assailants were not through punishing them. Longstreet reported that as the survivors of the 12th New York turned to the rear, a bayonet-wielding party of the 17th Virginia, two or more companies under Captain Morton Marye, crossed the run in a limited counterattack. One of Marye's men, stout, middle-aged private Edgar Warfield, caught up to a Yankee, called on him to surrender, and when the man refused "grabbed him by the collar." At such close quarters, firearms were useless, so the antagonists grappled wildly. In the struggle both "rolled down the hill into a spring branch, Yank on top and myself in the mud and water, face down." The venerable private was saved from drowning when a comrade came up and took the Federal prisoner. Warfield, however, had the honor of conducting the captive to the rear. En route he was seen by General Longstreet, who congratulated him on taking "the first prisoner—go back and get another!" Warfield, covered with mud and bruises, "respectfully declined."

Some of Marye's men counterattacked not with fists but with cold steel—bayonets and, reportedly in a few cases, Bowie knives— Warfield's comrade had captured his assailant at bayonet point. Until recalled, the Virginians slashed the rearmost bluecoats into greater speed and panic. Later the Federals, who considered the bayonet a terror weapon, conjured up atrocity stories. In his after-action report, Colonel Richardson claimed that by the orders of some Confederate officers, several wounded members of his brigade were bayoneted as they lay helpless on the field.[65]

Longstreet had not held Blackburn's Ford on his own. Between attacks on his position, the brigadier began to worry that he was roundly outnumbered. Uncertain how long he could stave off the Federals, whose force was plainly composed of several regiments, he dispatched a staff officer to Colonel Early, who had taken up a position in a stand of pines off the road leading from the McLean farm. Early—whose brigade of two and a half infantry regiments (this day it included only six companies of his own regiment, the 24th Virginia, under Lieutenant Colonel Peter Hairston) and three guns of the Washington Artillery under Lieutenant Charles W. Squires—was in good shape to lend assistance. He had just added two more pieces from the Washington Artillery under Captain Benjamin F. Eshelman and had also absorbed the section that Longstreet had sent to the rear under Lieutenant Garnett.

Before the firing began at Blackburn's, Beauregard had placed Early in position to support either Bonham or Longstreet as needed. Now the latter asked to borrow a single "reserve" regiment from the irascible and pugnacious Virginian. But before the colonel could respond, a courier from Beauregard ordered him to send Longstreet two regiments and two cannons. Early began complying by ordering up at the double-quick Colonel Harry T. Hays's 7th Louisiana. Hays would reach Longstreet after Richardson's third advance had been repulsed, but he was in time to blunt and hurl back the final assault. So too were the reserve companies of the 1st Virginia, which Longstreet had called to the firing line.[66]

With the Yankees retiring from their every position, Longstreet determined to cross the run and pursue. Four companies of the 1st Virginia and a small contingent of the 17th responded to his call. As one of their number recalled, "like a pack of hounds after a fox, we got across." To lend the counterattack staying power, Longstreet asked Early for the balance of his command, but before it could arrive, he changed his mind. The stream was so narrow and crossing it so difficult "that I soon found it would be impossible to make a simultaneous movement, and ordered the troops that had succeeded in crossing to return to their positions."[67]

Unaware that the crisis had passed, Early hastened his 7th Virginia and as much of his own outfit as was on hand toward Blackburn's, trailed by his artillery pieces. Passing General Beauregard en route, the Virginians heard him shout: "Keep cool, men, and fire low, shoot them in the legs!" The advice, though well intended, seemed to rattle the rookies' nerves. Upon reaching Longstreet's position, Early attempted to calm them down, assuring the men that "if you don't run, the Yankees will!" In hopes of lending Longstreet quick support, he ordered them to load quickly and fire at will. One of his company commanders responded by telling his men to "load in nine times." An exasperated Early exclaimed: "Hell and damnation! Load in the most expeditious manner possible!"[68]

After the war Longstreet criticized his colleague for not properly supervising his trigger-happy troops. He seems to have had a point. Upon reaching the ford, the 7th Virginia passed between Longstreet's field headquarters and the enemy shore, placing the brigadier, mounted on his war horse, in its line of fire. When some Yankees across the water opened on them, the newcomers panicked. Early admitted that the regiment "was momentarily thrown into confusion by this fire, and discharged many of its own guns over a portion of our own troops in front; fortunately, however, doing them no damage, as I believe."[69]

At the time he wrote, Early must have known that some of Longstreet's men were felled by the friendly fire and that it nearly killed their commander, who had to dive from the saddle to avoid being hit. Shaken but not badly hurt, Longstreet regained his feet once the errant firing subsided, collected the pieces of the expensive pair of field glasses he had been carrying, and went looking for his mount, which had bolted to safety, frightened but uninjured.[70]

Many others had failed to escape injury. When the casualty count was tabulated, Longstreet and Early found that their brigades had suffered a combined total of sixty-three killed or wounded. The injured included the Irish-born Colonel Moore, whose severe head wound would prevent him from continuing in command of the 1st Virginia. Among the dead was Major Carter H. Harrison of the 11th Virginia, shot twice while leading his men across the water near the close of the fighting. By a margin of inches, Longstreet had missed having his name added to the unhappy list.[71]

An opportunity to strike a stunning and dramatic blow for his army, his nation, and himself having gone by the boards, General Tyler ordered Richardson to withdraw his physically and psychologically shaken troops to the far rear under a covering fire from Brethschneider's skirmishers. There was no denying that the attack on Blackburn's Ford had been a botch, but Tyler was determined that the blame not adhere to him. In his postbattle report he disclaimed responsibility for ordering the 12th New York to attack. Ayres's shelling of the south bank, which eventually provoked a response from the Rebels, "accomplished the object I desired, as it showed that the enemy was in force and disclosed the position of his batteries, and had I been at hand the movement would have ended here." By implication, his ranking subordinates, Richardson and Walrath, were the culprits. Six months later, when testifying before Congress, Tyler would go further, insisting that his men had not attacked at all. If so, he never explained how his division had accumulated so many casualties—nineteen men killed, thirty-eight wounded, and twenty-six missing.[72]

Richardson was embarrassed by his brigade's performance and angered by reports that Colonel Walrath had given the initial order to retreat without consulting his superior. To restore his command's good name, after the firing had largely ceased on both sides, Richardson begged Tyler to advance him again to the ford, insisting that if Sherman's brigade were brought up in support they would "clear out those fellows from the [creek] bottom in two hours." Tyler, convinced that Longstreet's position could not be carried and perhaps intimidated by the presence of the clearly disapproving Major Barnard and Captain Fry, refused the request.[73]

Richardson acceded to the general's decision but did not like it much. In a "scornful sort of manner," he ordered his next closest regiment, the 2nd Michigan, to head for the rear before a newly detected body of Confederate horsemen could charge it. The Wolverines wheeled about and marched off; the rest of the brigade followed, its men muttering about a lack of competent leadership. But Tyler was not through with the enemy who had gotten the best of him. For nearly an hour after the infantry withdrew, Ayres and Benjamin dueled with the artillery that Early had placed along the right side of the road to Manassas Junction. The long-range encounter consumed a combined total of more than seven hundred shells but inflicted few casualties on either side, one being the severe wounding of Captain Eshelman.[74]

Although unwilling to confront the enemy at close range, Tyler desired a continuing presence north of Blackburn's Ford. Around two o'clock, as Richardson began his withdrawal, a divisional staff officer galloped to Colonel Sherman's headquarters on the outskirts of Centreville with orders to occupy the position being evacuated. Sherman had been expecting the summons but did not welcome it. He wrote his brother John, "I felt uneasy—The firing was quite sharp at times . . . though my duty was plain[ly] to stand fast" until ordered up.[75]

The reluctant colonel put his men in column and started them toward the battlefield at an extended gait. One participant called the experience "an hour's rushing" through "choking clouds of dust and under that broiling sun," which left men panting and wheezing long before they reached their assigned position. En route they were treated to the horrors of the battlefield, being passed by a line of ambulances bearing shattered men and many walking wounded, some of whom displayed ghastly injuries. All were heading for the field hospital that the army's medical director, Surgeon King, had established in a hotel, a stone church, and a large home in Centreville. Sherman's men also encountered demoralized fugitives who warned that Richardson's brigade had been cut to pieces and that the Rebels were in hot pursuit. "We met too many, far too many straggling soldiers," Sherman wrote, though an exodus of disheartened combatants would be a feature of every battlefield in this war.[76]

Sherman's men reached the front just as the last of Richardson's men departed. Tyler, his combativeness quenched, held the newcomers well back from Bull Run. The position did not spare them from exposure to a thirty-minute cannonade that killed four or five, prompting their colonel to hustle the rest into wooded areas on either side of the ford road. Even there, shells sought them out, sending tree limbs and branches down on heads and bodies. Sherman rode conspicuously through their ranks, doing his utmost to calm frayed nerves. He loudly explained that when a man heard a shell explode, it was too late to duck and cover, so he should not bother doing so. Even as he spoke a thunderous blast struck the top of the tree under which he sat his horse, showering him with foliage. The colonel instinctively hugged his saddle before bobbing up to find the men grinning at his self-protective reflex. Sherman, his face suddenly as red as his hair, declared that on second thought, "you may dodge the big ones." The incident would become one of the most enduring anecdotes of Sherman's celebrated career.[77]

Once Richardson had completely disengaged, around 4:00 P.M., Tyler, who had remained on the scene throughout the artillery contest, moved Sherman's troops out of shelling range. The brigade eventually returned to its bivouac outside Centreville. Sherman was not pleased with the way his men had stood fire; their behavior, he complained, showed "a great want of Discipline." He told his brother ruefully, "Twill take time to make soldiers of them." An enlisted man in the 2nd Michigan had a different perspective on the troops' participation: "The men generally behaved well. I am not so certain ab[ou]t the officers."[78]

When describing the fighting to Ellen, Sherman ran his criticism up the ladder of command. His once-strong faith in General Tyler, largely the product of the man's prewar reputation, had been shaken. He admitted that victory belonged to the enemy—Longstreet's men had had "the best of it," and Tyler had produced "a Blunder!" That view would be shared by many of those who had taken part in the glorified skirmish and one who had not—Irvin McDowell. Thus ended an engagement that the Confederacy would call (logically enough) the Battle of Bull Run but which the Union would dub the Battle (or Skirmish) of Blackburn's Ford.[79]

DUELING OFFENSIVES

F or hours the Confederate capital had strained to catch the report of cannons at Blackburn's Ford. Eighteen-year-old Constance Cary, daughter of one of Virginia's most prominent families, described the experience as "a long, long day of waiting, of watching, of weeping, of praying, of rushing out upon the railway track to walk as far as we dared in the direction whence came that intolerable booming of artillery."

Richmond remained uncertain of the result for hours after the shelling ceased. Late in the day wounded soldiers began to arrive at the depot of the Virginia Central Railroad to be admitted to the general hospitals of the city. They brought news that the first American engagement of any size involving "civilized white men" since the Mexican War had been a complete and glorious victory. The glad news quickly made its way to Miss Cary's doorstep, enabling her to resume normal breathing. Even so, she understood that the terrible suspense would return once the larger, more decisive engagement everyone believed imminent would get underway. Until then, all she could do was to pray for guidance and deliverance from the deity whom she and every other pious Southerner knew to favor Confederate triumph.[1]

Sometime after the shooting ceased at Blackburn's Ford—Tyler recalled the time as five o'clock—General McDowell reached the field of battle. The army commander arrived in style, accompanied by a retinue that included not only staff officers but also Governor Sprague of Rhode Island, who had fallen in with the army ostensibly to keep an eye on his state's regiments but in fact to indulge his lifelong fascination with war. It appears that McDowell was not in the saddle but was riding in a special conveyance, a "covered hackney coach" that reminded one observer, Lieutenant Averell of the Mounted Riflemen, of Napoleon during his European campaigns: "After setting his Marshals in motion he would be driven in a comfortable carriage to some distant and unthought of" place that would give him a unique vantage point from which to observe the working of his own genius. Presumably, the hackney had accompanied the general from Alexandria. It would have been delicious irony had McDowell, the scourge of looters everywhere, appropriated it from a local resident.[2]

As the spike-helmeted officer alighted from his coach, bystanders, including Sherman, saw that he was in a grim mood. Almost at once he began throwing out sharply worded questions—first to his on-scene emissaries, Fry and Barnard, who provided unsettling answers. Everything else he needed to know was evident in the faces and the body language of the subordinates who had controlled the afternoon's fighting. McDowell had wanted Tyler to reconnoiter, not to attack, and Tyler knew it—there had been no miscommunication. Avoiding a clash along Beauregard's right flank was important to McDowell's strategy, which included a decisive strike in that same sector with a considerable portion of the army. Now the Rebels had been alerted to strengthen that flank; McDowell would have to revamp his planning on short notice.

By some accounts, even when he discovered the magnitude of Tyler's blunder, the army commander managed to curb his temper, quietly asking the division leader for an operational report and ordering him to reoccupy the high ground where Richardson had been engaged. (This was a repetition of an order he had sent earlier that day, which Tyler had ignored.) Despite the air of calm, it was apparent to Sherman and other onlookers that McDowell was vastly displeased with his senior lieutenant. Tyler, who believed himself guiltless, resented the general's attitude. The bad blood that sprang up between the two men on this occasion would never diminish; it would exert far-reaching effects on the Army of Northeastern Virginia.[3]

Tyler may have had a point. McDowell's anger over the bungled skirmish seems to have been something of an overreaction. After all, the movement, clumsy as it was, had gained information of value—specifically, the locations of Longstreet's, Bonham's, and Early's forces. Recognizing this, McDowell might have reproved Tyler in a more private setting. News of their simmering confrontation spread quickly throughout the ranks and even inside Confederate lines; one of Beauregard's staff officers was later heard to exclaim, "Poor Tyler, his decapitation has come early." Still, McDowell had ample reason to be displeased. Through heavy-handedness and overweening ambition, Tyler had damaged the army's blueprint of operations beyond repair.[4]

Whether or not McDowell appreciated it, there was a human dimension to Tyler's repulse, one that promised to affect the psyche of the troops engaged. Though the fighting consumed only a few hours, the army had suffered fairly heavily, and it showed. A semi-literate member of the 2nd Michigan called this first battlefield of the war "the awfulist site that I ever sawe," some of the dead having "their legs off, some with an arm off some with now [no] hed some with there face off, one in partickler with . . . a hole throught him Big enough to stick your head in." Survivors were suddenly aware of what might happen to them the next time they encountered a Rebel battle line, especially if braced with artillery.[5]

The dead would provide a grim reminder for some time to come. The Confederates would complain that the retreating enemy had made little effort to inter their fatalities. According to one local civilian, "more than sixty men were found rotting in the field." A correspondent with the *Charleston Mercury* traveling with the Army of the Potomac lamented that while some bodies were doubtless carried off, "it argues a singular want of humanity that they should permit those [others] to be unburied." Days after the fight the victors, no doubt with the help of slave labor, interred the dead, a chore that for the rest of the war would generally be left to those who held the field at battle's end.[6]

The casualty roll would pale in comparison to those of later actions, including the one only three days away—officially, the fighting at Blackburn's Ford would be designated a mere skirmish. Yet that list was long enough to lower the Federals' morale, which until that afternoon had been stratospheric. Lieutenant Averell was shocked to hear that Tyler's men had "acted badly." Colonel Willcox remarked, "we felt chilled on hearing the result, particularly as a New York regiment behaved shamefully." As Captain Fry put it years later, "the depressing effect of the repulse [of Tyler's troops] was not confined to them; the whole army felt it." The affair, wrote a Connecticut soldier who had not taken part, "had a disheartening effect upon our soldiers, especially those who thought the rebels would not fight." A member of Sherman's 79th New York agreed that the fighting of the eighteenth proved that "the 'Johnnies' *would fight!* And our dreams of a 'walk over' were dispelled." If McDowell's army had ever dared believe itself invincible, it did no longer.[7]

Conversely, the victory, small as it would appear a few days hence, buoyed up the spirits of Beauregard's army. Its leader bestowed effusive praise on Longstreet's and Early's brigades and made sure word of it was disseminated far and wide. He also wired the happy news to Jefferson Davis, who telegraphed back an expression of his gratification. Longstreet's exemplary conduct in this, his first spate of combat since taking a musket ball in the thigh at Chapultepec, presaged the success and acclaim he would win in numerous latter battles.[8]

Amid soldiers' shouts that "the Valley Boys have come," the train bearing Jackson's brigade lurched to a halt at Manassas around four o'clock on the afternoon of Friday, July 19. Later trains unloaded half of Bartow's brigade at the depot soon after dawn of the twentieth, and two regiments and two companies of Bee's brigade, accompanied by General Johnston, around noon of that same day. Bee's 6th North Carolina would not arrive until midday of the twenty-first after recovering from its mishaps en route. These units—about 50 percent of the Army of the Shenandoah—thus reached the field of battle in ample time to take part in the coming fight. Because Elzey's brigade did not leave Piedmont Station until almost 3:00 A.M. on the twenty-first, its ability to take part would remain a matter of conjecture well after the battle commenced in the early morning of that torrid summer Sunday.[9]

Generations of scholars have cited the Manassas Gap Railroad's ability to get enough of Johnston's men to Manassas in time for action as critical to the outcome of the first large land battle of the conflict. It would seem, however, that too much importance has been placed on the value of the troop transfer by rail. It is true that Johnston's army moved glacially after leaving Winchester (it took Jackson's men eighteen hours to cover the twenty-three miles to Piedmont Station), but had they maintained that pace the rest of the way, they would have reached Beauregard in time to join the fight. In fact, had Johnston's army marched the thirty-four miles to Beauregard's headquarters in a little over twenty-four hours—which would have been entirely possible even with periodic rest halts— Smith's brigade could have reached Manassas by sundown on the twentieth or shortly afterward. The latest arrivals still would have enjoyed some hours to rest and regain their stamina before being committed to battle. And even if fatigued when the shooting started, the accompanying adrenalin rush would have quickly restored their physical and emotional strength.

Not only would it have been possible for all of Johnston's troops to march to Manassas in time to meet McDowell's attack, but they also would not have been kept idle for long periods en route. As it was, at Piedmont and thereabouts Bartow's and Bee's men spent ten to twelve hours waiting for the return of the trains that had transported Jackson's troops ahead of them, hours they could have spent more profitably on the move. In fact, they would have had to march only partway to Manassas; the returning train could have met them on the road and carried them the rest of the way in much quicker time than a full trip from Piedmont would have taken.

To be sure, the additional marching would have left the men footsore, but the journey would not have made undue demands on their health. After the war one of Bee's aides, Major William P. Shingler, insisted that his boss believed his men could have marched to Manassas in good time and without ill effect—in fact, he would have preferred that they had done so. Bee put his men aboard trains for two reasons: Johnston ordered him to do so, and Bee was concerned that his route of march, so near to Charles Town, might tempt Patterson to attack him in transit.[10]

Another advantage to traveling by foot was that Bartow's and Bee's brigades would have been assured of reaching the battlefield intact instead of at half strength. The additional men thus brought into the battle would have more than compensated for the loss of Elzey's brigade, which having made the slowest time on the roads from Winchester, would not have made it to Manassas by shank's mare before the fighting ended. Finally, by making the entire journey on foot, Johnston would have avoided not only the vexing delays caused by lazy or treasonous crewmen but also the mechanical problems that almost cost the 6th North Carolina the chance to see action on the twenty-first.

Any argument that seeks to downplay the role of the Manassas Gap Railroad in this campaign may appear unconvincing to present-day readers, but at the very least it provides food for thought. The delays and difficulties Johnston experienced en route to Beauregard's headquarters call into question the advisability of his commitment to an obsolete, underfunded, and overburdened transportation system. The little railroad may have gotten almost half an army to the field of battle, but the reliance Johnston placed on it may well have been counterproductive rather than essential to victory.

When Johnston alighted at Manassas around noon on July 20, he was dead tired, having been awake—on his feet or in the saddle— for almost seventy-two hours. Upon debarking, the Alabamians and Mississippians who had accompanied him were guided to bivouac areas in the fields south of Bull Run, where they could catch some sleep. Johnston did not have that luxury; as soon as he set foot on solid ground, he was provided with a mount and, trailed by his staff, escorted to Beauregard's headquarters at the McLean house.

After exchanging salutes, the two men would have studied one another more or less intensely. They had seen little of each other since their years in the old army, one of their last encounters having been at Chapultepec, where they had made a bet on Beauregard's ability to slay Mexicans at long range—or perhaps afterward in a cantina where, according to Beauregard, Johnston, the loser in the bet, paid for the evening's drinks. Now the two were placing a bet at even longer odds: that by joining forces, they could defeat an enemy that would still outnumber them.

Beauregard was of course happy and relieved to have Johnston finally on hand. Even after Richmond forwarded his plea for assistance to Winchester, the Louisianan had reason for concern that his colleague would arrive too late, if at all. Years later he would cite a telegram from General Cooper, dated July 19, explaining that as of that date, Richmond was in the dark about Johnston's response to the request for help and adding that "if the enemy in front of you has abandoned an immediate attack, and General Johnston has not moved, you had better withdraw your call upon him, so that he may be left to his full discretion." Having received this news immediately following Tyler's attack on Blackburn's Ford, Beauregard suspected that another, larger, assault was in the offing. Cooper's suggestion that he rescind his request for reinforcements left him flabbergasted and angry as well as fearful that help was not on the way.[11]

On one count Johnston's arrival may have displeased Beauregard, for it confirmed Jackson's statement that the Army of the Shenandoah was coming entirely by train. The knowledge that Johnston had rejected the plan for a double strike against McDowell may have peaked Beauregard's suspicion that his colleague was as cautious and unimaginative as Davis and Cooper. Obviously, the

Virginian shared the government's inability to appreciate classical Napoleonic thinking as served up by a highly knowledgeable disciple of the great captain.

Of course, the importance of arriving reinforcements overrode Beauregard's disappointment that another of his brilliant ideas had been ignored. The Bull Run line would now be held by an additional 2,400 men under Jackson and a combined total of 2,700 under Bee and Bartow. While Beauregard could not be certain these would suffice to check McDowell—now believed to be have at least 30,000 men—they would certainly help even the odds. Before Johnston's arrival, Beauregard had been reinforced from Fredericksburg (Holmes's brigade), Leesburg (Hunton's 8th Virginia), Richmond (Colonel Duncan K. McRae's 5th North Carolina), and Lynchburg (Colonel William Barksdale's 13th Mississippi). Beauregard would assign Hunton's eight companies to Philip St. George Cocke's brigade, McRae's men to Longstreet's brigade, and Barksdale's eventually to Early's. The battalion-size contingent of infantry in Hampton's well-regarded legion was also on the way from the Confederate capital, although it was making excruciating progress on a couple of overburdened railroads.[12]

Although excessively fatigued, Johnston would have taken the measure of his fellow army commander who, thanks to his success at Charleston and the newspaper coverage given his assignment to command at Manassas, had become the public face of Confederate military leadership. This must have rankled Johnston at least to some degree, for he was acutely aware that he himself had been relegated to a secondary theater of operations, one that lacked the attention and support Richmond had given Beauregard. Johnston thought of himself as untainted by such base emotions as jealousy and envy, but he could never completely suppress his conviction that Beauregard had been the unworthy recipient of high-level favoritism.

His view of Beauregard as a soldier was generally favorable, but he would have perceived some faults and limitations. From long-distance communication with him and from what knowledgeable observers had told him, Johnston knew of the Creole's outsize ego, his tendency to pose and preen, his unflagging effort to curry favor with politicians and editors, his habit of dispensing unsolicited advice to both peers and superiors, and his penchant for grandiose planning. Johnston, of course, had been the recipient of more than one of those plans, which he, along with Davis and Lee, had regarded as out of touch with reality. His latest refusal to accept Beauregard's Napoleonic vision may have created some tension, for the latter would now have to revamp his most recent idea for taking the battle to McDowell.

Although perhaps tempted, Johnston was not inclined to take Beauregard down a peg or two. Yet he was insistent that from the outset of their association, the official nature of their relationship would be recognized and observed. Although both he and Beauregard commanded armies, and even though the latter's was larger, Johnston wanted no question to exist as to who exercised overall command. Ever concerned with rank and preference and wishing to avoid any confusion over seniority, en route from Winchester Johnston had cabled Richmond for guidance on the subject. On the day that the Valley army reached Manassas, President Davis had replied that Johnston, like Lee and Cooper, had been elevated to the rank of full general in the Provisional Army of the Confederacy and was "possessed of all the powers attached to that rank."[13]

This was what Johnston wanted to hear, and he made sure to repeat it to Brigadier General Beauregard. The latter appeared to accept the ruling with equanimity, but something about the whole thing, perhaps the way Johnston went about promoting it—publishing an official order in which he named himself commander of the united armies—appears to have nettled him. Recalling the incident years later, the Louisianan wrote that he had never dreamed of disputing Johnston's seniority. He felt not "the least jealousy about rank" and insisted that his efforts were uniformly "directed to the one purpose of success in the fateful struggle at hand."[14]

It is difficult to believe that Beauregard was not resentful of Johnston's seniority. When he wrote after the war, he could not refrain from noting that he had been appointed a Confederate general almost two months before Johnston resigned his U.S. Army commission "and seventy-five days before he was made a Brigadier General in the Confederate army." Even so, he duly submitted to the Confederate Congress's March ruling that enabled officers who resigned their commissions in the U.S. Army to enter Confederate service at their old rank. Thus Johnston had joined the Provisional Army as a general officer, Beauregard as a full-rank captain.[15]

Other incidents during this first meeting may have irritated or displeased Beauregard. Johnston, the hard-to-please perfectionist, was predisposed to find fault with anything that his subordinate had planned or achieved prior to his arrival. When Beauregard gave him a general understanding of his six-mile-long line of defense, Johnston found the position lacking. He observed, as he later wrote, that the army's overall posture was "too extensive, and the ground, much of it, too broken, thickly wooded, and intricate, to be studied to any purpose in the brief space of time at my disposal." Johnston may have eluded Patterson, but he doubted he had left him so far behind as to prevent him from pursuing either via Leesburg or through the gaps in the Blue Ridge; thus he had reached Manassas "impressed with the opinion that it was necessary to attack the enemy next morning, to decide the event before the arrival of General Patterson's forces." One can readily imagine that Beauregard would not have appreciated this implied criticism of his logistical ability, but Johnston's view that the army's position was not advantageous for defense reactivated the Creole's preference for a bold offensive.[16]

Then Johnston's host showed him a map drawn by his engineer officers that gave the positions of the army's major elements. Few had changed following the fracas at Blackburn's Ford, though certain improvements had been made largely to accommodate the addition of the Shenandoah troops. Ewell's brigade still held the far right at Union Mills Ford, where it was now supported in rear by Holmes. Jones's troops remained at McLean's Ford, but Early's brigade, with Barksdale's regiment added, had been shifted to the rear of Jones's position. Longstreet continued to defend Blackburn's Ford; Beauregard would order the troops of Bee and Bartow to mass within supporting distance of him.

Mitchell's Ford was still in Bonham's hands. Jackson's brigade was behind Bonham but would be extended so that it also covered Blackburn's. Cocke patrolled the three fords between Mitchell's and Stone Bridge. Because these men covered so many fords and were also responsible for defending the Warrenton Turnpike, Beauregard had bolstered them with Hunton's regiment, three companies of Colonel William Smith's Virginia infantrymen, two four-gun batteries, and a company of cavalry. At and adjacent to Stone Bridge was Major Evans's little brigade, which both Beauregard and Cocke regarded as an element of the latter's command. This arrangement seemed in keeping with Evans's lowly rank.[17]

As for the cavalry and artillery of the combined armies, most of Radford's command had been fragmented and attached to numerous brigades on the front line; two additional companies were posted in rear of Mitchell's Ford. It appears that Beauregard considered the cavalry less valuable as a security force or for gathering intelligence than as a reserve for his infantry. Stuart's recently arrived horsemen —some three hundred members all told—were encamped on a plain extending between Bonham's and Cocke's positions, connecting with the left flank of the former and the right of the latter. Also in reserve were five guns of Walton's battalion and the several batteries of Pendleton's (or Imboden's) artillery, positioned, respectively, behind the right flank of Bee's brigade and in rear of Bonham's far left.[18]

The way Beauregard had distributed his manpower troubled his new commander. Johnston was struck by the lopsided concentration of men and guns along the army's right, to which Beauregard had also committed Jackson, Bee, and Bartow. Beauregard would claim that he had intended to stiffen the left with the remainder of Johnston's army, which he had expected to follow closely behind Bee's brigade. Yet all three of Johnston's brigades on the scene were placed in bivouac behind and equidistant from McLean's and Blackburn's Fords. Johnston, who placed stock in field works, looked askance at the scarcity of earthworks and rifle pits along Bull Run and the absence of heavy artillery positions beyond those at the rail junction. He considered the depot's armament inadequate, consisting as it did of "fourteen or fifteen old twenty-four pounders on naval carriages . . . under the command of naval officers." This was a reference to Captain Isaac S. Sterrett of the C.S. Navy, who had assumed command of the entrenched batteries around Tudor Hall.

Johnston also faulted Beauregard for permitting his engineers to compose a map that showed roads and streams but not contours and elevations. Beauregard's map did, however, include the assumed positions of McDowell's army and the roads—five of which converged at Centreville—by which it would probably advance to the attack come morning. Those same roads, the Louisianan pointed out, would facilitate a Confederate counterstrike.[19]

Beauregard then outlined a plan that he had developed early in the month and had since refined in light of the engagement at Blackburn's Ford and other considerations. It was still predicated on the belief that McDowell would strike heavily at the Confederate line at and near Mitchell's Ford. According to the plan, while Bonham's large brigade, bolstered by cavalry and artillery, held on at Mitchell's, Longstreet's brigade would cross Blackburn's Ford to batter McDowell's left while Jones's brigade would wade the run at McLean's Ford and strike the Union rear, supported farther south via Union Mills Ford by the troops of Ewell and Early. Johnston's newly arrived troops and those expected to follow would augment the attack and, once the Union line had come unhinged and McDowell sent reeling backward, would join the brigades of Cocke and Evans in pursuing the enemy to Centreville and cutting off his retreat to Washington.[20]

The plan was characteristic of its author—bold, sweeping, and dependent on circumstances beyond his ability to control. But it had no chance of being executed because by the evening of the twentieth, while Johnston slept in a grove near Beauregard's headquarters, the Creole had gained some information that undercut its chances of success. It now appeared that at least some of the troops that had been expected to follow Bee and Bartow from Winchester would not reach Manassas in time to fight. Of even greater concern, "reliable sources" (actually exaggerated rumors) had McDowell, commanding as many as 55,000 troops of all arms, already moving west on the Warrenton Turnpike or at least poised to do so.[21]

The information persuaded Beauregard that his opponent was not going to strike his center after all. But the report also strengthened his faith in the effectiveness of attacking the left of McDowell's army and threatening its rear. Thus he quickly had a new plan put on paper, one that he delivered to Johnston at about 4:00 A.M. on the twenty-first. It called for a direct attack on Centreville by four brigades, two from Beauregard's army and two from the Army of the Shenandoah. Bonham, supported by Bartow, was to advance by crossing the run at Mitchell's Ford, while Cocke, with Elzey in close support, was to move to the attack via Stone Bridge and adjacent fords. Meanwhile, Ewell, supported by Holmes, would stand ready to support the attack on Centreville or, if so ordered, to move east to Sangster's Cross Roads, near the depot of the same name. Via McLean's Ford, D. R. Jones, supported by Early, would join the attack on Centreville or move to Fairfax Station or the nearby courthouse, whichever appeared more desirable. Finally, the brigade of Longstreet, supported by that of Jackson, would cross at McLean's and gain the Union Mills–Centreville road. There both forces would be "held in readiness either to support the attack on Centreville or to move in the direction of Fairfax Court House, according to circumstances."[22]

Beauregard's revised strategy provided for movements to be made "after the fall of Centreville," presumably in pursuit of a beaten foe. This part of the offensive would be entrusted to General Holmes, who would have overall command of Bonham's, Ewell's, and Jones's operations, while Longstreet's and Cocke's brigades would be controlled by an unnamed "second in command." Early's operations were not covered by these instructions; presumably, the brigade would form part of a reserve force that also included Jackson, Bee, Bartow, and Elzey and that, commanded personally by Beauregard, would "move upon the plains between Mitchell's Ford and Stone Bridge."[23]

The new plan assigned a forward movement to every brigade except Evans's and Bee's. By all indications, if McDowell was in fact heading in his direction, Evans would have enough on his plate, while Bee, along with the 1st Virginia Cavalry, the recently arrived artillery of Johnston's army, and still another brigade thought to be en route from the Valley, would be relegated to a mobile reserve. When apprised of the plan, Bee was vastly disappointed with the secondary role assigned him, but like the good soldier he was, he did not vocalize his feelings for fear of impairing brigade morale.[24]

When presented with the new plan, Johnston would be taken aback by what he considered to be its several flaws. Historians have raised objections of their own, especially to the confusing and indefinite language in which the plan was written and the questionable strategy that underlay it. In his 1913 study of the campaign, R. M. Johnston declares, "it would be difficult to conceive a worse drawn-up order." William C. Davis, writing six decades later, notes, "No more ambiguous or confusing battle plan would come forth from this war."[25]

To be sure, the proposal had many faults. The terminology used throughout is vague and contradictory as well as confusingly ungrammatical. In places, Beauregard accurately refers to the various components of his army as brigades, elsewhere as divisions. When addressing operations following the seizure of Centreville, he even contemplates the formation of a corps. These, however, were semantic, not substantive, deficiencies; his subordinates knew the size and function of their commands, inconsistencies of nomenclature notwithstanding. More serious was Beauregard's habit of assigning objectives to forces he could no longer assume would be on hand to join the attack. These included not only Elzey's brigade but also a phantom command under Colonel Cadmus Wilcox, whose

9th Alabama had joined Johnston barely two days before his army left Winchester. It would not make the trip to Manassas in time to fight; while still at Piedmont Station on the twenty-first, it would become part of Smith's Fifth Brigade, Army of the Shenandoah, temporarily commanded by an officer senior to Wilcox, Colonel John H. Forney.[26]

Beauregard's grand design had other flaws as well. His assignment of pursuit forces to T. H. Holmes, an officer barely familiar with the position he had not seen until July 20 and who, presumably for that reason, would play a minor role in the proposed operations, defies logic. The plan failed to fix a starting time for the various attacks. The only instruction given to Ewell, Jones, Longstreet, and their supporting forces was to form abreast of one another and "be held in readiness" for an indefinite period until the word to go into action was received from Johnston. Only the brigades of Bonham, Bartow, and Cocke were ordered to march directly on Centreville, the focal appoint of Beauregard's offensive, though all were urged to adapt their movements to "the nature of the country and of the attack," whatever that meant.

Some criticism of Beauregard's plan seems overdrawn or misleading. R. M. Johnston's complaint that it was not a proper attack order misses the point: it was merely a battle plan. Beauregard's orders of 4:30 told his subordinates merely to stand by because he did not expect the offensive to begin until around 7:30 that morning. William C. Davis's criticism that the plan gave up the inherent advantages of the defensive, while correct on its face, does not address the situation as the Confederate commanders saw it. General Johnston, believing (naively but firmly) that Patterson was on his heels, considered an all-out attack the only alternative available to the combined Confederate armies, and Beauregard, given his predilection for offensive warfare, agreed with this for his own reasons. At bottom, the dearth of fortifications along Bull Run and the many shallow points at which an attacker could cross limited the position's defensive potential. A preemptive strike was the Confederates' best option, perhaps their only option.

By the time Johnston awoke from his slumber, several copies of Beauregard's revised blueprint of operations had been made by his staff. Its creator was proud not only of its strategic and tactical strengths but also of the speed with which he had been able to reshape his thinking and put it on paper. His pride of authorship survived the war; thus more than twenty years later when Johnston was publicly critical of the original plan, took credit for making it workable ("as fought, the battle was made by me"), and claimed that he had wanted an even earlier attack than his subordinate did, Beauregard was properly offended. Johnston's ego was such that he could not admit he did not shape, or at least reshape, the Confederate plan of battle. Because that plan was overtaken by events and thus never implemented, he could make a case for a critical role in developing it. Had it been put to the test and found to fail, one imagines that Johnston would never have claimed paternity.

In his postwar writings Beauregard struck back by arguing in print that the plan was his, that Johnston's revisions once the fighting began were mere responses to unforeseen circumstances, and that he had wanted to attack the Union left soon after Johnston reached him but that "subsequent inquiry" made it advisable to defer the movement until dawn of the twenty-first. He would also claim that the Virginian's supposed avidity for an early and sweeping offensive was a sham. He notes, "our systems of warfare are different. I believe in risking a battle at times to accomplish great ends," while Johnston was basically defensive minded, hesitant to strike, and willing to abandon any position when pressed. Thus Beauregard believed that his superior was taken aback by his emphasis on bold action but thought it best to make no issue of it.[27]

Though he considered it seriously flawed, Johnston agreed to the plan as summarized by Beauregard late on July 20 "without hesitation." The next morning, however, he hesitated. He found the plan, as committed to paper, substantially different from the original version. Johnston noted that under the first plan, "all of our forces would have been concentrated near Centreville, to attack the Federal army." The orders he was shown after awakening called for only four brigades to attack toward the village, one and a half of which (Elzey's and the second half of Bartow's) had yet to arrive from the Valley. He doubted that what remained could prevail against McDowell's numbers, especially as the troops Beauregard had designated to support them on the right would start from points too distant to ensure timely help. Johnston approved the written plan because it at least promised to set the combined armies into motion; once that occurred, their movements could be altered as conditions warranted.

Another troubling discovery drew a brief objection from the senior general. Copies of the order had been signed by Beauregard as if he held overall command, "my sanction," Johnston recalled, "to be written on each copy." Though the implication that his subordinate outranked him was grating, Johnston realized the matter "was too immaterial to be worth correction" as well as too time consuming given battle's imminence. Still, Beauregard received another black mark in the Virginian's book of military custom and procedure.[28]

A final issue remained to be worked out before the generals gave undivided attention to executing an attack order. Before he took his rest, Johnston had made a decision that would have a major effect on the conduct of operations. Although he, by virtue of seniority, had the right to make tactical decisions, he would delegate it—a large share of it at any rate—to Beauregard, who had a much better understanding of the ground upon which the battle would be fought as well as a knowledge of the strengths and capabilities of the units that would make the fight and those of their officers. Johnston would exercise overall strategic direction while giving Beauregard the benefit of his experience through advice and support.

On the face of it, this arrangement was a logical one, but it created a win-win situation for Johnston. Should Confederate arms prevail, he, as senior commander, should receive the majority of the credit and glory. If the army met defeat—a possibility Johnston could not discount even should the opposing forces be of equal size—Beauregard, as tactical coordinator, would probably absorb most of the blame. Later he would deny entrusting field command to his subordinate, but this is essentially what happened.[29]

Johnston understood that by the morning of the twenty-first, it was too late for him to nitpick any aspects of the plan, much less demand major changes. But it was not too late for a tweak or two. He recommended shifting Jackson and Bee into position to support the suddenly endangered left flank. Beauregard not only concurred with this revision but displayed his shared concern for that sector by declaring that when it arrived, the Hampton Legion would be added to the forces to move in that direction.[30]

Sometime after 4:30, only minutes before sunrise, Beauregard finally distributed copies of the order to his commanders, advising them to stand ready to "move at a moment's notice"—that is, as soon as the supposed intention of the enemy would be sufficiently apparent. It became sufficiently apparent within the hour.

By five o'clock or shortly after, McDowell was moving to envelop the Confederate left beyond Stone Bridge. His plan of attack was eerily similar to Beauregard's, but he had beaten his adversary to the punch. Beauregard would have to react to his operations, not vice versa.[31]

Irvin McDowell has been pilloried by historians for wasting two days at Centreville, giving Johnston time to arrive at Manassas and Beauregard time to plan a preemptive strike. For a variety of reasons, however, the Union commander had little choice. Having arrived at Centreville without a tactical plan, he had to improvise one. His initial intention, to move around the Rebel right by crossing the Occoquan River at Wolf Run Shoals and breaking the Orange & Alexandria southwest of Manassas, had been thwarted by Tyler's repulse at Blackburn's Ford. The enemy would be alert to another strike in that same area, making it seem as if McDowell must now move against the enemy's center or left. But that could be risky, for Beauregard might anticipate the need to strike those sectors.[32]

Planning anew was not the extent of McDowell's time-consuming chores, for he had to tend to matters involving morale, logistics, casualties, and public affairs. By the evening of the eighteenth, his soldiers were in declining spirits, partly due to the weather. That night the Centreville vicinity was swept by a series of thundershowers. Denied tents and dry firewood, the army was more or less miserable in its various positions. Tyler's division crowded both sides of the turnpike one mile west of Centreville; Hunter's bivouacs sprawled about two miles east of the place; Miles's command occupied the village itself; and the cheerless camps of Heintzelman's division stretched off to the southeast along the Braddock Road. Meanwhile, the New Jersey volunteers and militia under Runyon remained beyond supporting range of the main army, having been brought forward only as far as needed to guard communications. The Fourth Division's advance echelon was fully seven miles in rear of Centreville.[33]

In their sodden bivouacs McDowell's troops were assailed by hunger pangs. The original plan for the campaign had called for three days' rations carried in the men's haversacks, but by the evening of the eighteenth, for the most part, these had been consumed. Subsistence trains would not accompany the army but would follow it to its forward positions. Unlike the grossly inadequate

Confederate commissariat at Manassas, the Army of Northeastern Virginia had abundant edibles to draw upon—the trick was getting them to where they were needed.

McDowell had envisioned the manning of two supply trains, one to move from Alexandria via the O&A or the Little River Turnpike. The other, to be parked at Vienna, was intended to supply Tyler's column should it fail to reach the larger train before the fighting started. It had been expected that either or both trains, a total of almost 250 wagons, would be ready to move the day the troops began their movement to Fairfax Court House and thus would be at the front before the marching rations were gone. But not until the fifteenth were the trains—now three in all—assembled; only then did the loading of five days' extra rations begin. As McDowell's commissary of subsistence later reported, the transportation process was slowed appreciably by a last-minute shortage of wagons as well as by "many worthless teamsters and green teams."[34]

The first train, commanded by Lieutenant John P. Hawkins, consisted of nearly sixty wagons carrying beans, rice, bread in the form of hardtack, coffee, and sugar and trailed by ninety cattle capable of furnishing almost 50,000 meals of fresh beef. Soon after starting out, the convoy was halted by large bodies of slowly marching troops. Forced to use secondary roads that wandered across the landscape and abruptly petered out at stream beds and inside woods, Hawkins appeared to have little chance of meeting McDowell's timetable. But the thirty-year-old Hoosier, an energetic and resourceful officer who would rise to brevet major general by war's end and a quarter century later to commissary general of the army, managed to push through to Fairfax Court House by 7:00 A.M. on the eighteenth. There he hoped to distribute his wares, but just as he arrived, the army began to move to Centreville (all but the 4th Michigan of Willcox's brigade, which McDowell ordered to hold the village while also occupying Fairfax Station). Hawkins was forced to remain at the courthouse until late that afternoon, when his wagons rolled on through and finally reached his eager customers.

At once Hawkins began doling out rations to the commissary sergeants of the various regiments in the commands he had been assigned to supply, the divisions of Hunter and Miles. The other trains, intended for the succor of Tyler's and Heintzelman's divisions and including 135 head of cattle, did not make contact with the army that morning. As an expedient, the approximately 70,000 rations in Hawkins's train were doled out to regiments in every division. When the other trains finally reached Fairfax Court House, they were at once ordered up to Centreville, where they supplied the regiments that had failed to draw on Hawkins's cargo.[35]

Not until the evening of the nineteenth were most of the nearly 200,000 packaged dry rations and many of the 120,000 fresh beef rations distributed. For hundreds of famished soldiers, the edibles arrived not an hour too soon. A Massachusetts enlisted man reported that his outfit had been reduced to a single piece of hardtack per soldier, a situation typical of the army as a whole. Having thwarted mass starvation, some of the wagons made for Fairfax Station, where an advanced commissary depot was under construction. Others trundled back to Alexandria to reload prior to a return trip to the front.[36]

Historians such as R. M. Johnston have concluded that the delay caused by the need to succor his army was insufficient to have prevented McDowell from attacking on July 20. Supposedly, the freshly delivered rations were in the soldiers' hands (or their stomachs) by midday on the nineteenth. This is unlikely, however, for the last of the commissary trains did not reach Centreville until late on the morning of the nineteenth. It is not farfetched to assume that the unloading and allotting of the dry rations and the time-consuming process of butchering the cattle to provide the army's meat ration extended into the afternoon of July 20. In sum, the army was not fully fed until sometime on the twentieth, making that day unsuitable for the full-scale attack McDowell contemplated.[37]

While at Centreville, the Union commander probably took the time to familiarize himself with the physical condition of his army. He would have consulted with Captain Fry, others members of his staff, and perhaps with Tyler via courier to learn the extent of the losses at Blackburn's Ford. He may also have spoken with Medical Director King, who had been doing all in his power to relieve what one historian has called "the almost utter chaos" that enveloped the army's medical service in the aftermath of the July 18 skirmish. This situation was probably unpreventable, for the army's surgeons were woefully unprepared for ministering to wounded men under battle conditions. For a typical surgeon, Lieutenant Charles Carroll Gray of the 2nd U.S. Cavalry, Blackburn's Ford had been "the first time I was ever under fire—the real article," and even considering the limited scope of the fight, the experience had been almost overwhelming.[38]

The medical chaos encompassed not only the treatment of the wounded and disabled but also the neglect and abuse many of them suffered at the hands of their own officers. When Tyler's division withdrew to Centreville after the fight, two of the army's black-topped, two-wheel ambulances, both crammed to overflowing with casualties, were prevented from reaching the nearest field hospital by troops who clogged the only road; the delay consumed several hours. On the twentieth those wounded men whose condition had sufficiently stabilized were evacuated to Fairfax Court House prior to being transported by rail to a newly established general hospital at Alexandria. There, finally, they would receive the level of attention and care that should have been available to them at the front.[39]

At Centreville McDowell lost additional time when forced to pay court to a throng of civilian visitors. Noncombatants had accompanied the Army of Northeastern Virginia since its first day's march from Washington. These were not just newspaper reporters and the usual camp followers but also dispossessed unionists who hoped to reoccupy the homes from which they had been driven by violence or intimidation. Other civilians hoped to profit from a close association with the army, one being Matthew Brady. The bespectacled New Yorker, one of the North's leading portrait photographers, kept pace with the troops in a wagon that contained his camera, a supply of wet plates, and various photographic chemicals. Brady had visions of making history by recording images of a battlefield still drenched in blood, something no other American had accomplished. He would observe the blood but experience not a shred of glory.[40]

Then there were the war observers of the nonprofessional variety. By July 19–20, swarms of curious Washingtonians had descended on the moving army, accompanying it in carriages and in a few cases omnibuses, all hoping for a ringside seat from which to observe at a safe distance the battle they knew to be imminent. They thronged the camps of the regiments at Fairfax Court House and Centreville, making a nuisance of themselves as well as a possible impediment to military mobility. Captain Fry described the uninvited visitors as "under no military restraint" and "so numerous that as they . . . passed to and fro among the troops, the camp fairly resembled a monster military picnic ground."[41]

The boisterous throng included a number of distinguished men, including civilian officials to whom McDowell was compelled to grant an audience. Among those who sought his views on the campaign while dispensing unsolicited advice were Simon Cameron and Senator Wilson, Rose Greenhow's intimate companion and unwitting confidant. On the twentieth the secretary of war spent several hours at McDowell's field headquarters, during which he reviewed and addressed some of Tyler's regiments. If he had his druthers, the secretary might have lingered another day, but his visit was cut short when another guest at headquarters, Governor Sprague, informed him that based on the latest reports, Beauregard's army, 75,000 strong, was moving on Centreville. Cameron suddenly decided that his services were needed back in Washington.[42]

For his part, Sprague would stay on as a volunteer aide to Colonel Burnside, a position he hoped would permit him to take an active part in the fighting to come. Though Burnside seems to have regarded the governor as unwanted baggage, McDowell thanked him for overestimating Beauregard's forces—the report might shock Cameron into reinforcing the army. In fact, according to some sources, upon decamping, the secretary had promised to rush fifteen new regiments to Centreville. If so, he never delivered on the pledge.[43]

On the twenty-first, more high officials put in an appearance. These included members of Congress who were becoming known as Radical Republicans; among them were Senators Ben Wade of Ohio and Zachariah Chandler of Michigan and Representatives William M. Dunn of Indiana, Albert G. Riddle of Ohio, and Charles B. Hoard and Alfred Ely of New York. Riddle and Ely had come to support and share the fortunes of the regiments that had been raised in their home districts—respectively, the ninety-day 1st Ohio and the two-year 13th New York (the Rochester Regiment). The majority of the notables were on hand in the role of spectators. Safely ensconced with the rear guard at Centreville, they expected to observe what would surely be a great Union victory. But events would not play out as anticipated, especially in the case of Congressman Ely, who much to his surprise and chagrin, would become a participant in the fighting and in consequence would suffer a long interruption to his political career.[44]

Secretary Cameron was not the only visitor of high station to address the troops around Centreville. On the afternoon of the twentieth, McDowell found himself obliged to appeal to the patriotism and fidelity of two units whose terms of service were scheduled to expire within twenty-four hours; the majority of their officers and men had declared themselves unwilling to soldier one minute longer.

McDowell's situation in this regard was a great improvement over that of his colleague in the Shenandoah Valley. Whereas some 90 percent of Robert Patterson's regiments had threatened to melt away before they confronted the Rebels at Winchester, only sixteen of McDowell's fifty-one volunteer and militia regiments had enlisted for three months; these included the four under Runyon that would not see front-line action. One of the short-term outfits, Burnside's 1st Rhode Island, aware that battle was imminent and unwilling to embarrass their old commander, had vowed to stay and fight. Other ninety-day outfits, if pressed, would probably have made the same pledge. Then too, McDowell's forces included a far greater number of regular-army units than at Patterson's disposal: eight companies of infantry, seven of horsemen, nine artillery batteries or portions thereof, and a battalion of marines. These units were not going anywhere except where McDowell pointed them.[45]

The army leader had to work hard to try to retain Colonel John F. Hartranft's 4th Pennsylvania, part of Franklin's brigade, and the battery of light artillery attached to the 8th New York Militia (also known as Varian's Battery, after its commander, Captain Joshua M. Varian), an element of Andrew Porter's brigade. In addressing both units McDowell made the obligatory argument that the army and the nation required the services of every soldier. Colonel Hartranft had made a similar appeal to his regiment as had Secretary Cameron before he left for home.

All efforts were unavailing. The next morning when the army advanced to engage the enemy, Hartranft's and Varian's men remained behind. Later in the day they struck their bivouacs and marched to Fairfax Court House even as the roar of battle rent the air and shook the ground. Not every Pennsylvanian or New Yorker agreed with his comrades' decision to depart or appreciated being bound by it. Sergeant Joseph Corson of the 4th Pennsylvania recalled that "a feeling of shame came over me and I doubt not of most of the command, that we should be marching to the rear to the sound of the enemy's cannon."[46]

Corson's embarrassment only deepened when his outfit passed others moving to the front. Burnside's brigade met the 4th Pennsylvania near the Cub Run crossing of the Warrenton Pike. A Rhode Islander recalled that the departing troops were the recipients of "comments from our men not in the highest degree complimentary to them as men and soldiers." When carriages full of civilians passed, by word or gesture the passengers condemned the 4th as sneaks and cowards. "For myself," wrote one, "I felt as though they all deserved shooting when they got to Washington." The regiment was especially chagrined that so many reporters saw it march off, ensuring that its defection would receive maximum notoriety. William H. Russell was not particularly surprised by the regiment's leave-taking. He would comment that "perhaps the Fourth Pennsylvania were right, but let us hear no more of the excellence of three months' service volunteers."[47]

Though many of its officers accompanied the 4th Pennsylvania to the rear, others contrived to remain behind as volunteer aides to brigade commanders. The highest ranking of these, Hartranft, had his services accepted by Colonel Franklin. For his refusal to turn his back to the enemy, the future brevet major general would be awarded (in 1886) a Medal of Honor. One of his company commanders, disgusted that only half a dozen of his men had been willing to stay and fight, marched to the camp of the New York Fire Zouaves and offered to enlist in the regiment as a private. He too received a staff position at brigade headquarters.[48]

Though its men joined the 4th Pennsylvania in going to the rear, Varian's Battery would officially participate in the fighting to come. The six cannons its gun crews left behind were appropriated by Colonel Blenker of Miles's division. The German immigrant, whose brigade consisted of hundreds of foreign veterans, induced McDowell to reconstitute the battery with "experienced artillerists" from the 8th and 29th New York under Captain Charles Bookwood. The revamped unit would serve so effectively that after its guns were released to the state of New York, it would be rearmed, mustered in for two years, and renamed the 2nd New York Independent Battery.[49]

Much of the time McDowell spent at Centreville was taken up by a series of reconnaissances of various points on the Confederate main defensive line. Ever since framing his campaign strategy weeks earlier—and right up to the debacle at Blackburn's Ford—the general had intended to advance by his left flank against Beauregard's right. Prior to Tyler's skirmish he made a personal inspection of the ground looking toward the presumed location of the enemy's far right near Union Mills.

Around nine o'clock on the morning of the eighteenth, just after reestablishing contact with Heintzelman's errant division,

McDowell set out with a small escort to study the roads toward Wolf Run Shoals. On the way he encountered Major Barnard. Naturally enough, he invited his chief engineer to join him, but due to a miscommunication, Barnard declined. Believing his superior was still trying to locate Heintzelman, the major opted to join General Tyler near Centreville for a proposed reconnaissance of Blackburn's Ford. Apparently unconcerned by Barnard's absence, McDowell went ahead with his errand, which satisfied him that "the roads were too narrow and crooked for so large a body to move over, and the distance around too great to admit of it with any safety. We would become entangled, and our carriages would block up the way." So ended his preference for moving toward Wolf Run Shoals.[50]

When McDowell reached Blackburn's Ford in the aftermath of Tyler's fight, he informed Barnard that he now intended to move the army by its right flank against the Rebel left, which was believed to extend as far west as Stone Bridge. Barnard offered to examine the ground in that area and locate the best route for the new movement. McDowell approved the mission, in so doing deferring (and eventually repressing) an impulse to launch a reconnaissance in force against Bull Run—a sharp penetration of the enemy's position in order "to examine it more closely than we have been able to do." Considering the lengths to which he had gone to keep the enemy ignorant of his intentions, it seems curious that McDowell contemplated such a provocative move. An extensive reconnaissance would have alerted the Confederates to points of evident interest to him, perhaps forcing yet another revision of his strategy.[51]

Early on the sultry morning of July 19, Major Barnard, escorted by a company of regular cavalry, set out on his errand. He rode with a trusted subordinate, Captain Daniel P. Woodbury, as well as with the ubiquitous and irrepressible Governor Sprague. The party cantered out the turnpike as far as Cub Run, at which point, to avoid contact with Rebel pickets, it took a northward track through the little valley formed by that stream.

Persistent rumors had Stone Bridge defended by heavy abatis, at least four guns, and "several thousand men." According to another report, the span was mined with explosives to be detonated as soon as McDowell's vanguard drew near. Thus it could not be relied on as a crossing point. Barnard, however, had heard that a ford two or three miles north of the bridge, marked on the army's inadequate maps as "Sudley Springs," offered a lightly guarded shallow stretch of Bull Run, one that might enable the army to skirt the Rebel left. Moreover, a second accessible crossing, known locally as Poplar (or Red House) Ford, was said to exist midway between Sudley Springs and the bridge. The rub was that no known road connected either crossing to any of the routes available to the army.

According to Barnard, there was some indication that a trail left the turnpike a short distance beyond Cub Run, "by which, opening gates and passing through private grounds, we might reach the fords." This route the major and his subordinate strove mightily to locate, and they believed they found it at a point about four miles from Centreville. But no sooner had they begun to follow it than an enemy patrol appeared in the near distance. Not wishing to bring on an engagement that might disclose McDowell's plans and convinced of "the perfect practicability of the route," Barnard's party turned back to Centreville.[52]

Once back with the army, Barnard and Woodbury talked over what they had learned and what information they lacked. Perhaps the major was not as certain of the fords' accessibility as he later claimed, for he subsequently approved a proposal by Woodbury to make a night reconnaissance along with two other engineer officers and a team of Michigan pioneers with the idea of mapping Sudley Springs and Poplar Fords. When McDowell learned of the expedition, he ordered out a second reconnaissance party comprising not only other subordinates of Barnard but also the officer of topographical engineers attached to the headquarters staff.

Despite the high hopes entertained for the missions, neither accomplished anything of value. Soon after starting out, one or both parties found bodies of Confederate infantry and cavalry barring their path. Reflecting that "it was not our policy to drive in his [Beauregard's] pickets until we were in motion to attack," Barnard terminated both operations. It would prove a fateful decision.[53]

CHAPTER II

"STRANGE MUSIC" BEGINS

Convinced that he had all the topographical information he was likely to get, McDowell early on the twentieth began to commit his revised plan to paper. Because the ford halfway between Sudley Springs and Stone Bridge might be defended, he based his strategy on crossing Bull Run at Sudley, gaining the rear of the enemy guarding Poplar Ford and Stone Bridge, occupying the turnpike as far west as possible, and then sending a substantial force to destroy the Manassas Gap Railroad in the vicinity of Gainesville.[1]

He intended to attain these objectives through a complex operation that included two false attacks and a major assault by a column two divisions strong. One feint would be conducted against Blackburn's Ford by Richardson's brigade, which had been left in the position it had occupied late on the eighteenth. It would be supported by Miles's division, to which it was now attached, charged with protecting the Union rear in and around Centreville. The second diversion would be entrusted to the remaining three brigades of Tyler's division, which would move against Stone Bridge from its current position north of the Warrenton Pike and on both sides of Centreville ridge. Upon reaching the bridge, Tyler was to demonstrate conspicuously as if intending to cross there and deliver the main attack. Instead, that blow would be dealt by the two divisions to follow Tyler on the turnpike: Hunter's, moving from its bivouacs one mile east of Centreville, and Heintzelman's, advancing in Hunter's rear from its camps south of the decrepit little village.

A short distance beyond the Cub Run bridge, near a blacksmith shop, Hunter was to turn off the pike onto the northwestward-leading road that Barnard had attempted to examine. His division would follow the road to Sudley Ford, there to cross Bull Run. A short distance farther south, he would find it necessary to cross a tributary, Catharpin Run, at Sudley Springs Ford. Then he would descend to and below the turnpike, sweeping around the enemy's line and gaining its rear.

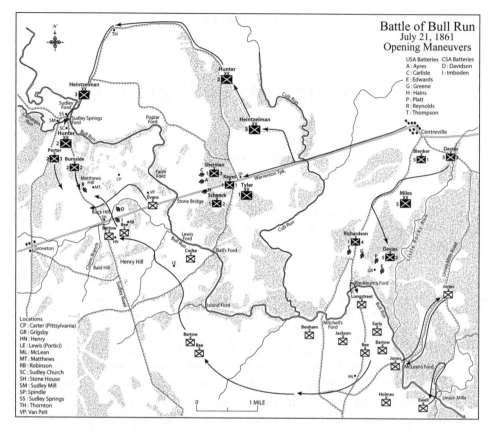

Battle of Bull Run, July 21, 1861: Opening Maneuvers. *Map by Paul Dangel.*

Heintzelman would follow Hunter only as far as the path leading to Poplar Ford, where he was to cross "after the enemy should have been driven out by Hunter's division." In McDowell's mind the dual crossings would not only crumple the enemy's left but put heavy pressure on his center as well. Meanwhile, the presence of Richardson and Miles between Centreville and Blackburn's Ford would hold the troops on the opposite end of Beauregard's line in place, preventing them from reinforcing the points of defense.

McDowell's plan, formalized as General Orders No. 22, called for Tyler to hit the turnpike at 2:30 A.M. on the twenty-first and to begin his noisy demonstration at "full daybreak." Hunter, who had farther to travel, was to break camp at two o'clock; Heintzelman would follow beginning at 2:30. McDowell set no schedule for the

operations below Centreville, where Richardson would be supported by Davies's brigade; Blenker's troops would remain in reserve,
guarding the army's rear. Mindful that Richardson had exceeded
his orders on the eighteenth, McDowell enjoined his new superior,
Miles, to open on the defenders of Blackburn's Ford "with artillery
only" and to "bear in mind that it is a demonstration only." Much
like Winfield Scott warning Patterson that a false step could bring
disaster, McDowell concluded the orders by cautioning his subordinates that "there must be no failure. . . . After completing the movements ordered the troops must be held in order of battle, as they
may be attacked at any moment."[2]

Military analysts have spent the last 150 years taking McDowell's
plan apart piece by piece, scrutinizing its every detail, and declaring
that it could do nothing but fail. Maximum attention is given to the
complexity of the undertaking—the many moving parts that must
operate in precise sequence to ensure coordination and mutual support. This criticism is understandable, for it would appear unlikely
that so many objectives could be achieved by an army of amateur
warriors. In so planning, however, McDowell had few options and
little flexibility.

Even so, he was up to the challenge of formulating a wide-ranging
offensive on short notice. Although he had never planned a battle
in twenty-three years of military service, he had observed enough
combat to perceive that frontal attacks across a meandering stream,
even one with many shallow crossings, would prove as ineffective as
they would costly. The unfavorable terrain along the enemy's right
and Tyler's blundering had made a successful attack in that sector
unlikely. And yet he had sufficiently bolstered the left of his line to
rivet Beauregard's attention on a possible strike out of Centreville.
This buildup at least partially deflects historians' criticism that
a heavy Federal demonstration on the Confederate center would
ease Beauregard's concern about a strike on the right. McDowell's
unwillingness to launch a heavy assault on Blackburn's Ford and
vicinity is usually ascribed to the fear that had been struck in his
heart by Tyler's fiasco. Yet no convincing proof has ever buttressed
the paralysis-of-will argument or the charge made by another venerable historian that Blackburn's Ford had produced "a want of confidence in his soldiers."[3]

To be sure, McDowell's strategy had its share of flaws and deficiencies. The long turning movement of Hunter and Heintzelman

would prolong the Union line of operations, exposing the forward flank and center. The routes of both columns, being at right angles to the main body's line of advance, would cause problems of command and control. The fact that part of the army would remain on one side of Bull Run for an extended period while the rest attacked south of the stream posed another challenge to overall control of the offensive. The turning movement would have other unintended but probably unpreventable consequences. As one historian has written, the operation would result in "cutting off the turning column almost as completely as if it had been the only Federal force on the field" and cause "the line of battle to face almost to the original rear," leaving its right flank vulnerable to attack from Manassas Junction should additional troops of Johnston's army arrive in time to join the fight. These were concerns of some substance, but the primary defect of McDowell's plan was not the complexity of the movements it called for or the dangers they invited. The principal flaw was the reliance it placed on incomplete information about the location of the fords where the flanking columns would cross and the roads leading to them.[4]

As for the oft-repeated accusation that McDowell was making troops unused to heavy marching travel too far to launch an energetic assault, he had originally intended to have Tyler, Hunter, and Heintzelman, at 6:00 P.M. on the twentieth, advance "a few miles" toward the point of divergence from the turnpike, thus shortening the distance they would travel after sunup on what was expected to be another excessively warm day. The army leader canceled the head start only after some of his subordinates objected to the idea of two marches only a few hours apart. A principal opponent was Burnside, whose brigade would lead the turning movement and thus have the farthest to march—a little more than ten miles, although Barnard had advised him that it was more like six. Dropping the idea made sense for another reason: if as Barnard's people had discovered, the roads and the adjacent fields and woods were well guarded, any move down the turnpike, even in the dark, would surely have been detected, tipping off Beauregard.[5]

Theoretically, Burnside and the other subordinates had the opportunity to study and comment on McDowell's battle plan. Around eight o'clock that evening, every division and brigade leader was called to army headquarters for a tactical briefing. Major Barry of the artillery was also summoned as were Major Barnard, Captain

A. W. Whipple of the topographical engineers, and the army's chief signal officer, Major Albert J. Myer.

It took two hours for everyone to assemble in McDowell's candlelit tent—a worrisome reminder of the army's inability to adhere to timetables. Apparently, the meeting was also attended by some of the civilian officials who had been visiting the army. Numerous regimental and staff officers had congregated outside the tent but were not privy to the discussion inside, if discussion is the right word. Colonel Keyes recalled the meeting as "a very short one. It was not a council of war exactly; it was a mere specification of the time in which we should all proceed the next day. The plans appeared to have been digested and matured before that meeting was called."[6]

Although McDowell sought no one's advice or opinion, the meeting was somewhat more substantive than Keyes remembered. The general outlined the army's operations and movements while adding a few details not embedded in the general orders. One concerned Tyler's operations once he reached Stone Bridge. If he found it mined as rumor had it and should the Confederates blow it up, Tyler's engineers had available the tools and materials required to rebuild it. Once the defenders had been displaced, Tyler would cross his infantry and the large number of guns assigned to him. These included the giant 30-pounder siege rifle, whose weight would limit its mobility and therefore its usefulness in battle.

At one point in the war council, McDowell entertained a few questions in hopes of clearing up any ambiguities or misunderstandings. One query must have irked him, though he tried to not let it show. Still smarting from the reprimand, overt and implied, he had received at Blackburn's Ford, Tyler made bold to question the strength of the enemy they would oppose in the morning. When McDowell replied that Tyler knew as much about the matter as he did, the division leader announced that over the past twenty-four hours he and many other officers clearly heard the sound of not-distant locomotives in the direction of Manassas. There could be only one explanation: "General, we have got the whole of Joe Johnston's army in our front, and we must fight the two armies." Giving the impression that he had factored this possibility into his planning, Tyler's superior ignored him and went on with the briefing.[7]

The extent to which McDowell was prepared to face a reinforced opponent remains unknown. His planning thus far had not been based on fighting only Beauregard's troops. By now he had heard rumors that Patterson had failed in his mission to keep Johnston away from Bull Run and that at least some Rebels were en route to Manassas, if they had not already arrived—in fact, he had informed Washington of this prospect. McDowell had long supposed that by the time the army was ready to advance, Beauregard's original force would have added several thousand reinforcements. As he testified before Congress, "I expected they would bring into Manassas every available man they could find."[8]

He had enough soldiers to fight on equal terms a force almost twice as large as the Army of the Potomac, and this should have given him confidence that he could prevail against another 10,000 from the Army of the Shenandoah. Of course, when opponents of near-equal size clash, the advantage normally goes to the defender, but McDowell had faith in the efficacy of his offensive plan despite its eleventh-hour formulation. In any case, he had no choice but to attack and fight the enemy, whatever his size and composition.

McDowell had not wanted to commit to battle an untried army— he had fought forcefully and articulately against the public demand to smash through the Bull Run defenses and take Richmond before the Confederate Congress could assemble there—but his efforts had been unavailing. He had drawn up some promising plans, and despite unexpected setbacks at Fairfax Court House and Blackburn's Ford, they remained viable and executable. Now it was time to put them to the test. A few hours after the meeting in McDowell's tent broke up, the army would be in motion.

For the soldiers under Johnston and Beauregard, especially those forced to remain awake on the front lines, it had been a long and fearful night under a full moon. A reporter who had attached himself to Bonham's brigade wrote that on the eve of battle, the fields and woods on either side of Bull Run lay wrapped in "the stillness of death." The silence was not total: opposing pickets were "hourly having affrays along the whole line, which is now upward of eight miles in length. Except [for] these occasional shots, however, all is quiet." The correspondent knew that this racket would be dwarfed by the noise to come, for assuredly dawn would "break upon a bloody battlefield."[9]

Awaiting the storm, many a Confederate's imagination got the best of him. Lieutenant G. Campbell Brown, a kinsman of Dick Ewell's and his recently appointed aide-de-camp, recalled that "the nerves of all were strained to their highest tension listening for the beginning of the conflict." It had been that way for many hours. The previous afternoon a young lieutenant in Ewell's 6th Alabama whose company was on picket a few miles below Union Mills Ford rode up to Second Brigade headquarters "pale & breathless with excitement." He gasped out the news that the Yankees were crossing a heavy force of all arms from the base of a hill near the ford. "He described it minutely," Brown wrote, and "said that the hill was steep & they had two bridges, one above the other below [the ford] and were then crossing rapidly." Through field glasses the lieutenant had seen "infantry and artillery and an officer on a pure white horse" directing the operation. Asked about the condition of his picket post, the officer admitted that in his haste to sound the alarm, he had forgotten it entirely and feared it had been cut off and its men captured.

Finding the man's story difficult to believe in the absence of evidence, Ewell sent him back to the ford accompanied by a trusted aide. "With a confident air," the lieutenant led the way to the stream, where he pointed out the bridge, the Yankee artillery then crossing it, and the pale rider. Ewell's aide saw only a quiet and intact picket post. It was obvious that the episode had been a "pure fantasy of [a] heated brain." Because the lieutenant was a man of good character, was not known to imbibe, and "showed intense mortification at his error," Ewell attributed the whole thing to the effect of tension and anxiety on a worried, imaginative mind. Brown added charitably that there was some insanity in the man's family, "but not much."[10]

Anxiety gripped not only those on the battlefield but also the residents of two capitals less than one hundred miles apart. For days the people of Washington had been "look[ing] for a *battle in earnest.*" Sensing that it was now only hours away, soon after dawn on the twenty-first they began to congregate in the streets, seeking word, any word, from the front. They importuned army officers passing to and from the War Department and collared newsboys hawking special editions of the city's papers. For some reason the largest body assembled at the construction site on Fifteenth Street and Pennsylvania Avenue where the Treasury Building was undergoing enlargement. A sizable group gathered in front of Willard's Hotel, one block from the White House, where dispatches from the front were read aloud as soon as they were received.[11]

Waking from another restless sleep, President Lincoln, the dream of a portentous journey fresh in his mind, tried to shed the anxiety gnawing at him by attending church services. Afterward he spent hours in the cramped War Department telegraph office poring over reports from McDowell's headquarters relayed from Fairfax Court House, terminus of the military telegraph. Nothing of importance having been received, early in the afternoon he paid a call at the Sixth Street residence of General Scott, whom he awoke from one of his obligatory naps. The venerable soldier assured his visitor that all was well with the army and predicted battlefield success. As if to demonstrate his unconcern, Scott fell back to sleep as soon as Lincoln departed.[12]

That afternoon the president, accompanied by Attorney General Edward Bates of Missouri, took a carriage ride to the Washington Navy Yard to chat with its commander, Admiral John A. B. Dahlgren, the inventor of naval ordnance. The ride seems to have calmed Lincoln's nerves, although he may have borrowed some apprehension from his companion. The border-state politician foresaw the coming battle as the opening phase of a long struggle that would rent his family. Already one of Bates's sons wore Confederate gray; in coming months three other sons would be fighting for the Union.[13]

The high level of anxiety that beset Lincoln and Bates also permeated the capital of an infant nation struggling for survival. For the literary-minded Constance Cary as well as for thousands of her fellow citizens, July 21 was "another unspeakably long day, full of the straining anguish of suspense." Those who could not stand the wait and enjoyed a means of transportation planned to flee the city for the front. While not in the same numbers as their Union counterparts, Confederate officials had already left for Manassas. There they joined small groups of civilians, many of whom had assumed a seat on high ground northwest of the Warrenton Pike–Sudley Road intersection.[14]

Some were on the field not merely to gawk at the combatants. There too was Edmund Ruffin, who had taken up arms in defense of Virginia and hoped to demonstrate his resolve in the hours ahead. Correspondents of such newspapers as Richmond's *Dispatch* and *Enquirer*, the *Mercury* and the *Courier* of Charleston, the *Savannah Republican*, the *Montgomery Advertiser*, the *Columbus Times* of Georgia, and the *New Orleans Picayune* found observation perches that would enable them to glimpse the battle from afar. Late in the afternoon the crowd would be joined by President Davis, who, unable to endure the distance between Richmond and the battlefield, had taken a special train to Manassas. He left behind an equally nervous General Lee, who from his War Department desk had to glean whatever information was available from second- and thirdhand sources.[15]

All of Richmond was in a state of agitation and uncertainty. Government officials, including members of Davis's cabinet, seeking the latest news from the front, had gathered in the offices of Lee, General Cooper, and Secretary Walker. Outside, crowds clustered around the Spottswood Hotel, hoping to get a glimpse of and hear some words from the hostelry's high-profile clientele, which included Senators Wigfall and Chesnut, Secretary of the Navy Stephen Mallory, and former secretary of state Robert A. Toombs. Other groups milled about Mechanics Hall at the corner of Franklin and Ninth Streets, straining to catch the distant thunder of the opening guns. John W. Daniel, editor of the *Richmond Examiner,* observed that "the deepest anxiety that can overwhelm the human heart is settled on this city."[16]

Richmond knew all too well that while the North might survive a defeat in the battle to be fought this day, the army, the government, and the people of the South might not. As the day progressed, what Miss Cary called the "burning excitement over the impending general engagement" grew hotter. It seemed inevitable that the events of July 21 "would decide the fate of the young Confederacy."[17]

Those Confederates "listening for the beginning of the conflict," if close enough to the Warrenton Turnpike to hear the shuffle of soldiers' feet, the clatter of horses' hooves, and the crunch of battery wheels, would conclude that almost an hour before sunrise—just shy of 5:00 A.M.—the battle was effectively underway. By 5:30 these sounds had become clearly discernible to every Rebel along the pike, and increasingly portentous. Intermingled with these warlike noises, however, were more soothing sounds, although their meaning was ambiguous. A worried Virginian on picket at Lewis Ford heard the shouts and cheers of Yankee soldiers as Tyler's division began its noisy demonstration. These were suddenly accompanied by music from a band belonging to one of Schenck's regiments. Under ordinary circumstances the picket would have enjoyed the tuneful strains, "yet just then they were extremely saddening, because they

indicated defeat to us." A less fatalistic South Carolinian nevertheless admitted to being "a little uneasy" at this melodic harbinger of
coming violence.[18]

At 6:15 an unearthly blast, quickly followed by two others just
as loud and as violent as the first, signified the commencement of
the day's fighting. Three four-inch percussion shells flew from the
barrel of the 30-pounder Parrott attached to General Tyler's division, almost a mile east of Stone Bridge. The first round sailed harmlessly over the heads of the nearest Confederates to land a mile and
a half away in the open fields of a farm owned by one Abraham Van
Pelt. The other shells came closer to taking human life, striking the
ground around a signal station that E. P. Alexander had established
on a hill near Van Pelt's house, penetrating a tent the captain had
just vacated.[19]

The source of this consternation—officially a component
of Lieutenant John Edwards's Company G, 1st U.S. Artillery of
Richardson's brigade, then on loan to General Schenck—was a technological marvel. A sergeant from Maine who had a close-up view
considered the 6,000-pound monster "as spectacular and burdensome as a mock dragon at the head of a Chinese parade." The physical enormity of the piece, whose predawn passage of Cub Run had
nearly caused the suspension bridge to cave in, made the soldier
wonder "if it was intended to frighten away the evil spirit of masked
batteries," those that had dealt Schenck's troops blows material
and psychological five weeks ago. A correspondent of the *New
York World*, observing the initial discharge of the gun, wrote that
"the reverberation was tremendous, shaking through the hills like
the volley of a dozen plebian cannon, and the roar of the revolving
shell indescribable."[20]

The firing of the Parrott, the care and feeding of which had been
entrusted to a young West Pointer, Lieutenant Peter C. Hains of the
2nd U.S. Artillery, signaled to the far-flung elements of the army that
McDowell's offensive was underway. It was, but only to the extent
that Tyler's entire artillery contingent was soon in action. Captain J.
Howard Carlisle's four-gun battery of the 2nd Artillery, also attached
to Schenck's brigade, opened up and kept firing at intervals for about
an hour, though with no discernable effect. The nearest enemy was
the tiny brigade under Major Evans, which, though lacking artillery of its own, had gained the timely support of two 6-pounders of
Captain H. Grey Latham's Lynchburg battery, on loan from Cocke's

brigade. Command of the section was divided between Lieutenants George S. Davidson and Clark Leftwich. Neither Evans's infantry (outside of a few skirmishers) nor Latham's cannons answered Carlisle's salvos, confounding Tyler and—whether he admitted it or not—calling into question the effectiveness of his demonstration. In fact, the only Rebels his division had seen thus far were a couple of mounted sentinels, who by the feeble light of dawn had fired a few shots toward the head of Schenck's column before galloping off.[21]

Carlisle's guns eventually attracted counterbattery fire from Latham's section as well as from four cannons of Captain Arthur L. Rogers's Loudoun Artillery, also attached to Cocke's brigade. One of Rogers's sections, commanded by Lieutenant Henry Heaton, responded to Carlisle from the position Cocke had assigned it within defensive range of Lewis Ford. Rogers's other section, under his direct command, was originally stationed near Portici, the Lewis family's plantation house, but about 11:00 A.M. was moved to a closer-in position just south of Stone Bridge, from which, according to its commander, it successfully answered the Union batteries. Not so, according to a Northern correspondent on the scene, who reported that following a "terrific cannonading" lasting no longer than thirty minutes, the Confederate guns were silenced. Rogers's explanation was that his pieces had been forced to the rear to replenish ammunition chests. For his part, Captain Latham claimed to have silenced and disabled "one or more of their pieces." His assertion is dubious—the Federals reported damage to a single limber of Carlisle's battery. But the claim was willingly endorsed by Beauregard, who in his report of the battle praised the Lynchburg Artillery for beating down the fire of the enemy's more powerful batteries.[22]

During the cannonade, some of Tyler's infantrymen moved up and occupied a spot from which they could add their weight to the demonstration. The going had been slow, for many obstructions had to be cleared. Since the morning of the eighteenth, Evans's men had been felling "every tree that was near enough to the road [Warrenton Turnpike] to fall across it, from the Stone Bridge to the hill near the Van Pelt house."[23]

At length, the Confederates began to show themselves. As the advance element of Schenck's brigade, the 2nd Ohio of Lieutenant Colonel Rodney Mason, crossed the fields toward Stone Bridge, it encountered a skirmish line from Evans's command, which formed astride the turnpike just west of the bridge. Suddenly, a Union officer rode up from the rear on what Captain George M. Finch of the 2nd considered a fool's errand. Finch identified the newcomer, whom he described as a "stern-looking man, with fiery red hair and whiskers," as Sherman. The commander of Tyler's Third Brigade had galloped into full view and rifle range of Evans's skirmishers, "all of whom took a shot at him as he passed. While I admired his bravery, with ready assurance I condemned him for his recklessness." Sherman's gallop to the front had a rational purpose—he was seeking a shallow spot where he might cross his troops over Bull Run— but it is doubtful that Finch had a close enough view to make the identification. His regiment's position was on the left of the pike, while the rider passed "rapidly off to the right" at a considerable distance. Learning later of Sherman's presence in the area, the captain cast himself as an eyewitness to a soon-to-be-famous soldier's early days in command.[24]

Slowly, with difficulty, Schenck's men gained the crest of a ridge perpendicular to the pike and from which Stone Bridge was visible except in those places where heavy foliage blocked the view. Carlisle's battery was advanced to the front of the division, where it unlimbered in a meadow north of the turnpike, while Tyler's other artillery unit, Ayres's Company E, 3rd U.S., dropped its trails along a farm track where it could cover the rear of the entire command. Within minutes the batteries were blasting away at the artillery supporting Evans.[25]

As the artillery duel heated up, Tyler listened intently for word that the army's turning columns had gotten into position to envelop the Confederate left. Seven o'clock had been designated as the hour for those columns to strike. In fact, Hunter's division had filed off the turnpike onto the wayward road to Sudley Ford only minutes before Hains's signal gun began firing. The unanticipated delay in getting into position could be laid at Tyler's feet, though as was the case with his blunder of the eighteenth, he would never accept blame for it.

Although Tyler would claim that Schenck's and Sherman's brigades had moved up the pike as far as the blacksmith shop sometime before 4:00 A.M., only an hour and a half after breaking camp at Centreville, this was patently untrue. He got his men up in time to wolf down a breakfast before forming for the march more or less at the appointed hour, but in the predawn gloom there was a great deal of confusion in the ranks, which continued well after the march got underway. An officer at the front of the division described the darkness as "so intense that, literally, you could not see your hand before your face. We had to feel our way, keeping up our alignment at right angles with the road, as best we could, by the voice of the next man on the right. We never knew where a fence or tree was located in front of us until we ran slap against it. Many of the skirmishers had bloody noses and bruised limbs from such collisions." The delay thus caused had a cumulative effect throughout the turning column. As David Detzer puts it, "during the next five hours, McDowell's 30,000 men functioned less like an army, more like a traffic jam, their convolutions almost as random as thousands of sports fans departing a venue at the same time."[26]

Confusion and disarray were especially characteristic of Schenck's march from Centreville. In his after-action report, the brigadier claimed to have left the bivouac area one mile south of Centreville promptly at 2:30 A.M. He admitted, however, that once underway he proceeded "slowly and carefully," so much so that he did not fully clear the Centreville area until after three o'clock. When it finally gained the Warrenton Turnpike, the brigade continued to make scant progress, feeling its way in the murk like a blind man in a briar patch. Perhaps the root of the problem was that Schenck had assigned to lead the march McCook's 1st Ohio, seven hundred of whose men had been ambushed, terrified, and humiliated outside Vienna. That encounter had taken place in bright daylight; advancing toward enemy territory in the dark was even more unnerving. Another impediment to progress was the 30-pounder Parrott, whose mobility was compromised not only by its girth but also by the ten-horse team that hauled it—none of the animals had worked with the others prior to this day. When crossing hills and ridges, the gun required the motive power of dozens of soldiers tugging on cables fixed to its undercarriage.[27]

It should be no surprise that Schenck's brigade failed to reach the turnoff for Sudley Ford until close to sunrise or to come within sight of Stone Bridge for another hour. As the men moved in a stop-and-start fashion, the sun rose and the temperature—initially in the low eighties—began a steady climb. Men took frequent swigs from their canteens, mopped their faces with dirty handkerchiefs, and discarded what they took to be excess baggage, including clothing they would wish they had hung on to. Those adorned with havelocks, which cooled as well as protected the neck, thanked the English officer who had popularized the item (and given his name to it).

The commanders of the troops moving in rear of Schenck's brigade appear to have broken camp just as late as he and to have marched their men just as slowly. Sherman reported that his brigade struck the turnpike around 2:30, but at least one of his regiments did not break camp for another hour. Keyes's brigade, which had bivouacked on the eastern slope of the Centreville ridge, must have departed no earlier than 3:30, though probably much later.[28]

All of this was distressing but also predictable, indicating the army's weak grasp of logistics. By withdrawing his initial intention to start the march early in the evening, McDowell had made a major error. As Detzer puts it: "McDowell's timetable had built-in flaws. Worse, it left no room for snafus. These should have been expected—and of course they arose."[29]

Sometime before six o'clock, one hour after Tyler drew within sight of Stone Bridge, both he and McDowell, whose covered coach was moving amid the division column, finally began to worry about the lack of progress made by the flanking column. Desperate to expedite progress, Tyler—who was responsible for the most vexing delay, having spent an hour reconnoitering the bridge and surrounding terrain—pulled Schenck's men off the south side of the turnpike to permit Sherman to move more quickly into position on the other side. Although Tyler later claimed that Keyes's brigade, bringing up the rear, was operating under McDowell's personal instructions, he also ordered Keyes to halt and clear the turnpike.

Keyes stopped a couple hundred yards beyond Cub Run bridge, where the road from Ball's Ford came up from the south to meet the turnpike. On the other side of the pike, the road leading in the direction of Sudley Ford branched off to the northwest. The removal of Keyes's troops to the left side of the pike opened this path to the turning column, but Keyes, fretting over the delay forced on him, sent a galloper to army headquarters asking that the brigade be allowed to proceed. McDowell, who was suffering from intestinal upset (a few historians have speculated without evidence that it was the result of overeating), was in no mood for a subordinate seeking to countermand orders during a battle. He told Keyes's messenger that the brigade must remain off the road until Hunter and Heintzelman overtook him.[30]

Those two divisions—a combined total of some 13,500 men and twenty-four guns—appear almost as culpable as Tyler for the army's inability to make acceptable time. Hunter's command, although

bivouacked just to the east of Centreville, did not form a marching column until 4:30, some two hours behind schedule. Finally
gaining the turnpike, the division—Burnside's brigade in front, followed by Porter's—moved so deliberately that not until 6:00 A.M.
was Heintzelman able to get started. This was only about an hour
before the time McDowell had set for the columns to begin crossing
Bull Run. Only now (according to Porter, about an hour after sunrise) was Hunter veering off the pike in pursuit of the path to Sudley
Ford. It had taken the army's vanguard four hours to march three
miles. Even for pea-green troops, this was wholly unacceptable.[31]

Heintzelman's belated departure did not leave Centreville deserted.
Dixon Miles had been expected to get the Fifth Division into its
assigned position soon after 2:30, but the colonel lodged a popular
complaint: he was "prevented from doing so by other divisions blocking up the road." After fuming impotently for some time, Miles discovered a way to pass Davies's brigade to the west and, by marching
it cross-country through early morning darkness, to clear the traffic
jam. Guided through farmland and open fields by one of Barnard's
officers, Lieutenant Frederick E. Prime, Davies's men eventually
struck the road to Blackburn's Ford, where they made contact with
the long-in-place brigade of Richardson. According to the latter, the
union occurred shortly after Tyler's signal gun fired, the sound of
which clearly carried across those four miles of ground. As soon as
Miles heard its thunderous report, he commenced firing toward Bull
Run from some of the twenty cannons at his disposal this day.[32]

Because the Fifth Division covered the army's rear and its escape
route through Centreville, it was rich in artillery support. Richardson
and Davies would be bolstered by portions of three batteries, but ten
other guns, attached to Blenker's command, covered both brigades
at long distance. One of the German's regiments had taken possession of the Artillery Hill defenses that their builders had so thoughtfully abandoned; these the Federals enlarged and improved. The
rest of his brigade—one regiment stationed west of the town on the
Warrenton Pike, the other two along the ridge that sloped toward
Bull Run—dug rifle pits, built breastworks, and erected a two-gun
redoubt north of the village that could sweep the Braddock Road.

The regiments on the ridge were protected not only by the
four guns and howitzers assigned to Blenker's command—Captain
John C. Tidball's Company A, 2nd Artillery—but also by the six

6-pounder guns of Varian's Battery, which Blenker's European veterans had manned under the direction of Captain Bookwood. At Miles's order Blenker had placed half of Bookwood's cannons east of Centreville, its other three farther south, thus covering both sides of the road to Fairfax Court House. Tidball's pieces unlimbered on top of a knoll one mile from town on the west side of the turnpike, facing toward Richardson's rear.[33]

Though his position appeared secure, Colonel Miles was a troubled man. He was not well physically, apparently suffering from intestinal distress, an affliction he was treating with long pulls on a flask that contained "medicine," also known as brandy. The job of safeguarding the army's left and rear and its connection with points north was a worrisome burden even for an officer in the peak of health. Longstreet's Confederates were assumed to be present in force around Blackburn's Ford and posed an imminent threat to Miles's sector as did Bonham's troops and the other Confederates holding the lower fords.[34]

Never known for his steely nerves, Miles felt insecure and threatened. Thus he concentrated much of his energy on fortifying his area of operations, giving special attention to Blenker's brigade in and around Centreville. Symptomatic of his state of mind was an order given to Lieutenant Prime that morning. Before the engineering party that Barnard had assigned his subordinate could complete a several-hundred-foot abatis to shield Richardson's exposed left flank, Miles peremptorily ordered the group to Centreville to refine Blenker's defenses.[35]

The work there was laborious in the extreme. Blenker's fatigue parties had a difficult enough time digging in the rising heat; occasionally they attracted a bullet or two from Mitchell's and Blackburn's Fords. Thus far Blenker's men had not "seen the elephant"—that is, had not been under fire. They had sat out the fighting on the eighteenth, having reached Fairfax Court House the previous day too late to shoot at anything except wild game. Now for the first time, members of the immigrant-laden brigade heard the spiteful whine of the minie ball as it flitted past, what Blenker later called the "strange music" of combat.[36]

The guns that began Miles's assigned diversion—a section of brass 12-pounders under Lieutenant James Thompson—had been placed to cover Richardson's position near the fork of the roads leading to Mitchell's and Blackburn's Fords. Thompson's unit, along with a section commanded by Lieutenant Edward R. Platt, belonged to one of the army's newest artillery units, Company M, 2nd U.S. Artillery. The battery was manned largely by raw recruits, but its commander was a twenty-two-year veteran of the Mexican War, garrison duty on the Atlantic Coast, and service on the southwestern plains. Brevet Major Henry Jackson Hunt was a West Pointer (he had graduated one year behind Beauregard and McDowell) who had forged a reputation as one of the army's most respected artillerists, his expertise encompassing both administration and tactics. Under his guidance the cannons on the Union left, notwithstanding the rawness of their personnel, would be well served.[37]

At Hunt's direction, beginning at about 6:45, Thompson's section shelled the area south of Blackburn's Ford that Longstreet's brigade had defended on the eighteenth. As the major later noted, a few rounds were "dropped into the woods and amongst the buildings which were supposed to contain the enemy, but no answer was returned, and the shelling ceased." Soon afterward, however, Hunt through his field glasses spied a column of infantry stirring amid the trees on the south bank. He had Thompson advance one of his guns with positive results: "After a few rounds, they disappeared."[38]

They would return soon enough, as Hunt's infantry support would discover. The ground occupied by Richardson's brigade stretched for a half mile from the west side of the Mitchell's Ford road to a hill about six hundred yards east of the road to Blackburn's Ford; both ends of this line were covered by Cowdin's 1st Massachusetts. Three of the regiment's companies guarded the left fork; two had been in position since the previous day, the third, which Richardson had placed in a ravine leading toward Longstreet's position, had been added that morning. Richardson had deployed the remainder of the outfit on his far right, with Colonel Daniel McConnell's 3rd Michigan Infantry between the detachments, drawn up in line of battle. The regiment, which constituted the brigade's principal strike force, had not been engaged and therefore not demoralized on the eighteenth. Five hundred yards to the rear stood the 12th New York and 2nd Michigan, whose men had met the elephant on that occasion and did not appear keen about renewing acquaintances.[39]

Originally, Richardson's line extended far enough to the east to occupy two barns on the farm owned by a Mr. Grigsby. Early that morning, however, Fighting Dick constricted his position upon the arrival farther east of Davies's brigade. According to Richardson,

Davies at once sought him out, inquired about his date of commissioning, and announced that because he was ten days Richardson's senior, he was assuming command of the entire sector (Davies would later claim that Miles directed him to supersede Richardson). Davies was anxious to firm up his position with artillery; upon his inquiry, Richardson recommended placing a battery near the Grigsby farmhouse. Davies thanked his colleague by appropriating both of Hunt's sections and moving them to his own sector.[40]

In shifting east Hunt rejoined a section of Edwards's Company G, 1st Artillery, which the previous day had been temporarily attached to his own unit. Fire direction of its two 20-pounder rifles reposed with Lieutenants Samuel N. Benjamin and Lawrence S. Babbitt, veterans of Tyler's botched demonstration of the eighteenth. Given the almost Herculean effort required to move it about, Edwards and his subordinates were probably glad they were no longer saddled with the 30-pounder Parrott that, attached to Carlisle's company, had "opened the ball."

Once satisfied that his position was effectively supported, Davies constructed a battle line on the Grigsby farm facing east, apparently with a view to keeping watch over Jones's brigade at McLean's Ford. He positioned the 18th New York Infantry of Colonel William A. Jackson to support his new-found artillery. Farther south he placed the 16th and 31st New York, commanded respectively by Lieutenant Colonel Samuel Marsh and Colonel Calvin E. Pratt, along a road that branched off the main route from Centreville, the 16th on the right of the road and the 31st still farther to the right. He left his fourth regiment, Colonel Roderick Matheson's 32nd New York, in the rear as a reserve. These dispositions were not permanent, as the colonel would discover before the morning was over.[41]

Richardson, who was confronting an enemy force at closer range than Davies, could not hold his position without artillery. To compensate for Hunt's and Edwards's detaching, he ordered up from the reserve at Centreville Company G, 2nd U.S. Artillery, commanded by Lieutenant Oliver D. Greene. Upon arriving Greene, with Richardson's approval, moved his four 10-pounder Parrotts down the road toward Bull Run, passing the Butler farm and unlimbering on a hill about six hundred yards from Blackburn's Ford.

Greene's sector quickly came alive with activity that the lieutenant interpreted as an effort to turn Richardson's flank. Longstreet had thrown out skirmishers, sheltered by a woods, on the north bank of the run. Though the Rebels had "congregated in consider-able force," they were not advancing just yet. The sharp-eyed Greene discerned in the skirmishers' rear two batteries, one masked, the other partially so; he opened against both with shrapnel. The shell-ing appeared to have an immediate effect: within minutes the Confederates had scrambled back to the south bank.

For an hour or more, Greene's guns hammered away at Longstreet's wooded enclave. Eventually, the barrage flushed out an enemy force that Richardson, through his field glasses, esti-mated at 2,500 or more. Most of these troops crossed to the north bank but did not advance, and a standoff ensued. Sometime later Richardson also discovered that two columns, at least a regiment apiece, appeared to have reinforced Longstreet's position on the south bank, "which lines," he reported, "already appeared full to overflowing." Fearing an attack against his front or left, Richardson put his pioneers to work digging an earthen parapet across the road to the ford, with embrasures to accommodate three guns; the pio-neers further strengthened the flank by felling trees to form an aba-tis. Greene's guns were soon advanced to the new position, where they again opened fire.[42]

At this point Colonel Miles appeared on the field and busily assumed command on Richardson's front. As if having forgotten McDowell's injunction to avoid a major confrontation, he appeared intent on crossing Blackburn's Ford in order "to cut the line of travel pursued by retreating and advancing detachments of the enemy." He was dissuaded from this only when Richardson showed him a written order from army headquarters that his brigade should "not attack at all."[43]

Miles contented himself by directing that a skirmish line be shaken out in Longstreet's direction. Richardson complied by ordering up two companies of the 3rd Michigan, some 160 men. This force, accompanied by Lieutenant Prime and supported in rear by the light infantry battalion of Captain Brethschneider, advanced through the ravine along Richardson's flank. When within rifle range of the ford, the skirmishers encountered a like force of Con-federates deployed north of the run. Since Richardson was pro-hibited from attacking, almost as soon as contact was made, the Michiganders were recalled. The Confederates pursued for some distance until driven back by rounds of short-range ammunition from Greene's battery.

The disjointed actions of the Rebels suggested that they were uncertain of their role in their army's plans. Their withdrawal gave Richardson the time he needed to complete the strengthening of his position on both sides of the ford road. For the balance of the afternoon, "no enemy appeared in force at my front with a disposition to assault." Thankful for the inactivity, the colonel hunkered down behind his improved works and let his cannons carry on the fight.[44]

At about this time, action heated up along Davies's line. Major Hunt had not liked the position the sector commander had selected for his guns, mainly because it skirted a deep ravine that could shelter any attackers; if he voiced his discontent, however, it was ignored. Although the order came from Miles, Davies also incurred the artilleryman's displeasure by having all the batteries on his front shell Blackburn's Ford without cessation. Like Tyler's opening barrage of the eighteenth, this fire attracted little or no response from the troops under Longstreet. A stickler for efficiency, Hunt considered excessive expenditure of ammunition a "besetting sin" of commanders unattuned to the proper functioning of field batteries. He was somewhat mollified when, at about ten o'clock, Davies, having discovered that shot and shell were running low, had Edwards's guns cease firing.[45]

If the colonel believed he had a firm grasp on his position, he was badly mistaken. He must have spent some time in advance of his line because he did not become aware that his brigade was being redeployed until about eleven o'clock, when Miles appeared at his field headquarters to announce that he had moved forward of their original positions three of Davies's regiments as well as both sections of Company M. The 16th and 31st New York had been sent out the farm road through heavy woods toward the Union Mills Road, while the 18th and 32nd had been pulled back three-quarters of a mile to the rear.

Miles further antagonized Davies—and especially Hunt—by ordering all of the brigade's guns to resume shelling Longstreet's position "without regard to ammunition." The combined barrage went on for two hours with no discernible result until Miles finally ordered it stopped. "As soon as Colonel Miles left me again in command," Davies spent the balance of the morning and some of the afternoon rehabilitating his haphazardly altered line. He also oversaw his pioneer corps as it took down trees along the road formerly guarded by the 16th and 31st New York, via which the colonel feared the Confederates might take his position in rear.[46]

By now it had become obvious to everyone who encountered Miles that he was drunk. His aborting of Lieutenant Prime's mission on Richardson's front—the importance of which Major Barnard had impressed on his subordinate—suggested an unbalanced appreciation of tactical priorities. The Rebels at the fords had been found in some force, but none had been detected anywhere close to Centreville. Miles's repeated repositioning of Davies's regiments without the latter's knowledge or consent, and his gyrating impulses to attack and withdraw, provided further proof that he could not be relied on to safeguard the rear of the Army of Northeastern Virginia.

Blenker's men in and around Centreville spent most of the day digging rifle pits, throwing up earthworks, and constructing parapets for the guns of Tidball and Bookwood. Through morning and afternoon, they performed these arduous duties before a growing audience of civilians.

By midmorning, a hill west of the village had become an observation post for visitors from Washington and Alexandria, including a number of prominent politicians. Ben Wade and Henry Wilson were joined this day by Republican senatorial colleagues James W. Grimes of Iowa, Lyman Trumbull of Illinois, John P. Hale of New Hampshire, and James H. Lane, Lincoln's friend and bodyguard from Kansas. The Senate's newly appointed sergeant at arms, George T. Brown, was also on hand. Members of the House had arrived at an early hour, prominent among them Elihu Washburne of Illinois and Schuler Colfax of Indiana. Representative Albert G. Riddle of Ohio, like Governor Sprague, came ready to fight, having armed himself and his traveling party, which included three other congressmen, with several pistols, including four Navy Colt revolvers. Like the other solons on the hill, Riddle was intent on gaining a glimpse, albeit from afar, of a Union victory he had helped shape through his involvement in the creation and sustenance of McDowell's army.[47]

A large segment of the crowd consisted of war correspondents from the papers of the big-city North, most of whom had been with the army since it left Washington. Ignorant of matters tactical and strategic, many asked questions of the officers whose units were clustered about Centreville. Captain Tidball was especially responsive, though his grasp of the unfolding battle was as limited as any civilian observer's. Around noon the gentlemen of the press were joined by one of the few true celebrities of their profession when

William Russell alighted from a two-horse gig. Clad in a khaki "Himalayan" suit, a brown felt hat, and an old pair of boots, the flamboyant scribe was surprised to find the hills and ridges around Centreville crowned not only with political and diplomatic officials but also with ordinary civilians—men of all walks of life, some in cutaway coats and top hats, others in working men's clothes. Moving among them were a few officers and enlisted men who, having straggled from their regiments, "pretended to explain the movements of the troops below."

Russell also observed specimens "of the fairer, if not gentler sex," including some resourceful vendors who were offering meats, fruits, and pies for sale. The dress and demeanor of other women marked them as society matrons. One followed the distant goings-on through opera glasses; when a particularly fierce blast reverberated from the battlefield, Russell heard her exclaim: "That is splendid. Oh my! Oh my! Is not that first-rate? I guess we will be in Richmond this time to-morrow." Among those who shared her hope was the daughter of Thurlow Weed, New York's most powerful political boss. Miss Weed was carrying a U.S. flag emblazoned with a one-word battle slogan: *Richmond.* As she told others, she intended to fly the banner from the roof of the Virginia Capitol some time the following day.[48]

Another interested observer, one with a professional interest in the battle unfolding a few miles away, was Matthew Brady. Outfitted in his favorite ensemble—rumpled linen duster, baggy trousers, and straw hat—the eminent photographer had been trying to imagine a way to capture war on emulsified glass, but at such a distance he could see none of what he hoped to record. His opportunity would come, however, once the day was won; then he intended to go forth with his horse-drawn studio to the blood-stained field, training his lens on the dead of both armies. By introducing the ignorant but ever-eager public to the realities of modern war, he would create a sensation, one that would christen Brady as the country's foremost photohistorian.[49]

In the weeks ahead, the spectacle of civilians sampling the thrills and horrors of war at a safe distance would become a national scandal. Stories would emerge of hundreds of carriages and wagons parked on the fringes of the battlefield from which picnickers of both sexes sallied forth to spread tablecloths on the ground and while away the day devouring not only reports from the front but also grapes, sweetmeats, and wine.

As latter-day historians have noted, for the most part these were lurid exaggerations. A majority of the spectators appear to have come not to indulge a fascination with war or an obsession with death and destruction, but to witness history in the making; they brought food only because they could not expect to procure it on the battlefield. A considerable number had a personal connection to the day's events and believed that they had a right to be there. Parents and spouses of soldiers in the fight included the anxious wife of Colonel Richardson and the elderly father of two members of General Tyler's 1st Ohio Infantry, Colonel Alexander M. McCook and eighteen-year-old Private Charles McCook. The latter, who had left college to serve in his brother's regiment, would die before the sun went down. Even so, the image of a bacchanal just off the battlefield would outrage public opinion North and South. Politicians, editors, and clergymen would condemn what appeared an attempt to reduce war to a spectator sport. And bards would attack them with doggerel such as the following:

> Have you heard of the story, so lacking in glory,
> About the civilians who went to the fight?
> With everything handy, from sandwich to brandy,
> To fill their broad stomachs, and make them all tight.[50]

Almost two hours before Hains's signal gun cued the fighting, Beauregard sent out copies of his attack plan. He anticipated no difficulty gaining his immediate objective, the overthrow of the Union left. As he wrote after the war, "Richardson, pressed in front by Longstreet and outflanked by Jones, Early, Ewell, and Holmes, must have been instantly routed, exposing still more fatally the flank of Davies' brigade which must have dissolved in turn; and Blenker's, under the full stress of the flight of these forces and the advance of superior numbers, would have been quickly stampeded." He envisioned a snowball-like effect that would roll up McDowell's line on the turnpike: "Schenck's, Sherman's, and Keyes' forces, demoralized by the unexpected sound of conflict on their rear, and enveloped, must have been overcome and scattered or captured."[51]

Validating von Moltke's adage that no battle plan survives contact with the enemy, nothing worked as Beauregard intended or expected. That morning about five-thirty, when Major Evans reported to army headquarters the advance of Tyler's division ("in all,"

Beauregard estimated, "over nine thousand men and thirteen pieces of artillery"), the Creole had to shift his strategic focus quickly and radically. At once he ordered Evans as well as the nearby troops under Colonel Cocke "if attacked, to maintain their position to the last extremity."[52]

Upon receiving word of Tyler's advance, Beauregard must have spent some time reconsidering his objectives. But any dithering was short lived. A commander less confident of his military instincts might have scrapped the offensive to concentrate on defending his imperiled left. Instead, Beauregard determined to proceed with his drive on Centreville. As he later wrote, "the most effective method of relieving that flank was by a rapid, determined attack with my right wing and center on the enemy's flank and rear at Centreville, with due precautions [taken] against the advance of his reserves from the direction of Washington." What these precautions consisted of no one knows, but the general claimed that when he presented the idea to Johnston, the latter "fully approved of it, and orders were forthwith issued for its execution."[53]

In his *Narrative of Military Operations*, Johnston remarks that Beauregard now envisioned "a vigorous attack on the left flank of the troops assailing our left, by the six brigades of our centre and right, while Cocke's, Jackson's, and Bee's brigades, and Hampton's legion, were meeting their [the Federals'] assault." When preparing his article on the battle for *Century* magazine a few years later, Johnston stressed to his editor that the plan Beauregard devised upon hearing from Evans was no longer aimed at Centreville because by then it was either known or suspected that the bulk of McDowell's army had cleared the village on its way out the Warrenton Pike. In his memoirs the Virginian confirms that he endorsed the plan but gave no opinion as to its effectiveness. In fact, he appears to dissociate himself from it: "The orders for this [modified plan], like those preceding them, were distributed by General Beauregard's staff officers, because they were addressed to his troops, and my staff knew neither the positions of the different brigades, nor the paths leading to them."[54]

The success of Beauregard's newest plan depended on the prompt advance of Dick Ewell, whose brigade, given its position, would have the farthest to march. All other forces earmarked for the operation— Longstreet's, Bonham's, and Jones's brigades, along with those elements of Johnston's army designated to support them—were not to move until they received word that Ewell had crossed Union Mills Ford. The cavalry would be called up to offer support when "deemed necessary." Seven companies of Radford's 30th Virginia Cavalry had been attached to the various maneuvering forces, or would be by morning. Meanwhile, the five companies of Stuart's 1st Virginia, bivouacked about two miles in rear of Ball's Ford, would support Jackson's brigade once the latter was called into action.[55]

The revised offensive demonstrated both Beauregard's ability to improvise and his tendency to fall back on old ways of thinking. In the end this mattered not at all, for due to unforeseen circumstances, his mighty thrust at the Union left never happened. Around five o'clock Ewell had received Beauregard's original order to hold his command "in readiness to take the offensive on Centreville at a moment's notice" as a diversion to relieve anticipated pressure on the Confederate center and perhaps the left as well. By then Ewell had been alerted to a threat from the northwest posed by the Federals under Davies. This news had come to him from Oceola Mason, daughter of a local physician, who had spied on the enemy's lines around Grigsby's before galloping off to Union Mills Ford to deliver a breathless report. Ewell thanked the young lady for the warning but seems to have considered it not worth the danger she had put herself in when delivering it.[56]

The subsequent order Ewell expected—the notice to get moving—never arrived, but it reached two of his colleagues. Shortly after seven o'clock, with the battle on the Confederate left apparently fully joined, D. R. Jones heard from Beauregard that Ewell had been ordered to advance and that Jones was to expand the offensive by crossing McLean's Ford "at once." (It appears that Jones had not received the order that reached Ewell—and also Longstreet—at 5:00 A.M. to stand ready to move.) At once he placed his troops in marching order, informed Longstreet on his left that he was moving out, and sent an aide to confirm Ewell's advance. No reply being forthcoming, Jones crossed the run and marched his men toward the Virginian's assumed position on the road from Union Mills.

Jones would claim that he spent two and a half hours awaiting word that Ewell had gone forward. A little after ten o'clock he received instead "a somewhat discretionary order" from Beauregard, the contents of which he did not reveal. To add to the confusion, a few minutes later Colonel Chisolm of the army headquarters staff handed him a positive order to resume his position of early morning.

Beauregard had decided that "on account of the difficulties in our front it is thought preferable to countermand the advance of the right wing."[57]

Ewell never received notice to change his posture from "wait to hear" to "go ahead." "No orders, no orders," a subordinate recalled him muttering as he paced back and forth at his field quarters. All the general got was a copy of the 7:00 A.M. dispatch to Jones, relayed by Jones himself. The message indicated that Ewell's troops had been put in motion and that Jones's own should follow as soon as the Second Brigade closed up on his right. Before receiving this copy, Ewell, at perhaps 9:30, directed that a rider be sent to army headquarters to clear up the misunderstanding. When the horseman reported for orders, Ewell managed to make a bad situation worse. A bystander noted that he began "slashing away with tongue and finger, delivering his directions with such rapidity and incompleteness that the young man's thoughts were dancing through his brain in inescapable confusion." When the would-be courier begged to inform the general that he did not understand, Ewell exploded, angrily dismissed him, and had members of his own staff run the errand.[58]

As soon as he saw the copy of Jones's attack directive, Ewell—confused by the contradictory orders and stressed by the possibility that the evident miscommunication was somehow his fault—began to throw his brigade across Bull Run. The operation was barely begun when he was met by a courier from Beauregard with an order to return his men to the south side. A bewildered Ewell did as told, but almost as soon as he regained his original position, he received another message from headquarters, this one relayed by Colonel Benjamin F. Terry, a volunteer aide-de-camp to Ewell, "to cross again, proceed up the run, and attack a battery of the enemy upon its flank and rear, regulating my movements upon the brigades of Generals Jones and Longstreet."

Wearily, Ewell again crossed the stream. By a little after three o'clock, his brigade had moved about a mile and a half toward the enemy; at this point the balding brigadier received yet another order to return to the south side. Once there, he should prepare to move to the far left in company with Holmes's brigade. This latest summons, even more so than the conflicting orders preceding it, made Ewell tremble: "*My feelings then were terrible* as such an order could only mean that we were defeated and I was to cover the retreat."[59]

Ewell's nightmare ended with his brigade, like Holmes's, failing to reach the embattled flank in time to help defend it. No longer at Union Mills Ford, he was not in a position to support the afternoon operations north of Bull Run by Longstreet and Jones, both of whom had advanced without reference to him. Six hours of marching and countermarching had brought Ewell no commitment to battle, no opportunity to win fame and glory—only grief.

The brigade leader was mortified by his involvement in the mammoth snafu, which he feared would sully his reputation. He had been anxious to launch his assigned move against Centreville and had made preparations to do so, carefully reconnoitering the area over which he expected to advance. His efforts may not have been known to those who would whisper that Ewell had been derelict in meeting his responsibilities. In the aftermath of the battle, he learned that unidentified critics were accusing him of gross negligence, or worse. At least one Southern newspaper issued thinly veiled accusations of treason, though its editor later retracted the charge.[60]

It took some time for the facts to come to light, but once revealed, they appeared to exonerate him of charges of incompetence or foot-dragging. After the fight Ewell claimed to have learned that the foul-up had been a classic case of a battle nearly lost for want of a horse and rider. In his official report he tried to explain why an aide-de-camp from Beauregard never reached him with important orders; the man's steed had given out. Others who looked into the communications snarl claimed that a courier who might have brought Ewell definitive orders had aborted his errand out of carelessness or cowardice. One Union veteran, writing years later, reported having heard that the rider got drunk and ran into a tree, incapacitating him for further service.[61]

After the battle an agitated Ewell pressed Beauregard for details of the errant order, but the army commander could not provide them—no copy of the communiqué had survived, and he had forgotten the courier's name. Under the circumstances he had no choice but to try to soothe his subordinate's wounded pride. On July 26 he wrote Ewell: "I do not attach the slightest blame to you for the failure of the movement on Centreville, but to the guide, who did not deliver the order to move forward, sent at about eight A.M. to General Holmes and then to you. . . . I am fully aware that you did all that could have been expected of you or your command."[62]

Yet Beauregard did not consistently and unambiguously exonerate his lieutenant. In the company of others, he reportedly accused Ewell of idling at Union Mills long after learning that the movement he was to lead was—or should have been—underway. In his battle report, which was not publicly released until mid-October, the army commander acknowledged that his order for Ewell to advance had "miscarried," but he also expressed "profound disappointment" over the Virginian's failure to act once battle had been joined. Campbell Brown, his relative's most vocal defender, fumed that the Creole's supposed exoneration of Ewell's inactivity "was so vague and unsatisfactory that . . . nine out of ten who read it would still impute blame to him when in fact it belonged to Beauregard."[63]

The historical consensus on this chaotic episode is twofold. The system by which Beauregard delivered orders to his subordinates on July 21 was abysmally flawed. As R. M. Johnston observes, Beauregard's "staff arrangements were as crude as his orders." After the battle the general attempted to blame his couriers, "the worst set I ever employed." In large measure, however, he himself was responsible for this and many another breakdown of communications, the result of his inability or unwillingness to focus on those seemingly minor details that if ignored can scuttle a battle plan no manner how adroitly conceived or effectively presented. But Ewell does not deserve to be absolved of all blame. Given his awareness of what his superior expected of him, he ought to have advanced even in the absence of explicit orders.[64]

Whoever was more blameworthy, Ewell's failure to begin the attack against McDowell's left and rear effectively doomed Beauregard's cherished offensive. With battle already joined in a sector he had neglected to secure, this was probably for the best. Yet Beauregard never completely forgave his flustered and frustrated subordinate for robbing him of the opportunity to demonstrate that his tactical planning was on a par with his brilliant but unappreciated efforts at grand strategy.

CHAPTER 12

"WE ARE IN FOR IT!"

E dward Porter Alexander would find his niche in the Confederate artillery, finishing the war as one of only three men to have attained general rank in that arm, but on July 21, 1861, he would excel in the role of chief signal officer of the Army of the Potomac. Since being assigned to Beauregard's staff on June 29, the resourceful Georgian had established four signal stations at strategic points along his army's lines. They extended from the hill on the Van Pelt farm on the far left to Wilcoxen's Hill, an eminence in the army's right rear a mile and a half east of Manassas Junction and six miles from the Van Pelt station. The post at Wilcoxen's, known as Signal Hill, afforded an extended and almost unobstructed view of the countryside on both sides of Bull Run. Alexander had located one of his other stations near Wilmer McLean's homestead, where Beauregard had maintained his headquarters since giving up his original base of operations at Liberia. The fourth station, set up in Centreville, was now of course in Union hands. Each of the remaining three was served by a detachment of couriers ready to carry messages to any of the others. None of these positions was in fact a "tower," as many reports of the campaign have it; each was situated on existing high ground, its operations shielded from enemy view by trees and vegetation.[1]

From these stations, Confederate signalmen communicated with one another by "wigwagging." In good weather the process involved waving a single color-coded flag fastened to a twelve-foot staff. After dark or during periods of rain, fog, or overcast, lanterns or kerosene torches were substituted. These simple devices furthered visual communication across distances of eight miles or more via a quasi-binary system of codes, similar in concept to Morse, in which letters, numbers, and other characters were represented by a unique sequence of waves.

The system had been developed on the prewar frontier by a former surgeon, Albert J. Myer. During the late 1850s, when he began

to test his creation under War Department auspices (the board established to consider the system was headed by Lieutenant Colonel
Robert E. Lee), Myer had been assisted by a small coterie of junior
officers, the most astute of whom was Alexander. The success of the
tests led to Myer's appointment to head the newly organized U.S.
Army Signal Corps. Because his expertise was considered critical to
field operations, the major had been named chief signal officer of the
Army of Northeastern Virginia. Thus teacher and star pupil were in
a position to pit their skills against one another on opposite sides of
Bull Run.[2]

Much has been made of the handicaps and deficiencies Alexander
(officially a member of the Confederate engineer corps) labored under
while attempting to build an effective visual-intelligence capabil-
ity for Beauregard. It is true that he had to cope with inadequate
resources, including a team of private soldiers who exasperated him
by their slowness to learn the duties assigned them and their clum-
siness in carrying out his orders. Although supplies arrived from
Richmond only intermittently, over time Alexander gained the
wherewithal to establish as many stations as he believed necessary
and enough flags, torches, field glasses, and other optical equipment
to crown his efforts with success. He himself operated a "fine glass,"
probably a standard 30-power signal telescope with a twenty-six-inch
focal length. Its tube would have been encased in leather, its joints
bronzed in black to prevent a gleam of sunlight from exposing the
operator's position.[3]

On the morning of the twenty-first, Alexander had left the Van
Pelt station minutes before the signal gun found his tent, narrowly
escaping becoming the first casualty of the battle. From the Van Pelt
hill, Alexander rode across the length of Beauregard's lines to Signal
Hill, where he gained a long, elevated view of General Tyler's skirmishers east of Stone Bridge, apparently preparing to launch an all-
out attack on Nathan Evans's insecure position. Alexander, fearing
that the major surely would be overrun and uprooted, kept a close
watch on the proceedings.

But if he was in trouble, "Shanks" Evans was not showing it.
Although handily outnumbered and soon to be outpositioned as
well, he was holding his ground by the bridge with remarkable equanimity, refusing to be drawn into a general engagement. His stand
against Tyler's mighty host would become one of the many legends
of the battle. Yet although Evans is usually accorded great credit for

his calm, quiet response to the enemy's provocation, it is easy to heap excessive praise on him. In his situation—clearly opposed as he was by several times as many troops as he could muster—Evans had little choice but to lay low lest he give his opponent cause and opportunity to attack and crush him.

For two hours after the Federals began shelling the ground around Stone Bridge, Evans feared that he was facing a real attack and quite possibly the extinction of his command. Thus he kept his troops—Colonel Sloan's 4th South Carolina and Major Wheat's Louisiana Zouaves—behind cover. Fortunately, the hills west of the bridge shielded them from enemy view and, to an extent, enemy missiles.

Evans simply refused to oppose the Yankee artillery for some time, but then he discovered that Tyler had deployed a "considerable force" of skirmishers south of the turnpike, which had begun to advance on his suddenly vulnerable position. At once the major formed his own skirmish line, consisting of two companies of Sloan's regiment and a company of Wheat's "wharf rats," and spread it out until it covered his entire position.

Evans noted that "the skirmishers were soon engaged, and kept up a brisk fire for about an hour." Having shown his hand at last, he must have feared that Schenck's brigade would cross the bridge and strike him head on, scattering his tiny force. This of course was the impression Schenck wished to create. A master poker player should have been able to bluff his opponent, especially one with such a poor hand, into folding. But Evans was alert and stone-cold sober this morning, and he was not about to throw in his cards. After a couple of hours of loud but static opposition from the other side of the run, he perceived that his opponent was waging a staying action. Evidently, Tyler's faux attack was a diversion—but in whose favor? The question appeared to be answered around 8:30, when a scouting party reported a Yankee column advancing from the north via the Sudley–Manassas Road or a farm path farther east.[4]

Confirmation of this intelligence came minutes later. At about 8:45 Captain Alexander, from his perch on Wilcoxen's Hill, saw something ominous through his glass, which he continued to train on the Stone Bridge vicinity. As he recalled years later,

> suddenly a little flash of light in the same field of view but far beyond them [Evans and Tyler] caught my eye. I was looking to

the west and the sun was low in the east, and this flash was the reflection of the sun from a brass cannon in McDowell's flanking column approaching Sudley Ford. It was about 8 miles from me in an air line and was but a faint gleam, indescribably quick, but . . . I knew at once what it was. And careful observation also detected the glitter of bayonets all along a road crossing the valley [that is, the Sudley Road], and I felt sure that I was "on to" McDowell's plan and saw what was the best part of his army.

Aware that Evans was in mortal danger, Alexander had a warning wigwagged to the Van Pelt station. It translated as: "Look out for your left. You are turned." Then the captain scribbled a note and had a rider rush it to Beauregard's headquarters: "I see a column crossing Bull Run about 2 miles above Stone Bridge. Head of it is in woods on this side; tail of it in woods on other side. About a quarter of a mile length of column visible in the opening. Artillery forms part of it."[5]

In his report of the battle, Major Evans made no mention of this timely warning. He implied that he was expecting a movement against him from the north—if not by David Hunter then someone else. Word of the Yankees' coming may already have reached him either from one of his scouts or from an English-born civilian whose plantation lay a mile north of Centreville. Whoever his informant, Evans quickly took action. By now he was sure that Tyler was not going to attack. One indication of the division leader's intent to remain on the defensive was the sight and sound of his men felling trees on both sides of the turnpike. Undeterred by the enemy's feeble ruse, "I at once decided to quit [my] position and to meet him in his flank movement."[6]

As he prepared to move out, Evans decided to leave behind his skirmishers, augmented by two other companies of the 4th South Carolina. This force, about two hundred strong, he judged sufficient to hold the feckless Tyler in place. Private B. B. Breazeale of the 4th South Carolina recalled that his unit—curiously designated as Company J—was held on the bank of the run while the three other companies were deployed on the turnpike between Van Pelt's house and across Young's Branch to the southwest toward the Robinson home. The skirmishers would hold their position until early in the afternoon, when their timid opponents, as Breazeale noted, finally "took off their knapsacks and prepared for action." When the Yankees were about two hundred yards off, the South Carolinians, cut off from the balance of their regiment, quit their post, crossed the run, clambered up adjacent Henry Hill, and joined the many comrades who had gathered around the Lewis house.[7]

When informing Sloan and Wheat of the threat from above, Evans had them turn their men in that direction, the Louisiana Tigers in the lead. He guided them, along with the guns of Davidson and Leftwich and a small force of cavalry, across the fields toward the assumed location of the enemy. He also sent a courier galloping to Lewis Ford, half a mile away, to apprise Colonel Cocke of the change of position. Perhaps his immediate superior would rush reinforcements to his endangered position. This, however, did not happen.[8]

Evans has been universally lauded for his quick and bold decision to disengage most of his 1,100 men and meet the Union flanking column. He might instead have fled to save his command, although a fighting retreat might have cost him heavy casualties should Tyler decide to pursue. The major's intention was to fall back to the intersection of the Warrenton Turnpike and "the Manassas roads"—not necessarily the Sudley–Manassas Road. He took his men back down the turnpike to the Van Pelt property and then northwest along a farm road leading to Pittsylvania, the manor house of the plantation owned by the family of the late Landon Carter, Jr., one of the area's wealthiest landowners.

By or before 9:00 A.M., Evans had formed a line of battle shielded by a grove of scrub oaks just south of Bull Run, which at this point meandered east to west. He placed Sloan's companies on the right, with Wheat's Zouaves—many of them attired in red battle shirts, off-white trousers, white canvas leggings, and broad-brimmed straw hats—father west. The flanks of Wheat's line, much of which ran the length of a split-rail fence some four hundred yards north of the Carter mansion, were protected by Companies A and I, 30th Virginia Cavalry—respectively, the Clay Dragoons of Captain William R. Terry and the Campbell Rangers under Captain John D. Alexander. Davidson's and Leftwich's guns had unlimbered on high ground one hundred yards northeast of Pittsylvania, their muzzles pointing north in front of Evans's infantry line.[9]

When Evans left the turnpike, Tyler might have been expected to advance and crush the couple of hundred skirmishers left behind to keep him occupied. Instead, undoubtedly mindful of the trouble he had gotten himself into at Blackburn's Ford, the New Englander remained in diversionary mode even though he detected no signs that Stone Bridge had been rigged to explode and despite the frustration and chagrin of subordinates such as Sherman who wished to plow ahead. The weak-kneed reaction of Tyler, son of a veteran of the Battle of Bunker Hill, reflected poorly on his family's long and proud military history.[10]

But his was not the only example of Union lethargy this morning. While Tyler dithered and temporized, Hunter's vanguard moved so slowly down the road from Sudley Ford that it was not in range to fully engage Evans until sometime after ten o'clock (although in his report, the major for some reason placed the time as an hour earlier). When the Yankees began shooting, the Rebels responded in kind. Evans would report: "My command opened a vigorous fire . . . which caused the enemy to halt in confused order. The fire was warmly kept up until the enemy seemed to fall back."[11]

The retrograde, however, was brief. Once Hunter's advance regained its composure and surged forward, the struggle to break or secure the Confederate left began in earnest.

It had been an unexpectedly long and frustrating journey for the soldiers of Hunter and Heintzelman. Beauregard, who knew the ground, described the path of the flanking column as "a narrow, deep-cut road, hedged on both sides by a dense second-growth forest, over a distance of six miles up to Sudley Ford." This was far more ground than the marchers had supposed they would have to cover, and the conditions under which they labored made the experience an ordeal from first to last. "The dust under our feet," recalled a New Yorker in Heintzelman's column, "was thrown into the air and filled our eyes and mouths, and the fierce July sun blazed remorselessly down upon us."[12]

The going was especially slow for the men of Ambrose Burnside's brigade in the forefront of Hunter's column. The wild undergrowth that clogged the road onto which the men had squeezed themselves caused innumerable halts, during which the pioneer corps of the 2nd Rhode Island hacked away at thickets, bramble bushes, overhanging limbs, and a multitude of fallen trees that the Confederates had thoughtfully strewn across the path. "What a toilsome march it was through the woods," recalled one New Englander, and "what wearisome work" to clear the barriers the enemy had erected. In a repeat performance of the march to Fairfax Court House, each time the march ground to a halt, men broke ranks to fill canteens from streams and ponds; others slaked their thirst by foraging among clumps of fluid-rich blackberries. Hunger pains could not be alleviated so easily. A soldier farther back in the column recalled that "the men soon getting fatigued threw their blankets and many their haversacks away, which left them without a morsel to eat."[13]

Another reminder of the first day out of Washington was the wariness with which some regiments, fearful of being ambushed, lurched ahead, stopping frequently to send out scouts. This was the height of uselessness since the nearest armed Rebel was three or four miles away. But the men had no way of knowing this, and they suspected that their equally ignorant officers were leading them into a trap.[14]

This blanket criticism did not extend to the commander of the 2nd Rhode Island. Thirty-six-year-old Colonel John Slocum had the respect and confidence of his men as well as the warm affection of his many friends, among whom he was known for his "peculiarly sanguine temperament and light heartedness." But not even Slocum could compel his regiment to remain in ranks, move at a steady pace, and refrain from cursing at the top of their voices.[15]

The meager pace distressed Colonel Hunter, especially when, a little more than an hour after he turned off the Warrenton Pike, the blasts from Hains's 30-pounder penetrated the forest cover. At this point Hunter's men had almost four hours of marching ahead of them. The remaining distance was largely the result of a miscalculation by the division's civilian guide, who had shunted the troops onto a northwest-leading road to Sudley Ford instead of having them take the more direct route that Major Barnard had located. The reason given was that the shorter path would have led the head of the column so close to Bull Run that the Confederates—presumably Evans's pickets—would have detected its approach. This may have been true, but Hunter, especially after hearing Tyler's signal gun, knew that speed was of paramount importance, even though he did not realize that the detour would add six miles to his march. The division leader had the authority to overrule the guide; why he did not remains unexplained.[16]

Further delay occurred after the 2nd Rhode Island, just short of nine o'clock, broke out of the woods near Thornton's house, within sight of Sudley Ford and a good three miles from the point where the enemy would finally be encountered. When the column reached the ford, Hunter called a half-hour halt to allow men and horses to drink from Bull Run, which at this point ran three feet deep and about twenty yards wide.[17]

When the column finally turned south on the road to Manassas, it covered less than two hundred yards before forced to wade Catharpin Run at Sudley Springs Ford. At that point, the site of a popular health resort now closed, the enemy finally came into view but at considerable distance. From the high ground north of the mineral springs, Andrew Porter, whose brigade was closing up on Burnside's, could see "a vast column on our left, moving rapidly towards our line of march in front." He watched as Burnside, to meet the threat, threw out a skirmish line from Slocum's regiment. Porter noted with some concern that the skirmishers, who formed ranks inside a woods, were made to advance before their flanks were secured. As it was, it took another thirty minutes for the men to clear their wooded shelter, advance into the fields beyond, and engage the enemy. At that point, Porter observed, "the rattle of musketry and occasional crash of round shot, through the leaves and branches of the trees in our vicinity betokened the opening of battle."[18]

It was now a few minutes past ten o'clock, three hours after McDowell had intended to throw more than one-third of his army across Bull Run, enveloping Beauregard's left. McDowell, having transferred his headquarters from Tyler's column to Hunter's, was personally attempting to hasten his troops. The men of Major Joseph Balch's 1st Rhode Island, directly behind Slocum's regiment, were abreast of Sudley Church, a whitewashed Methodist Episcopal meetinghouse overlooking Sudley Springs Ford, when the army leader rumbled past in his carriage. He was shouting at the top of his lungs, calling upon the marchers for greater speed, his urging prompted by receipt of disturbing news from the front: "The enemy is moving heavy columns from Manassas!"[19]

Although Beauregard had been assigned direct command of the field of battle, the "heavy columns" of reinforcements dispatched to Evans's sector were the product of Johnston's concern that the left flank must not become a casualty of the revamped offensive against Centreville. By 10:30, the sounds of fighting at and above Stone Bridge had grown so intense that they might have originated a few yards from Lookout Hill, a post of observation behind Mitchell's Ford that the army commanders had occupied about two hours earlier. The racket could not be ignored, but it seemed to trouble Johnston more than Beauregard, who even at this late hour believed the supposedly ongoing effort against Centreville would relieve the pressure on Evans. Captain Alexander recalled that Johnston dispatched to the scene of the fighting a half-dozen couriers and then a series of staff officers, including Captain Walter H. Stevens of the engineers, with orders to send back reports every ten minutes or so.[20]

Johnston's interest in securing the left flank derived not only from the evident intensity of the fighting but also from Alexander's continuing reportage of the activities in that sector. Shortly after 10:30, Beauregard and Johnston got another warning from Wilcoxen's Hill, this delivered in person by Alexander. Having shifted his telescope farther to the northwest, the signal officer spied what Johnston later described as a "heavy cloud of dust, such as the marching of an army might raise about ten miles from us . . . in the direction of the road from Harper's Ferry." Having failed to shake his concern that Patterson would pursue him to Manassas, Johnston now feared that his opponent was finally arriving at the head of enough Federals to decide a battle barely underway. His anxiety did not abate until, hours later, it became clear that the dust had been churned up not by soldier's feet but by wagon wheels and horses' hooves, the motive power behind the belatedly arriving supply train of Johnston's own army.[21]

Increasingly doubtful about Beauregard's offensive, Johnston insisted that the ongoing transfer of forces to the left flank be expedited. Around seven o'clock, the brigades of Bee and Bartow—a combined four regiments and two companies of infantry plus the Staunton Artillery of Captain Imboden—had been ordered from their positions near Mitchell's, Blackburn's, and McLean's Fords to the ground where more immediately needed. One might suppose that Bee would have relished his relief from the thankless and inglorious job of guarding the army's rear, but not so. Apparently believing that his brigade as well as Bartow's (both under Bee, as senior officer) would be relegated to another backwater of the battle, he curtly replied to Imboden's complaint about having to move without stopping to feed his hungry artillerymen: "You will have plenty of time to cook and eat, to the music of a battle in which we shall probably take little or no part."[22]

Bee was mistaken; as soon as it reached Evans's portion of the field, his brigade would be in the thick of the fighting and very much in harm's way. Fortunately, it would not bear the danger alone. It would be followed to the left by Jackson's five regiments of Virginians, the four guns of the Rockbridge Artillery under

Lieutenant John B. Brockenbrough, and the two sections of Stanard's Thomas Artillery. Farther to the rear would come the Wise Artillery, another four cannons, under John Pelham. All would be preceded by the infantry battalion of the Hampton Legion, only recently arrived at the depot at Manassas.[23]

The coming help was desperately needed. Evans had no illusions of holding on against an ever-widening enemy front. Even should reinforcements reach him in time to engage them, Hunter's troops were in such numbers that retreat was probably a matter of time. Even so, Evans made a stout fight of it, determined to sell his life and those of his men as dearly as possible.

He made his initial stand on the grounds below Pittsylvania, where he had the audacity to launch a preemptive blow. To deliver it he sent forward one of Wheat's companies, the colorfully named Catahoula Guerrillas. The men of this unit—the sons of New Orleans merchants and lawyers in contrast to their less privileged comrades, clad in dark gray shirts and blue kepis—quickly encountered Burnside's imperfectly formed skirmish line. In so doing they discovered something that surprised Evans, who still supposed that the Federals would confront him via the extension of the farm lane he had taken from Stone Bridge. Wheat or one of his men reported that a body of bluecoats was coming down the road from Sudley Ford, a mile to the west of Evans's position.[24]

Immediately, Evans ordered a shift in that direction, while moving his artillery into positions from which to cover the expanding field. He sent Wheat's battalion, followed by Sloan's men, at the double-quick westward about three-quarters of a mile. The movements of both units were shielded by high ground that extended from the Carter plantation to the road the enemy was using. Upon reaching their assigned positions, the winded troops formed in a line on the rear slope of a ridge known locally as Matthews Hill. The Louisianans deployed to cover the right flank; Evans moved the South Carolinians farther west until their left abutted the Sudley Road.

While the infantry moved west, Evans sent his two guns south. At his order Davidson, the ranking lieutenant, set up both on open ground two hundred yards north of the turnpike and almost a mile west of Stone Bridge. Soon after unlimbering, however, he was directed to send the 6-pounder under Leftwich down the pike, then up a lane parallel to and east of Sudley Road to provide closer support to the 4th South Carolina. The junior lieutenant emplaced his piece on Buck Hill, approximately five hundred yards north of the Stone House. From their new positions, both guns opened on the enemy, Leftwich at a distance of almost three-quarters of a mile, Davidson at longer range. As the Yankees came into range, both guns inflicted what Davidson called "considerable injury" on their targets, although he credited his subordinate with doing most of the damage.[25]

Then trouble broke out in the form of friendly fire. Along the Sidley Road, Sloan's regiment was no longer in touch with Wheat's battalion—a rectangular neck of pine trees separated them. When Wheat moved one of his companies, the Tiger Rifles, forward as skirmishers, their South Carolina comrades mistook them for the enemy and opened fire. Before the mistake could be corrected, at least two Tigers had been mortally wounded. Wheat shouted for his men to refrain from returning the fire, but only those near enough to hear him obeyed. Even some of those who heard the major yell retaliated out of anger. The deadly exchange compelled Wheat to risk his life by galloping between the units and personally stopping it. Chagrined by its mistake, the 4th South Carolina moved farther right to help close the gap that had caused the bloodletting.[26]

Once order had been restored, Wheat put himself at the head of the Catahoula Guerrillas and led them to the crest of Matthews Hill. Because the internecine shooting had prevented him from taking the position sooner, his men were not dug in when the skirmishers of the 2nd Rhode Island crossed the open field beyond the woods where they had formed and charged the hill. Wheat's men barely had time to unleash a ragged volley, but it was sufficient to halt the Rhode Islanders, many of whom dropped to the ground to escape the fire. But the skirmishers were not stymied for long; joined by comrades from the main body of their regiment, they scrambled to their feet and began to follow Colonel Slocum up Matthews Hill. Heavily outnumbered, Wheat ordered his guerrillas back down the ridge. Their retreat was helter-skelter, suggesting that the day's opening round had gone to their adversaries.[27]

At this point the rest of Evans's command opened on the Federals, who atop Matthews Hill with the rising sun at their backs made inviting targets. The 2nd Rhode Island absorbed what Corporal Sam English described as "a perfect hail storm of bullets, round shot and shell . . . tearing through our ranks and scattering death and confusion everywhere." The beleaguered regiment somehow managed to hold on to the crest and north slope but found further progress nearly impossible. Glancing rearward, the men anxiously awaited the appearance of the 1st Rhode Island, but they looked in vain. The 1st was somewhere back in the woods as if unaware it was needed at the front.[28]

For a considerable time, Colonel Slocum's only assistance came from the battery attached to his regiment, six 13-pounder James rifles commanded by Captain William Reynolds. Rocking and bouncing over the uneven ground north of Matthews Hill, Reynolds's pieces unlimbered east of the Sudley Road, in the left rear of the 2nd. Soon they were laying an intense shelling on all points of Evans's position. Davidson's and Leftwich's fewer and smaller cannons returned the fire as best they could. The uneven duel went on for half an hour or longer before the Confederates unlimbered and retired to the high ground east of the Lewis house, where they rejoined Captain Latham and the first section of the Lynchburg Artillery. Their survival probably owed to the length of time it took Reynolds to get their range. To one critically inclined infantryman, it appeared that the captain's objective "was to make as much noise as possible, and to get an immense quantity of iron into the enemy's line in the shortest possible space of time, without regard to whether it hit anything or not."[29]

The competing cannonades and fusillades made havoc among every unit involved. Union losses included an unusually high number of senior officers. Colonel Hunter, who had ridden to the head of his column to gain a better view of the unfolding contest, stopped a rifle ball, variously described as striking him in the neck, throat, and jaw; another missile disabled his warhorse. The wound may or may not have been severe; Hunter would survive it. It bled more or less profusely, but one who had a close up view of it some hours later pronounced it "a flesh wound and not dangerous." Even so, Hunter was through for the day—his fifty-ninth birthday—and soon evacuated by carriage to Washington. (His wounded mount would also survive the battle. Upon recovering, he would be sold to then-captain George Meade. The bright bay, whom Meade renamed Baldy, would carry the victor at Gettysburg through the rest of the war.)[30]

Before departing the field, Hunter temporarily turned his division over to Burnside, his nearest subordinate, telling him: "I leave the matter in your hands. Slocum and his Regiment went in handsomely and drove the scoundrels." But the matter would not rest with the bald-headed colonel with the memorable sidewhiskers.

Hunter thereafter dispatched an aide to inform Colonel Porter, whose men were pushing forward on the Sudley Road, that as the senior brigade commander, he was now in charge of the Second Division. Though at first stunned by the news of his enforced promotion, Porter shook off the psychological effect and rode forward to direct the next phase of the fight. By custom if not by regulation, he ought to have passed command of his brigade to his ranking subordinate, Colonel Henry W. Slocum of the 27th New York (no relation to the 2nd Rhode Island's commander). Instead, perhaps because the New Yorker was himself soon shot down and Porter was unfamiliar with or did not trust the brigade's other colonels, both of whom led militia outfits, he made an unorthodox selection of his successor: Lieutenant Averell, his longtime subordinate in the prewar regulars. According to Averell, shortly before Porter spurred off to assume division command, he told the twenty-eight-year-old subaltern, "Look after this brigade yourself." Averell's appointment to command may not have been by the book, but it did not matter— he would oversee the positioning of Porter's brigade for the balance of the day, his orders obeyed, apparently without question or hesitation, by the numerous officers who outranked him in the volunteer service.[31]

Shortly before he was crowned an acting brigadier, Averell had returned to Porter's side from an errand that had taken him to the front, where the colonel himself was now heading. Upon reaching the leading edge of the battlefield, the lieutenant had dismounted, climbed a fence, and through field glasses discerned "a long, moving column" off to the south and east. These were the troops Johnston had ordered to Evans's support and about which McDowell had warned Hunter's column. The newcomers included Bee's 4th Alabama and 2nd and 11th Mississippi and the 7th and 8th Georgia of Bartow's brigade, the combined force soon to be joined by Hampton's legionnaires. The approaching forces enjoyed artillery support as well; Averell would never forget the "whizzing and hurtling of the first solid shot from the enemy through the trees and tearing along the ground." In rather overripe prose he would describe the result as "the welcome of the spirits of all evil . . . an instantaneous expression of infinite wickedness."[32]

His observations complete, Averell had reported, as ordered, to Hunter. He was surprised by the picnic-like ambience he encountered at division headquarters, where Hunter was sharing a leisurely dinner with Colonel Burnside. He was further surprised to find Hunter not in the least concerned by the news that the enemy was advancing on him. As if dealing with a minor issue, he casually directed a staff officer to accompany Averell back to the front.

The two rode forward without incident. Breaking out of the trees along the Sudley Road, they climbed a hill—perhaps Averell's recent perch—from which they "made out distinctly the approaching column and its flags." After a few minutes' observation, the riders returned to Hunter's side. Upon receiving the aide's report, the division leader, just as casually as before as if extra caution was unwarranted, issued an order for Burnside's brigade to continue down the road in support of the soon-to-be-committed 2nd Rhode Island.

Leaving Hunter, Averell again rode south, this time to locate the best place for the rest of Burnside's command to exit the woods on its way to support Colonel Slocum. En route he met Slocum, an acquaintance from prewar days when the latter served in the 9th U.S. Infantry. The lieutenant remained with him for a few minutes as Slocum moved his regiment east of the Sudley Road and toward Matthews Hill, then turned to leave. The colonel, he recalled, was calmly "lighting a cigar as I saw him for the last time."[33]

Slocum assumed a conspicuous presence in order that his men—a large number of whom remained flat on their faces—could see him and heed his commands. Advancing on foot to the base of the ridge, sword and pistol upraised, he strode toward a rail fence that separated his regiment from the enemy. Shouting "now show them what Rhode Island can do," he threw a leg over the top rail and waved for his men to follow. Despite their respect for him as a leader, few got to their feet. Writing after the war, Private Elisha Hunt Rhodes implied as much when he wrote that the colonel "advanced nearer to the brow of the hill than the line occupied by the Regiment. As he returned and was in the act of climbing the fence, he fell on the side next to the Regiment." Slocum had been struck by at least three rifle balls, one penetrating his skull.

Rhodes and a comrade jumped up, ran to the fallen officer, lifted him, and carried him to the rear. Briefly conscious but mortally wounded, Slocum was borne to a temporary aid station set up in a farmhouse on the left end of the battle line. There he lapsed into a coma and in that condition was evacuated by ambulance to Sudley Church, whose spacious interior and location well behind the front had recommended it to Assistant Surgeon D. L. Magruder for conversion to a field hospital. For two days Slocum lay on a litter stretched across a pew before succumbing to his wounds, never having regained consciousness.[34]

Many of the colonel's men shared his fate, felled in their exposed position by musketry and shell now coming not only from Evans's men but also from those of Bee and Bartow. Some historians have laid their predicament at the feet of David Hunter, who has been criticized for mismanaging his column's deployment. It is true that while the 2nd Rhode Island struggled, Hunter retained in the rear the balance of Burnside's brigade—not only the 1st Rhode Island but also the 2nd New Hampshire, the 71st New York Militia, and the latter's two boat howitzers (bronze weapons with wrought-iron carriages designed in the 1840s by then-lieutenant John Dahlgren for service on sea and ashore). But Hunter left the field too early in the action to deserve all the blame. Before Porter could succeed to command, Burnside did little as acting division leader to improve the situation. He tried to form the New Hampshire and New York regiments into a line of battle on the 2nd Rhode Island's right, but the rookie outfits collided, got mixed up, and failed to untangle.[35]

Their missteps uncovered Reynolds's artillerists and exposed them to Evans's skirmish fire. Burnside had made the mistake of entrusting the guns' welfare to his ubiquitous, energetic, but inexperienced superior Governor Sprague. The one thing His Excellency showed himself to be good at this day was being shot off his horse. This happened three times in quick succession, one mount being decapitated by a shell fragment. Each time the plucky official remounted on a spare battery horse, aboard which he rode about shouting incoherent directions and otherwise making a nuisance of himself.[36]

At length, Burnside galloped off to locate Porter, whose brigade had begun to form on the west side of the Sudley Road. He found the colonel riding in his direction, intending to place himself at the head of his newly expanded command. Lieutenant Averell, who was riding with him, recalled that Burnside "came tearing up on a foaming charger, and saying with hysterical excitement, 'Porter, for God's sake let me have the regulars. My men are all being cut to pieces!'" Although Averell had alerted Porter to Bee's and Bartow's approach, the new division leader had been unaware of the gravity of the situation. Thus he replied: "Colonel Burnside, do you mean to say that the enemy is advancing on my left?" Burnside nodded emphatically, adding, "and you will be cut to pieces if you can't stop him."[37]

With great reluctance, Porter ordered Averell to bring to the head of the column the eight companies of regulars under Major Sykes of the 14th Infantry. Averell obeyed the order, one of the last he would answer that day—he would spend the rest of the battle giving orders of his own. With admirable aplomb, the professionals marched down from their position on the right of the brigade line and moved toward the position of Reynolds's battery. Averell did not think much of the maneuver, considering the shift of Sykes's position "one of the fatal errors of the day." The regulars, he believed, should have been held in the right rear of the division, where they could have served as a bulwark against the stampede of volunteer troops. Burnside, however, was relieved and elated by their appearance; riding up to their commander, he exclaimed: "Good God! Major Sykes, your regulars are just what we want; form on my left and give aid to my men who are being cut to pieces!"[38]

Farther west, Porter's brigade, now firmly in Averell's hands, moved to cover Burnside's right flank. From southwest to northeast, Averell's line comprised the 8th New York, the 14th Brooklyn, the battalion of U.S. Marine recruits under Major John G. Reynolds (not to be confused with the Rhode Island battery commander), and H. W. Slocum's 27th New York. Later in the morning, around 11:30, Captain Charles Griffin's Company D of the newly formed 5th U.S. Artillery, consisting of four 10-pounder Parrott rifles and two 12-pounder howitzers, unlimbered in front of the brigade line and began hurling shot and shell at Evans's men and their fast-arriving reinforcements.[39]

Hastening back to his own brigade, Burnside tried to get his New Hampshiremen and New Yorkers into the fight but failed miserably. Neither regiment had maintained order or cohesion. The formation of Colonel Henry P. Martin's 71st New York had been broken by the unheralded passage through its ranks of two of Griffin's cannons. The confusion afflicting the 2nd New Hampshire was partly attributable to a severe wound in the shoulder suffered by its colonel, Gilman Marston. The doughty ex-congressman, a graduate of both Dartmouth College and Harvard Law School, refused to go to the rear. Despite the wracking pain, he remained on horseback, his mount led about by an orderly, until blood loss forced him to leave on a litter. His regiment's ordeal also owed to a scathing fire directed at its left flank by enemy forces that, as Marston's second in command wrote, "appeared as if they had sprung out of the ground."[40]

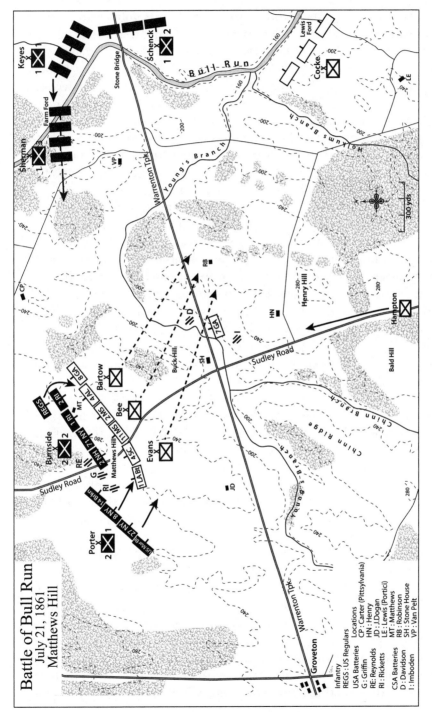

Battle of Bull Run, July 21, 1861: Matthews Hill. *Map by Paul Dangel.*

Frustrated by his inability to get his units fully into action, Burnside was forced to order up the well-aligned 1st Rhode Island, which he had hoped to preserve for rearguard duty. To make way he ordered Martin's New Yorkers to lie down and let the Rhode Islanders through. The desperate expedient permitted the newcomers to squeeze into the space between the 71st and the 2nd Rhode Island father east. Once the 1st reached the front, its men opened with their rifles (one of the companies was armed with easily reloadable carbines), and the pressure on the 2nd Rhode Island began to ease. To give their comrades room, the 2nd shifted left while also attempting to re-form its left flank to meet an expected attack.[41]

With Colonel Slocum out of the fight, the maneuver was overseen by his executive officer, Lieutenant Colonel Frank Wheaton, and the next in command, Major Sullivan Ballou. When the latter ushered his men into their new position, he turned his back momentarily to the enemy. As he did, a shell delivered by the Lynchburg Artillery exploded beside him, crushing his right leg and killing his horse, Jennie. Ballou also was transported to Sudley Church, where he joined his dying colonel. His shattered leg was later amputated, but the operation failed to save his life. On July 28 Ballou, his tragic premonition fulfilled, went on ahead to await his beloved wife and children.[42]

When Major Wheat, from his defensive position on the reverse slope of Matthews Hill, observed the 2nd Rhode Island's change of position, he believed it indicated either a Union withdrawal or an opportunity to precipitate one. At his order (and apparently without authority from Major Evans), Wheat led the way back to the summit of the ridge through an extensive field of corn that sheltered the right flank of the Rhode Islanders' position. His Tigers, following close behind, bent low as they filed through the cornrows. Then at their leader's shouted command, they bobbed up and charged the Yankees.

As they ran, many veering to the right instead of the left as intended, the Zouaves fired a final round before tossing aside their rifles to brandish the Bowie knives they had brought with them from New Orleans and that until now had served more often as cooking utensils than as fearsome weapons. Few, however, got close enough to the enemy to use cold steel; when twenty yards off, they absorbed a withering volley from the Rhode Islanders, who then let loose with something approximating a Yankee yell. At the same time, Reynolds's 13-pounder rifles dropped a murderous barrage on the Louisianans, who fell right and left.

The major later confessed that the attack had been a botch. He had intended to move to the cover of a hill beyond the corn, but "a part of my command, [by] mistake, crossed the open field and suffered severely from the fire of the enemy." Bob Wheat suffered alongside his men, dropping from a rifle ball that passed through his body, piercing at least one lung. Lugged off the field on a litter fashioned from his men's muskets, he was carried to the base of the hill. There he was united with the survivors of the charge, most of whom had withdrawn to safety in rear of the 4th South Carolina, from which they would sally forth as if never driven from the field. An army surgeon informed Wheat that his wound was fatal. This diagnosis did not faze the deeply religious major (son of an Episcopalian rector), but he replied cheerfully, "I don't feel like dying yet." Eventually he would recover, a feat attributable as much to force of will as to hearty constitution.[43]

Without his leadership, the Tigers rebounded from their heavy losses to fight throughout the day from successive positions. They gave a strong account of themselves in the thickest of the fight— their flag was pierced by at least fifteen bullets—and they remained contemptuous of the enemy to the last. As one of Wheat's lieutenants, shot through one thigh, shouted to his men as they swept past him to confront the enemy: "I'll be great gloriously God damned if the sons of bitches can ever whip the Tigers!"[44]

Major Wheat was similarly defiant. When describing in his official report his gallant but doomed assault—which historians have described as ill considered and ill timed—he insisted, "I was enabled to damage the enemy very much." Later he would claim to have led no fewer than three charges, all of which were in some fashion successful.[45]

His superior, Evans, made note of the charge in his own report but refused to characterize it as helpful to his situation. In fact, the Tigers' repulse fueled his growing anxiety that even with supports arriving, his position was unstable and perhaps untenable. From his vantage point just north of the Warrenton Pike–Sudley Road intersection, Evans could clearly observe the many forces moving into position to confront him: Porter's foot soldiers and Griffin's battery on the left; on the right, Burnside's brigade at last stabilizing its battle line. Burnside was being supported not only by Sykes's regulars but by no fewer than eight guns: the six of Captain Reynolds augmented by the navy howitzers. Already outnumbered roughly five-to-one, Evans could envision even greater trouble ahead. From all appearances, the enemy troops within his range of vision were not the extent of his opposition. He was right. Within an hour, in fact, McDowell would have twice as many men on the Confederate side of Bull Run.

Evans would have been swept off Matthews Hill long before the last of these forces reached his position were it not for the even more timely arrival of Bee and Bartow. A few minutes before eleven o'clock, the head of the relief column made its appearance. Bee halted it atop Henry Hill, about eight hundred yards short of Evans's position. This was a misnamed plateau about three hundred yards wide and a half mile long, most of it south of the Warrenton Pike and east of Sudley Road, which rose some one hundred feet above Bull Run. Near its northwestern brow stood the two-story frame house of eighty-four-year-old Judith Carter Henry, a member of the family that owned Pittsylvania and the widow of a naval surgeon, the namesake of the hill. The eminence featured long, gradual slopes and an apparently level summit. The impression of flatness was, however, deceptive: the ground concealed an array of rises, hollows, ravines, and on its eastern and southern sides, belts of oak and second-growth pine—all would serve well as defensive positions.[46]

Other landmarks of Henry Hill included not only elegant Portici, the Lewis family home, but also the modest clapboard house of James Robinson, a free African American, which sat on high ground overlooking the turnpike northeast of the Henry house. Like many another resident caught between warring armies (dozens of others had taken refuge at the old resort hotel at Sudley Springs), Robinson had evacuated the area. But the Widow Henry, borne down by years and bedridden, remained in her house, attended to by a son, a daughter, and a black servant. Her decision to ride out the fighting to come would prove a fatal mistake.[47]

Barnard Bee wanted nothing so much as to get into the thick of the battle as soon as possible. Before the general received his orders to move to the left flank, Captain Imboden, his army's de facto chief of artillery, found him in a truculent mood, chaffing at the inactivity he had been relegated to ever since arriving at Manassas. Bee did not believe he would gain the physical and emotional release he craved by being sent to the Confederate left. Aware of Beauregard's plan to attack from the right and center, he suspected that Jackson's brigade, which remained in its original position for some time after Bee and Bartow departed, would see far more action than he.[48]

The forced march from the lower fords toward Stone Bridge only made the South Carolinian more irritable. Conducted at a frenetic pace for nearly four miles over almost every imaginable feature of terrain, it was a hellish ordeal, especially for those afoot. James G. Hudson of Company D, 4th Alabama Infantry, which led Bee's column, described the march as "in a northwesterly direction through pine thickets and cedar hammocks, over ditches, gullies, briar patches, fences, swamps, hills and valleys, at about 1/2 double quick." Another Alabamian wrote, "we did not stop even for fences, but when we came to one, we would with one shove level it with the ground, and on we'd go."[49]

The movement ended with Bee's men "much exhausted" at the summit of Henry Hill east of Mrs. Henry's home. Bee now realized that he was going to see a great deal more fighting this morning than he had expected. While the infantry sought shelter behind one of the plateau's many rolling hills, the four smoothbore 6-pounders of the Staunton Artillery went into battery about 150 yards north of the widow's abode. Just before they deployed, Bee told Captain Imboden, "Here is the battle-field, and we are in for it!"

Soon Imboden's cannons were firing across the turnpike at the Federals on Matthews Hill. As the only artillery unit on Henry Hill just then, the battery might have made an inviting target. For its deliverance from "utter destruction," Imboden credited Bee. The sharp-eyed brigadier had assigned it a position where it was "sheltered by a swell in the ground to our front five or six feet high."[50]

As far as he was from the scene of the struggle on Matthews Hill, Bee could be of only so much help to his fellow South Carolinian. Afforded a full view of the fighting to the north, he could see that Evans, his front and flanks under increasing pressure, would be forced to give up his position sooner rather than later. Evans did not agree. When Bee sent a courier to bring word of his arrival on the high ground, Evans petitioned him to cross Young's Branch and join him in fending off the Yankees. Believing his own position more defensible, Bee advised Evans to disengage and withdraw to the plateau. The hard-pressed major would have none of it. As Beauregard wrote after the war, "Evans, full of the spirit that would not retreat, renewed his appeal that the forces in rear would come to help him hold his ground."[51]

Against his better judgment, Bee ordered the 4th Alabama of Colonel Egbert Jones to hasten to Evans's position, which it was to expand and secure. The regiment descended Henry Hill and, under fire from the Union batteries on Matthews Hill, crossed the turnpike above the Stone House. Beyond the pike the Alabamians climbed Buck Hill and dashed under a hail of rifle and artillery fire toward the exposed right flank of Evans's line. Imboden's smoothbores covered the movement with a steady barrage of long-range ammunition. The regiment was further assisted by a single 6-pounder that had accompanied the regiment from Henry Hill. According to Captain Thomas Goldsby, the little gun "did much to divert the attention of the enemy from our advance movement. Even in that hour of peril we could not fail to admire the accuracy and effect of its aim."[52]

Upon reaching Matthews Hill, the newcomers spread out to extend Evans's line to the north and east. They took up a position to the right of the copse of trees that sheltered Sloan's 4th South Carolina, within one hundred yards of the main Union line. Under fire from Reynolds's battery, many Alabamians took cover behind a fence line that bordered a field of tall corn, but it offered almost no protection. In time the 4th would be joined by the rest of Bee's brigade and one of Bartow's regiments, but for what must have seemed a lifetime, the outfit faced enemy bullets and shells virtually alone. "Our brave men fell in great numbers," wrote Captain Goldsby, "but they died as the brave love to die—with faces to the foe, fighting in the holy cause of liberty." The 4th was fated to absorb a casualty rate of almost 40 percent, the highest of any regiment, Union or Confederate, on this field.[53]

Even after the rest of Bee's command and the regiments of Bartow crossed the pike to assist Evans, the defenders were in a tight spot, not only opposed by the brigades of Burnside and Porter but soon also threatened by the approach of enemy troops from the north (where Heintzelman's division was belatedly reaching the battlefield) and the east (where Sherman's brigade was maneuvering toward a crossing of Bull Run). Despite the lengthening odds, Bee, the on-scene commander, believed that he could not afford to remain on the defensive, enduring the shells and rifle balls that were taking a steady toll of the 4th Alabama. Realizing that Jones's men could not remain rooted to its position, he galloped to its commander, waved his sword arm, and shouted, "Up, Alabamians!" In response Jones rode to the head of his outfit and called on his men to follow him through the fence and into the cornfield on the other side.[54]

Known for his diffidence ("as bashful as a timid young lady," in the words of one acquaintance) and soft-spoken ways, the six-foot-three-inch colonel was determined to show a different side of his personality today. Repressing their misgivings about his leadership, which had prompted some officers and men to petition him to resign his commission, the troops rose up and followed him into the corn-rows. While they moved they raised their own version of the newly minted Rebel yell. "We set up such a yell of hatred and defiance," one man wrote, "that it was heard a mile above the roar of battle."[55]

The decision to take the fight to the enemy may have been a necessity, but it only produced more bloodshed. As soon as the 4th topped the fence, rounds from a dozen artillery pieces shred-ded the cornfield beyond. Alabamians and cornstalks alike were mowed down by the rifle fire of Burnside's troops, including the 71st New York, which had recovered from its initial confusion to fight with "bravery and steadiness." In the face of this metallic blizzard, Colonel Jones's men appeared powerless. Unable to go forward, they obeyed the shouted orders of the colonel and their company offi-cers to lie flat among the rows as hundreds of missiles streamed overhead. As Colonel Richardson's men had discovered on the eigh-teenth, it was virtually impossible to deliver an accurate fire from a prone position, and those who risked their lives by bobbing up to shoot found their vision blocked by the ubiquitous stalks.

It was even more dangerous for anyone on horseback as Colonel Jones soon learned. While sitting his horse "as calm as a statue," he was struck by bullets that penetrated both of his thighs. His men left him where he fell from the saddle, some of them hastening to the rear in panic and confusion. Seeing this, Jones, unable to move, cried out futilely, "Men, don't run!" Minutes later his position was overrun, and he was captured inside the woodlot he had defended so stoutly. "Gentlemen, you have got me," he told some of Sykes's regulars who surrounded him, "but a hundred thousand and more await you!" Eventually forced to withdraw, the Federals left him to be recovered by his men and carried from the field for hospitaliza-tion. His wounds were mortal, though it would take him six weeks to succumb to them. Given the emphasis he and his men placed on honor and personal conduct, Jones may have felt his redeemed repu-tation worth the sacrifice it had extracted.[56]

While many Alabamians remained pinned down, others snaked their way back to the relative safety of the rear. Private Hudson recalled that when Lieutenant Colonel Evander M. Law and Major Charles L. Scott saw that the regiment was on the verge of being surrounded and cut off, they ordered a retreat, "which was made in 'double quick' but in good order, after having maintained their position for one hour and forty minutes against *ten thousand* of the enemy." Hudson may have exaggerated the odds his outfit faced, but he was right to be proud of the service it had rendered against such adverse conditions. Moreover, the 4th was not done fighting; it would engage the enemy through the balance of the day from one position after another.[57]

With Jones's outfit still in dire straits, Bee called up his Mississippians and Bartow's Georgians and advanced them to the firing line. Many of those moving up were happy to quit their former position some four hundred yards to the rear, where they had been pounded by Porter's and Griffin's guns. Incoming shells had dosed almost every point on Bee's line, but Lieutenant Colonel William M. Gardner's 8th Georgia appears to have received special attention. When shells tore through a grove of apple trees in which several members of the 8th had perched, a comrade saw them "drop like shot bears, and scrambled on hands and knees for their places in the line."[58]

Responding with alacrity to Bee's orders, the thirteen companies of the 2nd and 11th Mississippi hustled into line on the southwestern flank of the 4th Alabama. The brigade leader formed the 2nd in a patch of woods and then ordered the regiment to move up and occupy the position formerly held by Evans's 4th South Carolina, whose men were now falling back. The deployment was a hectic affair, but a Mississippi captain "with a great fondness for oratory" thought he could squeeze in a little speech that would fire the enthusiasm of his company. Shouting above the din, the officer reminded the men that they were facing "a most bitter and damaging enemy, and one that does not only propose to rob you of your property but to deprive you of your constitutional rights and privileges for which your ancestors fought, bled, and died." Warming to his subject as the battle heated up, he urged everyone to stand firm against all odds, showing his face, not his back, to the foe, when a shell burst over his head "and down went the captain flat on his face." He picked himself up, wiped the dirt from his mouth, and announced, "I will finish my remarks when this thing is over." His undignified sprawl seemed a bad omen for a regiment going into its first fight.[59]

While Bee put his entire brigade into line, Bartow deployed only half of his command at the front. Gardner's regiment he moved from its exposed position near the Robinson house across the turnpike and up Matthews Hill until it gained the dubious shelter of a thicket on the left flank of the 4th Alabama. Colonel Lucius J. Gartrell's 7th Georgia did not advance as far; Bartow held the regiment just south of the turnpike, covering the rear. Although many accounts place Gartrell's men on Matthews Hill, coordinating their operations with their fellow Georgians, the 7th never made it to the front but formed a link between Bee's reinforcements and Imboden's perpetually firing guns on Henry Hill.[60]

The 8th Georgia advanced to its designated position—a gnarly thicket of pine trees and blackberry bushes—under what one of its men called a perfect storm of bullets: "We gained the thicket and commenced firing the enemy returning the fire with all there arms (they had about 6000 we about 600)." Ten-to-one odds notwithstanding, the 8th applied mounting pressure to the left flank of Burnside's brigade, which the repositioned 2nd Rhode Island now held. The two regiments blazed away at each other for several minutes, casualties mounting on both sides. By day's end, the Rhode Islanders would suffer more than seventy casualties, the Georgians upward of two hundred.[61]

Well dug in around the Edgar Matthews farmhouse, the Federals had the tactical advantage; they shattered the front and flanks of the 8th Georgia while hacking away at their woodland sanctuary, which one defender dubbed "the place of slaughter." Captain Robert Grant of the 8th recalled that "many officers of the regiment were down— some killed, some wounded, and every step you were called on to stop and assist some poor fellow who was down or hobbling off." One who barely managed to hobble off was Colonel Gardner, his ankle shattered by a bullet The thirty-seven-year-old West Pointer's wounding had occurred only minutes after he delivered a succinct pep talk to his troops: "Remember that you are Georgians. Keep [in] your ranks, do your duty, and we'll whip 'em!"[62]

Minutes after Gardner went down, his adjutant, Lieutenant John Branch, was mortally wounded by a rifle ball in the chest. The staff officer's younger brothers, Sanford and Hamilton, also members of the 8th, were in the thick of the fight, the latter being wounded but not fatally. Sanford Branch stayed with the dying officer after his outfit withdrew; fidelity ensured his capture. Writing five days later from a prison near Washington, "Santy" told their mother that John "died in my arms. His last words were about you and Hamilton."[63]

Like the 4th Alabama inside its cornfield, the 8th Georgia was trapped by its supposed refuge. "In this jungle," Captain Grant wrote, "many of our boys got scattered, and some of them falling in, fought with other regiments." Yet the Georgians not only clung to their exposed position but also began to shift to the right in an effort to overlap the 2nd Rhode Island. It was this threat that had prompted Burnside to declare his need for reinforcement by Sykes's battalion.[64]

Although Burnside's plea had a decisive effect on the fight for Matthews Hill, he has been roundly criticized for overreacting to the threat to his flank. Supposedly, his premature commitment of the regulars robbed Porter's division of a steadying influence and a core of professionalism better used elsewhere. In truth, Sykes's force, only recently recruited back to manpower levels that had dropped precipitously during peacetime, contained more than a smattering of raw recruits, some of whom fired wildly as they advanced on Bee's battle line. Yet despite some brief confusion in their ranks, the regulars moved ahead steadily and resolutely, their main body preceded by three companies skilled in skirmisher tactics. The confident demeanor of veterans and rookies alike had a calming influence on the volunteers they were supporting.

The regulars' we-mean-business attitude also had a decisive effect on their enemy, still outnumbered two-to-one. Weak from blood loss and exhausted from two hours or more of fighting an ever-growing antagonist, the gray lines gradually began to give, and retreat became a matter of time. Averell, looking on from the rear, gave full credit to Sykes's men, whom, he wrote, "carried the grove in front of Burnside, driving the enemy out." The decisive blow, however, may have been self-inflicted. According to Major Whiting of Johnston's staff, who would later gain command of Bee's brigade, the coup de grace was delivered not by Sykes but by a column of unidentified Confederate troops that Bee ordered to confront the regulars and silence the battery supporting their advance. By Whiting's secondhand account, "the column refused to move," an unexpected resistance that "deprived our troops of selected positions, exposed them to severe and disastrous fire . . . , and naturally disheartened them by the backward movement."[65]

No one knows who first raised the cry, but shouted orders to retreat ran up and down the wavering line. Before twelve noon, the men of Bee, Bartow, and Evans were in full flight across Young's Branch. Dozens of fugitives crossed the turnpike to find temporary refuge behind the Robinson house; many others did not halt until securely atop Henry Hill. They were partially covered by Imboden's guns, still firing and quickly exhausting their supply of projectiles, as well as by the 7th Georgia and the just-arrived Hampton Legion.

As yet no body of reinforcements had secured the plateau where Mrs. Henry, her family, and her servant cowered inside a house that would soon be a target of both armies. Jackson's brigade, however, was now coming up as were Generals Johnston and Beauregard, seeking to take charge of the fighting in a sector they had not expected to have to hold at all costs. Having accepted that the offensive against Centreville was a dead letter, Beauregard embraced his superior's desire to concentrate on shoring up the opposite end of the battle line. "The battle is there," Johnston had announced with uncharacteristic decisiveness, and there, he told Beauregard, "I am going." Moments later he was galloping down Lookout Hill and heading northwest at breakneck speed. Unwilling to be left behind, Beauregard dashed after him, his staff trailing behind. En route both commanders tried to round up additional support for what had become the most critical point on the battlefield.[66]

The question that nagged Johnston, and presumably his senior subordinate as well, was whether time remained to shore up the flank before it came apart altogether. When the generals on their ride encountered fugitives from Matthews Hill—bloodied, exhausted troops, many having thrown away their muskets in their haste to outrun pursuit—and heard the wails of doom and disaster coming from these men, they must have wondered if the battle—and perhaps the war, and with it the dream of Southern nationhood—had already been lost.

CHAPTER 13

VICTORY ASSURED?

Forty-three-year-old Wade Hampton III of Columbia, South Carolina, was a cotton Croesus. Having inherited vast landholdings in four states, including two sprawling plantations worked by hundreds of slaves, he was rightly considered one of the richest men in all the South. Although a political moderate and a conciliatory voice during the secession debate of the late 1850s, when his state left the Union in December 1860 and went to war four months later, Hampton threw himself into the Confederate war effort. From his own pocket he paid the greater part of the cost of organizing a legion. This was a combined-arms organization with roots in European and eighteenth-century American history, composed of units of infantry, cavalry, and artillery—in effect, a small private army of which Hampton was elected colonel.[1]

A novice soldier but a born leader, the South Carolina grandee drilled alongside his raw recruits on one of his Columbia-area properties under the tutelage of experienced drillmasters, including his rotund but energetic lieutenant colonel Benjamin J. Johnson. By mid-July he was ready to lead his command off to war. A lack of rail accommodations meant that when he reached Manassas Junction around two-thirty in the morning of the twenty-first, Hampton had at his disposal only the infantry component of his army: six companies, about 620 men. Though reduced to its basic element, the Hampton Legion was eager to join in the battle that gave every indication of being hours away. The much-interrupted journey from Richmond had taken twenty-six and a half hours, and the cramped passengers were in a surly—and fighting—mood.

After devouring a meager breakfast, the legionnaires hoisted the English-made Enfield rifles their patron had armed them with and about 6:00 A.M. commenced a three-hour hike toward Colonel Cocke's field headquarters at the Lewis family plantation, one mile south of Stone Bridge. Hampton was in the saddle, but the march was fatiguing for his men on foot. They appeared to be animated, however, by the omnipresent signs that their baptism of fire was imminent, although its venue was uncertain. Shortly before eleven o'clock, Hampton, still far from his objective, was met by a scout from Beauregard's headquarters redirecting him to where Bee and Bartow were fighting for their lives. The colonel immediately turned his column to the left and started it at the double-quick "at a right angle to the course I had been pursuing, and guided by the sound of a heavy fire which had just opened."

Hampton's revised course carried his troops up Henry Hill. At the top he cast about for a position from which he could lend his heavily engaged comrades the most support. At first he formed his men on the flanks of Imboden's battery, which continued to pound Matthews Hill in the face of diminishing ammunition. Even in his hollow, Imboden's presence was conspicuous enough to draw counterbattery fire in profusion. One shell struck the ground only a few feet from Hampton, showering horse and rider with dirt and rocks. Only the colonel's exceptional seat kept him in the saddle.[2]

The legion's commander remained "for some time near the battery, but seeing that the enemy were closing in on [the] right flank," he moved his men down the slope and into a wooded patch southeast of the Robinson house. In this position his men lay down along a fence line behind and to the left of Bartow's rear guard, the 7th Georgia. For a time Hampton's infantry joined the Georgians in covering the fighting farther north, but as the enemy moved closer, descending Matthews Hill and threatening to overlap Bee's and Bartow's combined line on both ends, Hampton rode forward of his battle line, took a good look at the advancing Yankees through his field glasses, then rode back to his command and announced, "Men of the Legion, I am happy to inform you that the enemy is in sight!"[3]

Even before the Federals reached Hampton's position, the South Carolinians came under intense shelling. Hampton identified the source as Captain James Brewerton Ricketts's Company I, 1st U.S. Artillery, one of the best-manned, best-mounted, and best-equipped batteries in either army. Ricketts's guns were aiding Heintzelman's division, which was finally coming onto the battlefield, further extending the Union line. To escape the shelling, Hampton ordered his men toward the Warrenton Pike. En route they met a mass of troops rushing the other way, having been forced back across Young's Branch by the seemingly implacable advance of Porter's division, now supported by Heintzelman. "We rushed on toward the

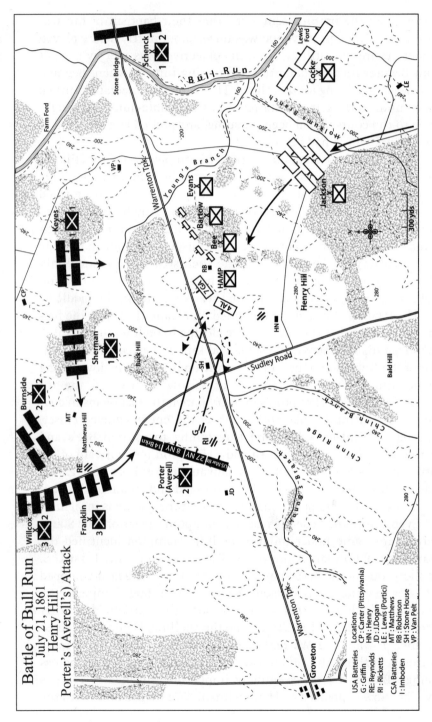

Battle of Bull Run, July 21, 1861: Henry Hill, Porter's (Averell's) Attack. *Map by Paul Dangel.*

Robinson house," wrote sixteen-year-old private Johnny Coxe, "and as we went we met many retreating stragglers and saw our artillery still firing near the Henry house." Entering the Robinson property through a garden gate, the legionaries took shelter around the front driveway of the house "while Federal bullets and shells were dropping thick and fast."[4]

The movement may have seemed a prudent one, but it was a case of out of the frying pan, into the fire. No sooner had the legion huddled along the drive than the head of the brigade now commanded by Lieutenant Averell opened on them at a range of 200 yards. The powerfully concentrated volley took down numerous legionnaires, including several who had not even gained the flimsy protection of the fence. Hampton had his horse shot from beneath him; he rose dazed and bleeding, his leg injured but otherwise unhurt. His second in command was not as fortunate. Lieutenant Colonel Johnson was, an admirer wrote, "a cool soldier" but corpulent enough to make a good target, especially in the saddle. A bullet passed through his skull, sending his "portly form" tumbling onto the dusty road. Hampton termed the demise of his principal drillmaster "a great loss" to the army and "an irreparable misfortune" for the legion itself.[5]

Hampton rallied and realigned his disordered ranks. Turning to the right, he led them down the slope in front of Robinson's house to the edge of the turnpike. Cover here was as scarce as it had been behind the little dwelling, but despite being rocked by Averell's initial fire, the legion held its ground and slowly gained the upper hand.

The principal assailants were members of the 27th New York Volunteers. An Elmira regiment, the pride of western New York, they were led by an officer destined to rise to high station; this day, however, he would lack an opportunity to display the ability that would make his reputation. Colonel Henry Warner Slocum's troops had surged ahead of the forces pursuing those Confederates who, after hours of stout fighting, had been forced off Matthews Hill and across Young's Branch and the turnpike. According to one source, an aide from Colonel Porter's staff (quite possibly Lieutenant Averell) had pointed Slocum toward the pike and told him that "you will find the enemy down there somewhere." Slocum needed no more specific instructions. Shouting a volley of orders, he led his New Yorkers in the general direction indicated.[6]

En route to their enemy's fallback position, the 27th crossed the croplands of John Dogan's farm in the northwest quadrant of the Warrenton Pike–Sudley Road intersection and angled toward the Stone House. Caught on the open ground behind the house, they came within range of Imboden's 6-pounders and lost upward of sixty men under a shower of shrapnel and canister. To escape the rain of iron, Slocum took his men to the left for a few hundred yards. By now the regiment's lines were becoming strung out and its men nervous and anxious to get back at the enemy. According to Averell, "excited and enraged by its casualties [it] rushed madly down the slope upon the enemy."[7]

Upon reaching the base of the hill, the men halted abruptly. Heading toward them via a brushy ravine on their right was a body of infantry—the remnant of the 4th Alabama—attempting to make a stand after being forced off Matthews Hill and losing almost every field officer. Thanks to the heavy underbrush, the newcomers could not be identified at such a distance, nor could their banners. Because they did not immediately open fire on the 27th, they had the potential to be friendly, so the Federals did not shoot.

The difficulty in discerning regimental colors had arisen almost with the day's first shot; it would recur time and again, on many parts of the battlefield, over the next five hours. The problem lay not only with those flags specific to regiments Union and Confederate, which were of various hues and designs, but also with the national colors of both armies. A degree of nostalgia for the old Union prevailed even in those states heavily supportive of secession. A typical Confederate who fought at Manassas, Private T. L. Wragg of the 8th Georgia, was saddened by his first glimpse of "the once glorious stars and stripes floating over the enemy." Perhaps not surprisingly, the first official flag of the Confederacy—a seven-star design adopted by the Provisional Congress in March 1861 and subsequently modified to include nine and then eleven stars—was strikingly similar to the Stars and Stripes borne by every Federal regiment. Until unique colors and devices were developed and approved, many a soldier would fall to friendly fire. Other men would suffer because their officers forbade them from firing until too late on enemy units thought to be carrying the colors of their own army.

The inconsistency of uniform colors was, of course, another source of confusion and casualties. At first the 27th supposed the advancing Alabamians were comrades—members of the 8th New York Militia of their own brigade also wore gray. For this reason the sons of Elmira hesitated, withholding fire, until the unknown force was almost within pointblank range.[8]

The Confederates, who were just as uncertain of their opponents' identity, would claim they were fired upon first. Private John Fowler of the 4th Alabama recalled that "the adjutant of the 27th New York reg. rode towards us with a flag of truce in his hand. He approached to within seventy or eighty yards of us, then rode back to his reg. and they opened fire upon us. Up to this time, we were of the opinion, that this was one of our reg[iments] sent to our assistance."[9]

Regardless of who squeezed off the first shots, the New Yorkers appeared to get the best of it. The 4th Alabama's sergeant major, Robert T. Coles, recalled that Slocum's men "poured a deadly volley into our already shattered ranks, which sent us retreating across the valley of Young's Branch beyond musket range." The fusillade left the 4th bereft of its remaining field officers, Lieutenant Colonel Law being disabled by a broken arm and Major Scott by a bullet in the leg. Coles added that "the men dragged themselves wearily back, feeling that they had been disgraced for showing their backs to the despised Yankees, and sad over the loss of comrades." The Alabamans, however, had no reason to feel ashamed; they had fought manfully until overwhelmed, in the process suffering most of the 196 casualties they would take this day, the second highest recorded loss rate of any Confederate regiment engaged in the battle.[10]

Slocum's troops closely pursued, expecting to make prisoners of many demoralized Rebels. The path they took carried them to the edge of the turnpike, where they unexpectedly encountered the Hampton Legion. The South Carolinians had been covering the 4th Alabama's retreat from their position in the lane of the Robinson house. Unprepared to meet a second body of assailants, the 27th staggered backward under a deadly shower of musketry and began to lose cohesion. Slocum's executive officer, Major J. J. Bartlett, reported that because of the confusion, "we lost many killed and wounded, besides the opportunity of capturing a large number of prisoners."[11]

Fired into from the right as well as from the front, the 27th grudgingly withdrew, first to, and then beyond, the Stone House. While leading the survivors back up Buck Hill, Slocum was dropped by a musket ball that passed through his right thigh. Taking command, Bartlett succeeded in rallying most of the men as well as some two hundred members of the 8th New York, which had suffered on Buck Hill what its commander, Colonel George Lyons, charitably called "a temporary break." The stampede—for that is what it was—had occurred when the 8th, while attempting to dislodge a body of Rebels that had been hitting Slocum's left, was subjected to a galling fire from artillery newly arrived on Henry Hill.[12]

By the time it topped Buck Hill, the 27th New York was in a "perfectly exhausted condition." One of Slocum's last acts before being carried from the field was to march his tired men into a woods for a respite from the nearly incessant enemy fire. Under Major Bartlett's direction, the regiment spent a good half hour in its leafy refuge. Even there, however, it attracted fire, principally from Hampton's troops. It also drew rifle balls from the men of Bee, Bartow, and Evans, who had battened down to defend the marshy ground south of Young's Branch.

Concerned that the First Brigade's advance had lost momentum, Lieutenant Averell rode into the woods and ordered Bartlett to join in "a united charge to be made against the enemy's strongest position by all the regiments not actually engaged at that moment." Though his ranks had been thinned dramatically, the major quickly got the rest ready for the attack (a sign that despite the disparity in rank, Bartlett considered Averell effectively in charge of the brigade). Having arranged the regiment in four ranks, Bartlett marched all four down Buck Hill and into the shallow, tree-lined valley of Young's Branch. The men covered the entire distance under fire not only from Hampton and the units chased off Matthews Hill but also the guns of the Staunton Artillery, which had a clear shot at them from atop Henry Hill. The banks of the little valley were just high enough and sufficiently brushy to afford the New Yorkers some shelter from the storm. Bartlett kept them there for some time, awaiting word of Averell's general assault—and never getting it.[13]

The lieutenant was fast learning the hard facts of brigade command, where plans could go awry with stunning suddenness. Instead of combining to deliver a cohesive, powerful attack toward Henry Hill, the two militia regiments he had chosen to execute his plan—the 8th New York and the 14th Brooklyn—faltered, one of them disastrously, and an opportunity to seize the crest of the strategic plateau was lost. According to Averell, both regiments started south "in fine style, perfectly cool and in good order. They were going so rapidly that the enemy could not keep the range." But when they reached the turnpike, "by some misunderstanding, an order was sent to them to turn up that road instead of keeping on according to the previous purpose." Averell never identified the guilty officer—perhaps he never learned his name.

By shifting to the left, both outfits drew a heavy shelling from the top of the hill as well as what the acting brigade commander called "a desultory fire from those running rebels [Hampton's men and the 7th Georgia], which broke them up." The Brooklynites, under Colonel Alfred M. Wood (later wounded and captured) and Lieutenant Colonel Edward B. Fowler, retired in tolerable order, retained their organization, and remained available for subsequent service. The 8th New York, however, was scattered to the winds and never re-formed. Averell believed that "there were only two officers in that regiment who afterwards displayed any courage and coolness at all," one being its quartermaster.[14]

With Averell's cherished offensive dead on arrival, Major Bartlett realized that if he committed his 27th New York, it would be caught up in the debacle. "Believing that no assistance I could render would avail in restraining the troops or stay their flight," he gave in to the entreaties of his junior officers. Carefully disengaging from his protective valley, he marched the men to the rear. On the way they were met by General McDowell, who personally found a more defensible position for them—one that, once the army leader rode off, Bartlett abandoned. This time the 27th withdrew from the field altogether.

The major's refusal to join in what he considered a forlorn-hope assault may have been wise, but it connoted a certain irresolution. And yet he would receive warm praise for his actions on this part of the field. Colonel Porter commended him for "his enthusiasm and valor," which kept his outfit "in action and out of the panic." Averell obviously agreed, referring in his memoirs to "the gallant Major J. J. Bartlett." In a letter written from his hospital bed, Colonel Slocum would claim that under Bartlett, the 27th had "covered itself with glory . . . not a man showed the white feather."[15]

Having sent three regiments of New Yorkers into retreat, the Hampton Legion found itself forced to withdraw from its suddenly untenable position on the Warrenton Pike. A new Yankee column—a substantial one, stretching beyond the range of Hampton's field glasses—was advancing over the ground the 8th New York and 14th Brooklyn had vacated. Yet another force was moving toward the turnpike well to the east of the legion's initial assailants. "We were nearly surrounded," Hampton reported, "the enemy being on three sides of us." His men were nearing exhaustion; as one observed, "we were reduced in number, & worn out by fatigue & thirst, & . . . in a most bewildered state, without a general & without the slightest notion of what was expected of us."[16]

The legion's plight only worsened when Imboden's battery, which had been covering Hampton from its assigned location near the Henry house, began to withdraw from the plateau with empty ammunition chests and a greatly reduced supply of horses. His left flank exposed by the artillery's departure and his front extending salient-like toward the enemy, the colonel was compelled to order everyone to the rear. Collecting his scattered troops and carrying off his wounded, he led the way back up the turnpike for about one hundred yards and deployed behind and to the east of the Robinson house. His new line, which faced north, was at a right angle to his last position, which had pointed westward. But his men had been fighting for an hour under such adverse conditions that many had lost interest in which direction they were facing. "By this time," recalled Private Coxe, "we didn't care much as to what happened." Their senses, especially their hearing, had deadened: "Our rifle fire sounded like the popping of caps, our throats were choked with powder, and we were burning up with thirst."[17]

Even in its new position, the legion faced an arduous task. A seemingly endless succession of Yankee units were pouring down Matthews Hill and preparing to cross Young's Branch toward the Robinson house. Hampton could not have identified every potential antagonist, but they represented an influx of fresh, battle-ready opponents. Large segments of Porter's division had been fought out and, like most of Burnside's men, had retired from the fight. To an increasing degree, however, they had been supplanted by the troops of Heintzelman's division as well as by those elements of Tyler's command that, in defiance of their leader's studied inactivity, had crossed Bull Run nearly a half mile above the Stone Bridge.

It had been Heintzelman's vanguard, Franklin's brigade, advancing from the northwest that had imperiled Hampton's left, and now Keyes's brigade was moving against the legion from the north. The coming of these forces indicated that McDowell's offensive had entered a new phase, one in which he appeared to be committing nearly his entire army. The future looked bleak for the Confederates on and just south of the turnpike. One of Hampton's men, Private W. H. Manghum, described the crisis as "a dreadful moment for our country; we had been beaten at all points & were almost surrounded & nothing was required of the enemy but a vigorous use of the bayonet to decide the day."[18]

Colonel Heintzelman's soldiers had suffered through a morning at least as difficult and exasperating as the one Hunter's troops had endured—in some ways more so—and they were feeling ill used and put out. Their march was not designed to be as long or as circuitous as Hunter's, for Heintzelman's column, after leaving the turnpike beyond the Cub Run bridge, was supposed to have taken the direct road to Poplar Ford and to have crossed there, a mile and a half east of the ford Hunter would use. Heintzelman had been accompanied on his roundabout journey by Captain Horatio G. Wright of the engineers, who had joined Major Barnard's reconnaissance on the nineteenth that supposedly located the path to the assigned crossing. This morning Wright, to his surprise and chagrin, failed to locate that path. It did exist, though; later in the day Heintzelman would find it and take it—but in retreat.[19]

Having missed the turnoff, Franklin's brigade, followed by Willcox's, plodded on in Hunter's wake. Assailed by the familiar irritants—temperatures climbing toward the mid-eighties, a road turned into dust clouds, and the scarcity of potable water—the men muttered and grumbled with increasing intensity, but there was no help for it. Heintzelman dutifully reported his revamped course to McDowell, who suddenly realized that his three-pronged offensive across Bull Run was about to lose its centerpiece, upon which the success of the other two columns largely depended.

As a result of this misfortune, the Third Division's vanguard failed to reach Sudley Ford until around 11:00 A.M. At that late hour Hunter's division was still crossing, so Heintzelman had the men of Franklin's brigade fill their canteens in the run while he went forward "to see with my glass what was going on." As the grizzled old colonel rode south, the rising din of musketry told him that the head of Hunter's column had become engaged; the worry that Hunter might lack supports at a critical time began to throb like a sick headache.[20]

En route to the field of battle, Heintzelman tried but failed to locate McDowell but near the end of his march was met by the latter's brother and staff officer. Major Malcolm McDowell informed the new arrival that Hunter's troops were in danger of being outflanked, and to prevent this, the colonel should rush two regiments to the front. At once Heintzelman called up the 11th Massachusetts and 1st Minnesota of Franklin's brigade. Both were hastened forward, the 11th via the Sudley Road, the Minnesotans down a byroad farther to the left. Heintzelman chose to accompany the Bay Staters while leaving orders to rush the rest of the division forward. Captain Richard Arnold's Company D, 2nd U.S. Artillery was placed a short distance below Sudley Ford to cover the division's rear, supported by the 1st Michigan of Willcox's brigade.[21]

When, shortly before noon, Heintzelman reached the edge of the battlefield, he placed his main body in position to shore up Hunter's embattled left. He found that Colonel Franklin, having preceded him, had sent Ricketts's battery up a hill on the opposite flank of Porter's (Averell's) brigade, where it united with Captain Griffin to form a continuous line twelve guns strong. Heintzelman was surprised to discover that only Averell's troops appeared to be actively engaged, firing on and periodically advancing against the Rebels who had been chased across Young's Branch to Henry Hill. Of Burnside's troops, only the 2nd New Hampshire appeared intact and in a fighting mood—even the thrill-seeking Governor Sprague had decamped for the rear. When Heintzelman's Second Brigade came up, it passed an oak thicket on Matthews Hill in which, Colonel Willcox noted rather sharply, "Burnside's glorious brigade was resting & caring for their wounded."[22]

Succoring its casualties was not a censurable act, but the brigade's next move was. After at least two hours among the trees, and probably longer, Burnside led his command, virtually en masse, to the rear. Ostensibly, he did so because his men were exhausted as was their ammunition. To be sure, they had suffered heavily in the early hours of the battle—more than three hundred casualties all told—but by disengaging from the fighting so early, Burnside's soldiers would incur the criticism of comrades who stayed and fought throughout the day. The brigade was also condemned for refusing Captain Fry's request (apparently not a direct order from McDowell) to return to the fight in midafternoon when the battle began to turn against the Union. Rhode Island sources confirm that such a suggestion was made but that rejoining the battle at that point was a sheer impossibility. Historian Bruce Catton notes that Burnside's idleness cost McDowell a chance to accomplish a critical task; instead of resting, his troops "could have marched downstream almost unopposed, uncovering the [stone] bridge and linking the two halves of the army."[23]

With or without assistance from Burnside, Sam Heintzelman was obliged to pitch in. Under his direction, Franklin began deploying his regiments with an eye to supporting Ricketts's guns. He placed the 1st Minnesota west of the Sudley Road, in front and to the left of the battery, while for a time holding the 5th and 11th Massachusetts in the rear as reserves. All held their ground while, for about twenty minutes, Ricketts's cannoneers joined those of Griffin's in plastering the crest of Henry Hill.

Their primary target, fifteen hundred yards to the southeast, was the Staunton Artillery, which had been covering, virtually by itself, the withdrawal of Evans and his supports across Young's Branch. Until Ricketts and Griffin could fix Imboden's position, their shells passed high over the heads of the Rebel crewmen. Observing the poor effect, General Bee, just then standing beside the captain, ordered him, as Imboden recalled, to "fire low and ricochet our shot and shrapnel on the hard, smooth, open field that sloped toward the Warrenton turnpike in the valley between us. We did this, and the effect was very destructive to the enemy."[24]

The ricochet fire may have inflicted damage on the Union infantry—primarily the New York regiments under Averell that had been threatening Imboden's position—but it failed to have an effect on the enemy artillery, now free to move forward to get a better line of sight on the Confederate battery. With some trepidation, Imboden watched as Griffin's guns suddenly rolled five hundred yards closer to his position. At that distance they ought to have done a great deal of damage but surprisingly failed to do so. With the exception of Company D's two howitzers, which, wrote Imboden, "hurt us more than all the rifles of both batteries," the enemy's shells exploded all around the battery but not in its midst. The shells bore "so deep in the ground," Imboden recalled, "that the fragments never came out. After the action the ground looked as though it had been rooted up by hogs." Finally, a round struck the Rebel position, breaking the axle on a gun carriage and dropping the piece to the ground with such force that it was no longer operable. Then other shells began to fall perilously close, and Imboden began to fear for the continued existence of his battery.[25]

The increasingly uneven duel continued until the last Confederate unit had been driven to the south side of Young's Branch. At this point the Staunton Artillery was in real peril. Its commander would claim that for more than an hour, his unit had been providing the only artillery support the infantry rallying on Henry Hill had received. He would appear to contradict himself by recollecting that a single section of the Washington Artillery had come to his assistance early in the fighting but, for unknown reasons, had withdrawn after firing a few rounds. In his report of the battle, Beauregard confirmed that he augmented Imboden with a section of the famous militia unit but made no mention of its quick departure.[26]

By now more than half of the horses of Imboden's battery had been killed and its ammunition chests were almost bare. General Bee had directed the captain to hold his position "till you are ordered away," but no such orders had reached him. (The following day he learned that Bee had sent a staff officer to tell him to retire, but the man had been disabled by a severe wound before able to complete the errand). To his regret, he saw only "one way to save our guns, and that was to run them off the field." Dividing up the remaining animals so that each gun and caisson could be hauled off, Imboden ordered his men to clear the hill.[27]

Under a continuing shelling, the three remaining smoothbores limbered up and were soon in motion, their drivers lashing the reduced teams mercilessly. The battery crossed the summit of the hill to the edge of a pine forest halfway between the Robinson and Henry houses, where it shuddered to a halt. Coming up the southeastern side of the hill at the double-quick was a strung-out column of Confederate infantry—the first cohesive body of foot soldiers Imboden had seen since taking position on the crest. It proved to be the Virginia brigade of T. J. Jackson. From the general himself Imboden learned that additional artillery was on the way to the hill, including at least a section of Stanard's Thomas Artillery.

Instead of expressing relief at the arrival of badly needed support, Imboden complained vehemently to Jackson about having been left so long on his own to defend the plateau. As he later admitted, he made his feelings known "with some profanity, which I could see was displeasing to Jackson." Imboden was never reluctant to admit his "rough 'cussin' ways," to which he gave full expression whenever excited or upset.

Jackson abruptly halted the captain's profanity-laden tirade with a raised hand and a promise to support his battery. He told Imboden, "Unlimber right here." Impressed by the firmness in the man's voice and demeanor and given time to reposition his guns thanks to a sudden lull on this part of the field, Imboden vowed to defend Jackson's Virginians to his last shell.[28]

Jackson's arrival on Henry Hill was the culmination of a flurry of orders that for several hours had moved the brigade in what Sergeant Henry Kyd Douglas of the 2nd Virginia called "a meaningless way." Jackson detailed these successive changes of position in a personal letter written a few days after the battle:

> About four o'clock A.M., on the 21st, by request of General Longstreet, I sent him a reinforcement of two regiments. Subsequently I received an order from General Beauregard to reenforce General Bonham. Afterward I received an order from the same officer to reenforce General [sic] Cocke. Finally, I was instructed by him to take such a position as would enable me to reenforce either General Bonham or General Cocke. These instructions were executed in the order in which they were given. About an hour after . . . I received a message from General Cocke, who requested me to guard the Stone Bridge. I promptly moved in the direction, and halted at a place indicated by the guide. While in that position, I had reason to believe that General Bee was hard pressed by the enemy, and I accordingly moved in the direction of the firing and at the same time sent a message to the general that I was reenforcing him.

Jackson, who better than his superiors knew where his 2,400 men were needed, acted without first notifying either Beauregard or Johnston of his intentions.[29]

Jackson's decision required his soldiers to exert themselves to the utmost. One recalled that when the brigade hastened to Henry Hill, "a burning July sun almost melted us, as [we were] enveloped in woolen garments and weighted down with musket and accoutrements." A more dramatic comrade claimed that the movement from one flank to the other, a distance of six miles or more, left the men "like panting dogs with flopping tongues, with our mouths and throats full of the impalpable red dust of that red clay country, thirsting for water almost unto death, and worn and weary indescribably."[30]

As soon as he reached a defensible-looking slope of the plateau about one thousand yards southeast of the Henry house, Jackson judiciously deployed his Virginians. To guard his right flank, he chose Colonel Harper's 5th Virginia, which had performed ably at

Falling Waters despite being handily outnumbered. Adhering to the contours of that section of the crest, Harper took position a considerable distance from, and almost at a right angle to, the rest of the brigade. Jackson placed the 4th Virginia of Colonel James F. Preston farther south and west to provide immediate support to the approaching artillery and had Colonel John Echols deploy his 27th Virginia in close order directly behind Preston. Colonel James W. Allen's 2nd Virginia and the 33rd of Arthur Cummings went into line still farther south, the 33rd on the far left of the brigade.

Cummings's regiment in its entirety and a portion of Allen's were sheltered in a grove of pines, which as one soldier wrote, "entirely concealed us from the enemy as well as the enemy from us, for we could not see ten yards beyond the line." At the opposite end of Jackson's five-hundred-yard front, the 5th Virginia also enjoyed the shelter of a pine thicket. The general deployed each of his regiments in two lines, each line two ranks deep. Because those of the 4th and 27th overlapped to some extent, their ranks appeared as one body eight-deep.[31]

While the infantry formed, Captain Imboden unlimbered in front of Jackson's fast-expanding position, but he did not expect to remain long. He had informed the brigade commander that he was down to three rounds of ammunition per gun. When first meeting Jackson, he had suggested going to the rear to restock, but the reply was, "No, not now." Jackson explained that in addition to Stanard's battery, other guns were coming up behind him, including the four of the Rockbridge Artillery, which was attached to his brigade. Once they arrived, Imboden could withdraw and grant his men ("exhausted from want of water and food, and black with powder, smoke, and dust") some rest.[32]

Jackson's pledge of artillery augmentation—most of it ordered up by General Johnston even as he and Beauregard galloped to Henry Hill—was quickly redeemed. Within about a half hour of the brigade's arrival, a veritable surfeit of cannons was on hand to supplant Imboden's badly depleted unit. In addition to Stanard's section, the new arrivals included the four guns of the Rockbridge Artillery under Lieutenant Brockenbrough, the Wise Artillery's four guns under Lieutenant Pelham, and five pieces of the Washington Artillery, three of them commanded by Lieutenant Squires, who had performed well at Blackburn's Ford. About an hour after the other units arrived, Lieutenant Heaton's section of Rogers's Loudoun

Artillery, which had spent the morning covering Cocke's brigade by opposing Tyler's Federals at the Stone Bridge, was also unlimbering on top of Henry Hill. If one includes the three still-serviceable pieces in Imboden's battery, the number of guns on the embattled plateau at this point in the day exceeded twenty.[33]

Imboden was of course grateful for the arrival, however belatedly, of additional cannons. He was surprised, however, that Colonel Pendleton had not accompanied any of them. Imboden, who had not seen Johnston's artillery chief all morning, grew suspicious when Pendleton's former unit, the Rockbridge Artillery, showed up without him. Apparently, others also looked askance at the colonel's absence. When Imboden inquired of his whereabouts, Lieutenant Brockenbrough supposedly replied with "a remark I would rather not put on paper."[34]

With the coming of the initial reinforcements, Imboden, with Jackson's permission, fired off his last rounds. He personally rammed the first charge down the barrel. Wishing to observe the effect of the shot, the captain failed to step back far enough to ensure safety. When the gun discharged, a burst of pent-up gas escaped from the muzzle and struck him in the side and head with enough force to propel him twenty feet through the air. The blast not only drew blood and caused cuts and abrasions but also left Imboden permanently deaf in his left ear.[35]

About 10:30, with the fighting on Matthews Hill going at full blast, McDowell perceived a chance to strike the Rebel defensive line from a second direction. Aware that General Tyler was facing a skeleton force at Stone Bridge, he ordered his senior subordinate to end his demonstration, cross Bull Run, and "press the attack" toward the Confederate right flank. In his official report Tyler would fail to note the receipt of this order, delivered by Lieutenant H. W. Kingsbury of the army headquarters staff. Instead he implied that he himself set in motion the forward movement based on personal observation of the battle's progress. At his direction one of his staff officers—a daring and physically fit fellow—shimmied fifty feet up a pine tree with a field glass. From this excellent but precarious vantage point, the aide provided his superior a fairly clear picture of Hunter's and Heintzelman's operations. Tyler reported, "I was promptly notified as to any change in the progress of their columns up to the time when it appeared that the heads of both were arrested, and the enemy seemed to be moving heavy re-enforce-ments to support their troops."[36]

Upward of ninety minutes after he was told to press on, Tyler finally ordered Sherman's brigade, followed by Keyes's, to cross the run and link with the turning column. Perhaps distrustful of the politician-general's abilities, Tyler ordered Schenck and his men to remain behind to occupy the Rebels near Lewis Ford. Only if the lat-ter withdrew would the Second Brigade join in the general advance. This relegated Schenck, who continued to demonstrate east of the Stone Bridge long after most of Evans's Confederates had left his front, to an indefinite period of stasis. This did not appear to upset him. In his battle report, however, he tried to portray himself as put out by his enforced inactivity, informing his superior, "here we lay, in pursuance of your orders, for, perhaps, two and a half or three hours with no evidence of our nearness to the enemy except the occasional firing of musketry by our skirmishers in the wood in front."

Schenck spent the balance of the day trying to look busy. He extended his flanks toward the assumed position of the enemy. He deployed and redeployed his regiments as if preparing to attack someone, somewhere, though keeping at least one of them, the 2nd New York Militia, well to the rear. When his tentative movements toward Lewis Ford attracted the notice of a Rebel battery (that sec-tion of the Loudoun Artillery personally commanded by Captain Rogers) that treated his 1st Ohio to "a heavy fire of shells and round and grape shot," Schenck yanked Colonel McCook's regiment out of range. He refrained from further provoking Rogers, who having exhausted his ammunition, was content to cease firing. Schenck also claimed to have kept an eye out for a "stampede of the enemy" that never materialized. With the possible exception of Blenker's troops at Centreville, who although not pressed at any point dur-ing the day did a reasonably effective job of guarding the army's rear and communications, Schenck's brigade was less actively engaged and thus contributed less to Federal fortunes than any other ele-ment of McDowell's army.[37]

The rest of Tyler's division was heavily involved in the after-noon's fighting and suffered accordingly; in the end, however, its participation counted for little. Thanks to its position in front of Keyes's brigade, Sherman's command was the first element of Tyler's column to see action. About noon, when he finally received per-mission to wade Bull Run, Sherman knew exactly where to cross, having studied the country north of Stone Bridge for almost three hours. Around nine o'clock he had located a ford near a nondescript farm some eight hundred yards above the bridge. It had been brought to his attention by a Rebel horseman who crossed from the opposite bank to challenge some Union skirmishers, or as he called them, "damned black abolitionists." Unverified accounts identify the bold rider as Major Wheat, who was an ardent white supremacist—the epithet credited to the horseman could certainly have come from his lips. When fired on, the man rode off, his route carefully tracked by the brigade commander. Sherman thus crossed the run at Farm Ford, doing so without opposition, a pleasant surprise since the banks on that stretch of the stream were steep enough that defenders could have made things tough for the Third Brigade. In fact the bluff was too high to permit the passage of artillery; Ayres's battery was forced to remain on the east bank with Schenck.[38]

Tyler's original plan for Sherman was that he "sustain" Schenck's demonstration at Stone Bridge. By the time his brigade crossed the run, though, it had become obvious that even if supported, Schenck would accomplish precious little. Tyler therefore ordered Sherman to join in the attacks that Porter and Heintzelman were then mounting or were about to mount.

Once over the run Sherman, eager to get into the fight after hours of vexing delays, marched his brigade across the high ground by the Van Pelt farm and onto Matthews Hill. Leading the way was the 69th New York, one of Manhattan's premier militia outfits, heavily Irish in its membership and fiercely pugnacious in its approach to fighting Rebels. The regiment was commanded by the celebrated anti-British émigré Michael Corcoran, namesake of the fort outside Arlington, who the previous year had been court-martialed for refusing to parade his troops for the visiting Prince of Wales. Corcoran's trial was still pending, but upon the coming of war he had been permitted to rejoin the officers and men whose esteem and loyalty he wore like a badge of honor. Behind the Hibernians came the Scotsmen of Cameron's 79th New York (their officers' kilts mothballed for the duration in favor of regulation pants), the gray-clad 2nd Wisconsin, under Lieutenant Colonel Harry Peck; and Colonel Isaac Quinby's 13th New York. Determined to link with Hunter as soon as possible, Sherman hustled across the shell-pocked, corpse-strewn ground from which most of the Rebels under Evans, Bee, and Bartow had been driven, heading for the Sudley Road.[39]

En route to the army's right, Corcoran's Irishmen encountered a party of the enemy amid a cluster of pines—a detachment of Wheat's Tigers or perhaps some 8th Georgians—that had been cut off while fleeing Matthews Hill. Without orders, Captain Peter Haggerty, serving today as Corcoran's second in command, rode in front of the regiment in hopes of personally bagging a straggler or two and toppled from his saddle with a bullet through the heart. The previous day the captain had joked with a New York reporter about his newspaper's claim that Haggerty had been killed at Blackburn's Ford, remarking that he "felt very warlike for a dead man, and good for at least one battle more."[40]

Enraged by the death of their acting lieutenant colonel, the head of the 69th opened on his assailants, who stubbornly returned fire. Sherman, though upset by the loss of the impetuous subordinate, quickly broke off the fight and resumed the march. Sweeping across farmland and open fields, at about 12:30 the head of his column finally "succeeded in attracting the attention of our friends"—that is, the men of Heintzelman's division, then coming down the Sudley Road. Taking position on the west side of the dusty thoroughfare, the colonel placed his men in the right rear of Willcox's brigade and awaited orders to advance.[41]

In his new position it appeared to Sherman that the battle was moving toward Henry Hill and that the Confederates were on the run. The habitually nervous brigade commander was anxious to contribute to what he supposed was a full-scale enemy retreat. His impression of impending triumph was strengthened by the vocal optimism of General McDowell and some of his staff officers, whom Sherman found galloping up and down the lines waving hats and swords and shouting: "Victory! Victory! The day is ours!" Those pronouncements were having an effect on the lower ranks. "It looked then," one of Sherman's officers wrote, "as though the whole rebellion was conquered."[42]

Although they would follow Sherman across Bull Run, Keyes's soldiers would not continue on to the Sudley Road. While the Third Brigade moved to join the fighting on the far right, Tyler, without informing McDowell or getting his permission, determined that the all–New England First Brigade should gain "the best possible position" on the left, "when we should have driven the enemy off, to join Schenck's brigade and the two batteries left on the opposite side."

To make certain Keyes followed orders and took maximum advantage of the apparently disorganized condition of the Confederates south of Young's Branch, Tyler accompanied him, evidently with a view to directing his movements. It may have seemed like a good idea at the time, but because neither man enjoyed a strategic vision, their teaming was a near-classic case of the blind leading the blind.[43]

Keyes's attempt to break the Rebels' fragile hold on the eastern half of Henry Hill was challenged from the start. Sherman had encountered no resistance at Farm Ford, but his colleague's crossing was made in the face of a shelling from a battery that had unlimbered on the opposite bank. The twenty-five or thirty rounds fired in Keyes's direction caused, as he admitted, "a temporary confusion" as well as the wounding of several members of his lead regiments, Lieutenant Colonel John Speidel's 1st Connecticut Volunteers and Colonel Alfred Howe Terry's 2nd Connecticut. Once order was restored, Keyes crossed his men over the stream, marched them to Van Pelt hill, and halted them just north of Young's Branch. Here he and Tyler found themselves within striking distance of the north end of the enemy's line on Henry Hill, a position that Jackson's newly arrived brigade had yet to secure.

The only opposition the First Brigade encountered south of Young's Branch was provided by a small force of foot soldiers and cavalrymen trying to cover Jackson's right flank, which lacked a natural anchor such as a stream or a forest. Though the Rebels were outpositioned as well as outnumbered, "some severe struggles" were required of Keyes's vanguard to drive them away and enable the brigade to wade the marshy watercourse. By the time the New Englanders reached the Warrenton Pike, about 12:15, enemy resistance had stiffened. Keyes observed a fairly sizeable force of infantry and artillery in position behind the Robinson dwelling. The colonel believed he had enough men to put the infantry on the run, but because he lacked guns of his own, the artillery posed a problem.

Keyes's opponents consisted mainly of the Hampton Legion, supported by clots of Evans's, Bee's, and Bartow's brigades, whose men were seeking refuge in a wooded ravine south of the Robinson property. The legion deserved credit for having vigorously covered their comrades' retreat from Matthews Hill under heavy fire and at great cost. Years later South Carolinian Charles Hutson wrote that "never have I conceived of such a continuous, rushing hailstorm of shot, shell, and musketry as fell around and among us for hours together.

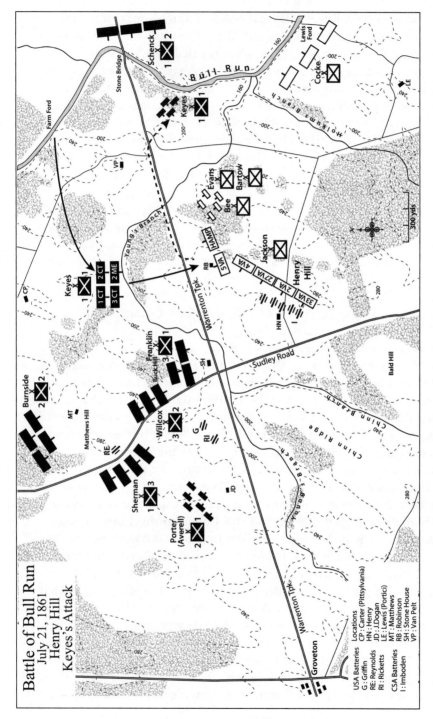

Battle of Bull Run, July 21, 1861: Henry Hill, Keyes's Attack. *Map by Paul Dangel.*

We who escaped are consistently wondering how we could possibly have come out of the action alive."[44]

Having taken so many blows, including an incessant shelling from the batteries on and near Matthews Hill, and now running low on ammunition, Hampton's little army appeared to be teetering on the brink of dissolution. Quite possibly if hard pressed, it might have given way altogether, exposing the flank the South Carolinians had so long secured. Behind them at the top of the hill, Jackson's soldiers were hunkering down, but their attention was drawn to Heintzelman's advance farther west; a vigorous push by Keyes could have taken them by surprise. Only Harper's 5th Virginia, supported by Captain Latham's Lynchburg Battery, now four guns strong, was available to help Hampton hold his ground. But the Virginians were outgunned, and they remained unaware of Keyes's approach until after he had crossed the turnpike, leaving little time for a robust defense.[45]

When Harper's men finally reacted to the threat from the north, it was almost too late. Keyes, who had reversed the marching order of his regiments, had double-quicked his leading regiments—the gray-clad 2nd Maine and 3rd Connecticut marching abreast, the former on the left of the line—across the turnpike. After a brief halt to steady the line and allow the men to catch their breath, Keyes pressed onward at the same speed to Robinson's house and then up the rise behind it. A Connecticut man wrote that "we went up that hill shouting and yelling as if two thousand demons had been suddenly let loose from Pandemonium." Their officers tried to silence the men, who resented the effort: "They didn't seem to realize that when a man is charging on a battery that is blazing grape and canister into his very face . . . it is one of his dearest privileges to be allowed to yell like a loon."[46]

The 2nd Maine nearly reached Harper's and Hampton's positions before the defenders realized they were confronting Yankees in gray, not comrades coming to reinforce them. The 5th Virginia rectified the mistake, unleashing an abrupt but effective volley in which Hampton's men joined. At first their combined response had minimal effect; the attackers kept coming on, stopping only long enough to reload before getting off another shot on the run. Repeated fusillades finally slowed Keyes's assault and then halted it, at least temporarily. Colonel John L. Chatfield of the 3rd Connecticut reported that "the regiment made a fine charge, but was obliged to fall back (the enemy being in very much larger force of infantry, beside their battery), which we did in good order." (The soldier who described shouting his way up Henry Hill would claim that Chatfield dissuaded Tyler from making a second attempt—so too did several enlisted men who told the division commander to his face that they were through attacking batteries.)[47]

One reason for the pullback was yet another case of mistaken identity: suddenly, the New Englanders were just as unsure of who they were opposing as Harper and Hampton had been. A portion of the 2nd Maine had become separated from the rest of the regiment; officers in Keyes's other outfits, fearing they were shooting at the Mainers, began to call on their men to cease firing on the Rebels. The resulting confusion caused the attack to stall while giving their real adversaries time to fall back to more defensible positions. At Colonel Harper's command the 5th Virginia abandoned its position behind the Robinson home and scrambled about one hundred yards up the slope of Henry Hill and inside a stand of trees. Colonel Hampton, although convinced his worn-down legion was on the cusp of being surrounded, needed outside urging to join the retreat. This came in the form of advice—presumably transported by mounted couriers—from both General Bee and Major Evans.[48]

The South Carolinians retired up Henry Hill "in good order," as Hampton wrote, "bearing off our wounded." Some comrades, especially Virginians, would quarrel with his characterization. As the legion scurried uphill, a shell exploded in its midst, killing several men and stampeding unhurt comrades. John Mosby of Stuart's cavalry, a portion of which had been assigned to cover the right flank of Jackson's command, described the fugitives as retreating "most disgracefully." Oblivious to or unimpressed by the fact that the legionnaires had lost almost 20 percent of their number in killed or wounded, Mosby added: "When we arrived on the field we met them running. . . . Captain [William E.] Jones told them they were a set of d—d cowards and all of us begged them to return."[49]

Captain Imboden, then preparing to take his guns off Henry Hill, took it upon himself to stem what he considered the legion's panicky rout. With sword in hand, he stood cursing the speeding troops, occasionally swiping at them with his blade. Then a burly rifleman whose path Imboden attempted to block lunged at him with his bayonet, raking the artilleryman's left arm "from wrist to shoulder. The blow knocked me sprawling on the ground, and the fellow got away."[50]

Hampton re-formed his survivors on the summit near the recently arrived Washington Artillery. "Here," he reported to Beauregard, "after indicating the place you wished me to occupy, you directed me to remain until you sent for me." He and his men would be sent for in due time. Despite having spent two bloody hours on the firing lines, "the d—d cowards" were not through fighting.[51]

With the dubious assistance of his division leader, Erasmus Keyes tried to restart his once-promising advance. But critical momentum had been lost; as Tyler would report, the brigade managed to occupy the grounds around the Robinson house but held on there for "a moment" only. Behind the house they came under a blistering musketry from the woods in which the 5th Virginia had re-formed while also attracting shells from the right of the artillery line now forming in front of Jackson's brigade.[52]

Without attempting to reinforce Keyes's brigade with Schenck's and unwilling to ask McDowell for support, Tyler decided to call off the assault. Nor did he augment the 2nd Maine and 3rd Connecticut with Keyes's rear regiments, which having suffered little from balls and shells, might have made a difference if committed to the action. One possible reason was a lack of confidence in Lieutenant Colonel Speidel's ability to command, he having been forced on short notice to replace Colonel George S. Burnham, a learned soldier but also a habitual drunkard. Yet the 2nd Connecticut was led by a superb officer—Alfred Terry would close an achievement-filled war career as a major general of volunteers. The inescapable inference is that neither Tyler nor Keyes had either the brains or fortitude to press an attack that appeared to have every chance of breaking the Confederate right flank on Henry Hill.[53]

With the division commander peering over his shoulder, Keyes ordered the men of Connecticut and Maine to retire by the left flank across a field that exposed them to shot and shell until sheltered by the valley of Young's Branch. From there the march resumed in the general direction of Stone Bridge. Tyler contended that the movement was made "with a view to turn the battery which the enemy had placed on the hill." He further claimed that it forced those Rebels who had opposed Keyes to "retire" when in fact it was he who was retreating. He also noted that the brigade's later movements permitted an engineering officer assigned to the division to tear down an enemy-built abatis near Stone Bridge, an accomplishment that paved the way for Schenck and the batteries of Ayres and Carlisle to cross Bull Run—something that never occurred. Back across the turnpike went Tyler's First Brigade as if content to drift off the battlefield. As a *New York Tribune* correspondent later reported, "Colonel Keyes soon vanished with his four regiments."[54]

But not every member of the brigade quit the field entirely. Several wounded members of the 2nd Maine having been left behind, presumably to fall into the enemy's hands, Colonel Charles D. Jameson formed a squad of volunteers for the purpose of retrieving them. Jameson personally led the party back up Henry Hill under fire; somehow they managed to bring off six of the casualties without additional loss. Their act of mercy gained the colonel and his men the commendation of the rest of the regiment, while two of the volunteers would receive the Medal of Honor for exceptional valor.[55]

Despite the inhibiting presence of Tyler, Colonel Keyes summoned up the will to make a new effort to secure a foothold on Henry Hill. Even after falling back north of the turnpike, where he rested those of his men who had been engaged around Robinson's house, the brigade posed a decided threat to Jackson's right flank. About 2:00 P.M., evidently with Tyler's concurrence, Keyes recrossed the turnpike, this time about a half mile west of the Stone House, and headed toward Bull Run in the vicinity of Stone Bridge.

The largely uncontested march eventually placed the First Brigade in rear of Jackson's right flank on Henry Hill—the only Union force to gain a position inside the enemy's lines at any point during the battle. It is not known whether either Tyler or his subordinate fully grasped the strategic advantage thus attained, but they had taken so long to gain this critical position—it was now midafternoon—that exploiting it was another matter entirely. Keyes was about to order an attack that would slice in behind the unsuspecting 5th Virginia and the exhausted troops of Hampton, Evans, Bee, and Bartow when his vanguard suddenly recoiled from the fire of a couple of guns atop that sector of the plateau.

Keyes was determined to weather the storm and push ahead, but at that moment he was flagged down by Lieutenant Emory Upton of Tyler's staff (apparently the general was no longer with Keyes's column), who informed him that McDowell's army was in retreat and ordered the colonel to withdraw his troops by the right flank. The news confirmed a foreboding of Keyes, produced by the recent diminution of the Union artillery firing on Henry Hill. Reportedly, he was crushed by the order to withdraw north of the turnpike yet again, this time to help cover a retreating army. An enlisted man in the 1st Connecticut saw Keyes "with the tears running down his cheeks" and heard him tell a subordinate, "My God, the whole day is lost!"[56]

No one would know if Keyes's second attempt to scale Henry Hill and wrest the summit from its tired defenders would have turned the tide, but a number of students of the battle think so. John Hennessey observes that "Keyes' attack represented the Federals' best opportunity to achieve a tactical victory that day." Military historian Ethan Rafuse calls Keyes's failure to uproot Jackson's flank and clear Henry Hill of most if not all of its defenders the loss of "the opportunity of a lifetime."[57]

Such claims rest on the premise that four inexperienced regiments, worn down by marching and countermarching (though only the 2nd Maine had experienced anything approaching hard fighting), would have displaced a greater number of Confederates, many of them relatively fresh and commanded by an officer soon to become famous for his tenacity. This outcome appears wholly improbable. Then too, even had Keyes gained a solid enough foothold on its crest to secure the plateau, one cannot imagine Jackson and his supporting forces failing to make a successful stand upon any number of hills and ridges farther south. Keyes's potential overthrow of the soon-to-be-christened Stonewall Brigade ranks as a tantalizing but unlikely might-have-been. This war would be replete with them.

Around 12:30, a half hour after Jackson arrived, he was joined on Henry Hill by Johnston and Beauregard. Once persuaded that the critical action was taking place southwest of Stone Bridge, the generals had covered the four miles to the embattled position "at full gallop." Johnston believed that they had reached the field "not a moment too soon." Beauregard agreed; in typical prose he would contend that upon their arrival, "danger stared us in the face. Our men seemed to have accomplished all that could be accomplished against such overpowering numbers; and depression, added to exhaustion, was about to destroy their over-taxed endurance."

The commanders proceeded to do what they could to revive morale. Beauregard rode among the scattered units of Evans, Bartow, and Bee, calling on the officers and men to rise above their afflictions and stand firm. He instructed their commanders to make conspicuous display of their regimental colors and to call on the troops to rally around them. "This was done," he added with a hint of self-satisfaction, if with dubious veracity, "and proved a complete success."[58]

While his subordinate orated and gesticulated, Johnston took action. Noticing that a particular unit on the hill appeared to be milling about in confusion, he rode up to its color-bearer and found him holding the flag of the 4th Alabama. Its ranks diminished by bullets and shells, its senior officers dead or disabled, the regiment had staggered back from Matthews Hill under the command of Captain Goldsby. By the time they reached Henry Hill, many survivors had completely broken down, their legs aching from hastening to and from Matthews Hill, their throats parched. "The thirst of the men," Goldsby wrote, "was intense and almost intolerable."[59]

Displaying his characteristic rapport with the common soldier, Johnston went among the Alabamians, inquiring what had become of their officers. According to Sergeant Major Coles, the collective answer was, "Left on the battle field." The few remaining line officers asked Johnston to place the regiment in a better position from which to reorganize and return to the fight. According to Coles, the general merely stated that he would find such a position "as soon as he learned the condition of affairs" on the plateau.

Other, more dramatic and thus more frequently cited sources have Johnston riding up to the 4th's standard bearer, Sergeant Robert Sinclair, and ordering him to hand over the colors—he would hold them aloft as a guide while repositioning the regiment. Sinclair is supposed to have replied, "General, I cannot give up my flag, but I will put it wherever you command." Another account has the sergeant imploring him: "Don't take my colors from me. Tell me where to carry them, and I will plant them there."[60]

What appears to have happened is that Johnston, rather than personally leading the 4th Alabama back into action, placed what remained of the outfit in the care of Colonel S. R. Gist, a volunteer aide to General Bee. In his *Narrative of Military Operations*, Johnston makes no mention of an exchange with Sergeant Sinclair, though he confirms the delegation of authority to Gist, an accomplished soldier who was to become a Confederate brigadier. In an article published more than a decade after penning his memoirs, however, Johnston confused matters by claiming that he, not Gist, "easily marched" the 4th Alabama "to its place."[61]

Following this incident, Johnston returned to Beauregard's side, conferred with him, and—at least according to the latter—reached an agreement on their respective roles in the fighting to come. Beauregard claimed that he urged his superior "to leave the immediate conduct of the field to me" while Johnston repaired to the Lewis house, a central position from which to take charge of, and give directions to, reinforcements for Henry Hill. According to Beauregard's postwar recollections, he made this proposal because the presence of both officers on the same ground, "instead of being of advantage, might impede prompt action—often necessary—by either commander." What he probably meant was that he did not want any decision he made to be second-guessed or countermanded by his superior within earshot of his subordinates, an understandable attitude but one he could hardly admit to in print.[62]

Johnston's version of the proposal conflicted with his subordinate's understanding of it. "At first he was unwilling," Beauregard added, "but reminded that one of us must do so, and that properly it was his place," the senior general acquiesced and immediately left for Portici, a mile away. Johnston's postwar explanation, however, was that Beauregard was assigned "command of the troops immediately engaged, which he properly suggested belonged to the second in rank, not to the commander of the army," while he "returned to the supervision of the whole field"—that is, he retained overall command, including the sector Beauregard occupied, should he wish to make changes or suggestions to its director. Yet according to Beauregard, his superior "never gave me one order or instruction during the whole progress of the battle."[63]

After some further discussion, Johnston left Beauregard and galloped off to expedite the previously directed transfer to the left flank of several commands, including all or portions of Holmes's, Early's, and Bonham's brigades. He was not convinced that the agreed-upon division of responsibilities would of itself produce victory: "The aspect of affairs was not encouraging, yet I had strong hope that Beauregard's capacity and courage, the patriotic enthusiasm of our Southern volunteers, would maintain the fight until adequate reinforcements could be brought to their aid."[64]

After Johnston departed, Beauregard continued to make motivational speeches to any unit and soldier who could hear his voice above the roar of battle. To the commander of the Washington Artillery he shouted: "Colonel Walton, do you see the enemy? Hold this position and the day is ours." A South Carolina infantryman heard him implore the troops to "fight for General Beauregard. When they put their heads over that hill they are ours!" Lieutenant Robert M. English of the 2nd Virginia made bold to ask the general how long Jackson's brigade had to remain in its present position—that is, until the men were permitted to charge. Beauregard chose to interpret the question differently. His terse reply: "Till death!"[65]

Spying the shot-torn flag of one of Francis Bartow's regiments, Beauregard rose in the stirrups, doffed his headgear (a straw hat, as Lieutenant Squires of the Washington Artillery remembered), and called out: "I salute the gallant Eighth Georgia Regiment!" Then he encountered Bartow himself at the head of Gartrell's 7th Georgia. The colonel, begrimed with sweat and powder residue, was bleeding and limping from a painful wound to his foot received following the disabling of his horse. According to one source, Bartow had already importuned Beauregard's superior: "General Johnston, I am hard pressed on my right and I cannot hold my position without reinforcements." It may be supposed that he said something similar to the Creole, who himself was now afoot, a Yankee shell having decapitated his mount. Johnston's response to the Georgian's plea went unrecorded, but Beauregard, according to his official report, ordered the complainant to post what remained of his brigade in a belt of pine trees on the right of Jackson's line of battle. He must have given Bartow a pep talk as well, for when the colonel returned to his troops, he told them: "General Beauregard expects us to hold this position, and, Georgians, I appeal to you to hold it!"[66]

The understrength brigade responded by steeling itself for yet another attempt to stave off attacks that seemed to be coming from every direction. Its men made such a worthy effort that at one point the nearest Yankees appeared to fall back. Seeing an opportunity to press an advantage, Bartow placed himself at the head of Gartrell's ranks and seized its colors as a rallying symbol. He led the regiment—now reduced to a few hundred able-bodied men—in what some considered a suicidal effort. One of his staff officers later wrote that Bartow's "big heart was full to bursting for his own regiment, cut to pieces . . . , and he prayed for death."[67]

While it seems unlikely that Bartow had a death wish, he had long suspected that he would die in battle, perhaps his first battle. Handing the flag back to its assigned color-bearer, he unsheathed his saber and waved the men forward with the cry, "Follow me, boys!" Then a minie ball thudded into his left breast and knocked him down. Carried to the rear and laid upon the ground with a knapsack for a pillow, Bartow was found to have been mortally wounded. Those who gathered around heard his final words: "Boys, they have killed me, but *never* give up the field."[68]

Bartow was not the only high-rankling supplicant on Henry Hill this day. According to Captain Thomas L. Preston, Johnston's cousin and adjutant general, soon after the Virginian sought to rally the 4th Alabama, Barnard Bee rode up and tearfully exclaimed, "General, my command is defeated and scattered, and I am alone," to which Johnston replied, "I know it is not your fault, General Bee; but don't despair, the day is not lost yet." Per this account, the commander gave Bee the only advice possible: rally your men and lead them back into the fight. Johnston makes no mention of this incident in either his postwar writings or his official report, although the latter cites his awareness that "the long contest against fivefold odds and heavy losses, especially of field officers, had greatly discouraged the troops of General Bee" and presumably their leader as well.[69]

Even before appealing to Johnston, Bee had sought the help of another general officer from Virginia. Not long after Jackson's brigade ascended the southeastern slope of Henry Hill, the general went looking for its leader. Viewing this fresh command as potential reinforcements for his own brigade, many of whose men continued to cling desperately to ever-precarious positions south of Young's Branch, Bee pleaded with his fellow brigadier for assistance, but it was all in vain.

The South Carolinian was under immense emotional strain. Not only was his brigade on the brink of destruction—even those of its units that retained their fighting spirit were in some confusion and disarray—but amid the chaos along Young's Branch, command relations were breaking down. According to Colonel Jordan of Beauregard's staff, shortly before Bartow's fall, the two brigade leaders had had a "violent" confrontation during which they nearly came to blows. The clash appears to have resulted from an unfortunate misunderstanding. Bartow may have seized a flag belonging to one of Bee's regiments, which nettled the brigadier. Another possible cause is that Bee made a derogatory reference to one of Bartow's outfits, which he mistakenly believed had evacuated a position with undue haste (a comment for which Bee quickly apologized). Regardless how the fracas began, up and down the chain of command morale was eroding, with potentially disastrous repercussions.[70]

Thus Bee was understandably distraught when he sought out Jackson. "General," he cried, "they are beating us back." Jackson's reply was not what his colleague wanted to hear: "Sir, we'll give them the bayonet," meaning that he would give them the bayonet from where he stood, not where Bee's men were struggling for survival.[71]

Jackson fully appreciated the defensive features of the ground he now occupied. Having been moved about promiscuously earlier in the day, his men left foot-weary, thirsty, and suffering from exposure to a merciless sun, Jackson had no intention of giving up this, his most defensible and most strenuously gained position. He had chosen it with utmost care. To avoid silhouetting his troops against the noontime sun, he had deployed them along a lower elevation on the pine-shrouded reverse slope of the plateau. From this "tactical crest" the Virginians were hidden from Union infantry, though artillery could and did still locate them. The position provided cover for Jackson's own guns while leaving open a long stretch of plateau that an exposed enemy would have to cross to come within rifle range of the Virginians. He would not forfeit these advantages no matter how earnestly Bee begged him to trade Henry Hill for Young's Branch.[72]

If Bee was upset by Jackson's refusal to succor his command, he undoubtedly felt he had a right to be. More than an hour ago he had come to Nathan Evans's assistance, willingly relinquishing the advantageous terrain that Jackson now claimed for himself. It seemed right and fair that his fellow brigadier should make the same gesture. Bee's valiant troops had already been shoved off Matthews Hill; a second, even more ignominious retreat was to be avoided at all costs. But Jackson understood something his colleague did not. Bee's rush to Matthews Hill had merely prolonged Evans's hold on a fundamentally untenable position. Should Jackson emulate Bee, it would not prevent a full-scale abandonment of the Young's Branch line, something that the Virginian knew to be imminent.

At some point following the Bee-Jackson exchange—it is impossible to construct a definitive chronology of events at this point in the battle—a legend was born atop Henry Hill, where a title destined for enduring fame was bestowed upon a brigade, its leader, or both.

By now Bee had reached an arrangement with Jackson. It was not one he had wanted or sought, but it represented his only chance to stave off the annihilation of his command: his troops would break contact with the Yankees threatening to surround them at the foot of Henry Hill and, along with the remnants of Evans's and Bartow's brigades, would retreat to the high ground occupied by Jackson and his still-arriving artillery supports. Descending the northern slope of the plateau, Bee rode back to his dwindling ranks and tried to gain the attention of as many officers and men as possible. He gave them the order to disengage and fall back. Then, pointing his sword toward the ground from which he had come, he supposedly shouted: "There is Jackson standing like a stone-wall. Let us determine to die here and we will conquer. Follow me!" With that, he started toward the hill's forward slope, his fought-out soldiers streaming behind him.[73]

Exactly what Bee said and when he said it has been lost to history. The words ascribed to him were recorded by a Richmond-based correspondent of the *Charleston Mercury*, published four days after the battle and copied by numerous other papers, including at least one in Richmond. It is virtually inconceivable that in the thick of the fighting, the reporter got close enough to overhear Bee. At least one historian has pointed out that the scribe arrived on the field of battle too late to have heard the South Carolinian say anything. It seems more likely that some of Bee's soldiers, perhaps members of his staff, repeated what they had heard or thought they had heard. Some students of the battle doubt that anything of the sort was actually said; R. M. Johnston contends that "the words ascribed to Bee smack less of the battlefield than of the editorial sanctum."[74]

In the days and weeks following the battle, several variations of Bee's phrasing were circulated inside the army. Writing to his wife on the twenty-fourth, Colonel Chesnut referred to the "stone wall" comment as if its exact wording had been authenticated. E. P. Alexander, however, claimed to have heard General Johnston on the evening of the battle use the same figure of speech to describe the formidable stand made by one of Jackson's regiments—a curious coincidence unless the term enjoyed more currency in the Confederate ranks than is generally supposed.[75]

Speculation as to the origins and meaning of Bee's remark has occupied historians for the past century and a half. Most, if not all, accept the conclusions of two celebrated chroniclers of Confederate history: Douglas Southall Freeman, writing in the first volume of his trilogy, *Lee's Lieutenants*, published in 1942; and James I. Robertson, Jr., author of what is generally considered the definitive biography of Jackson, *Stonewall Jackson: The Man, the Soldier, the Legend*, published in 1997. Both authors endorse, with minor misgivings, the *Mercury's* account of how the appellation was bestowed. They further agree that Bee was describing Jackson's brigade, not its leader, although they note that over the years the words became attached to commander as well as command; both conclude that Bee's intent was to praise the man and his troops for their steadfast defense of Henry Hill. Freeman and Robertson construct defensible arguments to bolster their claim that Bee was lauding the Virginians and thanking them for the support they were to provide his hard-pressed troops.[76]

Well-presented arguments notwithstanding, a case can be made for a pejorative connotation. Although Bee lauded the stand-up fortitude of Jackson's men, few of them were on their feet. As John Opie of the 5th Virginia recalled, "history does not explain this discrepancy: instead of standing, we were lying flat upon the ground, by order of General Jackson." Opie added, "The firing in our front was terrific, and why we did not render immediate and timely assistance to Bee I could never learn." Conceivably, some of the private's comrades who did not record their impressions wondered the same thing.[77]

Bee himself might have cleared up this discrepancy had he lived long enough to address it. When his troops began to depart Young's Branch for Henry Hill, the brigadier happened upon the officer-poor 4th Alabama, which Johnston had supposedly entrusted to Colonel Gist. Whether Gist had yet to take command or failed to make his presence known, Bee decided that the 4th was still in deep trouble. In fact, it had been so whittled down by battle losses that at first the general did not recognize it as one of his own. Riding up to Captains Richard Clarke and Porter King, he called out, "What regiment is this?" One of the two officers replied, "Why, General, don't you know your own men—this is what is left of the 4th Alabama." Supposedly, Bee cried, "Come with me!" and began to lead the tiny force up Henry Hill.

After reaching the summit, the brigadier appeared to change his mind. Perhaps concerned that not enough troops had been able to disengage from Young's Branch, he turned the 4th Alabama about and prepared to lead it back down the heights. Before he could do so, however, the regiment was cut in two by the passage through its ranks of a light battery and its train; multiple regimental sources identify the offender as John Pelham and the Wise Artillery. The larger part of the 4th filed off to the left, the remainder—little more than twenty men—were shunted off in the other direction. Undeterred by the mishap, Bee rode to the head of the smaller group and, "cheering them onward to victory and inspiring them with fresh courage and heroism," faced them toward the oncoming enemy.[78]

If Bartow's valiant but futile effort to engage the Federals with a depleted force can be considered suicidal, so too must Bee's attempt to turn the tide of his brigade's defeat virtually singlehandedly. According to at least one source, he was leading the remnant of the 4th across the yard of Mrs. Henry's house when he was knocked from the saddle by a minie ball that struck him in the left groin and passed out above the right hip. Taken up and carried from the field, the general "suffered dreadfully" until he breathed his last the next morning.[79]

Bee's demise did nothing to quell a growing controversy over the tenor of his reference to Jackson's demeanor on Henry Hill. After the battle a rumor sprang up that before he died, Bee, in the presence of Major Thomas G. Rhett, Johnston's adjutant general, excoriated Jackson for remaining rooted to the high ground, in the guise of an immovable barrier, instead of coming to his aid. John Cheves Haskell, a South Carolina artillery officer, claimed to have heard the story not only from Rhett but also from Major Whiting of Johnston's staff and Lieutenant James H. Hill, Bee's adjutant and brother-in-law.[80]

Perhaps Bee did intend his words to be construed as critical of Jackson. By the time he offered his dramatic description of the Virginia brigade and its leader, his own command had been evicted from Matthews Hill, an embarrassment for all involved. To retreat a second time so soon afterward would have been a grievous affront to Southern honor—Bee may have blamed Jackson for his having to endure this humiliation.

To this day the general's descendants rebuff any attempt to characterize their famous forebear's statement as anything less than laudatory. Their convictions may be sincere—yet one can understand why the Bee family would not wish to be caught on the wrong side of Confederate lore. The only source that could have provided a definitive answer to this 150-year-old question was lost to history late in the afternoon of July 21. Cut down by a Yankee bullet, Barnard Elliott Bee, the South Carolinian with the heart of a soldier and the soul of a poet, could shed no light on the meaning of his immortal but ambiguous simile.[81]

CHAPTER 14

ATTACK AND COUNTERATTACK

Around noon, when Jackson began to deploy on Henry Hill, a lengthy period of relative inactivity set in. During this time, only Keyes's advance on Jackson's far right broke the lull, and he was operating without McDowell's sanction or, for a time, his knowledge. For the next two hours, McDowell, with victory virtually within his grasp, unaccountably hesitated to order a general advance with the intent of clearing the lightly defended plateau, crumpling the enemy's left flank, and rolling up his line like a frayed gray carpet. He gave few or no orders to his senior subordinates, though due to his unpredictable movements from one part of the field to another, he was rarely in a position to communicate with them. A Minnesota officer would complain that throughout this period, "no one [was] in command." Lieutenant Averell agreed that "there was a want of a headquarters somewhere on the field."[1]

After Keyes's repulse by Hampton, Harper, and their supports, the fight was carried on mainly by the opposing artilleries, and it was McDowell's that finally ended the inactivity. Since clearing the Rebels from Matthews Hill and Young's Branch, most of the Union guns had remained planted to the high ground north of the Warrenton Turnpike. But just short of two o'clock, some of them rumbled forward, precipitating a final assault on Jackson and his comrades. McDowell had been sounding the victory chant for hours, but now he was determined to remove all doubt that the end of the contest was at hand. It was, but when it arrived it would not meet his expectations.

In seeking to prove his confidence warranted, the officer who had risen overnight from major to brigadier general made the most fateful decision of his long military career. Convinced that mobile ordnance was the key to seizing the enemy's most critical position, he directed Major Barry to order two batteries—one each from Porter's and Heintzelman's divisions—some eight hundred yards forward of their present locations west of the Sudley Road and up the nearest slope of Henry Hill. McDowell believed that from carefully chosen positions around the Henry house, the guns could shatter the head and flanks of Jackson's command.

Given their current positions in advance of most of his other guns, McDowell or Barry—or both—considered Ricketts's and Griffin's batteries the logical choice to make the move. Once on Henry Hill, they would be opposed by the almost two dozen guns shielding Jackson's men, but the Union batteries could bring to bear on their adversaries only eleven pieces—nine rifles and two howitzers (one of Griffin's 10-pounders had jammed during the morning's battle and had been abandoned on the Dogan farm). Most of their guns fired heavier rounds more accurately at longer distances than the Rebel batteries, relatively few of whose guns were rifled.

McDowell's preference for an "artillery charge" would have a major effect on the fighting to come. It would spawn a furious succession of attacks and counterattacks, of charges launched and repulsed, of guns and positions lost, recaptured, and lost again. Over the next two hours, fifteen Union and thirteen Confederate regiments would clash, for the most part one or two at a time as though adhering to a gentleman's agreement against ganging up. The result would be chaotic—one historian has described it as "a whirlpool of obscurity." Afterward, few combatants could determine the exact hour—none the minute—they attacked or how long they fought. Nor could they reconstruct the sequence of events that unfolded when they charged, countercharged, withdrew, or forced their opponent to withdraw.

The confused grappling on Henry Hill prevents a coherent timeline from being established and leaves in doubt some salient aspects of the contest. Given the importance this battle-within-a-battle assumed in the minds of both armies and in the eye of the public North and South, perhaps no other engagement of the war—Gettysburg not excluded—has been so heavily documented. Yet no other action remains so frustratingly opaque as the one that swirled across the plateau south of the Warrenton Pike and east of the Sudley Road between 2:00 and 4:00 P.M. on July 21, 1861.

If left to the commanders of the batteries that precipitated it, the struggle would not have taken place at all. When McDowell's artillery chief informed them of what the general had in mind, neither Griffin nor Ricketts was in favor of it. According to some sources, both protested the order, arguing that they could not long survive so near an established battle line even if they received close infantry support—something they doubted untried volunteers could provide. Months later when he appeared before the Joint Committee on the Conduct of the War, Griffin testified, "I hesitated about going there [Henry Hill] because I had no support." He insisted that he had made his views known to Major Barry, suggesting as an alternative that his battery be moved to the top of a smaller hill five hundred yards short of the position McDowell wished occupied.

Having been given his marching orders, Barry could not agree to this, nor could he grant Griffin's request that the infantry supports assigned to him precede rather than follow his guns to Henry Hill. Barry assured his subordinate that he would be fully supported, but the captain claimed to have told him, "I will go; but mark my words, they will not support us." Griffin shared his feelings with his subordinates, all of whom were, as Lieutenant Charles E. Hazlett later testified, "averse to going there." Hazlett suggested that Griffin make an issue of his reluctance but was told that "it was no use, and we had to go."

When appearing before Congress, Captain Ricketts, who composed no report of his participation, stated that the orders given him to advance came not from Barry but from McDowell himself as relayed by his aide Lieutenant Henry W. Kingsbury. Ricketts testified that by moving so far in advance of the army, he feared, "I was going into great peril for my horses and men." In his testimony, however, he denied a published report that he later told other officers as well as President Lincoln that in moving to the heights, he was going to certain destruction. "I made no remark at all," he insisted, "except that I wanted the place clearly indicated to which I was to move." For one thing, he was concerned that the ground ahead had not been reconnoitered. He could see that it included a shallow ravine that would impede his move to the top. Still, "I did not hesitate to obey the order."[2]

Barry must have appreciated the dangers inherent in the move, but he supposed they would be relieved by adequate assistance. Employing authority invested in him by McDowell, he later claimed to have ordered two infantry regiments, the 11th New York and the 14th Brooklyn, to furnish this protection. Barry considered both outfits hard fighting, tenacious, and dependable. He was impressed by the Fire Zouaves' reputation for daring and courage (the regiment had been the talk of Washington since its dramatic role in extinguishing a blaze in a tailor's shop that threatened the city's leading hotel, Willard's, in early May) and was probably also encouraged by the oft-expressed eagerness of "Ellsworth's Pet Lambs" to avenge the death of their beloved founder. Yet the indecorous escapades of some Zouaves, played up by the sensationalistic periodicals of the day, had given the regiment a reputation for lawlessness that embarrassed comrades hoped to eradicate through gallant deeds in combat. As for the young men of Brooklyn, Barry would have been aware of their earlier repulse along Young's Branch, although by all accounts the regiment had not disgraced itself. The men in the red trousers appeared to have regained their composure and spirit, and they seemed ready to reengage the foe.

Dutifully but with misgivings, the battery commanders led their guns, caissons, and limbers across Young's Branch at a small ford and up the northwest slope of Henry Hill. Ricketts's Company I had the lead, with Griffin's Company D more or less closely behind. The latter, however, got off to a false start; Lieutenant Hazlett, leading the way, was ordered by an unidentified superior to cross farmland belonging to a family named Chinn and to climb the eponymous ridge adjacent to it. Halfway up, the mistake was discovered; turning left, Hazlett led Griffin's way to the designated position. One can imagine that Griffin, whose normally volatile temper was more heated than ever this day, responded with some well-chosen epithets. If Hazlett was the target, he shrugged off the rebuke, for he was glad to have avoided topping Chinn Ridge. Indications were that an enemy force of some size was "just on the other side . . . waiting for us."[3]

After correcting his course, Griffin had no difficulty following Ricketts. Less than a half hour after the latter's arrival on the hill, Griffin unlimbered to his colleague's left, north of the Henry house. Ricketts too had experienced some difficulty getting into position; he had thrown down some farm fences that Griffin thus avoided. That ravine in Ricketts's front had also posed problems. While crossing it, one of Battery I's guns lost a wheel, though it was readily replaced.

Soon enough, Ricketts found himself confronting greater obstacles. Within minutes of unlimbering, his battery was fired on by sharpshooters holed up in the Henry house; a couple of cannoneers were wounded and several horses were killed. Over the next few minutes, additional animals were cut down, making Ricketts fear that he would be unable to vacate his exposed position even if ordered to do so.

Not realizing that the sharpshooters' nest was also occupied by noncombatants, the captain immediately trained his guns on the unimposing house and "literally riddled it." The results were devastating, especially for the Henry family. Earlier in the day, before the plateau was heavily occupied, an errant shell or two had landed on the property, prompting the widow's son and daughter to place their mother on a litter and attempt to move her, with the aid of her servant, to Portici, which though also in the line of fire was considered a safer venue. When the partial lull in the local fighting ended, however, the children found it impossible to move Mrs. Henry; they carried the bedridden octogenarian to the spring house on the southwest side of the property, "only to have her beg to be taken back to her own bed."

Minutes after she was returned to her home, a shell from one of Ricketts's guns came crashing through the roof to burst in the hallway where she had been lain. The shot shattered her bed, threw her to the floor, mutilated one of her feet, and wounded her in two other places; the same shell struck the servant, Lucy Griffith, in the arm. To escape the bombardment, Ellen Henry took shelter in the chimney, where she became permanently deafened by the concussions produced by the shell blasts. She would otherwise recover, but her mother succumbed to her injuries later that day and was buried in her garden, the only civilian fatality of the battle.[4]

Some students of the fight believe that after the batteries reached the top of Henry Hill, they coordinated their operations. Ricketts, however, would testify that for much of the afternoon he was unaware of Griffin's presence. His ignorance may have resulted from the fact that early in the fight the batteries were hundreds of yards apart and Ricketts's view of Griffin's position was blocked by the Henry house; once they unlimbered, each operated independently of the other. While Ricketts rooted out the sharpshooters, Griffin traded shots with the smaller but more numerous guns covering the newly christened Stonewall Brigade.[5]

Though in their new positions they had a clear shot at the nearest Confederates, Ricketts and Griffin were so close to their targets as to be almost on top of them. This complicated the process of calculating distance and range. In contrast, the gray-clad gunners, whose smaller-caliber pieces were accurate at shorter distances, enjoyed enhanced accuracy. "The [return] fire was exceedingly hot," recalled Lieutenant Hazlett, "and being in such close range of the enemy we were losing a great many men and horses." The subaltern perceived that the Federal batteries "were in full relief on top of the hill, while they were a little behind the crest of the hill. We presented a better mark for them than they did for us."

Soon the Southerners began to home in on Hazlett's position. To evade being struck, he gained Griffin's permission to move farther to the left. The lieutenant then suggested that the entire battery relocate to a more sheltered position. He assumed that his superior agreed with him, but when Lieutenant George Kensel and he began to shift two cannons to the rear, Hazlett was startled to behold the rest of the battery "flying all around." It took him some time to ascertain the cause of the frantic activity. For reasons not clear to Hazlett, Griffin was moving the pair of howitzers across the rear of Ricketts's position via the Sudley Road and was placing them on the right and well to the front of Company I. This was by far a more precarious spot than the one Griffin had abandoned, and Hazlett feared for the howitzers' survival.[6]

Jackson's Virginians may have held their position on the lower crest of Henry Hill with the strength and rigidity of a wall, but even stonework gives way under two hours' worth of cannonading. Although many of Ricketts's and Griffin's rounds passed harmlessly overhead, enough struck the earth around the brigade and its comrades farther to the rear to inflict gruesome casualties and scare the life out of those as yet unharmed. Once some of the Union guns moved to within three hundred yards of Jackson's left flank, "then the strife was fiercest," a member of the 4th Virginia recalled, "and the thunder of the battle was loudest." Every time a cannonball landed anywhere near him, one pious Virginian would exclaim: "Oh Lord! Have mercy upon me! Have mercy upon me!" A comrade lying beside him would immediately follow with: "Me too, Lord! Me too, Lord!"[7]

Those who survived the holocaust described their deliverance as miraculous and grieved for comrades who had not been spared. A youngster in Company I, 4th Virginia—the Liberty Hall Volunteers, composed mostly of students from Washington College in Lexington and assigned to support Stanard's battery—lost six of his friends: "William Paxton shot fairly in the heart with a cannon ball through his breast killing him instantly. Ben Bradley struck on the right hip with a piece of bomb shell, he lived five or six minutes; his last words were, 'Oh, Lord have mercy on me a poor sinner. Boys pray for me.' Charlie Bell who was killed with a part of the same bomb, lived about two hours, his whole right shoulder was torn off. William B. Ott, who was shot in the heart with a musket ball, killed instantly. Henry Wilson . . . was shot in the hip with a musket ball, killed instantly. The last was Calvin Utz, struck on the head with a piece of a bomb, he died the next day."[8]

Jackson rode among the men, steadying them with word and gesture, urging them to remain calm, withstand the incoming shells, and prepare for the attack of the enemy's infantry that was sure to come. He too was weary of the brigade's long exposure to shot and shell without the ability to return fire. At one point he sent word to his regimental commanders that as soon as the Yankee infantry reached the top of the hill, "let the whole line rise, move forward with a shout and trust to the bayonet. I'm tired of this long-range work!"[9]

His brigade's ordeal was worsened by the troops of Bee and Bartow, who continued to stream up the hill seeking refuge. "At first a few wounded men appeared," wrote John Opie, "then squads of men without order or organization. Some of them, carrying their dead and wounded, rushed headlong through our ranks to the rear."[10]

Nonchalantly sitting his horse, Jackson made a tempting target. At one point he halted to speak with Captain Imboden, who was finally taking what remained of his battery to the rear. To emphasize a point he was making, Jackson thrust his left arm skyward, palm forward. Suddenly he grimaced—a bullet or piece of shell had broken his middle finger. Calling the wound a mere scratch, he wrapped a handkerchief around it and rode off down his line. The finger would not be treated till battle's close.[11]

Equally defiant of the enemy's fire was G. T. Beauregard, who, having remounted, was making a conspicuous show of his presence atop Henry Hill. His arrival moved Private Sam Wright of the 2nd Virginia to break ranks, reach up, and take the Creole's hand. In addition to bolstering morale with his trademark oratory, Beauregard helped solidify Jackson's position by placing along his flanks and to the rear squads and companies of newly arrived reinforcements. At the same time, Jackson himself ordered up elements of Stuart's and Radford's cavalry to guard those same flanks. At his request, Stuart halved his command to support each end of the brigade line, albeit at some distance. One of those battalions would perform dramatic service, attacking two regiments of enemy infantry, but Radford's horsemen would serve less conspicuously, for the most part forced to endure hours of artillery shelling. They too mounted a couple of charges against Yankees imperiling Jackson's brigade, but neither achieved much, and one ended with several horses and riders tumbling into an undetected ditch. Nevertheless, the added support convinced Jackson that he could hold his ground against any infantry assault.[12]

Major Barry would claim that in fulfillment of his pledge to Griffin, he collected the Fire Zouaves and ordered them up Henry Hill, while Colonel Heintzelman, who had reached the base of the plateau at the head of his 9,500-man division, sent the 14th Brooklyn to Company D's support. In his congressional testimony, however, Heintzelman stated that he told the 1st Minnesota, stationed on the west side of Sudley Road, to assist the batteries, just then going into position on the summit.[13]

After putting the Minnesotans in motion, Heintzelman rode to the top of the hill, where he "made inquiries as to what was going on." He spied McDowell riding about on the edge of the crest but apparently did not speak to him. Instead, his attention was drawn to the movements of Ricketts and Griffin, whose guns he considered unduly exposed to the enemy's own batteries. Perceiving that despite his efforts, infantry support was lacking, Heintzelman followed the guns for a short distance, whereupon he saw the 11th New York coming across the fields from the Sudley Road. He appears not to have noticed Barry riding at the head of the regiment, for as he later testified, he took it upon himself to send orders for it to hasten to the top and form behind Ricketts's battery. Lieutenant Averell, coming forward to the crest of the hill at this same time, would also take credit for ushering up the Fire Zouaves as well as the battalion of marines attached to his command. His claim is dubious, however, since the 11th New York was an element not of his brigade, but of Willcox's.[14]

For some time Averell had been trying to shape the attack against Henry Hill, which he considered "the key-point of the enemy's position . . . , [one that] must be taken before the battle would be given up." Concerned by McDowell's apparent reluctance to make a climactic push, with input from Captain W. D. Whipple of the division's staff, Averell had crafted a plan to organize a strike column consisting of the 14th Brooklyn and several fresh regiments of Heintzelman's division: the 11th New York, 5th and 11th Massachusetts, 1st Minnesota, and 38th New York. These units—to be covered by Arnold's Company D, 2nd Artillery north of the turnpike—would be thrown forward without reference to Ricketts and Griffin. Averell and Whipple had broached the idea to Colonel Franklin and also Major Wadsworth of McDowell's staff and, as the lieutenant claimed, received their approval and pledges of support.

Before the acting brigade commander could put his plan in motion, he saw the guns of Companies I and D advancing toward and then up Henry Hill without visible infantry support. The movement threatened to put the kibosh on everything he, Whipple, Franklin, and Wadsworth had contemplated. Averell promptly galloped up to the moving batteries, asked what was going on, and was told where they were heading and why.

Concerned that the artillery would be sacrificed, Averell looked about for McDowell. Other subordinates had been seeking the peripatetic commander without finding him, but Averell spied him on a small hill in a field beyond the turnpike. Catching up with his superior, who had traded his carriage for a warhorse, he summarized the plan that he and Whipple (who minutes before had been unhorsed by a roundshot that had eviscerated his horse) had put together and "pointed out the danger the batteries were incurring." He described the general as replying in a weary voice, "Go and give any orders you deem necessary, Mr. Averell." Though Averell did not comment on it then or later, McDowell's apathetic response suggested that he was abdicating his responsibilities as army commander and chief architect of Union strategy. He appeared willing to endorse any plan that any subordinate—even a lieutenant of mounted troops—came up with.[15]

Perhaps McDowell was losing his grip on the battle. If so, it is hard to understand why. At this point the Army of Northeastern Virginia enjoyed substantial advantages of manpower and position. With the arrival of Heintzelman and the advance of half of Tyler's division (Sherman's and Keyes's brigades), McDowell had at his disposal almost 20,000 troops with which to oppose perhaps one-fourth as many enemy effectives.

It was true that the army's situation had deteriorated somewhat due to missteps by some of McDowell's subordinates, officers whose operations he had failed to oversee, at least in part, perhaps, because of his continuing debility. Hunter's and Porter's tactics had produced piecemeal, unsupported assaults. Upon taking charge of the Second Division, Porter had allowed his units to become fragmented and scattered between Matthews and Henry Hills while permitting Burnside to drop out of the fight for spurious reasons.

Porter had also erred by extending the army's right beyond the Sudley Road in violation of McDowell's intention to keep everyone facing south toward the enemy. From that extreme position, Porter's division had to curve eastward in order to confront the Rebels. As R. M. Johnston notes, the result was that McDowell "was fast tending to face backwards towards Centreville," while the constant elongation of his line raised the prospect of its breaking at one or more points. And, of course, Tyler had misused two-thirds of his division available to him today. Although he quite properly sent Sherman to reinforce Porter, he had led Keyes in an unauthorized and mismanaged assault against Jackson's detached right while permitting Schenck to idle away the afternoon on the far side of Bull Run.[16]

But McDowell was not the only commander to delegate control of the fighting to subordinates. His opponents had too, but their lieutenants had used the discretion granted them judiciously and in timely fashion. Because they had remained so long on the opposite end of the Confederate line, Johnston and Beauregard had exerted little or no control over the early, critical phase of the fighting. Evans, Bee, and Bartow had selected their own positions; so too had Jackson, who seized the critical initiative when he came to their assistance. While not truly a soldier's battle—in which individual troops or small units shape the course of combat—management of the struggle thus far had descended to the brigade and, in some cases, the regimental level.

Although they moved belatedly, and in some cases erratically, up Henry Hill, numerous units of foot soldiers were eventually on hand to protect the flanks and rear of Ricketts's and Griffin's guns. Regardless of who was responsible for ordering them up, the Zouaves of the 11th New York led the way up the western slope of the plateau, heading at the double-quick toward the rear of Ricketts's battery. At approximately the same time, the 1st Minnesota, apparently at Heintzelman's direct order, trudged up the heights on the right of the Fire Zouaves.[17]

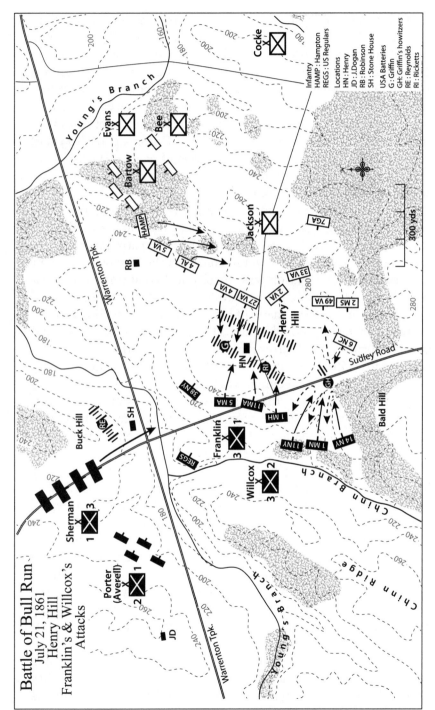

Battle of Bull Run, July 21, 1861: Henry Hill, Franklin's and Willcox's Attacks. *Map by Paul Dangel.*

Additional support for the artillery was on the way too. Lieutenant Averell claimed to have assembled the 14th Brooklyn, which he found "collecting in little masses" along the Sudley Road, and to have placed it in a small hollow within supporting distance of Griffin's position. The energetic Averell also called up the marine battalion and moved it to the left flank of the Fire Zouaves. Once in position the marines, in response to an order from their own officers, assumed a prone position within supporting range of Griffin's guns. To guard the far flank of this entire force, a squadron of regular cavalry under Brevet Captain Albert V. Colburn cantered down the Sudley Road, looking for targets of opportunity.[18]

The 11th New York and 1st Minnesota were the first of this disparate grouping to see action on the plateau. The 11th, the pride of McDowell's army, led the way, eagerly anticipating its first battle action, but the outcome would confound the Zouaves and their many admirers. One reason was the physical condition of the regiment this day. Its colonel, Noah Farnham, had fled a sickbed to lead the regiment into battle; many of his men were also feeling unwell, the result of having double-quicked from the regiment's original position north of the Warrenton Pike. Physical fitness was a prerequisite for a Zouave recruit, but by the time he climbed Henry Hill even the hardiest specimen was panting and sweating profusely under an afternoon sun that, as Private Lewis Metcalf recalled, "blazed remorselessly down upon us." In deference to the conditions, Farnham had permitted the men to strip off their jackets, allowing their colorful overshirts to show.[19]

While no longer the paragons of style that Ellsworth had made them, the Zouaves appeared more fashionable than the black-hatted comrades to their right. The 1st Minnesota Volunteers had traveled farther than any other combatant to reach this battlefield—more than a thousand miles from Fort Snelling on the Mississippi River. Though directed to cover Ricketts's battery, the scions of the Old Northwest would not be content to stand guard over inanimate objects. Two of their companies—A and F, under Captain Alexander Wilkin—were so anxious to engage the enemy that they forged ahead of the balance of the regiment, heading straight for the far left flank of Jackson's position.[20]

Sheltered by the back slope of the hill and the pines trees along it, the 33rd Virginia watched the Minnesotans advance to within fifty yards of its position. Apparently without orders, some Virginians loosed a volley that brought the westerners to a halt. At once Colonel Cummings, who could not identify these newcomers who wore no tunics or jackets, called on his men to stop shooting, suggesting that "you are firing on friends." After taking a closer look at the advancing troops, however, John Casler shouted, "Friends hell," and resumed shooting; numerous comrades followed his lead.[21]

The confusion over uniforms extended to the Minnesotans: many of their assailants appeared to be wearing civilian clothes. Moments after they began to return the Virginians' fire, Colonel Willis Gorman yelled for everyone to stop for fear of downing friends. He too was shouted down by more-discerning riflemen as well as several subordinates. One of the 1st's many German-born enlisted men kept firing while exclaiming, "Dem is secessers!" Private Jasper Searles wrote that the colonel "was soon undeceived for they suddenly gave us such a volley that had they not fired too high, [they] would have brought down two thirds of the Regt."[22]

It may have been pitched a bit too high, but the "deadly fire" was just that. Lieutenant Louis Muller later estimated that the fusillade killed 50 Minnesotans and wounded 125, the latter including Muller himself. He appraisal was not far off the mark: casualty returns would reveal that his outfit lost 42 killed and 108 wounded, the heaviest loss of any Federal regiment in the fight. According to a couple of accounts, some of the wounded left on the field when the 1st later retreated were bayoneted by the "savages" into whose hands they fell—one of a number of unfounded but widely credited atrocity stories to emerge from the battle.[23]

With the 1st Minnesota frozen in a state of shock, Heintzelman hastened to commit the Fire Zouaves, which had reached the rear of Ricketts's guns. Relieving them of their support role, the colonel ordered the New Yorkers to charge Jackson's position in the direction of the 2nd Virginia, on the 33rd's right. As the Zouaves swept forward, bayonets pointing toward the enemy, Captain Ricketts rode toward the head of their column and shouted, "For God's sake, boys, save my battery!"

He plead in vain. Almost as soon as they passed his guns, the Zouaves recoiled from volleys delivered by the 2nd and 33rd Virginia as well as scattered elements of Bee's and Bartow's brigades that had re-formed in Jackson's left rear. "Down, every one of you," cried Colonel Farnham, and his men hit the dirt, their first charge already a thing of the past. Farnham himself failed to duck quickly enough; a rifle ball thudded into the left side of his skull, leaving a mortal wound. The multidirectional fire also ravaged the 1st Minnesota, whose men joined their comrades in pressing their faces to the ground.[24]

From their prone position, both regiments squeezed off about four or five rounds per man without noticeable effect. When increasing numbers of Confederates trained muskets on them, the New Yorkers and Minnesotans saw that they could not remain stationary. Although to retreat was just as risky as to advance, dozens of men regained their feet, turned their backs to the enemy, and ran for their lives. Some whirled about and fired on the run, thereby posing a greater threat to their friends than to the Rebels. In his official report Heintzelman observed that these men fired, "fortunately for the braver ones, very high in the air—compelling those in front to retreat." The historian of the 1st U.S. Artillery would write that Ricketts's and Griffin's supports "wavered, broke, and fled. The panic had begun. On came the enemy, solid and determined, pouring in their volleys of musketry."[25]

Some of the officers, including Colonel Gorman of the 1st Minnesota, raced the enlisted men to the rear. After the fight a sarcastic Private Searles commented that Gorman's conduct "did not characterize him as a *very* brave man—not *his* conduct, but that of his horse which he could not keep on the field, not even by sinking his spurs into his sides & pulling with a will."[26]

The Minnesotans' actions may not have been as blameworthy as it appeared at the time. Although admitting that the regiment had been roughly handled, Heintzelman asserted that it headed to the rear with some semblance of formation. It withdrew primarily in two groups. The left wing retreated swiftly, but as Captain Wilkin insisted, only at the order of one of Heintzelman's aides. The right wing, which included Wilkin's unit, retired grudgingly under the direction of Lieutenant Colonel Stephen A. Miller and "fought like tigers." To keep the regimental colors from capture, Lieutenant Nathan S. Messick brought them off by tearing them from their flagstaff and wrapping them around his waist.

Given the numerical odds against them and their inability to tell friend from foe until almost too late, it seems unfair to condemn the citizen-soldiers of New York or Minnesota for quitting the battlefield either precipitately or reluctantly. Participants in the retreat would argue that neither fell back until ordered to do so multiple times, at least once by a member of McDowell's staff who shouted at them: "Retreat! God damn you, retreat! What do you stand there for? I never saw such men to fight!"[27]

Even in retreat, many gave a good account of themselves. When returning to the starting point of its advance, the 1st Minnesota was assailed by a regiment apparently not previously involved in the fighting: the 2nd Mississippi of Bee's brigade, which having retained its formation after being dislodged from Young's Branch, had found a rallying place a short distance beyond Jackson's left flank. Members of the 1st responded to the sudden strike by pivoting in the Mississippians' direction and "knocking them down right and left." The Rebels pulled back, giving up some of their number as prisoners, including Lieutenant Colonel Bartley Boone. The officer surrendered to an armed civilian, Javan Irvine, a resident of Saint Paul who had attached himself to Captain Wilkin's company. (Upon his parole and release, the humiliated Boone would be dropped from the rolls of his regiment.)[28]

In further exculpation of his regiment's eventual turn to the rear, Searles noted that "the regulars even retreated before we did." The reference was to Major John G. Reynolds's 350-man battalion of U.S. Marines, which Averell had unwisely committed to the fight. While the regiments on Jackson's left and the artillery shielding them fired on the New Yorkers and Minnesotans moving to Ricketts's support, other Confederates targeted Griffin's guns. At one point the marines, while seated in rear of Company D, attracted a scattered fire from the center of Jackson's line. It inflicted few casualties, but one of them—a junior officer decapitated by a ricocheting cannonball—was shocking enough to disrupt unit cohesion and tenacity. Some accounts have the marines running as soon as fired upon; others have them falling back and re-forming three times before a fourth, irreparable break.

Their scramble to the rear could have been predicted. Formed only a few weeks earlier, the battalion had received little training—not nearly enough to prepare the men for actual combat. Reynolds described his command as being "composed entirely of recruits, not one being in service over three weeks, and many had barely learned their facings [that is, basic maneuvers], the officers likewise being but a short time in service." Their commitment to the battle indicates Averell's ignorance of the caliber of the personnel he had inherited upon Porter's succession to division command.[29]

Even if improperly employed, the marines had stained the proud history of their corps. The officers keenly felt the sting of the battalion's disgraceful behavior. Averell described Reynolds's second in command, Brevet Captain Jacob Zeilin, as mired in "grief and mortification." Unable to rally the panicky fugitives, Zeilin, who had received a slight wound, was walking to the rear alone, sword drawn. Whenever he passed a clump of tall weeds he would "cut off its head with a right or left cut, accompanying the blow with a half audible curse."[30]

Although the Rebels declined to pursue either regiment, the ordeal of the 11th New York and 1st Minnesota was not over. As they scrambled down Henry Hill toward the Sudley Road, the battle-scarred troops were set upon by horsemen wielding pistols and sabers. The assailants were the 150 members of J. E. B. Stuart's 1st Virginia guarding Jackson's far left flank from recently assumed positions south of the Federals' escape route. Since the battle's earliest hours, Stuart, for whom idleness was a curse, had been relegated to scouting and picketing between Portici and Manassas Junction. Desperate to see action, he had repeatedly petitioned his superiors to permit him to unleash his troopers' potential.

Stuart's plight was reflective of Johnston and Beauregard's misuse of their mounted arm. At first chained to the Confederate right, the troopers had been unable to detect McDowell's turning movement, which if discovered early enough, might have changed the complexion of the battle. Nor had other mobile forces—Radford's regiment or the several independent companies attached to Beauregard's army—been in a position to discern, report, or resist McDowell's offensive. The Union cavalry had been similarly ineffective. Those troopers McDowell had assigned to Hunter's and Heintzelman's columns were so few and their utilization so faulty that their infantry comrades had been unprepared to confront Evans's brigade on Matthews Hill. Later in the battle the horsemen had scored a few successes, helping break up Stuart's attack on the 11th New York and 1st Minnesota and capturing at least one high-ranking Confederate. At other times they had become enmeshed with the foot soldiers they had been assigned to support, charging through their ranks, breaking up their formations, and inflicting casualties. Moreover, they had largely failed in their primary mission, reconnoitering the enemy's positions. Late in the day the horsemen had been shunted to the far right flank, where they saw little activity of consequence but were less likely to cause trouble. By day's end their leader, Major Palmer, had been reduced to "a woeful state of mortification," so upset by his command's misadventures that he broke down in tears.[31]

But Stuart's cavalry had finally been positioned to contribute to the fight following Jackson's noontime arrival on Henry Hill. Its orders to feel the Yankees in that sector and if possible assail one or the other of their flanks had originated with Johnston. In his report Stuart claimed that he rode at once toward the Union left, "but finding that it would be easier to attain the right flank, I immediately returned and marched rapidly toward the heaviest fire." This route brought him into contact with Jackson, who urged that the cavalry cover both ends of his battle line "but particularly his left flank." Stuart decided to tackle that task at the head of half his command; the other 150 troopers he sent to Jackson's right under command of Major Robert Swan.

To reach its preferred position, Stuart's detachment passed through a skirt of woods and across farm fields, throwing down a succession of fences, until striking the Sudley Road. Peering north, the lieutenant colonel spied a regiment "running in disorder towards a skirt of woods where the fire had been heaviest." Through his field glasses he saw that some of the scramblers wore red. Perhaps these were the Fire Zouaves, whose gaudy attire was familiar to Southerners as well as Northerners. But Stuart recalled that Bob Wheat's men wore red shirts too, and at first he took the fugitives for comrades, shouting to them, "Don't run, boys; we are here!" (Stuart should have appreciated how appearances could deceive, for he, like many other high-ranking Confederates, was wearing his blue prewar army uniform this day.) The men paid no heed but continued to hotfoot it up the road. Riding closer, Stuart identified their colors as those of the enemy. At once he ordered a charge in hopes of foiling what he supposed to be a flanking movement against Jackson.

Hearing the approaching thunder of horses' hooves, many of the New Yorkers and Minnesotans—if they had not already done so—gave way to panic. Here was a nightmare come true for every Federal familiar with the typical "black horse" Confederate, a fearsome combination of cavalier, Cossack, and Comanche. Thus it was no surprise that when set upon by Stuart, the cry of "Black Horse!" went up from officers and men alike, even though, as more than one survivor of the encounter observed, not one of Stuart's men rode a steed of that color.

Minutes before they could be ridden down, several Federals whirled about and leveled their rifles at the galloping horsemen. Officers discharged pistols at the head of Stuart's column—one Minnesotan emptied his revolver, then threw it at the nearest Confederate. Though poorly aimed, the resulting volley could not fail to be effective at such range. Several saddles immediately emptied, but unhurt riders rampaged through the infantry's broken ranks, flailing about with cold steel. Their attack fell primarily on the Fire Zouaves, a few of whom immediately fell beneath slashing hooves. A Union surgeon who had shimmied up a nearby tree observed "a grand melee . . . horses rearing, sabres glistening, and revolvers flashing; the only approach to a hand to hand conflict" he witnessed that day.[32]

At the outset the attackers had the advantage over their scattered, demoralized prey. William W. Blackford singled out two Yankees and deliberately rode them down. He had intended to leap the first man but his horse was "going too fast to rise higher than the breast of the man, and he struck him full on the chest, rolling him over and over under his hooves and knocking the rear rank man to one side. As Comet rose to make the leap, I leaned down from the saddle, rammed the muzzle of the carbine into the stomach of my man and pulled the trigger. . . . [T]he carbine blew a hole as big as my arm clear through him."[33]

It was not, however, the one-sided affair that Stuart and some of his troopers would later claim. Private Metcalf of the Zouaves recalled that the Rebels "rode through us cutting right and left with their sabers but hitting no one." Once they finally recovered from the shock of the assault, the Federals fought back with an abandon they had not displayed on Henry Hill. As their assailants thundered past, they fired into them and slashed about with bayonets. One New Yorker claimed that "in an instant . . . men and horses fell like ten-pins." Casualties included at least nine troopers and almost twenty of their animals. Concerned by his mounting losses and denied maneuvering room once the Federals took cover in roadside woods, Stuart called off the attack, turned his column about, and led it back the way it had come. Another reason for his hasty withdrawal—rarely reported in accounts of the battle—was a countercharge by Colburn's squadron of regulars, which according to Colonel Heintzelman, killed and wounded several more cavalrymen.[34]

In the end, Stuart failed to add materially to the damage suffered by the 11th New York and 1st Minnesota on Henry Hill or to destroy their capacity for further fighting. By this point his opponents had suffered greatly (the 11th New York would lose 123 men killed or wounded during the day, only 27 fewer than their Minnesota comrades). Although many of their men had been driven to the rear in panic, determined survivors of both regiments would make their way back up Henry Hill to provide belated support to their embattled artillery. Their ranks may have been broken up and cast about, but their fighting spirit had not been extinguished.[35]

Once their infantry supports took flight, the guns, men, and horses of Griffin and Ricketts became easy prey for Jackson's brigade. As a result, all but one 10-pounder rifle and one howitzer limber fell into enemy hands during a hectic and extremely bloody ninety-minute period on Henry Hill. The artillery's loss changed the course of the battle and made its denouement inevitable.

Misidentification and resulting confusion played a role in the outcome. It had begun even before the attack and repulse of the 11th New York and 1st Minnesota. As those regiments clambered uphill to support the guns, Colonel Heintzelman rode forward to the position recently taken up by Captain Griffin's howitzers. Peering eastward, the division commander made out a body of men "drawn up at a shoulder-arms, dressed in citizen's clothes." He was staring at the troops holding the left of Jackson's line, but their mixture of civilian and military attire confused him—for how long is a matter of some dispute. Heintzelman claimed that "in an instant" he saw that "they were a party of the enemy's troops." According to Lieutenant Averell, who had joined Heintzelman and Griffin on the summit after positioning the 14th Brooklyn, the colonel's confusion lasted much longer. He recalled finding him "by the side of Griffin, discussing with him the character of a line of men forming not over two hundred and fifty yards in front in the edge of the woods. Griffin's men were at the lanyards and he wished to give the command 'fire.' Heintzelman thought they were our own troops in front and appealed to me."[36]

Averell recalled that a little crest—one of those devilishly deceptive undulations in the half-mile-long plateau—"swelled up a little between the batteries and the line in question, so that the men in line could not be seen below their knees." From the waist up, however, they looked like Rebels to him, especially when he saw them dress ranks and sidestep as if preparing to charge Griffin's howitzers. The lieutenant make a quick decision and advised Griffin to open fire. Heintzelman, however, remained conflicted; grasping Averell's right arm as if to stay his impulsiveness, he shouted: "No, no! They are our men!"

Even as Heintzelman mouthed the words, the unidentified troops proved he had been deceived. "At that instance," Averell wrote, "down came the line of small arms of the enemy to a level; we heard the command 'fire,' and . . . Heintzelman gave an expression of pain as a ball passed through his wrist near my arm and it seemed to me that every horse in the batteries sank down with many of the men." The colonel fell back to have his wound treated but briefly returned to the front after having a surgeon carve the ball out of his upper right arm. The gesture suggested fortitude, but sources agree that Heintzelman played a negligible role in the rest of the fighting.[37]

Because disaster followed Griffin's decision to withhold fire, the identity of the person or persons who persuaded him that he was facing friends, not foes, became the focal point of a postbattle controversy. In his official report, composed two days later, Griffin stated that "an officer on the field" had identified the advancing force as "a regiment sent by Colonel Heintzelman to support the battery." Six months later, when testifying before the Joint Committee on the Conduct of the War, the artilleryman was no longer uncertain of the informant's identity. He now claimed that Major Barry rode up to him as he was about to shower canister on an enemy force that was scaling a fence to get at him, shouting, "Captain, don't fire there; those are your battery support." Griffin's claim was partially backed up by one of his subordinates, Lieutenant Horatio B. Reed, who told the committee that "some one" ordered the captain to withhold his fire. Although Reed was "under the impression" that Barry gave the order, he refused to testify that he heard him do so. Undoubtedly, however, he had heard his superior identify Barry as the culprit.

Griffin further testified that he suspected the unit in question was Confederate and told Barry so but that the latter repeated the order to withhold fire. Griffin dutifully unloaded his short-range ammunition, by which time the force in his front had cleared both fence and trees and was bearing down on him. At a distance of forty yards, the approaching troops halted, raised their muskets, and delivered a devastating fire. By then Griffin had begun taking steps to limber up his howitzers in the event of being attacked, but he lacked the time to complete the process.[38]

There are holes in Griffin's account of this critical turn of events. Why he failed to name Barry immediately after the battle but did so without hesitation when his role in the fight came under congressional scrutiny suggests an effort to evade personal blame. If Griffin initially remained silent about Barry's involvement for fear of jeopardizing his career, why indict the man six months later while still under his command? For that matter, why blame Barry at all? Averell, who was with Griffin when the Rebel force appeared in his front, firmly declared that Heintzelman stayed the artillery-man's hand. Heintzelman, by admitting that he initially failed to identify the approaching force as Confederate, appears to corroborate Averell's claim.

The colonel was not the only observer who failed at once to identify the troops as Confederate. Barry attested before the committee that he mistook the inconsistently clad troops for Federals too. Perhaps some of the troops wore trousers that appeared red at a distance—he supposed they were members of the 14th Brooklyn, which Averell had positioned in the hollow along the far left of Jackson's line minutes before the Confederates broke from those same trees. Barry categorically denied restraining Griffin: "I gave no orders not to fire." Indeed, he attested to having given no orders of any kind either to Griffin or Ricketts, both of whom he considered equipped to know when to fire or to withhold it. He further testified that had he immediately recognized the approaching troops as Confederates, there "would have been no time to do anything before they delivered their fire. . . . It was almost instantaneous after I saw them." Ricketts, when appearing before the committee, confirmed that Barry gave him no orders—in fact, "I did not see him" at any time during the afternoon.[39]

Griffin's dramatic testimony before Congress (the Rebels "opened fire upon us, and that was the last of us") has resonated with generations of military observers. When writing about the battle, they have declared Major Barry culpable, in large degree, for the loss of two splendidly mounted units of light artillery. Yet there is reason to believe that Griffin deliberately defamed a superior he had long disliked and resented. (Before and after the battle, Griffin admitted, he and Barry "were never on good terms.")[40]

Historians acknowledge that Griffin was a "hard case" who suffered fools neither gladly nor quietly—and he found them almost everywhere he looked. He had a contentious disposition and a volatile temper and was given to profane criticisms of colleagues and superiors he considered slow witted, obtuse, or incompetent. More commendable traits, including tactical skill and leadership ability, would gain him high rank—he would finish the war as a major general of volunteers and an acting corps commander. But in infantry command Griffin too often allowed his discontent to boil over. It happened during the Chancellorsville Campaign of mid-1863 and again a year later in the Virginia Wilderness. On the latter, well-publicized occasion, he threw such a tantrum, so spitefully criticizing another division commander, that the newly appointed commanding general of U.S. forces, Lieutenant General Ulysses S. Grant, wanted to place him under arrest for behavior bordering on mutinous.[41]

Griffin's attack on Barry may have served to divert scrutiny of an egregious tactical error by the battery commander. Before Congress, he admitted that McDowell, not Barry, was responsible for sending him into a risky position without adequate support. He never acknowledged, however, that he himself was to blame for advancing his howitzers so close to the enemy's lines as almost to hand them over to Jackson. In his battle report Griffin failed to detail his decision to detach those two pieces from Ricketts's left flank, pass them behind his colleague, and place them on exposed ground beyond the latter's right. Undoubtedly, Griffin made the move because, as Jackson had observed, direct artillery fire on the Confederates was having little effect—an enfilading fire would have been more productive. And Griffin would have understood that a howitzer, which has a more arching trajectory than a gun, would better achieve this effect.

In his testimony Griffin matter-of-factly described the move he made without orders from Barry or anyone else, but he did not address the risks it involved. He noted only that the new position brought his howitzers to within about 250 yards of a battery that had been supporting Jackson. As Averell mentioned, the ground swell prevented Griffin from discovering that Confederate infantrymen were within rifle range of his new position. Thus Griffin made the move without proper observation of terrain or an awareness of the enemy's proximity. What followed was primarily his fault, not his superior's.

The 33rd Virginia was the redheaded stepchild of Jackson's brigade. It had been assigned to the command only three days before Johnston's army left Winchester to join Beauregard and thus had yet to be fully integrated into it. With the exception of the seven-company 27th Virginia, the 33rd, only eight companies of which had made the march from the Valley, was the smallest of Jackson's regiments. As observers including Heintzelman and Averell had discovered, it was also poorly dressed. In contrast to the other units of the brigade, the 33rd wore a variety of clothing, although probably not the blue uniforms that some Union observers and latter-day historians have described. Yet at least one of its companies, which had joined the regiment only a few days before it started for Manassas, may have lacked uniforms of any cut and color. This may explain Heintzelman's description of the enemy before his eyes as wearing civilian clothes.

In addition to unfashionable attire, the regiment had a reputation for lax hygiene. While Jackson's other outfits would gain such nicknames as "The Fighting Fifth" and "The Bloody Twenty-Seventh," Cummings's regiment, which had experienced an early infestation of "graybacks" (head and body lice), had already been dubbed "The Lousy Thirty-Third." Nor did it enjoy the distinction, shared by the rest of the brigade, of having been recruited in those corners of Virginia considered bastions of Confederate loyalty. Of the six southwestern counties from which the 33rd drew its personnel, two would secede from their state in 1863 to help form West Virginia.[42]

Populated as it was by numerous Irishmen given to drinking, brawling, and carousing, the 33rd would become known for its general unruliness. Its commander, who had graduated from the Virginia Military Institute and had fought in Mexico, lamented the fact that his regiment, new to service and lacking instruction, was "raw and wholly without the advantage of discipline." Less than a year later, when the outfit gained the right to elect its officers, Colonel Cummings, whose strict notions of deportment had made him unpopular with the rank and file, returned to civilian life.[43]

From its position on Jackson's left, the 33rd was sheltered from enemy view not only by the clump of pines it occupied but also by a multirail fence in front of the trees. Only 150 to 200 yards from the nearest Union guns—which were now aiming slightly toward the north, not directly at the 33rd—the outfit was within range of attacking and seizing the howitzers before they could fire down the length of the brigade. Noting that infantrymen were coming up the hill in rear of Griffin and Ricketts and fearing that his entire position might become untenable, Jackson ordered Cummings to maintain his position until the Yankees were within thirty paces of his woods. Then he was to direct a concentrated fire at them, followed by an all-out assault. One account has the general telling not only Cummings but also each of his regimental commanders to wait until the enemy was within fifty yards, then "charge with the bayonet."[44]

For his part, Cummings had misgivings about following these orders. Doubtful that his undisciplined troops could stand their ground so long against advancing infantry, especially if under artillery fire, the colonel saw no reason to delay his attack. He believed, and hoped, that Jackson would understand. Brandishing his sword, he placed himself at the head of his regiment, whose men had been lying down per their brigade leader's instructions, and called for a charge. Virtually instantaneously, four hundred men got to their feet and started forward, yelling in a manner Old Jack would have approved of.

Scaling or detouring around the fence in front of them, the Virginians raced down a sharp incline on a southwesterly path to Griffin's howitzers. When seventy yards off, Cummings shouted "Fire!" and an uneven but powerful volley of musketry lashed the artillery's position. The result was devastation. Not only were the battery horses shot down by the dozens but also, as Averell noted, "the horses attached to the line of caissons in rear started down the slope at a frightening pace." Minutes later the attackers were flooding over Griffin's position, laying hands on both of the howitzers and dispatching their gunners with rifle, bayonet, and pistol. The cannoneers fought back fiercely, but although the melee continued for several minutes, its result was never in doubt: Griffin's howitzers became prizes of war. Whether they could be held for any length of time, however, remained to be seen.[45]

Their captors included not only Cummings's men but also members of the three-company 49th Virginia, which Beauregard had guided toward the far left from its original station north of the Lewis house. The truncated regiment was led by one of the most colorful characters in the political history of the Old Dominion. Known as "Extra Billy" for his ability to wring additional fees from the U.S. Post Office by adding routes to his prewar mail-coach service, sixty-three-year-old William Smith was an unlikely soldier, lacking as he did experience and familiarity with arms. But military service had a certain appeal, and his political clout and the notoriety he had won by helping repulse the June 1 raid on Fairfax Court House had gained him a commission.[46]

Although only a couple hundred of Smith's men had reached Manassas in time to see action, his command had been expanded by the addition of the two companies of the 11th Mississippi of Bee's brigade and a company of South Carolinians from Evans's command to a total of perhaps 450. The force remained undersized like the man himself, but Smith intended to make the most of an opportunity to add martial glory to his record of commercial and political achievement. He was proud to be leading a viable though little-heralded element of Beauregard's army. As the unit marched toward Jackson's left, it passed regiments who asked its name. "Smith's regiment" was the reply. Because many by that name held positions of command, the logical follow up was "Which Smith?" The colonel himself replied in a thunderous voice: *"Extra Billy, by God!"*[47]

Upon gaining the position Beauregard had assigned it—a pine thicket slightly to the south and west of Jackson's flank—Smith's battalion lurched into action. Minutes after the 33rd Virginia jumped to its feet and charged Griffin's howitzers, the 49th went in behind or beside it, though not before Extra Billy, in approved Beauregard style, delivered an oration calculated to activate the men's enthusiasm and determination. It seems to have worked, for minutes later his men joined Cummings's in delivering a volley that left Griffin's howitzers ripe for capture.

Some accounts, including Smith's own, have his men attacking side by side with the 33rd, their forces closely aligned. Yet it seems clear that, especially considering the time Smith took to fire up his troops, they followed rather than accompanied their fellow Virginians. Other sources deserving of more credence suggest that some of the charging Rebels, probably members of Cummings's regiment, also took Ricketts's battery in flank, temporarily seizing some of its cannons. It may have been these troops who seriously wounded the battery commander and left him for dead.[48]

For several minutes the Confederates had their way with Griffin's howitzers. Inexperienced in infantry tactics to say nothing of artillery employment, Cummings's and Smith's men were unable to maneuver the pieces to fire upon those Federals still moving up the hill. Some of the Confederates capered among the guns, almost giddy over their unexpected accomplishment. Their officers, however, suspected that their success would be short lived.

Because the retreat of the 11th New York and 1st Minnesota threatened to unhinge their army's newly established line on Henry Hill, reinforcements were hustled there from north of the turnpike and west of the Sudley Road. Led by the 14th Brooklyn, the supports also included the 5th and 11th Massachusetts of Franklin's brigade and Willcox's 38th New York and 1st Michigan. Though belatedly launched and not aligned with Griffin and Ricketts as originally intended, Lieutenant Averell's hastily improvised offensive was going forward at last. It would create the impetus for a series of desperate strikes and counterstrikes that would gyrate crazily across the now-littered plateau. By determining who would hold and who would relinquish the high ground, these actions would decide the critical phase of the battle.

Minutes after the 33rd and 49th Virginia took Griffin's howitzers, the red-trousered 14th Brooklyn rushed up through the shattered ranks of the 11th New York and broke into a charge. The chasseurs were returning to the fight for the first time since their repulse in the valley of Young's Branch two hours earlier. When about forty yards from the captured guns, Colonel Alfred M. Wood had the men halt, aim, and shoot. A torrent of rifle fire inundated the ranks of the 33rd and 49th Virginia, many of their men toppling beside the guns they had sized.

Survival instincts kicked in immediately; unhurt men turned and fled back to the trees out of which they had charged. Many did not halt till they were off the field entirely. In a postwar letter Cummings, whose regiment would suffer the greatest loss of any Confederates defending Henry Hill—45 men killed, more than 100 wounded—admitted, "I could not have collected together as many as twenty men" for further service. Even so, Southern scribes would heap praise on the regiment, insisting that "never in the annals of war was a braver charge made by raw troops."[49]

In their headlong flight Cummings's fugitives collided with the left-flank companies of Allen's 2nd Virginia, dislodging a large chunk of that regiment. Private Alex Shepherd of the 2nd wrote that the men of the 33rd, in their confused retreat, "were firing into us through mistake & that made the confusion so much worse, then there was no such thing as getting a line formed there." Shepherd

and many of the comrades caught up in the stampede were carried
to the rear, where they took refuge behind Jackson's artillery. The
chaos was compounded following Allen's wounding. Having lost an
eye in a childhood accident, the colonel was temporarily blinded
when struck in his good eye by a pine limb torn off by a cannon firing from north of the turnpike.[50]

To avert disaster, Jackson took personal charge of the left flank.
At first he met with adversity; his attempt to re-fuse the left flank
of Allen's regiment failed. When the 14th Brooklyn reloaded and
sent additional volleys their way, many of those who had held
their ground to that point suddenly took off for the rear. The regiment's unhinging greatly complicated Jackson's efforts to hold
firm. It appeared that the 14th Brooklyn had accomplished what
Keyes's brigade had failed to achieve against the opposite flank of
that line—the displacement of the entire Confederate position on
Henry Hill.

Though crisis loomed, Jackson refused to panic or to allow
others to do so. While rushing to the rear, an officer of the 33rd
unexpectedly encountered his brigade commander, to whom he
cried, "The day is going against us!" "If you think so, sir," Jackson
replied calmly, "you had better not say anything about it." Then
he went to work to shore up the line. The 5th Virginia was too far
detached to provide immediate support, so he turned to the 4th and
27th Virginia, telling their men, "Reserve your fire till they come
within fifty yards, then fire and give them the bayonet, and when
you charge, yell like furies!" His goal was to stun the Yankees into
mobility, then "drive them to Washington!"[51]

In a sense, they did just that. Charging by companies, the 4th
and 27th, accompanied by members of the 2nd (and a few of the
33rd) who had rallied and returned to the front, went up and over
the crest, shouting, as Jackson wished, the new Rebel yell. They
directed their assault not only at the Federals who had recaptured
Griffin's howitzers but also at Ricketts's guns, which, though
silenced, were still in Union hands. After discharging a volley or two,
the 4th Virginia crashed into the 14th Brooklyn. The result was an
especially vicious hand-to-hand grapple in which bayonets inflicted
an unusually high number of casualties on both sides. Outnumbered
and somewhat strung out, the Brooklynites gave ground at first but,
under Colonel Wood's steadying influence, regrouped and renewed
the fight at close range.

Some of the New Yorkers directed their fire not at Jackson's men but at the Rebel cannoneers who had been covering their position. A prominent target was the four-gun Wise Artillery. Its commander, Lieutenant Pelham, wrote that "rifle balls fell like hail around me. Shells bursted and scattered their fragments through my Battery." Even so, "my men were cool and brave and made terrible havoc on the enemy." Pelham, a boyishly handsome Alabamian who had left West Point shortly before graduation to offer his services to the Confederacy, had joined Captain Alburtis's battery as a drillmaster, but his tactical knowhow had gained him a field commission. Through some miracle, he would survive the battle to become the most celebrated officer in Stuart's horse artillery. But Pelham's penchant for exposing himself to enemy fire would erode his good fortune, leading to his mortal wounding less than two years hence. (When informed of his loss, Stuart would weep unashamedly.)[52]

Though hard pressed on all sides, the 14th Brooklyn held its ground till the last. At the height of the frenzied action, Colonel Wood was disabled by a severe wound; left on the field, he was destined for capture. His outfit absorbed another blow when suddenly attacked on the right by Colonel Fisher's blue-clad 6th North Carolina, which had just reached the field after a frantic race from Manassas Junction, where it had arrived about eight o'clock, then from the Lewis house, which it had left about noon. As if insufficiently challenged, the 14th was fired into by Billy Smith's collection of Virginians, Mississippians, and South Carolinians, while Jackson's artillery, including Pelham's battery, dosed the regiment with ricochet shelling.

Upon Wood's wounding, Lieutenant Colonel Edward Brush Fowler took charge of the 14th. Seeing no hope of holding his position, he ordered a fighting withdrawal to the Sudley Road. He later regretted the result, which he called "not a retreat or a falling back, it was a stampede." The men from Brooklyn left behind a field strewn with dead and wounded, who like the regiment as a whole, had shown conspicuous determination and endurance until overwhelmed. Three times Wood and Fowler had led their men in a desperate attempt to retake Griffin's howitzers; the third time they had gotten to within a few feet of their objective. Even had they reached the guns, however, the piles of dead horses, most still enclosed in their traces, would have made the pieces all but impossible to drag off.[53]

Jackson's men would never forget the stubbornness the regiment had shown when made to give ground and the ferocity with which it had fought. One Virginian would write that the 14th "charged us to a most uncomfortable nearness, pouring upon us their deadly fire, while their own loss was so great in actual dead it has often been said, one could walk on their dead bodies over a space of several acres without touching a foot upon the ground." The regiment would cherish the nickname given it this day by an equally formidable adversary: "The Red-Legged Devils of Brooklyn."[54]

At midafternoon of an increasingly torrid Sabbath, all suddenly and briefly turned quiet. For a few moments the crest of Henry Hill appeared free of Yankee infantry. Thus unencumbered, the men of the 4th and 27th Virginia swarmed over Griffin's defenseless guns. Lieutenant Elisha Paxton, who was destined to rise to command the Stonewall Brigade, planted the colors of the 4th between a pair of Ricketts's 10-pounder rifles. The soldiers from Brooklyn had made his accomplishment an ordeal. Paxton would write his wife: "I received a ball through my shirt sleeves, slightly bruising my arm, and others, whistling 'Yankee Doodle' around my head, made fourteen holes through the flag which I carried in the hottest of the fight. It was a miracle that I escaped with my life, so many falling dead around me."[55]

But the struggle for supremacy on the bloody plateau was far from over. As John Hennessy notes, for another hour or more, "it was bedlam, a maelstrom of surging and retreating men, acrid smoke, rattling muskets, and exploding shells. Regiments came onto the field one by one, and generally went into position as each particular colonel saw fit. And then, once in the fight, trim and polished ranks quickly degenerated into seething mobs of frightened men— men who knew what they wanted to do, but who had little idea of how to go about doing it."[56]

The frenzy resumed almost as soon as the 14th Brooklyn left the field. A few minutes later, the redlegs were spelled by the 1st Michigan of Willcox's brigade, coming from the right. Aware that the 6th North Carolina had helped recapture Griffin's howitzers and not fooled by the color of their garb, the Wolverines drew a collective bead on the regiment and shredded it with a close-quarters fusillade. The many who were cut down included the highly respected Colonel Fisher, killed instantly by a bullet in the head. The majority of his men broke and fled, leaving the 12-pounders open to recapture. Apparently, some abandoned Henry Hill altogether; one of Fisher's lieutenants complained that too many "stopped not till safe behind the works of Manassas." Some of the fugitives huddled around Fisher's second in command, who in a "fit of jealousy" had refused to accompany the regiment in its attack. An argument with Fisher at the outset of the charge had prompted Lieutenant Colonel Charles E. Lightfoot to remain out of the fight at the head of three companies of the regiment. Lightfoot's conduct would cost him the respect of his men and a promotion to succeed his fallen superior.[57]

Captain Isaac E. Avery—like Fisher a former railroad man—stepped into the leadership void to rally the other seven companies of North Carolinians. He had the men reload, then led most of them back into action against the newly arriving Yankees. They attacked without artillery support—most if not all of the Confederate batteries had recently gone to the rear, perhaps at Jackson's order but more likely at Beauregard's. The guns had begun to leave at about the time the Rockbridge Artillery limbered up, immediately following the attack of the 33rd Virginia. Although it may appear odd to leave the plateau thus uncovered, once Jackson, Smith, and Fisher began charging, the cannons could not have targeted the enemy for fear of striking their own troops. Moreover, their continued presence on the crest would have invited capture by counterattacking Federals. The guns withdrew by the road to the Lewis house; they would return to the front by that same route after the struggle for Henry Hill had been decided.[58]

The 6th North Carolina's renewed assault was a study in costly valor. Avery's seven companies succeeded in retaking Griffin's howitzers, but success was fleeting. During the charge, Avery fell with a wound as did fifty of his men; twenty-three others added their names to the roll of killed or mortally wounded. The casualties were so many because not only was the 6th struck in front by the 1st Michigan and also the remnants of apparently fought-out Union outfits that had gathered in wooded areas west of the Sudley Road; it was also shot up by an unidentified force in the regiment's right rear. It would appear that this was friendly fire delivered by members of one of the units under Evans, Bee, or Bartow that had been repositioned to support Jackson's left. Some participants in the charge, including Avery, believed the shots came from a gray-clad Yankee outfit such as the 11th Massachusetts, then advancing up the hill in rear of the 1st Michigan. It seems unlikely, however, that an entire enemy regiment, even in the chaos of battle, could have slipped behind the North Carolinians undetected.[59]

From behind a fence along a stretch of the Sudley Road, the 1st Michigan, under Major Alonzo F. Bidwell, poured successive volleys into the 6th North Carolina and, farther north, the 27th Virginia, which had replaced the scattered 33rd on the far left of Jackson's line. Under this pounding, Captain Avery led his Carolinians, dazed and bloodied, to the rear, but as they retired the 27th Virginia surged forward and forced most of Bidwell's men back beyond the Sudley Road under a "heavy and well-directed fire . . . from every quarter." In the melee the Wolverines' color-bearer was killed, and the regiment's flag was captured by a private in the 27th. The Virginians suffered heavily in return; by day's end they would have only 19 men killed but 122 wounded, the heaviest loss of any of Jackson's regiments. The "Bloody Twenty-Seventh" had fairly earned the appellation it would carry through the rest of the war.[60]

The circumstances surrounding the retirement of the 1st Michigan remain muddled. According to Bidwell, most of his men fell back as the result of "some little confusion" and "an order given at this time not clearly heard." Colonel Willcox, the regiment's original commander, would complain that the right wing of the regiment—seven companies—retreated at Bidwell's order. Assuming personal command, Willcox rode back to the road, collected the largely undemoralized regiment, and returned most of it to the firing line.

Eventually, the 1st's left wing—Companies B, G, and K—found shelter in a ravine inside a patch of woods on the southern edge of the plateau well to the left and rear of the 27th Virginia. There, according to Colonel Heintzelman, Willcox established "the most advanced position we [presumably, the entire Army of Northeastern Virginia] occupied that disastrous day." The 1st was enabled to hold that position thanks to the support it received from members of the 11th New York, 1st Minnesota, and 14th Brooklyn who had refused to quit the fight despite the defeat of the main bodies of their regiments.

Willcox's success was short lived, for the Wolverines' left flank quickly recoiled from the fire of Confederate reinforcements. The newcomers included the 5th Virginia, the Hampton Legion, and other troops that Beauregard had shifted from Jackson's right to shore up the still-imperiled left and center. Discovering his men on the verge of being surrounded, Captain Ira C. Abbott, who had assumed command of the left wing, called on them to retreat, "every man for himself." In the confusion, Abbott admitted, "the regt. went to pieces." The captain himself went to the rear at a measured gait, carrying off the national colors. He left behind Colonel Willcox and a small group of men, accosted in the woods by still other enemy reinforcements.[61]

Once again Griffin's and Ricketts's cannons were available for seizure. With a touch of desperation, Heintzelman committed his last reserves—the 5th and 11th Massachusetts of Franklin's brigade—with orders "to try to get back the guns" of Ricketts's battery. The 5th, a three-month militia outfit, moved to the task smartly enough, but the sight of grimy, dazed, and bloody fugitives stumbling to the rear crumpled its morale. Advancing ahead and to the left of the 11th Massachusetts, the regiment penetrated as far as the southwestern edge of the Henry farm. There Colonel Samuel C. Lawrence halted the men and ordered them to fire by companies, "every company," wrote a member of the 5th, "advancing in turn to the summit," where it "fired deliberately and then filed to the rear." Soon, in fact, the entire regiment was filing to the rear to escape what another man called "the most galling fire of the enemy, mowing our men down like grass." The regiment's antagonists—the 4th Virginia and other units along the right center of Jackson's line—wounded Colonel Lawrence and flung his once-well-aligned ranks back to the Sudley Road, thus preserving the capture of Ricketts's pieces.[62]

Now it became the 11th Massachusetts's turn to "try to get back the guns." Under Colonel George Clark, Jr., the three-year men did their best to erase the memory of their comrades' quick collapse. Advancing through the militiamen's fractured ranks, the 11th stormed up Henry Hill. In the face of successive fusillades from Jackson's line, the outfit succeeded in reaching Ricketts's guns and taking them back after a brief but vicious clash in which bayonets were used promiscuously. Unable to withstand the 11th's momentum, elements of the 2nd, 4th, and 27th Virginia pulled back toward their original positions.

Repossession of the batteries was a matter of minutes. Because Heintzelman had exhausted his readily available manpower, the 11th Massachusetts stood alone as a fresh wave of Confederates rolled toward it. Sent in by Beauregard with orders to "give them the bayonet," the counterattackers included the 5th Virginia and the Hampton Legion, which had rushed up from near the Robinson house. The relatively fresh Virginians attacked straight ahead, while to their right the legionnaires, in their commander's words, "advanced as rapidly as their worn-out condition would allow."[63]

Weakened or not, Hampton's men delivered an effective fire from their powerful Enfields. Clark's men absorbed it admirably as well as the final rounds from Beauregard's withdrawing artillery, some of which landed with devastating effect. Sergeant Henry N. Blake wrote that "the shells struck [our] rifles with such force, that some were twisted into the form of circles. A cannon-ball severed the arm of a sergeant, and threw it into the face of a soldier, who supposed, from the blow and the amount of blood upon his person, that he was dangerously wounded. One man stumbled over some briers . . . and a solid shot passed over him and killed his file-leader."[64]

For Blake's gray-clad regiment, the end came when its right flank began to take an enfilading fire from one of Jackson's regiments and, at the same time, confused comrades fired into its rear. That was enough—the 11th finally broke and raced helter-skelter to the Sudley Road. But the outfit had taken a severe toll of its opponents, including Colonel Hampton, who while riding near the Henry house was struck by a slug that imbedded itself under his left eye. Dazed and nearly blinded, the Carolina grandee was ushered to the rear, his introduction to war at an end. A captured Union surgeon who later examined the wound observed that it "lacked a few lines only of being a finisher." Though in pain, the colonel left the field in good spirits. A correspondent of the *Charleston Mercury* found him "exhilarated at the thought that his men had exhibited surpassing intrepidity."[65]

While the men of Massachusetts were charging, withdrawing, charging again, collapsing, and fleeing, pockets of fighting broke out farther to the left, where shards of regiments that had been forced off the hill—among them the 11th New York, 14th Brooklyn, 1st Minnesota, and 1st Michigan—returned to the summit in a truculent mood. They were opposed by equally fragmented units of Evans's, Bee's, and Bartow's commands, including an ad-hoc battalion composed of four companies that Johnston had entrusted to one of his aides, Colonel Francis J. Thomas. Like the majority of the encounters today, the combat in this sector was formless and largely leaderless. It produced no breakthroughs, no decisive tactical success, but it exacted a steep price in casualties, including Colonel Thomas, killed while leading a charge gone wrong.[66]

Here it was too that Barnard Bee was shot out of the saddle while leading a remnant of the eviscerated 4th Alabama in what some observers considered a suicide attack. "Suffering terribly," the brigadier was borne to a pine thicket in the rear, then transported by litter to a log cabin about a mile northeast of Manassas Junction. Early the next morning John Imboden, who had long been separated from his superior, learned of Bee's presence at the place where little more than twenty-four hours earlier the two officers had discussed the coming battle. Imboden found Bee unconscious, and "in few minutes, while I was holding his hand, he died."[67]

This time it appeared that both Union batteries were firmly in the hands of the enemy. Their losses were extreme, preventing most of the guns from being rescued, though a few were later dragged off to temporary safety. Ricketts's casualties were not tabulated; he would testify to Congress that he had no idea how many men he lost. Assuredly, they were numerous, including Lieutenant Douglas Ramsay, who was killed late in the day while exhibiting "cool and determined bravery." Lieutenant Edmund Kirby of Griffin's battery reported a loss to Company I of one officer and eleven enlisted men killed and one officer and fourteen men wounded. Fatal to the unit's mobility was the death of dozens of battery horses.[68]

For all the carnage the batteries suffered, most of their crews managed to get off Henry Hill alive, as did Griffin himself. Another escapee was Lieutenant Adelbert Ames of Company D. Ames (like his superior a future major general, though by brevet) had been badly wounded in the thigh early in the fight but refused to go to the rear for medical attention. By remaining with his section despite continuing blood loss, issuing orders, and shouting encouragement from a precarious perch aboard a caisson, the young West Pointer would gain official commendation, the respect of his superiors and subordinates, and—thirty-two years after the battle—a Medal of Honor.[69]

Captain Ricketts was not so fortunate. When the 5th Virginia chased off the 11th Massachusetts and swarmed over Company I, the captors found its commander lying helpless amid his guns, suffering from four wounds, including one to the thigh. Exposed to the continued firing of both armies, Ricketts might have been hit yet again, perhaps fatally, had not a Mexican War comrade, Lieutenant Colonel William H. Harman of the 5th Virginia, recognized him, ministered to him, and saw to his evacuation via one of his regiment's ambulances.

Though spared additional harm on the battlefield, Ricketts would spend the next five months recuperating in Richmond's squalid and noisome Libby Prison. The pain and privation he endured, however, would be alleviated by the attentions of his wife, Fanny, who from the moment she learned of his imprisonment was determined to share his fate. Acceding to the persistent demands of this remarkable woman, Confederate authorities permitted her to join her husband throughout his confinement, during which she also nursed to health many another wounded or sickly prisoner.[70]

Immediately following the repulse of Heintzelman's reserves, an eerie quiet blanketed Henry Hill. As was true of the longer lull that had preceded it, this pause would not endure, and the fighting, when it resumed, would be especially bitter and bloody. The seemingly endless succession of assault and counterassault over the past hour or more had littered the field with hundreds of bodies and carcasses, many piled atop one another. Enough wounded men were thrashing about to give the plateau, as William Averell would write of a future battlefield, "a singular crawling effect." Yet nothing had been resolved. Although the adversaries were nearing complete exhaustion, the outcome remained very much in doubt.[71]

Logically, the initiative remained with the attacker. General McDowell knew full well that to secure victory, he must wrest the summit of Henry Hill once and for all from its defenders. Yet too much of his army was no long capable of sustained fighting. With the exception of a single brigade (Howard's) that was not in position to contribute to this climactic effort, Porter's and Heintzelman's divisions had been effectively fought out. Most of Tyler's division was unbloodied, but Keyes's men had taken themselves off the board and Schenck's remained rooted to the ground east of Bull Run they had occupied for nine hours.

This left only the brigade of Colonel Sherman, approximately 3,000 officers and men, to launch a final drive up the hill against the well-established troops of Jackson and his many and various supports. Holding his breath, shortly after 3:00 P.M. McDowell ordered the Ohioan into action, praying that his as-yet-uncommitted troops would succeed where all who had gone before had failed. It may have been a gesture of desperation, but McDowell saw it as his only hope of salvaging a victory that he and his subordinates had considered assured short hours ago.

CHAPTER 15

McDowell's Last Stand

The four regiments under W. T. Sherman had been awaiting orders to engage the Rebels on Henry Hill since crossing Bull Run. Held relatively idle for nearly four hours since then and enraged by the losses it had suffered that morning, especially the death of Captain Haggerty, the brigade was nearly frantic to be committed to the climactic phase of the battle.

Its nerve-wracking wait came to an end at about 3:30, when Sherman sought out General McDowell and received orders to advance to the front. The colonel responded promptly, sending his lead regiment, Colonel Quinby's 13th New York, down the high ground above the Warrenton Pike, across Young's Branch, and toward the Sudley Road, the jumping-off point for the assault. Behind Quinby came Lieutenant Colonel Peck's 2nd Wisconsin followed by Colonel Cameron's 79th and Colonel Corcoran's 69th New York.[1]

Sherman went forward with the idea of sparking a final, full-scale enemy retreat. Because Jackson's men and their supports had been beaten back from Ricketts's and Griffin's guns more than once, McDowell believed that the defenders were on the verge of collapse. When giving Sherman his orders, he directed him to "join in the pursuit of the enemy." This was so much wishful thinking, but the colonel, as impressionable as his superior, believed the Rebels were on their last legs, if not in fact on the run. His view was not shared by the commander of the regiment bringing up the rear of the brigade. Michael Corcoran, a burly six-foot-six, was not one to shy from a fight. But since early morning he had been dogged by a sense of impending disaster, "which, try as I might, I could not shake off." Soon enough, it would become evident whether he or his superior was the more prescient soldier.[2]

The brigade leader supposed the Rebels were "falling back to the left of the road by which the Army had approached from Sudley Springs." The banks of that byway, rising high above a roadbed worn away by decades of wagon travel, sheltered Sherman's troops from enemy fire as the column closed up and awaited the word to advance. To get into position for the attack, the men squeezed themselves between the bodies of the dead and wounded and those able-bodied comrades who had taken refuge there after being chased off the hill. The crush of soldiers, many of them in distress, was a horror; writing after the battle, a Wisconsin enlisted man assured his correspondent, "I will not sicken [you] with a description of this road."[3]

Sherman began his advance by sending Quinby's regiment up the northwestern slope in the general direction of the Henry house. The other regiments remained in place as their comrades went forward, ready to join them in taking the hill. This would not happen, however, for Sherman was wedded to the tactic of committing his command piecemeal, one regiment—or portions of one regiment—at a time. It was a mistake that almost every commander who had preceded him had already made. Of them all, only Franklin had deployed his Massachusetts regiments in tandem, adding breadth, width, and weight to an assault that nevertheless had no chance of succeeding. The tactic had failed in this instance due to the unsteadiness of Lawrence's regiment, but the theory behind it was sound. Properly executed, such an assault might have had a significant effect on the fighting on almost every part of the field.[4]

The red-haired Ohioan cannot be faulted for a lack of tactical vision. The war now beginning marked the first time in American history that sizable bodies of infantry had become available to a field commander. In Mexico, the only operational proving ground in national memory, most of the fighting had been accomplished in regimental and small-unit strength. Thus mid-nineteenth-century infantry-assault tactics (most of them predicated on attacking fixed works rather than an enemy force in line of battle) suggested that larger formations would prove unmanageable, exceeding the control of a single commander. Military theory also limited the size of an attacking force by recommending that fully half of it be assigned to the reserve rather than to the front line.[5]

Thus the 13th New York clambered up Henry Hill bereft of close support. Under Colonel Quinby's determined leadership, the Rochester Regiment pressed to within seventy yards of the Henry house, at which point the combined fire of the Hampton Legion and some artillery that had not yet left the front stopped it in its tracks. "Their shot fell short of us at first," reported Private Samuel Partridge, "but we had to get inside their range—so that they would go over us." The effort failed: "Before we could do that we were raked badly—a six pounder passed through the [regiment] taking off the legs of two of Capt. [Adolph] Nolte's men," one of whom died instantly.

A depression in the ground offered a measure of shelter from the cannonading. There the attackers, at Quinby's order, went to earth and began shooting from the prone position. Their contorted posture limited the effect of their return fire, and when a familiar cry rose up from an unknown source ("You're firing on friends!"), the volume slackened and nearly ceased. The New Yorkers later suspected that they had been the victim of an enemy ruse. Only when the flag of Hampton's battalion suddenly became visible among the powder smoke did the Rochester boys resume shooting as a unit. By then the damage had been done; the 13th was trapped in its position north of the Henry house, unable to advance or withdraw without any assurance of safety. The regiment hugged the ground, hoping that reinforcements would draw fire from it and thus grant it a chance to escape.[6]

Sherman tried to provide help for Quinby's men but too late— the effort was doomed from the outset. At his command the 2nd Wisconsin rose up from its protective bank and advanced well forward and to the right of the New Yorkers. The unusual configuration of the ground at the point where the 2nd climbed the hill suddenly and unexpectedly broke its formation. Captain Thomas Allen wrote that "the crest of the hill in front of us . . . was of a semicircular form, so that when our regiment pushed on to the summit, our left and center were facing south, while our four right companies [A, D, F, and I] faced east and south-east." Due to the regiment's misalignment, "no command could be heard along the whole line, nor was more than half the regiment visible at the same time." The larger detachment attacked toward the Henry house and, beyond it, the line held by the Hampton Legion and various Virginia units. Meanwhile, the other four companies veered off course and came into rifle range of the 4th Alabama, 7th Georgia, and other miscellaneous defenders on the far Rebel left.[7]

Another factor that worked against the regiment was its cadet gray uniforms, which while not protecting them against enemy missiles from the front and flank, attracted some from the rear, the work of confused members of the 11th Massachusetts and the 38th and 79th New York. Assailed simultaneously from so many angles, it

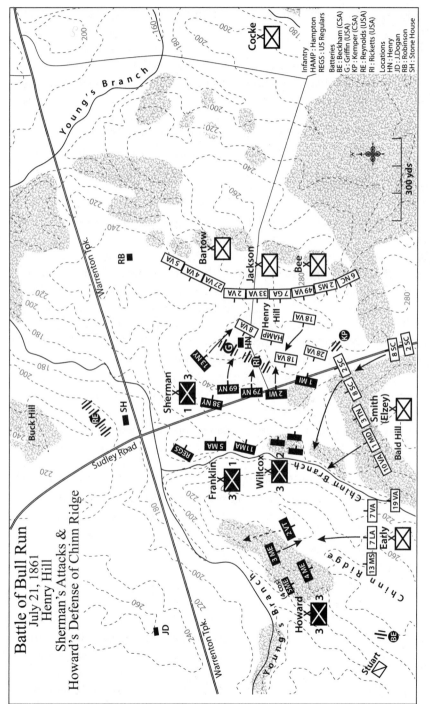

Battle of Bull Run, July 21, 1861: Henry Hill, Sherman's Attacks and Howard's Defense of Chinn Ridge. *Map by Paul Dangel.*

was little wonder that the larger segment of the 2nd quickly dropped to the ground in the manner of the 13th New York. "It was impossible," one Badger wrote, "to push our line forward against the evidently superior forces massed in our front."

Like the Rochester regiment, the 2nd was confounded by a flag in the hands of an approaching color-bearer that appeared to display stars and stripes. Then an officer in a blue uniform screamed at the Wisconsin men to cease firing on comrades. Some members of the 2nd complied; others kept firing, though uncertain whether targeting friend or foe. At some point the weight of so much confusion caused both wings of the regiment to withdraw, leaving behind numerous casualties. At the urging of Lieutenant Colonel Peck and some of his subordinates, the reunited regiment regrouped and attempted another advance only to be forced back to the Sudley Road under an even heavier multidirectional fire than before.[8]

Half of his command having become scattered or stymied, Sherman tried to salvage the offensive by calling up the 79th New York. Simon Cameron's brother led his outfit—originally composed predominantly of militiamen of Scots ancestry but filled out with volunteers of various ethnic origins—across the Sudley Road and headed toward the opening between the Henry house and what remained of Ricketts's and Griffin's batteries. As they trudged slowly uphill, defeated members of the 2nd Wisconsin streamed past on their right and left.[9]

Reaching the crest in advance of his vanguard, Colonel Cameron turned around to urge the men forward: "Come on my brave Highlanders." They responded with alacrity, but as soon as they came in sight of the enemy and began firing, they encountered the same obstacles that had hamstrung their luckless comrades: reported sightings of U.S. flags and shouted warnings that they were shooting at friends, quickly followed by volley after volley of decidedly unfriendly fire. It "swept our ranks," wrote one Highlander, "like a quick darting pestilence."

For a time the outfit not only stood resolutely against the torrent but also managed to advance as far as Ricketts's silent battery. Then rifle fire from many angles staggered it, inflicted casualties, and caused the rest of it to melt away. Cameron attempted to rally the men while also endeavoring to obtain ammunition to feed some of the cannons that had not yet been drawn off by the enemy. "Not succeeding in this," the regiment's historian recorded, the colonel "again rushed into the hottest fire." He did so alone, for no one was willing to follow his suicidal example.

Cameron's predicament elicited admiration and pity from his opponents. Wade Hampton, just before being carried from the field, lamented, "isn't it terrible to see that brave officer trying to lead his men forward, and they won't follow him." Not every Rebel was overcome with sympathy; Cameron, pressing ever forward, had nearly reached the Henry house when a rifleman sent a minie ball through his breast. By the time the colonel was carried from the field and placed in an ambulance, he was dying. His loss effectively ended the 79th New York's first battle.[10]

That Cameron had penetrated so deeply into the enemy's lines indicated that the Confederates were wearing down. The defenders, especially Hampton's South Carolinians, were reeling from repeated body blows and running perilously low on ammunition. To some observers, including Sherman, they seemed primed for a final push that would break their hold on the western side of the plateau and salvage victory at the eleventh hour.

A first glance it appeared that only Corcoran's Irishmen remained to deliver that thrust. But appearances deceived, for another regiment that had not been heavily engaged was in a position to offer support to the 69th New York and possibly strike on its own. This was the 38th New York Volunteers, part of Willcox's brigade in Heintzelman's division. Commanded by Colonel John Henry Hobart Ward, the regiment (also known as the Scott Life Guard) had been assigned the same task as many of its sister outfits, supporting the artillery on Henry Hill. It had gotten off to a good star but had been unable to sustain any momentum. Early in the afternoon Ward's men had left their position north of the turnpike and east of Sherman's brigade and moved toward Griffin's guns. "In gallant style and in double-quick time," they drove off an enemy regiment that crossed its path. Soon, however, Rebel artillerymen noticed the regiment, turned their guns on it, and forced it to scurry back down the hill.[11]

How long the 38th remained at the base of the heights is unknown, but it must have been at least an hour, for when the regiment was finally prodded back to the high ground, it discovered that Griffin's cannoneers had managed to drag their three 10-pounder rifles off the summit and down the hill. Under a "spiteful and destructive fire from the enemy's batteries," Lieutenant Colonel Addison

Farnsworth, who was now in charge of the New Yorkers, ordered the men to again retire. Farnsworth would later claim that the withdrawal left no stigma on the regiment because there were no more guns for the 38th to support. General McDowell appears to have disagreed with this self-serving assessment. Coming upon the regiment in its new position, he personally ordered it for the third time back to the summit of Henry Hill.[12]

While Ward's people went up and down, up and down, Sherman concluded his piecemeal attacks by ordering his last regiment into the fight on the heights. The 69th New York responded with a mighty shout, half in English and half in Gaelic. Having shucked their heavy uniforms to fight in shirt sleeves, the men charged upward, following their emerald-green flag. The voice of Captain Thomas Francis Meagher, like Corcoran a prominent disciple of Irish liberty and a future general officer, could be heard above the din shouting to his Irish Zouaves, "Come on, boys, you've got your chance at last!"[13]

In his report Sherman described the 69th's effort as brief and ineffective. Corcoran, he wrote, "led his regiment over the crest, and had in full open view the ground so severely contested. The firing was very severe, and the roar of cannon, muskets, and rifles incessant. It was very manifest the enemy was here in great force, far superior to us at that point." In fact, the Irishmen made excellent progress, thanks largely to effective artillery and infantry support.

The first was supplied by a section of Reynolds's Rhode Island battery under Lieutenant J. Albert Monroe, who had refused to accompany Burnside's brigade in quitting the battle. Much of the battery, however, had been put out of commission or was beyond Sherman's reach. One of the its James rifles had been disabled, a second had run out of ammunition, and two others positioned near the Dogan house could offer only long-range support to the attackers on Henry Hill. At the urging of Governor Sprague, Monroe and his guns had crossed Young's Branch and ascended Henry Hill to offer more immediate assistance. Sources give a contradictory account of the section's effectiveness. Writing seventeen years later, Monroe recalled that he arrived on the plateau too late to take much part in the fighting. Other sources have his guns making life difficult for the Rebels occupying the Henry homestead.[14]

Corcoran received infantry help from a variety of sources, including those largely leaderless but still pugnacious detachments of New Yorkers, Badgers, and Wolverines east of Sudley Road. The most concentrated source of support, however, was Farnsworth's 38th New York, which after topping Henry Hill for the third time, had obliqued toward Ricketts's nearest assailants. In combination with the fire of Corcoran's Irishmen on its left, the Scott Life Guard spent thirty minutes or more blasting away at the steadily weakening 5th Virginia and the temporarily leaderless Hampton Legion.

The Confederates found themselves increasingly unable to withstand the pounding of two relatively fresh regiments of New Yorkers. When the combined fire became too much to bear, the gray line finally gave way. Firing as they went, South Carolinians and Virginians fled across the Henry property, uncovering the guns they had been holding so tenaciously for an hour or more. Upon its retreat, as Farnsworth succinctly noted, Ricketts's pieces "fell into the hands of my regiment." He would report that parties of the 38th manhandled three of the guns—apparently those closest to the Henry house—some three hundred yards to the rear, where they were "left in a road [presumably, the Sudley Road], apparently out of the reach of the enemy." Although some historians have accepted the colonel's claim, it would appear that the 10-pounders never reached the road. Short of their objective, the would-be rescuers found their path blocked by Union troops retreating from the fight as well as by Confederate infantry and cavalry bursting out of the woods to the south of the present-day Manassas National Battlefield Park Visitor Center. By no means were Ricketts's guns beyond possibility of recapture, nor were the rifles Griffin's men had removed from the left of the artillery line.[15]

The determined efforts of the 38th and 69th New York had swept the crest of Henry Hill clear of defenders—so at least some chroniclers have contended. Many attackers believed so too. Colonel Farnsworth reported that the Federals appeared "to have complete possession of the field." A wounded but still combative enlisted man of the 1st Minnesota wrote, "to all appearances we had gained the day." The truth was that although the Confederate left flank appeared to have disappeared, Rebel forces farther to the right, including the majority of Jackson's men, remained in position to prevent the entire line from giving way. And it was at this point that Beauregard and Johnston were summoning up fresh troops to strengthen all points of that line.[16]

One who believed that the Rebels' hold had been decisively broken was the officer who would benefit the most from it. According to an enlisted man of the 69th New York, a jubilant Irvin McDowell galloped up Henry Hill, halted at the 69th's firing line near the Henry house, and personally congratulated Colonel Corcoran on his perceived success. Since this sector remained a dangerous place, McDowell's sudden appearance might appear foolhardy, if it occurred at all. Yet in a postwar article, Captain Fry places his boss on the hill at about this time and describes him as climbing the stairs to the second floor of Mrs. Henry's dwelling to obtain an extended view of the field. If Fry's account is correct, the general was basking in what he believed to be his army's final triumph. He had predicted this hours earlier, only to discover that his boast had been premature. Now, suddenly, his pronouncement appeared justifiable.[17]

Johnston and Beauregard deserve equal credit for shoring up shaky sectors of the line on Henry Hill at critical times and for mounting a series of counterattacks late that afternoon that rocked McDowell's troops as well as his peace of mind. By three o'clock Beauregard had sent into the fray Hampton's South Carolinians, Fisher's North Carolinians, and the Virginians of William Smith. He had rallied what remained of the regiments and battalions under Evans, Bee, and Bartow, most of which he had moved from the rear of Jackson's line to extend its left flank in the direction of the Sudley Road. Early in the afternoon he had also ordered to the left of the Henry Hill line three units from Bonham's brigade— Kershaw's 2nd South Carolina, the 8th South Carolina of Colonel E. B. C. Cash, and Kershaw's Alexandria Light Artillery—the whole under Colonel Kershaw as senior officer. Beauregard would never receive full recognition for these efforts; it was Johnston, who had officially assumed the task of directing late-arriving units to the front, who would come to be regarded as the savior of Confederate fortunes at Bull Run.[18]

Not that the Virginian failed to make a contribution in this regard. Sometime after 2:00 P.M. he visited Colonel Cocke's position overlooking Lewis Ford and the adjacent crossings. Beauregard's recent detaching of the 49th Virginia along with Heaton's section of the Loudoun Artillery had weakened this position, but Colonel Cocke believed the troops' departure had gone unnoticed by the enemy. The nearest Federals, Schenck's men, were not particularly observant, and Smith's march had been screened by "a thicket of willows and other trees skirting the edge of Bull Run at this point."

Earlier in the day, when Johnston first broached the idea of reinforcing the line on Henry Hill, Cocke had begged off, citing threats
from the Yankees below Stone Bridge; the general had agreed to leave
his brigade intact and in place. This time around, probably because
of the gravity of the situation on the left flank, Cocke was more amenable to bolstering that sector. In fact, he claimed to have suggested
to Johnston the propriety of sending off all, or nearly all, of his command. The general gave his approval, and Cocke immediately dispatched a succession of units: Colonel Robert Enoch Withers's 18th
Virginia followed by the Lynchburg Artillery (now four guns strong,
Davidson's and Leftwich's pieces having rejoined Captain Latham),
the 28th Virginia under Colonel Robert T. Preston, and the 19th
Virginia of Lieutenant Colonel John B. Strange. Since early morning, Withers's and Preston's men had been stationed on the north
side of Bull Run; presumably, it took some time for them to recross
the stream. On the south side they unslung their knapsacks, placed
them on the ground, and formed marching columns. Within minutes they were passing the Lewis house and the orchard south of it
and winding along the farm road that led to Mrs. Henry's place.[19]

Cocke failed to identify the units retained to cover Bull Run. He
appears not to have removed the three troops of cavalry he had held
in reserve north of the Lewis house as well as Captain Schaeffer's
three companies of infantry, which had been protecting Strange's
left flank along both sides of Lewis Ford. Nor did Cocke mention
the removal of those skirmishers of Evans's brigade who, about
1:00 P.M., had abandoned Stone Bridge to take position just north
of Portici. Presumably, these troops—perhaps also detachments of
some or all of the units rushed to the left—remained behind to cover
the fords assigned to Cocke and to keep tabs on Schenck's operations, such as they were.[20]

The troops of Withers, Preston, and Strange were eager to quit
their static posture of the morning and enter the critical fighting
of the afternoon. "The men are so anxious to get at the Yankees,"
wrote Private Harry Wooding of the 18th Virginia, "that it is impossible to keep them in line." Reaching Jackson's position, which they
passed behind, the men of the 18th, as Wooding recorded, "began to
draw the fire of the artillery of the enemy stationed on the heights
near the Stone Bridge. Marching by the right flank, the line was
exposed to this fire for a mile. . . . [T]he steadiness of the men, for
the first time under fire, was severely tried."

Arriving south of the Henry house, the regiment now endured what its colonel called "a hot fire of musketry, and could not clearly distinguish friends from foe." An open field before them bloomed with a rich crop of death—dozens of red-legged Yankees of the 14th Brooklyn, whose uniform may have confused Withers as to whom he was facing in his new position. Until able to sort things out, he had his men take cover in one of the numerous shallow depressions on the summit of Henry Hill. They remained there for some minutes, dodging rifle fire, until Lieutenant Samuel Wragg Ferguson of Jackson's staff located them and, with several choice words, ordered them forward.[21]

When it finally moved up, the 18th came in on the far left flank of the Hampton Legion, now in the hands of its senior line officer, Captain James Conner. Conner or another subaltern contacted Colonel Withers, explained the legion's weakened condition but touted its fighting spirit, and asked for directions. Incredibly, the South Carolinians, although having fought long and hard, suffering terribly on so many parts of the field, were ready to charge the enemy. Withers had the legionnaires close up on his flank and then the two units went forward together, angling toward what remained of Griffin's battery position.[22]

Covered by the shelling of Captain Latham's just-arrived battery, the attackers caught the nearest Federals—portions of the 38th and 69th New York—flatfooted. The power of the assault was substantially enhanced by a simultaneous strike against the left flank of the 69th by the 8th Virginia. Colonel Hunton's regiment, like Withers's, had been itching to become involved in the critical fighting. Its colonel used as his excuse to attack a request from Beauregard to help halt and rally some troops retreating "in great confusion" across his regiment's front. In some circles Hunton's heroics would earn him a hyperbolic title: "The man who saved the Confederate army from defeat."[23]

The multipronged assault swept all before it, shoring up the hitherto sagging fortunes of the Henry Hill position. The 38th New York offered little resistance before breaking and scrambling down the hill (for the third time that day) in the direction of the Stone House. At about the same time, the first of Sherman's regiments to enter the fight, the 13th New York, decided the time had come to relinquish its precarious foothold on the left of its brigade line. Under a blizzard of rifle and artillery fire from three sides, the Rochester boys scurried off the hill. A typical fugitive, Sam Partridge, later wrote, "I got up and ran like thunder amid a perfect shower of balls." He noted that unlike some officers who retired with head bowed and spirit broken, Colonel Quinby withdrew in a fighting mood, cutting down several pursuers with a borrowed rifle: "Everytime he fired, he dropped a man." Partridge nevertheless admitted that the Rebels "beat us like the very devil."[24]

According to its senior company commander, Captain James Kelly, the 69th put up a good fight before being overwhelmed, twice resisting attacks on its right flank and center and counterattacking both times. Finally, it was forced to give ground, "owing principally to the panic of the regiment which preceded us." A Rebel soldier agreed that the 69th, as was true of Sherman's brigade in the aggregate, "fought bravely, dying almost to a man around their cannon." Captain Meagher offered a succinct analysis of his regiment's fortunes: "We beat their men—their batteries beat us. That is the story of the day."[25]

Thrown off Henry Hill, the disorganized and demoralized Federals reached safety, some north of the Warrenton Pike, others west of the Sudley Road. In both locales they became intermingled with the units under Franklin and Willcox that had preceded Sherman's men in attacking and then fleeing. Sherman had a difficult time sifting order from near chaos. He admitted that despite strenuous efforts, he managed to "partially" reform Corcoran's ranks. Even this minor success proved temporary: "It was manifest they would not stand." With a sigh of resignation—"I saw we were gone"—he directed the regiment's leader to form a rear guard to cover the rest of the command, which with some difficulty withdrew to his brigade's preattack position. Like many another commander who had fought and failed this day, Sherman's first taste of war (he had missed seeing combat in Mexico) had been bitter indeed. All in all, the experience "was as disgraceful as words can portray."[26]

A finishing touch of sorts to the Union effort to hold Henry Hill had been added shortly before Sherman's withdrawal when the second regiment in Cocke's column, the 28th Virginia, reached the field of battle. Getting that far had been an ordeal: moving out the farm road leading from Portici, Colonel Preston's regiment had been slowed not only by the lead-footed 18th Virginia but also by the passage to the front of Latham's battery and the simultaneous movement to the rear of the Washington Artillery. After clearing these roadblocks, the regiment advanced another half mile under a torrid sun before entering a patch of pine trees from which its vanguard drew enemy fire.[27]

The Virginians had stumbled upon the hiding place of the segment of the 1st Michigan that had been left behind when the bulk of its regiment withdrew under fire. Accompanied by its brigade commander, Colonel Willcox, the isolated force—strength unknown but certainly smaller than a normal battalion—had moved up the other end of the road Preston's men had taken with the unrealistic objective of circumventing the far Rebel left and, once in the rear, creating a degree of havoc out of proportion to its meager numbers. Earlier Willcox, at the head of one hundred or so Fire Zouaves, had entered a patch of woods closer to the Sudley Road and, according to the colonel, "killed, wounded, and captured about thirty of the enemy." His second foray among the trees would not end so successfully.[28]

The 1st Michigan's volley downed a half-dozen unsuspecting members of Company B, Colonel Preston's advance. The rest of the company promptly returned fire, killing or wounding several Michiganders. When Preston sent parties to outflank Willcox's group, they cut off and surrounded an exposed band that included the brigade leader and members of his staff. Willcox had been wounded in the right arm, and his dapple gray stallion had been disabled by musketry; with his good arm he handed over his sword while seeking consideration, as "an officer and a gentleman," for himself and his men. His words seemed to have little effect, for he was soon accosted by a furiously angry Preston, shouting "loud oaths, pointing his revolver, & demanding our surrender." Over the next thirteen months, Willcox would share confinement in Libby Prison with some of his subordinates as well as with James and Fanny Ricketts. He would be succeeded in command of the Second Brigade, Third Division by Colonel Ward.[29]

After corralling Willcox's detachment, the 28th Virginia continued through the woods for about half a mile. The regiment descended the hill and reached the Sudley Road, both sides of which were occupied by the two South Carolina regiments under Kershaw and the battery under Kemper that Beauregard had hustled up from Lewis Ford. Kershaw's men were busily opposing a heterogeneous force of Yankees that included the portion of the 1st Michigan that had not accompanied Willcox into the woods. Preston's men moved up in the South Carolinians' rear to offer assistance as needed.[30]

The tactical situation, so recently in the Federals' favor, had shifted nearly 180 degrees in a matter of a half hour or less, and it appeared on the brink of tilting even farther in the Confederates' direction. The units that Johnston and Beauregard were rushing to the hill appeared to be in sufficient strength and in the proper position to relinquish the defensive and take the initiative. This could be done, however, only if the far left flank were secure. Kershaw's and Kemper's presence there suggested that it was, but in fact one last hurdle had to be cleared before the Confederates could celebrate a stunning and glorious victory.

Like every other Union brigade that had marched many miles to get into position to join the fighting, the four regiments of Oliver O. Howard's brigade had had an exhausting and exasperating day. Although forced to reach the battlefield by the same long and wayward trail that had conveyed the rest of Heintzelman's division, Howard's men had not completed the ten-mile journey until midafternoon. In order to provide a ready reserve for his army, McDowell had detached the command soon after the rest of the Third Division crossed Cub Run and headed north and west. For several hours the troops had sat idle, leaving their leader "fidgeting," the result of McDowell's uncertainty over how to employ them. Historians would fault the general for not committing the brigade—his last readily available source of manpower—to the struggle for Henry Hill when it might have tipped the balance in his favor.

McDowell did not recall the brigade until just before noon, when without explanation he ordered Howard to rejoin Heintzelman on the march. The result was a hot and dusty journey that consumed more than two hours, though the exact route the brigade took is open to dispute. Some scholars state that the men followed the same trail as the rest of their division, crossing Bull Run at Sudley Ford. R. M. Johnston suggests that while on the march, Howard discovered the path to Poplar Ford; he implies that the unit crossed there, cutting a couple of miles off its march. This seems unlikely—taking the initiative under such circumstances would not have served the colonel well in the eyes of his superiors. Howard himself failed to clear up the matter; in his official report he mentioned turning left at some point and taking a crossroad to reach a third road that Captain Whipple of McDowell's staff had pointed out to him. He did not, however, identify these routes, probably because their names were unknown to him.[31]

Wherever he crossed Bull Run, Howard found that his journey to battle was just beginning. Upon reaching an "open plain" below the stream, he was met by the brigade's quartermaster, who had ridden on ahead to report to Colonel Heintzelman. According to this officer, the division commander—still on horseback after having his wounded arm tended to—had ordered Howard to move at the obligatory double-quick toward the far right of the line. As the man from Maine pointedly remarked in his after-action narrative: "I gave the order, and we marched nearly a mile at this pace, when I found the men so much exhausted that they could march no longer. . . . Many [had] dropped out and fainted from exhaustion." Colonel Mark H. Dunnell of the 5th Maine believed that "none but an immediate eye-witness can fully realize the sufferings of the men during the march." One of Dunnell's men recalled that after being pushed so relentlessly toward their assigned position, "we were ready to lay down when we got there."[32]

At this point another of McDowell's aides, whom Howard failed to identify, met the head of the brigade and, under orders from Captain Fry, guided it cross-country to the west side of the Sudley Road. Upon reaching the assigned position—undoubtedly having lost additional stragglers en route—Howard received an order to pass through a thicket and up a ridge a quarter mile beyond. This stretch of high ground, perhaps five hundred yards west of Henry Hill, overlooked a tributary of Young's Branch that watered the farm of one Benjamin Chinn. This was the position mistakenly occupied by Charles Hazlett while guiding Griffin's battery toward the Henry house more than an hour earlier.

Since Fry was involved in Howard's positioning, he was following McDowell's orders. But just what the army commander intended the colonel to accomplish on the Chinn farm remains unclear. John Hennessy theorizes that by attacking west of Sudley Road, Howard was supposed to bypass the enemy's left flank, gain the Confederate rear, and uproot the defenders of Henry Hill once and for all. Since McDowell did not disclose his motives, Hennessy infers this from Howard's report, but the latter is equally silent on the subject. If this was in fact McDowell's intention, one wonders why he did not act upon it when the fighting on Henry Hill was at its height rather than winding down. And how he expected Howard to evict the Rebels from their position with four regiments, each exhausted by hard marching on a hot day, challenges the imagination.[33]

Howard moved up Chinn Ridge in two lines, the 4th Maine and 2nd Vermont in front, followed by the 3rd and 5th Maine. When Lieutenant Hazlett had climbed the ridge, he had found the opposite side held in some force by the enemy; it still was when Howard's leading ranks went up the slope. Delayed by the thicket at the foot of the ridge, the 4th Maine fell to the rear; thus the 2nd Vermont was the first regiment to reach the top and draw enemy fire, which emanated from at least one battery and a force of infantry of unknown size in support. As Howard observed, the storm of shells and minie balls "made it rather warm work for new men; but they stood well, or rallied to fire between twenty and thirty rounds per man."

Supported on the right by the 4th Maine, Howard's first rank went to earth, its men appropriating every physical feature of the ridge that offered any shelter. Satisfied that the line was in good hands—Hiram G. Berry of the 4th, one of the most capable colonels in the army, was general-officer material—Howard went to the rear to bring up the remaining troops. To his horror he discovered that less than half of the 5th Maine remained within his reach, six of the regiment's ten companies having retreated without orders after being "discomfited by our own cavalry and by a cannon ball striking their flank." These were not lame excuses; a detachment of Major Palmer's cavalry, which had ranged ahead of the rest of its battalion into an untenable position, had indeed retreated through the ranks of the 5th Maine, scattering its men. Those who did not at once flee were exposed to a heavy shelling, one that rookie troops could not endure for long. The 3rd Maine suffered terribly from the combination of shelling and musketry. As one of its men, seventeen-year-old George S. Rollins, wrote, "we made a stand and fought the best we could with that battery raking us on the right and musketry playing upon us in front."

Howard placed what was left of the 5th on his far right, but in a matter of minutes it too took off for parts unknown, "an order for a wing to retire being understood for the whole." The brigade commander's refusal to censure the regiment and its colonel, who had gone to the rear complaining of exhaustion, suggests that he felt to some extent responsible for the error that depleted his command of a quarter of its strength and eroded the extreme right flank of its army at a critical time.

The 5th's skedaddle—and the suddenly increased volume of enemy opposition—cost Howard any chance of securing Chinn

Ridge. "Our men fought well and stood like heroes," wrote Private Rollins, "but it was of no use. All the other troops had left, and the rebels were coming upon us in overpowering numbers." Even the heroics of Colonel Berry, who carried aloft the flag of the 4th Maine in an effort to spur regimental tenacity, failed to secure a lodgment on the ridge. Gradually but steadily, the brigade lost its footing and began to fall back in groups large and small. "Many officers strove to reform ranks," Howard recalled, "but we could not [do so] under fire, so I gave the order to retire under cover and form." As he fell back, the colonel heard reports from the rear that a general retreat had been ordered. Only then did he realize that the difficulties he had experienced in keeping his men on the firing line and in fighting trim had also afflicted numerous colleagues and superiors.[34]

The 5th Maine's precipitate retreat aside, Howard's withdrawal from Chinn Ridge connoted no disgrace, for he had been outnumbered and outpositioned from the start, and his opposition had increased exponentially as the fight wore on. Even so, the young colonel had comported himself well in his first battle, an experience that would soon start him on the path to distinction, acclaim, and high rank. (He would end the war as a major general in command of an entire army.) In a letter to his mother eight days after the battle, the theologian-turned-soldier reflected that while Chinn Ridge had been "a pretty hot place" and the air around it "full of whistling bullets, I felt at peace in my heart. You should think that a battle would be horrible & sickening, but the sense of personal danger & the effort necessary to master it, make one feel very differently from what he would anticipate."[35]

Howard could not have foreseen the resistance his attempt to hold a position on Benjamin Chinn's land would attract. By the time his men began to scale the ridge, the ground west of the Sudley Road was firmly in the hands of Kershaw and Kemper, supported on the other side of the road by the 28th Virginia and the final vestiges of the Hampton Legion, which had seen more action on this field than almost any other unit of comparable size but still was not of a mind to retire and rest. As a private in the 8th South Carolina wrote after the battle, Kershaw's and Cash's regiments, which provided the lion's share of Howard's opposition, had gotten into rifle range of Chinn Ridge after a debilitating march from Lewis Ford, "many falling out of the ranks from fatigue."[36]

While the fighting raged, these forces were augmented by two full brigades of foot soldiers, one dispatched by Beauregard from the far right, the other rushed up by Johnston from Manassas Junction. The newcomers not only made it impossible for Howard to hold his position but also provided enough strength to attack and smash the Union right. First to arrive on the scene was the Fourth Brigade, formerly commanded by Arnold Elzey and now led by Edmund Kirby Smith. Apparently due to the breakdown of a locomotive on the Manassas Gap line, Smith's Fifth Brigade had been unable to reach the battlefield; it remained at Piedmont Station awaiting engine repairs. Smith, however, had not been willing to share his men's inertia—to ensure participation in the imminent fight, the brigadier had pulled rank on Elzey and appropriated his command for the duration of the campaign.[37]

A little past one o'clock, Smith's overburdened train had wheezed to a halt a few hundred yards short of Manassas Junction. The passengers piled out of the cars, stacked knapsacks, and prepared to hasten to the field of battle. Before they marched, the general detached the four companies of A. P. Hill's 13th Virginia to guard the depot and the lower fords of Bull Run against a possible Federal flank attack. The assignment rankled the young and ambitious colonel, whose fighting spirit would power his rise, by mid-1863, to corps command in the main Confederate army in the East. At once the balance of the brigade—Colonel Simeon B. Gibbons's 10th Virginia, Colonel J. C. Vaughn's 3rd Tennessee, and Elzey's own 1st Maryland—began the six-mile march to Portici, where it expected to receive orders from Johnston. Like the Hampton Legion and other units that had preceded it, much of the way was covered at a killing pace—the double-quick and, at intervals, even faster.[38]

Smith could not get to the scene of action fast enough. Like every one of Elzey's men, he had undergone a long and stressful journey from the Valley, during the last few hours of which the sounds of battle grew ever louder, increasing the anxiety of every listener. The trip had frayed the temper of at least one private who appears to have disapproved of Smith's superseding of Elzey. The previous day, while waiting to board the train at Piedmont Station, the man had accosted Smith upon some matter that the latter did not care to discuss. Rebuffed, the soldier retorted, "I asked you a civil question, sir, and if you were disposed to act the gentleman you would give me a civil answer." An aggravated Smith went for his sword, whereupon the private drew a pistol and threatened to shoot. Before he could pull the trigger, he was overpowered and placed under arrest, but the confrontation must have shaken Smith's legendary aplomb, if only briefly.[39]

As the men hightailed it toward Portici, some managed to cheer and shout until they grew hoarse and their throats filled with the dust that rose in clouds from the well-traveled road. According to Sergeant McHenry Howard, whose 1st Maryland led the column, thirst-wracked men dropped out of the line of march and, laying aside their .69-caliber "buck and ball" rifles, greedily consumed the fluid-laden berries they found growing all along their route. Other parched soldiers drank from pools of water left by recent rains and muddied by the passage of horses and wagons; some resorted to drinking from a brook whose waters were tinged with blood. Once satiated, most of the men resumed the grueling pace, although assailed not only by heat and dust but also by the wails of wounded and demoralized men. Some of these urged the newcomers to "go in" but they refused an invitation, conveyed "in strong language," to turn about and join in. Elzey would have none of it. "Pay no attention to those miserable cowards and skulkers!" he shouted from the head of the column. Heartened by his admonition, and by Smith's reassumed composure, the men surged forward, leaving their unworthy comrades behind. Even so, the sights and sounds of battle, and the dire predictions of defeat, continued to bother many Marylanders. As one of them later wrote, "I cannot think there was ever a regiment of young & new men who went upon a field of battle under more distressing circumstances than ours."[40]

Shortly before Smith's arrival, Joe Johnston had also been visibly agitated. At this point the battle not only continued to hang in the balance but appeared to be expanding westward. The senior commander feared that the combined armies lacked the numbers necessary for a successful counterattack. A Richmond reporter heard him exclaim in a tone of near despair, "Oh, for four regiments!" With Smith's and Elzey's men on hand, Johnston now had three of those regiments as well as the four guns of Lieutenant Robert F. Beckham's Culpeper Artillery (also known as the King and Queen Artillery).[41]

Although Johnston could not have known it, the coming of Elzey's brigade—the last to reach the battlefield from Winchester in time to fight—brought the number of Confederate troops on the field to almost 31,000, only a few thousand short of the number available to McDowell, who had frittered away his strength to the point that, on the most critical parts of the field, his army was the decided underdog. Just as the Washington authorities had feared, Patterson's failure to hold the Army of the Shenandoah to its Valley home had created a dramatic reversal of fortune for the forces vying for supremacy along Bull Run. Early in his planning McDowell had taken into account the prospect that he would have to fight more than just Beauregard's army, but he had not necessarily anticipated opposing as many troops as Johnston actually brought to the field.[42]

About a mile short of the Lewis house, Smith was met by one of Johnston's aides who conveyed an order starkly simple. Johnston remembered it as to turn west by the most expeditious route, "form on the left of the line, with his left thrown forward, and to assail the enemy's right flank." He could have been no more specific, for as Beauregard would be quick to point out in later months, the Virginian had an imperfect understanding of the terrain. Johnston, who soon after joined Smith on the march, confessed as much to him: "The ground is new to me, and I cannot direct you exactly." Although Johnston would receive credit in some circles for placing the new arrivals in exactly the right place at precisely the right time, this last arrival's positioning hinged on Smith's ability to locate the point where his men were most needed.[43]

The sprint to Chinn Ridge was shorter than the race from Manassas to Portici, but it took an additional toll of Smith's panting and heaving troops. Following a wooded path that had been taken by Kershaw's men, at length the 1st Maryland came up in the South Carolinians' rear. The left of Kershaw's line, held by Cash's regiment, extended southwest from the Sudley Road, while the 2nd South Carolina straddled the road; farther to the right, Delaware Kemper's guns had unlimbered and were firing furiously at the Yankees on Chinn Ridge. Kershaw, until now the senior officer on the scene, met Smith upon his arrival and suggested that the Fourth Brigade extend the line farther left so as to make Howard's position even less tenable. The brigadier, eager for action, readily agreed.

As soon as Smith moved up on the left, his vanguard drew fire from Howard's men, which told him he had reached the place from which to fight. When some of his troops staggered under the sudden blow, he decided to make a conspicuous show of leadership. Waving his sword, he trotted forward, thus placing himself squarely in the line of fire. Seconds later a minie ball tore through

Smith's body from shoulder to shoulder, knocking him senseless to the ground.[44]

Seeing him fall, Elzey, who was following close behind on foot, let loose an exclamation that emphasized his resentment at having lost his brigade to a usurper: "God is just; Smith is dead!" In fact, Smith would survive his wound—the bullet narrowly missed his spine—although widespread reports of his death would plunge his family in Florida into mourning. Reassuming command, Elzey delegated control of his 1st Maryland to his senior subordinate, Major Bradley T. Johnson. (Lieutenant Colonel George H. Steuart had been captured minutes earlier by a detachment of the 2nd U.S. Dragoons, roving up the Sudley Road.) As he mounted Smith's horse, Elzey confronted two prospects: he too might fall to a Yankee bullet, but should he survive, he would win promotion to brigadier general. As he told Major Johnson, "this means for me six feet of ground or a yellow sash!"[45]

Adhering to the route Kershaw had suggested, Elzey led his brigade along an oblique path to the northwest. He crossed Sudley Road and, just short of Chinn Branch, ascended Bald Hill, which offered a good view of Howard's position across the stream. From the shelter of a woods on the hill, his men began to fire on as many Yankees as poked their heads over the top of the ridge. They were ably assisted by Beckham, who had moved his battery across the stream to the vicinity of Hazel Plain, the Chinn farmhouse, where he could enfilade Howard's right flank. In that exposed position the lieutenant was supported by Stuart's cavalry, which had been hovering on the west side of the Sudley Road since its encounter with the 11th New York and 1st Minnesota.[46]

When the 1st Maryland and 3rd Tennessee started up the ridge, the fire from Howard's position suddenly slackened. Mindful that the Yankees might have shifted position—perhaps mindful too of those six feet of dirt—Elzey ordered a staff officer to peer over the crest and report his findings. The aide saw no Federals on the summit except for the dead and dying, although a group of fugitives had taken shelter in a stand of pines a few hundred yards away.[47]

Elzey was not going to be denied a parting blow. He whipped his regiments into line—the 3rd Tennessee on the right, connecting with Cash's South Carolinians; the eight-company 1st Maryland farther left; and the 10th Virginia in the left rear of the Marylanders. By now Kershaw's men had taken a decisive toll of the defenders on Chinn Ridge; already Howard had received orders to disengage and join the rest of Heintzelman's division in retreat. Perceiving that the enemy was faltering, Elzey located an object to serve as the point of an attack, a stand of U.S. colors still waving from the top of the ridge. "Stars and Stripes!" he called to his men. "Give it to them, boys!" His men responded with a volley that swept the crest. Then Elzey called for a charge at bayonet point. Marylander Winfield Peters recalled that "immediately the two regiments— numbering together some 1,200—well aligned, charged out of the woods at 'Double-quick,' 'Charge bayonets,' with a ringing yell." Exhilarated Confederates swept forward, angling toward the position that Beckham's gunners were lathering with shot and shell.[48]

To get at Howard's men, the attackers splashed across Chinn Branch, cleared the ditch beyond, and then crossed a field dotted with blackberry bushes. Numerous soldiers, their canteens empty and their throats coated with dust and gunpowder residue, halted in midattack, broke ranks, and grabbed for the fruit heedless of the briars enclosing them. "For days afterward," Sergeant Howard recalled, "I was occupied extracting the thorns from the palms of my hands." When the 1st Maryland and 3rd Tennessee started uphill, the enemy's fire slackened further. According to Private Peters, "after we clambered out of the ditch they disappeared down the hill, the top of which we reached as speedily as possible." Before the assault could hit home, however, the enemy broke from the trees, loosed a few rounds in Elzey's direction, and then ran, stumbled, and fell down the ridge toward the Warrenton Pike.[49]

At first their assailants could not believe their eyes, then someone shouted, "There they go, they're breaking!" Moving forward on the far left to get a good view, William Blackford of Stuart's regiment discovered the fields beyond Chinn Ridge filled with "a confused swarm of men, like bees, running away as fast as their legs could carry them, with all order and organization abandoned."

When the realization set in that the Yankees were in full flight, infantrymen, troopers, and cannoneers split their throats with what one South Carolinian called "a yell that seems to shake the tree-tops." A Virginia artilleryman wrote his sister, "I never saw anything like the enthusiasm manifested when we learned they [the Yankees] were in full retreat." Other Confederates celebrated quietly and privately. Randolph McKim of the 1st Maryland, a future Confederate chaplain, dropped to his knees to thank the Lord for his critical support: "It was truly the hand of Providence which gave us the victory."[50]

Elzey tried to mount a pursuit, though with indifferent success. More effective were the efforts of Jubal Early, whose brigade had been summoned hours earlier to this part of the field from the far right. After a hurried and stressful march, the colonel had arrived just in time to fill the gap between Elzey's infantry and Beckham's cannoneers with his own 17th Virginia and 7th Louisiana and the borrowed 13th Mississippi. The troop transfer to the far left was the work of Beauregard, who some time before noon, aware that every available unit was needed at Henry Hill, had directed D. R. Jones to march his brigade to the same sector. Jones had shown the order to Early, two of whose regiments had begun to cross McLean's Ford in hopes of silencing Hunt's artillery before being recalled by Beauregard. The communiqué contained a postscript in pencil: "Send Early to me."

Held in place by the enemy across the run from him, Jones felt unable to comply with the order, but Early quickly organized his brigade—less the six companies of his own 24th Virginia that he had attached to Longstreet's brigade at the latter's request—into a marching column and started west, heading for the Lewis house. It took the men almost three hours to cover the six miles over farm lanes clogged with troops and vehicles before breaking out into more open country.[51]

Early had expected to report to either Beauregard or Johnston but found neither; he learned that both had gone to the front. His approach, however, caused consternation at the former's relocated field headquarters. Distracted by the tactical situation, the Creole had forgotten that he had summoned the brigade. At first he failed to identify the fast-moving command, whose colors were hanging limp in the breezeless heat. Then Captain Alexander wigwagged a warning that a large body of troops, identity unknown, was approaching the Confederate left. Like Johnston on a previous occasion, Beauregard for a time feared—in defiance of all logic—that Patterson was arriving from the Valley at the head of enough troops to snatch victory from the jaws of defeat. A rumor that the Pennsylvanian had already joined McDowell had come to the attention of some of Beauregard's troops. Should it prove true, their commander would have no choice but to abort his counterattack and fall back out of harm's reach. Thus he let out an almost audible sigh when finally able to distinguish the approaching banner as that of the 13th Mississippi.[52]

As he neared the scene of Kershaw's and Howard's struggle, Early was met by a member of Beauregard's staff, who told him to march to the place where the firing was the loudest. Soon afterward the Virginian heard "a heavy fire of musketry" from west of the Sudley Road. He "immediately inclined to the left . . . and soon met with General Johnston, who directed me to proceed to the extreme left of our line and attack the enemy on their right flank." Another mile or more had to be covered at the quickstep before Early reached Elzey's position, passed behind it, and debouched from a patch of woods east of Stuart and Beckham. "Here," Early reported, "I turned to the front, and a body of the enemy soon appeared in front of my column on the crest of a hill." He countered by forming James Kemper's 7th Virginia (depleted by sickness and casualties to fewer than four hundred effectives) in an open field facing the enemy's skirmish line. Hays's Louisianans went into line on Kemper's left, with Barksdale's Mississippians extending the line westward, all covered by Stuart's cavalry, which had sidled far enough to the left "to command a view of a very large portion of the ground occupied by the enemy." In his high-pitched voice, Early ordered everyone forward, intending to coordinate the movement as much as possible with Elzey's advance farther east.

Almost at the outset, however, Early's movement began to falter, the result of the battle's most vexing bollix, the inability to tell at a distance comrades from antagonists. Spying some of Howard's gray-clad Mainers in and around the Chinn house, the brigade leader screeched out a warning not to fire on "our friends." A nearby captain in the 7th Virginia, who had a better view of the field in that direction, shouted, "They may be your damned friends, Col[onel], but they are none of ours; fire, men!" The suddenly disabused Virginians surged forward and poured a volley into the lines opposite them.[53]

This, the final Confederate advance of the day, had the potential to reduce the Union right to atoms. But a climactic blow would not be needed. When his forward ranks gained the crest of Chinn Ridge, there were no Yankees left to overwhelm. Looking off into the distance, Early was surprised and disappointed to see a ragged column of bluecoats moving eastward on the turnpike. The spineless enemy had refused to stay and meet his thrust. So believing, the prideful and disputatious colonel would forever assert that he and his men deserved a heaping share of the credit for overcoming the last stand of McDowell's army.

To be sure, there appeared enough credit to go around, although Kershaw's foot soldiers and Kemper's cannoneers, who had provided the bulk of Howard's opposition prior to Elzey's and Early's arrival, appeared to have a stronger claim to clearing Chinn Ridge. In the end, however, the distinction would be awarded by turns to Smith and Elzey, each of whom would be christened "Blucher of Manassas" in reference to the Prussian field marshal whose eleventh-hour arrival at Waterloo tipped the scales of battle against Napoleon. Supposedly, Beauregard personally conferred the title on Elzey soon after Smith's wounding, but Smith, as Elzey's superior, felt justified in appropriating it. Over the years the two appeared unwilling to share the honor, which neither truly deserved.[54]

At the start, the Union withdrawal was a deliberate and, in the main, orderly affair. There was no widespread panic or chaos, for the army was not then threatened with a vigorous pursuit. Virtually as a body, its soldiers had come to an understanding that, having exhausted themselves in one fruitless attack after another, they could not seize, let alone secure, the most critical sectors of the battlefield. They had driven the Rebels from Matthews Hill to Young's Branch and then to the top of Henry Hill, but bedeviled by heat, thirst, hunger, and blood loss, they could push them no farther. As one bewildered Federal later put it, wherever he and his comrades turned, the enemy appeared to rise "up out of the ground to fight" them. Having exhausted strength, spirit, and ammunition, suffering hundreds of casualties during one piecemeal and unsupported assault after another, they had been unable to surmount the fanatical, almost superhuman, resistance of the enemy. Their officers could not persuade them otherwise. Colonel Heintzelman found this out early in the retreat. Although he made the most strenuous efforts to halt and redeploy his demoralized troops, "not one would form, or advance. . . . not a Regt could be rallied nor even a company." In unison with many another Federal officer, he declared that "such a rout I never saw before."[55]

Studying the facial expressions and body language of the retreating troops, Surgeon Gray of the 2nd Cavalry decided that "they could not be urged forward but loitered along or sat down as though the war—or their part in it at least—was over. They did not seem frightened but stupid [that is, benumbed], tired, & indifferent" and thoroughly beaten. A Michigan infantryman agreed that initially the retreat was an orderly affair: "As a matter of fact, I saw no running where the fight took place but the men fell back in a sullen, dogged manner until they had got away from the presence of the enemy." The man knew why so many of his comrades turned their back to the battlefield: "Our army were all raw, green men and were pretty well played out. Some of them needed only an excuse to quit the game and here they had it."[56]

The initially recumbent soldiers eventually regained their feet and began heading for the rear. They moved off in groups large and small, carrying off their weapons as if willing to take them up again under more favorable conditions. Captain Fry observed "no special excitement except that arising from the frantic efforts of officers to stop men who paid little or no attention to anything that was said." The majority waded the same Bull Run fords that had led them to the field of battle that morning. After crossing, Porter's and Heintzelman's troops headed out the same extended, looping route that had so exhausted and aggravated them almost twelve hours earlier. Tyler's regrouped brigades marched up the Warrenton Pike, the direct route to the rear echelon at Centreville. The routes converged on the turnpike between Stone Bridge and Cub Run, where the flanking column had branched off at 6:00 A.M.

Although consumed by nervous exhaustion, still suffering from indigestion, and fearing the worst, General McDowell had not relinquished the hope that he could reverse his losses and salvage some form of victory or perhaps at least a drawn battle. Upon reaching Centreville, he consulted with some of his division and brigade commanders as to whether they should attempt to turn the men about and reengage the enemy or accompany them to Washington. As Fry noted, "the verdict was in favor of the latter, but a decision of officers one way or the other was of no moment; the men had already decided for themselves and were streaming away to the rear, in spite of all that could be done. They had no interest or treasure in Centreville, and their hearts were not there. Their tents, provisions, luggage, and letters from home were upon the banks of the Potomac, and no power could have stopped them short of the camps they had left less than a week before."[57]

Lieutenant Averell, who was wrestling with "uncontrollable indignation and mortification at the failure of our army to win the battle," observed McDowell, whom he described as "broken down" mentally and physically, bow to the inevitable, instructing various subordinates to cover the withdrawal of the army. That delicate and risky process had already begun. When Howard abandoned Chinn Ridge, the only troops in position to assist him were George Sykes's regulars. Supported on the left by a scattering of volunteers, including a company of the 1st Minnesota and a larger portion of the 2nd New Hampshire, the regulars ascended the ridge just as Howard's troops were clambering down the other side. Lieutenant Robert G. Carter of the 8th Infantry wrote that the battalion moved "where these regiments were retreating to, and tried to form them, or at least cover their retreat." A few of Howard's men rallied, but "the rest were panic stricken and nothing could save them. We formed line of battle, and then deployed . . . as skirmishers."[58]

Mistaking for Confederates the few New Englanders who were belatedly leaving the ridge—probably the gray-uniformed 3rd or 5th Maine—Sykes's men opened on them, the last recorded instance of friendly fire in a day replete with it. Suddenly, the Stars and Stripes became visible in the hands of a color-bearer. "We saw our mistake very quickly," Carter recalled, and the firing ceased, only to resume upon the approach of three regiments clearly displaying the Star and Bars. Upon giving them "a dose of lead they will long remember," Sykes noticed that the entire army seemed to be leaving the field and the battalion was at risk of being surrounded. Taking steps to ensure that his ranks were smartly aligned, the major led the men back down the ridge and then up the turnpike in the role of rear guard.[59]

When the regulars moved off, their rear and flanks became exposed to a harassing fire from the forces of Kershaw, Elzey, Early, and (after some dithering as to "whether this was a general or a partial rout"), Jeb Stuart. By hard marching, the regulars outdistanced the infantry, but Stuart, perceiving another opportunity to create havoc among retreating Yankees, led one hundred of his men through the woods west of Chinn Ridge and bore down on the regulars. Without missing a beat, Sykes formed the men into a hollow square, the preferred defense against a mounted charge. The sight of this formation made Stuart realize two things: not only was he outnumbered but he also was challenging professionals, some of them raw recruits, but the majority experienced and pugnacious soldiers on a par with their commander. One of the regulars noted that before a collision took place, the cavalry halted, fell back, "and kept out of the range of our rifles." No longer hard pressed, Sykes returned his men to marching formation and resumed his withdrawal, thereafter virtually unmolested.[60]

With the exodus of Howard and Sykes, the retreat was fully underway, though its success was not assured. His rear echelon having disengaged, McDowell must now ensure that his vanguard would not be cut off before it cleared Centreville. An unencumbered Warrenton Pike was the key to a timely escape from this field of ruined plans and dashed hopes. To see to its safeguarding, in advance of reaching Centreville, he had sent aides and couriers pounding up the pike to alert Dixon Miles to be alert for Rebel attempts to turn their flank and smite their rear. Should the troops around and below Blackburn's Ford drive back the Fifth Division and push north to block the passageways to Washington via Fairfax Court House, the Army of Northeastern Virginia would face total destruction.

After its indecisive skirmishing of the morning, Davies's brigade of Miles's division, supported by Richardson's brigade of Tyler's division as well as two batteries and an attached section, the artillery all under the supervision of Major Henry J. Hunt, had guarded the roads leading to Blackburn's and Mitchell's Fords. Davies, the senior officer on the field, was intent on keeping the Confederates at the lower fords—the brigades of Longstreet, Ewell, Early, and Jones—from crossing and striking the Union left even as the heavier fighting raged a half-dozen miles to the west. But by early afternoon Davies's and Hunt's operations were becoming increasingly complicated thanks to the erratic behavior of an intoxicated Colonel Miles, who had begun to issue contradictory and obstructive orders.

Davies and Hunt were being aided, however, by the confusion evident in the ranks of their enemy. The Confederates' foul-ups had begun with Ewell's failure to receive Beauregard's early morning order to cross the run at Union Mills and initiate the offensive against McDowell's left flank and rear. That order, copies of which were received shortly after seven o'clock by Longstreet and Jones, had sent their brigades across the run at Blackburn's and McLean's Fords, respectively, but when Ewell, who was to lead the offensive, did not advance, his colleagues remained immobile on the north bank.

For nearly an hour, Longstreet's five regiments were pounded by Hunt's artillery, suffering more or less heavily. Sometime after eight o'clock, a reconnaissance conducted by two of Longstreet's volunteer aides-de-camps told the general that the Yankees below Centreville appeared to be moving away from the lower fords. Longstreet relayed the news to army headquarters. Soon afterward he returned his men to the right bank in response to an order from Beauregard, presumably in anticipation of sending his and perhaps other commands to the left.

Shortly after noon Longstreet also forwarded to higher head-quarters information that his resourceful aides had gathered on the positions of Hunt's artillery. The brigadier added a suggestion that his men be returned to the Yankees' side of the run and an effort made to capture their guns. At least an hour passed before he heard from Beauregard. Longstreet's proposal having been approved, he was again ordered across the stream and directed to advance on the enemy, though not by himself. On the left bank he was to await Jones's advance from McLean's Ford and coordinate operations with him.

Expecting action this time, Longstreet crossed his brigade and on the far side again awaited orders to advance. He kept his men on the north side for "some time," all the while hearing nothing sug-gesting that Jones (who had not been notified to go forward) had crossed at McLean's in cooperation with him. Occupying mostly open ground, Longstreet's regiments again came under artillery fire. This was bad enough, but soon after, to the general's manifest dis-gust, another courier-borne message ordered him to defer attacking and hold his position.

This he did despite his growing frustration and the continuing discomfiture of his troops until, between 5:00 and 6:00 P.M., yet another courier from Beauregard ordered the brigade to advance and attack. The messenger announced that McDowell's army had been routed and was in full retreat; it was hoped that Longstreet would cut it off short of Centreville. Slightly confused but relieved that his long, fruitless waiting was apparently over, the South Carolinian began "advancing to the attack of the routed column" with the 1st Virginia under Major Frederick G. Skinner; Garland's 11th Virginia; Corse's 17th Virginia; Hairston's 24th Virginia; Lieutenant J. J. Garnett's 3rd Company, Washington Artillery; and Company E, 30th Virginia Cavalry under Captain Edgar Whitehead. No one in the column, least of all Longstreet, could have known that none of these units would see further action this day.[61]

Ewell's and Early's transfer to the left and Longstreet's enforced hours-long inactivity meant that the only offensive north of Bull Run would be conducted by Jones's brigade. Thanks to the unconscionable lack of communication between Beauregard's headquarters and the army's right—and also to the power and tenacity displayed by Davies, Richardson, and Hunt—that operation would end in disaster.

Despite being ordered to coordinate with Jones, Longstreet reported hearing nothing from his fellow brigadier throughout the day. Because Jones did not go forward when expected, Longstreet supposed that he had not received Beauregard's order to advance. In his battle report, however, Jones stated that late in the morning Longstreet sent him a request to "make a demonstration in his favor on my front," followed soon after by an order from Beauregard to advance north and west through the valley of Little Rocky Run in cooperation with both Longstreet and Ewell. Jones would claim that after crossing Bull Run, he informed both generals of his action— apparently neither replied. With no other course open to him, Jones went ahead on his own and attacked unsupported.

The long, difficult march the Third Brigade made to get into position to strike the Union left was severely hampered by the weariness of the men, who that morning had spent two and a half hours on the enemy side of the run waiting fruitlessly for word to attack before recalled to their original position. In his report Jones stressed not only the men's exhaustion but the fact that many were "just convalescing from the measles." The movement to Little Rocky Run appears to have taken more than three hours, for not until shortly before four o'clock was the brigade in column along the Union Mills Road.

From his staging area at Croson's farm, Jones started the men westward across terrain obstructed by trees that had been felled that morning by Davies's pioneer teams. The Confederates advanced in two lines, the first consisting of the 5th South Carolina of Colonel Micah Jenkins, and farther left, the 18th Mississippi of Colonel Erasmus Burt. To the left rear came Colonel Winfield Scott Featherston's 17th Mississippi, its flanks covered by Captain J. W. Flood's company of Radford's cavalry. Flood's small force also supported the two guns of the 2nd Company, Washington Artillery, commanded by Captain Merritt B. Miller.[62]

Jones's brigade was made of good stuff, but he had failed to reconnoiter the ground ahead of him, an inexcusable failing considering

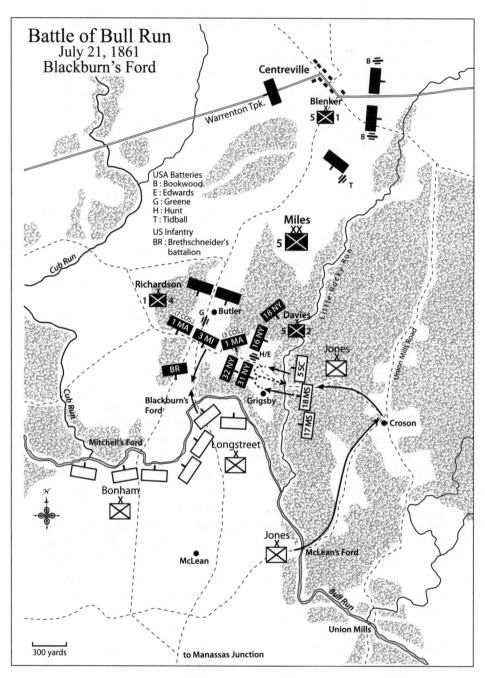

Battle of Bull Run, July 21, 1861: Blackburn's Ford. *Map by Paul Dangel.*

the lengthy preparations he had made. The hilly, heavily wooded terrain broke up his formations and prevented communication among the units. The advance guard had a difficult time locating the enemy, for Major Hunt had persuaded the foot soldiers supporting his flanks to shield themselves behind the trees and underbrush that grew heavily in that sector.

Only minutes after the Confederates made contact with Hunt and Davies, their assault began to collapse. Already Jones had lost his artillery support; in his report he blamed Captain Miller for placing his section in an "impracticable" position, one that drew a converging fire from the Federal guns and such a strong infantry advance that both pieces had to be withdrawn. Left on its own, the Rebel infantry provided easy targets for Hunt's cannons. Even before it reached Little Rocky Run, Colonel Jenkins's regiment, now in advance of the others, was blasted by canister and shrapnel. At the same time, it absorbed musketry from the 18th Mississippi, whose men had plunged into a woods that prevented them from seeing clearly either friend or foe. The fire in the rear quickly ceased, but by now the 5th South Carolina had taken enough casualties to be thoroughly demoralized.[63]

Colonel Burt's outfit compounded its error when suddenly stymied by an impassable ravine. The barrier, in the words of sixteen-year-old private George Gibbs, "changed the result of our attack from a certain victory to a repulse." Gibbs wrote that the enemy "were protected from our bullets by the embankment on the other side, while we were exposed to their fire, and a good many of our men were killed and wounded on the edge of the ravine. At last the order was given to retreat, and we went down the hill as fast as we had gone up it."[64]

In his own report Colonel Burt strongly implied that the entire attack had been a botch, having been made "without any knowledge of the ground over which the regiment was to pass, and continued in the face of a terrific fire of canister, shell, and shot from the battery of the enemy." When his regiment withdrew, its comrades in the 17th Mississippi began to waver. According to Colonel Featherston, "standing thus, unable to advance, and exposed to a heavy fire from the enemy, the Seventeenth fell back with the Eighteenth Regiment." Like Burt, Featherston argued that although Hunt's fire was blistering, only the physical obstacles in their path prevented his men from topping the high ground and silencing the guns.[65]

Though deserted by their supports, Jenkins's men briefly continued their advance, but by the time they reached Grigsby's Knoll, only a few hundred yards from their objective, their ranks had been shredded by what Major Hunt, who had seen much action during the Mexican War, considered "the most rapid, well-sustained, and destructive fire I have ever witnessed." In turn, Jenkins's men took a toll of their infantry assailants while killing Hunt's brother-in-law, Lieutenant Presley Craig of the 2nd Artillery. Finally, the South Carolinians could advance no farther, and Jenkins decided "unwillingly to withdraw," leapfrogging his regiment by companies to the rear. At this point General Jones called it quits, opting to regroup his shot-torn ranks beyond the range of Hunt's and Davies's weapons.[66]

The repulse of Jones's assault marked the only sustained Union success on any part of the battlefield. Technically, credit went to Dixon Miles as the ranking officer in that sector. But within an hour of Jones's overthrow, the division leader found himself relieved of his command and sent to the rear in disgrace, a blow from which his career would never recover.

Throughout the morning, Miles had had run-ins with the commanders of both of the brigades south of Centreville. Early in the afternoon, before Jones's attack, he had a confrontation with Colonel Richardson, who had reported that at least some of the Confederates in his front had slipped back across the run. He feared that they had withdrawn to add their weight to the fighting farther west. Miles was not convinced, but nothing was done to determine the accuracy of Richardson's surmise.

Later in the afternoon, at about the time Jones advanced on Davies and Hunt, Miles rode to Centreville, where he received word of the pending collapse of the Union right flank. The news came from one of McDowell's staff officers, who carried a request from the army leader that two brigades be sent down the turnpike toward Stone Bridge in the event that they were needed to support a general retreat. At first Miles, befogged by liquor, refused, but eventually he consented to advance Blenker's brigade toward the Cub Run bridge. Because of the crush of soldiers retreating along the turnpike, Blenker's column progressed only a half mile from Centreville before it could proceed no farther. Toward sundown, however, Blenker repulsed a cautious advance by a party of Virginia cavalry, the Albemarle Troop under Major John Scott, which had outdistanced its pursuing comrades in a frenetic effort to scoop up prisoners and booty.[67]

In response to McDowell's request, Miles also sent a courier to the telegraph terminus at Fairfax Court House to plead for reinforcements from Washington. The message that went out under Miles's name connoted panic: "Send on immediately all the troops that can be spared." This was a futile gesture given the time it would take to organize a relief column and place it in position to protect a general withdrawal.[68]

One might suppose that McDowell, in his frantic quest for support, would have considered calling up Runyon's reserve division. He knew full well, however, that the New Jersey volunteers and militia were a hollow force. They had been armed with antiquated muskets, lacked sufficient ammunition, and had spent even less time training than most of the units that had accompanied McDowell to Manassas. Moreover, the division had been fragmented to guard depots between Fairfax Station and Alexandria. It would have taken twenty-four hours or more to group, organize, and dispatch the full division to the rescue.[69]

The nearest element of Runyon's command—portions of the 1st and 2nd New Jersey Volunteers—did advance to Centreville late on the twenty-first, toting their obsolete firearms. Soon after arriving, the 2nd, appreciating the futility of the effort, turned about and without orders headed for Washington. The more tenacious 1st New Jersey remained at Centreville until 2:00 A.M. on the twenty-second, when permitted to head north in company with McDowell's fugitives. Early that evening a third regiment of Runyon's division, Colonel Leopold Von Gilsa's 41st New York, came down to Centreville from Fairfax Court House as did the companies of the 4th Michigan that had been stationed there with them. None of the late arrivals could stem the tide of retreat, which they duly joined.[70]

Thus McDowell had to cover his retreat with the troops available around Centreville. Not long after Jones was repulsed, Miles ordered Richardson, Davies, and Hunt to fall back upon the "strongest position" available, Centreville heights. Richardson was operating under orders from McDowell to hold his position in front of Blackburn's Ford "at all hazards," but being under Miles's authority he felt that he "could not disobey the order" and so began to move his brigade north. En route conferring with Davies, he learned that his colleague also had been ordered to Centreville but without explanation.

About half a mile from the village, one of McDowell's staff officers halted Richardson and ordered him to form a battle line facing toward both Blackburn's Ford and Union Mills. Anticipating enemy attempts to pursue, the colonel readily obeyed, but while positioning his brigade he discovered that some of his troops had been shifted elsewhere without his consent. Upon inquiry, he learned from a subordinate that a drunken Miles had ordered the redeployment.

Soon after Miles's latest interference, Richardson was met by Captain Barton S. Alexander, one of McDowell's engineer officers. Alexander explained that by the general's express order Richardson now had command of the troops in his immediate area. (It remains unclear whether these included Davies's men, though the latter reported that some time afterward, he was ordered by McDowell to "take command of the left wing.") Whatever the extent of Richardson's authority, the order suggests that McDowell bore no grudge against him for any mistakes he may have made during the fiasco on the eighteenth.

Richardson complained to Alexander of Miles's repeated interference with the positioning of his brigade—his most recent handiwork being the construction of a crooked and discontinuous line on low ground outside Centreville. Alexander replied that McDowell knew of the old regular's physical condition and that the matter "would soon be attended to." With the engineer's assistance, Richardson went to work to undo Miles's interference. He filled the gaps in the wayward line, moved some of Hunt's guns onto higher ground, and deployed infantry units inside woods and behind prepared works.

Amid Richardson's efforts, General McDowell, recently arrived at Centreville, rode up and inquired why his brigade had fallen back from Blackburn's Ford. When the colonel explained that he had done so at Miles's direct order, the army commander said nothing except to confirm that Fighting Dick had charge of all units in his sector.[71]

While this was going on, Miles had been checking on Blenker's dispositions along the turnpike. Upon returning to Centreville, he was furious at finding "all my defensive arrangements changed." Davies's brigade, like Richardson's, had not withdrawn as near to Centreville as the division commander desired—in fact, two of Davies's regiments had taken position behind Richardson's new line. Miles could not immediately locate Davies, but he angrily confronted Richardson about the changes made in his absence. His subordinate tried to explain, but when Miles, who "was reeling in the saddle" and using "incoherent language," attempted to reposition his troops, Richardson stopped him cold and explained that by McDowell's order he was now in command locally. Waving him off, Miles threatened to arrest him for insubordination, but Richardson simply ignored him and rode off. When Miles returned to Centreville, he did so as a division commander without a division.[72]

The successful defense of the Union left ensured that the route of retreat to Washington would remain open long enough for McDowell's troops to outdistance any pursuers. But by the time the fighting in that sector wound down, the day was done, and so was the Army of Northeastern Virginia. The struggle to break the Rebels' hold on northern Virginia and carry the war on to Richmond had been irretrievably lost.

CHAPTER 16

A STUNTED PURSUIT

Within minutes of Howard's withdrawal, if not earlier, Beauregard and Johnston moved to follow up their extraordinary victory. The stand made by the defenders of Centreville, which stymied Longstreet and demolished Jones, suggested that the Confederates would not be able to sever the head of the retreating column. Yet opportunities for attacking, or at least harassing, sections of the Union army presented themselves well before the last Yankee abandoned the battlefield. Targets of opportunity were plentiful. These were seized upon by some of the cannoneers who had withdrawn from the plateau during the attacks on Ricketts's and Griffin's batteries and had returned to the crest to help speed the Yankees on their way with shell, shrapnel, and canister.[1]

Johnston, who had returned to Portici after meeting Smith's brigade on the march, commenced the pursuit by ordering Radford's cavalry to smite the Federals' flank and rear and directing Bonham and Longstreet to squeeze off their escape route via Centreville. Yet it would appear that the first troops to try to get at the retreating enemy were those on the far left, already in the most advantageous position to overtake the enemy rear. Nevertheless, they failed to do so thanks to a tentative, fragmented, and uncoordinated effort.

Jubal Early's brigade started after Howard's fugitives shortly after they abandoned Chinn Ridge. From atop the captured height, Early reported, "we saw the evidences of the flight all along the march, and unmistakable indications of the overwhelming character of the enemy's defeat, in the shape of abandoned guns and equipments." Joined on the ridge by Colonel Cocke with Strange's 19th Virginia, Early squinted into the lowering sun and made out a large body of Yankees crowding the turnpike near the Dogan house.

Supposing the retreating troops to be demoralized and perhaps incapable of defending themselves, Early set out to overtake them. But his resolve to strike a parting blows appears to have waned with every step. Accompanied by Cocke and Strange and covered by the fire of some cannons (probably Beckham's), his troops descended Chinn Ridge, crossed the turnpike west of Dogan's, and marched— with extreme slowness, it would appear—in rear of the fleeing enemy. Then, for unexplained reasons, Early turned off the pike and proceeded to a point north of the Carter plantation house, about a mile above the Stone Bridge. Here he appears to have been within striking distance of the column heading for Farm Ford, but he never got close enough to Bull Run to deliver even a parting blow. Instead, he halted on the west side of the stream, where he put his command in bivouac for the night. Early never explained his feckless, hesitant movement, nor did he indicate whether he did any damage at all to the Federals he was supposedly chasing, even to taking prisoners. Rather than pursuing the enemy, Early had escorted them from the field.[2]

Colonel Cocke performed just as timidly in pursuit, perhaps more so. With Strange's outfit in tow, he struck the turnpike west of Early and, parting company with him, led the 19th Virginia directly north in the wake of Heintzelman's column. At the close of a two-mile march made at a desultory pace, Cocke and Strange crossed Bull Run "below and in sight" of Sudley Mill. By the time they reached the mill, the Federals were out of sight. Considering the numbers at his disposal, Cocke may not have been displeased by the outcome. At Sudley Church he did take some prisoners—almost all of them wounded, including the intensely suffering Sullivan Ballou. With night coming on and unable to proceed, Cocke again crossed the run and guided the 19th Virginia—minus one company left behind to make prisoners of the ambulatory wounded—to its original position near the Lewis house, thereby ending another effort unworthy of being called a pursuit.[3]

In Early's and Cocke's defense, the Yankees were making good time on their divergent routes to Centreville. Perhaps half of McDowell's army was retreating up the Warrenton Pike, which was perceived to be the quickest route to a place of safety. Many had begun their retreat by crossing Stone Bridge, in their haste forgetting or ignoring reports that the span had been mined. The rest of the army had withdrawn by the routes they had taken to the battlefield early that morning: the long, semicircular trail via Sudley Ford and the less roundabout path to Farm Ford. It is likely that some troops withdrew not by these well-used lines of travel but by the recently discovered road to Poplar Ford. It is impossible to determine, however, which organizations retreated in which direction.

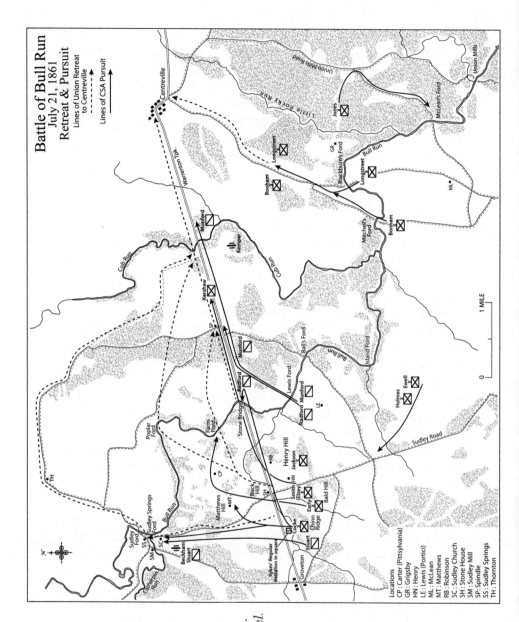

Battle of Bull Run,
July 21, 1861:
Retreat and Pursuit.
Map by Paul Dangel.

450

Other forces along the Confederate left flank followed the lead of Early and Cocke, although belatedly and with no greater accomplishments to show for their efforts. Colonel Elzey, for example, was ordered by Beauregard to withdraw his somewhat scattered troops to Bald Hill, presumably to re-form and ready them for pursuit. The colonel complied as quickly as possible but only after surmounting the confusion stemming from an erroneous report that some of his men had fired on Early's brigade atop Chinn Ridge, making a forward movement risky. After a halt of indeterminate length—by which time the Federals were long gone from the western reaches of the turnpike—Elzey moved out but quickly halted near Stone Bridge. He advanced no farther, probably because, as Captain Alexander of the signal corps noted upon meeting him on the turnpike, it was nearly 7:00 P.M., only forty-five minutes before sunset. It is hard to describe Elzey's "pursuit" as anything more than a change of position.[4]

At least he got his men in motion. Most of the forces atop Henry Hill, including Jackson's brigade, pursued briefly or not at all. Instead, while Jackson had his wounded hand tended to by his medical staff, his men moved to a new position around Johnston's headquarters, where they slept on their arms throughout the night. They would not need those weapons on the morrow. By morning the Yankees would be miles away and would not be coming back.[5]

Their mobility made Radford's and Stuart's troopers capable of staging a highly effective pursuit. Both commands were sicced on the enemy almost simultaneously but by widely divergent paths. In view of their relatively small numbers, neither probably expected to achieve more than helping speed the bluecoats on their way. This pretty much describes Radford's achievements, although his colleague in the 1st Virginia accomplished much more.

Stuart had expected to pursue as soon as Howard's brigade gave way, but he asked for and received Beauregard's formal approval. According to Adjutant Blackford, who carried Stuart's request to army headquarters, when starting out the troopers rode parallel to and about a half mile from the Sudley Road. Choosing to follow the Yankees who crossed Bull Run at Sudley Ford, Stuart got off to a rough start when, short of the stream, an errant shell from Latham's Lynchburg battery landed uncomfortably close to the head of the column. Stuart appeared unruffled, but his adjutant was indignant. "It was bad enough to be killed by the enemy," Blackford complained, "but that could not be helped; but to be bowled over by our own people, and hit in the back at that, was disgusting."[6]

Once across the run, Stuart's cavaliers pounded north, detouring around the human and inanimate debris that lined and sometimes blocked their path. Sergeant Otho Lee recalled, "we went in a gallop through hundreds of dead, wounded, and dying soldiers, the wounded calling for water, men with stretchers gathering up the wounded, and ambulances being loaded for field hospitals." With these exceptions, "the sight on the road was wonderful to behold. Abandoned wagons, camp chests, ambulances, and artillery wagons left behind by the fleeing Federals."[7]

Four or five miles into the ride, Stuart struck what Blackford described as "a broad stream of stragglers, extending forty or fifty yards on each side of the road. The main body had just passed. . . . We struck it crossing a meadow and my men went wild. They were like a pack of hounds when they see a fox, and I turned them loose. There were at least a hundred foxes in sight and a most exciting chase began." Though many Yankees escaped by hurtling roadside fences, dozens were made prisoner. Stuart, as he reported, became "so much encumbered with prisoners, whom I sent as fast as possible back to the infantry, that my command was soon too much reduced to encounter any odds." Although the cavalry chieftain had a penchant for exaggeration and self-aggrandizement, which he here displayed in print for the first time, he was undoubtedly telling the truth. He had started out with fewer than 150 sabers and surely lost a considerable number to prisoner-escort duty. But his claim to having been reduced by nightfall to a single squad of horsemen is dubious.[8]

Stuart's ride, which covered fully twelve miles, was not uncontested. He reported being opposed by various coherent and semicoherent forces, including a section of Arnold's battery as well as by at least five companies of regular cavalry under Major Palmer, the whole of McDowell's mounted arm. Though destined to attract little attention for its role in the battle, earlier in the day Arnold had fired more than four hundred rounds in futile support of his beleaguered colleagues Ricketts and Griffin. Conversely, Palmer's troopers merited little recognition, but through no fault of their own. Permitted to stage a few offensive maneuvers such as Colburn's counterattack on Stuart following the latter's assault on the Fire Zouaves and their comrades from Minnesota, through most of the day the Union horsemen had been chained to Heintzelman's headquarters. Like many another infantry commander, especially at this stage of the conflict, Heintzelman had little appreciation for the tactical value of cavalry. Believing the terrain in his sector "unfavorable" for mounted operations, he had withheld the troopers from combat so that they might spend their time covering his flanks and rear.

It appears that Palmer did little to stifle Stuart, who claimed to have cut off "a great many squads" of Union horsemen, while Beckham's battery, which accompanied him part of the way, dueled with Arnold. The Virginian's ride effectively ended at the Union hospital at Sudley Church, which he would have reached well in advance of Colonels Cocke and Strange. Presumably, he made prisoners of Surgeon Magruder, his staff, and the more than three hundred wounded and dying being cared for there—if time did not permit, Stuart would have entrusted the task to his slower-moving infantry comrades.[9]

Although unable to overtake a sizeable portion of McDowell's army, Stuart's battalion had done considerable physical and psychological damage to what the alliterative Beauregard called "the fast-fleeing, frantic Federalists." Moreover, Stuart had done so on the cheap, having lost one man killed and one wounded during the course of his ride. The disparity between captives and casualties hinted at the damage that cavalry, properly handled and supported, could inflict in pursuit of a beaten enemy. Yet only a few army commanders, North or South, would learn this lesson and apply it effectively over the course of the conflict.[10]

While Stuart headed north from the battlefield, Colonel Radford, at the head of five companies of his 30th Virginia as well as Captain Williams C. Wickham's company of independent cavalry, crossed Bull Run and galloped along the turnpike in hopes of catching up to the enemy somewhere between the Bull Run and Cub Run crossings. Radford had been set in motion by an order handed him by Colonel George W. Lay, adjutant general of Bonham's brigade, within minutes of the collapse of the Union right. His instructions for dealing with the Federals were simple enough: "Charge upon them and cut off their retreat" short of Centreville. When the colonel relayed the order to his men, it was received "with enthusiasm, they having remained the whole day patiently under the enemy's fire."

Radford's Rangers splashed across Bull Run at Lewis Ford and headed for Stone Bridge, looking for demoralized Federals and sluggish supply vehicles. One trooper wrote that he and his comrades had been ordered "to shoot all the horses drawing the artillery and wagons." The disabled vehicles were to be left behind, allowing the pursuit to continue at top speed; they would be hauled to the rear when convenient.[11]

Radford's primary target was the southern flank and rear of Daniel Tyler's division, most of which—especially Schenck's uncommitted brigade and the lightly engaged troops of Keyes—was moving east at a deliberate pace and in good order. Farther to the rear, Sherman's brigade, which had suffered heavy losses, was more vulnerable. When Radford's men appeared on their flank just short of the Cub Run bridge, Sherman's troops panicked at the vision of being ridden over by hundreds of horses and cut down by the pistols and sabers of their riders. Again the fearsome cry—"Black Horse Cavalry!"—went up, and the column began to accordion upon itself, the rearmost troops rampaging through the ranks of comrades in front. Those swept up in the frenzy included members of Captain Reynolds's battery of Burnside's brigade. As they ran, a harried young cannoneer asked his commander what the Rebels, having already beaten them, intended to do. Reynolds shouted back, "They are trying to kill every mother's son of us!"[12]

The Confederate vanguard met the turnpike at the whitewashed abode of one Mrs. Spindle, roughly midway between Bull Run and Cub Run. Here the troopers plowed into a mass of demoralized Federals. Lieutenant William B. Newton of Wickham's company reported: "We came suddenly on a detachment of the enemy concealed in the [roadside] bushes, with their pieces leveled. The Colonel ordered the charge and the boys rushed on."[13]

Radford's men struck so quickly that those who had failed to heed their comrades' warning were taken by surprise. Lieutenant Hains, whose men were struggling mightily to drag their 30-pounder Parrott to safety, was one of the few at the rear of the column to detect the cavalry's approach before it struck home. He tried to alert others to the danger but failed to arouse enough men to take action. Captain Carlisle, whose battery was bringing up the rear of Tyler's column, managed to swing about two of his guns, but the rounds of canister they fired passed above the cavalrymen's heads. The blasts managed, however, to stir fear in the hearts of the many stragglers who were crowding around a well on the Spindle property to grab a drink and fill their canteens. Firmly in the grip of panic, they began running in all directions.[14]

Against minimal opposition, Radford's men swarmed over Carlisle's guns, which were hemmed in by roadside woods. The captain and his men—those not rendered *hors de combat*—hastily abandoned their charges and fled into the trees. Little else could have been done; as one of Carlisle's lieutenants reported, "Our men were shot down and sabered. The wheels broke down in all the pieces and caissons of my section. I halted to see if they could be fixed, amidst a perfect shower of pistol bullets, but finding they could not be, [I] moved forward with the pieces on a jump without wheels until every trace broke."[15]

The horsemen seized numerous prisoners, between sixty and eighty by Radford's count. The majority appear to have been members of the 69th New York, which had retreated by way of the turnpike rather than Farm Ford, where they had crossed Bull Run five hours ago. The cavalrymen's captures included a wounded Colonel Corcoran, whom they scooped up along with one of his regiment's banners near the Spindle place. According to a member of the 69th, Corcoran had advised his men, once attacked, to "cut and run, every man on his own hook, as well as he could."[16]

Though his attack was profitable in terms of numbers of men and guns captured, Radford made the mistake of attacking through a narrow gap between bodies of retreating troops. As his advance struck home, his rear was fired on by a force he estimated at 5,000 men "posted on each side of the road in thick woods, supported by a battery of three pieces, blocking up the road." The cannons, probably those of Ayres's battery, opened on the riders in unison, killing or mortally wounding seven officers and men, including the colonel's brother, Captain E. Winston Radford; wounding four others; and downing a dozen horses. One of Radford's subordinates later admitted that two more horses and men were wounded by the accidental discharge of the shotguns they and many of their comrades carried. Cowed by this resistance, the cavalry's rear echelon galloped off across the fields south of the pike.

The extent of Radford's accomplishments—beyond making prisoners of dozens of exhausted, panic-stricken Yankees—is open to dispute. Six companies of troopers would appear too few to have inflicted as much damage as the colonel claimed in his postaction report. He asserted, for instance, that his initial assault caused a massive traffic jam on the Cub Run bridge, resulting in the capture of no fewer than fourteen pieces of artillery, countless supply wagons and ambulances, and forty or fifty horses. Radford based his claims "on the fact that we were in advance of all our forces, and by our charge the enemy were thrown into wild confusion before us, their vehicles of all sorts going off at full speed and in the greatest disorder."

These appear gross exaggerations. Joseph B. Kershaw, whose ad-hoc brigade of infantry and artillery approached Cub Run following Radford's attack, reported that before he arrived, the cavalry had been forced to retire. If so, Radford would have lacked the time to gather up as many spoils as he claimed. As Kershaw pointed out, the chaos at Cub Run was less the result of the cavalry's efforts than the simple fact that too many soldiers tried to cross the bridge at the same time: "The reserve [rear guard] which we were pursuing, meeting the main body of the enemy coming by the other road [from Sudley Springs] just at the entrance of the bridge, completely blocked it."[17]

Captain Finch, whose 2nd Ohio formed a part of Tyler's rear guard, would claim that while a small body of horsemen bore down on the Federals just short of Cub Run, "they were easily driven off, to appear no more." The brigade of which the regiment was a part, Schenck's, lost only two men killed when sparring with the cavalry, suggesting that Finch was justified in downplaying Radford's accomplishments.[18]

Schenck would claim that his brigade ably warded off a pursuit by several thousand Confederates, but at day's end his ability to avoid contact with the enemy remained intact. Upon first learning of his army's retreat, Schenck might have remained at Stone Bridge to form a shield behind which the rest of the army could reach Centreville without molestation, but he was intent on getting to the rear as quickly as possible. Upon reaching Washington, he proudly informed his family that although hard pressed, his command remained "altogether unscathed."[19]

If Radford's cavalry accomplished anything of substance, it appears to have been the work of a battalion-size detachment under Lieutenant Colonel Thomas T. Munford. This provisional organization included only one squadron from Munford's regiment, the 30th Virginia Cavalry: Companies D (Captain Giles W. B. Hale) and

F (Captain John S. Langhorne) plus two companies of independent Virginia horsemen led by Captains Dulany Ball of the Chesterfield Light Dragoons and William Henry Fitzhugh Payne of the legendary Black Horse Troop. This command did not accompany Radford or coordinate operations with him. According to some sources, Munford began his pursuit—at the order of Colonel Lay of Bonham's staff—from a location near the original position of Cocke's brigade; other, less credible accounts have him starting out from the Sudley Road. Munford himself stated that he received Lay's order just after 5:00 P.M., a short time after the six companies under Radford had taken up the chase.[20]

Captain Langhorne reported that Munford's pursuit was conducted "with spirit and alacrity." The battalion reached the turnpike in advance of Kershaw's infantry and Kemper's artillery, about a half mile east of where Radford had attacked. There the troopers plowed into a disorganized mass of stragglers. According to a Black Horse trooper, "the attack threw the Federals, already in confusion, into greater terror, caused them to abandon several pieces of artillery, many wagons, and several carriages in which congressmen and others had come out from Washington to see the promised Federal walk over."

The distressed Yankees offered up some twenty prisoners before a volley from some roadside woods wounded two cavalrymen and disabled four horses, persuading Munford to abandon the turnpike. Only now did he discover the presence of Kershaw and Kemper farther west. At first he mistook them for enemy forces, making him fear that he had been cut off from his own army. It would seem that the error was a shared one; the volley that ripped into Munford's column appears to have come from one of Kershaw's regiments, whose men had mistaken the cavalry for Yankees. Upon discovering the source of the error, Munford collected his well-scattered command, regained the turnpike, and reported to Kershaw, whose artillery had begun shelling the Cub Run bridge. At this point Munford had direct charge of only Payne's and Ball's companies. The whereabouts of the other units remain uncertain, although at least some troopers had proceeded toward Cub Run, apparently without orders.

Munford held Payne and Ball in check until Kemper's battery had ceased firing, whereupon the lieutenant colonel cautiously approached the bridge, Kershaw's infantry covering his rear. Captain Payne later wrote that the squadron advanced more than a mile "in front of any other arm of the service at the time." Nearing the west side of the run in falling darkness, Munford was surprised to come upon Major John Scott.[21]

A cofounder of the Black Horse Troop, Scott held a nebulous position in the Confederate ranks, having severed his connection with the unit at war's commencement. As far as Munford knew, the man was not affiliated with the 30th Virginia in any capacity. Yet by someone's authority Scott had taken charge of Company K of the Radford Rangers, commanded by Captain Eugene Davis. Munford supposed that Scott had gone to the bridge in hopes of laying claim to many of the weapons, especially the cannons, that had been abandoned there. In his report of the affair, he criticized the major for having "lost or dismissed his command before I arrived." Yet one of Munford's own men later reported that Scott, with twenty members of Davis's company, had already crossed Cub Run in hopes of extending the pursuit. The horsemen had returned rather abruptly after a sizeable body at the end of the retreat column turned around and leveled a volley that doused Scott's enthusiasm for chastising the enemy.[22]

Assuming command of Scott's unit and all other horsemen on the scene, Munford found little to do except gather up a king's ransom in spoils, including not only miscellaneous arms and equipment but also entire batteries of artillery complete with caissons, limbers, wagons, forges, and other resources. The greatest prize was Lieutenant Hains's Parrott rifle. Hains and his crew had managed to haul the monster gun across the bridge only to lose it on the other bank. Hoping to avoid the crush of soldiers and overturned wagons jamming up the turnpike, the lieutenant attempted to pull the gun up a wooded hillside. Halfway to the top, it sank in the spongy earth and could not be extricated. Frustrated beyond measure, Hains spiked and abandoned a weapon that should never have been brought on the battlefield in the first place. The 30-pounder had been fired at intervals throughout the day but had failed to inflict damage commensurate with its range and power. Tapping its potential would now rest with the Confederate artillery.[23]

There seemed to be enough spoils to go around, but Munford would complain that Major Scott appropriated several of the abandoned cannons and carried them off (by what means no one knows) before he could be stopped. Munford managed to seize additional ordnance, including the 30-pounder, which should have been sufficient compensation for any other prizes denied him. The work of

maneuvering these and more moveable captures to the rear continued under evening darkness long after the last able-bodied Yankee
had raced off to Centreville.[24]

While the troops on the Confederate left enjoyed opportunities to
harass and harm their fleeing adversaries, comrades on the far right,
within striking distance of Centreville, were in an even more advantageous position to overtake the Yankees short of a safe haven. In
this sector too, no substantial damage was inflicted on McDowell's
fugitives, partially as the result of the timidity and perhaps even
cowardice of a pursuit commander.

After having been ordered across Blackburn's Ford and then back
again with infuriating frequency, James Longstreet had been told by
army headquarters to "hold my position *only*." When, sometime
after four o'clock, word reached him that the Federals were in retreat,
his brigade was once again ordered forward, this time in pursuit.
Crossing Bull Run for the fifth time that day, he advanced toward
Centreville in hopes of finally seeing some action. Longstreet moved
at the head of his four Virginia regiments, the 5th North Carolina
having been left behind to guard the ford and the brigade's bivouac.
Garnett's section of artillery and Whitehead's cavalry "were at once
put in pursuit, followed as rapidly as possible by the infantry."

Since Jones had not yet returned from the valley of Little Rocky
Run, and because the brigades of Ewell, Early, and Holmes were long
gone from the right flank, only Longstreet and, to his left, the brigade of Milledge Bonham—that part of it that had not gone to the
left flank under Kershaw—were available to spearhead the pursuit.
According to Longstreet's postwar account, Bonham was supposed
to advance on a parallel road toward Cub Run, a path he diverged
from upon encountering "some obstructions to his march." Instead
of going ahead on his own, Bonham joined Longstreet on the
Centreville road, which thereby became quite crowded and hardly
conducive to mobility. For his part Bonham claimed to have been
ordered not to Cub Run but to Centreville. Upon reaching the direct
road to the village, he as senior officer took charge of Longstreet's
troops as well as his own.[25]

Almost as soon as they crossed the run, the combined force
discovered that Davies, Richardson, and Hunt had evacuated their
positions of the morning and early afternoon and had pulled back
closer to Centreville. "We set out in double quick time with a shot

at every step," wrote one of Bonham's officers, "and we went up to the ground where the enemies guns had been planted and from where they had been shooting at us all day—but they had made good their escape with the exception of a few poor fellows who I suppose were scared too bad to run and who we made prisoners."[26]

Obviously, the Federals had departed in some haste. The camps they had abandoned, wrote Longstreet, contained "pots and kettles over the fire, with food cooking; quarters of beef hanging on the trees, and wagons by the roadside loaded, some with bread and general provisions, others with ammunition." Some of Bonham's men broke ranks to wolf down an unexpected dinner or replenish empty haversacks. It is doubtful that the strict disciplinarian Longstreet had the same problem with his men, at least not to the same degree.

Their ranks now somewhat thinned by stragglers, both brigades pressed onward in the fading light. Eventually, they approached the new Union line that faced toward both the Mitchell's Ford and Blackburn's Ford roads. Longstreet, determining that he was within artillery range of the enemy, had Garnett's gunners take up an advantageous position while deploying his foot soldiers on the right side of the Centreville road. He was about to open with his guns when a courier reached Bonham with a report—from whose headquarters Longstreet does not say—warning that, instead of fleeing, the Yankees were moving to attack the extreme Confederate right. Longstreet, who knew a retreat when he saw one, denounced the report as absurd, and it was. No Union attack was underway on any part of the battlefield; the Army of Northeastern Virginia had fought itself into a stupor.[27]

Historians seem to agree that the phantom attackers were D. R. Jones's troops returning from their unfortunate encounter with Major Hunt and his infantry friends. Given the myriad movements of Union troops within sight of the lower fords on Bull Run, however, it is impossible to categorically accept the long-held view that the misidentification of this brigade is what halted pursuit efforts. The overeager observers on the Confederate right may have been reacting not to Jones's movements, which should have been easily identified as those of a friendly force, but to those of the Federals below Centreville in response to the conflicting orders of Miles and McDowell.

When discussing the incident in his *Military Operations*, Beauregard, perhaps unwittingly, deepens the mystery. He states that the initial report—that McDowell's reserves "in considerable force, had penetrated our lines at Union Mills Ford, and were marching on Manassas"—originated with Jones's adjutant general, who relayed it to Major Rhett of Johnston's staff, who in turn alerted Beauregard. If the source of the report was one of Jones's aides, his brigade could not have triggered the rumor of an attack toward Union Mills—it had to have come from an outside source never positively identified.[28]

Before Longstreet could persuade Bonham that the report of a Yankee offensive was false, Major Whiting of Johnston's staff rode up and ordered Garnett not to fire. When a skeptical Longstreet asked if the army commander himself had issued the order, Whiting replied, "No; but I take the responsibility to give it." Longstreet was inclined to shell the enemy regardless of Whiting's interference when Bonham ordered him not to. Since he was "the ranking officer present," Longstreet realized that "this settled the question."[29]

According to his aide G. Moxley Sorrel, Longstreet did not acquiesce with a quiet sigh but flew into "a fine rage. He dashed his hat furiously on the ground, stamped, and bitter words escaped him." Returned to their former positions along Bull Run, both brigades "slept on our arms the balance of the night." Upon hearing the details of the incident, Lieutenant Goree pinned the failure to strike Centreville on the unprofessionalism of Bonham, "who could not realize that the enemy was so completely routed and disorganized." Longstreet, Goree wrote, knew "from experience how utterly impossible it was to rally a demoralized army . . . , [but] Bonham (being a civilian and politician) could not understand it." Less charitable commentators faulted Bonham for faintheartedness rather than inexperience. Captain Alexander opined that the South Carolinian was paralyzed by the heavy responsibility that had come to rest on his shoulders: "From all accounts of the condition of the enemy at this time, had Bonham even stood still and fired blank cartridges to make a great roar and pretend that he was coming, the panic at Centreville would have been doubled."[30]

Although the incident rankled him severely, in his after-action report Longstreet downplayed its significance. Bonham's report contained no mention of it. In explanation of his inaction in the face of the enemy's retreat, the senior brigadier stated that by the time his and Longstreet's men were in position to menace Centreville, it was too dark to do so effectively. After about a half hour, he ordered both brigades back to their camps "to refresh themselves." Some regiments were more refreshed than others. The 3rd South Carolina bivouacked at midnight in an oak grove in which the civilian specta- tors of the battle had parked their carriages. Many vehicles remained on the field, some of them loaded with good things to eat and drink. "We were tired and hungry," recalled an enlisted man in the 3rd, "and imagine what a feast we had that night!"[31]

Though the aborted pursuit had a happy ending for some of Bonham's men, their commander had squandered a precious and irrecoverable opportunity to check the flight of McDowell's army in midcareer and bottle it up before it could escape.

Of all the forces involved in running the Army of Northeastern Virginia to earth, perhaps the most persistent were Kershaw's two regiments of infantry and Kemper's Alexandria Light Artillery. Once it became evident that not only the Union right flank but McDowell's entire line had given way, Kershaw set out to cut off the Federals on the turnpike before they could cross Stone Bridge. His own 2nd South Carolina and the 8th South Carolina of Colonel Cash trudged along the pike, stopping repeatedly to clear it of obstructions and seize abandoned arms and equipment.

Kershaw was accompanied briefly by Colonel Preston's 28th Virginia, which had supported the South Carolinian's operations against Chinn Ridge. Within minutes of starting out, however, Preston's regiment veered off the pike, and Kershaw forged onward without it. Under orders from Beauregard to "scour the woods beyond," the 28th marched to the Stone House, which had been con- verted into a field hospital. After making prisoners of the wounded, two surgeons, and thirty-six other able-bodied occupants, Preston led his regiment as far north as the scene of Evans's early morning fight with Burnside. Of course this sector was now free of Federals except their dead. Finding no one to fight, the white-bearded colonel returned his men to Stone Bridge and then to Mitchell's Ford, where they spent a night of regret over their inability to further chastise the fleeing, frightened enemy.[32]

After Preston's troops went their own way, Kershaw's column crossed Stone Bridge. Just beyond, it was joined by another element of Cocke's brigade, the 18th Virginia, which had been advancing ahead of and parallel to the South Carolinians. Accompanying Colonel Withers was what remained of the Hampton Legion, which despite thinned ranks and all manner of battle scars, continued to soldier on.

A little farther up the road, the suddenly enlarged force encountered a "reserve of the enemy," including at least one cannon, sheltered in a woods. Kershaw promptly formed line of battle, his and Cash's outfits in front, Captain Conner's legionnaires on their left, and Withers's Virginians in rear. As the self-promotive Kershaw noted in his operational report (which he managed to publish in a Charleston newspaper before submitting it to Beauregard), he had pursued the Yankees strictly on his own enterprise, consumed with the thought of halting them short of Centreville. Now, however, his will began to weaken just a bit. Suddenly, he decided that he required orders from the high command; to this end he sent a courier to locate Colonel Chesnut, Beauregard's aide and Kershaw's close friend, explaining his situation and asking how he should proceed.

While awaiting word, Kershaw skirmished with the enemy at long range. At this time he unexpectedly gained support from the cavalry company that Major Scott had appropriated (he mistook Scott's unit for a squadron). The horsemen had been conducted to the forefront of the pursuit by Major Clement D. Hill, a supply officer on Beauregard's staff who wanted a taste of combat. In addition to reinforcements Hill brought word that his boss had "authorized the pursuit of the enemy with a view to cut them off." Kershaw claimed that he immediately formed a "column by company" and resumed the advance.[33]

The delay had enabled most of Tyler's division, including the reserve force that had halted Kershaw, to move up the turnpike and across Cub Run. Soon after starting up again, Kershaw was stopped a second time, now by an order from Beauregard delivered by E. P. Alexander. About 6:00 P.M., presumably in reply to the colonel's request for instructions, the army commander had told his signal chief to cross Stone Bridge, locate the South Carolinian, and "order him to advance very carefully and not to attack." To make sure he understood correctly, Alexander asked if Kershaw should withhold attacking "under *any circumstances, no matter what* the condition of the enemy in his front?" Beauregard supplied a clarification: "Kemper's battery has been ordered to join him. Let him wait for it to come up. Then he can pursue, but cautiously, and he must not attack unless he has a decided advantage."

Alexander caught up with Kershaw at or near Mrs. Spindle's house. Kershaw had halted again, this time under artillery fire from unionists on the far side of Cub Run. The colonel's force now consisted of the two South Carolina regiments and the Hampton Legion, Withers's regiment having been left near Stone Bridge. (After idling there for a time, the 18th Virginia would be called to Manassas Junction to defend against an expected attack that never materialized.) After hearing from Alexander, Kershaw agreed to hold his position until Kemper arrived—the only thing to do under the circumstances.

Beauregard's desire for caution had a familiar source. After leaving Kershaw to return to army headquarters, Alexander met Lieutenant Ferguson of Beauregard's staff, who explained that the Creole had been reacting to Major Rhett's report of a Union advance toward Union Mills. Ferguson, like Longstreet, doubted the accuracy of the report, but as he reminded Alexander, orders were orders.[34]

Upon reaching Mrs. Spindle's, Kershaw captured a field hospital the Federals had set up there. He also came upon the littered field where Radford's Rangers had clashed with the Union rear guard; Radford's wounded brother was there, barely clinging to life. There too, Kershaw, peering eastward, spied a wealth of potential targets: hundreds, perhaps thousands, of fugitives pouring into the turnpike at the end of their extended journey from Sudley Springs.

Artillery was the preferred instrument to exploit this opportunity; it arrived shortly after six o'clock in the form of Captain Kemper and a section of his battery. At Kershaw's order Kemper unlimbered on a hill about a mile south of the pike that commanded the Cub Run bridge. To protect the guns, Kershaw advanced a company of his regiment as skirmishers under the immediate command of the bellicose quartermaster, Major Hill. The skirmishers made contact with the rear of the retreating army, taking a few prisoners and in turn freeing a Yankee captive, Lieutenant Colonel Steuart of the 1st Maryland.

When the Federals surged eastward, Kershaw moved the rest of his regiment, along with Cash's outfit in its entirety and the Hampton Legion, onto the hill Kemper occupied. The captain had trained one of his guns on the Cub Run bridge, the other on the troops emerging into the turnpike from the north. An admiring Kershaw remarked that both delivered a "most disastrous" fire on the enemy.[35]

Another legend of the battle was born when Kemper permitted Edmund Ruffin, who had attached himself to the battery in hopes of getting a crack at the damned Yankees, to fire the first shot. Yanking a lanyard, the white-maned Virginian who only three months earlier had ceremoniously fired on Fort Sumter, sent a shell arching toward the bridge. Not having aimed the shot, Ruffin could not take credit for its accuracy, but he gloried in the result. It exploded in the air above the heads of foot soldiers and wagon teamsters, killing a horse and causing the wagon it had been pulling, loaded with barrels of rations, to overturn. A Confederate who later examined the scene concluded that after the wagon went sprawling, the rest of its team became unmanageable, turned about, and ran backward, dragging the vehicle for some distance: "This cut the wagon squarely across the road with its front end up Cub Run."[36]

According to a vastly pleased Ruffin, the resulting bottleneck "effectually precluded any other wheel-carriage or horse, from moving on. The whole mass of fugitives immediately got out of track, & all escaped who could, on foot & as quickly as possible." As soldiers bunched up on the pursuers' side of the span, they created further chaos, forming, as Kershaw wrote, "a barricade with cannon, caissons, ambulances, wagons, and other vehicles. . . . Many of the soldiers threw their arms into the creek, and everything indicated the greatest possible panic."[37]

As Ruffin stepped back, Kemper's gunners sent a dozen more shells at the bridge. One Federal called the result "utmost consternation." Many struck human targets, killing and maiming soldiers who had jumped into the waist-high stream in hopes of paddling to safety. "The slaughter of men and horses here was terrible," wrote Private Partridge of the 13th New York. The 2nd Rhode Island's Elisha Rhodes was horrified to see the upper body of a comrade, struck by a direct hit, fly through the air. Captain Otis H. Tillinghast of McDowell's staff, a former artilleryman who had voluntarily served with Griffin's battery on Henry Hill, lay bleeding on the approach to the bridge, crying hysterically to a wife he would never see again.[38]

Erasmus Keyes would pen one of the most evocative descriptions of this retreat turned to rout: "Cavalry horses without riders, artillery horses disengaged from the guns with traces flying, wrecked baggage wagons, and pieces of artillery drawn by six horses without drivers, flying at their utmost speed and whacking against other vehicles, soldiers scattered everywhere, running, some without guns or caps. I saw men throw down their muskets with a gesture as violent as they would throw off a venomous snake. The rush produced a noise like a hurricane at sea."[39]

Kemper fired for less than a half hour before he and most of Kershaw's infantry fell back, at Beauregard's order, to Stone Bridge. The panic caused by the shelling had not abated, however, it had merely shifted eastward. The special correspondent of the *Times* of London, whose breathless coverage of the battle and its aftermath would gain him the nickname "Bull Run" Russell, reported that "all the road[s] from Centreville for miles presented such a sight as can only be witnessed in the track of the runaways of an utterly demoralized army. Drivers flogged, lashed, spurred, and beat their horses, or leaped down and abandoned their teams and ran by the side of the road; mounted men, servants, and men in uniform, vehicles of all sorts, commissariat wagons, thronged the narrow ways." The traffic snarl only increased the all-consuming panic: "Men literally screamed with rage and fright when their way was blocked up."[40]

Russell's American colleagues also expressed outrage at the sight of soldiers trampling one another in their panicky search for safety. A *New York Tribune* reporter declared that in the mad dash to the rear, "all sense of manhood seemed to be forgotten." A correspondent for the *New York World* heard officers cursing their fleeing men as cowards and skulkers, but the same epithets could be applied to the men with shoulder straps: "Majors and colonels, who had deserted their commands pass[ed] me galloping as if for dear life." That evening it was rumored that a Massachusetts colonel was found three miles in advance of his routed regiment.[41]

It may be assumed that the great majority of McDowell's officers did not join their men in terror-stricken flight. Even so, they keenly felt the guilt that accompanied defeat and demoralization. Colonel Sherman spoke for a host of colleagues when he wrote home: "I was under heavy fire for hours, touched on the knee and shoulder . . . and cannot imagine how I escaped except to experience the mortification of retreat, rout, confusion and abandonment by whole regiments. . . . I have read of retreats before, have seen the noise and confusion of crowds of men at fires and shipwrecks, but nothing like this. It was as disgraceful as words can portray, but I doubt if volunteers from any quarter can do better." When his fellow brigade commander Keyes reached Washington after twenty-seven hours in the saddle and threw himself down on his cot, "Sherman came into my tent. His countenance was that of a disappointed man. After resting in silence twenty minutes, he arose and departed. I am not certain whether Sherman had troops or company with him or not."[42]

Other soldiers—those caught up in the rout and those who had avoided it but heard lurid accounts of it—adopted a more understanding and forgiving view of the phenomenon. "When men get stampeded," a Michigan corporal observed, "they have no more reason than a dumb animal, not even as much as some animals. They become mere selfish brutes." Colonel Sylvanus Thayer, former superintendent of the U.S. Military Academy, who learned of the retreat from some of his former students, observed: "Let one division be driven to rout and the whole pack will run like children from an apple orchard when set upon by dogs." Writing to his brother a few days after the battle, the wounded Lieutenant Ames of Griffin's battery tried to put a historical context to the army-wide skedaddle: "The best European troops have time and again been panic-stricken and fled in the most disorderly and cowardly manner."[43]

Combatants were not the only ones who fled in terror and despair. Correspondent Russell, for one, lingered on the fringes of the battlefield until caught up in the retreat. Belatedly turning to depart, he discovered that the buggy, team, and driver he had left behind at Centreville had bolted for Washington. Astride a borrowed horse, he made his way through the throng of soldiers, wagons, and civilian conveyances to Fairfax Court House. From there he cantered "up hills, down valleys, with the silent grim woods forever by my side," until by eleven o'clock, he made his way to Washington. He entered the city via Long Bridge after a testy confrontation with an officer of Runyon's rear guard. The circumstances surrounding his leave-taking would inspire some controversy. Russell claimed that he departed the battlefield with composure and dignity intact. Northern correspondents, envious of his reputation and angered by his condemnation of Union-army ineptitude and cowardice, would contend that he fled in the same state of panic and dishevelment as those he accused of showing the white feather.[44]

Matthew Brady was also swept up in the flood of escapees. Some accounts portray him as becoming separated from his companions, helplessly lost in unfamiliar surroundings, and wandering alone without food or water for three days. But a self-portrait of Brady, taken in his Washington studio, bears the date July 22, 1861. Other reports of his postbattle activities are similarly dubious. He would claim that by the time he fled, most of the photographic equipment he had hauled to Bull Run had been damaged, forcing him to leave it behind. Supposedly, the lost items included wet plates of views taken of the battlefield. Present-day scholars caution that little is known of what apparatus he may have brought from Washington, and they doubt that he had the time and opportunity to make any images at all. All that is certain is that the artistic ambition of the little man in the goatee and spectacles was forced to wait until a battle fourteen months later provided him with a Union-held battlefield whose horrors he could record at his leisure. The resulting public exhibition in his New York studio of these views, mostly of Confederate corpses, entitled "The Dead of Antietam," would gain him initial recognition as America's first photohistorian.[45]

The experiences of the members of Congress among the spectators at Centreville were, like Brady's, physically and psychologically distressing. Not content to observe the proceedings at a distance, at some point early in the day a coterie of senators and congressmen took up a vantage point on an elevation overlooking Stone Bridge. These adventurous souls, later joined by small groups of less distinguished spectators, included Senators Wilson, Wade, and Lane; Congressmen Riddell, Washburne, and Ely; and Judge McCook and his son. Although its numbers would later be exaggerated, the group, no more than fifty in all, represented less than 10 percent of the war watchers at and near Centreville. But as the afternoon wore on and the fighting heated up in tune with the temperature, some of the politicos assumed extramilitary duties in the mode of Governor Sprague. Congressman Washburne, for one, took it upon himself to reconnoiter for those troops of Schenck's brigade positioned nearest the bridge.

Some of the august gentlemen retained their perch near the bridge even after the army began to retire. Thus they had a close-up view of the chaos that subsequently erupted. Some, including Senator Wilson and Congressman Riddle, were so outraged that they shouted for the fugitives to halt and turn back, even attempting to block their escape. Their efforts went for naught, for no fear-crazed soldier was prepared to respond to the upbraiding of a civilian no matter how lofty his station. Eventually, senators and congressmen gave up the effort and joined the surging tide of defeat.[46]

Among the congressional delegation, Alfred Ely suffered the most ignominious fate. Having assumed an exposed position in advance of his colleagues, the New York representative found himself cut off and surrounded when, about six o'clock, Kershaw's pursuers advanced up the turnpike. Found huddling behind a tree,

Ely was taken captive by a member of the 8th South Carolina and hauled before his colonel. E. B. C. Cash was plainly outraged that a Republican official—especially one armed with a small revolver—had come out (as Johnston and Beauregard would later express it in their victory proclamation) "to witness the immolation of this Army and the subjugation of our people." Having just delivered Beauregard's order for Kershaw to pursue with caution, Captain Alexander was on hand to witness the "red headed, red faced" Cash screaming at his prisoner and threatening to shoot him: "You infernal son of a bitch! You came to see the fun did you? God damn your dirty soul I'll show you."

Cash tried mightily to get a bead on his prisoner, who, "scared almost into a fit," tried to hide behind the sergeant in whose custody he had been placed. Only when Alexander and other officers begged the colonel not to harm the prisoner and warned him of the consequences did he agree to turn Ely over to the provost detail. The congressman's devout wife had warned him against having anything to do with a battle fought on a Sabbath. Ely would not see her again for nearly six months, the length of his confinement in Libby Prison.[47]

The war-watchers of Bull Run would be pilloried not only for sharing in the panic that had produced the disgraceful rout but also for helping produce, or at least worsen, it. The public's perception of noncombatants munching sandwiches and sipping wine on a bloody battlefield helped promote the myth that the civilians impeded the army's withdrawal, worsening traffic jams and spreading terror throughout the retreating column. A Confederate officer heard that "the stampede among the ladies and Congress members was as great as it was among the soldiers. . . . [T]he screams of the ladies was frightful indeed for so eager were the men to get off that they ran off and left the ladies to shift for themselves." In their haste to depart, another Rebel reported, the female spectators left dignity behind along with "many hoop skirts on the way side."[48]

These sensationalistic charges, while in tune with their general portrayal of the civilians at Centreville, were unfounded. The majority of the spectators (including the few females among them) left the battlefield in orderly fashion before the real terror set in. After extensive study, John Hennessy has found that "the panic was a military, not a civilian, event. . . . The civilians in fact affected (or were affected by) events that day very little indeed."[49]

When McDowell's troops fled, they threw aside every imaginable species of impedimenta. Years later a Virginia officer recalled: "I was on many a hard-fought field afterwards, but never saw I a scene like that. Musket, knapsack—everything in fine that impedes flight—was thrown away." Riding with Stuart, John Mosby described the countryside for miles around the battlefield as "very much like Egypt after a flood of the Nile . . . strewn with the debris of McDowell's army." The amount of booty came as a shock to many lightly equipped Confederates. Lieutenant Pitts of the 3rd South Carolina marveled at the "provisions of all kinds" he scooped up from the ground in the enemy's path, "in fact everything that an invading army needed." McDowell's troops, he decided, were "much better prepared for care and comfort than we are."[50]

Many pursuers had not eaten at any time during the day; they greedily appropriated the rations they found in the castoff haversacks that seemed to appear magically every hundred feet or so. Officers' baggage—trunks full of fancy edibles and garments of all kinds—were found in some overturned wagons. Ragged Rebels were soon sporting new or lightly used hats, shirts, brogans, and boots, which they eagerly appropriated without regard to size, color, or the "U.S." markings stamped on belt buckles and knapsacks. That night many slept in "good oil cloths, blankets, &c."[51]

Officers' discards included official documents; General Bonham discovered an annotated map of the Bull Run crossings left behind by Major Barnard or one of his staff officers. Piles of personal correspondence also fell into the hands of the pursuers. Three days after the battle, Mosby observed, "we have been very much amused reading their letters—they were confident of wiping us out." Captain Alexander sent examples of such letters to his wife: "All varieties of them, some from *wives* to husbands," which he thought "Prish" would find especially interesting. According to Confederate congressman (and later brigadier general) Thomas R. R. Cobb of Georgia, many correspondents boasted of "hellish schemes of rapine, lust, and murder. . . . Such a set of devils never were [let] out of Hell." Other captured correspondence elicited a different reaction. A South Carolina lieutenant was impressed by those wives and sweethearts who urged their menfolk to fight until victory was won. "The language," he observed, "was that of the uneducated, but the spirit was simple, earnest, and pure, and would have done credit to our Southern women."[52]

Along with their rations, equipment, and personal items, hundreds of weary and demoralized Federals fell into enemy hands, in many cases more than their captors could properly handle. An English-born Confederate reported, with perhaps a dash of exaggeration, that a majority of those taken "were more dead than alive, men so pale and exhausted I never saw [before]. Their uniforms were in tatters; they were, for the most part, shoeless, hatless, and literally gasping for water. With hair disheveled, powder-begrimed and dusty faces, bloodshot eyes, and unstrung nerves, they were more the object of pity than derision."[53]

More pitiful still were the wounded and dying found in the field hospitals scattered around the battlefield. Especially gruesome was the scene at Sudley Church, where Surgeon Magruder and his assistants struggled to treat an overflow of patients who continued to pour in long after the battle wound down. "Blood trickled from the ambulances like water from an ice cart," wrote one visitor, "and directly in front of the church door was a large puddle of blood." Several Union surgeons volunteered to stay with the wounded and thus became prisoners of war. Allowed to continue to minister to their patients, in later days they were duly released and returned to their own army along with many of their charges. Those captured at Sudley Church included Assistant Surgeon George M. Sternberg, who thirty-two years hence would become surgeon general of the U.S. Army.[54]

From a purely military perspective, the most important spoils were not prisoners, edibles, or items of clothing but firearms and, to a lesser degree, swords and bayonets. Although 4,000 rifles and muskets, 500,000 rounds of small-arms ammunition, and 4,500 sets of accoutrements lay scattered about the field, the most substantial prize was the immense cache of heavy ordnance—twenty-seven guns of various types, models, and calibers, including the two 12-pounder boat howitzers of the 71st New York (the Federals would claim that no more than twenty-five guns were lost). Taken with them were almost 3,000 shells, thirty-seven caissons, six forges, four battery wagons, and sixty-four artillery horses.[55]

The sight of a field strewn with jettisoned armaments and dead horses paled in comparison to the acres of corpses in every species and color of clothing—so many bodies that it took six days to commit all of them to the earth. "I went over the field," a Georgia infantryman informed his father, "and I never saw the like of dead men in my life." A Virginian found corpses scattered "miles down the road beside[s] those that was lying in the battle field." Another Georgian wrote his sister, "Lizzie I saw Yankeys buried that was not covered up so but what you could [still] see them." A late-arriving Alabamian, taking his first tour of the ghastly field, was sickened by the smell of blood.[56]

A preponderance of bodies wore blue. They lay sprawled across almost six miles of blood-stained earth, in fields and pastures, under trees and in ditches, along fences and around farm buildings, and inside the field hospitals in rear of both armies. Under the summer sun, the bodies quickly became stiff and bloated, their skin blackened to the same hue as the slaves pressed into service as burial teams. To an enlisted man of the 3rd South Carolina, their faces appeared "quite different from those of ours, theirs having a haggard look, as of fear."[57]

The sight of still-living but suffering Federals evoked perhaps the strongest emotions in the observers. A Georgian wrote that "although they were our enemies the sight of the wounded men was enough to melt my heart in pity for them." Even Edmund Ruffin, who consigned every Yankee to hell, was unprepared for the sights he encountered when examining the field on July 22. Most of the fallen, he wrote in his journal, "lay quiet and motionless," many in grotesque postures of distress, feasted on by blowflies and other carrion. "Clotted blood, in what had been pools, [was] under or by every corpse. From bullet holes in the heads of some, the brains had partly oozed out. The white froth covering the mouths of others was scarcely less shocking." While revulsed, he was also unexpectedly moved by those bluecoats he found clinging to life, moaning softly or begging for water. Encountering a group of soldiers berating a wounded Federal, the rabid secessionist rebuked them. Though no one detested "the Northerners as a class" more than he, his hatred had been "silenced for the wounded, seen in this long continued and wretched state of suffering."[58]

It fell to the victors, who held the field at battle's close, to dispose of the dead. "We have to burry the Yankees today," a Confederate wrote, "to keep them from stinking us to death." This need posed an almost insurmountable problem. An Alabama enlisted man wrote that "there were so many Yankees that it was impossible for us to bury them very decently. Sometimes they would bury 40 or 50 in one grave." At other times even more would be interred as a group. On July 27 Captain Alexander watched as the last eighty-three corpses ("principally those red breeched New York Zouaves") were dumped in a single grave.[59]

When finally tabulated, the casualty counts for July 21 would drive home the intensity—indeed, the savagery—of the fighting on every part of the field. The reports prepared by McDowell and his subordinates show that out of about 13,000 troops engaged throughout the day, their army lost 481 officers and men killed, 1,011 wounded, and 1,216 missing. Many historians caution that these figures are incomplete and understated—for one thing, a careful count of prisoners of war by the Confederates came to more than 1,400 men.

Confederate figures, which lack full statistics for at least sixteen units, are even less complete and accurate. The numbers we have suggest that out of 14,000 troops engaged, the combined Rebel armies suffered 387 killed, 1,582 wounded, and 13 missing. (As Johnston was quick to point out in his official report, his army had absorbed nearly twice as many casualties as Beauregard's, indicating that the latecomers to Manassas had done the majority of the fighting and suffering on the twenty-first.) Despite their incompleteness, the numbers suggest that the Federals suffered almost 1,000 more casualties than their adversaries, a not-uncommon outcome for a pea-green army forced to fight on the offensive on ground of their enemy's choosing. The combined figures, modest enough in comparison to the battles to be waged in various theaters over the subsequent four years, were sufficient to shock both North and South into the realization that the country had embarked on a critical life-or-death struggle that would consume more blood and treasure than either section could afford.[60]

Late that afternoon—the consensus of historical opinion puts the time at about 5:00 P.M., though Johnston would insist it occurred hours after the fighting had ceased—a special train from Richmond arrived at Manassas Junction and deposited Jefferson Davis on the southern edge of the battlefield. Accompanied by his nephew and aide-de-camp Joseph R. Davis and an entourage of government officials, the president started on horseback for Johnston's headquarters, escorted by a cavalry troop. Though hopeful that he had arrived in time to witness victory, he began to fear the worst upon passing a seemingly endless procession of fugitives from the front, few of whom showed signs of having been wounded. The skulkers were wailing piteously that their comrades were being cut to pieces, and that all was lost. An ashen-faced Davis muttered to the escort leader: "Fields are not won where men desert their colors as ours are doing."[61]

Well before reaching the Lewis house, Davis's troubled mind was relieved. Met by several high-ranking officers, including Beauregard's adjutant Thomas Jordan, the president was assured that the Yankees had been beaten and were in full retreat. Made jubilant by the news, Davis tipped his hat to nearly every officer and man he encountered and shook hands with many. He profusely congratulated a number of organizations, supposedly including every regiment in Early's brigade. Its leader reported that in return the president "was received with great enthusiasm."[62]

Davis received an even-heartier reception from the six companies under Colonel Radford, who had returned to Portici following their exploits on the Warrenton Pike. An onlooker noted that "the cavalrymen, in great spirits, rode around the President, wrapped their flags bout him and almost pulled him off his horse in their enthusiasm." His Excellency experienced a different kind of thrill when Lieutenant Colonel Munford ceremoniously presented him with six of the cannons his men had carried off, including the 30-pounder Parrott.[63]

When Davis's party topped Henry Hill, it happened upon General Jackson, then having his wounded finger treated by a surgeon. "We have whipped them!" the newly christened Stonewall exulted. "They ran like sheep!" Supposedly, Jackson added, "Give me 5,000 fresh men, and I will be in Washington City to-morrow morning!" Few historians believe that Jackson's boast was sustainable, but none doubt that he uttered it.[64]

At the Lewis house Davis found Beauregard as well as Johnston. The trio shared in a round of congratulations, the generals gave their visitor a quick summary of the action, and everyone agreed to reconvene at a later hour, presumably to discuss ways in which the victory might be followed up. The president then resumed his ride and, guided by Colonel Chesnut and other members of Beauregard's staff, visited various parts of the battlefield. He later claimed that the group encountered an enemy battle line, which his escort charged and dispersed. Johnston would deny this could have happened, Davis having reached Portici long after the nearest Yankees had departed. It is possible that Davis witnessed at some distance the day's final actions when Confederate horsemen, rather than inflicting additional blows, were repulsed on the Warrenton Turnpike by Blenker's rear guard.[65]

After visiting with and orating before numerous other regiments, companies, and batteries, their men begrimed with sweat and powder stains and many spattered with blood (their own, their comrades', or their enemy's), but all in high spirits, Davis returned to Portici for a late-night conference with his commanders, whom he promised to shower with honors and Beauregard with a promotion to full general. The major topic of discussion was the viability of a large-scale pursuit of the beaten foe. Davis could see that the victorious armies were exhausted and in a disorganized state, although he did not seem to share his generals' view that they were in no condition to pursue anyone.

Davis desired that a concerted attempt be made to consolidate the victory, and he inquired which units were in the best shape and position to follow the enemy. He later claimed that when told that Bonham's troops were best positioned to do so, he directed that they be sent forth at once and even dictated an order to that effect. Neither Johnston nor Beauregard favored a nighttime march, so, according to Davis, the starting time was changed to "early dawn." Both generals, however, would later insist that no such agreement was reached and that no order was either modified or issued. Beauregard's impression was that the president dictated it to Colonel Jordan but that the adjutant destroyed it upon discovering "a unanimous decision against it." Jordan later confirmed this version of events.[66]

At some point the conference was interrupted by word that one of Beauregard's artillery officers, Lieutenant Robert C. Hill, had found Centreville—from which he had just returned after conducting a personal, unauthorized reconnaissance—free of the departing enemy. Brought to Portici, Hill reported that the Yankees, now totally demoralized, were making haste for Washington and warned that time to overtake them was slipping away. At first his high-level audience was impressed. As soon as the lieutenant was excused, Davis intended to order an immediate pursuit until someone in attendance—Johnston himself, as Davis recalled—mentioned that the informant had such a reputation for eccentricity and exaggeration that his nickname in the army had been "Crazy Hill." Called to the conference, Captain Alexander, who had attended West Point with Hill, reluctantly confirmed the characterization. He would always regret that when he had finished speaking, everyone "laughed heartily" at the man's expense. From then on, no one was willing to act on Hill's word. For his part, Alexander never believed that his schoolmate scouted as far as Centreville, although later he decided that the town had been evacuated within hours of Hill's report.[67]

The aggressive pursuit that Davis claimed he urged on his generals never materialized. His modified order was not issued, although he would claim that a draft similar in content went out to General Bonham and Colonel Cocke. Supposedly, Bonham was directed to dispatch toward Centreville two infantry regiments supported by a strong force of cavalry and a battery "as early as practicable in the morning." Cocke was to send a force about equal in size across Bull Run at Stone Bridge and a second column by the road to Sudley Ford.

In later years Davis cited this order as a basis for his claim that he had directed a general pursuit. Beauregard agreed that some such document had been drafted but denied that it was anything but a directive to reconnoiter toward Sudley Ford and Centreville, gathering up the wounded and the spoils of victory. None of this mattered in the long run, for early on the morning of the twenty-second, a heavy rain "extraordinary for its violence and duration" began to fall. The storm continued through the day, burying the roads in enough mud to impede any movement. A few units started out in hopes of locating any Federals lingering in the area, only to be recalled and returned to camp.[68]

A second war council, convened by the president that evening, failed to produce additional progress. Davis recalled that both Johnston and Beauregard were opposed to a large-scale pursuit, fearing the time for it had passed. The Washington defenses, Johnston argued, were too strong to attack with any hope of success. Beauregard agreed that the army had exhausted itself "by marches and countermarches" and lacked enough supplies to press a pursuit and enough wagons to transport what was on hand. Davis claimed that one or both generals even raised the possibility, however remote, that Patterson would aid McDowell in holding the capital. At last persuaded that nothing more could be done, the president made plans to return next day to Richmond, there to spread the glad tidings of victory and to advocate legislation to increase the size and efficiency of the Confederate forces in Virginia.[69]

CHAPTER 17

THE FRUITS OF VICTORY
AND DEFEAT

For years afterward, legions of Southerners believed, or at least argued, that the war would have been won had the Confederate hierarchy nerved itself to deliver a finishing blow to a critically wounded adversary. One early proponent of this view, Colonel Gibbons of the 10th Virginia, wrote his sister six days after the battle: "I should like to hear the order to march to Washington for I don't believe until that place is taken, or leveled in ashes, that we can hope for peace." A company-grade officer, also a Virginian, agreed that only a movement on the Federal capital would leave "the Lincoln administration . . . paralyzed in its tracks" and amenable to suing for peace. Yet not every soldier looked forward to carrying the war inside Yankeedom. A member of the 7th Georgia, whose regiment had suffered dreadfully in the battle, wrote his sister: "The truth is there is none of us is . . . anxious to get into another fight (officers not excluded)." Lieutenant Pitts of the 3rd South Carolina told his fiancée that the army's next move appeared to be an advance against Arlington Heights or Alexandria, "and if so I tremble for the result for I assure you that many, very many of us have seen our homes and friends for the last time."[1]

Ubiquitous signs indicated that the Confederates were incapable of anything more than savoring their triumph. They might reestablish their communication links to Fairfax Court House and perhaps Fall Church, but they were in no condition to range beyond those outposts. Colonel Richard Taylor, whose 9th Louisiana Infantry joined Beauregard a few days after the battle, recalled that "the confusion that reigned about our camps for the next few days was extreme. Regiments seemed to have lost their colonels, colonels their regiments. Men of all arms and all commands were mixed in the wildest way. A constant fusillade of small arms and singing of bullets were kept up, indicative of a superfluity of disorder, if not of ammunition."

As late as ten days after the fighting, E. P. Alexander reported, "our army is nearly disorganized now for any offensive movements."[2]

Postwar opinion as to whether the Confederates should have, or could have, advanced on the enemy's lines along the Potomac was decidedly mixed. When he wrote his memoirs, Captain Alexander seems to have forgotten his earlier assessment of his army's postbattle capabilities. In a lengthy recounting of his war service not published until 1989, Alexander roundly criticized the Confederate high command for not assuming the offensive as soon as possible:

> The battle was treated as over as soon as the Federals retreated across Bull Run. It should have then been considered as just beginning—our part of it. It was, up to that time, the *enemy's fight*. They began it & were aggressive & we defended. Now it was the time for our aggression, & there was plenty of time to do a lot before dark & a good moon to help after dark. One of our two generals should have crossed Bull Run at Stone Bridge with every man he could raise in that vicinity, & the other gone to Mitchell's Ford & crossed with all the forces in that vicinity & pushed for Centreville. Then they would have promptly discovered how utterly demoralized the enemy was. As it was they never realized it fully at least for a day.[3]

In later years James Longstreet believed that "a favorable aspect for fruitful results" existed had the army been equal to the opportunity: "The supplies of subsistence, ammunition, and forage passed as we marched through the enemy's camps towards Centreville seemed ample to carry the Confederate army on to Washington. Had the fight been continued to that point, the troops, in their high hopes, would have marched in terrible effectiveness against the demoralized Federals." In later weeks the Confederates established outposts as far north as Munson's and Mason's Hills, within easy reach of Falls Church, but Longstreet regretted that they had not been extended to Abraham Lincoln's front door.[4]

Other ranking officers were just as convinced that a movement on Washington would have failed. A well-considered argument against a drive to the Potomac was advanced by Jubal Early, albeit long after the war when hindsight was its clearest. The feisty Virginian, who normally favored aggressive action, had adopted the view of Joe Johnston that the victorious armies were too inefficient, too poorly supplied, and insufficiently mobile to undertake such an operation. Then too, the defenses of Washington were manned by more troops than Johnston and Beauregard could have hurled against them. Early believed the defenders numbered as many as 50,000 men, including numerous elements of McDowell's army that had retained their organization and recent reinforcements. The most any attack might have achieved was occupation of the capital's suburbs: "Alexandria would probably have fallen into our hands without a struggle, and we might have forced the enemy to evacuate his works south of the Potomac, but very likely not until after a fight in which our loss would have been greater than the object to be accomplished would have justified. We might have transferred our line to the banks of the Potomac, but we could not have held it, and would eventually have been compelled to abandon it."[5]

Whether the Washington fortifications of the time were truly strong enough to withstand attack would generate much heat but little light in the days, weeks, and years after the battle. When he wrote (or cowrote) his *Military Operations*, Beauregard claimed that Washington was "entirely unprotected," its fortifications too few and too weak to prevent capture by a well-organized, well-armed, and well-supplied force—something, however, that the Confederates in Virginia lacked at the time. Writing in 1868, his adjutant, Colonel Jordan, advanced the argument that while the forts guarding Washington might have been vulnerable to a well-coordinated assault, the Potomac bridges that gave access to the capital were heavily guarded. Even should the Confederates find a way to cross, the wooden structures could easily be taken up or set afire before an attack hit home.[6]

Sixteen years after Bull Run, General Bonham, who had hoped to be among the first Confederate officers to enter Washington, opined in a letter to Beauregard that although the capital's defenses were too strong to be taken by direct attack, they might have fallen to a strike from the rear via an invasion of Maryland, a move the victors at Manassas should have attempted. This was a reversal of the point he had made to Governor Pickens a month before the battle: "I am by no means certain that we ought to attempt to take Washington, we have no use for it, do not want it, can not keep it, & ought not to destroy it."[7]

The military and political leaders who had the power to order an "On to Washington" movement seemed to have agreed, at least at the time of their postbattle conferences, that a general advance was neither feasible nor in the best interests of the Confederacy. Twenty years later, however, when historians attempted to determine when and where the Lost Cause had been lost, Jefferson Davis suggested that he had expected a more aggressive pursuit of the enemy. At least one of his early biographers, who had received the president's assistance with, and approval of, his work, stated that before leaving Manassas to return to Richmond, Davis had advocated the most vigorous pursuit possible, a claim that Johnston in his *Narrative of Military Operations* vehemently denied. In his own memoirs Beauregard insisted that Davis neither opposed nor hindered plans for a rapid and concerted pursuit; in fact "he desired it." But the president had not pressed the issue or set in motion any forward movement.[8]

At the same time, Beauregard tried to distance himself from Johnston's categorical assertion that a movement on Washington would not have succeeded. In his *Military Operations* he states that for at least three days after the battle, he had considered it feasible to march on the Yankee capital. Yet it would appear that his opinion was derived not from reconnaissance or observation but from "all accounts"—whatever that means.[9]

Johnston never wavered from his oft-stated belief that the decision to forgo direct pursuit, especially one aimed at Washington, was the only one that could have been made under the prevailing conditions. He did not doubt the superiority of his troops over those of the enemy, which he ascribed to "the difference between men fighting for independence . . . & those who hire for eleven dollars a month." But the Confederates suffered from too many disadvantages, one being a woeful insufficiency of cavalry. As he notes in his memoirs, "infantry, unencumbered by baggage, can easily escape pursuing infantry." (In his postbattle report, he had written that "our victory was as complete as one gained by infantry and artillery can be. An adequate force of cavalry would have made it decisive.")[10]

References by Johnston in the aftermath of battle to an even more pernicious obstacle to a general advance helped spark a renewal of the feud between the field commanders and the Richmond-based officers in charge of supply. On July 28 the senior general at Manassas complained to Adjutant General Cooper's office of the woeful lack of transportation that had hamstrung postbattle operations, a failing he laid at the feet of Colonel Northrop and his assistants. In later years Johnston would insist that for three weeks after the battle, "we never had rations for more than two days, and sometimes none." Other army officers familiar with the logistical situation at Manassas would voice the same criticism, often in the harshest terms.[11]

In the weeks after the battle, Beauregard, who had suffered from supply shortages long before Johnston's army joined his, went even further with his condemnation. By making his complaints public, he deliberately created a storm of controversy that roiled the bureaucratic waters inside Richmond. In an intemperate letter read on the floor of the Confederate Congress by political supporters including Senator (erstwhile Colonel) Chesnut, the Creole blasted Northrop and also Lieutenant Colonel Myers, the acting quartermaster general (who despite the acrimony heaped on him, would soon gain the permanent post). In the letter Beauregard claimed that "the want of food and transportation had made us lose all the fruits of our victory. We ought at this moment to be in or about Washington. . . . God only knows when we will be able to advance; without those means we can neither advance nor retreat." These and other high-level accusations produced a resolution that an official inquiry should be made into the workings and policies of the government's supply bureaus; a standing committee of the Congress was appointed to do so. Its investigations, which did not receive the sanction or assistance of President Davis, failed to produce findings that supported widespread claims of "great imbecility or shameful neglect" on the part of Northrop, Myers, or their subordinates.[12]

Beauregard's enmity toward the supply chiefs would outlast the war. In later years he went so far as to spread patent falsehoods that Northrop deliberately withheld supplies to prevent the army from carrying the war beyond the Potomac. Northrop fired back in a series of postwar letters to leading periodicals such as *Century*, accusing Johnston, Beauregard, and the latter's own commissary of subsistence, Lieutenant Colonel Richard Bland Lee, of incompetence and "incapacity." In particular he blamed Beauregard for failing to distribute properly the resources stockpiled at Manassas and neighboring depots, which Northrop considered ample to support an offensive. The bitter back-and-forth continued virtually until the deaths of the principal antagonists.[13]

Even before discussing with Johnston and Beauregard the possibility of a vigorous pursuit, Davis had telegraphed to Richmond reports of "a glorious though dear-bought victory." Dispatches subsequently conveyed to General Cooper at the War Department included details of a battle in which "the enemy was routed and fled precipitately." The news relieved the anxiety of many officials, military and political, who had been anxiously awaiting word from the front, not the least of whom was Robert E. Lee. Throughout the day, the commanding general of Virginia forces had heard rumors of a Confederate defeat and a Union march on Richmond. Finally, he could exhale, settle back, and take pride in having placed at Bull Run a substantial number of the victorious forces. He sent a letter of congratulations to Johnston: "I almost wept for joy at the glorious victory achieved by our brave troops." Similar missives went to Beauregard. And Lee warmly greeted his superior when Davis—accompanied by 675 Yankee prisoners of war and the bodies of Barnard Bee, Francis Bartow, and other leading lights sacrificed on the altar of victory—returned to the capital on the evening of the twenty-third.[14]

Richmond celebrated the victory Davis had announced with fireworks, church bells, minute guns, and train whistles. Speeches by the president and other officials, public gatherings, and impromptu parades stoked public enthusiasm for the war effort, while religious services enabled the devout to thank the Creator for his role in the city's deliverance. On the twenty-second the Confederate Congress passed a resolution recognizing "the hand of the most High God, the King of Kings, and Lord of Lords, in the glorious victory with which He has crowned our arms at Manassas."[15]

The morale of the populace soared above the rooftops and spires, but only until the first trainloads of wounded pulled into the Virginia Central station, reminding the city anew of war's horrors. Before long, upward of 1,500 Confederate wounded and sick were being treated at a dozen Richmond-area hospitals, and military funerals were a daily occurrence. Mary Boykin Chesnut, wife of Beauregard's aide, noted in her diary: "We are never out of the sound of the Dead March in Saul. It comes and it comes, until I feel inclined to close my ears and scream."[16]

Some experienced the darker side of victory more immediately than others. Constance Cary, who had passed another "unspeakably long day" of battle "full of the straining anguish of suspense," was given a personal tour of the battlefield only days after the Yankees abandoned it. She would never forget the grisly sights that met her eyes at almost every turn, including a hand extending from an imperfectly dug grave. "We were glad enough," she wrote, "to turn away and gallop homeward."[17]

Harsh reality aside, Richmond, all of Virginia, and the South as a whole hailed the glorious victory. Most of those who had played a direct role in it limited their observations to the army's extraordinary performance in the face of near-crippling odds, though many considered what the battle revealed about the physical and moral strength of the victors. A typical comment was that of a lieutenant in the 8th Georgia: "Our troops never were so confident of . . . [their ability to] repell any force that may invade Confederate soil." An Alabamian wrote that "the result of this battle will teach the North a lesson that will not soon be forgotten . . . , that we are in earnest and that we mean what we say and that in attempting our subjugation the North have undertaken a herculean task." Taking a cue from soldiers such as these, Southerners who had done nothing to influence the result considered the victory proof of the inherent moral superiority of the South. The editor of the *Richmond Examiner* crowed: "The enemy now know that when they go forth to the field they will encounter a master race. The consciousness of this fact will cause their knees to tremble beneath them on the day of battle."[18]

Soldiers and civilians alike believed that the outcome of July 21 would have decisive effects. In a letter to his family, Elisha Paxton of the 4th Virginia expressed a conviction that his wife must have received with mixed emotions. The day of battle, he wrote, was "the happiest day of my life, our wedding day *not* excepted. I think the fight is over forever." To one prominent Virginia civilian, "this great victory, dearly bought as it has been . . . , has virtually established our Independence. . . . [T]he tide will rush in our favor now." Congressman Cobb of Georgia echoed the sentiment, writing his wife on July 24, "It is one of the decisive battles of the world and . . . has secured our Independence." An enlisted man in Cocke's brigade agreed that enough blood had been shed to convince "the northern Congress to take time by the forelock and acknowledge our Independence."[19]

Three days later Cobb again expressed his conviction that the battle would produce "a cessation of active hostilities in a few months." Should the Yankees refuse to sue for peace, the Confederacy now enjoyed an opportunity to gain moral and material support from Europe. Cobb had learned of William Russell's presence on the battlefield: "I am very glad of it, as he can give the English now some idea of the difference between the North and South when it comes to a fight." Other commentators believed that the victory would resonate far and wide. As the *New Orleans Picayune* put it in a July 23 editorial, the peal of victory would sound "in every corner of this land, and at every capital in Europe." A Charleston merchant believed that the victory "will have a decided influence on the English & French governments, & prove to them that we are a government not only in name, but in deed." Many unionists feared this to be true. Charles F. Adams, Jr., whose diplomat father had the task of persuading Britons to remain neutral in America's struggle, failed to see "how foreign nations can refuse to acknowledge the Confederacy now, for they are a government *de facto* and this result [the triumph at Manassas] looks very much as though they could maintain themselves as such. Their ultimate independence is I think assured."[20]

Southerners versed in international affairs shared this view. A Virginian assured his sister that the economic interests of French and England would align both nations firmly with the Confederacy. An officer in the 7th South Carolina opined that "when the Fall opens, and the abundant cotton crop which God seems determined to grant us, is prepared for market, the whole of Europe will be arrayed against our enemies." Even before Fort Sumter, the Confederacy had been avidly purchasing munitions from England and France, for which they paid in cash. After July 21, Confederate state-department officials hoped to secure more foreign aid by manipulating Europe's voracious appetite for certain Southern products, especially bale after bale of raw cotton. Even the U.S. government realized that that appetite had not weakened with the coming of war. Banker-diplomat August Belmont, then traveling in London, wrote Treasury Secretary Chase three weeks after the battle about his recent conversation with the British prime minister: "One of the closing remarks of Lord Palmerston was: 'We do not like Slavery but we want Cotton & we do not like your tariff.'"[21]

If the South could create a cotton shortage in Europe while cementing the impression that Confederate arms would prevail, perhaps the Powers could be induced to intervene militarily in its behalf or at least take steps to challenge the Union shipping blockade that for three months had been threatening to starve the South of imported goods critical to its war effort. Many observers believed that the results of July 21 would go far toward attaining these goals.

Soon enough, they would learn that Europe was not prepared, on the basis of single battle, to insert itself into a civil war fraught with social, political, and economic repercussions. While impressed by Johnston and Beauregard's success, the crowned heads would refuse to grant their victory international significance. Should the South continue to win battles, Europe might be tempted to help broker a peace between the warring sections. Failing this, to grant diplomatic recognition to an insurrectionary government, especially one that owed its existence to the institution of chattel slavery, would be perilous in the extreme.

And yet the effects of Bull Run rippled through the international community. As French historian Auguste Laugel has written, in the aftermath of its defeat, "the North doubted of itself, and from that day Europe never ceased to doubt the North." Many foreign commentators applauded the South's victory as a harbinger of political and diplomatic change. The editor of the *Westminster Review* hoped that a divided Republic would limit the excesses of American democracy and curb its tendency to mob rule. Conversely, some European liberals, shocked by the poor showing of the Federal military establishment, feared the battle betokened the downfall of Western civilization itself. Still other observers believed the battle merely emphasized the realities of mid-nineteenth-century warfare, one lesson being that the complex military technology of the age demanded better training and leadership than the army beaten at Manassas had received.[22]

Southern realists also doubted that one victory would gain Confederate independence. They feared the victory would produce instead an unhealthy mindset. Stonewall Jackson, for one, was never enthusiastic over the results of the battle. In later months he suggested that defeat would have benefited the Confederacy in the long run as it would have saved the army and its civilian support base from an insidious sense of overconfidence. Even as he joined Beauregard in composing a grandiose congratulatory address to the troops, Johnston understood that the vanquished troops would rebound from their drubbing to renew the struggle with restored will, better leadership, and increased resources. He could only hope that their opponents would, in like measure, rise above their triumph.[23]

Although most exercises of this kind tend to raise hackles rather than awareness, an especially tantalizing "what-if" spawned by the battle and campaign appears to deserve some consideration: the effect of a Union victory on the military and political fortunes of the Confederacy. Over the past forty years, historians have speculated about the fragility of Southern morale and will, and—fiery nation-alistic rhetoric to the contrary notwithstanding—the inadequacy of the Confederacy's determination to do everything necessary to win the war. Indeed, some have cited the failure of the Southern peo-ple to develop a viable sense of nationhood as the main reason for their section's defeat in 1865. If this theory has validity, it stands to reason that early reverses on the battlefield would have seriously damaged, perhaps even ended, the South's attempt to develop "a feeling of oneness, that almost mystical sense of nationhood," able to sustain its military forces through the trials of 1862 and beyond. Viewed in this light, a defeat at Manassas might have ended prema-turely a perhaps unrealistic experiment in Southern nationalism and led to a much earlier downfall of the Confederacy.[24]

Because Manassas was not a defeat, the Confederate South—whether or not it achieved a necessary degree of unity—lived on for almost four years. But not all its people saw the result as anything but a reprieve from an inevitable fate. One who feared the worst was Judith Brockenbrough McGuire, daughter of a justice of Virginia's supreme court and mother of two Rebel soldiers. Upon learning of the battle's outcome, the fortyish matron confided in her diary her hope that the defeated Yankees "would now consent to leave our soil, and return to their own homes!"

Having been driven from her native Alexandria and now forced to board with relatives in the Shenandoah Valley, the well-heeled refugee declared, "I do not desire vengeance upon them, but only that they would leave us in peace, to be forever a separate people." But she suspected that she was asking too much: "It is true that we have slaughtered them, and whipped them, and driven them from our land, but they are people of such indomitable perseverance, that I am afraid that they will come again, perhaps in greater force." McGuire was prescient—she would not return to her home until war's end, when compelled to add to her diary a tear-stained entry: "My native land, good-night!"[25]

While jubilation swept the Confederacy, the ranks of the defeated were mired in gloom and despondency. In the immediate aftermath of the battle, however, most of the survivors were too tired or too frightened to dwell on their misery. For these soldiers, the pressing issue was not how badly they had been beaten, but how to ensure their survival by placing themselves beyond the possibility of being butchered by diabolical pursuers. Many found it hard to believe that they had come out of the fight unscathed. An old woman who lived outside Centreville would tell of two Yankees who stumbled across her yard, oblivious to its owner: "They didn't have no arms and mitely little clothes on. One of them was bareheaded and barefooted." This man turned a full circle in front of his comrade and asked him: "Bill, take a good look. Do you see any holes in me?" Bill assured him there were none, whereupon the man exclaimed: "Thank heaven! I am still alive!"[26]

By the time the greater part of McDowell's army reached Centreville, the panic that had driven it from the battlefield had largely subsided thanks in part to the comforting presence of the rear guard, Sykes's regulars. Then there was Blenker's brigade, which through the evening remained under arms and in good order on the high ground west of the village—standing "firm as the hills," in the words of one retreater. By all accounts the much-maligned immigrants who predominated in this brigade did an able job of calming the minds of their fleeing comrades, especially after 9:00 P.M., when they repulsed a last-ditch effort by Confederate horsemen to disrupt the retreat.

Much of the work was shouldered by the 8th New York (the 1st German Rifles), which, positioned a mile and a half southwest of Centreville, held the turnpike firmly and resolutely. The 29th New York did a similarly effective job guarding the gap between the 8th and the village itself, while the Garibaldi Guards of the 39th New York stood tall in rear of the 29th. Not until midnight would Blenker's brigade turn about and follow the troops whose escape to Fairfax Court House and points north it had secured. Another source of confidence to a frightened and bewildered army was the artillery that Major Barry deployed to cover the retreat. Supported closely by Blenker's and Davies's soldiers, no fewer than twenty guns from the batteries of Ayres, Hunt, Tidball, Edwards, Greene, and Bookwood commanded the turnpike until sometime after midnight. By then all but the slowest soldiers had made their way inside the safety net of Centreville.[27]

Through that pitch-black night and into the small hours of the twenty-second, what remained of the Army of Northeastern Virginia returned, in streams and driblets, to its camps and bivouacs on the Potomac. Some of the units that trudged north—companies, regiments, even portions of brigades—had maintained a semblance of organization. Most of the soldiers, however, made their way home in inchoate clumps or on their own—exhausted, disconsolate men who, separated from their outfits, looked for a safe place to collapse from bone-weariness. Negotiating the route to Fairfax Court House was a difficult task even for the undemoralized and self-composed. Not only was the road, like the fields on either side, awash in mud, but it also presented, as one Minnesotan wrote, "a perfect havoc of destruction. . . . For 6 miles there was nothing but wagons, broken down guns, haversacks, blankets, omnibuses, here and there a dead horse, and all of this [sure] to fall into the hands of the enemy." A Michigan man found that those who had preceded him had thrown aside "everything to lighten them up. Even musical instruments and drums were scattered along the road. Some officer had even dropped his sword, which I picked up and brought with me to camp."[28]

Many fugitives expected that the retreat would end at the court-house, but a rumor ran the length of the disheveled column that General McDowell or Tyler had ordered the march to continue all the way to Washington. The men cursed and plodded on, though many dropped abruptly in the mud and lay there, dead to all sensation. Then around seven o'clock came reports of the Black Horse Cavalry rampaging in the rear. A secondary panic set in as men, wagons, ambulances, artillery vehicles, and private conveyances resumed the frenzied pace of hours earlier. The reports were unfounded, but for a time an unreasoning fear worked its will on officers, men, and civilians. A nearly exhausted youngster from Maine, calling upon his last reserve of energy in hopes of keeping pace with his spooked comrades, could never bring himself to tell his family "what I suffered that night."[29]

The army's ambulatory wounded experienced perhaps the greatest ordeal, forced to keep moving, although in pain and distress, to avoid being left behind to fall into enemy hands. One soldier whose arm had been amputated above the elbow walked—sometimes ran—the more than twenty miles to his regiment's Washington-area camp. A comrade with "a hole through both cheeks, a broken jaw, and his tongue nearly off" also endured the twelve-hour journey to the Potomac. So did a soldier "with a large hole through both thighs and the scrotum."[30]

From Fairfax Court House, the rain-soaked column straggled up the turnpike to Falls Church, where it branched off onto several roads that carried it across the district line within sight of the capital's defenses. Here the men could believe they were finally safe from being overtaken and captured or cut down. Even the most zealous pursuer would quail at the sight of the cannons protecting Forts Runyon and Ellsworth and adjacent installations.

But was the capital truly secure? Contemporary opinion on this vital issue was divided. Sherman, for one, doubted that the few forts then standing would have deterred an all-out attack. So too did the assistant adjutant general, E. D. Townsend. Even Major Barnard, McDowell's chief engineer, who ought to have been in a position to know, described the half-dozen incomplete works around the city as "far from constituting a defensive system" that would secure "the long line from Alexandria to Georgetown or even . . . the heights of Arlington."[31]

Others familiar with the strength of the various redoubts, redans, lunettes, and blockhouses shielding the capital did not doubt their ability to withstand assault. General Scott placed complete faith in their effectiveness; General Mansfield went so far as to assure the commander of the guard at the Chain Bridge, "We are amply able to whip the enemy if he will give us a chance here." Present-day historians seem to agree that the existing defenses, though incomplete, would have withstood attack, supported as they were by unstampeded portions of McDowell's army, a continuous wave of reinforcements, and a fleet of gunboats in the Potomac. Even so, had Johnston and Beauregard fashioned a determined pursuit, they might well have seized Arlington Heights and imposed a partial siege on Washington. Even those who in the aftermath of the battle professed faith in the deterrent effect of the capital's works must have breathed a sigh of relief once it became evident that the enemy did not contemplate an assault on the Federal seat of government.[32]

The rain was coming down in torrents as McDowell's fugitives began to cross the river into Washington in the darkness of early morning on July 22. The guards at the bridges had orders to halt and turn back all traffic except civilian conveyances, but resourceful soldiers found ways to enter the city and stalk its muddy streets. The returnees found the capital enveloped in "an oppressive silence," though one that did not endure. William Russell, who had fallen into bed upon reaching his rented quarters, awoke at 6:00 A.M. to the drumming of the rain on his window, but louder than all, came a strange sound, as if of the tread of men, a confused tramp and splashing, and a murmuring of voices. I got up and ran to the front room, the windows of which looked on the street, and there, to my intense surprise, I saw a steady stream of men covered with mud, soaked through with rain, who were pouring irregularly, without any semblance of order, up Pennsylvania Avenue towards the Capitol. A dense stream of vapor rose from the multitude; but looking closely at the men, I perceived they belonged to different regiments, New Yorkers, Michiganders, Rhode Islanders . . . mingled pell-mell together. Many of these men were without knapsacks, cross belts, and firelocks. Some had neither great-coats nor shoes; others were covered with blankets.[33]

The eminent journalist was shocked to see exhausted soldiers drop to the cobblestones as if shot. He watched others go door to door, begging food, water, and in some cases clothing. Moved by their plight, citizens came forth with pails of water and pots of coffee; some carried worn-out, sick, or wounded men inside their homes. Many soldiers favored stronger drink; some attempted to break into grog shops and grocery stores. The scene had all the earmarks of a lawless city, a prospect that frightened Russell: "Now and then shots are heard down the street or in the distance, and cries and shouting, as if a scuffle or a difficulty were occurring." The danger had not abated by midday of the twenty-second, when Rose Greenhow pronounced the capital "paralysed with fear." While engaged in composing a dispatch for his paper, Russell was interrupted "by soldiers clamoring for drink and for money, attracted by the light in my windows." A few managed to gain entrance to his rooms but were persuaded to leave empty handed.

Enlisted men were not the only seekers of strong drink. The day after the battle, Russell and other disapproving observers found the city's saloons crowded with officers of all arms of the service. Separated from their regiments but apparently unconcerned by that fact, men with eagles and leaves on their shoulders drank long and deep while cursing the Rebels, their own men, and their fate—being caught up in a debacle had the potential to ruin budding military careers. When Walt Whitman, a Brooklyn-based former journalist with a genius for free verse, found the first-floor bar at Willard's Hotel "thick, crush'd, creeping with shoulder-straps," he exploded in indignation: "Where are your companies? Where are your men? Incompetents! Never tell me of chances of battle, of getting stray'd, and the like. I think this is your work, this retreat, after all."[34]

Making his way through the streets of the city late on the twenty-second, Russell was privy to "all kinds of rumors respecting the advance of the enemy, the annihilation of Federal regiments, the tremendous losses on both sides, charges of cavalry, storming of great intrenchments and stupendous masked batteries, [all] circulated under the genial influence of excitement, and by the quantities of alcohol necessary to keep out the influence of the external moisture." Another rumor gaining currency was the imminent arrival of the Confederate army and the fall of the Lincoln government.

The war correspondent doubted the accuracy of these stories, believing them fueled by "the influence of excitement and alcohol," but many residents hoped they proved true. Though slow to publish the news of McDowell's retreat and defeat, local newspapers were quick to condemn the capital's numerous prosecessionists for publicly rejoicing and proclaiming the city's forthcoming capture and occupation. According to the *Washington Star*, Rebel sympathizers exhibited "inhuman joy" at the sufferings of the passing wounded. The boldest specimens of this ilk attempted to fly the new Confederate national flag from their windows and rooftops. Taking umbrage, soldiers ripped down the banners, offered to beat those who made public display of their allegiance to the enemies of the Union, and threatened to attack Confederate prisoners of war being herded through the streets to Old Capitol Prison. Such scenes disturbed and alarmed Russell; late on the twenty-second, he noted that "there is no provost guard, no patrol, no authority visible in the streets." It would be another twenty-four hours before law and order was fully restored in the heart of the nation's capital.[35]

While returning the borrowed horse that had borne him "nobly and well" from the fringes of the battlefield, Russell had a brief conversation with the manager of the livery stable at Willard's. Although less than twelve hours had passed since McDowell's army had begun its retreat, the man had heard "such news! such news! Twenty thousand of them killed and wounded." Rubbing his hands anxiously, he cast a glance up the street and wondered aloud if "they're not having fits in the White House to-night!"[36]

The liveryman was no seer, but it did not take one to make such a prediction. For most of the twenty-first, the principal resident of the

Executive Mansion had found no reason to worry about the outcome of the fighting whose rumblings could be clearly heard twenty miles away. After spending some hours in the War Department telegraph office, where incoming message traffic gave no hint of a reverse to the army, and especially after his reassuring visit to General Scott's quarters, the president took his usual afternoon drive.

He set out at about five-thirty, only minutes before the telegrapher at Fairfax Court House relayed General Miles's panicky request for reinforcements. An hour or so later Lincoln returned to the White House, where he found Secretary of State William Henry Seward waiting with telegrams recently received from Fairfax reporting that the battle had been lost, McDowell was in full retreat, and General Scott had been called on to save the capital. The president's secretaries, John G. Nicolay and John Hay, recalled that while the messages were read to him, Lincoln "listened in silence, without the slightest change of feature or expression," then, accompanied by Seward and Attorney General Bates, calmly walked down Pennsylvania Avenue to Seventeenth Street, where army headquarters was located.

At Scott's office the trio joined the commanding general, General Mansfield, Lieutenant Colonel Townsend, and other members of Scott's staff. The group quickly expanded to include Simon Cameron, Salmon Chase, Secretary of the Navy Gideon Welles, and Assistant Secretary of War Thomas Scott, who had charge of the commercial telegraph systems around Washington. All poured over the latest bulletins, which confirmed the initial reports of overthrow and flight.[37]

While trying to understand this rapid reversal of fortune, most of the officials remained remarkably calm. General Scott, however, at first appeared perplexed by the unfolding disaster, professing not to credit the incoming reports. Believing that the army had experienced a temporary setback, at 9:00 P.M.—much too late to affect the course of events—he wired McDowell of his expectation that the troops would regroup at Centreville or, failing that, at Fairfax Court House.[38]

When finally convinced of the magnitude of the defeat and the impossibility of rallying the troops, Scott took action. One of his first moves was to order that the grim details be suppressed. Official censorship extended not just to the military telegraph: all comment about the reverse was to be expunged from the "special dispatches" that war correspondents were sending to their editors via the American Telegraph Office on Pennsylvania Avenue.[39]

The commanding general then issued a stream of orders, not all of them practical or timely. He directed Mansfield, through Assistant Secretary Scott, to "man all the forts and prevent soldiers from passing over to the city." Mansfield was also to inquire into reports that General Runyon's regiments had returned to their camps at Alexandria "without [firing] a shot." He cabled Andrew Curtin of Pennsylvania and the governors of neighboring states to expedite the previously arranged shipment of reinforcements to the capital. He wired General McClellan at Beverly, Virginia, "to come down to the Shenandoah Valley with such troops as can be spared." As the beaten soldiers began to pour into the city, he took steps to restore municipal order by clearing the streets of the rowdy, drunken element.[40]

A growing appreciation of the enormity of the still-unfolding disaster began to make Scott fearful of its effects on his position and reputation. During one conference with Lincoln, a few senators and representatives, and Secretary of War Cameron—who had just been informed of the mortal wounding of his brother—the general called himself a coward for having given in to political pressure to advance on Manassas: "I have fought this battle, sir, against my judgment." A visibly upset Lincoln asked him to clarify his remarks, which made it sound as if "I forced you to fight this battle." The general refused to give a direct answer, replying only, "I have never served a President who has been kinder to me than you have been."

Despite the attempt to backtrack, severe damage had been done to the Lincoln-Scott relationship. From this point on, the two were never as close as they had been prior to July 21. To make matters worse, a Democratic congressman from Illinois who overheard Scott's outburst later charged Lincoln, from the floor of the House, with forcing a premature offensive on an unwilling commanding general.[41]

Suddenly feeling the weight of bad tidings, the president left Scott's office, returned to the Executive Mansion, and stretched out on a lounge in the cabinet room. He remained recumbent while a steady stream of visitors, including senators and representatives who had been swept up in McDowell's retreat, recited tales of travail and woe. All seemed convinced that the army had dissolved and that Washington's seizure and occupation was a matter of time. Daylight of the twenty-second found Lincoln, physically and emotionally spent, still on his sofa.[42]

With the cessation of the rain, however, prospects appeared to improve generally. The armies of the streets grew less boisterous.

Teams of provost guards began patrolling the city, breaking up mobs, collaring drunks and looters, and guarding private homes against vandalism and invasion. It was noted that "colonels, even, are compelled to show their passes and consequently do not lounge as much as they used to do around bars and corners." Rations were furnished to stragglers and placards posted to direct them to their regiments' rendezvous.[43]

At Scott's orders, a steady stream of newly arrived units, including cavalry and artillery, were moved across the river to bolster and build up the existing forts and erect new ones. In this work the general received timely support from subordinates, including a rejuvenated William T. Sherman. Regardless of whether he had the requisite authority, the Ohio colonel proposed to strengthen the garrisons of Fort Corcoran as well as those of some outworks on the Arlington road. The news gratified and impressed Scott, who told an aide, "thank God there is one man on the other side of the river who has his wits about him." Upon their return from Bull Run, officers who were reported to have served faithfully and well in the fight were called to the commanding general's office to receive his personal thanks.[44]

By the morning of the twenty-third, almost every straggler was back in his assigned camp or en route to it, and the capital had resumed its normal rhythm. With prospects for an enemy attack fading, Scott had recovered his equanimity. Colonel Townsend heard him exclaim, in response to an unverified report of a Confederate advance: "It is impossible, sir! We are now tasting the first fruits of a war, and learning what a panic is. We must be prepared for all kinds of rumors. Why, sir, we shall soon hear that Jefferson Davis has crossed the Long Bridge at the head of a brigade of elephants."[45]

Lincoln too had overcome the temptation to despair that Russell believed had beset him forty-eight hours earlier. Early that afternoon, accompanied by Secretary Seward, the president took the Georgetown ferry to visit some of the troops. He stopped by several camps, including that of Sherman's brigade. Pleased to see the president, with whom he had spoken privately on at least one prior occasion, Sherman turned out his entire command and placed it at parade rest facing the commander in chief. Lincoln, standing up in his carriage so that all could see him, delivered what Sherman considered "one of the neatest, best, and most feeling addresses I ever listened to, referring to our late disaster at Bull Run, the high duties that still devolved on us, and the brighter days yet to come." At one point the soldiers began to cheer, but the president politely asked for quiet. Sherman had requested him to discourage "all cheering, noise, or any sort of confusion; that we had had enough of it before Bull Run to ruin any set of men . . . no more hurrahing, no more humbug."

Lincoln agreed with the colonel's view that from here on out, the war would be prosecuted through deeds, not boasts. In later days, as often as he could get away, he visited the camps at Arlington and Alexandria. He wanted the soldiers to know that their government intended to give them the support they needed to win the war; he also wanted to display his personal regard for every one of them. To this end he would leave his carriage to walk along the ranks of men assembled on the parade grounds, shaking hands, patting shoulders, and constantly adding, "God bless you, God bless you."[46]

A great battle having been lost, the soldiers who had fought it, the military and civilian leaders who had overseen it, the politicians and editors who by molding public support had helped bring it about, and the people of the North who to one degree or another were affected by it, all demanded to know what had gone wrong. Why had lofty but realistic expectations not been met? How could a magnificently equipped and armed force been beaten so soundly by a most unprepossessing opponent? How could certain victory have so quickly degenerated into abject, humiliating defeat? In the days and weeks after Bull Run, numerous theories were advanced in the hope of answering these questions, no two of them exactly alike. They fell into three general categories: the superior strength of the Confederates, the failure of Union leadership from top to bottom, and the unpreparedness of the army to wage a fight forced on it by external pressures too powerful to resist.

One of the most popular explanations was that McDowell's troops were fatally outnumbered, though to what extent was a matter of debate. Charles B. Haydon of the 2nd Michigan Infantry believed that the defenders of Bull Run were "double our numbers," while a member of the 1st Minnesota insisted that the Confederates had a three-to-one advantage. A New Jersey clergyman, a future army chaplain, gave credence to a rumor that Johnston's and Beauregard's forces exceeded 90,000 men. A soldier from Maine and one from Minnesota each put the enemy's numbers at more than 100,000. Even the usually sensible *New York Times* declared that 60,000 troops had defended the Bull Run line, nearly twice the actual number. Few of those who commented publicly on the defeat admitted, as did the *Philadelphia Press*, that the Federals had underestimated not the Rebels' numbers but their fighting ability.[47]

Those who did not blame superior enemy strength faulted Union leadership. The most convenient target was the man at the top, and Irvin McDowell made a perfect scapegoat. Largely unfamiliar to the public at large and beloved by virtually no one, his image was that of a political appointee promoted beyond his limited ability. In the minds of his beaten troops, the general became a fool, an incompetent, or worse, a traitor to the cause, the latter an inexplicable accusation that would dog the staunch unionist throughout his war career. Other rumors, perhaps originating with McDowell's stomach ailment, had the strict teetotaler as drunk and stuperous throughout July 21 as Dixon Miles. During their retreat and long after their return to Washington, soldiers cursed their commander— sometimes within earshot—for leading them to rout and ruin.

William Russell visited McDowell two days after he returned to his headquarters at Arlington and found the "kindly, honest soldier" far from despondent, or at least intent on appearing so. The journalist was pleased to see that although his host "was not proud of being 'whipped,' there was no dejection other than that a man should feel who has been beaten by his enemy, but who knows he has done his duty." Even so, by the time Russell visited him, McDowell had been punished for "the unhappy termination to his advance." Not surprisingly, he had been replaced as army commander. Early on the twenty-second, with Lincoln's and Cameron's approval, the War Department had ordered George McClellan to report at Washington without delay. General Scott had followed with a personal note instructing Little Mac to "bring no troops with you." His intent was clear: the officer who had won small but well-publicized victories in a backwater of the war would inherit the Army of Northeastern Virginia. Henceforth the responsibility for saving the Union would rest with a general unblemished by adversity and censure.[48]

McDowell was not the only candidate to bear the blame for defeat. Numerous critics (with the conspicuous exception of the editors of Philadelphia newspapers) vented their wrath on Robert Patterson, as if the disgraced Pennsylvanian had not been punished enough. The general's own troops led the chorus of condemnation. When he learned of the defeat at Bull Run, an artillery officer who had retreated under Patterson to Harpers Ferry lamented that McDowell had been beaten "by the arrival of Johnson's [sic] army at Manassas, the very thing we were here to prevent." Patterson too was accused not only of incompetence but also of treason. By this line of reasoning, any commander who failed in active operations did so intentionally through a secret allegiance to the enemy's cause.[49]

Winfield Scott appears to have absorbed less blame than either of his senior subordinates, perhaps because he did not command in the field. Many observers believed the battle had been lost because the commanding general's strategy had been executed improperly or not at all. "I think the generalship was very bad on our side," wrote one Minnesotan. "I don't think it had been Scott's design to attack them on Sunday and I am certain that his plan was not carried out." A comrade in the same regiment opined that "the whole conduct" of the campaign "was against the orders of Gen Scott," who would not have attacked the Bull Run works until they had been leveled by Union artillery. To be sure, Lincoln received a proportionate share of public criticism, principally for appointing the field commanders who had failed and for sending an unprepared army to its downfall. As one might expect, critiques of his performance had a partisan tinge, with Democrats, even those supportive of the war effort, being his most vocal critics.[50]

Some commentators blamed the army's defeat not on McDowell or Patterson personally but on every officer regardless of rank. A New York enlisted man believed that the battle had been mismanaged "by the *Brigade* commanders. They had no (with few exceptions) experience & the Col[onels] (some exceptions to be made) were not fitted to take their men into action, nor withdraw them. . . . Even once in action, they found they could scarcely get their comp[anie]s to change their position & move with any precision, from lack of promptitude & presence of mind of the company officers."[51]

The militia generals who commanded under Patterson received especially harsh criticism. As early as mid-June, a *New York Times* editorial had asked: "Is this a war we are engaged in, or merely an immense national militia parade, wherein all the posts of honor are to be assigned on political and personal grounds, without the slightest reference to capacity, fitness, or past military education?" The editor of *Harper's Weekly* decried the performance of militia and volunteer officers alike, concluding that "Bull Run must rid us of cowardly, or imbecile colonels, majors, and captains." The *Baltimore*

American agreed that the nation required a "clean sweep" of lax, lazy, and incompetent civilians in command positions and "precipitate action" to revamp and improve an "indifferently officered" army.[52]

Other critics of the campaign blamed not ignorant or uneducated officers but an untutored and unmotivated enlisted force. Private Haydon was not surprised by the results of July 21: "Our army is large & full of good material but it is loosely put together. Not one man in 50 ever saw a battle before this war. Not one in 10 knew the simplest elements of military drill. . . . Where rough & tumble fighting & personal bravery are needed they are great but for steady movements in line & on retreat they are not reliable." In far-off Detroit, Captain George Gordon Meade, an officer of topographical engineers who would come east to play a major role in the fighting ahead, observed that "the shameful disaster at Bull's run . . . resulted entirely from our army not being efficiently *officered* & organized. . . . [Soldiers] can not be made by merely putting uniforms on men & arms in their hands—You might just as well try to work a ship in a gale of wind with a lot of [land]lubbers." To Meade's mind, only the most extensive training would produce an army capable of redeeming its recent debacle.[53]

McDowell heartily agreed with Meade's observations. Weeks before the battle he had lamented to his friend John Bigelow that while he commanded several thousand men, they did not constitute an army in the true sense. Having returned to Arlington in defeat, he considered his suspicions confirmed. The crux of his downfall, as he saw it, was the lack of polish and professionalism in his ranks, not only among the three months' outfits but in the long-term regiments as well. The way in which volunteer troops had been recruited and organized was, as he told Bigelow, "a vicious system" that had to change. Many of these units, including the highly touted Zouaves that had figured to be the backbone of McDowell's command, had proven themselves unreliable and uncontrollable—in sum, "worthless."[54]

All this would change upon the coming of the army's new commander. Willing and able to learn from his predecessor's mistakes, McClellan would not take the field at the head of his newly christened Army of the Potomac until many months of training turned raw recruits into soldiers who viewed war as a dirty job that had to be done rather than a glorified militia muster or an exercise in the manly arts. Bull Run had much to do with that change in the corporate mentality. One of Charles Haydon's comrades in the 2nd Michigan, looking back on the battle years later, wrote that "with its unhappy termination, went out forever the effervescence and impulsiveness of the service in the war."[55]

During his postbattle chat with John Bigelow, McDowell remarked that although criticism was coming at him from all sides, the newspapers "have dealt fairly with me, and where they have erred, have not done so intentionally." Such a pronouncement may seem unduly charitable considering that the general and his overlords had been, in the words of New York diarist George Templeton Strong, "teased into action" by the power of the press. Not surprisingly, few Northern journals admitted to having pressured the army to advance. The *Albany Journal,* whose editorial reach did not extend to Washington and thus had exerted undue influence on no one, was almost alone in censuring its big-city colleagues for effectively "assuming command of the army" and making "open aspersions and denunciations" of Lincoln, Scott, McDowell, and other officials.[56]

Other critics were equally unwilling to let the policymaking journalists off the hook. Soldiers railed that defeat had come from "yielding to the importunities of an ignorant press." Even foreigners, such as Major (later Field Marshal) Garnet Wolseley of the British army, who would visit America the following year to study the Virginia campaigns, identified the agent of defeat at Bull Run as "Public Opinion" fashioned into a whip by the press.[57]

The gentlemen of the Fourth Estate attempted to have it both ways. The same editors who had demanded quick action and expected early success were the first to castigate the defeated army and declare that not only the battle but also the war had been lost and the Union dismantled. In banner headlines the *New York Times* announced on July 23 the "DISASTER TO THE NATIONAL ARMY." Horace Greeley's *Tribune* affirmed that "the agony of this overwhelming disgrace can never be expressed." Let there be "another 'Manassas,'" wrote the *Cincinnati Gazette,* "and all would be lost." Other editors feared the results of the battle "will alienate thousands from the cause" while not only eroding foreign support but actually enlisting England and France on the side of the Confederacy.[58]

These gloomy assessments filled only a few editions. Within three days of the army's return to Washington, and with no pursuers in sight, the leading journals recovered their composure and reevaluated their dire predictions. In so doing, they anticipated Russell's pronouncement in the *Times* that the consequences of Bull Run were more political than military and that "the North will, no doubt, recover [from] the shock." The *Boston Daily Advertiser* assured its readers that the North would "rise above its misfortune." The *Boston Courier* now found "no reason to despond." The *New York Express* predicted that the specter of defeat would arouse unionists "to unparalleled exertions and call forth their full strength." The *Providence Journal* regarded the outcome of the battle as "only an argument for [a] new effort."[59]

Certainly, the rank and file shared these sentiments. Even the officer under Patterson who had been shamed by his army's performance affirmed that he and his comrades "are not at all disheartened, only chagrinned." Though disappointed by the disaster in which he participated only peripherally, a New Jersey officer predicted that within a couple of months, "our army will be swelled to a tremendous size and will be well-drilled. Then we will take up our line of march and see Centreville again. . . . Let the people and the press leave Genl. Winfield Scott have his own way and don't hurry him until he is fully ready, and you will not hear of a defeat." Private Rhodes of the 2nd Rhode Island spoke for many a comrade when he wrote that while hardships and dangers lay ahead, "I will not turn [my] back on a good cause. . . . I enlisted during [that is, for the duration of] the war unless sooner discharged & I mean to stand in my bargain let the discharge come in what form it may."[60]

Given time for reflection, a number of soldiers, as well as many opinion makers, began to view the results of Bull Run in a new light. Rather than a disaster, as one New York infantryman wrote, the battle was "a blessing in disguise." Although a "costly experience, [it] was really worth all it cost," for it would force the North to see the war for what it was, "a reality and not [a] shadow." Colonel (later Major General) Franklin came to believe that the defeat "taught our people to be a little patient, and not to expect the army to be ready to move next week." Public spokesmen, including legions of clergymen, called on the North, in the wake of the fiasco, to rededicate itself to winning a war it could not afford to lose. Typical was the sermon delivered on the Sunday following the battle by the Reverend Horace Bushnell of Hartford, Connecticut. In measured tones the prominent theologian called on the congregation of North Church to acknowledge that "our

spirit as a people is not quelled, but that we find ourselves beginning, at once, to meet our adversity with a steady and stout resolve.
. . . The flash feeling is burst, but the fire of duty burns only the
more intensely."[61]

Bushnell's underlying theme—that an early defeat served an
army and a nation better than a victory—permeated the writings
of Northern intellectuals, who viewed the battle as a necessary prelude to a cultural and moral transformation of a restored Union.
Speaking to the alumni of his institution, the president of Yale
College argued, "we have no reason to suppose or to hope that we,
more than other nations, can fulfill a great destiny without passing,
like them, through a baptism of suffering." Henry David Thoreau,
poet, naturalist, and civil libertarian, envisioned Bull Run as leading
inevitably to "the moral regeneration of the nation."[62]

New England abolitionist Wendell Phillips and many others like
him considered the defeat a godsend because it would commit the
North to do whatever was necessary to win the war, the inevitable result being the downfall of the slaveocracy. Reverend Henry
W. Bellows, editor of the *Christian Examiner,* spoke of the "moral
necessity of the late defeat," while the historian Francis Parkman
informed the readers of the *Boston Advertiser* in the wake of the
battle that "the time may come, when, upheaved from its depths,
fermenting and purging itself, the Nation will stand at length clari-
fied and pure in a renewed and strengthened life."[63]

Although he never considered himself an intellectual and had
little in common with New England philosophers, Abraham Lincoln might well have endorsed these sentiments. The outcome of
the war's first campaign would give the president and his political
and military subordinates a mandate to wed the people of the North
to an effort capable of changing the political, cultural, economic, and
moral fabric of the country. Henceforth the North would no longer
fight by half measures; the full resources of the region and the capabilities of its people would be enlisted in the struggle. The deep pool
of manpower available to the armies of the Union would be tapped.
Legislation ushered through Congress would bring hundreds of long-
term regiments into the field via recruiting bonuses and, eventually,
conscription. The War Department would set up examining boards
to weed out incompetent officers. The blockade of Southern ports
would be tightened until it strangled the region's economy. Through
trial and error, those able to be entrusted with the tools of victory

would be found, and they would be given the power and support to apply a total-war strategy devastating to the enemy.[64]

None of this would have been possible had the fighting of July 18–21 ended in Union victory. A quick defeat of the Rebels in Virginia and an early advance on their seat of government might well have resulted in a negotiated peace, leaving in limbo the legality of secession and chattel slavery. America's advancement on the world stage depended on resolving these and other critical issues—a final determination would only come through additional bloodshed and suffering. As Lincoln clearly understood, anything short of a final resolution would constitute a tragedy far greater than the one played out on the blood-stained banks of Bull Run.

The Antagonists

Confederate Forces

Army of the Potomac (Brig. Gen. P. G. T. Beauregard)

First Brigade (Brig. Gen. Milledge L. Bonham)
        8th Louisiana [six companies]
        11th North Carolina
        2nd South Carolina
        3rd South Carolina
        7th South Carolina
        8th South Carolina
        Alexandria Light Artillery [four guns]
        First Company, Richmond Howitzers [four guns]
        30th Virginia Cavalry [three companies]
        Independent Virginia cavalry [four companies]
Second Brigade (Brig. Gen. Richard S. Ewell)
        5th Alabama
        6th Alabama
        6th Louisiana
        First Company, Washington Artillery [four guns]
        Independent Virginia cavalry [four companies]
Third Brigade (Brig. Gen. David R. Jones)
        17th Mississippi
        18th Mississippi
        5th South Carolina
        Second Company, Washington Artillery [two guns]
        30th Virginia Cavalry [one company]
Fourth Brigade (Brig. Gen. James Longstreet)
        5th North Carolina
        1st Virginia
        11th Virginia

        17th Virginia
        24th Virginia
        Third Company, Washington Artillery [two guns]
        30th Virginia Cavalry [one company]
Fifth Brigade (Col. Philip St. George Cocke)
        Schaeffer's Battalion [three companies]
        8th Virginia [eight companies]
        18th Virginia
        19th Virginia
        28th Virginia
        49th Virginia [three companies]
        Loudoun Artillery [two guns]
        Lynchburg Artillery [two guns]
        30th Virginia Cavalry [one company]
Sixth Brigade (Col. Jubal A. Early)
        7th Louisiana
        13th Mississippi
        7th Virginia
        Fourth Company, Washington Artillery [five guns]
Seventh Brigade (Maj. Nathan G. Evans)
        1st Special Battalion Louisiana Volunteers [five companies]
        4th South Carolina
        30th Virginia Cavalry [two companies]
Reserve Brigade (Brig. Gen. Theophilus H. Holmes)
        1st Arkansas
        2nd Tennessee
        Purcell Artillery [six guns]
Unbrigaded Infantry
        Hampton Legion (Col. Wade Hampton) [six companies]
Unbrigaded Cavalry
        30th Virginia Cavalry [two companies]
Reserve Artillery
        Camp Pickens Company [fifteen guns]

Army of the Shenandoah (Gen. Joseph E. Johnston)

First Brigade (Brig. Gen. Thomas J. Jackson)
        2nd Virginia
        4th Virginia

5th Virginia
27th Virginia [seven companies]
33rd Virginia [eight companies]
Rockbridge Artillery [four guns]
Second Brigade (Col. Francis S. Bartow)
7th Georgia
8th Georgia
Wise Artillery [four guns]
Third Brigade (Brig. Gen. Barnard E. Bee)
4th Alabama
2nd Mississippi [eleven companies]
11th Mississippi [two companies]
6th North Carolina
Staunton Artillery [four guns]
Fourth Brigade (Brig. Gen. Edmund K. Smith, Col. Arnold Elzey)
1st Maryland [eight companies]
3rd Tennessee
10th Virginia
13th Virginia
Culpeper Artillery [four guns]
Unbrigaded Artillery
Thomas Artillery [four guns]
Unbrigaded Cavalry
1st Virginia [five companies]

Federal Forces

Army of Northeastern Virginia (Brig. Gen. Irvin McDowell)

First Division (Brig. Gen.* Daniel Tyler)
First Brigade (Col. Erasmus D. Keyes)
1st Connecticut
2nd Connecticut
3rd Connecticut
2nd Maine

---

* = of State Volunteers

Second Brigade (Brig. Gen. Robert C. Schenck)
    2nd New York Militia
    1st Ohio
    2nd Ohio
    Company E, 2nd U.S. Artillery [seven guns]
Third Brigade (Col. William T. Sherman)
    13th New York
    69th New York Militia
    79th New York
    2nd Wisconsin
    Company E, 3rd U.S. Artillery [six guns]
Fourth Brigade (Col. Israel B. Richardson)
    1st Massachusetts
    2nd Michigan
    3rd Michigan
    12th New York
    Company G, 1st U.S. Artillery [two guns]
    Company M, 2nd U.S. Artillery [four guns]

Second Division (Brig. Gen. David Hunter)
    First Brigade (Col. Andrew Porter)
        8th New York Militia [with battery]
        14th New York Militia ("14th Brooklyn")
        27th New York
        2nd U.S. Infantry [two companies]
        3rd U.S. Infantry [five companies]
        8th U.S. Infantry [one company]
        1st U.S. Cavalry [two companies]
        2nd U.S. Cavalry [four companies]
        2nd U.S. Dragoons [one company]
        U.S. Marines [battalion]
        Company D, 5th U.S. Artillery [six guns]
    Second Brigade (Col. Ambrose E. Burnside)
        2nd New Hampshire
        71st New York Militia [with two guns]
        1st Rhode Island
        2nd Rhode Island
        2nd Rhode Island Battery [six guns]

Third Division (Col. Samuel P. Heintzelman)
    First Brigade (Col. William B. Franklin)
        5th Massachusetts Militia
        11th Massachusetts
        1st Minnesota
        4th Pennsylvania
        Company I, 1st U.S. Artillery [six guns]
    Second Brigade (Col. Orlando B. Willcox)
        1st Michigan
        4th Michigan
        11th New York
        38th New York
        Company D, 2nd U.S. Artillery [four guns]
    Third Brigade (Col. Oliver O. Howard)
        3rd Maine
        4th Maine
        5th Maine
        2nd Vermont

Fourth Division (Brig. Gen.* Theodore Runyon)
    First Brigade (Col.* A. J. Johnson)
        1st New Jersey Militia
        2nd New Jersey Militia
        3rd New Jersey Militia
        4th New Jersey Militia
    Second Brigade (Col. William R. Montgomery)
        1st New Jersey
        2nd New Jersey
        3rd New Jersey
        41st New York

Fifth Division (Col. Dixon S. Miles)
    First Brigade (Col. Louis Blenker)
        8th New York
        29th New York
        39th New York

---

* = of State Volunteers

           27th Pennsylvania
           Company A, 2nd U.S. Artillery [four guns]
           Bookwood's Company (formerly Varian's Battery)
           [six guns]
       Second Brigade (Col. Thomas A. Davies)
           16th New York
           18th New York
           31st New York
           32nd New York
           Company G, 2nd U.S. Artillery [four guns]

Army of Pennsylvania (Maj. Gen. Robert Patterson)

First Division (Maj. Gen.* George Cadwalader)
       First Brigade (Col. George H. Thomas)
           6th Pennsylvania
           21st Pennsylvania
           23rd Pennsylvania
           2nd U.S. Cavalry [three companies]
           First Troop, Philadelphia City Cavalry
           Company F, 4th U.S. Artillery [one section]
       Third Brigade (Brig. Gen.* Edward C. Williams)
           7th Pennsylvania
           8th Pennsylvania
           10th Pennsylvania
           20th Pennsylvania
       Fourth Brigade (Col. Henry C. Longnecker)
           9th Pennsylvania
           13th Pennsylvania
           16th Pennsylvania
       Siege Train (Maj. Abner Doubleday)

Second Division (Maj. Gen.* William H. Keim)
       Second Brigade (Brig. Gen.* George C. Wynkoop)
           1st Pennsylvania
           2nd Pennsylvania
           3rd Pennsylvania

---

* = of State Volunteers

Fifth Brigade (Brig. Gen.* James S. Negley)
  14th Pennsylvania
  15th Pennsylvania
  24th Pennsylvania
Sixth Brigade (Col. J. J. Abercrombie)
  4th Connecticut
  2nd Massachusetts
  11th Pennsylvania
  1st Wisconsin
  McMullin's Independent Rangers [company]
  Company F, 4th U.S. Artillery [two guns]

Third Division (Maj. Gen.** Charles W. Sandford)
  Seventh Brigade (Col. Charles P. Stone)
    District of Columbia Infantry [one company]
    1st New Hampshire
    9th New York Militia
    17th Pennsylvania
    25th Pennsylvania [six companies]
    Company F, 4th U.S. Artillery [section]
  Eighth Brigade (Col.** Daniel Butterfield)
    5th New York
    12th New York Militia
    19th New York
    28th New York

---

* = of State Volunteers
** = of State Militia

Notes

Abbreviations

C-CWC	Century–Civil War Collection
CW&M	College of William and Mary Library
DU	Duke University Library
ECU	East Carolina University Library
EU	Emory University Library
GDA&H	Georgia Department of Archives and History
GLC	Gilder Lehrman Collection, Gilder Lehrman Institute of American History
GTB	G.T. Beauregard
HR&D	Francis B. Heitman, comp., *Historical Register and Dictionary of the United States Army, 1789–1903*, vol. 1
HSP	Historical Society of Pennsylvania
IM	Irvin McDowell
JCCW	*Report of the Joint Committee on the Conduct of the War: Part I—Bull Run—Ball's Bluff*
JEJ	Joseph E. Johnston
LC	Library of Congress
MiHS	Minnesota Historical Society
MoHS	Missouri Historical Society
MNBP	Manassas National Battlefield Park
MSS	Correspondence, Papers
NYPL	New York Public Library
OR	*The War of the Rebellion: A Compilation of the Official Records of the Union and Confederate Armies* (unless otherwise noted, all references are to series 1, vol. 2; all others are from series 1)
RP	Robert Patterson
RU	Rutgers University Library
SHC	Southern Historical Collection
TSL&A	Tennessee State Library and Archives

UGA   University of Georgia Library

UNC   University of North Carolina Library

UND   University of Notre Dame Archives

USAH&EC   U.S. Army Heritage and Education Center

USC   University of South Carolina Library

UVA   University of Virginia Library

VHS   Virginia Historical Society

Prologue

1. Welles, *Diary*, 2:282–83.
2. Weigley, *Great Civil War*, 58–60.
3. Hopkins, *From Bull Run to Appomattox*, 31–33.
4. C. Adams, *Charles Francis Adams*, 120–21; Guillemin, *World of Comets*, 212–14.

Chapter 1

1. GTB to James G. Totten, Mar. 1, 1861, GTB MSS, LC.
2. T. Williams, *Beauregard*, 2–3, 51–52.
3. Ibid., 3–6.
4. Ibid., 6–7; Morrison, "*Best School in the World*," 94–97. A venerable but still valuable discussion of the extent of Jomini's influence on mid-nineteenth-century American commanders is included in Donald, *Lincoln Reconsidered*, 87–100. For an argument that Beauregard was never a true disciple of Jomini see Connelly and Jones, *Politics of Command*, 29–30. A thorough overview of the subject is Reardon, *With a Sword in One Hand and Jomini in the Other*.
5. For Beauregard's class standing, see *Register of Officers and Cadets* (1835), 15; (1836), 12; (1837), 9; (1838), 6. For his demerits, see *Roll of Cadets According to Merit* (1835), 21; (1836), 21; (1837), 21; (1838), 21. For Lee's academic record, see Freeman, *R. E. Lee*, 1:81–82.
6. T. Williams, *Beauregard*, 7.
7. *New York Times*, May 6, 1885; *Sixteenth Annual Reunion of the Association of Graduates*, 103; Cullum, *Biographical Register*, 1:712; Beatie, *Road to Manassas*, 36–37; W. C. Davis, *Battle at Bull Run*, 9–10.
8. Cullum, *Biographical Register*, 1:711. For McDowell's class, see *Register of Officers and Cadets* (1835), 16; (1836), 13; (1837), 10; (1838), 9. For his demerits, see *Roll of Cadets According to Merit* (1835), 23; (1836), 23; (1837), 23; (1838), 24.
9. *Sixteenth Annual Reunion of the Association of Graduates*, 103; Cullum, *Biographical Register*, 1:711. For the duties of the academy adjutant and the institution's academic board, see Morrison, "*Best School in the World*," 4, 25, 43–47, 74, 151.
10. *New York Times*, May 6, 1885; *Sixteenth Annual Reunion of the Association of Graduates*, 103; Longacre, "Fortune's Fool," 22. For John Wool, see Rezneck, "Civil War Role."

11. T. Williams, *Beauregard*, 8–11.

12. Ibid., 12–14; Bauer, *Mexican War*, 32–43.

13. Bauer, *Mexican War*, 232–37; T. Johnson, *Winfield Scott*, 149–70; GTB, *With Beauregard in Mexico*, 30–31; G. McClellan, *Mexican War Diary*, 56–57, 60–63.

14. GTB, *With Beauregard in Mexico*, 34–37, 109; Bauer, *Mexican War*, 263; Eisenhower, *So Far from God*, 276–77; D. Hill, *Fighter from Way Back*, 98–99.

15. T. Williams, *Beauregard*, 21–22; Bauer, *Mexican War*, 263; Freeman, *R. E. Lee*, 1:238–41. Beauregard's account of the fighting at Cerro Gordo is in *With Beauregard in Mexico*, 32–40.

16. T. Williams, *Beauregard*, 25–26; GTB, *With Beauregard in Mexico*, 41–59. General Twiggs's report of the battle at Contreras cites Beauregard for being "particularly active" in assisting an artillery unit. See U.S. Congress, House, *Message from the President . . .* , 322–25.

17. T. Williams, *Beauregard*, 28–30; GTB, *With Beauregard in Mexico*, 60–74; Bauer, *Mexican War*, 311–12; Eisenhower, *So Far from God*, 337–38; Smith and Judah, *Chronicles of the Gringos*, 250–51, 257. During the operations in advance of Mexico City, Beauregard received prominent mention in the reports of Major John L. Smith, his immediate superior in the corps of engineers. See U.S. Congress. House. *Message from the President . . .* , 349–53, 425–28.

18. GTB, *With Beauregard in Mexico*, 75–81. Beauregard's report of the fighting at Chapultepec is in U.S. Congress. House. *Message from the President . . .* , 190–91.

19. GTB, *With Beauregard in Mexico*, 84–98; U.S. Congress. House. *Message from the President . . .* , 190–91, 428; Reilly, *War with Mexico!*, 181.

20. Bauer, *Mexican War*, 145–46; Eisenhower, *So Far from God*, xx, 156.

21. Eisenhower, *So Far from God*, 156; Smith and Judah, *Chronicles of the Gringos*, 34.

22. Baylies, *Wool's Campaign in Mexico*, 10; Gregg, *Diary and Letters*, 217, 223–24, 261–63, 263n; Eisenhower, *So Far from God*, 156.

23. Smith and Judah, *Chronicles of the Gringos*, 93–95; Gregg, *Diary and Letters*, 218, 261–63; Lavender, *Climax at Buena Vista*, 136–37.

24. Baylies, *Wool's Campaign in Mexico*, 18–19, 28–39; Bauer, *Mexican War*, 150, 209–18; Eisenhower, *So Far from God*, 178–90. For a book-length study of the campaign in northern Mexico, see Lavender, *Climax at Buena Vista*.

25. U.S. Congress, Senate, *Message from the President . . .* , 144–53; IM to "My dear Mrs. Hart," Mar. 8, 1847, Folder 4, Box 21, John E. Wool MSS, New York State Library. Historian Russel Beatie intimates that in the aftermath of Buena Vista, McDowell was the object of rumors of cowardice. Beatie cites no source for his comment, and the record is silent on the subject. It seems doubtful that Wool would have praised McDowell's "gallant bearing" and so strongly recommended his promotion had there been a basis for any such claims. Beatie, *Army of the Potomac*, xxxii.

26. IM to "My dear Mrs. Hart," May 8, 1847, Wool MSS.

27. Ibid.; *HR&D*, 664; Edwards, *Campaign in New Mexico*, 145–46; Smith and Judah, *Chronicles of the Gringos*, 424–29; Bauer, *Mexican War*, 221–26; Baylies, *Wool's Campaign in Mexico*, 52, 66–78. Wool's receipt of the thanks of Congress and a presentation sword did not take place until January 1854, fully six years after his service at Buena Vista.

28. T. Williams, *Beauregard*, 32–33; *HR&D*, 204.

29. T. Williams, *Beauregard*, 32–36.

30. Ibid., 36–42; GTB, *With Beauregard in Mexico*, 106–12. Late in 1856 Beauregard considered resigning his commission and joining the ranks of South American filibusterer William Walker but was talked out of it by superiors loath to lose his services. He was thus spared the fate of the injudicious Walker, who died before a firing squad in Honduras.

31. T. Williams, *Beauregard*, 44–45.

32. Crackel, *West Point*, 131–32, 277, 322n; Roman, *Operations of General Beauregard*, 1:13–15; GTB to Joseph G. Totten, Jan. 25, 1861, GTB MSS, LC.

33. T. Williams, *Beauregard*, 47; GTB to D. D. Tompkins, Mar. 31, 1861, GTB MSS, LC.

34. Cullum, *Biographical Register*, 1:711; T. Johnson, *Winfield Scott*, 241–42.

35. Cullum, *Biographical Register*, 1:711; Thian, *Military Geography*, 36, 43, 59, 63, 98–99.

36. Cullum, *Biographical Register*, 1:711; *New York Times*, May 6, 1885; Dupuy and Dupuy, *Encyclopedia of Military History*, 829–30. The Franco-Italian-Austrian War spawned some military milestones, including the establishment of the International Red Cross. Anticipating First Bull Run, it was also one of the first major conflicts to feature the strategic use of railroads.

37. *OR*, 51(1):326; Leech, *Reveille in Washington*, 6–16, 32; Woodruff, "Early War Days," 91–92; Cooling, "Civil War Deterrent," 164; Stone, "Washington in 1861," 57.

38. *OR*, 51(1):322–24, 335; Cullum, *Biographical Register*, 1:711; Leech, *Reveille in Washington*, 71–73; Allaben, *John Watts de Peyster*, 2:25.

39. *Sixteenth Annual Reunion of the Association of Graduates*, 104; W. C. Davis, *Battle at Bull Run*, 10; Longacre, "Fortune's Fool," 22; Small, *Road to Richmond*, 20; Warren Hassler, *Commanders of the Army of the Potomac*, 4. Beatie's description of McDowell's character and personality is one of the best. *Army of the Potomac*, 165–66.

40. *New York Times*, May 6, 1885; Allaben, *John Watts de Peyster*, 2:28; Nevins, *War for the Union*, 159; Schuckers, *Life and Public Services of Salmon Portland Chase*, 451.

41. Strong, *Diary*, 179; Niven, *Salmon P. Chase*, 254; Longacre, "Fortune's Fool," 23.

42. T. Williams, *Beauregard*, 48–49; *OR*, 260–61.

43. *OR*, 260, 266; Francis W. Pickens to M. L. Bonham, July 7, 1861, Bonham MSS, USC.

44. *OR*, 271–85.

45. Ibid., 288–308; J. Davis, *Rise and Fall of the Confederate Government*, 264–72.

46. Detzer, *Allegiance*, 260–302; Swanberg, *First Blood*, 298–322.

47. J. Davis, *Rise and Fall of the Confederate Government*, 289; *Journal of the Congress of the Confederate States*, 1:108–109; Yearns, *Confederate Congress*, 60–61.

48. Leech, *Reveille in Washington*, 1–2; T. Johnson, *Winfield Scott*, 222–23.

49. Freeman, *R. E. Lee*, 1:349–51, 360–61, 377–78, 405–26, 429–36.

50. Ibid., 437–42, 463–65, 516–21.

51. *OR*, 51(1):341; Townsend, *Anecdotes of the Civil War*, 16; Thian, *Military Geography*, 103; Sivertsen, "McDowell and the Campaign of First Manassas," 15; *JCCW*, 54–55.

52. Beatie, *Army of the Potomac*, xxxii–xxxiv; W. Robertson, "First Bull Run," 88; Townsend, *Anecdotes of the Civil War*, 13–14; Chase, *Inside Lincoln's Cabinet*, 12–13; Niven, *Salmon P. Chase*, 254; Schuckers, *Life and Public Services of Salmon Portland Chase*, 450–51.

53. Townsend, *Anecdotes of the Civil War*, 14; Beatie, *Army of the Potomac*, 163–64.

54. T. Johnson, *Winfield Scott*, 223–25; Beatie, *Army of the Potomac*, 143–44.

55. T. Johnson, *Winfield Scott*, 226–28; Peskin, *Winfield Scott*, 249–52; Nevins, *War for the Union*, 151–52; Stone, "Washington in 1861," 59–61.

56. Sanger, *Statutes at Large*, 12:1260.

57. Fry, *McDowell and Tyler*, 7–9; Nicolay and Hay, *Abraham Lincoln*, 4:323; Niven, *Salmon P. Chase*, 254.

58. *HR&D*, 664; Beatie, *Army of the Potomac*, 164; *JCCW*, 37; Fry, *McDowell and Tyler*, 9–10; R. Johnston, *Bull Run*, 20–21.

59. IM, "Military Operations East of the Allegheny's [*sic*]," May 16, 1861, copy in Chase MSS, HSP.

60. Ibid.; Beatie, *Army of the Potomac*, 146–47.

61. Thian, *Military Geography*, 87; *OR*, 607, 611, 635; 51(1):330–31, 336.

62. *OR*, 7–9, 28–32, 600–601, 604–608, 611, 623–24, 627, 638.

63. Ibid., 23–26, 37–39, 48–52.

64. Ibid., 37–44; O. B. Willcox to Joseph K. F. Mansfield, May 24, 1861, GLC; *New York Times*, May 25, 1861; Willcox, *Forgotten Valor*, 260–67; Nicolay and Hay, *Abraham Lincoln*, 4:311–13; Randall, *Colonel Elmer Ellsworth*, 257–59; Anthony W. Smith to "Dear Brother," June 3, 1861, A. Smith MSS, MoHS.

65. *OR*, 768–69; Cooling, *Mr. Lincoln's Forts*, 1–2, 4–12, 48–50; J. M. Wilson, *Defenses of Washington*, 7–9; Beatie, *Army of the Potomac*, 557–58; Leech, *Reveille in Washington*, 115–16.

66. Details of the location, origins, structural composition, and condition of the Aqueduct, Chain, and Long Bridges can be found in the text accompanying the map entitled *Seat of War: Manassas and Its Vicinity*, published in an issue (date unknown) of the *Richmond Enquirer* following the First Battle of Bull Run.

67. *OR*, 653; *New York Herald*, May 28, 29, 1861; Thian, *Military Geography*, 81.

68. *OR*, 653–55; *New York Express*, May 30, 1861; Allaben, *John Watts de Peyster*, 2:25.

69. K. Williams, *Lincoln Finds a General*, 1:67; Bigelow, *Retrospections*, 1:360.

70. GTB to Leroy P. Walker, Apr. 17, 1861, GTB MSS, LC.

71. Roman, *Operations of General Beauregard*, 1:54–59; T. Williams, *Beauregard*, 63; GTB to Leroy P. Walker, May 1, 1861, GTB MSS, LC.

72. *OR*, 52(2):106.

73. T. Williams, *Beauregard*, 64–65; E. Thomas, *Confederate State of Richmond*, 45.

74. Warner, *Generals in Gray*, 28–29, 56–57; Dickert, *Kershaw's Brigade*, 51; Couper, *One Hundred Years at V.M.I.*, 2:127; W. C. Davis, *Battle at Bull Run*, 15–16.

Chapter 2

1. B. Johnson, *Memoir of . . . Johnston*, 2–7; Hughes, *General Johnston*, 6–8; Govan and Livingood, *Different Valor*, 12–13.

2. Symonds, *Joseph E. Johnston*, 11; Hughes, *General Johnston*, 10–12.

3. Hughes, *General Johnston*, 13.

4. Ibid., 14; Peter Johnston to JEJ, July 17, 1825, JEJ MSS, UVA; Benjamin R. Johnston to JEJ, Dec. 4, 1825, ibid.; JEJ to Louisa S. Johnston, June 30, 1825, JEJ MSS, CW&M.

5. For Johnston's fourth-year class standing, see *Register of Officers and Cadets* (1826), 13. For his fourth-year demerits, see *Roll of Cadets According to Merit* (1826), 3.

6. For Johnston's demerits, see *Roll of Cadets According to Merit* (1827), 19; (1828), 19; and (1829), 19.

7. *HR&D*, 259, 262, 394, 539, 577–78, 715, 796; Symonds, *Joseph E. Johnston*, 16.

8. Maddox, "Grog Mutiny," 32–36; Fleming, *West Point*, 58; Govan and Livingood, *Different Valor*, 14.

9. Symonds, *Joseph E. Johnston*, 19; Freeman, *R. E. Lee*, 1:55, 82–83; A. Long, *Memoirs of Lee*, 71.

10. *Register of Officers and Cadets* (1829), 6; Wainwright, "First Regiment of Cavalry," 153; JEJ to Louisa S. Johnston, Jan. 25, 1829, JEJ MSS, CW&M; Hughes, "Some Letters from Papers of Johnston," 319–20.

11. "Major General Robert Patterson, 1792–1881," 5–6, Patterson MSS, HSP.

12. Ibid., 6–7; *HR&D*, 775.

13. "Major General Robert Patterson," 7–8; Johnson and Malone, *Dictionary of American Biography*, 14:306.

14. "Major General Robert Patterson," 8–11; "The Patterson Mansion," HSP. For more on the general's home, see L. Patterson, "Old Patterson Mansion." For information on Patterson's wife and children, see "Robert Patterson (1792–1881)," Oct. 12, 2000, Find a Grave, http://www.findagrave.com/cgi-bin/fg.cgi?page=gr&GRid=12941.

15. *Mexican War and Its Heroes*, 2:145. For details of these civil disturbances, see C. Brown, *Buckshot War;* Feldberg, *Philadelphia Riots of 1844;* and Geffen, "Violence in Philadelphia in the 1840s and 1850s."

16. Symonds, *Joseph E. Johnston*, 23; A. Dyer, "Fourth Regiment of Artillery," 352.

17. Symonds, *Joseph E. Johnston*, 23–24, 86, 93; Longacre, *Worthy Opponents*, 9–11.

18. Hughes, *General Johnston*, 17.

19. Ibid., 17–19; Cullum, *Biographical Register*, 1:427–28; JEJ to Beverly R. Johnston, Jan. 9, Mar. 25, 1834, Feb. 18, 1836, JEJ MSS, CW&M.

20. Symonds, *Joseph E. Johnston*, 34; Hughes, *General Johnston*, 19; JEJ to Beverly R. Johnston, June 13, 1837, JEJ MSS, CW&M.

21. *Army and Navy Chronicle* 7 (1838): 125; Hughes, *General Johnston*, 20–21; B. Johnson, *Memoir of . . . Johnston*, 10–11; Buker, *Swamp Sailors*, 60–62.

22. Hughes, *General Johnston*, 21–23; B. Johnson, *Memoir of . . . Johnston*, 262–63; *HR&D*, 578; Cullum, *Biographical Register*, 1:428; JEJ to J. Preston Johnstone, May 30, Aug. 31, Oct. 17, 1839, Mar. 11, 16, July 12, Nov. 19, 1840, May 13, 21, June 2, 13, Sept. 16, 1841, May 13, Nov. 27, 1842, Apr. 4, 1843, JEJ MSS, CW&M.

23. "Major General Robert Patterson," 11.

24. Bauer, *Mexican War*, 52–57, 59–63, 85–89; Eisenhower, *So Far from God*, 111–12; U.S. Congress, House, *Mexican War Correspondence*, 418–19.

25. Eisenhower, *So Far from God*, 158; U.S. Congress, House, *Mexican War Correspondence*, 341.

26. Bauer, *Mexican War*, 85–90; Eisenhower, *So Far from God*, 112; F. Smith, *Mexican War Journal*, 19–20; U.S. Congress, House, *Mexican War Correspondence*, 461–62.

27. U.S. Congress, House, *Mexican War Correspondence*, 343–45, 381–84, 472–73; Eisenhower, *So Far from God*, 158–59; Lavender, *Climax at Buena Vista*, 124–39; Bauer, *Mexican War*, 232–36; D. Hill, *Fighter from Way Back*, 29.

28. Eisenhower, *So Far from God*, 159; Lavender, *Climax at Buena Vista*, 151–54; U.S. Congress, House, *Mexican War Correspondence*, 381–82, 385, 388, 848, 850, 852, 861, 879–80.

29. "Major General Robert Patterson," 14–16; U.S. Congress, House, *Mexican War Correspondence*, 368–69.

30. Symonds, *Joseph E. Johnston*, 54; Bauer, *Mexican War*, 8–9, 16–17, 46–48, 52–63, 86–101, 209–17, 232–42; *HR&D*, 578; Elliott, *Winfield Scott*, 455.

31. Bauer, *Mexican War*, 261–74; Elliott, *Winfield Scott*, 464; Hughes, *General Johnston*, 25–26; GTB, *With Beauregard in Mexico*, 32–33; Maury, "Reminiscences of Johnston," 172.

32. Hughes, *General Johnston*, 25; Bauer, *Mexican War*, 306–11.

33. Johnston's report of the storming of Chapultepec is in U.S. Congress, House, *Message from the President*, 210–13.

34. Ibid.; Bauer, *Mexican War*, 306–17; GTB, *With Beauregard in Mexico*, 78–81; B. Johnson, *Memoir of . . . Johnston*, 14–15; Hughes, *General Johnston*, 30–32.

35. *HR&D*, 578; Hughes, *General Johnston*, 31–32. For a concise explanation of how Johnston's brevet promotions for gallantry in Mexico hampered his later rise in the army, see Symonds, *Joseph E. Johnston*, 89–90.

36. U.S. Congress, House, *Mexican War Correspondence*, 369–70; Bauer, *Mexican War*, 235–36; T. Johnson, *Winfield Scott*, 157–59; Lavender, *Climax at Buena Vista*, 140–45.

37. U.S. Congress, House, *Mexican War Correspondence*, 367–69; Eisenhower, *So Far from God*, 164; "Major General Robert Patterson," 14–16.

38. G. McClellan, *Mexican War Diary*, 26, 31, 41, 43; F. Smith, *Mexican War Journal*, 35, 49, 70.

39. GTB, *With Beauregard in Mexico*, 25–26; Eisenhower, *So Far from God*, 257n; D. Hill, *Fighter from Way Back*, 73, 91; G. McClellan, *Mexican War Diary*, 56; Smith and Judah, *Chronicles of the Gringos*, 181, 181n; Bauer, *Mexican War*, 245–46.

40. GTB, *With Beauregard in Mexico*, 34–37; Eisenhower, *So Far from God*, 275–77, 282n.

41. U.S. Congress, House, *Mexican War Correspondence*, 936, 957, 1023.

42. Ibid., 1031, 1034, 1036; Eisenhower, *So Far from God*, 295–96, 350; D. Hill, *Fighter from Way Back*, 147; *HR&D*, 775.

43. Cullum, *Biographical Register*, 1:428; *HR&D*, 578; Symonds, *Joseph E. Johnston*, 72–83; JEJ to Edward W. Johnston, Jan. 6, 1851, JEJ MSS, CW&M; *HR&D*, 578; Wainwright, "First Regiment of Cavalry," 159; JEJ to Samuel Cooper, Feb. 24, 1855, JEJ MSS, DU; JEJ to George Cadwalader, Feb. 11, 1854, Mar. 7, 1855, Cadwalader MSS, HSP.

44. JEJ, "Diary of Survey of Southern Border of Kansas," May 16–Oct. 29, 1857, JEJ MSS, CW&M; Lash, *Destroyer of the Iron Horse*, 2–3.

45. Longacre, *Worthy Opponents*, 74–75; Parish, *American Civil War*, 123; Govan and Livingood, *Different Valor*, 30–31; Haskell, *Memoirs*, 6–7; Alexander, *Fighting for the Confederacy*, 82.

46. Cullum, *Biographical Register*, 1:428; Furniss, *Mormon Conflict*, 198–203; JEJ to Assistant Adjutant General, USA, May 27, 1858, JEJ MSS, CW&M; Govan and Livingood, *Different Valor*, 22–23; Symonds, *Joseph E. Johnston*, 90.

47. Govan and Livingood, *Different Valor*, 23, 25–26; *HR&D*, 40, 573; Symonds, *Joseph E. Johnston*, 90; Freeman, *R. E. Lee*, 1:411–12; R. E. Lee to JEJ, July 30, 1860, JEJ MSS, CW&M; Hughes, *General Johnston*, 33–34.

48. "Major General Robert Patterson," 8–9; L. Patterson, "Old Patterson Mansion," 81; Johnson and Malone, *Dictionary of American Biography*, 14:306.

49. "Major General Robert Patterson," 10–11; *HR&D*, 774. In April 1862 Frank Patterson rose to brigadier general of volunteers and took command of an infantry brigade in the Army of the Potomac, but his war service, like his father's, ended in controversy and disgrace. That

November, distressed by charges that he had abandoned a post in response to erroneous reports of approaching Confederates, Frank was found dead in his tent of a pistol wound. Warner, *Generals in Blue*, 362–63, 649n.

50. Beatie, *Road to Manassas*, 6, 224n.
51. Copy of General Orders No. 3, Apr. 19, 1861, Cadwalader MSS, HSP; *Philadelphia Inquirer*, Apr. 18, 1861; RP, *Narrative*, 26; *JCCW*, 78; *HR&D*, 272, 587, 742, 1040, 1064.
52. Beatie, *Army of the Potomac*, 101, 101n. Over the years historians have assumed that Patterson served only in the Pennsylvania state troops; thus, for instance, he is not represented in Warner, *Generals in Blue*. Beatie discovered Patterson's unorthodox transfer of rank while researching his study of the Army of the Potomac and its predecessor.
53. Symonds, *Joseph E. Johnston*, 91–93; Longacre, *Worthy Opponents*, 59.
54. Govan and Livingood, *Different Valor*, 26–27.
55. Ibid., 28; Milton, *Conflict*, 57.
56. Chesnut, *Mary Chesnut's Civil War*, 187.
57. Cullum, *Biographical Register*, 1:428; JEJ, *Narrative of Military Operations*, 10; JEJ, copies of resignation letter and Confederate-army appointment, JEJ MSS, CW&M.
58. JEJ, *Narrative of Military Operations*, 12–13; *OR*, 783–84, 787, 837, 844–45; James, "Storm Center of the Confederate Army," 347.
59. JEJ, *Narrative of Military Operations*, 13, 16; Downs, "Responsibility Is Great," 40–41; Perry, "Davis and Johnston," 93.
60. *OR*, 579, 51(1):331; Thian, *Military Geography*, 103.
61. *Philadelphia Inquirer*, May 4, 1861; Warner, *Generals in Blue*, 378–80; Beatie, *Army of the Potomac*, xxiv–xxvi, 106–108.
62. *Philadelphia Inquirer*, May 4, 1861; Beatie, *Army of the Potomac*, 102.
63. *OR*, 579–80, 585–87; Beatie, *Army of the Potomac*, 102–104.
64. RP, *Narrative*, 26–27; *OR*, 585–86. There is no record of John Sherman having been commissioned into the army. Although he is occasionally referred to in official correspondence as "Colonel" and "Major," these appear to have been honorary titles. See ibid., 692, 704.
65. *OR*, 600, 623–24; RP, *Narrative*, 27; Trefousse, *Ben Butler*, 66–69, 73; West, *Lincoln's Scapegoat General*, 52–57, 66–68; Lockwood and Lockwood, *Siege of Washington*, 229–30.
66. RP, *Narrative*, 27–28; Beatie, *Army of the Potomac*, 138–41.
67. *OR*, 607, 615–16, 635, 647; Thian, *Military Geography*, 87, 103.
68. *OR*, 615–16, 621; Fitz John Porter to George B. McClellan, May 1, 1861, McClellan MSS, LC.
69. *OR*, 579, 620, 622, 624–25, 627–28, 635, 637.
70. Ibid., 29–32, 637.
71. JEJ, *Narrative of Military Operations*, 13; *OR*, 784–85, 844–45; Symonds, *Joseph E. Johnston*, 102–103; Kellogg, *Shenandoah Valley and Virginia*, 12; Govan and Livingood, *Different Valor*, 34–35; Frye, *2nd Virginia Infantry*, 8; J. W. Jones, "Reminiscences of the Army of Northern Virginia . . . Early Days," 90–92.

72. OR, 871–72, 877; JEJ, *Narrative of Military Operations*, 14–15.
73. *HR&D*, 568; Warner, *Generals in Gray*, 151–52; Couper, *One Hundred Years at V.M.I.*, 2:95–98; OR, 784–85; Imboden, "Jackson at Harper's Ferry," 120–25; Hughes, *General Johnston*, 40–41; Conrad, "Manassas and . . . the Stonewall Brigade," 83; D. Hill, "Real Stonewall Jackson," 623–26; Charles Grattan memoirs, 6–7, USAH&EC; Bean, *Liberty Hall Volunteers*, 32; Douglas, "Stonewall Jackson and His Men," 645–47; E. Daniel, *Speeches of John Warwick Daniel*, 45.
74. Govan and Livingood, *Different Valor*, 35; Parks, *General Edmund Kirby Smith*, 126; Wert, *Cavalryman of the Lost Cause*, 48–49; JEJ, *Narrative of Military Operations*, 17–19.
75. Walker G. Camp to "Miss Lizzie Camp," June 1, 1861, Camp MSS, GDA&H; Downs, "Responsibility Is Great," 43; OR, 881, 910.
76. B. Davis, *They Called Him Stonewall*, 141; Wellman, *Harpers Ferry*, 33; J. W. Jones, "Reminiscences of the Army of Northern Virginia . . . Early Days," 93.
77. Chesnut, *Mary Chesnut's Civil War*, 268. Johnston's overriding concern for his reputation and his overweening regard for his military contributions only increased after the war. Thus his published recollections of the First Manassas Campaign, like Beauregard's, must be consulted carefully, preferably matched against other, more objective accounts of his service. Biographical treatment runs the gamut of the hero worshipping (Hughes, *General Johnston*, and B. Johnson, *Memoir of . . . Johnston*), the generally laudatory (Govan and Livingood, *Different Valor*), and the more highly critical (Symonds, *Joseph E. Johnston*).
78. OR, 646–47, 652, 657–58, 51(1):336; RP, *Narrative*, 29–30.
79. OR, 657–58, 660–62, 669; RP, *Narrative*, 31.
80. OR, 665.
81. Ibid., 670–71, 51(1):397; RP, *Narrative*, 33.

Chapter 3

1. Nineteenth-century descriptions of Bull Run (the stream) are numerous. They include Longstreet, *From Manassas to Appomattox*, 34; Pollard, *First Year of the War*, 96; Alexander, *Fighting for the Confederacy*, 39; Barnard, *C.S.A. and the Battle of Bull Run*, 43–44; and Roman, *Operations of General Beauregard*, 1:92.
2. Alexander, *Fighting for the Confederacy*, 39; R. Johnston, *Bull Run*, 38–41; W. C. Davis, *Battle at Bull Run*, 61–63. Johnston considered the land on either side of Bull Run to be too poor for farming. JEJ, "Bull Run: An Important Letter," 237. At least one latter-day historian disagrees. See Hanson, *Bull Run Remembers*, 25.
3. Perhaps the finest set of maps specific to the First Bull Run battlefield emerged from a study conducted in the late 1980s by technicians of the National Park Service and MNBP. The study team produced a historical base map and six troop-movement maps derived from contemporary and post–Civil War maps of the battlefield and adjacent areas found at MNBP, the Library of Congress, the National Archives, the library of

the U.S. Department of the Interior, and the U.S. Army Heritage and Education Center (copies of the troop-movement maps are available for a modest fee from MNBP). In order to plot battle movements, the study team compiled a book-length collection of after-action reports of "participants, unit histories of commands engaged in the campaign; journals, diaries, letters, and reminiscences of officers and enlisted men who fought at First Manassas and Blackburn's Ford." The work, as edited by Ed Bearss, was published in 1991 as *First Manassas Battlefield Map Study*.

4. Cooling, *Historical Highlights*, 23–24; R. Johnston, *Bull Run*, 41–42; GTB, "First Battle of Bull Run," 211. A member of the 18th Virginia provided a contemporary overview of the local road system. See William F. Cocke to Thomas L. P. Cocke, Aug. 7–11, 1861, Armistead-Cocke MSS, CW&M.

5. *OR*, 806; R. Johnston, *Bull Run*, 31–32.

6. Cooling, *Historical Highlights*, 24–26; Hanson, *Bull Run Remembers*, 26–27; R. Johnston, *Bull Run*, 42; W. C. Davis, *Battle at Bull Run*, 7. In the spring of 1861, Manassas and Strasburg were linked by rail, but due to prewar politics and lobbying, there was no rail connection between Strasburg and Winchester, which would prove a logistical handicap to the Confederates in the coming campaign. Kean, "Development of the 'Valley Line,'" 545.

7. Hanson, *Bull Run Remembers*, 26, 26n.

8. *OR*, 804–86, 817–18; Freeman, *R. E. Lee*, 1:505; Warner, *Generals in Gray*, 56–57. According to Beauregard's adjutant general, in postwar years Johnston, while acknowledging the contributions of Lee and Cocke, claimed credit for recommending the early occupation of the Manassas area. Thomas Jordan to R. U. Johnson, Sept. 12, 1884, Jordan MSS, C-CWC, NYPL.

9. *OR*, 817, 824, 841–42, 845–47, 51(2):79, 82; Freeman, *R. E. Lee*, 1:512–13.

10. *OR*, 836–37; W. C. Davis, *Battle at Bull Run*, 31.

11. Warner, *Generals in Gray*, 28–29; Dickert, *Kershaw's Brigade*, 51; A. H. Marston to M. L. Bonham, June 6, 1861, Bonham MSS, USC.

12. A. P. Aldrich to his wife, June 23, 1861, Bonham MSS, USC; David W. Aiken to his wife, Aug. 2, 1861, Aiken MSS, USC. Aldrich's letter has been published as Longacre, "On the Staff of the 'Dictator.'"

13. W. C. Davis, *Battle at Bull Run*, 26, 31–32; *OR*, 865–66, 879; Hanson, *Bull Run Remembers*, 36.

14. *OR*, 896; R. Johnston, *Bull Run*, 34; Cooke, *Wearing of the Gray*, 73; M. L. Bonham to GTB, Aug. 15, 1861, Bonham MSS, Gratz Collection, HSP; Warner, *Generals in Gray*, 29. Williams has Beauregard assuming command on the morning of June 3. *Beauregard*, 67.

15. Warfield, *Confederate Soldier's Memoirs*, 48; GTB, "First Battle of Bull Run," 219.

16. Hanson, *Bull Run Remembers*, 31; Thomas Jordan to Daniel Ruggles, May 29, 1861, Jordan MSS, Gratz Collection, HSP.

17. Hanson, *Bull Run Remembers*, 31–32.

18. Cooke, *Wearing of the Gray*, 73–74; Alexander, *Fighting for the Confederacy*, 38.
19. London *Times*, May 14, 1861.
20. *Battle-fields of the South*, 32; Cooke, *Wearing of the Gray*, 75; C. W. Truehart to "Cousin William," Oct. 26, 1861, MNBP.
21. *Battle-fields of the South*, 19.
22. Hanson, *Bull Run Remembers*, 34; *OR*, 901–902.
23. GTB, "First Battle of Bull Run," 197.
24. Ibid.; *OR*, 775, 865, 867, 907, 915, 917; Eppa Hunton to M. L. Bonham, June 21, 1861, Bonham MSS, USC.
25. M. L. Bonham to "Gernl.," Aug. 15, 1861, Bonham MSS, Gratz Collection, HSP; *OR*, 538; Coles, *From Huntsville to Appomattox*, 25; Bevens, *Reminiscences of a Private*, 11; C. Williams, "A Saline Guard," 346; R. A. Moore, *Life for the Confederacy*, 37–38; Hundley, "Beginning and the Ending," 297; F. B. Williams, "From Sumter to the Wilderness," 2; Gibbs, "With a Mississippi Private," 44.
26. Dickert, *Kershaw's Brigade*, 42; Louis P. Foster to his mother, June 19, 1861, Foster MSS, USC.
27. *OR*, 943–44; W. C. Davis, *Battle at Bull Run*, 54.
28. *OR*, 943–44; T. Williams, *Beauregard*, 72; R. Johnston, *Bull Run*, 111.
29. Warner, *Generals in Gray*, 84–85; Haskell, *Memoirs*, 18; G. Campbell Brown memoirs, 4–5, TSL&A; J. Gordon, *Reminiscences*, 40; Pfanz, *Richard S. Ewell*, 132, 137.
30. Warner, *Generals in Gray*, 163–64, 192–93; *HR&D*, 580; Johnson and Malone, *Dictionary of American Biography*, 10:166–67; W. C. Davis, *Battle at Bull Run*, 54, 57; Longstreet, *From Manassas to Appomattox*, 32–33.
31. Longstreet, *From Manassas to Appomattox*, 33; Sorrel, *Confederate Staff Officer*, 17.
32. *OR*, 23–26, 944, 51(1):27; *New Orleans Daily Delta*, Aug. 13, 1861; Donnelly, "District of Columbia Confederates," 208; L. A. Wallace, *1st Virginia Infantry*, 18–19; Couper, *One Hundred Years at V.M.I.*, 2:130.
33. Warner, *Generals in Gray*, 79–80, 83–84; Haskell, *Memoirs*, 18; Cooke, *Wearing of the Gray*, 99; R. E. Lee to N. G. Evans, June 20, 1861, GLC; Sorrel, *Confederate Staff Officer*, 93; *Battle-fields of the South*, 59. Virtually every history of the First Bull Run Campaign identifies Evans as a colonel at the time of the battle. But Evans, who is identified as a major in official correspondence, did not attain a colonelcy until some days after the fighting and held that rank only briefly before being appointed a brigadier general, largely on the strength of his achievements on July 21. That Evans was given command over Colonel Sloan of the 4th South Carolina is testimony to his West Point education and regular-army background, credentials that Sloan lacked: Silverman et al., *Shanks*, 6–61, 75–76, 119n.
34. Dufour, *Gentle Tiger*, 6–7, 123–25; Alexander, *Military Memoirs*, 22; Alexander, *Fighting for the Confederacy*, 119. Wheat's multifaceted prewar career is covered in A. Moore, *Old Bob Wheat*.

35. Driver and Howard, *2nd Virginia Cavalry*, 1–13; *OR*, 457–58, 852–53, 858, 926, 51(2):112, 123; Thomas T. Munford to Charles C. Jones, Jr., Nov. 11, 1875, Munford MSS, Gratz Collection, HSP.

36. Wise, *Long Arm of Lee*, 129–30, 155; R. Johnston, *Bull Run*, 112; Hanson, *Bull Run Remembers*, 17–18; Warner, *Generals in Gray*, 165–66; *OR*, 446.

37. On paper at least, Beauregard's nineteen regiments of infantry and his unbrigaded cavalry and artillery would combine to produce approximately 20,000 men, although the number of effectives in this force cannot be determined. Around this time, McDowell believed that Beauregard had between 23,000 and 25,000 at Manassas. *OR*, 718. The Northern press estimated the number as at least 30,000 men, with another 20,000 at Colonel Cocke's old bailiwick at Culpeper Court House. *Philadelphia Inquirer*, June 12, 1861. For Beauregard's "Beauty and booty" oration, see *OR*, 907; and Roman, *Operations of General Beauregard*, 1:73–74.

38. T. Williams, *Beauregard*, 68.

39. Myers, *Children of Pride*, 724–25; J. Reid, *Fourth Regiment of S.C. Volunteers*, 12–13; David W. Aiken to his wife, June 21, 1861, Aiken MSS, USC.

40. Martin, "Cotton [Family] Letters," 16; Huettel, "Letters from Private Richard C. Bridges," 361; J. McGuire, *Southern Refugee*, 25.

41. Eggleston, *Rebel's Recollections*, 73–74.

42. Francis W. Pickens to M. L. Bonham, July 7, 1861, Bonham MSS, USC.

43. Burnett, "Letters of Three Lightfoot Brothers," 389.

44. Bevens, *Reminiscences of a Private*, 10; J. Franklin, "Incidents at First Manassas," 291.

45. Walker G. Camp to "Miss Lizzie Camp," June 11, 1861, Camp MSS, GDA&H; "Soldiers of '61 and '65," 308–309; R. Lewis, *Confederate Boy*, 10–11; Reid, *Fourth Regiment of S.C. Volunteers*, 8.

46. K. M. Jones, *Heroines of Dixie*, 45.

47. Roman, *Operations of General Beauregard*, 1:71–75; T. Williams, *Beauregard*, 70.

48. Northrop, "Confederate Commissariat at Manassas," 261; Imboden, "Incidents of the First Bull Run," 239. Beauregard's complaints did not extend to his own commissary of subsistence, Lt. Col. Richard Bland Lee, a cousin of Robert E. Lee, whose efforts met with the Creole's "ample satisfaction." GTB to Benjamin Conrad, Aug. 21, 1861, GTB MSS, Gratz Collection, HSP.

49. Northrop, "Confederate Commissariat at Manassas," 261. Historians are divided as to whether Northrop was at fault in this matter. Richard D. Goff and Jeremy P. Felt are critical of the commissary general, while Thomas Robson Hay generally supports Northrop's claim that the army's supply problems were beyond his ability to control or correct. Goff, *Confederate Supply*, 21–25; Felt, "Lucius B. Northrop," 184–85; Hay, "Lucius B. Northrop," 7, 22–23.

50. F. Moore, *Rebellion Record*, 2:54–55.

51. Roman, *Operations of General Beauregard*, 1:76–77; OR, 922.

Chapter 4

1. Starr, *Bohemian Brigade*, 34; Warner, *Generals in Blue*, 540–41.
2. Starr, *Bohemian Brigade*, 35.
3. *New York Tribune*, June 26-July 20, 1861; Andrews, *North Reports the Civil War*, 80.
4. Starr, *Bohemian Brigade*, 36–37; J. Nicolay, *Outbreak of Rebellion*, 171–72.
5. OR, 653; R. Johnston, *Bull Run*, 22; JCCW, 38; W. Franklin, "First Great Crime of the War," 72.
6. John S. French to "Dear Parents, Brothers, and Sisters," July 14, 1861, French MSS, USAH&EC.
7. OR, 654–55.
8. Ibid., 653–54.
9. JCCW, 37.
10. Ibid., 38.
11. Russell, *My Diary North and South*, 395; Nevins, *War for the Union*, 160; K. Williams, *Lincoln Finds a General*, 1:67–68; Warner, *Generals in Blue*, 162–63; HR&D, 439.
12. OR, 322–23.
13. JCCW, 37.
14. OR, 51(1):389–90; Warner, *Generals in Blue*, 480–81; Longacre, "Charles P. Stone," 8–9, 38–41.
15. OR, 51(1):390; HR&D, 557; Miller, *Lincoln's Abolitionist General*, 28–58; Longacre, "Profile of Major General David Hunter," 4–6; Beatie, *Army of the Potomac*, xxxv–xxxvii.
16. Warner, *Generals in Blue*, 227–28; HR&D, 521; Beatie, *Army of the Potomac*, xcxxiv; Catton, *Mr. Lincoln's Army*, 30; Allaben, *John Watts de Peyster*, 2:29.
17. J. Thompson, *Civil War to the Bloody End*, 114–15.
18. Anthony W. Smith to "Dear Brother," June 3, 1861, A. Smith MSS, MoHS; George S. Rollins to his father, July 12, 1861, Rollins MSS, USAH&EC; Thomas H. Davis to "Mother & All," May 6, 1861, Davis MSS, in possession of Walter G. Lee; John S. French to "Dear Brother," July 6, 1861, French MSS, USAH&EC.
19. E. Tyler, *"Wooden Nutmegs" at Bull Run*, 27; Lyster, *Recollections of the Bull Run Campaign*, 17.
20. I. Adams, "Letters of James Rush Holmes," 112; John S. French to "Dear Parents, Brothers and Sisters," Apr. 30, 1861, French MSS, USAH&EC; Sullivan Ballou to Latimer W. Ballou, June 11, 1861, Ballou MSS, Rhode Island Historical Society.
21. *U.S. Infantry Tactics . . . May 1, 1861*, 137–38.
22. Dodd, "Making of a Regiment," 1033.
23. W. Robertson, "First Bull Run," 85; B. Lewis, *Notes on Ammunition*, ii, 7, 11; Bilby, *Civil War Firearms*, 43, 47–49.
24. Bilby, *Civil War Firearms*, 49–61.

25. McWhiney and Jamieson, *Attack and Die*, 48–58; W. Robertson, "First Bull Run,"85–86.

26. *JCCW*, 38.

27. Ibid.; Nevins, *War for the Union*, 162; *OR*, 654–55.

28. Finch, "Boys of '61," 248–49; Blake, *Three Years in the Army of the Potomac*, 11.

29. *OR*, 51(1):396.

30. Warner, *Generals in Blue*, 514–15; *HR&D*, 977; *New York Times*, Dec. 1, 1882; Birkhimer, *Historical Sketch of . . . the Artillery*, 239–42; W. T. Sherman to Ellen E. Sherman, July 15, 1861, Sherman Family MSS, UND; Andrew McClintock to Jane D. McClintock, July 1, 1861, McClintock MSS, USAH&EC; Fry, *McDowell and Tyler*, 12; Finch, "Boys of '61," 246; Staples, "Reminiscences of Bull Run," 131.

31. Warner, *Generals in Blue*, 422–23; *New York Times*, June 19, 1861; *OR*, 51(1):399. Schenck's letters covering the campaign have been published as Longacre, "Ohio Brigadier at Bull Run."

32. *OR*, 51(1):408–409.

33. Warner, *Generals in Blue*, 159–60, 377–78; *HR&D*, 434, 798; Garraty and Carnes, *American National Biography*, 8:403–404; Greene, *In Memoriam*, 9–10; Averell, *Ten Years in the Saddle*, 283; W. Robertson, "First Bull Run," 91.

34. Averell, *Ten Years in the Saddle*, 283–84; W. Robertson, "First Bull Run," 91–92; Warner, *Generals in Blue*, 558–59; *HR&D*, 1038; Garraty and Carnes, *American National Biography*, 23:419–20. See also Willcox, *Forgotten Valor*.

35. Sherman, *Memoirs*, 1:139. See also Marszalek, *Sherman*; L. Lewis, *Sherman, Fighting Prophet*; and Hirshon, *White Tecumseh*.

36. L. Lewis, *Sherman, Fighting Prophet*, 162; Special Orders No. 105 (copy), Adjutant General's Office, June 20, 1861, Sherman MSS, LC; E. D. Townsend to W. T. Sherman, June 28, 1861, ibid.; James B. Fry to W. T. Sherman, June 30, 1861, ibid.; W. T. Sherman to Ellen E. Sherman, July 6, 1861, Sherman Family MSS, UND; Sherman, *Memoirs*, 1:179–80.

37. *OR*, 64–74; Rafuse, *McClellan's War*, 103–14.

38. *OR*, 52–59, 77–104.

39. Ibid., 104–23, 163, 51(1):416.

40. Ibid., 59–61; *Philadelphia Inquirer*, June 3, 1861; J. McGuire, *Southern Refugee*, 23; George W. Latham diary, June 1, 1861, Latham MSS, UVA; Fry, "McDowell's Advance to Bull Run," 174. The last named is, for all intents and purposes, Irvin McDowell's version—a quarter century after the events—of his conduct in the campaign. He had declined an invitation from the editors of the *Century* Magazine (the original source of most of the pieces later published in *Battles and Leaders of the Civil War*) to write the article himself, instead suggesting Fry as the author. IM to "Editor, 'Century' Magazine," June 13, 1884, IM MSS, C-CWC, NYPL. It may be supposed that McDowell carefully vetted Fry's contribution, offering corrections and suggestions with a view to improving it as well as his historical standing.

41. *HR&D*, 964; *OR*, 61–64.
42. *OR*, 61.
43. Ibid., 60; W. C. Davis, *Battle at Bull Run*, 34.
44. *OR*, 662; R. Johnston, *Bull Run*, 24–25; *Philadelphia Inquirer*, June 5, 1861.
45. *OR*, 664–65; R. Johnston, *Bull Run*, 26–28; Fry, "McDowell's Advance to Bull Run," 173–74; Beatie, *Army of the Potomac*, 192–93.
46. *OR*, 666, 690.
47. Ibid., 695; E. Tyler, *"Wooden Nutmegs" at Bull Run*, 44.
48. *OR*, 695; Finch, "Boys of '61," 246.
49. Finch, "Boys of '61," 246.
50. Ibid., 247; D. R. Jones, "Acting Assistant Adjutant General, Camp Pickens," to M. L. Bonham, June 9, 1861, GLC; *OR*, 128–30; F. B. Williams, "From Sumter to the Wilderness," 3.
51. *OR*, 124–28; *New York Times*, June 19, 1861.
52. Glasgow, "General Was a Recruit," 159.
53. *JCCW*, 39; T. Allen, "Second Wisconsin at First Bull Run," 379; Small, *Road to Richmond*, 19; Joseph Corson memoirs, 9–10, Corson MSS, in possession of Dr. Joseph K. Corson; *OR*, 700, 713–15.
54. *OR*, 709, 711, 718, 726; R. Johnston, *Bull Run*, 57–60; Sivertsen, "McDowell and the Campaign of First Manassas," 33–34.
55. *JCCW*, 38.
56. Barnard, *C.S.A. and the Battle of Bull Run*, 45–46; Curtis, *From Bull Run to Chancellorsville*, 44.
57. Andrew McClintock to Jane D. McClintock, July 11, 1861, McClintock MSS, USAH&EC; G. Adams, *Doctors in Blue*, 13–20.
58. *JCCW*, 38; *OR*, 711.

Chapter 5

1. *OR*, 881, 889, 895–98, 901, 907–908; JEJ, *Narrative of Military Operations*, 18.
2. *OR*, 894; JEJ, *Narrative of Military Operations*, 20–21; Downs, "Responsibility Is Great," 41; JEJ, "Responsibilities of the First Bull Run," 242.
3. *OR*, 894; R. Johnston, *Bull Run*, 49.
4. *OR.*, 889–90, 907–908; Govan and Livingood, *Different Valor*, 35, 39; Symonds, *Joseph E. Johnston*, 106.
5. *OR*, 910.
6. W. H. C. Whiting to GTB, June 21, 1861, Whiting MSS, Gratz Collection, HSP.
7. Edmund K. Smith to Hugh L. Clay, May 29, 1861, Smith MSS, SHC, UNC; Smith to Frances M. Webster, June 2, 24, 1861, ibid.; Warner, *Generals in Gray*, 279–80; Heth, *Memoirs*, 168.
8. *OR*, 910; Freeman, *R. E. Lee*, 1:520.
9. *OR*, 668–69.
10. Ibid., 910.
11. JEJ, *Narrative of Military Operations*, 18–19, 22–23.

12. Ibid., 23; *OR*, 123–24, 676; J. W. Jones, "Reminiscences of the Army of Northern Virginia . . . Early Days," 93–95; J. Robertson, *General A. P. Hill*, 39; Stutler, *West Virginia in the Civil War*, 39–41.

13. J. Robertson, *General A. P. Hill*, 1–38; Warner, *Generals in Gray*, 134–35; JEJ, *Narrative of Military Operations*, 25.

14. JEJ, *Narrative of Military Operations*, 23; Symonds, *Joseph E. Johnston*, 107–108; Hughes, *General Johnston*, 44.

15. *OR*, 923–25.

16. Govan and Livingood, *Different Valor*, 39; Symonds, *Joseph E. Johnston*, 107; M. Jackson, *Life and Letters of Jackson*, 162; Mosby, *Memoirs*, 29.

17. J. B. Jones, *Rebel War Clerk's Diary*, 1:52–53.

18. *OR*, 684–86. Those three-months' regiments raised by Governor Curtin that were not assigned to Patterson were the 4th and 5th Pennsylvania, which went instead to the Army of Northeastern Virginia; the 12th Pennsylvania, which was retained in rear of Patterson's army to guard railroads; and the 18th, 19th, and 22nd Pennsylvania, which were posted to garrison duty at Baltimore.

19. Ibid., 672, 51(1):397–98.

20. *OR*, 51(1):397; Warner, *Generals in Blue*, 500–502; Strother, "Personal Recollections of the War," 153; Sherman and Sherman, *Sherman Letters*, 123; Shanks, "Recollections of [George H.] Thomas," 755–56.

21. Ibid., 697, 51(1):397; Bates, *Pennsylvania Volunteers*, 1:241–44.

22. *OR*, 51(1):398; *HR&D*, 708; Cullum, *Biographical Register*, 1:387; Beatie, *Army of the Potomac*, 345–49.

23. *OR*, 679.

24. Ibid., 679–81.

25. Ibid., 685–86.

26. Ibid., 686–91; RP, *Narrative*, 33; Beatie, *Army of the Potomac*, 176–78.

27. *OR*, 687–89; Beatie, *Army of the Potomac*, 177.

28. *OR*, 687–92.

29. Ibid., 691–92; RP, *Narrative*, 33–34.

30. *OR*, 693.

31. Ibid., 691–95; RP, *Narrative*, 34–35.

32. W. H. Keim to George C. Wynkoop, June 5, 1861, C. W. Unger Collection, HSP; *OR*, 693.

33. *OR*, 694–96.

34. RP, *Narrative*, 36; Detzer, *Donnybrook*, 61; K. Williams, *Lincoln Finds a General*, 1:75. In his closely reasoned and highly critical analysis of Patterson's campaign, Thomas L. Livermore concludes that Scott's claim of Washington and Alexandria being in need of security was a valid one. He also dismisses Patterson's postwar contention that he told Scott he could make no pursuit of the retreating Confederates only after learning that he was to be stripped of his regular units. Livermore, "Patterson's Shenandoah Campaign," 13–16.

35. R. Johnston, *Bull Run*, 55; Marvel, *Burnside*, 16.

36. *OR*, 695–98, 715; "Soldiers of '61 and '65," 308.

37. Strother, "Personal Recollections of the War," 142.

38. JEJ, *Narrative of Military Operations*, 23.

39. Ibid., 23–24; *OR*, 923–25.

40. Hughes, *General Johnston*, 50; GTB, *Campaign and Battle of Manassas*, 25–26.

41. *OR*, 924, 935.

42. Ibid., 929–30; Symonds, *Joseph E. Johnston*, 108–109.

43. JEJ, *Narrative of Military Operations*, 24–25; B. Johnson, "Memoir of First Maryland Regiment," 351.

44. JEJ, *Narrative of Military Operations*, 25–28.

45. *OR*, 949.

46. Lash, "Johnston and the Virginia Railways," 10–13. Johnston's self-defense is in *Narrative of Military Operations*, 28–29.

47. JEJ, *Narrative of Military Operations*, 27, 29–30; Imboden, "Incidents of the First Bull Run," 229.

48. Warner, *Generals in Gray*, 23–24; *HR&D*, 205; Heth, *Memoirs*, 137; Shingler, "Reminiscences of the Late Barnard Bee," in possession of Dr. Pat Wilson; Agnew, "General Barnard Bee," 4, 6–8, 44; Gaines Kincaid (Bee family genealogist) to the author, Jan. 3, 1976; James B. Agnew to the author, Jan. 26, 1976; Coles, *From Huntsville to Appomattox*, 24.

49. Warner, *Generals in Gray*, 82–83; *HR&D*, 404; Garraty and Carnes, *American National Biography*, 7:477–78.

50. Zettler, *War Stories*, 60; Myers, *Children of Pride*, 724; Wilkinson and Woodworth, *Scythe of Fire*, 14–16; C. McDonald, *Reminiscences of the War and Refugee Life*, 19–20; *Charleston Mercury*, July 25, 1861; Akin, *Letters*, 20.

51. JEJ, *Narrative of Military Operations*, 27; *OR*, 187; Wise, *Long Arm of Lee*, 127–28.

52. Warner, *Generals in Gray*, 296–97; *HR&D*, 933–34; H. McClellan, *Life and Campaigns of Stuart*, 31–32; Mosby, *War Reminiscences*, 11–12. At this point it would appear that Stuart's regiment had yet to acquire its designation as 1st Virginia Cavalry. See Thomas T. Munford to Charles S. C. Jones, Jr., Nov. 11, 1875, Munford MSS, Gratz Collection, HSP.

53. JEJ, *Narrative of Military Operations*, 16; *OR*, 185; H. McClellan, *Life and Campaigns of Stuart*, 32; E. Thomas, *Bold Dragoon*, 68–74; Wert, *Cavalryman of the Lost Cause*, 49–54; Kerwood, "His Daring Was Proverbial," 19–21.

54. Warner, *Generals in Gray*, 234–35; *HR&D*, 782; J. Robertson, *Stonewall Brigade*, 17; "General William N. Pendleton," 299; John D. Imboden to C. C. Buel, June 11, 1885, Imboden MSS, C-CWC, NYPL; Wise, *Long Arm of Lee*, 127.

55. *OR*, 698.

56. Ibid., 700–701, 703, 707–708.

57. Ibid., 702–703. An incomplete and unsigned reply to Sherman's letter, dated June 20 and undoubtedly written by Secretary of War Simon Cameron, is in ibid., 710–11.

58. Ibid., 703, 708; Barthel, *Abner Doubleday*, 79–80. Although originally ordered to Washington, Thomas was held back at the last minute,

apparently because the three companies of his regiment assigned to Patterson's army were awaiting remounting and thus could not travel.

59. RP, *Narrative*, 36; *OR*, 701–702, 707–708.
60. RP, *Narrative*, 37, 39; *OR*, 709; Beatie, *Army of the Potomac*, 180, 180n.
61. *OR*, 698, 704, 711.
62. RP, *Narrative*, 39; R. Johnston, *Bull Run*, 58.
63. *OR*, 725, 734.
64. Ibid., 727, 729, 732–34; Beatie, *Army of the Potomac*, 181–83.
65. *OR*, 725.

Chapter 6

1. Roman, *Operations of General Beauregard*, 1:76.
2. Ibid., 77; GTB, *Campaign and Battle of Manassas*, 148–49.
3. T. Williams, *Beauregard*, 71; W. C. Davis, *Battle at Bull Run*, 64; Detzer, *Donnybrook*, 87–92.
4. *OR*, 922–23; Freeman, *Lee's Lieutenants*, 1:39–40.
5. T. Williams, *Beauregard*, 73; John L. Manning to his wife, July 7, 1861, Williams-Chesnut-Manning MSS, USC.
6. Roman, *Operations of General Beauregard*, 1:79; GTB, "First Battle of Bull Run," 197; A. P. Aldrich to his wife, June 22, 23, 1861, Bonham MSS, USC; Thomas H. Pitts to "My dear Lizzie," July 11, 1861, Pitts-Craig MSS, EU; Dickert, *Kershaw's Brigade*, 46; Irby, *Nottoway Grays*, 10; *OR*, 722–23.
7. Craven, *Edmund Ruffin*, 216–17; B. Mitchell, *Edmund Ruffin*, 178–79.
8. Roman, *Operations of General Beauregard*, 1:79–80.
9. *OR*, 447–48; Roman, *Operations of General Beauregard*, 1:80; T. Williams, *Beauregard*, 72–73; Hennessy, *First Battle of Manassas*, 10–11.
10. Irby, *Nottoway Grays*, 10.
11. Goree, *Longstreet's Aide*, 21; J. Scott, "Black Horse Cavalry," 593.
12. Roman, *Operations of General Beauregard*, 1:81; E. P. Alexander to his wife, July 5, 10, 1861, Alexander MSS, SHC, UNC.
13. Roman, *Operations of General Beauregard*, 1:81–82.
14. Ibid., 82–83; *OR*, 969; T. Williams, *Beauregard*, 74.
15. Roman, *Operations of General Beauregard*, 1:83.
16. Ibid., 80; *OR*, 447–48. A copy of the order is in Alexander MSS, SHC, UNC.
17. W. C. Davis, *Battle at Bull Run*, xi–xiii, 65; Bakeless, *Spies of the Confederacy*, 7–10, 18–22; GTB to W. J. Marrin, Apr. 12, 1874, Civil War Miscellany Collection, HSP.
18. Sigaud, "Mrs. Greenhow and the Rebel Spy Ring," 175; Canan, "Confederate Military Intelligence," 35–36; Bakeless, *Spies of the Confederacy*, 24; George Donnellan [a go-between for Jordan, Greenhow, and Beauregard] to anon., July 14, 1861, GLC. Arguably the most authoritative source on the Confederate spy ring run from Washington downplays the effectiveness of Greenhow's efforts: "Those of Mrs. Greenhow's reports that survive are unimpressive. Two that do not survive are commonly credited with having had much to do with

Confederate victory at First Bull Run, but contemporary evidence indicates that Beauregard did not base his preparations on them to any great extent." Fishel, "Mythology of Civil War Intelligence," 352.

19. GTB to JEJ, July 13, 1861, JEJ MSS, DU; Roman, *Operations of General Beauregard*, 1:84, 87; Freeman, *Lee's Lieutenants*, 1:43; GTB, *Campaign and Battle of Manassas*, 26, 150.

20. Roman, *Operations of General Beauregard*, 1:84–87; M. L. Bonham to GTB, Aug. 28, 1877, Bonham MSS, USC; "Suppressed Part of Gen. Beauregard's Report," 259–60.

21. *OR*, 506–507, 515; Freeman, *Lee's Lieutenants*, 1:43.

22. T. Williams, *Beauregard*, 75; W. C. Davis, *Battle at Bull Run*, 66; R. Johnston, *Bull Run*, 86–87.

23. Roman, *Operations of General Beauregard*, 1:88.

24. *OR*, 718–19.

25. *JCCW*, 36.

26. *OR*, 718–19.

27. Ibid., 719–21.

28. R. Johnston, *Bull Run*, 61–67; W. C. Davis, *Battle at Bull Run*, 73–74.

29. Beatie, *Army of the Potomac*, 205–206.

30. Ibid., 207–209; *JCCW*, 36, 55, 62; Nicolay and Hay, *Abraham Lincoln*, 4:323–25.

31. *OR*, 720; *JCCW*, 40.

32. *JCCW*, 36, 55, 62. At least one historian faults McDowell for lacking foresight and his plan for being too limited, assuming responsibility for engaging only those forces then at Manassas: "Logical consideration should have been then, not just the force under Beauregard, but both Johnston's and Beauregard's armies." Sivertsen, "McDowell and the Campaign of First Manassas," 36–38.

33. *JCCW*, 55; R. Johnston, *Bull Run*, 70.

34. *JCCW*, 37–38.

35. Townsend, *Anecdotes of the Civil War*, 57.

36. J. Nicolay, *Outbreak of Rebellion*, 173; S. P. Heintzelman diary, June 29, 1861, Heintzelman MSS, LC; Weigley, *Quartermaster General of the Union Army*, 172–73; K. Williams, *Lincoln Finds a General*, 1:76.

37. *OR*, 51(1):413–14; Warner, *Generals in Blue*, 329–30; *HR&D*, 720, 851; Bilby and Goble, "*Remember You Are Jerseymen!*," 52–66.

38. Warner, *Generals in Blue*, 264–65; *HR&D*, 596; Beatie, *Army of the Potomac*, 8, 27–28. See also E. Keyes, *Fifty Years' Observations*.

39. Warner, *Generals in Blue*, 402–403; *HR&D*, 828; Elderkin, *Biographical Sketches and Anecdotes*, 142–43; Catton, *Mr. Lincoln's Army*, 204–205; Detzer, *Donnybrook*, 160.

40. Warner, *Generals in Blue*, 237–39; *HR&D*, 546–47; O. O. Howard to unidentified official, U.S. Military Academy, Feb. 26, 1861, Howard MSS, Gratz Collection, HSP.

41. Warner, *Generals in Blue*, 37, 113–14; Lonn, *Foreigners in the Union Army*, 188–89; Curtis, *From Bull Run to Chancellorsville*, 19–20; William H. Walling to "My Dear Sisters," July 30, 1861, USAH&EC.

42. S. P. Heintzelman diary, June 29, 1861, Heintzelman MSS, LC; Beatie, *Army of the Potomac*, 209; *JCCW*, 36.

43. D. Tyler, *Autobiography*, 49; S. P. Heintzelman diary, July 10, 1861, Heintzelman MSS, LC.

44. S. P. Heintzelman diary, July 15, 1861, Heintzelman MSS, LC; Beatie, *Army of the Potomac*, 213–14.

45. *OR*, 157, 720; F. Moore, *Rebellion Record*, 2:52; Russell, *My Diary North and South*, 403–404.

46. Beatie, *Army of the Potomac*, 272–73; L. Lewis, *Sherman, Fighting Prophet*, 172.

47. Snell, *From First to Last*, 59–60.

48. Young, *For Love & Liberty*, 17–19, 23, 28–30, 78–80, 89–90, 99–100, 249–53.

49. Sullivan Ballou to Sarah S. Ballou, July 14, 1861. The copy of this famous letter, consulted by the author and here transcribed verbatim, is from the Chicago Historical Society. When I obtained the copy in 1975, this institution had Ballou's name and hometown as Sullivan Bullen from Chicago, an error that found its way into Catton, *Coming Fury*, 473. There are many variant versions of the letter, and over the past fifteen years or so, some historians have questioned its authenticity and even its authorship. For a detailed account of its origins and history, see Young, *For Love & Liberty*, xxxi–xxxv, 764; and Evan C. Jones, "Sullivan Ballou: The Macabre Fate of an American Civil War Major," June 12, 2006, Historynet.com, http://www.historynet.com/sullivan-ballou-the-macabre-fate-of-a-american-civil-war-major.htm (originally published in *America's Civil War* [Nov. 2004]).

Chapter 7

1. *OR*, 727, 729, 735; Beatie, *Army of the Potomac*, 215.

2. *OR*, 160; "General Patterson's Campaign in Virginia," 259.

3. "General Patterson's Campaign in Virginia," 259–60; *OR*, 160, 179, 181. For a succinct account of the fight, see Shier, "Battle of Falling Waters."

4. *OR*, 160, 182; Hewett et al., *Supplement to the Official Records*, 1:127–28; Opie, *Rebel Cavalryman*, 21.

5. *OR*, 185–86; Hewett et al., *Supplement to the Official Records*, 1:128–29.

6. *OR*, 160, 180, 182–84; Locke, *Story of the Regiment*, 23–24; D. Keyes, "1861—The First Wisconsin Infantry," 96–98; Pierce, "Skirmish at Falling Waters," 290–94.

7. *OR*, 185–86; Hewett et al., *Supplement to the Official Records*, 1:128–29.

8. *OR*, 185–86; JEJ, *Narrative of Military Operations*, 30; Wise, *Long Arm of Lee*, 125–26; J. Robertson, *Stonewall Brigade*, 31; M. Jackson, *Life and Letters of Jackson*, 165–66; Opie, *Rebel Cavalryman*, 22.

9. *OR*, 180, 182, 186–87; JEJ, *Narrative of Military Operations*, 30.

10. Bates, *Pennsylvania Volunteers*, 1:142–43, 149; E. K. Smith to Hugh L. Clay, July 4, 1861, Smith MSS, SHC, UNC; E. Thomas, *Bold Dragoon*, 74–75.

11. *OR*, 185; H. McClellan, *Life and Campaigns of Stuart*, 33.

12. JEJ, *Narrative of Military Operations*, 30; E. K. Smith to Hugh L. Clay, July 4, 1861, Smith MSS, SHC, UNC; Hughes, *General Johnston*, 49.

13. *OR*, 160; *Philadelphia Inquirer*, July 4, 1861; *Philadelphia Press*, July 5, 1861; *New York Times*, July 4, 1861; *New York Tribune*, July 8, 1861.

14. Pierce, "Skirmish at Falling Waters," 290.

15. *OR*, 161–63; RP, *Narrative*, 49–50.

16. *OR*, 51(1):415–16; *JCCW*, 55–56; W. W. H. Davis, *Campaign in the Shenandoah*, 5–8.

17. Warner, *Generals in Blue*, 62–63; Garraty and Carnes, *American National Biography*, 4:114–16.

18. *OR*, 158–59, 161–63, 170, 760; L. Wallace, *Autobiography*, 1:310; F. Dyer, *Compendium of the War of the Rebellion*, 1122, 1248; *JCCW*, 99.

19. *OR*, 159.

20. Ibid., 170; RP, *Narrative*, 50; R. Johnston, *Bull Run*, 72; H. E. Emley to George Cadwalader, July 16, 1861, Cadwalader MSS, HSP.

21. Quint, *Second Massachusetts*, 14–15; Ralph A. Lanning to "My Darling Julia," July 12, 1861, Lanning MSS, NYPL; "General Patterson's Campaign in Virginia," 261.

22. *JCCW*, 66.

23. Boyd's own account is *Belle Boyd in Camp and Prison*, published in 1865 (see especially 135–36). More modern works on her life and career as a spy include Sigaud, *Belle Boyd, Confederate Spy*, and Scarborough, *Belle Boyd, Siren of the South*. For a more sober assessment of her role in Confederate espionage, see Fishel, "Mythology of Civil War Intelligence," 352–53.

24. Hudson, "Company D, 4th Alabama," 159; Sanford W. Branch to his mother, July 8, 1861, Margaret Branch Sexton Collection, UGA. The Branch family's letters covering the campaign have been published as Longacre, "Three Brothers Face Their Baptism of Battle."

25. *OR*, 161–62.

26. Ibid., 158–59; R. Johnston, *Bull Run*, 72–73. William C. Davis theorizes that Scott's suggestion that Patterson move toward Leesburg was intended as a feint to keep Johnston in the Valley. *Battle at Bull Run*, 87. It would seem, however, that a move by his adversary in the direction of Manassas would have lured Johnston eastward as well. Then too, Davis does not explain how a westward move toward Strasburg, as Scott also suggested, would affect Johnston.

27. *OR*, 161–62.

28. *JCCW*, 195.

29. Ibid., 99; *OR*, 163, 166–67.

30. Stewart, *Camp, March, and Battle-field*, 22.

31. RP, *Narrative*, 53–54; *JCCW*, 84–87.

32. *OR*, 163–64; RP, *Narrative*, 52–55; *JCCW*, 85–86, 193–94, 196, 236; Plum, *Military Telegraph*, 1:74; Beatie, *Army of the Potomac*, 224–26.

33. RP, *Narrative*, 55, 57; W. W. H. Davis, *Campaign in the Shenandoah*, 9.

34. *OR*, 164–65; RP, *Narrative*, 55–57.

35. *OR*, 969; JEJ, *Narrative of Military Operations*, 32–33; Symonds, *Joseph E. Johnston*, 110–11; Edmund K. Smith to his mother, July 4, 1861, SHC, UNC; Smith to Hugh L. Clay, July 4, 1861, ibid. Although its exact composition remains unknown, it appears that the Fifth Brigade, which would not reach Manassas in time to take part in the fighting of July 21, consisted of the 9th, 10th, and 11th Alabama and the 19th Mississippi; the 38th Virginia would be added later. *OR*, 51(2):188–89.

36. *OR*, 967, 969; JEJ to GTB, July 8, 1861, JEJ MSS, Gratz Collection, HSP.

37. JEJ to GTB, July 9, 1861, JEJ MSS, Gratz Collection, HSP; *OR*, 969.

38. *OR*, 962, 967, 969, 973–74; JEJ, *Narrative of Military Operations*, 31, 33; Wise, *Long Arm of Lee*, 127; Hamilton M. Branch to his mother, July 15, 1861, Margaret Branch Sexton Collection, UGA.

39. Chesnut, *Mary Chesnut's Civil War*, 607.

40. Francis W. Pickens to M. L. Bonham, July 7, 1861, Bonham MSS, USC.

41. *JCCW*, 56; Dwight, *Life and Letters*, 49; Strother, "Personal Recollections of the War," 154; Morse, *Letters*, 7; Quint, *Second Massachusetts*, 14–15; F. Moore, *Rebellion Record*, 2:303–304.

42. *JCCW*, 56, 132–33, 208–209; RP, *Narrative*, 70–71; Hall and Hall, *Cayuga in the Field*, 60; T. Livermore, "Patterson's Shenandoah Campaign," 35–36.

43. JEJ, *Narrative of Military Operations*, 32.

44. Ibid.; Longacre, *Lee's Cavalrymen*, 1–3.

45. *JCCW*, 195; *OR*, 163, 165, 203–10, 214–18; RP, *Narrative*, 69.

46. *JCCW*, 91, 100; Beatie, *Army of the Potomac*, 232; *OR*, 165.

47. RP, *Narrative*, 58–59; *Philadelphia Press*, July 27, 1861; RP to James R. Snowden, July 21, 1861, RP MSS, HSP.

48. *JCCW*, 56–57; Hall and Hall, *Cayuga in the Field*, 60.

49. *JCCW*, 191; Beatie, *Army of the Potomac*, 234–38.

50. *JCCW*, 100–101.

51. W. W. H. Davis, *Campaign in the Shenandoah*, 11; Bates, *Pennsylvania Volunteers*, 1:152, 186; L. Wallace, *Autobiography*, 1:320.

52. *JCCW*, 92, 98, 101, 236–37; *OR*, 166–67.

53. *JCCW*, 101–103, 111, 113; *OR*, 162–63.

54. *JCCW*, 59, 101, 110; *OR*, 165.

55. *JCCW*, 58.

56. Ibid., 89–90, 99, 113–14, 141, 208; *OR*, 169–71; Locke, *Story of the Regiment*, 34; Schaadt, "Company I, First Regiment Pennsylvania Volunteers," 548; *Philadelphia Press*, July 27, 1861.

57. *JCCW*, 91–93, 113.

58. *New York Times*, July 26, 1861.

59. It is not known why these letters (a sampling of which were published as Longacre, "'Come home soon and dont delay'") were not distributed to the troops. Because they repose in the George Cadwalader Papers, the logical inference is that the division commander took them home to Philadelphia when, along with Patterson, he was discharged from Federal service on July 19. Assumedly, Cadwalader was aware that

earlier letters, similar in content and tone, had had a deleterious effect on the morale of his command; perhaps he deliberately chose to censor this batch of mail.

60. C. W. Mark to G. W. Baskins, June 3, 1861, Cadwalader Papers, HSP.
61. "Sallie" to Charles B. Wainwright, July [?], 1861, ibid.
62. "Mely" to "My Dearest Henry," July 10, 1861, ibid.
63. Josephine Copeland to Robert Morris Copeland, July 8, 1861, ibid.
64. John Bartley to William B. Bartley, July 9, 1861, ibid.
65. Garet Pittinger to Henry Pittinger, [July 1861], ibid.
66. Melvina R. Buckman to "My dear husband," July 12, 1861, ibid; Sarah Bowman to "My dear Son," [July 1861], ibid.

Chapter 8

1. *OR*, 345; Russell, *My Diary North and South*, 423–24.
2. Gardner, "'Bull Run' Russell," 59, 78; Starr, *Bohemian Brigade*, 43–48; Andrews, *North Reports the Civil War*, 85–86.
3. *OR*, 304.
4. Fry, "McDowell's Advance to Bull Run," 176; Averell, *Ten Years in the Saddle*, 289.
5. *OR*, 303–304; William W. Averell diary, July 16, 1861, Averell MSS, GLC.
6. T. Livermore, *Days and Events*, 7.
7. Ibid.; J. McDonald, *"We Shall Meet Again,"* 3–5; R. Smith, *American Civil War Zouaves*, 57–58; Battillo, "Red-Legged Devils," 10–12. Detzer erroneously has the Fire Zouaves clothed in "bright red 'firemen's' shirts, each with a buttoned bib in the front." *Donnybrook*, 336.
8. Hall, "Volunteer at the First Bull Run," 147; Averell, *Ten Years in the Saddle*, 289.
9. *OR*, 305; Averell, *Ten Years in the Saddle*, 290; K. Williams, *Lincoln Finds a General*, 1:76–77.
10. Hanson, *Bull Run Remembers*, 17; K. Williams, *Lincoln Finds a General*, 76; R. Johnston, *Bull Run*, 100–101.
11. Warner, *Generals in Blue*, 22–23; *HR&D*, 195; Naisawald, *Grape and Canister*, 28–29; Beatie, *Army of the Potomac*, 541–42.
12. O. Howard, *Autobiography*, 1:147–48; O. O. Howard to Lizzie Howard, July 18, 1861, Howard MSS, Bowdoin College Library; Roe, *Fifth Regiment Massachusetts Volunteer Infantry*, 65; Shannon, "A Few Incidents," 323.
13. Barrett, *What I Saw at Bull Run*, 12.
14. James W. Carter to "Cousin Lydia Ann," July 20, 1861, Carter MSS, ECU; L. Swift, "Bully for the First Connecticut," 77.
15. Lloyd G. Pendergast to Lewis Harrington, July 26, 1861, Pendergast MSS, MnHS.
16. Fiske, "Second New Hampshire," 155; Barrett, *What I Saw at Bull Run*, 12.
17. *JCCW*, 39; F. Moore, *Rebellion Record*, 2:70; Small, *Road to Richmond*, 18; James Butler diary, July 17, 1861, NYPL. Another New Yorker, the

scribe of the 69th Militia, wrote that each day on the march hundreds of men would "break from the ranks whenever a farm-house held out to them the promise that water was at hand, and not merely disregarding, but defying, every effort of their officers to restrain them. . . . [I]n many instances the poor fellows were ruthlessly doomed to disappointment, the retreating Southerners having cut the ropes which held the buckets in the wells, or broken the chains." Meagher, *Last Days of the 69th*, 7. A member of Keyes's brigade recalled that "every well was suspected of being poisoned because we had found some that were and instead of occasionally filling our canteens, we had to post a guard at every well to keep the troops from using the water till a Surgeon had time to test it." L. Swift, "Bully for the First Connecticut," 77.

18. Small, *Road to Richmond*, 19.

19. *OR*, 304–305.

20. Alexander, *Military Memoirs*, 21.

21. Townsend, *Anecdotes of the Civil War*, 56; R. Johnston, *Bull Run*, 123.

22. Curtis, *From Bull Run to Chancellorsville*, 39–40.

23. Hewett et al., *Supplement to the Official Records*, 1:145–46; Meagher, *Last Days of the 69th*, 6; Catton, *Coming Fury*, 446.

24. GTB, "First Battle of Bull Run," 199–200; Roman, *Operations of General Beauregard*, 1:79, 89; Beymer, "Mrs. Greenhow," 564.

25. GTB, "First Battle of Bull Run," 200; Roman, *Operations of General Beauregard*, 1:89–90; *OR*, 440, 445, 449, 460, 520. A small Civil War earthwork, probably dating to 1861, survives atop an elevation overlooking the northeast corner of the Braddock Road–Ox Road intersection (today Fairfax County Road 620 and Virginia Highway 123) in a wooded part of George Mason University's main campus. Greg Wolf, MNBP, to the author, Mar. 27, 2013.

26. *OR*, 51(2):172–73.

27. *OR*, 473, 478; Roman, *Operations of General Beauregard*, 1:90; GTB, "First Battle of Bull Run," 200; JEJ, *Narrative of Military Operations*, 33.

28. *OR*, 545, 565, 980; R. Johnston, *Bull Run*, 149; Warner, *Generals in Gray*, 141; *HR&D*, 539; Castel, "Theophilus Holmes," 11–12.

29. *OR*, 980–81, 985–86.

30. Black, *Railroads of the Confederacy*, 62; Longacre, *Gentleman and Soldier*, 1–2, 47–48.

31. *OR*, 51(2):176; W. C. Davis, *Battle at Bull Run*, 104–105.

32. *OR*, 51(2):175–76.

33. *OR*, 450, 51(2):176.

34. William W. Averell diary, July 16, 1861, Averell MSS, GLC; S. P. Heintzelman, "Notes Taken on the Advance to Bull Run, July 16th 1861 to July 21st 1861," Heintzelman MSS, LC.

35. W. T. Sherman to John Sherman, July 19, 1861, Sherman MSS, LC; L. Swift, "Bully for the First Connecticut," 77.

36. Small, *Road to Richmond*, 20; E. Tyler, *"Wooden Nutmegs" at Bull Run*, 61–62.

37. Meagher, *Last Days of the 69th*, 6.
38. Ibid., 5; W. T. Sherman to Ellen E. Sherman, July 28, 1861, Sherman Family MSS, UND; Haydon, *For Country, Cause, & Leader*, 51–52; Crotty, *Four Years Campaigning*, 20; R. S. Ewell to "Lizzie," July 31, 1861, Ewell MSS, LC.
39. *OR*, 423; William W. Averell diary, July 17, 1861, Averell MSS, GLC; W. C. Davis, *Battle at Bull Run*, 97.
40. *OR*, 309; Willcox, *Forgotten Valor*, 287; R. C. Schenck to "My Dear Sally," July 13, 1861, Schenck MSS, Miami University (of Ohio) Library; *New York Leader*, Aug. 3, 1861; Dixon Miles to Frederick d'Utassy, July 17, 1861, d'Utassy MSS, New-York Historical Society.
41. *OR*, 310; R. Johnston, *Bull Run*, 121–22; J. Thompson, *Civil War to the Bloody End*, 120–21.
42. Goree, *Longstreet's Aide*, 25.
43. Thomas H. Pitts to "My Dear Lizzie," July 11, 17, Pitts-Craig MSS, EU.
44. Thomas H. Pitts to "My Dear Lizzie," July 20, 1861, ibid.; William F. Cocke to Thomas L. P. Cocke, Aug. 7–11, 1861, Armistead-Cocke MSS, CW&M; E. Rhodes, *All for the Union*, 24–25.
45. Thomas H. Pitts to "My Dear Lizzie," July 20, 1861, Pitts-Craig MSS, EU.
46. *OR*, 449–56, 458–59; Stiles, *4th Virginia Cavalry*, 5, 7; Dickert, *Kershaw's Brigade*, 56; Goree, *Longstreet's Aide*, 25; C. E. Henderson, "Just before First Bull Run," 262; William F. Cocke to Thomas L. P. Cocke, Aug. 7–11, 1861, Armistead-Cocke MSS, CW&M; H. A. Jackson to his father, July 30, 1861, USAH&EC.
47. E. Rhodes, *All for the Union*, 24–25; Cooke, *Wearing of the Gray*, 405; Whittemore, *Seventy-First Regiment N.G.S.N.Y.*, 43–44.
48. Edmund Ruffin diary, July 16–17, 1861, LC; Craven, *Edmund Ruffin*, 228; B. Mitchell, *Edmund Ruffin*, 191.
49. S. P. Heintzelman diary, July 20, 1861, Heintzelman MSS, LC.
50. J. J. Seibels to M. L. Bonham, Feb. 13, 1862, Bonham MSS, USC; R. S. Ewell to "Lizzie," July 31, 1861, Ewell MSS, LC.
51. Samuel L. West to his father, Aug. 8, 1861, West MSS, USAH&EC.
52. Collins, *Robert E. Rodes*, 85.
53. William F. Cocke to Thomas L. P. Cocke, Aug. 7–11, 1861, Armistead-Cocke MSS, CW&M; Irby, *Nottoway Grays*, 11.
54. Samuel W. Melton to his wife, July 20, 1861, Melton MSS, USC; Francis W. Pickens to M. L. Bonham, Aug. 12, 1861, Bonham MSS, USC.
55. Samuel L. West to his father, Aug. 8, 1861, West MSS, USAH&EC; F. B. Williams, "From Sumter to the Wilderness," 5.
56. John S. French to "Dear Father & all hands," July 20, 1861, French MSS, USAH&EC; James Butler diary, July 18, 1861, NYPL; Fiske, "Second New Hampshire," 155; Coffin, *Stories of Our Soldiers*, 19.
57. *New York Times*, July 18, 1861; Barrett, *What I Saw at Bull Run*, 13; Fiske, "Second New Hampshire," 155; Eugene B. Beaumont to his wife, July 23, 1861, Beaumont MSS, U.S. Military Academy Library; Woodbury, *First Rhode Island*, 81.

58. Burnett, "Letters of Three Lightfoot Brothers," 394; *OR*, 459–61; N. Cooper, "How They Went to War," 32–33; W. C. Davis, *Battle at Bull Run*, 109–10.

59. James Butler diary, July 17, 1861, NYPL.

60. *JCCW*, 199; OR, 312; John S. French to "Dear Father & all hands," July 20, 1861, French MSS, USAH&EC; Fiske, "Second New Hampshire," 155.

61. *OR*, 310, 312; D. Tyler, *Autobiography*, 51–52; Fry, *McDowell and Tyler*, 22–23; Barnard, *C.S.A. and the Battle of Bull Run*, 47–48.

62. *OR*, 310, 312; *JCCW*, 19–20, 199; W. T. Sherman to John Sherman, July 19, 1861, Sherman MSS, LC.

63. *OR*, 980.

64. Ibid.; Alexander R. Chisolm to G. P. Smith, Apr. 15, 1901, Chisolm MSS, New-York Historical Society.

Chapter 9

1. *OR*, 473, 478; JEJ, *Narrative of Military Operations*, 33.

2. GTB to JEJ, July 13, 1861, JEJ MSS, DU; GTB, *Campaign and Battle of Manassas*, 150.

3. JEJ, *Narrative of Military Operations*, 34.

4. Ibid., 34–35; *OR*, 982.

5. C. McDonald, *Reminiscences of the War and Refugee Life*, 28; Coles, *From Huntsville to Appomattox*, 18.

6. Conrad, "Manassas and . . . the Stonewall Brigade," 85–86.

7. Ibid., 86; Eisenschiml and Newman, *Eyewitness*, 48; W. C. Davis, *Battle at Bull Run*, 135.

8. Eisenschiml and Newman, *Eyewitness*, 48; Goldsborough, *Maryland Line*, 16; M. Howard, *Maryland Confederate*, 31.

9. M. Howard, *Maryland Confederate*, 32; Baylor, *Bull Run to Bull Run*, 20; E. Patterson, *Yankee Rebel*, 7; Conrad, "Manassas and . . . the Stonewall Brigade," 87; Robert Grant to his mother, July 24, 1861, printed in *Savannah Morning News*, July 21, 1892.

10. Coles, *From Huntsville to Appomattox*, 19; Cooke, *Stonewall Jackson*, 26.

11. M. Howard, *Maryland Confederate*, 32.

12. JEJ, *Narrative of Military Operations*, 36–37.

13. Lash, "Johnston and Virginia Railways," 13–14; Roman, *Operations of General Beauregard*, 1:91; GTB, "First Battle of Bull Run," 200. After the war Beauregard stated that he had worked closely with railroad officials to place rail transportation at Johnston's disposal. *Campaign and Battle of Manassas*, 31–32. In his official report of the campaign, however, he makes no such claim. He sent Colonel Chisolm to the Valley merely "to communicate my plan to General Johnston, and my wish that one portion of his forces should march by the way of Aldie, and take the enemy on his right flank and in reverse at Centreville." *OR*, 485–86.

14. Detzer, *Donnybrook*, 177; Coles, *From Huntsville to Appomattox*, 19; Hudson, "Company D, 4th Alabama," 165.

15. Hamilton M. Branch to his mother, July 20, 1861, Margaret Branch Sexton Collection, UGA; Sullivan, "Fowler the Soldier," 29.

16. J. Robertson, *Stonewall Jackson*, 256; Robert Grant to his mother, July 24, 1861, printed in *Savannah Morning News*, July 21, 1892.

17. John Fort to his mother, July 20, 1861, MNBP; J. W. Jones, "Reminiscences of the Army of Northern Virginia . . . First Manassas," 130; Casler, *Four Years in the Stonewall Brigade*, 22.

18. JEJ, *Narrative of Military Operations*, 37–38; Conrad, "Manassas and . . . the Stonewall Brigade," 87.

19. John Fort to his mother, July 26, 1861, MNBP; Hamilton M. Branch to his mother, July 20, 1861, Margaret Branch Sexton Collection, UGA; Bryan, "Letters of Two Confederate Officers," 170.

20. Coles, *From Huntsville to Appomattox*, 19, 199; JEJ, *Narrative of Military Operations*, 38; E. Patterson, *Yankee Rebel*, 7; Alfred L. Scott memoirs, 4, VHS; M. Brown, *University Greys*, 19.

21. W. Blackford, *War Years with Jeb Stuart*, 19; Thomason, *Jeb Stuart*, 102; Wert, *Cavalryman of the Lost Cause*, 57; Driver, *1st Virginia Cavalry*, 11–12; Driver, *Staunton Artillery*, 7; Crockett, "Battery That Saved the Day," 29; Imboden, "Incidents of the First Bull Run," 230; Woodward, *Defender of the Valley*, 34–35; S. Tucker, *Brigadier General John D. Imboden*, 49.

22. JEJ, *Narrative of Military Operations*, 37–38; JEJ, "Responsibilities of the First Bull Run," 250; Roman, *Operations of General Beauregard*, 1:91; GTB, *Campaign and Battle of Manassas*, 30–34.

23. JEJ, *Narrative of Military Operations*, 37–38.

24. Shingler, "Reminiscences of the Late Barnard Bee," in possession of Dr. Pat Wilson.

25. T. Williams, *Beauregard*, 77; Early, *War Memoirs*, 10–11; J. Robertson, *Stonewall Jackson*, 257; Detzer, *Donnybrook*, 181–82.

26. JEJ, *Narrative of Military Operations*, 38.

27. Clark, *Regiments . . . from North Carolina*, 1:341; JEJ, "Bull Run: An Important Letter," 233; Detzer, *Donnybrook*, 183–84.

28. E. K. Smith to his mother, July 31, 1861, Smith MSS, SHC, UNC; Cadmus M. Wilcox to his wife, Aug. 1, 1861, Wilcox MSS, LC; Goldsborough, *Maryland Line*, 18; *OR*, 51(2):188–89.

29. G. Gordon, *Brook Farm to Cedar Mountain*, 27; *Philadelphia Inquirer*, July 19–20, 1861.

30. "Captain Samuel A. Craig's Memoirs," 225; Quint, *Second Massachusetts*, 38.

31. *New York Times*, July 26, 1861; Quint, *Second Massachusetts*, 16–17; W. W. H. Davis, *Campaign in the Shenandoah*, 11; Hall and Hall, *Cayuga in the Field*, 61; L. Wallace, *Autobiography*, 1:319–20.

32. *New York Times*, July 26, 1861; Beatie, *Army of the Potomac*, 231–32; *OR*, 166; *JCCW*, 163; R. Johnson, *Soldier's Reminiscences*, 169.

33. Bates, *Pennsylvania Volunteers*, 1:152, 186; Morse, *Letters*, 9; Hall and Hall, *Cayuga in the Field*, 61; Boyce, *Twenty-Eighth Regiment New York State Volunteers*, 18.

34. *New York Times,* July 31, Aug. 2, 1861; Boyce, *Twenty-Eighth Regiment New York State Volunteers,* 18.

35. *OR,* 165; T. Livermore, "Patterson's Shenandoah Campaign," 31–32.

36. *OR,* 166.

37. Ibid., 167–68.

38. *JCCW,* 230; Beatie, *Army of the Potomac,* 240–41.

39. *JCCW,* 113.

40. *OR,* 168; RP, *Narrative,* 74; T. Livermore, "Patterson's Shenandoah Campaign," 39–41.

41. *OR,* 168–69, 172, 746; RP, *Narrative,* 77–83. After the campaign's end, Patterson would argue that, having informed Washington of Johnston's escape three days before McDowell attacked at Bull Run, Lincoln and Scott had ample time to call off the assault; they might have withheld it until the Army of Pennsylvania could link with the Army of Northeastern Virginia. General Scott, however, was unable to confirm Johnston's union with Beauregard and relay the information to McDowell until July 21.

42. *OR,* 171; Thian, *Military Geography,* 92.

43. *JCCW,* 232.

44. Ibid., 99–114. Patterson vigorously sought an official inquiry into his conduct during the campaign. Although both President Lincoln and Secretary of War Cameron assured him that they found no fault with his generalship, the convening of a court was considered "incompatible with the public interest." The underlying reason appears to be that neither the president nor the secretary wished to take the chance that public blame would shift to General Scott, who, having been retired from active duty on November 1, 1861, deserved to live out his remaining years in peace.

45. *OR,* 310, 312; *JCCW,* 199; D. Tyler, *Autobiography,* 52; Longstreet, *From Manassas to Appomattox,* 34; R. Johnston, *Bull Run,* 39.

46. *OR,* 310, 313.

47. Ibid., 310, 313, 449, 452–54, 458–59; W. T. Sherman to John Sherman, July 19, 1861, Sherman MSS, LC; Henry A. Jackson to his father, July 30, 1861, USAH&EC.

48. *OR,* 310.

49. Ibid., 311–13; Fry, *McDowell and Tyler,* 23, 28; D. Tyler, *Autobiography,* 53; *JCCW,* 46–47, 162.

50. *OR,* 311–12, 458, 461–62, 466; J. Franklin, "Incidents at First Manassas," 291.

51. GTB, "First Battle of Bull Run," 201; Cauble, "Wilmer McLean," 53; Alexander, *Fighting for the Confederacy,* 46; Longstreet, *From Manassas to Appomattox,* 40.

52. *OR,* 461–62; Longstreet, *From Manassas to Appomattox,* 34–35; George W. Latham diary, July 18, 1861, Latham MSS, UVA; C. Blackford, *Lynchburg Home Guard,* 52–53; Goree, *Longstreet's Aide,* 25; Samuel L. West to his father, Aug. 8, 1861, West MSS, USAH&EC.

53. *OR*, 311, 313; Fry, *McDowell and Tyler*, 23; "Letter from General Early," 54; Alexander, *Fighting for the Confederacy*, 45; *New York Times*, July 21, 1861; Comte de Paris, *Civil War in America*, 1:233.

54. Detzer, *Donnybrook*, 159.

55. D. Tyler, *Autobiography*, 54–55; Fry, *McDowell and Tyler*, 26–28.

56. *OR*, 311, 459; *JCCW*, 200; Wise, *Long Arm of Lee*, 128–29.

57. *OR*, 313; Richardson, "Report of Richardson's Brigade," USAH&EC; W. C. Davis, *Battle at Bull Run*, 117–18.

58. Samuel L. West to his father, Aug. 8, 1861, West MSS, USAH&EC; *Charleston Mercury*, July 25, 1861.

59. George D. Wells to "Dear S," July 19, 1861, Wells MSS, ECU; Wells to his mother, July 19, 1861, ibid.; Cudworth, *First Regiment [Massachusetts Volunteers]*, 44.

60. Haydon, *For Country, Cause, & Leader*, 52; W. C. Davis, *Battle at Bull Run*, 119; *JCCW*, 20; Fry, *McDowell and Tyler*, 35.

61. C. Blackford, *Lynchburg Home Guard*, 56, 62; D. Tyler, *Autobiography*, 54; *JCCW*, 20. When appearing before the joint committee, Richardson did not positively state that Tyler had ordered him to charge with the 12th New York. He testified that he himself placed the 12th in line of battle "on the left of the battery, and directed Colonel Walworth [*sic*] to make a charge into the woods." In his report of the engagement, Tyler claims that Richardson gave "an order for the Twelfth New York to deploy into line and advance into the woods." *OR*, 311.

62. Crotty, *Four Years Campaigning*, 22; *OR*, 313.

63. Morgan, *Personal Reminiscences*, 53; C. Blackford, *Lynchburg Home Guard*, 55; Longstreet, *From Manassas to Appomattox*, 39; Goree, *Longstreet's Aide*, 26–27.

64. Dickert, *Kershaw's Brigade*, 58; Coffin, *Drum-beat of the Nation*, 92. Other sources have the yell first raised during the fighting of July 21. See Conrad, "Manassas and . . . the Stonewall Brigade," 91–92; Morgan, *Personal Reminiscences*, 70; and Wiley, *Life of Johnny Reb*, 71.

65. Warfield, *Confederate Soldier's Memoirs*, 49–50; Longstreet, *From Manassas to Appomattox*, 40; *OR*, 313–14; K. M. Jones, *Heroines of Dixie*, 53.

66. *OR*, 462–64, 466, 468; Longstreet, *From Manassas to Appomattox*, 39; Early, *War Memoirs*, 7–8.

67. *OR*, 462; Alexander, *Military Memoirs*, 23–24; Alexander Hunter memoirs, 39, VHS.

68. D. Johnston, *Four Years a Soldier*, 76–77; Morgan, *Personal Reminiscences*, 58.

69. Longstreet, *From Manassas to Appomattox*, 39; *OR*, 462, 464.

70. Longstreet, *From Manassas to Appomattox*, 40; Goree, *Longstreet's Aide*, 27; Morgan, *Personal Reminiscences*, 60.

71. Longstreet, *From Manassas to Appomattox*, 41; *OR*, 462–63, 465; *Charleston Mercury*, July 25, 1861; J. Franklin, "Incidents at First Manassas," 292; S. Blackford, *Letters from Lee's Army*, 23.

72. *OR*, 311, 314; D. Tyler, *Autobiography*, 54; *JCCW*, 199–200, 205.

73. D. Tyler, *Autobiography*, 54.

74. Ibid.; *JCCW*, 20, 205; *OR*, 311, 467; C. Robinson, "My Experiences," 40. A member of Richardson's old regiment recalled that his commander's temper did not cool quickly: Fighting Dick "reared around a good deal during the next two or three days." Lyster, *Recollections of the Bull Run Campaign*, 9–10.

75. W. T. Sherman to John Sherman, July 19, 1861, Sherman MSS, LC.

76. Meagher, *Last Days of the 69th*, 9; Cunningham, *Field Medical Services*, 4; W. T. Sherman to John Sherman, July 19, 1861, Sherman MSS, LC.

77. James Butler diary, July 18, 1861, NYPL; Todd, *Seventy-Ninth Highlanders*, 25.

78. W. T. Sherman to John Sherman, July 19, 1861, Sherman MSS, LC; Haydon, *For Country, Cause, & Leader*, 53.

79. W. T. Sherman to Ellen E. Sherman, July 19, 1861, Sherman Family MSS, UND.

Chapter 10

1. C. Harrison, "Virginia Scenes in '61," 163–64.

2. Averell, *Ten Years in the Saddle*, 291.

3. W. T Sherman to John Sherman, July 19, 1861, Sherman MSS, LC; *JCCW*, 46; *OR*, 306–307; Meagher, *Last Days of the 69th*, 10.

4. R. Johnston, *Bull Run*, 136; *Battle-fields of the South*, 35.

5. Destler, "Second Michigan," 398, 398n.

6. *Charleston Mercury*, July 25, 1861.

7. *JCCW*, 39; William W. Averell diary, July 18, 1861, Averell MSS, GLC; Willcox, *Forgotten Valor*, 288; Fry, *McDowell and Tyler*, 35; E. Tyler, *"Wooden Nutmegs" at Bull Run*, 63; Todd, *Seventy-Ninth Highlanders*, 25.

8. Roman, *Operations of General Beauregard*, 1:94.

9. *History of the Seventeenth Virginia*, 23; W. C. Davis, *Battle at Bull Run*, 139–40; Detzer, *Donnybrook*, 183–84.

10. Shingler, "Reminiscences of the Late Barnard Bee," in possession of Dr. Pat Wilson.

11. *OR*, 983; Roman, *Operations of General Beauregard*, 1:94–95; GTB, "First Battle of Bull Run," 202.

12. Detzer, *Donnybrook*, 184; Hennessy, *First Battle of Manassas*, 34; Roman, *Operations of General Beauregard*, 1:97; GTB, *Campaign and Battle of Manassas*, 70.

13. Roman, *Operations of General Beauregard*, 1:91; GTB, "First Battle of Bull Run," 203; GTB, *Campaign and Battle of Manassas*, 34–38; *OR*, 985; JEJ, *Narrative of Military Operations*, 38–39.

14. GTB, "First Battle of Bull Run," 203; GTB, *Campaign and Battle of Manassas*, 18–19.

15. GTB, *Campaign and Battle of Manassas*, 20–21.

16. JEJ, *Narrative of Military Operations*, 39–40.

17. Roman, *Operations of General Beauregard*, 1:97.

18. Ibid.; E. Thomas, *Bold Dragoon*, 77; Driver, *1st Virginia Cavalry*, 12; Driver and Howard, *2nd Virginia Cavalry*, 14; *OR*, 458.

19. JEJ, *Narrative of Military Operations*, 39–40; Hanson, *Bull Run Remembers*, 31; GTB, *Campaign and Battle of Manassas*, 43–44, 53–54.

20. *OR*, 447–48; Roman, *Operations of General Beauregard*, 1:98; GTB, *Campaign and Battle of Manassas*, 54–56; JEJ, *Narrative of Military Operations*, 40; T. Williams, *Beauregard*, 78–79; Hennessy, *First Battle of Manassas*, 10–11.

21. *OR*, 486–87; Roman, *Operations of General Beauregard*, 1:98–99; GTB, *Campaign and Battle of Manassas*, 64; T. Williams, *Beauregard*, 81; Hennessy, *First Battle of Manassas*, 34.

22. *OR*, 479–80.

23. Ibid., 480.

24. Imboden, "Incidents of the First Bull Run," 231.

25. Roman, *Operations of General Beauregard*, 1:98; R. Johnston, *Bull Run*, 161; W. C. Davis, *Battle at Bull Run*, 146.

26. Cadmus M. Wilcox to his wife, Aug. 1, 1861, Wilcox MSS, LC; *OR*, 51(2):188–89.

27. JEJ, "Responsibilities of the First Bull Run," 250; GTB, "First Battle of Bull Run," 226–27; GTB, *Campaign and Battle of Manassas*, 39–40; GTB to W. J. Marrin, Apr. 9, 12, 1874, Civil War Miscellany Collection, HSP.

28. *OR*, 479–80; Roman, *Operations of General Beauregard*, 1:99; JEJ, *Narrative of Military Operations*, 40–41; W. C. Davis, *Battle at Bull Run*, 147.

29. JEJ, "Responsibilities of the First Bull Run," 245–48, 250, 258–59; JEJ, *Narrative of Military Operations*, 41–42, 49; GTB, "First Battle of Bull Run," 203, 226–27; GTB, *Campaign and Battle of Manassas*, 15, 17; Howell, "First Battle of Bull Run," 19; GTB to anon., Jan. 6, 1888, C-CWC, NYPL.

30. JEJ, *Narrative of Military Operations*, 41; JEJ, "Responsibilities of the First Bull Run," 246.

31. Roman, *Operations of General Beauregard*, 1:99.

32. Hennessy, *First Battle of Manassas*, 9; Howell, "First Battle of Bull Run," 32.

33. *JCCW*, 41; S. P. Heintzelman diary, July 19, 1861, Heintzelman MSS, LC; Bilby and Goble, "*Remember You Are Jerseymen!*," 64–65; *OR*, 747, 751.

34. *OR*, 324, 336; Hanson, *Bull Run Remembers*, 24–25.

35. *OR*, 343, 408; Warner, *Generals in Blue*, 218–19; *HR&D*, 513.

36. *OR*, 336–42; Kingsbury, *Hero of Medfield*, 15.

37. R. Johnston, *Bull Run*, 137–38.

38. Cunningham, *Field Medical Services*, 4; Charles C. Gray memoirs, 3, UNC.

39. Cunningham, *Field Medical Services*, 4.

40. Horan, *Matthew Brady*, 38.

41. Fry, "McDowell's Advance to Bull Run," 183.

42. Ibid.; D. Tyler, *Autobiography*, 57; Stedman, *Battle of Bull Run*, 14; Bradley, *Simon Cameron*, 178.

43. E. Rhodes, *All for the Union*, 35; Beatie, *Army of the Potomac*, 271; Belden and Belden, *So Fell the Angels*, 44–46.
44. Riddle, *Recollections of War Times*, 46–49; Ely, *Journal*, 11; Trefousse, *Benjamin Franklin Wade*, 150; Leech, *Reveille in Washington*, 102–103; Beatie, *Army of the Potomac*, 271.
45. In addition to the 4th Pennsylvania, the 1st Rhode Island, and the four militia outfits in Runyon's division, these regiments were nearing the expiration of their service terms: 1st Connecticut (July 31), 2nd Connecticut (August 7), 3rd Connecticut (August 12), 5th Massachusetts (August 1), 1st Michigan (August 1), 8th New York (July 20), 69th New York (August 3), 71st New York (July 30), 1st Ohio (August 2), and 2nd Ohio (July 31).
46. Joseph Corson memoirs, 10, Corson MSS, in possession of Dr. Joseph K. Corson.
47. Ibid., 10–11; C. Clarke, *Company F, 1st Regiment, R.I. Volunteers*, 54; Clement, *Bull-Run Rout*, 8; Barrett, *What I Saw at Bull Run*, 16; Russell, *Battle of Bull Run*, 9. The case for the 4th Pennsylvania's right to demand its discharge is laid out in Bates, *Pennsylvania Volunteers*, 1:42; and Cunliffe, *Soldiers & Civilians*, 8.
48. *Medal of Honor of the United States Army*, 105; Bates, *Pennsylvania Volunteers*, 1:42–43; *Philadelphia Inquirer*, July 26, 1861.
49. *OR*, 315n, 424n, 427, 769.
50. Ibid., 329; Barnard, *C.S.A. and the Battle of Bull Run*, 47.
51. *OR*, 307, 330.
52. Ibid., 308, 318, 330–31; Barnard, *C.S.A. and the Battle of Bull Run*, 49; Stedman, *Battle of Bull Run*, 11.
53. *OR*, 317, 331; *JCCW*, 160–61; R. Johnston, *Bull Run*, 142.

Chapter 11

1. *OR*, 318; Fry, "McDowell's Advance to Bull Run," 183.
2. *OR*, 318, 326–27.
3. G. F. R. Henderson, *Civil War—A Soldier's View*, 105.
4. Critiques of the battle plan include the following: R. Johnston, *Bull Run*, 145–47; Ropes, *Story of the Civil War*, 158; K. Williams, *Lincoln Finds a General*, 1:90–91; Howell, "First Battle of Bull Run," 32; Warren Hassler, *Commanders of the Army of the Potomac*, 19; Sivertsen, "McDowell and the Campaign of First Manassas," 79–80; Welsh, "McDowell's Offensive," 36–40; W. C. Davis, *Battle at Bull Run*, 156; Beatie, *Army of the Potomac*, 275–76; Rafuse, *Single Grand Victory*, 117; and Detzer, *Donnybrook*, 195–96. Most agree that, in contrast to Beauregard's plan, McDowell's was well conceived and clearly articulated, but it called for operations too complex to be executed by amateur soldiers and was too dependent on precise coordination among widely separated columns.
5. *OR*, 317; R. Johnston, *Bull Run*, 143–44; Marvel, *Burnside*, 22; Alexander, *Military Memoirs*, 569. Another possible reason for deferring the march until morning—the time needed to bring up additional ammunition—is advanced in Stedman, *Battle of Bull Run*, 12.

6. E. Keyes, *Fifty Years' Observations*, 432; *OR*, 151.
7. *OR*, 348; D. Tyler, *Autobiography*, 57; Beatie, *Army of the Potomac*, 272–74; *JCCW*, 207.
8. *JCCW*, 40; *OR*, 720.
9. Andrews, *South Reports the Civil War*, 81–82.
10. G. Campbell Brown memoirs, 5–6, TSL&A.
11. Jacob A. Camp to his wife, July 19, 1861, Camp MSS, Cornell University Library; Leech, *Reveille in Washington*, 122–25; Waterman, "Washington at the Time of the First Bull Run," 28–29.
12. Nicolay and Hay, *Abraham Lincoln*, 4:352; Plum, *Military Telegraph*, 1:75; Goodwin, *Team of Rivals*, 371–72.
13. Ibid., 372; Julia C. Bates diary, "This Day—August 15—1861" [recounting events of July 21], 2–3, E. Bates MSS, MoHS.
14. C. Harrison, "Virginia Scenes in '61," 164–65; Detzer, *Donnybrook*, 314–16.
15. F. Moore, *Rebellion Record*, 2:47.
16. Hendrick, *Statesmen of the Lost Cause*, 180; E. Thomas, *Confederate State of Richmond*, 49; *Daily Richmond Examiner*, July 22, 1861.
17. C. Harrison, "Virginia Scenes in '61," 164.
18. Irby, *Nottoway Grays*, 12; Breazeale, *Co. J, 4th South Carolina*, 11.
19. Hains, "First Gun at Bull Run," 389–91; Alexander, *Fighting for the Confederacy*, 50.
20. Small, *Road to Richmond*, 20; Stedman, *Battle of Bull Run*, 20.
21. *OR*, 361, 497, 553, 563; R. H. Moore, *Lynchburg Artillery*, 50–51.
22. *OR*, 361–68, 497, 554; Andrus, *Brooke, Fauquier, Loudoun, and Alexandria Artillery*, 45; *New York World*, July 23, 1861.
23. Breazeale, *Co. J, 4th South Carolina*, 5.
24. Finch, "Boys of '61," 256.
25. *OR*, 359, 361–62, 364–67, 372–73; Stedman, *Battle of Bull Run*, 22–23.
26. *JCCW*, 41–43, 200–204; Finch, "Boys of '61," 255; Detzer, *Donnybrook*, 206–207.
27. *OR*, 357; Detzer, *Donnybrook*, 209.
28. *OR*, 368, 371; *JCCW*, 43.
29. *OR*, 353; *JCCW*, 43; L. Swift, "Bully for the First Connecticut," 77.
30. *OR*, 348, 353; D. Tyler, *Autobiography*, 57–58; *JCCW*, 41, 43, 150, 202; E. Keyes, *Fifty Years' Observations*, 432; Detzer, *Donnybrook*, 205; Warren Hassler, *Commanders of the Army of the Potomac*, 20; W. C. Davis, *Battle at Bull Run*, 156; Stedman, *Battle of Bull Run*, 24; L. Lewis, *Sherman, Fighting Prophet*, 174.
31. *OR*, 383, 402.
32. Ibid., 334, 374, 424.
33. Ibid., 427; Tidball, "View from the Top of the Knoll," 183.
34. *OR*, 423, 439.
35. Ibid., 335.
36. *JCCW*, 76.
37. Warner, *Generals in Blue*, 242–43; *HR&D*, 556. The only full-length biography of this outstanding artillerist is Longacre, *Man behind the Guns*.

38. *OR*, 378, 544.
39. Ibid., 374; Haydon, *For Country, Cause, & Leader*, 56.
40. *OR*, 374, 429; *JCCW*, 24, 178.
41. *OR*, 378, 346, 348, 381–82, 429, 433–34.
42. Ibid., 374, 436; *JCCW*, 24–25; Nye, "Action North of Bull Run," 48–49.
43. *OR*, 375, 424; *JCCW*, 23–24.
44. *OR*, 335, 375, 429.
45. Ibid., 378, 429; *JCCW*, 178.
46. *OR*, 425, 429, 433–34; *JCCW*, 179; Curtis, *From Bull Run to Chancellorsville*, 42.
47. Hennessy, "War-Watchers at Bull Run," 42–44; Riddle, *Recollections of War Times*, 46; McMaster, *History of the People of the United States*, 83.
48. Tidball, "View from the Top of the Knoll," 184; Gardner, "'Bull Run' Russell," 59; Russell, *My Diary North and South*, 439, 448–49.
49. Horan, *Matthew Brady*, 28; Leech, *Reveille in Washington*, 100; W. C. Davis, *Battle at Bull Run*, 255.
50. Lyster, *Recollections of the Bull Run Campaign*, 15; Hennessy, "War-Watchers at Bull Run," 46–47; F. Moore, *Rebellion Record*, 2 (poetry section): 4.
51. GTB, *Campaign and Battle of Manassas*, 68.
52. *OR*, 487; Roman, *Operations of General Beauregard*, 1:99.
53. *OR*, 474, 487–88; JEJ, *Narrative of Military Operations*, 41–42.
54. JEJ, *Narrative of Military Operations*, 42; JEJ to R. U. Johnson, May 11, 1885, JEJ MSS, C-CWC, NYPL.
55. *OR*, 488; Roman, *Operations of General Beauregard*, 1:199; GTB, *Campaign and Battle of Manassas*, 65–66; GTB, "First Battle of Bull Run," 203.
56. *OR*, 536; Curtis, *From Bull Run to Chancellorsville*, 48; Cooling, *Historical Highlights*, 49–50; J. Gordon, *Reminiscences*, 41–42. Detzer suggests that Ewell's warning was delivered not by Miss Mason but by seventeen-year-old Sally Summers, whose home was close to Davies's position. *Donnybrook*, 402, 473n.
57. *OR*, 536–37; G. Brown, "General Ewell at Bull Run," 259n; R. Johnston, *Bull Run*, 173–74.
58. G. Campbell Brown memoirs, 8, TSL&A; G. Brown, "General Ewell at Bull Run," 259–61; Pfanz, *Richard S. Ewell*, 135–38; J. Gordon, *Reminiscences*, 38.
59. *OR*, 536–37; R. S. Ewell to "Lizzie," July 31, 1861, Ewell MSS, LC; William P. Miles to GTB, Aug. 4, 1861, GTB MSS, Gratz Collection, HSP.
60. G. Campbell Brown memoirs, 9, TSL&A; Andrews, *South Reports the Civil War*, 84, 90–91. Holmes's travail is recounted in *OR*, 565; and Hammock, *With Honor Untarnished*, 33–34.
61. *OR*, 536–37; Goree, *Longstreet's Aide*, 28; Lyster, *Recollections of the Bull Run Campaign*, 10–11.
62. G. Brown, "General Ewell at Bull Run," 260n. See also G. Brown, *First Manassas*.

63. *OR*, 491; G. Campbell Brown memoirs, 8–12, TSL&A; G. Brown, "General Ewell at Bull Run," 259–61; Casdorph, *Confederate General R. S. Ewell*, 119–20.

64. R. Johnston, *Bull Run*, 175; Alexander, *Military Memoirs*, 46; G. Harrison, "Ewell at First Manassas," 356–59; G. Brown, "General Ewell at Bull Run," 260n; Hennessey, *First Battle of Manassas*, 43; W. C. Davis, *Battle at Bull Run*, 169–70; GTB, "First Battle of Bull Run," 209; GTB, *Campaign and Battle of Manassas*, 83–85; Roman, *Operations of General Beauregard*, 1:102.

Chapter 12

1. *OR*, 51(2):150; Warner, *Generals in Gray*, 3–4; E. P. Alexander to his wife, July 1, 5, 10, 1861, Alexander MSS, SHC, UNC; Alexander, *Military Memoirs*, 16; Hanson, *Bull Run Remembers*, 27–28, 32; W. C. Davis, *Battle at Bull Run*, 67.

2. Detzer, *Donnybrook*, 241; Lord, "Flags, Torches, Rockets," 30–31.

3. Lord, "Flags, Torches, Rockets," 30–31; Cummins, "Signal Corps in the Confederate States Army," 93–107; E. P. Alexander to his wife, July 10, 1861, Alexander MSS, SHC, UNC.

4. *OR*, 559; Alexander, *Fighting for the Confederacy*, 50.

5. Alexander, *Fighting for the Confederacy*, 50.

6. *OR*, 559; Silverman et al., *Shanks*, 68; *Battle-fields of the South*, 38–39; Welsh, "McDowell's Offensive," 38.

7. *OR*, 559; Breazeale, *Co. J, 4th South Carolina*, 11–12; R. Lewis, *Confederate Boy*, 12.

8. *OR*, 559, 562, 564–65; R. H. Moore, *Lynchburg Artillery*, 48.

9. *OR*, 559; Hewett et al., *Supplement to the Official Records*, 1:194; William R. Terry to N. G. Evans, July 23, 1861, GLC; Dufour, *Gentle Tiger*, 136–37; Hennessy, *First Battle of Manassas*, 46; J. McDonald, "We Shall Meet Again," 2; Driver and Howard, *2nd Virginia Cavalry*, 15.

10. *OR*, 349, 358; D. Tyler, *Autobiography*, 58.

11. *OR*, 358, 383, 559.

12. Ibid., 489; GTB, *Campaign and Battle of Manassas*, 66.

13. *OR*, 395; E. Rhodes, *All for the Union*, 26; Rafuse, *Single Grand Victory*, 122; Christopher Heffelfinger to "Dear Sister," July 24, 1861, MiHS.

14. W. C. Davis, *Battle at Bull Run*, 167.

15. Strong, *Diary*, 179; Woodbury, *Second Rhode Island*, 25–26.

16. *JCCW*, 161.

17. *OR*, 383, 395; E. Rhodes, *All for the Union*, 26; Blake, *Three Years in the Army of the Potomac*, 16; Hall, "Volunteer at the First Bull Run," 152–53.

18. *OR*, 383, 395; William W. Averell diary, July 21, 1861, Averell MSS, GLC.

19. Ibid., 395; Woodbury, *Second Rhode Island*, 32.

20. *OR*, 475 488; Alexander, *Military Memoirs*, 34; JEJ, *Narrative of Military Operations*, 46; Hughes, *General Johnston*, 61; GTB, "First

Battle of Bull Run," 210; Roman, *Operations of General Beauregard*, 1:101.

21. Alexander, *Military Memoirs*, 32.

22. JEJ, *Narrative of Military Operations*, 47; JEJ, "Responsibilities of the First Bull Run," 248; Imboden, "Incidents of the First Bull Run," 231; *OR*, 488–89.

23. *OR*, 474–75, 491–92; Wise, *Long Arm of Lee*, 130–34; JEJ, *Narrative of Military Operations*, 48; R. H. Moore, *Lynchburg Artillery*, 37; R. H. Moore, *Miscellaneous Disbanded Artillery*, 30–31; Driver, *1st and 2nd Rockbridge Artillery*, 5–6.

24. *OR*, 559; Hewett et al., *Supplement to the Official Records*, 1:194; Dufour, *Gentle Tiger*, 137.

25. *OR*, 559–60, 563; Hewett et al., *Supplement to the Official Records*, 1:194; R. H. Moore, *Lynchburg Artillery*, 48.

26. *OR*, 561; Hewett et al., *Supplement to the Official Records*, 1:194.

27. *OR*, 383, 395; Dufour, *Gentle Tiger*, 137–38; T. Jones, *Lee's Tigers*, 51.

28. E. Rhodes, *All for the Union*, 33. A detailed study of Burnside's struggle for Matthews Hill is in Nosworthy, *Roll Call to Destiny*, 33–78.

29. *OR*, 396, 562–65; R. Johnston, *Bull Run*, 188; Monroe, *Rhode Island Artillery*, 14–16; R. H. Moore, *Lynchburg Artillery*, 48, 50–51.

30. Hunter, *Military Services*, 8; F. Moore, *Rebellion Record*, 2:371; Russell, *My Diary North and South*, 462; Miller, *Lincoln's Abolitionist General*, 69; Julia C. Bates diary, "This Day—August 15—1861" [recounting events of July 21], 4, E. Bates MSS, MoHS; "Famous Cavalry Mounts: Baldy," 16–17.

31. *OR*, 382, 395; Woodbury, *Second Rhode Island*, 33; William W. Averell diary, July 21, 1861, Averell MSS, GLC; Averell, *Ten Years in the Saddle*, 297.

32. Averell, *Ten Years in the Saddle*, 295–96; William W. Averell to anon., Oct. 31, 1887, Averell MSS, GLC.

33. Averell, *Ten Years in the Saddle*, 295–96.

34. *OR*, 396–400; E. Rhodes, *All for the Union*, 26–28; E. Rhodes, *First Campaign of Second Rhode Island*, 19–20; *Memorial of Colonel John Stanton Slocum*, 22, 67–68; Woodbury, *Second Rhode Island*, 34.

35. *OR*, 396, 401, 51(1):23–24; C. Clarke, *Company F, Regiment, R.I. Volunteers*, 57; Marvel, *Burnside*, 24. The boat howitzers were a unique infantry weapon. Company I, 71st New York Militia had been training in the use of these compact but highly serviceable pieces since late April, when assigned to duty at Dahlgren's navy yard. The only guns in either army not pulled by horses, the howitzers were hauled about by drag ropes in the hands and over the shoulders of a team of burly New Yorkers. *OR*, 346; Ripley, *Artillery and Ammunition of the Civil War*, 87–92.

36. Whittemore, *Seventy-First Regiment N.G.S.N.Y.*, 46; C. Clarke, *Company F, 1st Regiment, R.I. Volunteers*, 58; Detzer, *Donnybrook*, 275.

37. Averell, *Ten Years in the Saddle*, 297.

38. Ibid., 297–98; Parker, *Personal Reminiscences*, 13.

39. Averell, *Ten Years in the Saddle*, 298.

40. *OR*, 401, 51(1):23; Whittemore, *Seventy-First Regiment N.G.S.N.Y.*, 46; Haynes, *Second Regiment New Hampshire Volunteers*, 25–27; Fiske, "Second New Hampshire," 156. For Marston, see Warner, *Generals in Blue*, 312.

41. *OR*, 396; Marvel, *Burnside*, 24; C. Clarke, *Company F, Regiment, R.I. Volunteers*, 57; E. Rhodes, *All for the Union*, 33.

42. *OR*, 396, 400; Woodbury, *Second Rhode Island*, 34; Young, *For Love & Liberty*, 487–90, 631. In the aftermath of the battle, Confederate soldiers disinterred and desecrated the remains of Colonel Slocum and Major Ballou. The grisly details are spelled out in Evan C. Jones, "Sullivan Ballou: The Macabre Fate of an American Civil War Major," June 12, 2006, Historynet.com, http://www.historynet.com/sullivan-ballou-the-macabre-fate-of-a-american-civil-war-major.htm (originally published in *America's Civil War* [Nov. 2004]).

43. Hewett et al., *Supplement to the Official Records*, 1:194–95; Dufour, *Gentle Tiger*, 137–39, 141–42; T. Jones, *Lee's Tigers*, 51–53; "Major Chatham Roberdeau Wheat," 425, 427; *OR*, 561.

44. Dufour, *Gentle Tiger*, 140–41.

45. Hewett et al., *Supplement to the Official Records*, 1:194–95.

46. *OR*, 474, 489–90, 559; K. W. Jones, "Fourth Alabama Infantry," 43; Haskin, *First Regiment of Artillery*, 147; GTB, "First Battle of Bull Run," 206–207; Alexander, *Military Memoirs*, 35, 39.

47. E. Henry, "Life of Judith (Carter) Henry," 3, VHS; W. C. Davis, *Battle at Bull Run*, 204.

48. Imboden, "Incidents of the First Bull Run," 231; Hennessy, *First Battle of Manassas*, 42.

49. Hudson, "Company D, 4th Alabama," 166; Coles, *From Huntsville to Appomattox*, 20.

50. Imboden, "Incidents of the First Bull Run," 232; Hewett et al., *Supplement to the Official Records*, 1:175; Driver, *Staunton Artillery*, 8.

51. *OR*, 559; GTB, "First Battle of Bull Run," 207.

52. Coles, *From Huntsville to Appomattox*, 234n; Hennessy, *First Battle of Manassas*, 56; Hewett et al., *Supplement to the Official Records*, 1:172.

53. Hewett et al., *Supplement to the Official Records*, 1:172; K. W. Jones, "Fourth Alabama Infantry," 43–45; Shingler, "Reminiscences of the Late Barnard Bee," in possession of Dr. Pat Wilson; Warder and Catlett, *Battle of Young's Branch*, 19–20; Detzer, *Donnybook*, 294.

54. Coles, *From Huntsville to Appomattox*, 21.

55. Ibid., 27; R. K. Krick, *Lee's Colonels*, 213; Sullivan, "Fowler the Soldier," 29.

56. *OR*, 396, 398, 490; Hudson, "Company D, 4th Alabama," 166–67; K. W. Jones, "Fourth Alabama Infantry," 45; Coles, *From Huntsville to Appomattox*, 22; Hewett et al., *Supplement to the Official Records*, 1:173; *Addresses Delivered at the Unveiling of the Memorial Tablet . . . Seventy-First Regiment [New York]*, 4; Parker, *Personal Reminiscences*,

13; *Narrative of the Battles of Bull Run*, 15; Reese, *Sykes' Regular Infantry*, 37.

57. Hudson, "Company D, 4th Alabama," 167.

58. Zettler, *War Stories*, 62–63; Wilkinson and Woodworth, *Scythe of Fire*, 63.

59. Hewett et al., *Supplement to the Official Records*, 1:192–93; Hankins, *Simple Story of a Soldier*, 12–13.

60. J. McDonald, *"We Shall Meet Again,"* 73, 77–79.

61. Wilkinson and Woodworth, *Scythe of Fire*, 68; Hamilton M. Branch to his mother, July 23, 1861, Margaret Branch Sexton Collection, UGA; R. Johnston, *Bull Run*, 257, 261, 263.

62. T. L. Wragg to his father, July 23, 1861, Wragg MSS, LC; Robert Grant to his mother, July 24, 1861, printed in *Savannah Morning News*, July 21, 1892; Wilkinson and Woodworth, *Scythe of Fire*, 71–72.

63. Hamilton M. Branch to his mother, July 23, 25, 1861, Margaret Branch Sexton Collection, UGA; Sanford W. Branch to his mother, July 26, 1861, ibid.

64. T. L. Wragg to his father, July 23, 1861, Wragg MSS, LC; Zettler, *War Stories*, 61–63; Sanford W. Branch to his mother, July 26, 1861, Margaret Branch Sexton Collection, UGA; Robert Grant to his mother, July 24, 1861, printed in *Savannah Morning News*, July 21, 1892; Wilkinson and Woodworth, *Scythe of Fire*, 68.

65. Reese, *Sykes' Regular Infantry*, 35, 37; Carter, *Four Brothers in Blue*, 13–15, 20; Averell, *Ten Years in the Saddle*, 297–98; Parker, *Personal Reminiscences*, 28–29; Hewett et al., *Supplement to the Official Records*, 1:187–88; Hennessy, *First Battle of Manassas*, 58, 60.

66. *OR*, 475; JEJ, *Narrative of Military Operations*, 48; Alexander, *Military Memoirs*, 34; Hamilton M. Branch to his mother, July 23, 25, 1861, Margaret Branch Sexton Collection, UGA; Sanford W. Branch to his mother, July 26, 1861, ibid.; Robert Grant to his mother, July 24, 1861, printed in *Savannah Morning News*, July 21, 1892.

Chapter 13

1. Warner, *Generals in Gray*, 122–23; Longacre, *Gentleman and Soldier*, 7–43.

2. Longacre, *Gentleman and Soldier*, 1–7, 44–48; *OR*, 566.

3. *OR*, 491, 566; Hennessy, *First Battle of Manassas*, 42; *Charleston Daily Courier*, Aug. 8, 1861.

4. *OR*, 567; Coxe, "Battle of First Manassas," 25.

5. *Narrative of the Battles of Bull Run*, 16; unidentified enlisted man, Hampton Legion Inf., to anon., July 26, 1861, MNBP; *OR*, 566.

6. *OR*, 566; Coxe, "Battle of First Manassas," 25; Fairchild, *27th Regiment N.Y. Vols.*, 11; Merrell, *Five Months in Rebeldom*, 6.

7. Hennessy, *First Battle of Manassas*, 66; Hall, "Volunteer at the First Bull Run." 154–55; Averell, *Ten Years in the Saddle*, 298.

8. T. L. Wragg to his father, July 23, 1861, Wragg MSS, LC; Coski, *Confederate Battle Flag*, 4–10.

9. Sullivan, "Fowler the Soldier," 30; Fairchild, *27th Regiment N.Y. Vols.*, 12–13; Merrell, *Five Months in Rebeldom*, 7. Some historians have mistakenly identified the Confederates involved in this incident as the men of the Hampton Legion. The detailed contemporary account of Private Fowler and the careful recollections of Sergeant Major Coles make it clear that the troops the 27th New York mistook for friends were members of the 4th Alabama.

10. Coles, *From Huntsville to Appomattox*, 22–24, 200, 235n; K. W. Jones, "Fourth Alabama Infantry," 45; Hudson, "Company D, 4th Alabama," 167; R. Johnston, *Bull Run*, 261.

11. *OR*, 389; Fairchild, *27th Regiment N.Y. Vols.*, 12–13; Hall, "Volunteer at the First Bull Run," 155–56. Apparently, at one point the 27th New York was also assailed by the 8th Georgia, which had rallied after being driven from Matthews Hill. Merrell, *Five Months in Rebeldom*, 7.

12. An example of the difficulties inherent in establishing even simple facts: Charles Slocum claims that Colonel Slocum was wounded in the left thigh. *Henry Warner Slocum*, 14. According to Major Bartlett of Slocum's regiment, his superior was struck in the right thigh. *OR*, 389. Slocum's latter-day biographer agrees with Bartlett. See Melton, *Sherman's Forgotten General*, 48–52. See also H. W. Slocum to E. D. Townsend, Aug. 14, 1861, Gratz Collection, HSP. Colonel Lyons's report is in *OR*, 387–88.

13. *OR*, 389; Averell, *Ten Years in the Saddle*, 298.

14. *JCCW*, 214–15; *OR*, 386, 388. John Hennessy suggests that a junior officer gave the errant order. *First Battle of Manassas*, 67. Joanna McDonald states that "another Union officer sent them [the 8th New York and 14th Brooklyn] to engage Hampton's Legion" instead of directing them to Henry Hill. *"We Shall Meet Again,"* 80–81.

15. *OR*, 386, 389; Slocum, *Henry Warner Slocum*, 15.

16. *OR*, 566–67; unidentified enlisted man ("James") to "Dear Cousin Mattie," July 26, 1861, UVA.

17. *OR*, 567; Coxe, "Battle of First Manassas," 26; Hennessy, *First Battle of Manassas*, 68.

18. Unidentified enlisted man ("James") to "Dear Cousin Mattie," July 26, 1861, UVA.

19. *OR*, 402; *JCCW*, 30; R. Johnston, *Bull Run*, 184; J. Thompson, *Civil War to the Bloody End*, 124–25. Despite his misadventures this day, Wright would rise to major general of volunteers. By war's end he would be commanding the VI Corps, Army of the Potomac. Warner, *Generals in Blue*, 575–76.

20. *OR*, 402; S. P. Heintzelman diary, Sept. 1, 5, 1861 [recounting events of July 21], Heintzelman MSS, LC; *JCCW*, 30.

21. *OR*, 402, 405–406, 410; *JCCW*, 30; S. P. Heintzelman diary, Sept. 1, 5, 1861 [recounting events of July 21], Heintzelman MSS, LC.

22. *OR*, 402; Fiske, "Second New Hampshire," 158; Averell, *Ten Years in the Saddle*, 298; R. Johnston, *Bull Run*, 194–95, 210; W. C. Davis, *Battle at Bull Run*, 192; Willcox, *Forgotten Valor*, 289.

23. How long Burnside's brigade remained inactive is a matter of some debate. Union accounts claim the period was brief and that by then the fighting had moved to another sector. See, for example, Woodbury, *First Rhode Island*, 101. E. P. Alexander claims that Burnside dawdled under the trees for five hours. *Military Memoirs*, 37. For Burnside's refusal to return to the fighting when petitioned to do so by McDowell's adjutant general, see Fry, "McDowell's Advance to Bull Run," 190; and T. Vincent, *Battle of Bull Run*, 17. Marvel argues that by this point the colonel's brigade was too exhausted and ammunition-poor to return to the fight. *Burnside*, 25–26. Catton's comment is from *Coming Fury*, 457.

24. *OR*, 402–403; *JCCW*, 30; J. Thompson, *Civil War to the Bloody End*, 125; Snell, *From First to Last*, 62, 64; Imholte, *First Volunteers*, 52; Hutchinson, *Eleventh Massachusetts*, 22–23; Imboden, "Incidents of the First Bull Run," 233.

25. Imboden, "Incidents of the First Bull Run," 233; Hewett et al., *Supplement to the Official Records*, 1:176–78.

26. Imboden, "Incidents of the First Bull Run," 233; Hewett et al., *Supplement to the Official Records*, 1:177; Squires, "'Boy Officer' of the Washington Artillery," 10–13; Hennessy, *First Battle of Manassas*, 64; Driver, *Staunton Artillery*, 9–10; *OR*, 490, 516.

27. Imboden, "Incidents of the First Bull Run," 234; Hewett et al., *Supplement to the Official Records*, 1:176.

28. Imboden, "Incidents of the First Bull Run," 234–35; John D. Imboden to C. C. Buel, June 11, 1885, Imboden MSS, C-CWC, NYPL.

29. Douglas, *I Rode with Stonewall*, 9; R. Cook, *Family and Early Life of Stonewall Jackson*, 160–61; *Life of Stonewall Jackson . . . by a Virginian*, 27–28; Vandiver, *Mighty Stonewall*, 160–61; J. Robertson, *Stonewall Jackson*, 259–61.

30. "Jackson and His Brigade at Manassas," 537–38; J. Robertson, *Stonewall Jackson*, 260.

31. "Jackson and His Brigade at Manassas," 539; Caddall, "Pulaski Guards," 174; J. Robertson, *Stonewall Brigade*, 38.

32. Imboden, "Incidents of the First Bull Run," 235.

33. No one can say with any degree of certainty how many cannons supported Jackson's brigade on Henry Hill. General accounts of the fighting are no help, nor is a specialty source such as Wise, *Long Arm of Lee*. MNBP historians accept the figure of thirteen. See Kelly, "Plan to [Re]locate Artillery," 79–80. Yet the official reports of Johnston and Beauregard place the number at twenty-two (Imboden's three serviceable pieces, the four guns of Stanard's Thomas Artillery [two of them being the first guns to be placed on the hill after Imboden's arrival, around 11:30 A.M.], five of the Washington Artillery, two of the Loudoun Artillery under Lieutenant Heaton, four of the Rockbridge Artillery, and four of the Wise Battery under Lieutenant Pelham). Interestingly, although he claimed that Heaton had served under him two months earlier, Imboden misidentified his unit as the "Leesburg Artillery." "Incidents of the First Bull Run," 235–36.

34. John D. Imboden to C. C. Buel, June 11, 1885, Imboden MSS, C-CWC, NYPL. Imboden would claim that he did not know that Pendleton had been elevated to command of Johnston's artillery, supposing him still a captain in charge of the Rockbridge Artillery. "Incidents of the First Bull Run," 235–36, 236n. It should be noted that Johnston praised Pendleton's services. See *OR*, 475–77. He did the same about ten days after the battle upon learning that the artillery officer was considering retiring from the service. This suggests that Pendleton was aware his conduct at Manassas had attracted criticism. JEJ to W. N. Pendleton, [ca. July 31, 1861], JEJ MSS, DU.

35. Imboden, "Incidents of the First Bull Run," 235.

36. *OR*, 349; *JCCW*, 42, 206; Fry, "McDowell's Advance to Bull Run," 187; D. Tyler, *Autobiography*, 58–59.

37. *OR*, 349, 353, 357–59, 368–69; D. Tyler, *Autobiography*, 58; R. Johnston, *Bull Run*, 194; Andrus, *Brooke, Fauquier, Loudoun, and Alexandria Artillery*, 45.

38. *OR*, 369; W. T. Sherman to Ellen E. Sherman, July 28, 1861, Sherman Family MSS, UND; Hennessy, *First Battle of Manassas*, 62, 149n; Dufour, *Gentle Tiger*, 134, 136; Todd, *Seventy-Ninth Highlanders*, 33.

39. *OR*, 348–49, 369; W. T. Sherman to Ellen E. Sherman, July 28, 1861, Sherman Family MSS, UND; Sherman, *Memoirs*, 1:214; Meagher, *Last Days of the 69th*, 3–5; Warner, *Generals in Blue*, 93–94; Lonn, *Foreigners in the Union Army*, 200–201; Todd, *Seventy-Ninth Highlanders*, 33–34.

40. *OR*, 369; *New York World*, July 23, 1861; Stedman, *Battle of Bull Run*, 17; Wilkinson and Woodworth, *Scythe of Fire*, 77, 318–19n.

41. *OR*, 369, 398; *JCCW*, 206.

42. *OR*, 369; D. Tyler, *Autobiography*, 60; Todd, *Seventy-Ninth Highlanders*, 34; Blake, *Three Years in the Army of the Potomac*, 16; King, "Battle of Bull Run," 503; T. Allen, "Second Wisconsin at First Bull Run," 381, 385.

43. *OR*, 349, 353; D. Tyler, *Autobiography*, 59.

44. *OR*, 349, 353, 491, 566–67; Detzer, *Donnybrook*, 343; Hennessy, *First Battle of Manassas*, 74; E. Tyler, *"Wooden Nutmegs" at Bull Run*, 66–67; Wellman, *Giant in Gray*, 62.

45. E. Tyler, *"Wooden Nutmegs" at Bull Run*, 68; Rafuse, "Man Who Could Have Knocked Down Stonewall," 32–37.

46. E. Tyler, *"Wooden Nutmegs" at Bull Run*, 68.

47. Ibid., 70–71; Hewett et al., *Supplement to the Official Records*, 1:170; E. Keyes, *Fifty Years' Observations*, 433–34.

48. *OR*, 353, 566–67; Hennessy, *First Battle of Manassas*, 75.

49. *OR*, 567; R. H. Moore, *Lynchburg Artillery*, 51; John S. Mosby to his wife, July 24, 1861, Mosby MSS, UVA; Mosby, *Letters*, 11.

50. Imboden, "Incidents of the First Bull Run," 256.

51. *OR*, 567; Longacre, *Gentleman and Soldier*, 50.

52. *OR*, 349, 353–54; Rafuse, *Single Grand Victory*, 153–54.

53. L. Swift, "Bully for the First Connecticut," 76; Andrew McClintock to Jane D. McClintock, July 18, 1861, McClintock MSS, USAH&EC; Alexander, "Battle of Bull Run," 91.

54. *OR*, 349–50, 354; L. Swift, "Bully for the First Connecticut," 79; *New York Tribune*, July 26, 1861.

55. *OR*, 354, 357; Detzer, *Donnybrook*, 345–46.

56. *OR*, 350, 354; D. Tyler, *Autobiography*, 60–61; L. Swift, "Bully for the First Connecticut," 79.

57. Hennessy, *First Battle of Manassas*, 77; Rafuse, *Single Grand Victory*, 153; Rafuse, "Man Who Could Have Knocked Down Stonewall," 66. This view is convincingly refuted by Greg Wolf, MNBP, in a letter to the author, Jan. 17, 2013.

58. JEJ, *Narrative of Military Operations*, 48; Roman, *Operations of General Beauregard*, 1:102–103.

59. Hewett et al., *Supplement to the Official Records*, 1:173.

60. JEJ, *Narrative of Military Operations*, 48; Preston, "General Hill's Article," 155–56; JEJ to C. C. Buel, Aug. 5, 1884, JEJ MSS, C-CWC, NYPL; Coles, *From Huntsville to Appomattox*, 23; Chapman, "4th Alabama Regiment," 197.

61. JEJ, "Responsibilities of the First Bull Run," 248.

62. *OR*, 492; Roman, *Operations of General Beauregard*, 1:104.

63. *OR*, 475; JEJ, *Narrative of Military Operations*, 48–49; GTB to W. J. Marrin, Apr. 12, 1874, Civil War Miscellany Collection, HSP.

64. JEJ, *Narrative of Military Operations*, 49.

65. W. Owen, *Camp and Battle with Washington Artillery*, 38; "Jackson and His Brigade at Manassas," 539.

66. Squires, "'Boy Officer' of the Washington Artillery," 12; Wilkinson and Woodworth, *Scythe of Fire*, 83; K. W. Jones, "Fourth Alabama Infantry," 46–47; *Narrative of the Battles of Bull Run*, 19; Catton, *Coming Fury*, 455; *OR*, 492.

67. Robert Grant to his mother, July 24, 1861, printed in *Savannah Morning News*, July 21, 1892.

68. Akin, *Letters*, 20; T. L. Wragg to his father, July 23, 1861, Wragg MSS, LC; Wilkinson and Woodworth, *Scythe of Fire*, 84, 107; F. Moore, *Rebellion Record*, 2:373.

69. Preston, "General Hill's Article," 156. After the battle Colonel Gist excused Bee's retreat from Matthews Hill by claiming that it had been made "in consequence of the information given him by Evans, that a column of the enemy were cutting him off by the rear and right, which information was an entire mistake, as the column proved to be friends." Hewett et al., *Supplement to the Official Records*, 1:193.

70. Thomas Jordan to R. U. Johnson, Sept. 9, 1884, Jordan MSS, C-CWC, NYPL; Detzer, *Donnybrook*, 296, 465n; Wilkinson and Woodworth, *Scythe of Fire*, 80.

71. *Charleston Mercury*, July 25, 1861; "Jackson and His Brigade at Manassas," 538.

72. J. Robertson, *Stonewall Jackson*, 262; Hennessy, *First Battle of Manassas*, 69–70; R. Johnston, *Bull Run*, 198–99.

73. *Charleston Mercury*, July 25, 1861; *Richmond Dispatch*, July 29, Aug. 17, 1861. John Hennessy provides a good summary of the various accounts of Jackson's naming. *First Battle of Manassas*, 152n. In this

note Hennessy directs the reader to his MNBP typescript, "Jackson's Stone Wall: Fact or Fiction?"

74. Murfin, "How Stonewall Got His Name," 39–40; R. Johnston, *Bull Run*, 202.

75. W. C. Davis, *Battle at Bull Run*, 197; Alexander, *Fighting for the Confederacy*, 51. Interestingly, D. H. Hill, Jackson's brother-in-law, vehemently disagreed that the title was ever meant to be applied to Jackson himself. "Real Stonewall Jackson," 623.

76. Freeman, *Lee's Lieutenants*, 1:733–34; J. Robertson, *Stonewall Jackson*, 834–36nn. Couper points out that the nickname was first applied to Jackson personally in a February 1862 issue of the *Lexington (Va.) Gazette. One Hundred Years at V.M.I.*, 2:161n.

77. Opie, *Rebel Cavalryman*, 30; JEJ, *Narrative of Military Operations*, 48n.

78. Coles, *From Huntsville to Appomattox*, 23, 237n; Hudson, "Company D, 4th Alabama," 169–71; K. W. Jones, "Fourth Alabama Infantry," 47.

79. S. Blackford, *Letters from Lee's Army*, 27; M. Brown, *University Greys*, 967; Shingler, "Reminiscences of the Late Barnard Bee," in possession of Dr. Pat Wilson; Breazeale, *Co. J, 4th South Carolina*, 17–18.

80. Haskell, *Memoirs*, 22, 138n; Stutler, "'There Stands Jackson Like a Stone Wall!,'" 204–205; Murfin, "How Stonewall Got His Name," 40; James B. Agnew to the author, Jan. 26, 1976.

81. Gaines Kincaid (Bee family genealogist) to the author, Jan. 3, 1976.

Chapter 14

1. S. P. Heintzelman diary, Sept. 1, 5, 1861 [recounting events of July 21], Heintzelman MSS, LC; King, "Battle of Bull Run," 505; Averell, *Ten Years in the Saddle*, 298; *JCCW*, 214. Like many another aspect of the battle, the timing and duration of the lull in the action is a matter of opinion, if not of debate. Some participants recalled it as lasting for barely a half hour. See, for example, Conrad, "Manassas and . . . the Stonewall Brigade," 90; S. Blackford, *Letters from Lee's Army*, 28; and Blake, *Three Years in the Army of the Potomac*, 18. Others believed that the respite began as late as 3:00 P.M. See, for example, Woodbury, *Second Rhode Island*, 35; and King, "Battle of Bull Run," 499. As they often do, historians differ: William C. Davis has it lasting from one to two o'clock. *Battle at Bull Run*, 205. Joanna McDonald says 12:30 to 1:30. *"We Shall Meet Again,"* 84, 89. John Hennessy places it from noon to two o'clock. *First Battle of Manassas*, 72, 77. The last appears to be the consensus of battlefield historians. Greg Wolf, MNBP, to the author, Jan. 12, 2013.

2. *OR*, 345–46, 394; *JCCW*, 168–69, 220, 245. Artillery historian Gary Schreckengost argues that McDowell would have done better to place Griffin and Ricketts on Matthews Hill and Chinn Ridge. Then Tyler's division could have attacked Henry Hill from Stone Bridge while Heintzelman drove south across the turnpike and Porter from the west after swinging around Chinn Ridge. "'Fatal Blunder of the Day,'" 26.

But while this plan sounds less rash than McDowell's preference for an "artillery charge," it would not have won the battle. Even if driven from Henry Hill, Jackson most certainly would have continued the fight on some other field or hill to the south along the Sudley Road.

3. *JCCW*, 143, 219–20, 243; *OR*, 346–47, 394; Leech, *Reveille in Washington*, 91, 94.

4. *JCCW*, 243; E. Henry, "Life of Judith (Carter) Henry," 3–4, VHS; Breazeale, *Co. J, 4th South Carolina*, 24; W. C. Davis, *Battle at Bull Run*, 204–205. For a postbattle description of what remained of the house, see Dickert, *Kershaw's Brigade*, 69.

5. *JCCW*, 244; Detzer, *Donnybrook*, 353, 362.

6. *JCCW*, 219. John Hennessy and Ethan Rafuse agree that Griffin moved his guns from one position to another via the Sudley Road. Hennessy, *First Battle of Manassas*, 83; Rafuse, *Single Grand Victory*, 166. Detzer claims that the route remains unknown. *Donnybrook*, 362. Schreckengost further claims that once McDowell sent Ricketts and Griffin into Jackson's "apportioned kill zone," Beauregard should have moved at least some guns around the east face of Henry Hill and set up on Bald Hill so as to enfilade the Federals with solid shot. "'Fatal Blunder of the Day,'" 27. Yet such a move would have been rash and perhaps impossible. Confederate guns would have had to cross Young's Branch with no bridge available except the turnpike bridge immediately east of the Stone House, and the Federals had inundated that area. My thanks to Greg Wolf of MNBP for discussing this situation with me.

7. J. Robertson, *Stonewall Brigade*, 38.

8. Barclay, *Ted Barclay, Liberty Hall Volunteers*, 25. The original of this letter is in the Barclay MSS, Washington and Lee University Library.

9. Douglas, "Stonewall Jackson and His Men," 643; Douglas, *I Rode with Stonewall*, 10.

10. Opie, *Rebel Cavalryman*, 30–31.

11. Imboden, "Incidents of the First Bull Run," 236; M. Jackson, *Life and Letters of Jackson*, 178; J. Robertson, *Stonewall Jackson*, 263, 834n, 836n.

12. Baylor, *Bull Run to Bull Run*, 21; *OR*, 483, 532; Driver and Howard, *2nd Virginia Cavalry*, 16; Orson V. Hancock to his father, July 29, 1861, MNBP.

13. *JCCW*, 30, 143; *OR*, 347, 402–403.

14. *JCCW*, 30, 216; Averell, *Ten Years in the Saddle*, 298.

15. *JCCW*, 215–16; Averell, *Ten Years in the Saddle*, 298.

16. R. Johnston, *Bull Run*, 211; Sivertsen, "McDowell and the Campaign of First Manassas," 66; W. C. Davis, *Battle at Bull Run*, 193. Davis argues that the unintended extension of the Union right flank "hardly seemed to matter. The gathering strength here was overwhelming." The figure generally given is that McDowell placed no more than 17,000–18,000 troops—roughly half of his army—across Bull Run at any point on July 21. R. Johnston, *Bull Run*, 266.

17. *OR*, 385, 402–403, 408, 410, 51(1):20–21; S. P. Heintzelman diary, Sept. 1, 5, 1861 [recounting events of July 21], Heintzelman MSS,

LC; Imholte, *First Volunteers*, 45–47; Moe, *Last Full Measure*, 47–48; Barrett, *What I Saw at Bull Run*, 20–21; Metcalf, "So Eager Were We All," 34–36; Willcox, *Forgotten Valor*, 290–93; Hennessy, *First Battle of Manassas*, 78–81; W. C. Davis, *Battle at Bull Run*, 205–207, 216–17; Detzer, *Donnybrook*, 357, 364, 366–68; Rafuse, *Single Grand Victory*, 161–63.

18. *JCCW*, 215; Averell, *Ten Years in the Saddle*, 298; *OR*, 347. In their official reports both Heintzelman and Barry claimed that Heintzelman ordered up and accompanied the 14th Brooklyn on its way to support Griffin's battery. *OR*, 347, 403. This may have occurred after Averell posted the regiment in the woods in rear of Griffin's position.

19. Metcalf, "So Eager Were We All," 35.

20. Alexander Wilkin to Samuel J. Wilkin, July 23, 1861, Wilkin MSS, MiHS; A. Wilkin to Wescott Wilkin, July 30, 1861, ibid.; Imholte, *First Volunteers*, 46; Moe, *Last Full Measure*, 48–49, 52.

21. Casler, *Four Years in the Stonewall Brigade*, 26.

22. *OR*, 51(1):21; Hennessy, *First Battle of Manassas*, 80; Jasper N. Searles to "Friends at Home," July 25, 1861, Searles MSS, MiHS. Searles's Bull Run letters have been published as Longacre, "'Indeed We Did Fight.'"

23. R. Johnston, *Bull Run*, 258; Moe, *Last Full Measure*, 63; Louis Muller to "My dearest Cousin Brigitta and relatives," Oct. 14, 1861 [recounting events of July 21], MiHS. Atrocity stories were especially prevalent in the ranks of Muller's regiment. See Lloyd G. Pendergast to Lewis Harrington, July 26, 1861, Pendergast MSS, MiHS; Jerome B. Farnsworth to "Dear Friends," July 23, 1861, Farnsworth MSS, ibid.; Farnsworth to "My Dear Friends," July 26, 1861, ibid.; and Christopher Heffelfinger to "Dear Sister," July 24, 1861, MiHS. See also John S. French to "Dear Parents & Friends," July 25, 1861, French MSS, USAH&EC; R. McAllister, *Civil War Letters*, 48–49; Haydon, *For Country, Cause, & Leader*, 58; and Chesnut, *Mary Chesnut's Civil War*, 121.

24. Metcalf, "So Eager Were We All," 38.

25. *OR*, 403; Haskin, *First Regiment of Artillery*, 506.

26. Jasper N. Searles to "Friends at Home," July 25, 1861, Searles MSS, MiHS.

27. *OR*, 403; *JCCW*, 34; Hubbs, "Civil War and Alexander Wilkin," 176–78; Alexander Wilkin to Samuel J. Wilkin, July 23, 1861, Wilkin MSS, MiHS; Jasper N. Searles to "Friends at Home," July 25, 1861, Searles MSS, ibid.; Bassett, *From Bull Run to Bristow Station*, 7.

28. *OR*, 51(1):22; Searles, "First Minnesota Volunteer Infantry," 85–86; Imholte, *First Volunteers*, 54; Moe, *Last Full Measure*, 49.

29. Jasper N. Searles to "Friends at Home," July 25, 1861, Searles MSS, MiHS; *OR*, 391–92; Detzer, *Donnybrook*, 354; Sullivan, *Marine Corps in the Civil War*, 135; Sharp, "Reynolds' Regrets," 22, 24.

30. *OR*, 392; Sharp, "Reynolds' Regrets," 22, 24; Averell, *Ten Years in the Saddle*, 299.

31. *OR*, 393, 482–83; R. Johnston, *Bull Run*, 255; Brackett, *United States Cavalry*, 216; Charles C. Gray memoirs, 7, UNC.

32. Wert, *Cavalryman of the Lost Cause*, 58–59; Driver, *1st Virginia Cavalry*, 12–13; Blackburn, "Confederate Cavalry at First Manassas," 530; *JCCW*, 31; Charles E. Davis to anon., July 23, 1861, Davis MSS, MiHS; Davis to "Dear Bro[ther] George," July 24, 27, 1861, ibid.; Christopher Heffelfinger to "Dear Sister," July 24, 1861, MiHS; Moe, *Last Full Measure*, 55; Barrett, *What I Saw at Bull Run*, 20–21.

33. W. Blackford, *War Years with Jeb Stuart*, 30.

34. Metcalf, "So Eager Were We All," 37; *New York Leader*, Aug. 3, 1861; *OR*, 347, 403, 483; S. P. Heintzelman diary, Sept. 1, 5, 1861 [recounting events of July 21], Heintzelman MSS, LC.

35. *OR*, 51(1):22; R. Johnston, *Bull Run*, 258; Christopher Heffelfinger to "Dear Sister," July 24, 1861, MiHS.

36. *OR*, 328, 394; Averell, *Ten Years in the Saddle*, 298. Detzer suggests that Heintzelman never saw, let alone joined, Griffin's battery, though this seems unlikely given Heintzelman's congressional testimony. Detzer, *Donnybrook*, 364; *JCCW*, 30.

37. Averell, *Ten Years in the Saddle*, 298–99; S. P. Heintzelman diary, Sept. 1, 5, 1861 [recounting events of July 21], Heintzelman MSS, LC; J. Thompson, *Civil War to the Bloody End*, 130.

38. *OR*, 394; *JCCW*, 169, 220. In his testimony before the joint committee, Averell quoted Barry as stating: "I am to blame for the loss of that battery. I put Griffin there myself." Ibid., 217. But Barry testified that he never told the captain to withhold his fire. His statement to Averell, if indeed he uttered it as the latter recalled, seems to have been a lament that he had carried out an order from McDowell to place both batteries in untenable positions. Significantly perhaps, in his memoirs Averell does not mention this incident. In fact, his only reference to Barry relates to his relaying McDowell's order to the battery commanders.

39. *JCCW*, 145–46, 244.

40. Ibid., 169, 175.

41. Warner, *Generals in Blue*, 191; Lyman, *Meade's Headquarters*, 26, 90–91, 168n; Catton, *Stillness at Appomattox*, 66; Beatie, *Army of the Potomac*, 552.

42. J. Robertson, *Stonewall Brigade*, 38; J. Allen, "Thirty-Third Virginia at First Manassas," 368; Reidenbaugh, *33rd Virginia Infantry*, 1–6; Dennis P. Kelly, MNBP, to the author, June 18, 1979.

43. R. K. Krick, *Lee's Colonels*, 108; Reidenbaugh, *33rd Virginia Infantry*, 26; A. C. Cummings to JEJ, Dec. 27, 1870, JEJ MSS, CW&M.

44. J. Allen, "Thirty-Third Virginia at First Manassas," 367–69; Cooke, *Stonewall Jackson*, 508.

45. A. C. Cummings to JEJ, Dec. 27, 1870, JEJ MSS, CW&M; Averell, *Ten Years in the Saddle*, 299; J. Allen, "Thirty-Third Virginia at First Manassas," 369–70; "Jackson and His Brigade at Manassas," 540; Casler, *Four Years in the Stonewall Brigade*, 27; Reidenbaugh, *33rd Virginia Infantry*, 8–10; Naisawald, "Location and Fate of Griffin's and Ricketts' Batteries," 10–18, MNBP. A copy of Colonel Cummings's after-action report, which is missing from the *OR*, is in Cummings MSS, CW&M.

46. Warner, *Generals in Gray*, 284–85; Smith, "Reminiscences of the First Battle of Manassas," 436–37.

47. *OR*, 475, 500, 551–52; W. Smith, "Reminiscences of the First Battle of Manassas," 436; "Jackson and His Brigade at Manassas," 540. For more on Smith's service this day, see Mingos, *General William "Extra Billy" Smith*, 65–71.

48. *OR*, 552; Naisawald, "Location and Fate of Griffin's and Ricketts' Batteries," 11–12; Greg Wolf, MNBP, to the author, Jan. 24, 2013.

49. *OR*, 387, 392, 403, 410, 414; Tevis, *Fighting Fourteenth*, 228–29; S. P. Heintzelman diary, Sept. 1, 5, 1861 [recounting events of July 21], Heintzelman MSS, LC; Averell, *Ten Years in the Saddle*, 298; Hennessy, *First Battle of Manassas*, 97–99; Detzer, *Donnybrook*, 357, 373, 378; A. C. Cummings to JEJ, Dec. 27, 1870, JEJ MSS, CW&M; R. Johnston, *Bull Run*, 263.

50. Alexander H. Shepherd to "Dear Puss," July 25, 1861, West Virginia Department of Archives and History; Baylor, *Bull Run to Bull Run*, 21; Hewett et al., *Supplement to the Official Records*, 1:189–90; Cummings, "Thirty-Third Virginia at First Manassas," 365.

51. J. Robertson, *Stonewall Brigade*, 41; S. Randolph, *Life of Gen. Thomas J. Jackson*, 86–87.

52. R. H. Moore, *Miscellaneous Disbanded Artillery*, 31; William Hassler, *John Pelham*, 1–10.

53. Tevis, *Fighting Fourteenth*, 229–33; Hennessy, *First Battle of Manassas*, 97; Clark, *Regiments . . . from North Carolina*, 1:344–45; Iobst, *Bloody Sixth*, 21.

54. Fonerden, *Carpenter's Battery*, 13; Battillo, "Red-Legged Devils," 11–12.

55. E. Paxton, *Civil War Letters*, 11–12.

56. Hennessy, *First Battle of Manassas*, 99.

57. *OR*, 408–409, 476, 495; Benjamin F. White to James J. Phillips, Jan. 5, 1862, White MSS, North Carolina State Archives; J. McDonald, *"We Shall Meet Again,"* 117–19; Iobst, *Bloody Sixth*, 20–23; Clark, *Regiments . . . from North Carolina*, 1:344, 346.

58. Fishburne, "Rockbridge Artillery," 115; Driver, *1st and 2nd Rockbridge Artillery*, 6; Greg Wolf, MNBP, to the author, Jan. 16, 2013.

59. J. McDonald, *"We Shall Meet Again,"* 204n; Iobst, *Bloody Sixth*, 21–23.; Clark, *Regiments . . . from North Carolina*, 1:345.

60. *OR*, 411–12; R. Johnston, *Bull Run*, 263.

61. *OR*, 409–10, 412; Willcox, *Forgotten Valor*, 293, 687–88.

62. *JCCW*, 33–34; *OR*, 406; Roe, *Fifth Regiment Massachusetts Volunteer Infantry*, 81; Snell, *From First to Last*, 63–64; Hennessy, *First Battle of Manassas*, 100; Bennett, *Musket and Sword*, 17–19; F. Robinson, *Fifth Regiment, M.V.M.*, 13–14; Barrett, *What I Saw at Bull Run*, 25; James W. Carter to "Dear Cousin," July 25, 1861, Carter MSS, ECU.

63. *OR*, 406, 567; Hennessy, *First Battle of Manassas*, 100–101; Blake, *Three Years in the Army of the Potomac*, 23; Hutchinson, *Eleventh Massachusetts*, 24.

64. Blake, *Three Years in the Army of the Potomac*, 23–24.

65. Longacre, *Gentleman and Soldier*, 51, 54; Charles C. Gray memoirs, 21, UNC; *Charleston Mercury*, July 25, 1861. Some historians, including John Hennessy, have Hampton being wounded in the leg with a rifle ball, but his facial wound was observed by his sister, who visited the South Carolinian during his convalescence. Hennessy, *First Battle of Manassas*, 104; Mary Fisher Hampton to Mr. William Martin, Aug. 12, 1861, Hampton Family MSS, USC.

66. *OR*, 475, 478, 495, 561; A. Moore, *Louisiana Tigers*, 39; J. Reid, *Fourth Regiment of S.C. Volunteers*, 24–25.

67. Imboden, "Incidents of the First Bull Run," 230, 237.

68. *OR*, 405, 407, 410; *JCCW*, 244; R. Johnston, *Bull Run*, 259; Detzer, *Donnybrook*, 366.

69. *OR*, 394; Detzer, *Donnybrook*, 361; Warner, *Generals in Blue*, 5–6; *HR&D*, 162.

70. Opie, *Rebel Cavalryman*, 34–35; *JCCW*, 244; Willcox, *Forgotten Valor*, 302, 305; Chesnut, *Mary Chesnut's Civil War*, 136–37.

71. Averell, "With the Cavalry on the Peninsula," 432.

Chapter 15

1. *OR*, 369.

2. Ibid.; Corcoran, *Captivity of General Corcoran*, 22; F. Moore, *Rebellion Record*, 2:66.

3. *OR*, 369; GTB, "First Battle of Bull Run," 211; Hennessy, *First Battle of Manassas*, 102.

4. W. Robertson, "First Bull Run," 105. Lloyd Lewis suggests that Sherman was ordered to attack one regiment after another. *Sherman, Fighting Prophet*, 175. Yet there is no evidence to support the statement; at this point in the war, Sherman was no more prescient than the other brigade commanders who had attacked piecemeal before him.

5. H. Scott, *Military Dictionary*, 70–72. This reference work, compiled by the son and staff officer of Winfield Scott, includes a detailed discussion of 1861-style offensive tactics under the entry "Assault."

6. "Civil War Letters of Samuel S. Partridge," 80; Hennessy, *First Battle of Manassas*, 102–103.

7. T. Allen, "Second Wisconsin at First Bull Run," 385–90; J. McDonald, *"We Shall Meet Again,"* 135–38, 140.

8. *OR*, 369–70; W. C. Davis, *Battle at Bull Run*, 217; T. Allen, "Second Wisconsin at First Bull Run," 390–91.

9. *OR*, 370; Sherman, *Memoirs*, 1:187; Todd, *Seventy-Ninth Highlanders*, 34–37.

10. Todd, *Seventy-Ninth Highlanders*, 37–42; unidentified officer, 79th New York Inf., memoirs, 3–4, NYPL; Hanson, *Bull Run Remembers*, 91.

11. *OR*, 410, 413–14; Detzer, *Donnybrook*, 365, 385.

12. *OR*, 394, 414.

13. Ibid., 370, 372; Stedman, *Battle of Bull Run*, 26; Meagher, *Last Days of the 69th*, 13.

14. *OR*, 370; Monroe, *Rhode Island Artillery*, 19–22. R. M. Johnston claims that Monroe withdrew from Henry Hill because the battle was nearly over when he reached the summit. Detzer says the section retired when about to be attacked. *Donnybrook*, 353–54.

15. *OR*, 414; Hennessy, *First Battle of Manassas*, 106; Greg Wolf, MNBP, to the author, Jan. 15, 2013.

16. T. Allen, "Second Wisconsin at First Bull Run," 385; Hennessy, *First Battle of Manassas*, 106; T. Vincent, *Battle of Bull Run*, 16; *OR*, 415; Matthew Marvin to "Dear Brother," Aug. 1, 1861, MiHS.

17. *New York Times*, July 26, 1861; Fry, "McDowell's Advance to Bull Run," 188; R. Johnston, *Bull Run*, 214.

18. *OR*, 492–95. A typical example of downgrading Beauregard's efforts at shoring up critical points of the line on Henry Hill is W. Robertson, "First Bull Run," 103.

19. *OR*, 475–76, 546, 550, 51(1):24–29; Fields, *28th Virginia Infantry*, 7; Breazeale, *Co. J, 4th South Carolina*, 12.

20. *OR*, 51(1):27–29; Jordan and Thomas, *19th Virginia Infantry*, 8.

21. J. Robertson, *18th Virginia Infantry*, 6; *OR*, 547.

22. *OR*, 547–48, 566; J. Robertson, *18th Virginia Infantry*, 6–7; Hennessy, *First Battle of Manassas*, 104.

23. *OR*, 545, 553–54; unidentified enlisted man, 8th Virginia Inf., memoirs, 1, MNBP; "General Eppa Hunton at the Battle of Bull Run," 143–45.

24. *OR*, 415; "Civil War Letters of Samuel S. Partridge," 80–81.

25. *OR*, 372; Louis P. Foster to "My Dear Sister," July 27, 1861, Foster MSS, USC; Meagher, *Last Days of the 69th*, 13.

26. *OR*, 370; W. T. Sherman to Ellen E. Sherman, July 28, 1861, Sherman Family MSS, UND; Sherman, *Memoirs*, 1:215; Todd, *Seventy-Ninth Highlanders*, 41–42; T. Allen, "Second Wisconsin at First Bull Run," 390–91.

27. *OR*, 550; Fields, *28th Virginia Infantry*, 7.

28. *OR*, 408.

29. Ibid., 408, 550; Willcox, *Forgotten Valor*, 294–96.

30. *OR*, 550; Fields, *28th Virginia Infantry*, 7.

31. *OR*, 418, 421; O. Howard, *Autobiography*, 1:153–54, 157; Small, *Road to Richmond*, 20; Howell, "First Battle of Bull Run," 34; R. Johnston, *Bull Run*, 184, 223.

32. *OR*, 418, 421; John S. French to "Dear Parents & Friends," July 25, 1861, French MSS, USAH&EC.

33. Hennessy, *First Battle of Manassas*, 109, 154–55n. Joanna McDonald notes that Chinn Ridge is a modern term to describe farmland not otherwise identified at the time of the battle. *"We Shall Meet Again,"* 152n.

34. *JCCW*, 219; *OR*, 418–20, 422; O. Howard, *Autobiography*, 1:158–59; Small, *Road to Richmond*, 21–23; E. Gould, *Major-General Hiram G. Berry*, 62–63; Benedict, *Vermont in the Civil War*, 1:77–81; Bicknell, *Fifth Regiment Maine Volunteers*, 28–31; McIntyre, *Alonzo Palmer Stinson*, 5; J. Adams, *Letters of Rev. John R. Adams*, 28; Weston,

Christian Soldier-Boy, 8; George S. Rollins his father, July 26, 1861, Rollins MSS, USAH&EC; George S. Andrews to "Fred," Aug. 2, 1861, Andrews MSS, Brown University Library.

35. O. Howard, *Autobiography*, 1:160–62; O. O. Howard to his mother, July 29, 1861, Howard MSS, Bowdoin College Library.

36. Henry A. Jackson to his father, July 30, 1861, Jackson MSS, USAH&EC.

37. Goldsborough, *Maryland Line*, 18. It is well known that Smith's brigade did not arrive in time to join in the battle, but lesser known is the fact that the balance of Bee's brigade—at least the balance of his 11th Mississippi—reached Manassas by 5:00 P.M. on the twenty-first, nearly but not quite in time to see action. M. Brown, *University Greys*, 19.

38. M. Howard, *Maryland Confederate*, 35. One of Elzey's men claimed that the brigade reached Manassas as early as 10:00 A.M. W. Hollis to "My Dear," July [?], 1861, MNBP. Other accounts place the time as noon or shortly thereafter. Hennessy, *First Battle of Manassas*, 111. These estimates seem too early. Howard says the train halted a few hundred yards west of the depot; another account says it stopped at the depot itself. Coles, *From Huntsville to Appomattox*, 24. For the reasons for detaching the 13th Virginia, see J. Robertson, *General A. P. Hill*, 42; Riggs, *13th Virginia Infantry*, 6; Hewett et al., *Supplement to the Official Records*, 1:179–80; and Thomas S. Parran to his wife, July 26, 1861, CW&M.

39. J. W. Jones, "Reminiscences of the Army of Northern Virginia . . . First Manassas," 130.

40. M. Howard, *Maryland Confederate*, 35–36; McKim, *Soldier's Recollections*, 36; Goldsborough, *Maryland Line*, 19–20; Peters, "First Battle of Manassas," 170, 174–75; W. Hollis to "My Dear," July [?], 1861, MNBP.

41. *Richmond Dispatch*, Aug. 1, 1861; *Narrative of the Battles of Bull Run*, 21.

42. McDowell would tell the joint committee that by 11:00 A.M. he knew "beyond all doubt" that Johnston's army had joined Beauregard's. *JCCW*, 40.

43. JEJ, *Narrative of Military Operations*, 51; Hewett et al., *Supplement to the Official Records*, 1:180; B. Johnson, "Memoir of the First Maryland," 482–83; W. C. Davis, *Battle at Bull Run*, 225; N. Buck, "'Blucher of the Day' at Manassas," 108. Nina Buck, General Smith's daughter, quotes her father as saying that when Elzey's brigade reached the field, Johnston's staff was drawing up contingency plans for a full-scale retreat.

44. Henry Buist to Mrs. Frances K. Smith, July 22, 1861, Smith MSS, SHC, UNC; Hugh W. Cole to Mrs. Frances K. Smith, July 23, 1861, ibid.; E. K. Smith to his mother, July 31, 1861, ibid.; Parks, *General Edmund Kirby Smith*, 137–38; McKim, *Soldier's Recollections*, 36.

45. Peters, "First Battle of Manassas," 173–74; B. Johnson, "First Maryland Regiment," 482–83; *OR*, 393.

46. Hewett et al., *Supplement to the Official Records*, 1:180; *OR*, 483.

47. *OR*, 418; Hewett et al., *Supplement to the Official Records*, 1:180; Peters, "First Battle of Manassas," 171; M. Howard, *Maryland Confederate*, 39.

48. M. Howard, *Maryland Confederate*, 38.

49. Ibid.; Peters, "First Battle of Manassas," 171.

50. Metcalf, "So Eager Were We All," 41; W. Blackford, *War Years with Jeb Stuart*, 34; Varner, "Third South Carolina," 520; William H. Tatum to "Dear Louisa," July 22, 1861, Tatum MSS, VHS; McKim, *Soldier's Recollections*, 39.

51. *OR*, 496, 555–56; Osborne, *Jubal*, 61–66; J. Davis, *Rise and Fall of the Confederate Government*, 352.

52. Freeman, *Lee's Lieutenants*, 1:71–72; W. H. Hardy to his parents, July 21, 1861, MNBP; W. C. Davis, *Battle at Bull Run*, 227–28, 231. Another account has Beauregard mistaking the image of a pelican on the state flag of the 7th Louisiana for the eagle emblem of the United States. T. Jones, *Lee's Tigers*, 53–54.

53. *OR*, 556–58; Early, *War Memoirs*, 19–26; Riggs, *7th Virginia Infantry*, 3–4; D. Johnston, *Four Years a Soldier*, 80–83.

54. Peters, "First Battle of Manassas," 174; N. Buck, "'Blucher of the Day' at Manassas," 108–109.

55. *OR*, 403; S. P. Heintzelman diary, Sept. 1, 5, 1861 [recounting events of July 21], Heintzelman MSS, LC; Walker G. Camp to "Miss Lizzie Camp," July 25, 1861, Camp MSS, GDA&H.

56. Charles C. Gray memoirs, 8, UNC; R. Wallace, *Memories of a Long Life*, 7–9.

57. Fry, "McDowell's Advance to Bull Run," 191–92.

58. William W. Averell diary, July 22, 1861 [recounting events of July 21], Averell MSS, GLC; Averell to anon., Oct. 31, 1861, ibid.; Carter, *Four Brothers in Blue*, 14–15; Parker, *Personal Reminiscences*, 17.

59. *OR*, 390; Carter, *Four Brothers in Blue*, 15; Reese, *Sykes' Regular Infantry*, 38–39.

60. W. Blackford, *War Years with Jeb Stuart*, 35; *OR*, 390–91, 483; Carter, *Four Brothers in Blue*, 15; Parker, *Personal Reminiscences*, 18; Reese, *Sykes' Regular Infantry*, 39.

61. *OR*, 498, 543–45; Longstreet, *From Manassas to Appomattox*, 75; Goree, *Longstreet's Aide*, 28; R. Johnston, *Bull Run*, 244.

62. *OR*, 537–38; R. S. Ewell to "Lizzie," July 31, 1861, Ewell MSS, LC; Alexander, *Military Memoirs*, 46; R. Johnston, *Bull Run*, 173–75; Fontaine, *My Life and My Lectures*, 70.

63. *OR*, 378–79, 430, 538–42; Nye, "Action North of Bull Run," 49; Cudworth, *First Regiment [Massachusetts Volunteers]*, 65–66; unidentified enlisted man, 5th South Carolina Inf., to "Miss Irene," Aug. 3, 1861, MNBP.

64. Gibbs, "With a Mississippi Private," 45; Fontaine, *My Life and My Lectures*, 71–72.

65. *OR*, 540–41. A member of Ewell's staff later wrote that Jones "ran up against them [Davies and Hunt] as stupidly as if he were blindfolded." G. Campbell Brown memoirs, 11, TSL&A.

66. *OR*, 379, 542; unidentified enlisted man, 5th South Carolina Inf., to "Miss Irene," Aug. 3, 1861, MNBP; G. Campbell Brown to Henry J. Hunt, Jan. 27, 1885, H. Hunt MSS, LC; Longacre, *Man behind the Guns*, 87, 92. Proving his ability to turn a nice phrase, John Nicolay wrote that Hunt's shelling "scattered the attacking column as if by enchantment." *Outbreak of Rebellion*, 199.

67. *JCCW*, 24; *OR*, 335, 425, 427, 524; T. Vincent, *Battle of Bull Run*, 23–25; W. Randolph, "First Manassas . . . Cavalry Pursuit," 263; W. C. Davis, *Battle at Bull Run*, 241.

68. *OR*, 425, 747; R. Johnston, *Bull Run*, 238.

69. Baquet, *First Brigade, New Jersey Volunteers*, 7; Bilby and Goble, "*Remember You Are Jerseymen!*," 64–65.

70. *OR*, 321, 408, 437–38, 747, 751–52; Putnam, "Before and after the Battle," 239–41; Baquet, *First Brigade, New Jersey Volunteers*, 8; R. McAllister, *Civil War Letters*, 48n; Charles A. Hopkins memoirs, n.d., Hopkins MSS, RU.

71. *OR*, 375–76, 379, 425, 430–31; *JCCW*, 25–27, 183.

72. *OR*, 375–76, 425; *JCCW*, 27; *New York Times*, Aug. 5, 1861. The proceedings of an official inquiry into Miles's conduct on July 21 can be found in the National Archives; see Record Group 153, Entry II-498. Surprisingly—or perhaps not so surprisingly—the court found that "evidence cannot now be found sufficient to convict Colonel Miles of drunkenness before a court-martial; that a proper court could only be organized in this Army with the greatest inconvenience at present, and that it will not be for the interests of the service to convene a court in this case." *OR*, 438–39. Miles would continue to serve until killed in September 1862 while attempting to surrender Union-held Harpers Ferry to Stonewall Jackson. Some observers suspected that he was drunk at the time of his death.

Chapter 16

1. Driver, *1st and 2nd Rockbridge Artillery*, 6; R. H. Moore, *Lynchburg Artillery*, 51; *OR*, 554–55.

2. *OR*, 557.

3. Ibid., 51(1):30; Jordan and Thomas, *19th Virginia Infantry*, 8; Hundley, "Beginning and the Ending," 305.

4. Hewett et al., *Supplement to the Official Records*, 1:180; Alexander, *Military Memoirs*, 45; T. Murphy, *10th Virginia Infantry*, 9–10.

5. *OR*, 482; R. Johnston, *Bull Run*, 263. The accepted view is that Jackson's brigade received no orders to pursue. In his battle report the general claimed that he was merely directed "to act as circumstances might require." This seems logical: his command had been fought out, having lost almost 20 percent of its strength in the fighting, and its leader required medical attention for his wounded hand. After the battle, however, Colonel Harper of the 5th Virginia stated that he had received "the order to march in pursuit" and implied that his regiment, at least, had carried it out. Hewett et al., *Supplement to the Official Records*, 1:191.

6. W. Blackford, *War Years with Jeb Stuart*, 36; Blackburn, "Confederate Cavalry at First Manassas," 532; *OR*, 553–54; R. H. Moore, *Lynchburg Artillery*, 51.

7. Otho S. Lee memoirs, 3–4, Washington and Lee University Library.

8. W. Blackford, *War Years with Jeb Stuart*, 37; *OR*, 483–84.

9. *OR*, 393, 403, 416–17, 483; Wert, *Cavalryman of the Lost Cause*, 59–60.

10. *OR*, 497; JEJ, *Narrative of Military Operations*, 53.

11. *OR*, 532; Driver and Howard, *2nd Virginia Cavalry*, 18.

12. Aldrich, *Battery A, First Regiment Rhode Island Light Artillery*, 26–27.

13. Stiles, *4th Virginia Cavalry*, 6.

14. *OR*, 363–38; Naisawald, "Bull Run," 175; Hains, "First Gun at Bull Run," 395–96; Hennessy, *First Battle of Manassas*, 118–19.

15. *OR*, 363.

16. Ibid., 371–72, 532; Corcoran, *Captivity of General Corcoran*, 24; Coyle, "General Michael Corcoran," 113; William G. Terry to N. G. Evans, July 23, 1861, GLC; Blackburn, "Confederate Cavalry at First Manassas," 533; Coles, *From Huntsville to Appomattox*, 25; Russell, *My Diary North and South*, 459. Corcoran spent more than a year incarcerated at Richmond, then in a succession of prison pens in the Carolinas. In captivity he would serve as a pawn in a high-stakes diplomatic standoff between the belligerents, held hostage against the threatened execution of Confederate privateer crews whom the Federal government regarded as pirates. Finally released in August 1862, the patriot-soldier (acting head of the Fenian Brotherhood in America) returned to the field as a brigadier general in command of the Irish Legion, a brigade he had helped recruit and that included elements of the reconstituted 69th New York.

17. *OR*, 373, 524–25, 527, 532–33; Driver and Howard, *2nd Virginia Cavalry*, 18–20; S. Blackford, *Letters from Lee's Army*, 32.

18. Finch, "Boys of '61," 259; E. Tyler, *"Wooden Nutmegs" at Bull Run*, 74–75. R. M. Johnston agrees that "Radford's advance on the Cub Run bridge was not a very serious affair." *Bull Run*, 256.

19. R. C. Schenck to his family, July 22, 1861, Schenck MSS, Miami University (of Ohio) Library. Schenck reported a loss in his brigade of twenty-one killed and an equal number wounded, but as R. M. Johnston points out, the majority of the casualties occurred in a single regiment, the 2nd New York, which conducted "a demonstration . . . about eleven o'clock, toward Lewis' Ford that was checked by the Confederate artillery beyond Bull Run. . . . On the whole Schenck's brigade saw hardly any fighting." *Bull Run*, 256.

20. *OR*, 525, 532, 534; S. Blackford, *Letters from Lee's Army*, 31–32; Blackburn, "Confederate Cavalry at First Manassas," 532.

21. *OR*, 525, 534, 553; Stiles, *4th Virginia Cavalry*, 6.

22. *OR*, 534; J. Scott, "Black Horse Cavalry," 590–93; Driver and Howard, *2nd Virginia Cavalry*, 20; W. Randolph, "First Manassas . . . Cavalry Pursuit," 262–63.

23. *OR*, 350, 364, 367, 534; Hains, "First Gun at Bull Run," 395–99; Haskin, *First Regiment of Artillery*, 149; Naisawald, "Bull Run," 175; Breazeale, *Co. J, 4th South Carolina*, 24.

24. *OR*, 534.

25. Ibid., 543; Longstreet, *From Manassas to Appomattox*, 51.

26. Samuel L. West to his father, Aug. 8, 1861, West MSS, USAH&EC.

27. *OR*, 543–44; Longstreet, *From Manassas to Appomattox*, 51–52; F. B. Williams, "From Sumter to the Wilderness," 5–6; Dickert, *Kershaw's Brigade*, 65.

28. Roman, *Operations of General Beauregard*, 1:109–10.

29. *OR*, 544; Longstreet, *From Manassas to Appomattox*, 52; Alexander, *Fighting for the Confederacy*, 57.

30. Sorrel, *Confederate Staff Officer*, 20; Goree, *Longstreet's Aide*, 28–29; Alexander, *Military Memoirs*, 47–48. It would appear that army head-quarters came to agree with these low opinions of Bonham's competence. After the battle Beauregard and he were on poor terms, especially after the Creole announced that colleagues such as D. R. Jones, formerly junior to Bonham, now outranked him on the basis of added seniority. GTB to M. L. Bonham, Nov. 20, 1861, GTB MSS, Gratz Collection, HSP.

31. *OR*, 519, 529; Samuel L. West to his father, Aug. 8, 1861, West MSS, USAH&EC; Varner, "Third South Carolina," 520.

32. *OR*, 523–24, 531, 551; Fields, *28th Virginia Infantry*, 8–9.

33. *OR*, 524; J. Robertson, *18th Virginia Infantry*, 7; McDowell and Davis, "Joe Writes His Own Praise," 37; Hennessy, *First Battle of Manassas*, 119.

34. *OR*, 524–25; Alexander, *Military Memoirs*, 44–45; Alexander, *Fighting for the Confederacy*, 54–56; J. Robertson, *18th Virginia Infantry*, 7.

35. *OR*, 525, 531, 535–36; R. Johnston, *Bull Run*, 232.

36. *OR*, 525, 536; Alexander, *Fighting for the Confederacy*, 56; B. Mitchell, *Edmund Ruffin*, 194–95; Breazeale, *Co. J, 4th South Carolina*, 25.

37. Edmund Ruffin diary, July 21, 1861, LC; *OR*, 525.

38. Barrett, *What I Saw at Bull Run*, 28; "Civil War Letters of Samuel S. Partridge," 81; E. Rhodes, *All for the Union*, 39; *OR*, 323, 340–41, 386, 394; Ostrander, *Monument in Memory of the Men Who Fell*, 17.

39. E. Keyes, *Fifty Years' Observations*, 434–35.

40. *OR*, 525; F. Moore, *Rebellion Record*, 2:59. Alexander recalled that Kershaw did not completely withdraw but left one regiment and Scott's horsemen to unpile the traffic jam the retreating Yankees had created. *Military Memoirs*, 45.

41. *New York Tribune*, July 26, 1861; *New York World*, July 23, 1861; *Philadelphia Inquirer*, July 25, 1861.

42. W. T. Sherman to Ellen E. Sherman, July 24, 28, 1861, Sherman Family MSS, UND; Sherman, *Memoirs*, 1:215; E. Keyes, *Fifty Years' Observations*, 435.

43. R. Wallace, *Memories of a Long Life*, 9; Dupuy and Dupuy, *Military Heritage of America*, 222; Benson, "Adelbert Ames," 18.

44. Russell, *My Diary North and South*, 450–64; Russell, *Russell's Civil War*, 94; F. Moore, *Rebellion Record*, 2:62–64. Russell's alleged panic-stricken flight from the battlefield inspired numerous satirical poems, broadsides, and pamphlets such as *A Modern Gilpin: A Ballad of Bull Run* (New York, 1866).

45. Frassanito, *Antietam*, 29–30.
46. Hennessy, "War-Watchers at Bull Run," 46–47, 67, 69, 72; Riddle, *Recollections of War Times*, 47–52; Trefousse, *Benjamin Franklin Wade*, 150–51.
47. *OR*, 574; Ely, *Journal*, 14–18; "Civil War Letters of Samuel S. Partridge," 82; Alexander, *Fighting for the Confederacy*, 55; E. B. C. Cash to M. L. Bonham, July 31, 1861, GLC; Leech, *Reveille in Washington*, 127.
48. Samuel L. West to his father, Aug. 8, 1861, West MSS, USAH&EC; unidentified enlisted man, 5th South Carolina Inf., to "Miss Irene," Aug. 3, 1861, MNBP.
49. Hennessy, "War-Watchers at Bull Run," 69, 72.
50. W. Randolph, "First Manassas . . . Cavalry Pursuit," 261–62; Mosby, *Memoirs*, 50; Thomas H. Pitts to "My dear Cousin," July 28, 1861, Pitts-Craig MSS, EU.
51. Louis P. Foster to his mother, July 22, 1861, Foster MSS, USC.
52. M. L. Bonham to "Genl.," Aug. 27, 1861, Bonham MSS, Gratz Collection, HSP; John S. Mosby to his wife, July 24, 1861, Mosby MSS, UVA; E. P. Alexander to his wife, July 25, 1861, Alexander MSS, SHC, UNC; Chesnut, *Mary Chesnut's Civil War*, 108; Thomas R. R. Cobb to "Dearest Marion," July 27, 1861, Cobb MSS, UGA; Wiley, "Story of 3 Southern Officers," 8.
53. *Battle-fields of the South*, 53.
54. Barrett, *What I Saw at Bull Run*, 26; *OR*, 344–45, 391; *HR&D*, 921; Charles C. Gray memoirs, 9, UNC.
55. *OR*, 328, 571.
56. W. H. Manghum to his father, Aug. 28, 1861, Manghum MSS, GDA&H; John H. Barker to Mildred A. Barker, Aug. 8, 1861, Barker MSS, CW&M; Hiram W. Camp to "Miss Lizzie Camp," Aug. 3, 1861, GDA&H; E. Patterson, *Yankee Rebel*, 8.
57. Louis P. Foster to "My Dear Sister," July 27, 1861, Foster MSS, USC.
58. John Fort to his mother, July 26, 1861, Fort MSS, MNBP; B. Mitchell, *Edmund Ruffin*, 195; Craven, *Edmund Ruffin*, 231.
59. Austin, "Georgia Boy with 'Stonewall' Jackson," 315; "W. C. Tunstall, Co. D, 5th AL on the Aftermath of the Battle," *Bull Runnings* (blog), July 11, 2009, http://bullrunnings.wordpress.com/2009/11/07/w-c-tunstall-co-d-5th-al-on-the-aftermath-of-the-battle/; E. P. Alexander to his wife, July 27, 1861, Alexander MSS, SHC, UNC.
60. *OR*, 327, 570; R. Johnston, *Bull Run*, 253–55, 260–62; T. Livermore, *Numbers and Losses*, 77.
61. *Charleston Mercury*, July 25, 1861; JEJ, *Narrative of Military Operations*, 53–54; J. Davis, *Rise and Fall of the Confederate Government*, 327–28; Thomas R. R. Cobb to "Dearest Marion," July 27, 1861, Cobb MSS, UGA; Alexander, *Military Memoirs*, 42. In later life Alexander remembered Davis's comment somewhat differently. See *Fighting for the Confederacy*, 54.
62. J. Davis, *Rise and Fall of the Confederate Government*, 328; Early, *War Memoirs*, 27.

63. Breazeale, *Company J, 4th South Carolina*, 23; *OR*, 534.

64. Alexander, *Military Memoirs*, 42; H. McGuire, "General Thomas J. Jackson," 303; S. Randolph, *Life of Gen. Thomas J. Jackson*, 92; Mosby, *Memoirs*, 81. James Robertson doubts the incident happened exactly as here stated, "yet the basic circumstances have a ring of authenticity." *Stonewall Jackson*, 269.

65. J. Davis, *Rise and Fall of the Confederate Government*, 328. R. M. Johnston endorses the view that the battle had ended before Davis arrived on the field. *Bull Run*, 249n.

66. J. Davis, *Rise and Fall of the Confederate Government*, 332–35; Roman, *Operations of General Beauregard*, 1:115–19; JEJ, *Narrative of Military Operations*, 63–64; T. Williams, *Beauregard*, 89–90; Symonds, *Joseph E. Johnston*, 122–24; JEJ, "Responsibilities of the First Bull Run," 252–53; *OR*, 511–12. A good summing up of the controversy is Freeman, *Lee's Lieutenants*, 1:73–78.

67. J. Davis, *Rise and Fall of the Confederate Government*, 333; Roman, *Operations of General Beauregard*, 1:114; Alexander, *Fighting for the Confederacy*, 58.

68. J. Davis, *Rise and Fall of the Confederate Government*, 334–35; Roman, *Operations of General Beauregard*, 1:116–17; Hughes, *General Johnston*, 74–75.

69. J. Davis, *Rise and Fall of the Confederate Government*, 338–39; Roman, *Operations of General Beauregard*, 1:116.

Chapter 17

1. S. B. Gibbons to "Dear Sister," July 27, 1861, Gibbons MSS, MNBP; George W. Latham to his father, July 4, 1861, Latham MSS, UVA; Hiram W. Camp to "Miss Lizzie Camp," Aug. 3, 1861, GDA&H; Thomas H. Pitts to "My dear Cousin," July 28, 1861, Pitts-Craig MSS, EU.

2. Taylor, *Destruction and Reconstruction*, 10; *OR*, 1000; E. P. Alexander to his wife, July 31, 1861, Alexander MSS, SHC, UNC.

3. Alexander, *Military Memoirs*, 43; Alexander, *Fighting for the Confederacy*, 56–57.

4. Longstreet, *From Manassas to Appomattox*, 56–59.

5. Early, *War Memoirs*, 44.

6. Roman, *Operations of General Beauregard*, 1:117; Thomas Jordan to GTB, Feb. 23, 1868, Civil War Miscellany Collection, HSP.

7. M. L. Bonham to GTB, Aug. 15, 1861, Bonham MSS, Gratz Collection, HSP; M. L. Bonham to GTB, Aug. 28, 1877, Bonham MSS, USC; M. L. Bonham to Francis W. Pickens, June 23, 1861, ibid.

8. JEJ, *Narrative of Military Operations*, 63; Roman, *Operations of General Beauregard*, 1:119.

9. Roman, *Operations of General Beauregard*, 1:122.

10. JEJ, *Narrative of Military Operations*, 56, 60–62; JEJ to "My dear sir," Aug. 5, 1861, GLC; *OR*, 477; JEJ, "Responsibilities of the First Bull Run," 252.

11. *OR*, 1005–1006; JEJ, *Narrative of Military Operations*, 67; Goff, *Confederate Supply*, 22–23; Imboden, "Incidents of the First Bull Run," 239; Eggleston, *Rebel's Recollections*, 76.

12. Roman, *Operations of General Beauregard*, 1:121–22; T. Williams, *Beauregard*, 96–98; Goff, *Confederate Supply*, 23–24; Imboden, "Incidents of the First Bull Run," 239; Dufour, *Nine Men in Grey*, 204–205. In the weeks after the battle, Richmond's most influential diarist called Northrop "the most cussed and vilified man in the Confederacy." Chesnut, *Mary Chesnut's Civil War*, 124.

13. M. L. Bonham to GTB, Sept. 5, 1877, Bonham MSS, USC; Dufour, *Nine Men in Grey*, 205–206; Northrop, "Confederate Commissariat at Manassas," 261; Goff, *Confederate Supply*, 25; L. B. Northrop to editors of *Century*, Feb. 23, Nov. 27, Dec. 16, 1885, Feb. 19, 1886, Northrop MSS, C-CWC, NYPL.

14. *OR*, 986; Richardson, *Messages and Papers of the Confederacy*, 1:124–25; Freeman, *R. E. Lee*, 1:537–38; Akin, *Letters*, 19; E. Thomas, *Confederate State of Richmond*, 53. The captured Yankees who accompanied Davis to Richmond did not embrace the total number of prisoners taken in the battle, which—including wounded men unable to be evacuated from Manassas—was reported as exceeding 1,400. *OR*, 571. An Alabama soldier stationed in Richmond a week after the battle reported that the city then held some 900 prisoners of war, quite close to the official count (871) in the "return of captures and abstract of prisoners taken" compiled almost three months later. William W. Andrews to Mollie Buckelew, July 28, 1861, UVA.

15. Fletcher, *History of the American War, Vol. 1*, 140.

16. Cunningham, "Confederate General Hospitals," 376; Chesnut, *Mary Chesnut's Civil War*, 107.

17. C. Harrison, "Virginia Scenes in '61," 164–65.

18. Bailey, "Letters of Melvin Dwinnell," 199; E. Patterson, *Yankee Rebel*, 8; *Daily Richmond Examiner*, Sept. 27, 1861.

19. Elisha F. Paxton to his wife, July 23, 1861, C-CWC, NYPL; Angus Blakey to his brother, July 23, 1861, UVA; Coulter, *Confederate States of America*, 345; Henry J. Dobbs to Millie and Patty Barker, Aug. 7, 1861, CW&M.

20. Thomas R. R. Cobb to his wife, July 27, 1861, Cobb MSS, UGA; *New Orleans Picayune*, July 23, 1861; J. Adger Smythe to anon., July 26, 1861, South Carolina Historical Society; C. Adams et al., *Cycle of Adams Letters*, 1:22–23.

21. John H. Barker to Mildred A. Barker, Aug. 8, 1861, Barker MSS, CW&M; David W. Aiken to his wife, Aug. 2, 1861, Aiken MSS, USC; Leroy P. Walker to Caleb Huse and Edward C. Anderson, July 22, 1861, Records of War Department, CSA: Letters Sent, CSA Papers, LC; August Belmont to Salmon P. Chase, Aug. 15, 1861, Chase MSS, HSP; Crook, *North, South, and the Powers*, 16–21; Owsley, *King Cotton Diplomacy*, 64, 123.

22. Crook, *North, South, and the Powers*, 21–25, 89; Laugel, *United States during the Civil War*, 4; Owsley, *King Cotton Diplomacy*, 67; Luvaas,

Military Legacy of the Civil War, 63–64; "American Belligerents," 109–12, 121. For a sampling of European opinion on the battle and the military and diplomatic issues arising from it, as reported in leading journals, see *London Daily News*, Aug. 9, 1861; *Times* (London), Aug. 10, 1861; "Democracy on Its Trial," *Quarterly Review* 110 (1861): 247–88; "The Disruption of the Union," *Blackwood's Edinburgh Magazine* 90 (1861): 125–34; "The Convulsions of America," ibid., 91 (1861): 118–30; "The Disunion of America," *Edinburgh Review* 114 (1861): 556–87; "The Dissolution of the Union," *Cornhill Magazine* 4 (1861): 153–66; "The Civil War in America," *Punch, or the London Charivari* 41 (Aug. 17, 1861): 63–64; and "English and French View of the American Rebellion," *North American Review* 94 (1862): 408–35.

23. Douglas, *I Rode with Stonewall*, 11; JEJ, *Narrative of Military Operations*, 59. A copy of the address, dated July 25, 1861, is in JEJ MSS, Henry E. Huntington Library.

24. On the failure of Southern nationalism, see Beringer, Hattaway, Jones, and Still, Jr., *Why the South Lost*, 64–81, 424–28. I thank William C. Davis for suggesting that I speculate on this subject.

25. J. McGuire, *Southern Refugee*, 43, 360.

26. "Skirmish Line," 524.

27. *OR*, 335, 347, 427–28; E. Tyler, *"Wooden Nutmegs" at Bull Run*, 77; Cudworth, *First Regiment [Massachusetts Volunteers]*, 63; *Memoir of William A. Jackson*, 10–11.

28. Clement, *Bull-Run Rout*, 9–10; Christopher Heffelfinger to "Dear Sister," July 24, 1861, MiHS; R. Wallace, *Memories of a Long Life*, 8.

29. E. Keyes, *Fifty Years' Observations*, 435; Putnam, "Before and after the Battle," 241; George S. Rollins to his father, July 26, 1861, Rollins MSS, USAH&EC.

30. Cunningham, *Field Medical Services*, 18.

31. W. T. Sherman to Ellen E. Sherman, July 28, 1861, Sherman Family MSS, UND; Townsend, *Anecdotes of the Civil War*, 59; *OR*, 5:679.

32. *OR*, 757–58; Elliott, *Winfield Scott*, 729–30; Cooling, *Symbol, Sword, and Shield*, 60–61.

33. Putnam, "Before and after the Battle," 239; Woodruff, "Early War Days," 102; Russell, *My Diary North and South*, 467.

34. Russell, *My Diary North and South*, 469–70; Waterman, "Washington at the Time of the First Bull Run," 30; Greenhow, *My Imprisonment*, 17; Whitman, *Prose Works 1892: Volume I*, 28–29.

35. Russell, *My Diary North and South*, 470; Leech, *Reveille in Washington*, 130.

36. Russell, *My Diary North and South*, 465.

37. Nicolay and Hay, *Abraham Lincoln*, 4:352–54; Townsend, *Anecdotes of the Civil War*, 58; W. Wilson, *Leaf from History of the Rebellion*, 6–9.

38. *OR*, 747–48.

39. W. Wilson, *Leaf from History of the Rebellion*, 10.

40. Ibid., 11; *OR*, 749, 752, 754–55.

41. Nicolay and Hay, *Abraham Lincoln*, 4:358–59; Elliott, *Winfield Scott*, 730–31; Eisenhower, *Agent of Destiny*, 392.
42. Nicolay and Hay, *Abraham Lincoln*, 4:355.
43. Hoadley, *Henry Sanford Gansevoort*, 95; Townsend, *Anecdotes of the Civil War*, 59.
44. Fitzgerald, *In Memoriam*, 5; Francis E. Butler diary, July 23, 1861, RU; *OR*, 755; Noyes, "Few Guns before Bull Run," 417.
45. Townsend, *Anecdotes of the Civil War*, 58–59.
46. Russell, *My Diary North and South*, 471; *OR*, 758; W. T. Sherman to Ellen E. Sherman, July 23, 1861, Sherman Family MSS, UND; Sherman, *Memoirs*, 1:189–91; Tarbell, "Lincoln Gathering an Army," 230.
47. Haydon, *For Country, Cause, & Leader*, 60; Christian Heffelfinger to "Dear Sister," July 24, 1861, MiHS; Francis E. Butler diary, July 23, 1861, RU; John S. French to "Dear Parents & Friends," July 25, 1861, French MSS, USAH&EC; Jerome B. Farnsworth to "Dear Brother," July 23, 1861, Farnsworth MSS, MiHS; *New York Times*, July 23, 1861; *Philadelphia Press*, July 23, 1861.
48. George S. Rollins to his father, July 26, 1861, Rollins MSS, USAH&EC; Jasper N. Searles to "Friends at Home," July 25, 1861, Searles MSS, MiHS; Longacre, "Fortune's Fool," 26, 30; Andrews, *North Reports the Civil War*, 98; Russell, *Russell's Civil War*, 95; F. Moore, *Rebellion Record*, 2:69; *OR*, 753, 755.
49. Samuel S. Elder to "My Dear Friend," July 23, 1861, NYPL; *New York Times*, July 31, 1861.
50. Christopher Heffelfinger to "Dear Sister," July 24, 1861, MiHS; Jasper N. Searles to "Friends at Home," July 25, 1861, Searles MSS, ibid.
51. Jacob A. Camp to his wife, July 27, 1861, Cornell University Library.
52. *New York Times*, June 16, 1861; *Harper's Weekly*, Aug. 10, 1861, 499; *Baltimore American*, July 26, 1861.
53. Haydon, *For Country, Cause, & Leader*, 62; George G. Meade to "Dear Dort," Aug. 5, 1861, Meade MSS, HSP.
54. Bigelow, *Retrospections*, 1:361.
55. Lyster, *Recollections of the Bull Run Campaign*, 18.
56. Bigelow, *Retrospections*, 1:361; Strong, *Diary*, 170; F. Moore, *Rebellion Record*, 2:385.
57. Samuel S. Elder to "My Dear Friend," July 23, 1861, NYPL; Wolseley, *American Civil War: An English View*, 99.
58. *New York Times*, July 23, 1861; Starr, *Bohemian Brigade*, 50; Drell, "Letters by Richard Smith," 541; *Frank Leslie's Illustrated Newspaper*, Aug. 3, 1861, 179.
59. F. Moore, *Rebellion Record*, 2:52, 108–10; Russell, *Battle of Bull Run*, 5.
60. Samuel S. Elder to "My Dear Friend," July 23, 1861, NYPL; R. McAllister, *Civil War Letters*, 55; E. Rhodes, *All for the Union*, 60–61.
61. R. Wallace, *Memories of a Long Life*, 9–10; W. Franklin, "First Great Crime of the War," 72; Bushnell, *Reverses Needed*, 6–7.

62. "Lessons of Our National Conflict," 895; Fredrickson, *Inner Civil War*, 73.
63. Fredrickson, *Inner Civil War*, 73, 763.
64. J. Nicolay, *Outbreak of Rebellion*, 208–10; W. Robertson, "First Bull Run," 108.

Bibliography

Unpublished Documents

Correspondence, Diaries, and Memoirs

CONFEDERATE ADMINISTRATIVE AND FIELD COMMANDERS

Beauregard, P. G. T. Correspondence. Century–Civil War Collection. New York Public Library, New York, N.Y.

———. Correspondence. Columbia University Library, New York, N.Y.

———. Correspondence. Gratz Collection. Historical Society of Pennsylvania, Philadelphia.

———. Correspondence. Library of Congress, Washington, D.C.

———. Correspondence. New-York Historical Society, New York, N.Y.

———. Letter of July 13, 1861. Duke University Library, Durham, N.C.

———. Letter of July 17, 1861. Gilder Lehrman Collection, Gilder Lehrman Institute of American History, New York, N.Y.

Bonham, Milledge L. Correspondence. Gratz Collection. Historical Society of Pennsylvania, Philadelphia.

———. Correspondence. Library of Congress, Washington, D.C.

———. Correspondence. New-York Historical Society, New York, N.Y.

———. Correspondence. University of South Carolina Library, Columbia.

———. Letter of July 6, 1861. Chicago Historical Society, Chicago, Ill.

Cocke, Philip St. George. Correspondence. University of Virginia Library, Charlottesville.

Early, Jubal A. Correspondence. Historical Society of Pennsylvania, Philadelphia.

———. Correspondence. Library of Congress, Washington, D.C.

———. Correspondence. Virginia Historical Society, Richmond.

———. Manuscript Account of the Battle of Manassas. College of William and Mary Library, Williamsburg, Va.

Evans, Nathan G. Letter of June 28, 1861. Historical Society of Pennsylvania, Philadelphia.

Ewell, Richard S. Correspondence. Library of Congress, Washington, D.C.

———. Correspondence. Tennessee State Library and Archives, Nashville.

Holmes, Theophilus H. Letter of September 7, 1861. Historical Society of Pennsylvania, Philadelphia.

Jackson, Thomas J. Correspondence. Library of Congress, Washington, D.C.

Johnston, Joseph E. Correspondence. Century–Civil War Collection. New York Public Library, New York, N.Y.

———. Correspondence. College of William and Mary Library, Williamsburg, Va.

———. Correspondence. Duke University Library, Durham, N.C.

———. Correspondence. Gratz Collection. Historical Society of Pennsylvania, Philadelphia.

———. Correspondence. New-York Historical Society, New York, N.Y.

———. Letter of August 5, 1861. Gilder Lehrman Collection, Gilder Lehrman Institute of American History, New York, N.Y.

———. Letter of July 30, 1861. Chicago Historical Society, Chicago, Ill.

Johnston, Joseph E., and P. G. T. Beauregard. Address to "Soldiers of the Confederate States," July 25, 1861. Henry E. Huntington Library, San Marino, Calif.

Jones, David R. Correspondence. Historical Society of Pennsylvania, Philadelphia.

———. Letter of June 9, 1861. Gilder Lehrman Collection, Gilder Lehrman Institute of American History, New York, N.Y.

Lee, Robert E. Correspondence. Library of Congress, Washington, D.C.

———. Correspondence. University of North Carolina Library, Chapel Hill.

———. Correspondence. Virginia Historical Society, Richmond.

———. Letter of June 20, 1861. Gilder Lehrman Collection, Gilder Lehrman Institute of American History, New York, N.Y.

Longstreet, James. Correspondence. Duke University Library, Durham, N.C.

Northrop, Lucius B. Correspondence. Century–Civil War Collection. New York Public Library, New York, N.Y.

Smith, Edmund K. Correspondence. Southern Historical Collection. University of North Carolina Library, Chapel Hill.

———. Correspondence. U.S. Army Heritage and Education Center, Carlisle Barracks, Pa.

CONFEDERATE BATTERY, REGIMENTAL, AND STAFF PERSONNEL

Aiken, David W. (7th South Carolina Inf.) Correspondence. University of South Carolina Library, Columbia.

Alexander, Edward P. (staff officer). Correspondence. Library of Congress, Washington, D.C.

———. Correspondence. Manassas National Battlefield Park Library, Manassas, Va.

———. Correspondence. Southern Historical Collection. University of North Carolina Library, Chapel Hill.

Andrews, William W. (13th Alabama Inf.). Letter of July 28, 1861. University of Virginia Library, Charlottesville.

Armstrong, Ezekiel (17th Mississippi Inf.). Diary. Mississippi Department of Archives and History, Jackson.

Avery, Alphonso C. (6th North Carolina Inf.). Correspondence. University of North Carolina Library, Chapel Hill.

Bacon, Thomas G. (7th South Carolina Inf.). Letter of July 25, 1861. University of South Carolina Library, Columbia.

Baldwin, William G. (18th Virginia Inf.). Correspondence. Virginia Historical Society, Richmond.

Barclay, Alexander T. (4th Virginia Inf.). Correspondence. Washington and Lee University Library, Lexington, Va.

Barker, John H. (18th Virginia Inf.). Correspondence. College of William and Mary Library, Williamsburg, Va.

Barnsley, George S. (8th Georgia Inf.). Diary. University of North Carolina Library, Chapel Hill.

Baylor, George W. (2nd Virginia Inf.). Correspondence. University of Virginia Library, Charlottesville.

Bayol, F. Edward (5th Alabama Inf.). Correspondence. Manassas National Battlefield Park Library, Manassas, Va.

Bayol, Jules (5th Alabama Inf.). Correspondence. Manassas National Battlefield Park Library, Manassas, Va.

Bell, Isaac G. (11th Mississippi Inf.). Correspondence. Virginia Historical Society, Richmond.

Bidgood, Robert W. (15th Virginia Inf.). Correspondence. Virginia Historical Society, Richmond.

Blackford, William W. (1st Virginia Cav.). Correspondence. U.S. Army Heritage and Education Center, Carlisle Barracks, Pa.

———. Correspondence. University of Virginia Library, Charlottesville.

———. Memoirs. Virginia State Library, Richmond.

Booton, William S. (8th Georgia Inf.). Correspondence. Virginia Historical Society, Richmond.

Bouldin, James O. (6th North Carolina Inf.). Correspondence. Duke University Library, Durham, N.C.

Bowman, Ephraim (8th Virginia Inf.). Correspondence. University of Virginia Library, Charlottesville.

Branch, Hamilton M. (8th Georgia Inf.). Correspondence. Margaret Branch Sexton Collection. University of Georgia Library, Athens.

Branch, John L. (8th Georgia Inf.). Letter of July 14, 1861. Margaret Branch Sexton Collection. University of Georgia Library, Athens.

Branch, Sanford W. (8th Georgia Inf.). Correspondence. Margaret Branch Sexton Collection. University of Georgia Library, Athens.

Bratton, John (6th South Carolina Inf.). Correspondence. University of North Carolina Library, Chapel Hill.

Brown, G. Campbell (staff officer). Memoirs. Tennessee State Library and Archives, Nashville.

Bryant, Richard (18th Virginia Inf.). Letter of June 29, 1861. Virginia State Library, Richmond.

Buck, Richard B. (11th Virginia Inf.). Correspondence. University of Virginia Library, Charlottesville.

Burnley, William H. (30th Virginia Cav.). Correspondence. University of Virginia Library, Charlottesville.

Cain, William G. (4th North Carolina Inf.). Letter of August 13, 1861. Duke University Library, Durham, N.C.

Camp, Hiram W. (7th Georgia Inf.). Letter of August 3, 1861. Georgia Department of Archives and History, Atlanta.

Camp, Walker G. (7th Georgia Inf.). Correspondence. Georgia Department of Archives and History, Atlanta.

Campbell, James M. (5th Virginia Inf.). Diary. Gilder Lehrman Collection, Gilder Lehrman Institute of American History, New York, N.Y.

Carrington, Henry A. (18th Virginia Inf.). Correspondence. Virginia Historical Society, Richmond.

Cash, E. B. C. (8th South Carolina Inf.). Letter of July 31, 1861. Gilder Lehrman Collection, Gilder Lehrman Institute of American History, New York, N.Y.

Chamberlayne, Francis W. (Independent Virginia Cav.). Memoirs. Virginia Historical Society, Richmond.

Chisolm, Alexander R. (staff officer). Correspondence and Memoirs. New-York Historical Society, New York, N.Y.

Choice, William (5th South Carolina Inf.). Memoirs. Manassas National Battlefield Park Library, Manassas, Va.

Cocke, Edmund R. (18th Virginia Inf.). Armistead-Cocke Correspondence. College of William and Mary Library, Williamsburg, Va.

Cocke, William F. (18th Virginia Inf.). Armistead-Cocke Correspondence. College of William and Mary Library, Williamsburg, Va.

Conner, Henry C. (5th South Carolina Inf.). Correspondence. University of South Carolina Library, Columbia.

Conner, James (Hampton Legion [inf.]). Correspondence. University of South Carolina Library, Columbia.

Conway, Catlett F. (7th Virginia Inf.). Memoirs. Virginia Historical Society, Richmond.

Coons, Henry W. (Independent Virginia Cav.). Letter of November 22, 1861. Virginia Historical Society, Richmond.

Craven, P. H. (19th Virginia Inf.). Correspondence. University of Southern Mississippi Library, Hattiesburg.

Culpeper, Wesley (8th Georgia Inf.). Diary. University of Southern Mississippi Library, Hattiesburg.

Cummings, Arthur C. (33rd Virginia Inf.). Correspondence. College of William and Mary Library, Williamsburg, Va.

Cushwa, Daniel (1st Virginia Cav.). Correspondence. Virginia Historical Society, Richmond.

Dabney, Robert L. (18th Virginia Inf.). Correspondence. Virginia Historical Society, Richmond.

Dalton, A. H. (Hampton Legion [inf.]). Correspondence. U.S. Army Heritage and Education Center, Carlisle Barracks, Pa.

Daniel, John W. (27th Virginia Inf.). Correspondence. University of Virginia Library, Charlottesville.

Dasher, William B. (8th Georgia Inf.). Memoirs. Georgia Department of Archives and History, Atlanta.

Dawson, Nathaniel H. R. (4th Alabama Inf.). Correspondence. University of North Carolina Library, Chapel Hill.

Dearing, James (Washington Arty. of New Orleans). Letter of September 24, 1861. Historical Society of Pennsylvania, Philadelphia.

Dobbs, Henry J. (18th Virginia Inf.). Letter of August 7, 1861. College of William and Mary Library, Williamsburg, Va.

Doby, Alfred (staff officer). Letter of July 25, 1861. Manassas National Battlefield Park Library, Manassas, Va.

Duncan, Blanton (1st Kentucky Inf. Btn.). Letter of October 22, 1861. Virginia State Library, Richmond.

Dwinnell, Melvin (8th Georgia Inf.). Correspondence. Georgia Department of Archives and History, Atlanta.

Elkins, Joseph M. (49th Virginia Inf.). Correspondence. Virginia Historical Society, Richmond.

Evans, Maurice (Independent Virginia Cav.). Letter of July 19, 1861. Virginia Historical Society, Richmond.

Ferguson, Samuel W. (staff officer). Memoirs. Manassas National Battlefield Park Library, Manassas, Va.

Figures, Henry (4th Alabama Inf.). Correspondence. Gilder Lehrman Collection, Gilder Lehrman Institute of American History, New York, N.Y.

———. Diary. U.S. Army Heritage and Education Center, Carlisle Barracks, Pa.

Fishburne, Clement D. (Rockbridge Arty.). Diary. University of Virginia Library, Charlottesville.

Fisher, Charles P. (6th North Carolina Inf.). Letter of July 17, 1861. University of North Carolina Library, Chapel Hill.

Fort, John (9th Georgia Inf.). Correspondence. Manassas National Battlefield Park Library, Manassas, Va.

Fort, Tomlinson (3rd South Carolina Inf.). Correspondence. Manassas National Battlefield Park Library, Manassas, Va.

Foster, Louis P. (3rd South Carolina Inf.). Correspondence. University of South Carolina Library, Columbia.

Gallagher, William B. (1st Virginia Cav.). Correspondence. Virginia Polytechnic Institute and State University Library, Blacksburg.

Gardner, J. A. (5th Alabama Inf.). Correspondence. Duke University Library, Durham, N.C.

Garnett, James M. (Rockbridge Arty.). Correspondence. University of Virginia Library, Charlottesville.

Gibbons, Simeon B. (10th Virginia Inf.). Correspondence. Manassas National Battlefield Park Library, Manassas, Va.

Goodlett, William H. (3rd South Carolina Inf.). Letter of July 19, 1861. Duke University Library, Durham, N.C.

Grattan, Charles (staff officer). Memoirs. U.S. Army Heritage and Education Center, Carlisle Barracks, Pa.

Griffin, James (Hampton Legion [cav.]). Correspondence. U.S. Army Heritage and Education Center, Carlisle Barracks, Pa.

Grimes, Bryan (4th North Carolina Inf.) Correspondence. North Carolina State Archives, Raleigh.

Habersham, Richard W. (Hampton Legion [inf.]). Correspondence. Library of Congress, Washington, D.C.

Hall, N. D. (4th Alabama Inf.). Correspondence. Manassas National Battlefield Park Library, Manassas, Va.

Haller, Peter (10th Virginia Inf.). Letter of November 3, 1861. Duke University Library, Durham, N.C.

Hampton, Wade, III. (Hampton Legion). Correspondence. Duke University Library, Durham, N.C.

———. Correspondence. University of North Carolina Library, Chapel Hill.

———. Family Papers. University of South Carolina Library, Columbia.

Hancock, Orson V. (30th Virginia Cav.). Letter of July 29, 1861. Manassas National Battlefield Park Library, Manassas, Va.

Hands, Washington (1st Maryland Inf.). Memoirs. University of Virginia Library, Charlottesville.

Hardy, W. H. (2nd South Carolina Inf.). Letter of July 21, 1861. Manassas National Battlefield Park Library, Manassas, Va.

Harllee, Andrew T. (8th South Carolina Inf.). Letter of July 23, 1861. University of North Carolina Library, Chapel Hill.

Harper, Henry C. (8th Georgia Inf.). Diary. Emory University Library, Atlanta, Ga.

Haxall, Philip (Independent Virginia Cav.). Correspondence. Virginia Historical Society, Richmond.

Higginbotham, Joseph A. (19th Virginia Inf.). Diary. Manassas National Battlefield Park Library, Manassas, Va.

Hillhouse, Samuel P. (4th South Carolina Inf.). Correspondence. U.S. Army Heritage and Education Center, Carlisle Barracks, Pa.

Hinsdale, John W. (staff officer). Correspondence. Duke University Library, Durham, N.C.

Hite, Cornelius B. (1st Virginia Cav.). Correspondence. Museum of the Confederacy, Richmond, Va.

Hite, John P. (33rd Virginia Inf.). Diary. Manassas National Battlefield Park Library, Manassas, Va.

Hogan, Jeremiah (6th Louisiana Inf.). Letter of August 12, 1861. Manassas National Battlefield Park Library, Manassas, Va.

Hogue, A. J. (28th Virginia Inf.). Correspondence. Roanoke Historical Society, Roanoke, Va.

Hollingsworth, William T. (3rd Georgia Inf.). Correspondence. Gilder Lehrman Collection, Gilder Lehrman Institute of American History, New York, N.Y.

Hollis, Rufus (4th Alabama Inf.). Memoirs. Tennessee State Library and Archives, Nashville.

Hollis, W. (1st Maryland Inf.). Letter of July [?], 1861. Manassas National Battlefield Park Library, Manassas, Va.

Holmes, Michael (6th Alabama Inf.). Letter of June 2, 1861. U.S. Army Heritage and Education Center, Carlisle Barracks, Pa.

Hooke, Robert W. (1st Virginia Cav.). Correspondence. Duke University Library, Durham, N.C.

Hopkins, George W. (11th Mississippi Inf.). Correspondence. Mississippi Department of Archives and History, Jackson.

Howell, F. A. (11th Mississippi Inf.). Memoirs. U.S. Army Heritage and Education Center, Carlisle Barracks, Pa.

Hoyle, Alfred E. (23rd North Carolina Inf.). Letter of August 2, 1861. University of North Carolina Library, Chapel Hill.

Hudgens, Jesse F. (18th Virginia Inf.). Diary. Maryland Historical Society, Baltimore.

Hudson, James G. (4th Alabama Inf.). Alabama Department of Archives and History, Montgomery.

Humphries, William S. (5th Virginia Inf.). Memoirs. U.S. Army Heritage and Education Center, Carlisle Barracks, Pa.

Hundley, George J. (19th Virginia Inf.). Memoirs. Virginia Historical Society, Richmond.

Hunt, Nathan G. (11th North Carolina Inf.). Correspondence. Manassas National Battlefield Park Library, Manassas, Va.

Hunter, Alexander (17th Virginia Inf.). Memoirs. Virginia Historical Society, Richmond.

Hunton, Eppa (8th Virginia Inf.). Correspondence. Virginia Historical Society, Richmond.

Hutson, Charles W. (Hampton Legion [inf.]). Letter of July 24, 1861. University of North Carolina Library, Chapel Hill.

Imboden, John D. (Staunton Arty.). Correspondence. Century–Civil War Collection. New York Public Library, New York, N.Y.

———. Correspondence. University of Virginia Library, Charlottesville.

———. Correspondence. Virginia Historical Society, Richmond.

———. Correspondence. West Virginia University Library, Morgantown.

Jackson, Henry A. (8th South Carolina Inf.). Letter of July 30, 1861. U.S. Army Heritage and Education Center, Carlisle Barracks, Pa.

Jenkins, Micah (5th South Carolina Inf.). Correspondence. Duke University Library, Durham, N.C.

———. Correspondence. University of North Carolina Library, Chapel Hill.

Johnson, Bradley T. (1st Maryland Inf.) Correspondence. Duke University Library, Durham, N.C.

Jones, Iredell (Hampton Legion [inf.]). Correspondence. Duke University Library, Durham, N.C.

Jones, Samuel (staff officer). Letter of July 25, 1861. Gilder Lehrman Collection, Gilder Lehrman Institute of American History, New York, N.Y.

Jones, William H. G. (24th Virginia Inf.). Letter of July 29, 1861. Virginia Historical Society, Richmond.

Jordan, Thomas (staff officer). Correspondence. Century–Civil War Collection. New York Public Library, New York, N.Y.

———. Correspondence. Chicago Historical Society, Chicago, Ill.

———. Correspondence. Gilder Lehrman Collection, Gilder Lehrman Institute of American History, New York, N.Y.

———. Correspondence. Gratz Collection. Historical Society of Pennsylvania, Philadelphia.

Kearns, Watkins (27th Virginia Inf.). Diary. Virginia Historical Society, Richmond.

Keiley, John D. (1st Virginia Inf.). Letter of July 23, 1861. Virginia Historical Society, Richmond.

Kemper, James L. (7th Virginia Inf.). Correspondence. University of
    Virginia Library, Charlottesville.
———. Correspondence. Virginia Historical Society, Richmond.
Kern, Joseph M. (13th Virginia Inf.). Correspondence. University of North
    Carolina Library, Chapel Hill.
King, William (Thomas Arty.). Correspondence. University of Virginia
    Library, Charlottesville.
Langhorne, James H. (4th Virginia Inf.). Letter of July 21, 1861. Virginia
    Historical Society, Richmond.
Latham, George W. (11th Virginia Inf.). Correspondence and Diary.
    University of Virginia Library, Charlottesville.
Lee, Otho S. (1st Virginia Cav.). Memoirs. Washington and Lee University
    Library, Lexington, Va.
Lee, Richard B. (staff officer). Letter of July 29, 1861. Chicago Historical
    Society, Chicago, Ill.
Lee, Wills (Richmond Howitzers). Memoirs. U.S. Army Heritage and
    Education Center, Carlisle Barracks, Pa.
Lemmon, Robert (21st Virginia Inf.). Letter of July 26, 1861. Manassas
    National Battlefield Park Library, Manassas, Va.
Lowndes, James (Hampton Legion [inf.]). Letter of August 2, 1861.
    University of South Carolina Library, Columbia.
Manghum, W. H. (Hampton Legion [inf.]). Correspondence. Georgia
    Department of Archives and History, Atlanta.
Manning, John L. (staff officer). Correspondence. University of South
    Carolina Library, Columbia.
Maxey, William H. (8th Georgia Inf.). Letter of September 5, 1861.
    University of Georgia Library, Athens.
McGuffin, John B. (5th Virginia Inf.). Correspondence. University of
    Virginia Library, Charlottesville.
McGuire, Hunter H. (2nd Virginia Inf.). Correspondence. Virginia
    Historical Society, Richmond.
McIntyre, J. C. (16th Mississippi Inf.). Correspondence. Duke University
    Library, Durham, N.C.
Melton, Samuel W. (staff officer). Correspondence. University of South
    Carolina Library, Columbia.
Miley, George W. (10th Virginia Inf.). Correspondence. Virginia Historical
    Society, Richmond.
Morgan, T. J. (10th Alabama Inf.). Letter of August 11, 1861. Auburn
    University Archives, Auburn, Ala.
Mosby, John S. (1st Virginia Cav.). Correspondence. New York Public
    Library, New York, N.Y.
———. Correspondence. University of Virginia Library, Charlottesville.
Munford, Thomas T. (30th Virginia Cav.). Correspondence. Gratz
    Collection. Historical Society of Pennsylvania, Philadelphia.
Murray, W. H. (1st Maryland Inf.). Correspondence. Maryland Historical
    Society, Baltimore.
Newman, James S. (13th Virginia Inf.). Diary. Museum of the Confederacy,
    Richmond, Va.

Nicholson, Thomas A. (2nd Virginia Inf.). Correspondence. Manassas
    National Battlefield Park Library, Manassas, Va.
Norton, Charles B. (8th Georgia Inf.). Correspondence. Georgia
    Department of Archives and History, Atlanta.
Old, James W. (11th Virginia Inf.). Correspondence. In possession of
    Murray L. Brown, Lincoln, Neb.
Overcash, James (6th North Carolina Inf.). Letter of August 11, 1861. Duke
    University Library, Durham, N.C.
Owen, Henry T. (18th Virginia Inf.). Correspondence. Virginia State
    Library, Richmond.
Owen, William M. (Washington Arty. of New Orleans). Correspondence.
    New York Public Library, New York, N.Y.
Paine, Henry R. (Rockbridge Arty.). Diary. Virginia Historical Society,
    Richmond.
Palmer, W. M. (13th Mississippi Inf.). Correspondence. Manassas National
    Battlefield Park Library, Manassas, Va.
Parran, Thomas S. (13th Virginia Inf.). Letter of July 26, 1861. College of
    William and Mary Library, Williamsburg, Va.
Paxton, Elisha F. (4th Virginia Inf.). Letter of July 23, 1861. Century–Civil
    War Collection. New York Public Library, New York, N.Y.
Payne, William H. (30th Virginia Cav.). Letter of August 27, 1861. Virginia
    Historical Society, Richmond.
Pendleton, William N. (Rockbridge Arty.). Correspondence. University of
    North Carolina Library, Chapel Hill.
————. Letter of July 31, 1861. Duke University Library, Durham, N.C.
Perry, William H. (Richmond Howitzers). Correspondence and Diary.
    University of Virginia Library, Charlottesville.
Petty, James T. (17th Virginia Inf.). Diary. Museum of the Confederacy,
    Richmond, Va.
Pitts, Thomas H. (3rd South Carolina Inf.). Pitts-Craig Correspondence.
    Emory University Library, Atlanta, Ga.
Pleasants, James (Thomas Arty.). Letter of June 25, 1861. Virginia
    Historical Society, Richmond.
Poague, William T. (Rockbridge Arty.). Correspondence. Virginia State
    Library, Richmond.
Potts, Franklin (1st Virginia Inf.) Diary. Virginia Historical Society,
    Richmond.
Powers, Philip H. (1st Virginia Cav.). Correspondence. U.S. Army Heritage
    and Education Center, Carlisle Barracks, Pa.
Randolph, Robert L. (Independent Virginia Cav.). Correspondence. Virginia
    Historical Society, Richmond.
Reed, John (Hampton Legion [inf.]). Memoirs. Alabama Department of
    Archives and History, Montgomery.
Reeve, Edward P. (1st Virginia Inf.). Correspondence. University of North
    Carolina Library, Chapel Hill.
Richardson, Robert A. (24th Virginia Inf.). Correspondence. Manassas
    National Battlefield Park Library, Manassas, Va.
Robertson, Littleton T. (18th Virginia Inf.). Correspondence. Virginia
    Historical Society, Richmond.

Ross, G. W. (6th Alabama Inf.). Correspondence. Auburn University Archives, Auburn, Ala.

Rosser, Thomas L. (Washington Arty. of New Orleans). Correspondence. University of Virginia Library, Charlottesville.

Scott, Alfred L. (9th Alabama Inf.). Memoirs. Virginia Historical Society, Richmond.

Scott, Benjamin I. (18th Virginia Inf.). Letter of July 25, 1861. Virginia Historical Society, Richmond.

Sessions, Joseph F. (17th Mississippi Inf.). Letter of July 7, 1861. Mississippi Department of Archives and History, Jackson.

Shand, Robert W. (2nd South Carolina Inf.). Diary and Memoirs. University of South Carolina Library, Columbia.

Shanklin, Henry S. (27th Virginia Inf.). Correspondence. Virginia State Library, Richmond.

Shepherd, Alexander H. (2nd Virginia Inf.). Letter of July 25, 1861. West Virginia Department of Archives and History, Charleston.

Shingler, W. P. (staff officer). "Reminiscences of the Late General Barnard Bee." Transcription in Annie J. Bee scrapbook. In possession of Dr. Pat Wilson, Austin, Tex.

Simpson, James (Hampton Legion [inf.]). Correspondence. Duke University Library, Durham, N.C.

Simpson, William D. (17th Virginia Inf.). Correspondence. Duke University Library, Durham, N.C.

Singleton, James (Hampton Legion [inf.]). Correspondence. University of Virginia Library, Charlottesville.

Skinner, William H. (8th Georgia Inf.). Letter of August 23, 1861. Georgia Department of Archives and History, Atlanta.

Sloan, J. B. E. (4th South Carolina Inf.). Correspondence. Manassas National Battlefield Park Library, Manassas, Va.

Smith, Otis D. (6th Alabama Inf.). Letter of August 18, 1861. Manassas National Battlefield Park Library, Manassas, Va.

Smith, William R. (17th Virginia Inf.). Diary. University of Virginia Library, Charlottesville.

Stevens, Clement H. (staff officer). Letter of July 28, 1861. In possession of Dr. Pat Wilson, Austin, Tex.

Stone, William A. (Hampton Legion [inf.]). Letter of November 8, 1861. U.S. Army Heritage and Education Center, Carlisle Barracks, Pa.

Stuart, James E. B. (1st Virginia Cav.). Correspondence. Duke University Library, Durham, N.C.

———. Correspondence. Virginia Historical Society, Richmond.

Talley, Henry M. (38th Virginia Inf.). Correspondence. Virginia Historical Society, Richmond.

Tate, Jeremiah M. (5th Alabama Inf.). Correspondence. Gilder Lehrman Collection, Gilder Lehrman Institute of American History, New York, N.Y.

Tatum, William H. (Richmond Howitzers). Correspondence. Virginia Historical Society, Richmond.

Taylor, Murray F. (13th Virginia Inf.). Correspondence. U.S. Army Heritage and Education Center, Carlisle Barracks, Pa.

Terry, William R. (30th Virginia Cav.). Letter of July 23, 1861, Gilder Lehrman Collection, Gilder Lehrman Institute of American History, New York, N.Y.

Thurston, Charles H. (7th Louisiana Inf.). Diary. University of Virginia Library, Charlottesville.

Tracy, Edward D. (4th Alabama Inf.). Correspondence. U.S. Army Heritage and Education Center, Carlisle Barracks, Pa.

Trahern, William E. (6th Louisiana Inf.). Memoirs. Virginia Historical Society, Richmond.

Truehart, C. W. (Rockbridge Arty.). Letter of October 26, 1861. Manassas National Battlefield Park Library, Manassas, Va.

Turner, John R. (17th Virginia Inf.). Correspondence. Duke University Library, Durham, N.C.

Unidentified Enlisted Man (8th Georgia Inf.). Letter of July 21, 1861. Museum of the Confederacy, Richmond, Va.

Unidentified Enlisted Man (8th Virginia Inf.). Memoirs. Manassas National Battlefield Park Library, Manassas, Va.

Unidentified Enlisted Man (5th South Carolina Inf.). Letter of August 3, 1861. Manassas National Battlefield Park Library, Manassas, Va.

Unidentified Enlisted Man (Hampton Legion [inf.]). Letter of July 26, 1861. University of Virginia Library, Charlottesville.

Vairin, A. L. P. (2nd Mississippi Inf.). Diary. Mississippi Department of Archives and History, Jackson.

Walker, F. N. (3rd South Carolina Inf.). Diary. College of William and Mary Library, Williamsburg, Va.

Walker, James A. (13th Virginia Inf.). Correspondence. University of North Carolina Library, Chapel Hill.

Waller, David G. (30th Virginia Cav.). Correspondence. Manassas National Battlefield Park.

Watters, Richard (8th Georgia Inf.). Letter of July 28, 1861. Georgia Department of Archives and History, Atlanta.

West, Samuel L. (3rd South Carolina Inf.). Correspondence. U.S. Army Heritage and Education Center, Carlisle Barracks, Pa.

Wheat, Chatham R. (1st Louisiana Special Btn.). Letter of July 26, 1861. University of North Carolina Library, Chapel Hill.

White, Benjamin F. (6th North Carolina Inf.). Correspondence. North Carolina State Archives, Raleigh.

Whiting, W. H. C. (staff officer). Correspondence. Gratz Collection. Historical Society of Pennsylvania, Philadelphia.

Whitlock, Philip (1st Virginia Inf.). Memoirs. Virginia Historical Society, Richmond.

Wight, Charles C. (27th Virginia Inf.). Memoirs. Virginia Historical Society, Richmond.

Wilcox, Cadmus M. (9th Alabama Inf.). Correspondence. Library of Congress, Washington, D.C.

Wise, George N. (17th Virginia Inf.). Diary. Duke University Library, Durham, N.C.

Wooding, Henry (18th Virginia Inf.). Correspondence. Averett University Library, Danville, Va.

Wragg, Thomas L. (8th Georgia Inf.). Correspondence. Library of Congress, Washington, D.C.

Yarborough, Joel S. (8th Georgia Inf.). Memoirs. Georgia Department of Archives and History, Atlanta.

Young, John A. (4th North Carolina Inf.). Diary. North Carolina State Archives, Raleigh.

FEDERAL ADMINISTRATIVE AND FIELD COMMANDERS

Burnside, Ambrose E. Correspondence. Rhode Island Historical Society, Providence.

Cadwalader, George. Correspondence. Historical Society of Pennsylvania, Philadelphia.

Franklin, William B. Correspondence. Library of Congress, Washington, D.C.

Heintzelman, Samuel P. Papers. Library of Congress, Washington, D.C.

Howard, Oliver O. Correspondence. Bowdoin College Library, Brunswick, Me.

———. Correspondence. Gratz Collection. Historical Society of Pennsylvania, Philadelphia.

Keim, William H. Letter of June 5, 1861. C. W. Unger Collection. Historical Society of Pennsylvania, Philadelphia.

Mansfield, Joseph K. F. Correspondence. Library of Congress, Washington, D.C.

———. Correspondence. U.S. Military Academy Library, West Point, N.Y.

McClellan, George B. Correspondence. Library of Congress, Washington, D.C.

———. Correspondence. New Jersey Historical Society, Newark.

McDowell, Irvin. Correspondence. Century–Civil War Collection. New York Public Library, New York, N.Y.

———. Correspondence. Historical Society of Pennsylvania, Philadelphia.

———. Correspondence. John E. Wool Papers. New York State Library, Albany.

Patterson, Robert. Correspondence. Historical Society of Pennsylvania, Philadelphia.

Richardson, Israel B. "Report of Richardson's Brigade at First Bull Run." U.S. Army Heritage and Education Center, Carlisle Barracks, Pa.

Schenck, Robert C. Correspondence. Miami University Library, Oxford, Ohio.

Scott, Winfield. Correspondence. Historical Society of Pennsylvania, Philadelphia.

———. Correspondence. Library of Congress, Washington, D.C.

———. Correspondence. U.S. Military Academy Library, West Point, N.Y.

Sherman, William T. Correspondence. Library of Congress, Washington, D.C.

————. Correspondence. Ohio Historical Society, Columbus.

————. Correspondence. U.S. Military Academy Library, West Point, N.Y.

————. Letter of September 9, 1861. Gilder Lehrman Collection, Gilder Lehrman Institute of American History, New York, N.Y.

————. Sherman Family Papers. University of Notre Dame Library, South Bend, Ind.

Thomas, George H. Letter of August 31, 1861. U.S. Military Academy Library, West Point, N.Y.

Tyler, Daniel. Correspondence. Library of Congress, Washington, D.C.

Willcox, Orlando B. Letter of May 24, 1861. Gilder Lehrman Collection, Gilder Lehrman Institute of American History, New York, N.Y.

FEDERAL BATTERY, REGIMENTAL, AND STAFF PERSONNEL

Adams, Charles P. (1st Minnesota Inf.). Memoirs. Minnesota Historical Society, Saint Paul.

Allyn, Arthur W. (1st Connecticut Inf.). Correspondence. Connecticut Historical Society, Hartford.

Ames, Adelbert (5th U.S. Arty.). Correspondence. Manassas National Battlefield Park Library, Manassas, Va.

————. Correspondence. New York Public Library, New York, N.Y.

Andrews, George L. (2nd Massachusetts Inf.). Correspondence. U.S. Army Heritage and Education Center, Carlisle Barracks, Pa.

Andrews, George S. (3rd Maine Inf.). Correspondence. Brown University Library, Providence, R.I.

Averell, William W. (Reg. of Mounted Riflemen). Correspondence. New York State Library, Albany.

————. Correspondence and Diary. Gilder Lehrman Collection, Gilder Lehrman Institute of American History, New York, N.Y.

Bacon, James H. (2nd Maine Inf.). Correspondence. Manassas National Battlefield Park Library, Manassas, Va.

Ballou, Sullivan (2nd Rhode Island Inf.). Correspondence. Rhode Island Historical Society, Providence.

————. Letter of July 14, 1861. Chicago Historical Society, Chicago, Ill.

Bartlett, John S. (2nd Connecticut Inf.). Correspondence. Connecticut Historical Society, Hartford.

Bates, Albert C. (1st Rhode Island Inf.). Correspondence. U.S. Army Heritage and Education Center, Carlisle Barracks, Pa.

Bates, C. E. (4th U.S. Cav.). Letter of July 16, 1861. Virginia Historical Society, Richmond.

Beaumont, Eugene B. (staff officer). Correspondence and Diary. U.S. Military Academy Library, West Point, N.Y.

Brisbin, James S. (1st U.S. Dragoons). Letter of July 20, 1861. Gilder Lehrman Collection, Gilder Lehrman Institute of American History, New York, N.Y.

Bronford, John P. (4th New Jersey Militia). Correspondence. Rutgers University Library, New Brunswick, N.J.

Bulkley, William H. (13th New York Militia). Correspondence. Connecticut Historical Society, Hartford.

Burnham, George S. (1st Connecticut Inf.). "History of the First
    Connecticut Volunteers (Three Months)." Manassas National
    Battlefield Park Library, Manassas, Va.
Burrill, John H. (2nd New Hampshire Inf.). Correspondence. State
    Historical Society of Wisconsin, Madison.
————. Correspondence. U.S. Army Heritage and Education Center,
    Carlisle Barracks, Pa.
Bush, Ransom (4th Michigan Inf.). Letter of July 20, 1861. University of
    Michigan Library, Ann Arbor.
Butler, James (69th New York Militia). Diary. New York Public Library,
    New York, N.Y.
Callan, Henry H. (2nd New Jersey Inf.). Correspondence. Rutgers
    University Library, New Brunswick, N.J.
Carter, James W. (5th Massachusetts Militia). Correspondence. East
    Carolina University Library, Greenville, N.C.
Clark, Ruet (2nd Maine Inf.). Letter of June 20, 1861. U.S. Army Heritage
    and Education Center, Carlisle Barracks, Pa.
Cole, George W. (12th New York Inf.). Correspondence. U.S. Army
    Heritage and Education Center, Carlisle Barracks, Pa.
Corl, George W. (25th Pennsylvania Inf.). Correspondence. U.S. Army
    Heritage and Education Center, Carlisle Barracks, Pa.
Corson, Joseph (4th Pennsylvania Inf.). Correspondence. In possession of
    Dr. Joseph K. Corson, Plymouth Meeting, Pa.
Crane, Aaron D. (2nd New Jersey Inf.). Correspondence. Rutgers
    University Library, New Brunswick, N.J.
Crosby, Abner S. (7th Pennsylvania Inf.). Letter of August 12, 1861. Gilder
    Lehrman Collection, Gilder Lehrman Institute of American History,
    New York, N.Y.
Cumings, Harrison W. (11th New York Inf.). Memoirs. U.S. Army Heritage
    and Education Center, Carlisle Barracks, Pa.
Davis, Charles E. (1st Minnesota Inf.). Correspondence. Minnesota
    Historical Society, Saint Paul.
Davis, Norris A. (3rd Maine Inf.). Letter of July 31, 1861. U.S. Army
    Heritage and Education Center, Carlisle Barracks, Pa.
Davis, Ober R. (5th Massachusetts Militia). Correspondence. U.S. Army
    Heritage and Education Center, Carlisle Barracks, Pa.
Davis, Thomas H. (4th New Jersey Militia). Correspondence. In possession
    of Walter G. Lee, Chestnut Hill, Pa.
Dawson, S. W. (2nd Maine Inf.). Letter of July 31, 1861. U.S. Army
    Heritage and Education Center, Carlisle Barracks, Pa.
Denton, James (1st New Jersey Inf.). Correspondence. Rutgers University
    Library, New Brunswick, N.J.
Donovan, Joseph (2nd New Jersey Inf.). Correspondence. Rutgers
    University Library, New Brunswick, N.J.
Doubleday, Abner (1st U.S. Arty.). Memoirs. New-York Historical Society,
    New York, N.Y.
Eddy, Hiram (2nd Connecticut Inf.). Diary. Connecticut Historical Society,
    Hartford.

Elder, Samuel S. (4th U.S. Arty.). Letter of July 23, 1861. New York Public Library, New York, N.Y.

Ellinwood, Eli (2nd Vermont Inf.). Letter of July 28, 1861. U.S. Army Heritage and Education Center, Carlisle Barracks, Pa.

Erwin, Robert M. (28th Pennsylvania Inf.). Correspondence. U.S. Army Heritage and Education Center, Carlisle Barracks, Pa.

Farnsworth, Jerome B. (1st Minnesota Inf.). Correspondence. Minnesota Historical Society, Saint Paul.

Filbert, Peter A. (10th Pennsylvania Inf.). Diary. U.S. Army Heritage and Education Center, Carlisle Barracks, Pa.

Foster, Nathan (2nd Michigan Inf.). Letter of June 12, 1861. Western Michigan University Library, Kalamazoo.

Fowler, Frederick (5th New York Inf.). Correspondence. U.S. Army Heritage and Education Center, Carlisle Barracks, Pa.

French, John S. (5th Maine Inf.). Correspondence. U.S. Army Heritage and Education Center, Carlisle Barracks, Pa.

Giddings, Allan M. (2nd Michigan Inf.). Correspondence. Western Michigan University Library, Kalamazoo.

Goodridge, Allen (2nd Michigan Inf.). Letter of July 22, 1861. Gilder Lehrman Collection, Gilder Lehrman Institute of American History, New York, N.Y.

Gray, Charles C. (2nd U.S. Cav.). Memoirs. University of North Carolina Library, Chapel Hill.

Gregg, John C. (2nd Michigan Inf.). Correspondence. Western Michigan University Library, Kalamazoo.

Halpine, Charles G. (staff officer). Letter of July 2, 1861. Henry E. Huntington Library, San Marino, Calif.

Harrington, Thomas R. (3rd Connecticut Inf.). Letter of July 18, 1861. U.S. Army Heritage and Education Center, Carlisle Barracks, Pa.

Harrison, Charles A. (2nd New Jersey Inf.). Diary. U.S. Army Heritage and Education Center, Carlisle Barracks, Pa.

Hawley, Joseph R. (1st Connecticut Inf.). Correspondence. Connecticut Historical Society, Hartford.

———. Correspondence. Library of Congress, Washington, D.C.

Haydon, Charles B. (2nd Michigan Inf.). Diary. University of Michigan Library, Ann Arbor.

Heffelfinger, Christopher (1st Minnesota Inf.). Letter of July 24, 1861. Minnesota Historical Society, Saint Paul.

Herring, Charles P. (3rd Pennsylvania Inf.). Correspondence. War Library, National Commandery, Military Order of the Loyal Legion of the United States, Philadelphia, Pa.

Hill, George (16th New York Inf.). Correspondence. U.S. Army Heritage and Education Center, Carlisle Barracks, Pa.

Holmes, Phillip W. (13th New York Inf.). Diary. New York Public Library, New York, N.Y.

Hopkins, Charles A. (1st New Jersey Inf.). Correspondence and Memoirs. Rutgers University Library, New Brunswick, N.J.

Hunt, Henry J. (2nd U.S. Arty.). Correspondence. Library of Congress, Washington, D.C.
———. Correspondence. New York Public Library, New York, N.Y.
Irvine, John B. (1st Minnesota Inf.). Correspondence and Memoirs. Minnesota Historical Society, Saint Paul.
Johnston, George H. (1st Massachusetts Inf.). Correspondence. East Carolina University Library, Greenville, N.C.
Jones, Edward F. (6th Massachusetts Inf.). Diary. Manassas National Battlefield Park Library, Manassas, Va.
Jones, William T. (23rd Pennsylvania Inf.). Correspondence. Historical Society of Pennsylvania, Philadelphia.
Knox, Andrew (1st Connecticut Inf.). Correspondence. U.S. Army Heritage and Education Center, Carlisle Barracks, Pa.
Ladner, Louis B. (21st Pennsylvania Inf.). Letter of July 19, 1861. War Library, National Commandery, Military Order of the Loyal Legion of the United States, Philadelphia, Pa.
Lanning, Ralph A. (9th New York Militia). Correspondence. New York Public Library, New York, N.Y.
Leavitt, Joseph (5th Maine Inf.). Correspondence. U.S. Army Heritage and Education Center, Carlisle Barracks, Pa.
Littlefield, Daniel W. (3rd Michigan Inf.). Diary. University of Michigan Library, Ann Arbor.
Lockley, George (1st Michigan Inf.). Diary. University of Michigan Library, Ann Arbor.
Marvin, Matthew (1st Minnesota Inf.). Letter of August 1, 1861. Minnesota Historical Society, Saint Paul.
Mayo, Perry (3rd Michigan Inf.). Letter of July 23, 1861. Michigan State University Library, East Lansing.
McClintock, Andrew (1st Connecticut Inf.). Correspondence. U.S. Army Heritage and Education Center, Carlisle Barracks, Pa.
McCreight, Robert (1st New Jersey Inf.). Correspondence. U.S. Army Heritage and Education Center, Carlisle Barracks, Pa.
Meade, George G. (staff officer). Correspondence. Historical Society of Pennsylvania, Philadelphia.
Meloy, George (5th New York Inf.). Letter of June 11, 1861. U.S. Army Heritage and Education Center, Carlisle Barracks, Pa.
Miller, George W. (3rd Michigan Inf.). Letter of June 20, 1861. Western Michigan University Library, Kalamazoo.
Morey, Charles C. (2nd Vermont Inf.). Correspondence. U.S. Army Heritage and Education Center, Carlisle Barracks, Pa.
———. Diary. Gilder Lehrman Collection, Gilder Lehrman Institute of American History, New York, N.Y.
Muller, Louis (1st Minnesota Inf.). Letter of October 14, 1861. Minnesota Historical Society, Saint Paul.
Neff, Harmanus (2nd Pennsylvania Inf.). Correspondence. Union League Archives, Philadelphia, Pa.
Niblock, James (28th Pennsylvania Inf.). Diary. Manassas National Battlefield Park Library, Manassas, Va.

O'Brien, John (4th Connecticut Inf.). Correspondence. Connecticut Historical Society, Hartford.

———. Correspondence. U.S. Army Heritage and Education Center, Carlisle Barracks, Pa.

O'Connell, John (2nd Maine Inf.). Memoirs. U.S. Army Heritage and Education Center, Carlisle Barracks, Pa.

Orne, David J. (2nd Massachusetts Inf.). Correspondence. U.S. Army Heritage and Education Center, Carlisle Barracks, Pa.

Pardee, Ariovistus (28th Pennsylvania Inf.). Correspondence. U.S. Army Heritage and Education Center, Carlisle Barracks, Pa.

Pendergast, Lloyd G. (1st Minnesota Inf.). Correspondence. Minnesota Historical Society, Saint Paul.

Phillips, Marshall (5th Maine Inf.). Letter of July 24, 1861. Maine Historical Society, Portland.

Pine, Joshua (38th New York Inf.). Correspondence. Cornell University Library, Ithaca, N.Y.

Pollock, Cyrus C. (25th Pennsylvania Inf.). Correspondence. U.S. Army Heritage and Education Center, Carlisle Barracks, Pa.

Pomeroy, Willis A. (4th Connecticut Inf.). Correspondence. U.S. Army Heritage and Education Center, Carlisle Barracks, Pa.

Porter, Fitz John (staff officer). Correspondence. Historical Society of Pennsylvania, Philadelphia.

———. Correspondence. Library of Congress, Washington, D.C.

Pressnell, Thomas H. (1st Minnesota Inf.). Memoirs. Minnesota Historical Society, Saint Paul.

Randall, William H. (1st Michigan Inf.). Memoirs. University of Michigan Library, Ann Arbor.

Robbins, Jerome J. (2nd Michigan Inf.). Diary. University of Michigan Library, Ann Arbor.

Roberts, Charles (1st Connecticut Inf.). Letter of June 6, 1861. U.S. Army Heritage and Education Center, Carlisle Barracks, Pa.

Roberts, William (11th Pennsylvania Inf.). Letter of May 19, 1861. U.S. Army Heritage and Education Center, Carlisle Barracks, Pa.

Robertson, Judah T.(12th New York Inf.). Diary. Gettysburg College Library, Gettysburg, Pa.

Robison, Isaiah (28th Pennsylvania Inf.). Correspondence. U.S. Army Heritage and Education Center, Carlisle Barracks, Pa.

Rogers, Horace (3rd Connecticut Inf.). Correspondence. Connecticut Historical Society, Hartford.

Rollins, George S. (3rd Maine Inf.). Correspondence. U.S. Army Heritage and Education Center, Carlisle Barracks, Pa.

Rollins, Nathaniel (2nd Wisconsin Inf.). Diary. State Historical Society of Wisconsin, Madison.

Scott, George D. (8th New York Militia). Memoirs. U.S. Army Heritage and Education Center, Carlisle Barracks, Pa.

Scott, George I. (2nd New Jersey Inf.). Correspondence. Rutgers University Library, New Brunswick, N.J.

Searles, Jasper N. (1st Minnesota Inf.). Correspondence and Diary. Minnesota Historical Society, Saint Paul.

Seibert, David S. (15th Pennsylvania Inf.). Correspondence. U.S. Army Heritage and Education Center, Carlisle Barracks, Pa.

Setright, John T. (2nd Michigan Inf.). Letter of July 28, 1861. University of Michigan Library, Ann Arbor.

Shaw, Henry (2nd New Hampshire Inf.). Letter of July 18, 1861. Virginia Historical Society, Richmond.

Shaw, William H. (3rd Connecticut Inf.). Diary. Manassas National Battlefield Park Library, Manassas, Va.

Shepard, J. W. (71st New York Militia). Letter of May 16, 1861. U.S. Army Heritage and Education Center, Carlisle Barracks, Pa.

Sherman, John (staff officer). Correspondence. Library of Congress, Washington, D.C.

Slocum, Henry W. (27th New York Inf.). Letter of August 14, 1861. Gratz Collection. Historical Society of Pennsylvania, Philadelphia.

Smart, Benjamin F. (2nd Maine Inf.). Letter of July 23, 1861. Manassas National Battlefield Park Library, Manassas, Va.

Smart, Richard B. (1st Massachusetts Inf.). Correspondence. Duke University Library, Durham, N.C.

Smith, Anthony W. (District of Columbia Inf.) Correspondence. Missouri Historical Society, Saint Louis.

Smith, Charles W. (4th Connecticut Inf.). Diary. Connecticut Historical Society, Hartford.

Smith, Levi L. (28th Pennsylvania Inf.). Correspondence and Diary. U.S. Army Heritage and Education Center, Carlisle Barracks, Pa.

Stewart, James P. (28th Pennsylvania Inf.). Correspondence. U.S. Army Heritage and Education Center, Carlisle Barracks, Pa.

Taber, Joseph S. (23rd Pennsylvania Inf.). Diary. U.S. Army Heritage and Education Center, Carlisle Barracks, Pa.

Terry, Alfred H. (2nd Connecticut Inf.). Correspondence. Connecticut Historical Society, Hartford.

———. Correspondence. Yale University Library, New Haven, Conn.

Terry, Robert B. (7th Pennsylvania Inf.). Correspondence. Gilder Lehrman Collection, Gilder Lehrman Institute of American History, New York, N.Y.

Thomas, Edmund W. (3rd Maine Inf.). Letter of August 1, 1861. U.S. Army Heritage and Education Center, Carlisle Barracks, Pa.

Thompson, A. B. (2nd New Hampshire Inf.). Letter of July 24, 1861. Manassas National Battlefield Park Library, Manassas, Va.

Tidball, John C. (2nd U.S. Arty.). Diary. U.S. Military Academy Library, West Point, N.Y.

Unidentified Enlisted Man (2nd New Hampshire Inf.). Letter of July 24, 1861. Manassas National Battlefield Park Library, Manassas, Va.

Unidentified Officer (79th New York Inf.). Memoirs. New York Public Library, New York, N.Y.

d'Utassy, Frederick (39th New York Inf.). Correspondence. New-York Historical Society, New York, N.Y.

Vaill, George (4th Connecticut Inf.). Correspondence. U.S. Army Heritage and Education Center, Carlisle Barracks, Pa.

Wagner, Levi (1st Ohio Inf.). Memoirs. U.S. Army Heritage and Education Center, Carlisle Barracks, Pa.

Walling, William H. (16th New York Inf.). Letter of July 30, 1861. U.S. Army Heritage and Education Center, Carlisle Barracks, Pa.

Wells, George D. (1st Massachusetts Inf.). Correspondence. East Carolina University Library, Greenville, N.C.

Wells, John A. (14th New York Militia). Correspondence. Manassas National Battlefield Park Library, Manassas, Va.

Wells, William R. (12th New York Inf.). Letter of July 23, 1861. University of North Carolina Library, Chapel Hill.

Westervelt, William (27th New York Inf.). Diary and Memoirs. U.S. Army Heritage and Education Center, Carlisle Barracks, Pa.

Wild, Edward (1st Minnesota Inf.). Correspondence. Minnesota Historical Society, Saint Paul.

Wild, Edward A. (1st Massachusetts Inf.). Correspondence. U.S. Army Heritage and Education Center, Carlisle Barracks, Pa.

Wiley, John S. (1st Massachusetts Inf.). Correspondence. U.S. Army Heritage and Education Center, Carlisle Barracks, Pa.

Wilkin, Alexander (1st Minnesota Inf.). Correspondence. Minnesota Historical Society, Saint Paul.

Wilkinson, Frederick W. (2nd Michigan Inf.). Correspondence. Gilder Lehrman Collection, Gilder Lehrman Institute of American History, New York, N.Y.

Young, Henry H. (2nd Rhode Island Inf.). Correspondence. U.S. Army Heritage and Education Center, Carlisle Barracks, Pa.

CIVILIANS, NORTH AND SOUTH

Bates, Julia D. Diary. Edward Bates Papers. Missouri Historical Society, Saint Louis.

Belmont, August. Correspondence. Historical Society of Pennsylvania, Philadelphia.

Blakey, Angus. Letter of July 23, 1861. University of Virginia Library, Charlottesville.

Butler, Francis E. Diary. Rutgers University Library, New Brunswick, N.J.

Cameron, Simon. Correspondence. Historical Society of Pennsylvania, Philadelphia.

Camp, Jacob A. Correspondence. Cornell University Library, Ithaca, N.Y.

Chase, Salmon P. Correspondence. Historical Society of Pennsylvania, Philadelphia.

Cobb, Thomas R. R. Correspondence. University of Georgia Library, Athens.

Cocke, Thomas L. P. Letter of July 19, 1861. Armistead-Cocke Correspondence. College of William and Mary Library, Williamsburg, Va.

Croom, Elizabeth R. F. Correspondence. East Carolina University Library, Greenville, N.C.

Davis, Jefferson. Correspondence. Historical Society of Pennsylvania, Philadelphia.

———. Correspondence. New-York Historical Society, New York, N.Y.

———. Correspondence. Virginia Historical Society, Richmond.

Donnellan, George. Letter of July 14, 1861. Gilder Lehrman Collection, Gilder Lehrman Institute of American History, New York, N.Y.

Ellis, Margaret. Letter of July 20, 1861. Duke University Library, Durham, N.C.

Ewing, Hugh B. Diary. Ohio Historical Society, Columbus.

Finnell, Phoebe H. Memoirs. Manassas National Battlefield Park Library, Manassas, Va.

Fletcher, Laura. Memoirs. Manassas National Battlefield Park Library, Manassas, Va.

Galloway, James C. Letter of July 22, 1861. East Carolina University Library, Greenville, N.C.

Greenhow, Rose O. Correspondence. Duke University Library, Durham, N.C.

Hairston, Peter W. Correspondence. University of North Carolina Library, Chapel Hill.

Harrison, Burton N. Correspondence. Library of Congress, Washington, D.C.

Henry Family. Correspondence. Manassas National Battlefield Park Library, Manassas, Va.

Hollingsworth, William T. Letter of July 24, 1861. Gilder Lehrman Collection, Gilder Lehrman Institute of American History, New York, N.Y.

Hough, Franklin B. Correspondence and Diary. New York State Library, Albany.

Letcher, John. Correspondence. Library of Congress, Washington, D.C.

Lincoln, Abraham. Correspondence. Library of Congress, Washington, D.C.

———. Correspondence. New-York Historical Society, New York, N.Y.

Miles, William P. Correspondence. Historical Society of Pennsylvania, Philadelphia.

———. Correspondence. University of North Carolina Library, Chapel Hill.

Raymond, Henry J. Correspondence. New York Public Library, New York, N.Y.

Ricketts, Fanny. Diary. Manassas National Battlefield Park Library, Manassas, Va. .

Ruffin, Edmund. Diary. Library of Congress, Washington, D.C.

Russell, Earl John. Letter of June 15, 1861. Pennsylvania State University Library, University Park.

Smythe, J. Adger. Letter of July 26, 1861. South Carolina Historical Society, Charleston.

Stanton, Edwin M. Correspondence. Historical Society of Pennsylvania, Philadelphia.

Sumner, George. Letter of June 4, 1861. Pennsylvania State University Library, University Park.

Turnure, David M. Diary. New-York Historical Society, New York, N.Y.
Van Buren, Louisa D. M. Memoirs. University of Southern Mississippi Library, Hattiesburg.
Van Lew, Elizabeth. Correspondence. New York Public Library, New York, N.Y.
Welles, Gideon. Correspondence. Library of Congress, Washington, D.C.
Wright, Augustus R. Letter of July 22, 1861. Gilder Lehrman Collection, Gilder Lehrman Institute of American History, New York, N.Y.

Unpublished Records

Records of Court of Inquiry: Conduct of Colonel Dixon S. Miles at Bull Run, July 21, 1861. Record Group 153, Entry II-498. National Archives, Washington, D.C.
Records of Headquarters Department of Northeastern Virginia: Letters Sent, May–October 1861. Record Group 393, Entry 3684 (2 vols.). National Archives, Washington, D.C.
Records of Headquarters 4th Brigade, 1st Division, Army of Northeastern Virginia: Letters Received, July–August 1861. Record Group 393, Entry 3944. National Archives, Washington, D.C.
Records of War Department, Confederate States of America: Letters Sent, February–August 1861. Confederate States of America Papers, Vols. 109–10. Library of Congress, Washington, D.C.

Printed Materials

Newspapers

Army and Navy Chronicle
Baltimore (Md.) American
Charleston (S.C.) Daily Courier
Charleston (S.C.) Mercury
Daily Richmond (Va.) Enquirer
Daily Richmond (Va.) Examiner
Frank Leslie's Illustrated Newspaper
Harper's Weekly
Hartford (Conn.) Courant
New Orleans Daily Delta
New Orleans Picayune
New York Express
New York Herald
New York Leader
New York Times
New York Tribune
New York World
Philadelphia Daily Evening Bulletin
Philadelphia Inquirer
Philadelphia Press
Philadelphia Weekly Times

Providence (R.I.) Daily Journal
Providence (R.I.) Daily Press
Richmond (Va.) Dispatch
Richmond (Va.) Whig
Savannah Morning News
Times (London)
Washington Daily National Intelligencer

Battle and Campaign Studies

Addresses Delivered at the Unveiling of the Memorial Tablet . . . in Memory of Those Members of the Seventy-First Regiment [New York Volunteers] Who Were Killed or Wounded at the Battle of Bull Run, July 21, 1861. New York: privately issued, 1895.

"The Advantages of Defeat." *Atlantic Monthly* 8 (1861): 360–65.

Alexander, E. Porter. "The Battle of Bull Run." *Scribner's Magazine* 41 (1907): 80–94.

Allen, J. W. "Thirty-Third Virginia at First Manassas." *Southern Historical Society Papers* 34 (1906): 363–71.

Allen, Thomas S. "The Second Wisconsin at the First Battle of Bull Run." *War Papers: Read before the Commandery of the State of Wisconsin, Military Order of the Loyal Legion of the United States* 1 (1891): 374–93.

Barnard, John G. *The C.S.A. and the Battle of Bull Run.* New York: D. Van Nostrand, 1862.

Barrett, Edwin S. *What I Saw at Bull Run.* Boston: Beacon, 1886.

"The Battle at Bull's Run, Sunday, July 21." *Frank Leslie's Illustrated Newspaper* 12 (August 3, 1861): 177–78.

"The Battle of Bull Run: An Important Letter from General Joseph E. Johns[t]on." *Historical Magazine* 2, no. 2 (1867): 232–37.

Beatie, Russel H. *The Army of the Potomac: Birth of Command, November 1860–September 1861.* New York: Da Capo, 2002.

———. *Road to Manassas: The Growth of Union Command in the Eastern Theatre from the Fall of Fort Sumter to the First Battle of Bull Run.* New York: Cooper Square, 1961.

Beauregard, G. T. *A Commentary on the Campaign and Battle of Manassas of July, 1861.* New York: G. P. Putnam's Sons, 1891.

———. "The First Battle of Bull Run." In *Battles and Leaders of the Civil War*, edited by Robert U. Johnson and Clarence C. Buel, 4 vols., 1:196–227. New York, 1887.

Bird, W. D. "The Campaign of Bull Run, 1861." *Journal of the United Service Institution of India* 40 (1911): 25–53.

Blackburn, J. S. "Confederate Cavalry at the First Manassas." *Southern Bivouac* 2 (1884): 529–34.

Blackeney, Thomas O. "The Commander's Estimate and General McDowell." *Military Review* 33 (December 1953): 9–17.

"The Blunder at Bull's Run." *Frank Leslie's Illustrated Newspaper* 12 (August 3, 1861): 178–79.

Breazeale, B. B. *Co. J, 4th South Carolina Infantry at the First Battle of Manassas*. Manassas, Va.: Manassas Journal, 1912.

Britton, Rick. "Rush to Glory." *Civil War Times Illustrated* 35 (June 1996): 46–53.

Brown, G. Campbell. *The First Manassas: Correspondence between Generals R. S. Ewell and P. G. T. Beauregard to Which Are Added Extracts from a Letter of Gen. Fitz Lee*. Nashville, Tenn.: Wheeler, Osborn & Duckworth, 1885.

———. "General Ewell at Bull Run." In *Battles and Leaders of the Civil War*, edited by Robert U. Johnson and Clarence C. Buel, 4 vols., 1:259–61. New York, 1887.

———. "General Ewell at First Manassas: Colonel Campbell Brown's Reply to General Beauregard." *Southern Historical Society Papers* 13 (1885): 41–45.

Buck, Nina K. "'Blucher of the Day' at Manassas." *Confederate Veteran* 7 (1899): 108–109.

Bushnell, Horace. *Reverses Needed: A Discourse Delivered on the Sunday After the Disaster of Bull Run*. Hartford, Conn.: L. E. Hunt, 1861.

Caddall, J. B. "The Pulaski Guards, Company C, 4th Virginia Infantry, at the First Battle of Manassas." *Southern Historical Society Papers* 32 (1904): 174–78.

Carter, Robert G. *Four Brothers in Blue; or, Sunshine and Shadow of the War of the Rebellion . . . from Bull Run to Appomattox*. Austin: University of Texas Press, 1978.

Clement, Edward. *The Bull-Run Rout: Scenes Attending the First Clash of Volunteers in the Civil War*. Cambridge, Mass.: Wilson & Son, 1909.

Conrad, Daniel B. "History of the First Battle of Manassas and the Organization of the Stonewall Brigade: How It Was So Named." *Southern Historical Society Papers* 19 (1891): 82–92.

———. "The Stonewall Brigade at Bull Run." *Blue and the Gray* 4 (1894): 359–65.

Coxe, John. "The Battle of First Manassas." *Confederate Veteran* 23 (1915): 24–26.

Crockett, Cary I. "The Battery That Saved the Day." *Field Artillery Journal* 30 (1940): 26–33.

Cummings, Arthur C. "Thirty-Third Virginia at First Manassas." *Southern Historical Society Papers* 34 (1906): 363–71.

Cunningham, Horace H. *Field Medical Services at the Battles of Manassas (Bull Run)*. Athens: University of Georgia Press, 1968.

Davis, Peter, and H. John Cooper. *First Bull Run, 1861*. New York: Hippocrene Books, 1973.

Davis, W. W. H. *The Campaign of 1861 in the Shenandoah Valley*. Doylestown, Pa.: Doylestown Publishing, 1893.

Davis, William C. *Battle at Bull Run: A History of the First Major Campaign of the Civil War*. Garden City, N.Y.: Doubleday, 1977.

Detzer, David. *Donnybrook: The Battle of Bull Run, 1861*. New York: Harcourt, 2004.

Donnelly, Ralph W. "Federal Batteries on the Henry House Hill, Bull Run, 1861." *Military Affairs* 21 (1957): 188–92.

Elliott, Stephen. *God's Presence with Our Army at Manassas: A Sermon Preached . . . in Commemoration of the Victory at Manassas Junction, on Sunday the 21st of July, 1861.* Savannah, Ga.: W. T. Williams, 1861.

Field, Ron, and Adam Hook. *Lincoln's 90-Day Volunteers, 1861: From Fort Sumter to First Bull Run.* Oxford: Osprey, 2013.

First Bull Run Staff Ride Briefing Book. Washington, D.C.: U.S. Army Center of Military History, n.d.

"The First Manassas: A Man Who Was There Tells about the Great 'Skedaddle.'" *Southern Historical Society Papers* 30 (1902): 269–76.

1st Manassas (Bull Run) and the War around It. Manassas, Va.; First Manassas Corporation, 1961.

Fiske, Francis S. "At the Battle of Bull Run with the Second New Hampshire Regiment." *New England Magazine* 17 (1894): 153–63.

Folsom, William R. "Vermont at Bull Run." *Vermont Quarterly,* n.s., 19 (1951): 5–21.

"The 4th Alabama Regiment at the Battle of Manassas." *Alabama Historical Quarterly* 23 (1961): 208–10.

Franklin, James, Jr. "Incidents at the First Manassas Battle." *Confederate Veteran* 2 (1894): 291–92.

Fry, James B. *McDowell and Tyler in the Campaign of Bull Run, 1861.* New York: D. Van Nostrand, 1884.

———. "McDowell's Advance to Bull Run." In *Battles and Leaders of the Civil War,* edited by Robert U. Johnson and Clarence C. Buel, 4 vols., 1:167–93. New York, 1887.

Garnett, James M. "Harpers' Ferry and First Manassas: Extracts from the Diary of Captain James M. Garnett. . . ." *Southern Historical Society Papers* 28 (1900): 58–71.

"General Eppa Hunton at the Battle of Bull Run, July 21, 1861. . . . He Saved the Confederate Army from Defeat." *Southern Historical Society Papers* 32 (1904): 143–45.

"General Johnston before First Manassas." *Confederate Veteran* 23 (1915): 28.

"General Patterson's Campaign in Virginia." *Continental Monthly* 1 (1862): 257–63.

Gibbs, George Alphonso. "With a Mississippi Private in a Little Known Part of the Battle of First Bull Run." *Civil War Times Illustrated* 4 (April 1965): 42–47.

Glasgow, William M., Jr. "The General Was a Recruit." *Military Affairs* 23 (1959): 159–60.

Haight, Theron W. "After the First Bull Run." *War Papers: Read before the Commandery of the State of Wisconsin, Military Order of the Loyal Legion of the United States* 3 (1903): 215–25.

Hains, Peter C. "The First Gun at Bull Run." *Cosmopolitan* 51 (1911): 388–99.

Hall, H. Seymour. "A Volunteer at the First Bull Run." *War Talks in Kansas: A Series of Papers Read before the Kansas Commandery of the Military Order of the Loyal Legion of the United States* (1906): 143–59.

Hanson, Joseph Mills. *Bull Run Remembers: The History, Traditions, and Landmarks of the Manassas (Bull Run) Campaigns*. Manassas, Va.: National Capitol, 1953.

Harris, Shawn C. "Standing Like a Stone Wall." *America's Civil War* 3 (July 1990): 18–25.

Harrison, George F. "Ewell at First Manassas." *Southern Historical Society Papers* 14 (1886): 356–59.

Henderson, C. E. "Just before First Manassas." *Confederate Veteran* 23 (1915): 24–26.

Hennessy, John. *The First Battle of Manassas: An End to Innocence, July 18–21, 1861*. Lynchburg, Va.: H. E. Howard, 1989.

———. "War-Watchers at Bull Run." *Civil War Times Illustrated* 40 (August 2001): 40–47, 67–69, 72.

Henry, Hugh F. *Souvenir of the Battlefield of Bull Run*. Manassas, Va.: Manassas Journal, 1900.

"Historians' Forum: The First Battle of Bull Run." *Civil War History* 57 (2011): 106–20.

How Bull Run Battle Was Lost. New York: Tribune Association, 1863.

Howell, Willey. "The First Battle of Bull Run." *Journal of the United States Infantry Association* 6 (1909): 7–36.

Imboden, John K. "Incidents of the First Bull Run." In *Battles and Leaders of the Civil War*, edited by Robert U. Johnson and Clarence C. Buel, 4 vols., 1:229–39. New York, 1887.

———. "Jackson at Harper's Ferry in 1861." In *Battles and Leaders of the Civil War*, edited by Robert U. Johnson and Clarence C. Buel, 4 vols., 1:111–25, New York, 1887.

Jackson, H. B. "From Washington to Bull Run and Back Again in the Second Wisconsin Infantry." *War Papers: Read before the Commandery of the State of Wisconsin, Military Order of the Loyal Legion of the United States* 4 (1910): 233–50.

"Jackson and His Brigade at Manassas." *Southern Bivouac* 2 (1884): 537–41.

Johnston, Joseph E. "The Battle of Bull Run: An Important Letter from Joseph E. Johnston." *Historical Magazine* 2 (1867): 232–37.

———. "Responsibilities of the First Bull Run." In *Battles and Leaders of the Civil War*, edited by Robert U. Johnson and Clarence C. Buel, 4 vols., 1:240–59. New York, 1887.

Johnston, R. M. *Bull Run: Its Strategy and Tactics*. Boston: Houghton Mifflin, 1913.

Jones, Archer. *Civil War Command and Strategy: The Process of Victory and Defeat*. New York: Free Press, 1992.

Jones, J. William. "Reminiscences of the Army of Northern Virginia . . . First Manassas and Its Sequel." *Southern Historical Society Papers* 9 (1881): 129–34.

Jones, Kenneth W. "The Fourth Alabama Infantry: First Blood." *Alabama Historical Quarterly* 36 (1974): 35–53.

Jones, Virgil Carrington. *First Manassas: The Story of the Bull Run Campaign*. Harrisburg, Pa.: Historical Times, 1973.

Jordan, Frank B. "Retrospect: First Bull Run, July 16–22, 1861." *Infantry Journal* 33 (1928): 238–47.

Kearsey, Alexander. *A Study of the Strategy and Tactics of the Shenandoah Valley Campaign, 1861–62*. Aldershot: Gale & Polen, 1953.

King, Josiah R. "The Battle of Bull Run: A Confederate Victory Obtained But Not Achieved." *Glimpses of the Nation's Struggle: A Series of Papers Read Before the Minnesota Commandery of the Military Order of the Loyal Legion of the United States* 6 (1909): 497–510.

King, Kendall J. "From Montezuma to Manassas." *America's Civil War* 9 (September 1996): 48–53.

King, W. S. "Medical and Surgical Report [of the Battle of First Bull Run]." *Civil War History* 4 (1958): 36.

"The Lesson of Defeat." *Harper's Weekly* 5 (August 10, 1861): 499.

"Letter from General Early [Regarding Longstreet's Brigade at First Manassas]." *Transactions of the Southern Historical Society* 2 (1875): 71–74.

Livermore, Thomas L. "Patterson's Shenandoah Campaign." *Papers of the Military Historical Society of Massachusetts* 1 (1895): 3–58.

Lyster, Henry F. *Recollections of the Bull Run Campaign after Twenty-Seven Years*. Detroit: W. S. Ostler, 1888.

Manassas National Battlefield Park, Virginia. Washington, D.C.: National Park Service, 1967.

Masters, John. "The Day the South Could Have Won the Civil War." *Reader's Digest* 77 (November 1960): 159–68.

McComas, William R. "Ohio Troops at Bull Run." *G.A.R. War Papers: Papers Read before . . . Post No. 401* (1891): 190–202.

McDonald, Joanna M. *Give Them the Bayonet!: A Guide to the Battle for Henry Hill, July 21, 1861*. Shippensburg, Pa.: Burd Street, 1999.

———. *"We Shall Meet Again": The First Battle of Manassas (Bull Run), July 18–21, 1861*. Shippensburg, Pa.: White Mane, 1999.

A Modern Gilpin: A Ballad of Bull Run. New York: Historical Publishing, 1866.

Monroe, J. Albert. *The Rhode Island Artillery at the First Battle of Bull Run*. Providence, R.I.: Sidney S. Rider, 1878.

Munford, Thomas T. "Reply of General Munford [to Letter of William Fitzhugh Randolph]." *Southern Historical Society Papers* 23 (1895): 264–66.

Murfin, James V. "How Stonewall Got His Name." *Civil War Times Illustrated* 1 (July 1962): 39–40.

Murray, R. L. *"They Fought Like Tigers": The 11th New York Fire Zouaves, 14th Brooklyn, and the Irish 69th New York at First Bull Run*. Wolcott, N.Y.: Benedum Books, 2005.

Naisawald, L. Van Loan. "Bull Run: The Artillery and the Infantry." *Civil War History* 3 (1957): 163–77.

A Narrative of the Battles of Bull Run and Manassas Junction, July 18th and 21st, 1861. Charleston, S.C.: Evans & Cogswell, 1861.

Nofi, Albert A., ed. *The Opening Guns: Fort Sumter to Bull Run, 1861*. New York: Gallery, 1988.

Northrop, Lucius B. "The Confederate Commissariat at Manassas." In *Battles and Leaders of the Civil War*, edited by Robert U. Johnson and Clarence C. Buel, 4 vols., 1:261. New York, 1887.

Noyes, Henry E. "A Few Guns before the First Gun at Bull Run." *Journal of the Military Service Institution of the United States* 49 (1911): 413–18.

Nye, Wilbur S. "Action North of Bull Run: An Often Overlooked Phase of [the] Battle of First Manassas." *Civil War Times Illustrated* 4 (April 1965): 48–49.

Official Reports of Generals Johnston and Beauregard of the Battle of Manassas, July 21st, 1861. . . . Richmond, Va.: Enquirer Book, 1862.

O'Flaherty, P. D. "The 69th [New York Militia] Regiment at Bull Run." *Irish Sword* 7 (1965): 2–4.

"The Opposing Armies at the First Bull Run." In *Battles and Leaders of the Civil War*, edited by Robert U. Johnson and Clarence C. Buel, 4 vols., 1:194–95. New York, 1887.

Organization of the Union Army (Brigadier-General Irvin MacDowell [sic] Commanding) at the Battle of Bull Run, Va., July 21, 1861. Washington, D.C.: Government Printing Office, 1882.

Ostrander, Peter W. *A Narrative of the Work of the Commission . . . in Purchasing a Site and Erecting Thereon a Monument in Memory of the [New York] Men Who Fell in the Battles of the First and Second Bull Run*. Brooklyn, N.Y.: Eagle, 1907.

"Panic Terror." *Atlantic Monthly* 7 (1861): 492–505.

Parker, Daingerfield. "Personal Reminiscences: The Battalion of Regular Infantry at the First Battle of Bull Run." *Military Order of the Loyal Legion of the United States, Commandery of the District of Columbia, War Paper 36*. N.p., 1900.

Patterson, Robert. *A Narrative of the Campaign in the Valley of the Shenandoah in 1861*. Philadelphia: John Campbell, 1865.

Peters, Winfield. "First Battle of Manassas: Dash and Heroism of the Maryland Line." *Southern Historical Society Papers* 34 (1906): 170–78.

Pierce, James O. "The Skirmish at Falling Waters." *Glimpses of the Nation's Struggle: A Series of Papers Read before the Minnesota Commandery of the Military Order of the Loyal Legion of the United States* 2 (1890): 289–313.

Pohanka, Brian C., ed. "With the Fire Zouaves at First Bull Run: The Narrative of Private Arthur O. Alcock, 11th New York Volunteer Infantry." *Civil War Regiments* 5 (1997): 80–104.

Preston, Thomas L. "General Hill's Article on Stonewall Jackson." *Century Illustrated Monthly Magazine* 48 (1894): 155–56.

Putnam, G. P. "Before and after the Battle: A Day and Night in 'Dixie.'"
    Knickerbocker Magazine 58 (1861): 231–50.
Rafuse, Ethan S. "The Man Who Could Have Knocked Down Stonewall."
    Civil War Times Illustrated 40 (August 2001): 30–39, 65–66.
———. *A Single Grand Victory: The First Campaign and Battle of
    Manassas*. Wilmington, Del.: Scholarly Resources, 2002.
Ramirez, Thomas P. "Bull Run: Battle of a Summer's Day." *Mankind* 2
    (1969): 10–17, 49.
Randolph, William Fitzhugh. "First Manassas: The Closing Scenes of
    the Battle—Cavalry Pursuit." *Southern Historical Society Papers* 23
    (1895): 259–64.
*Report of the Joint Committee on the Conduct of the War: Part I—Bull
    Run—Ball's Bluff*. Washington, D.C.: Government Printing Office,
    1863.
"Report of the Operations of Early's Brigade in the Affair at Blackburn's
    Ford on Bull Run, the 18th of July, 1861." *Transactions of the
    Southern Historical Society* 2 (1875): 74–77.
Rhodes, Elisha Hunt. *The First Campaign of the Second Rhode Island
    Infantry*. Providence, R.I.: Sidney S. Rider, 1878.
Robertson, W. Glenn. "First Bull Run." In *America's First Battles, 1776–
    1965*, edited by Charles E. Heller and William A. Stofft, 81–108.
    Lawrence: University Press of Kansas, 1986.
Robins, William M. "The Sobriquet 'Stonewall': How It Was Acquired."
    Southern Historical Society Papers 19 (1891): 164–67.
Roman, Rita G. "Mastermind Maneuvers at Manassas: A Study in Strategy
    Operations." *OAH Magazine of History* 8 (Fall 1993): 48–53.
Russell, William Howard. *The Battle of Bull Run*. New York: Rudd &
    Carleton, 1861.
———. *Mister Russell on Bull Run, with a Note from the Rebellion
    Record*. New York: Rare Books Club, 2012.
Schreckengost, Gary J. "'The Fatal Blunder of the Day': Artillery
    Deployment at Bull Run." *Field Artillery Journal* 2 (July–August
    2001): 22–28.
Shier, Maynard J. "The Battle of Falling Waters." *Civil War Times
    Illustrated* 15 (February 1977): 16–26.
Sholes, Albert E. *Personal Reminiscences of Bull Run*. . . . Flushing, N.Y.:
    privately issued, 1910.
"The Significance of Bull Run." *Infantry Journal* 10 (1913): 173–77.
Smith, Gustavus W. *Generals J. E. Johnston and G. T. Beauregard at the
    Battle of Manassas, July, 1861*. New York: C. G. Crawford, 1892.
Smith, William. "Reminiscences of the First Battle of Manassas."
    Southern Historical Society Papers 10 (1882): 433–44.
Snell, Mark. "First Manassas, an End to Innocence: A Conversation with
    Historian John Hennessy." *Civil War Regiments* 5 (1997): 105–19.
Staples, Horatio. "Reminiscences of Bull Run." *War Papers: Read before
    the Commandery of the State of Maine, Military Order of the Loyal
    Legion of the United States* 3 (1908): 126–38.

Starbuck, Gregory J. "'Up Alabamians!': The Fourth Alabama Infantry at First Manassas." *Military Images* 8 (July-August 1986): 25–29.

Stedman, Edmund C. *The Battle of Bull Run.* New York: Rudd & Carleton, 1861.

Steele, Matthew Forney. *The First Battle of Bull Run.* Fort Leavenworth, Kans.: U.S. Infantry and Cavalry School, 1906.

"Strategic Importance of Manassas Evidenced in First Major Battle of the Civil War." *Pennsylvania Guardsman* 16 (July 1939): 22–25.

Stutler, Boyd B., ed. "Notes and Queries: 'There Stands Jackson Like a Stone Wall!'" *Civil War History* 7 (1961): 204–205.

Sullivan, David M., ed. "One Marine's Brief Battle." *Civil War Times Illustrated* 31 (March–April 1992): 14, 16, 18, 20–21, 57–60.

"Suppressed Part of Gen. Beauregard's Report of the Battle of Manassas." *Land We Love* 2 (1867): 259–60.

Swift, Eben, comp. *The Bull Run Campaign in Virginia, 1861.* N.p., n.d.

Telfer, William Duff. *A Reminiscence of the First Battle of Manassas: A Camp-Fire Story of the Seventy-First Regiment, N.G.I.N.Y.* [National Guard Infantry of New York]. Brooklyn, N.Y.: W. D. Teller, 1864.

"Thirty-Third Virginia at First Manassas." *Southern Historical Society Papers* 34 (1906): 363–71.

Tidball, Eugene C. "The View from the Top of the Knoll: Captain John C. Tidball's Memoir of the First Battle of Bull Run." *Civil War History* 44 (1998): 175–93.

Tucker, Glenn. "Bull Run: Signal for a Long War." *Civil War Times* 2 (June 1960): 4–5, 18–19.

Tyler, Elnathan B. *"Wooden Nutmegs" at Bull Run: A Humorous Account of Some of the Exploits and Experiences of the Three Months Connecticut Brigade, and the Part They Bore in the National Stampede.* Hartford, Conn.: George L. Coburn, 1872.

Vincent, Thomas M. "The Battle of Bull Run, July 21, 1861." *Military Order of the Loyal Legion of the United States, Commandery of the District of Columbia, War Paper 58.* N.p., 1905.

Voices of the Civil War: First Manassas. Alexandria, Va.: Time-Life Books, 1997.

Warder, T. B., and James M. Catlett. *Battle of Young's Branch or, Manassas Plain, Fought July 21, 1861.* Richmond, Va.: Enquirer Book, 1862.

Waterman, Arba N. "Washington at the Time of the First Bull Run." *Military Essays and Recollections: Papers Read before the Commandery of the State of Illinois, Military Order of the Loyal Legion of the United States* 2 (1894): 21–31.

Welsh, Charles E. "McDowell's Offensive." *Military Review* 33 (April 1953): 22–40.

Wheeler, Richard. *A Rising Thunder: From Lincoln's Election to the Battle of Bull Run.* New York: HarperCollins, 1994.

Wilkes, George. *The Great Battle, Fought at Manassas . . . Sunday, July 21, 1861.* New York: Brown & Ryan, 1861.

Wilshin, Francis F. *Manassas (Bull Run) National Battlefield Park, Virginia.* Washington, D.C.: National Park Service, 1955.

Winder, J. R. "Second South Carolina at First Manassas." *Confederate Veteran* 17 (1909): 28.

Woodbury, Augustus. *The Memory of the First Battle: A Discourse Preached . . . on the 28th Anniversary of Bull Run, July 21, 1889.* Providence, R.I.: E. L. Freeman & Son, 1889.

Autobiographies, Collected Correspondence, Diaries, Memoirs, etc.

CONFEDERATE

Alexander, E. Porter. *Fighting for the Confederacy: The Personal Recollections of General Edward Porter Alexander.* Edited by Gary W. Gallagher. Chapel Hill: University of North Carolina Press, 1989.

———. *Military Memoirs of a Confederate: A Critical Narrative.* New York: Charles Scribner's Sons, 1907.

Austin, Aurelia, ed. "A Georgia Boy with 'Stonewall' Jackson: The Letters of James Thomas Thompson." *Virginia Magazine of History and Biography* 70 (1962): 314–31.

Bailey, Virginia Griffin, ed. "Letters of Melvin Dwinnell, Yankee Rebel." *Georgia Historical Quarterly* 47 (1963): 193–203.

Barclay, Alexander Tedford. *Ted Barclay, Liberty Hall Volunteers: Letters from the Stonewall Brigade.* Edited by Charles W. Turner. Berryville, Va.: Rockbridge, 1992.

Barton, Randolph. *Recollections: 1861–'65.* Baltimore: privately issued, 1913.

Batchelor, Benjamin F., and George Q. Turner. *Batchelor-Turner Letters, 1861–1864, Written by Two of Terry's Texas Rangers.* Edited by Helen J. H. Rugeley. Austin, Tex.: Steck, 1961.

Baylor, George. *Bull Run to Bull Run; or, Four Years in the Army of Northern Virginia. . . .* Richmond, Va.: B. F. Johnson, 1900.

Beauregard, Pierre G. T. *With Beauregard in Mexico: The Mexican War Reminiscences of P. G. T. Beauregard.* Edited by T. Harry Williams. Baton Rouge: Louisiana State University Press, 1956.

Bevens, W. E. *Reminiscences of a Private, Company "G," First Arkansas Regiment Infantry.* Newport, Ark.: privately issued, 1913.

Blackford, Susan Leigh, comp. *Letters from Lee's Army; or, Memoirs of Life in and out of the Army in Virginia during the War between the States.* New York: Charles Scribner's Sons, 1947.

Blackford, William W. *War Years with Jeb Stuart.* New York: Charles Scribner's Sons, 1945.

Bosang, James N. *Memoirs of a Pulaski Veteran of the Stonewall Brigade, 1861–1865.* Pulaski, Va.: B. D. Smith & Brothers, 1930.

Brown, G. Campbell. *Campbell Brown's Civil War.* Edited by Terry L. Jones. Baton Rouge: Louisiana State University Press, 2001.

Bryan, T. Conn, ed. "Letters of Two Confederate Officers, William Thomas Conn and Charles Augustus Conn." *Georgia Historical Quarterly* 46 (1962): 169–95.

Buck, Samuel D. *With the Old Confeds: Actual Experiences of a Captain in the Line.* Baltimore: H. E. Houck, 1925.

Burnett, Edmund Cody, comp. "Notes and Documents: Letters of Three
    Lightfoot Brothers, 1861–1864." *Georgia Historical Quarterly* 25
    (1941): 371–400.
Casler, John O. *Four Years in the Stonewall Brigade*. Dayton, Ohio:
    Morningside, 1971.
Conner, James. *Letters of General James Conner, C.S.A.* Columbia, S.C.:
    State, 1933.
Cooke, John Esten. *Wearing of the Gray: Being Personal Portraits, Scenes,
    and Adventures of the War*. Edited by Philip Van Doren Stern.
    Bloomington: Indiana University Press, 1959.
Coward, Asbury. *The South Carolinians: Colonel Asbury Coward's
    Memoirs*. Edited by Natalie Jenkins Bond and Osmun Latrobe Coward.
    New York: Vantage, 1968.
Davis, Edwin A., ed. "A Louisiana Volunteer: Letters of William J. Walter,
    1861–62." *Southwest Review* 19 (1933): 78–88.
De Leon, T. C. *Four Years in Rebel Capitals*. Mobile, Ala.: Gossip Printing,
    1890.
Douglas, Henry Kyd. *I Rode with Stonewall: Being Chiefly the War
    Experiences of the Youngest Member of Jackson's Staff*. Chapel Hill:
    University of North Carolina Press, 1940.
Early, Jubal A. *War Memoirs: Autobiographical Sketch and Narrative of
    the War between the States, by Jubal Anderson Early, Lieutenant
    General, C.S.A.* Edited by Frank E. Vandiver. Bloomington: Indiana
    University Press, 1960.
Eggleston, George Cary. *A Rebel's Recollections*. New York: G. P.
    Putnam's Sons, 1887.
Ewell, Richard S. *The Making of a Soldier: Letters of General R. S. Ewell*.
    Edited by Percy G. Hamlin. Richmond, Va.: Whittet & Shepperson,
    1935.
Fontaine, Lamar. *My Life and My Lectures*. New York: Neale, 1908.
"From Manassas to Frazier's Farm: Recollections of a Soldier in Many
    Battles." *Southern Historical Society Papers* 35 (1907): 366–69.
Gallaher, DeWitt C. *A Diary Depicting the Experiences of DeWitt Clinton
    Gallaher in the War between the States*. Charleston, S.C.: privately
    issued, 1945.
Gordon, John B. *Reminiscences of the Civil War*. New York: Charles
    Scribner's Sons, 1904.
Goree, Thomas J. *Longstreet's Aide: The Civil War Letters of Major
    Thomas J. Goree*. Edited by Thomas W. Cutrer. Charlottesville:
    University Press of Virginia, 1995.
Graybill, John H. *Diary of a Soldier of the Stonewall Brigade*. Woodstock,
    Va.: privately issued, ca. 1909.
Handerson, Henry E. *Yankee in Gray: The Civil War Memoirs of Henry
    E. Handerson, with a Selection of His Wartime Letters*. Edited by
    Genevieve Miller. Cleveland: Press of Western Reserve University,
    1962.
Hankins, Samuel W. *Simple Story of a Soldier: Life and Service in the 2d
    Mississippi Infantry*. Tuscaloosa: University of Alabama Press, 2004.

Haskell, John C. *The Haskell Memoirs*. Edited by Gilbert E. Govan and James W. Livingood. New York: G. P. Putnam's Sons, 1960.

Heth, Henry. *The Memoirs of Henry Heth*. Edited by James L. Morrison, Jr. Westport, Conn.: Greenwood, 1974.

Hill, Daniel Harvey. *A Fighter from Way Back: The Mexican War Diary of Lt. Daniel Harvey Hill, 4th Artillery, U.S.A.* Edited by Nathaniel Cheairs Hughes, Jr., and Timothy D. Johnson. Kent, Ohio: Kent State University Press, 2002.

Hopkins, Luther W. *From Bull Run to Appomattox: A Boy's View*. Baltimore: Fleet-McGinley, 1908.

Howard, McHenry. *Recollections of a Maryland Confederate Soldier and Staff Officer Under Johnston, Jackson, and Lee*. Baltimore: Williams & Wilkins, 1914.

Huettel, William L., ed. "Letters from Private Richard C. Bridges, C.S.A., 1861–1864." *Journal of Mississippi History* 33 (1971): 357–72.

Huffman, James. *Ups and Downs of a Confederate Soldier*. New York: William E. Rudge's Sons, 1940.

Hundley, George A. "Beginning and the Ending: Reminiscences of the First and Last Days of the War." *Southern Historical Society Papers* 23 (1895): 294–313.

Hunter, Alexander. *Johnny Reb and Billy Yank*. New York: Neale, 1905.

Hunton, Eppa. *The Autobiography of Eppa Hunton*. Richmond, Va.: William Byrd, 1933.

Jackson, Mary Anna. *Life and Letters of General Thomas J. Jackson (Stonewall Jackson)*. New York: Harper & Brothers, 1892.

Johnston, David E. *Four Years a Soldier*. Princeton, W.Va.: privately issued, 1887.

Johnston, Joseph E. *Narrative of Military Operations Directed, during the Late War between the States, by Joseph E. Johnston, General, C.S.A.* New York: D. Appleton, 1874.

Jones, J. William. "Reminiscences of the Army of Northern Virginia . . . Early Days of the War." *Southern Historical Society Papers* 9 (1881): 90–95.

Kibler, James Allen. "Letters from a Confederate Soldier." *Tyler's Quarterly* 31 (1949–50): 120–27.

Lee, Robert E., Jr. *Recollections and Letters of General Robert E. Lee*. Garden City, N.Y.: Garden City Publishing, 1924.

"Letters of Three Lightfoot Brothers, 1861–1864." *Georgia Historical Quarterly* 25 (1941): 371–400.

Lewis, Richard. *Camp Life of a Confederate Boy . . . Letters Written by Lieut. Richard Lewis, of Walker's [4th South Carolina Infantry] Regiment, to His Mother, during the War*. Charleston, S.C.: News and Courier, 1883.

Longacre, Edward G., ed. "On the Staff of the 'Dictator.'" *Manuscripts* 36 (1984): 224–27.

———. "A South Carolinian Awaits 'Abraham's Forces.'" *Manuscripts* 30 (1978): 21–29.

———. "Three Brothers Face Their Baptism of Battle, July 1861." *Georgia Historical Quarterly* 61 (1977): 156–68.

Longstreet, James. *From Manassas to Appomattox: Memoirs of the Civil War in America.* Philadelphia: J. B. Lippincott, 1896.

Martin, Abbott C., comp. "The Cotton [Family] Letters." *Virginia Magazine of History and Biography,* 37 (1929): 12–22.

McKim, Randolph H. *A Soldier's Recollections: Leaves from the Diary of a Young Confederate.* New York: Longmans, Green, 1911.

Moore, Robert A. *A Life for the Confederacy, As Recorded in the Pocket Diaries of Pvt. Robert A. Moore.* Edited by James W. Silver. Jackson, Tenn.: McCowat-Mercer, 1959.

Morgan, William Henry. *Personal Reminiscences of the War of 1861–5.* Lynchburg, Va.: J. P. Bell, 1911.

Mosby, John Singleton. *Letters of John S. Mosby.* Edited by Adele H. Mitchell. N.p. Stuart-Mosby Historical Society, 1986.

———. *The Memoirs of Colonel John S. Mosby.* Edited by Charles Wells Russell. Bloomington: Indiana University Press, 1959.

———. *Mosby's War Reminiscences and Stuart's Cavalry Campaigns.* New York: Dodd, Mead, 1887.

Myers, Robert Manson, ed. *The Children of Pride: A True Story of Georgia and the Civil War.* New Haven, Conn.: Yale University Press, 1972.

Opie, John N. *A Rebel Cavalryman with Lee, Stuart, and Jackson.* Chicago: W. B. Conkey, 1899.

Owen, Henry T. *The War of Confederate Captain Henry T. Owen . . . Company C, 18th Virginia.* Edited by Kimberly A. Owen. Westminster, Md.: Willow Bend Books, 2004.

Patterson, Edmund D. *Yankee Rebel: The Civil War Journal of Edmund DeWitt Patterson.* Chapel Hill: University of North Carolina Press, 1966.

Paxton, Elisha Franklin. *The Civil War Letters of General Frank "Bull" Paxton, C.S.A., a Lieutenant of Lee & Jackson.* Edited by John Gallatin Paxton. Hillsboro, Tex.: Hill Junior College Press, 1978.

Pender, William Dorsey. *The General to His Lady: The Civil War Letters of William Dorsey Pender to Fanny Pender.* Edited by William W. Hassler. Chapel Hill: University of North Carolina Press, 1965.

Pendleton, William N. *Memoirs of William Nelson Pendleton, D.D.* Edited by Susan P. Lee. Philadelphia: J. B. Lippincott, 1893.

Pogue, William T. *Gunner with Stonewall: Reminiscences of William Thomas Poague. . . .* Edited by Monroe F. Cockrell. Jackson, Tenn.: McCowat-Mercer, 1957.

Shotwell, Randolph A. *The Papers of Randolph Abbott Shotwell.* Edited by J. G. R. Hamilton and Rebecca Cameron. 3 vols. Raleigh: North Carolina Historical Commission, 1929–36.

Simpson, Richard, and Tally Simpson. *"So Far from Home": The Wartime Letters of Dick and Tally Simpson, Third South Carolina Volunteers.* Edited by Guy R. Everson and Edward W. Simpson. New York: Oxford University Press, 1994.

Sorrel, G. Moxley. *Recollections of a Confederate Staff Officer*. Edited by Bell I. Wiley. Jackson, Tenn.: McCowat-Mercer, 1958.

Squires, Charles W. "The 'Boy Officer' of the Washington Artillery—Part I of a Memoir." *Civil War Times Illustrated* 14 (May 1975): 11–17, 19–23.

Stuart, Meriwether, ed. "The Military Orders of Daniel Ruggles, Department of Fredericksburg, April 22–June 5, 1861." *Virginia Magazine of History and Biography* 69 (1961): 149–80.

Taylor, Richard. *Destruction and Reconstruction: Personal Experiences of the Late War*. Edited by Charles P. Roland. Waltham, Mass.: Blaisdell, 1968.

Vance, Zebulon B. *The Papers of Zebulon Baird Vance*. Edited by Frontis W. Johnston. 2 vols. Raleigh, N.C.: State Department of Archives and History, 1963.

Warfield, Edgar. *A Confederate Soldier's Memoirs*. Richmond, Va.: Masonic Home, 1936.

Williams, Charles G., ed. "A Saline Guard: The Civil War Letters of Col. William Ayers Crawford, C.S.A., 1861–1865." *Arkansas Historical Quarterly* 31 (1972): 328–55.

Williams, Frank B., Jr., ed. "From Sumter to the Wilderness: Letters of Sergeant James B. Suddath, Co. E, 7th Regiment, S.C.V. [South Carolina Volunteers]." *South Carolina Historical Magazine* 63 (1962): 1–11.

Withers, Robert E. *Autobiography of an Octogenarian*. Roanoke, Va.: Stone, 1907.

Wood, William N. *Reminiscences of Big I*. Edited by Bell I. Wiley. Jackson, Tenn.: McCowat-Mercer, 1956.

Zettler, Berrien M. *War Stories and School-day Incidents for the Children*. New York: Neale, 1912.

FEDERAL

Adams, Charles F. *Charles Francis Adams, 1835–1915: An Autobiography*. New York: Russell & Russell, 1968.

———— et al. *A Cycle of Adams Letters, 1861–1865*. Edited by Worthington Chauncey Ford. 2 vols. Boston: Houghton, Mifflin, 1920.

Adams, Ida Bright, ed. "The Civil War Letters of James Rush Holmes." *Western Pennsylvania Historical Magazine* 44 (1961): 105–27.

Adams, John Ripley. *Memorials and Letters of Rev. John R. Adams, Chaplain of the Fifth Maine*. Cambridge, Mass.: University Press, 1890.

Averell, William W. *Ten Years in the Saddle: The Memoir of William Woods Averell, 1851–1862*. Edited by Edward K. Eckert and Nicholas J. Amato. San Rafael, Calif.: Presidio, 1978.

Bassett, M. H. *From Bull Run to Bristow Station*. St. Paul, Minn.: North Central, 1964.

Bennett, Edwin C. *Musket and Sword; or, Camp, March, and Firing Line in the Army of the Potomac*. Boston: Coburn, 1900.

Blake, Henry N. *Three Years in the Army of the Potomac*. Boston: Lee & Shepard, 1865.

Campbell, Robert. "Pioneer Memories of the War Days in 1861–1865." *Michigan Historical Collections* 30 (1906): 567–72.

"Captain Samuel A. Craig's Memoirs of Civil War and Reconstruction." *Western Pennsylvania Historical Magazine* 13 (1930): 215–36.

"Civil War Letters of Amory K. Allen." *Indiana Magazine of History* 31 (1935): 338–86.

"Civil War Letters of Samuel S. Partridge of the 'Rochester Regiment' [13th New York Infantry]." *Rochester Historical Society Publications* 22 (1944): 77–90.

Coffin, Charles C. *Stories of Our Soldiers: War Reminiscences*. Boston: Journal Newspaper, 1893.

Conwell, Russell H. *Magnolia Journey: A Union Veteran Revisits the Former Confederate States*. Edited by Joseph C. Carter. University: University of Alabama Press, 1974.

Cook, Frederick N. *Cook's War Journal*. New York: privately issued, ca. 1861.

Corcoran, Michael. *The Captivity of General Corcoran . . . the Hero of Bull Run*. Philadelphia: Barclay, 1862.

Cronin, David E. *The Evolution of a Life*. New York: S. W. Green's Son, 1884.

Crotty, D. G. *Four Years Campaigning in the Army of the Potomac*. Grand Rapids, Mich.: Dygert Brothers, 1874.

Custer, George A. *Custer in the Civil War: His Unfinished Memoirs*. Edited by John M. Carroll. San Rafael, Calif.: Presidio, 1977.

DeTrobriand, Regis. *Four Years with the Army of the Potomac*. Boston: Ticknor, 1889.

Doster, William E. *Lincoln and Episodes of the Civil War*. New York: G. P. Putnam's Sons, 1915.

Dwight, Wilder. *Life and Letters of Wilder Dwight, Lieut.-Col. Second Mass. Inf. Vols.* Boston: Little, Brown, 1891.

Eaton, James R. *Sixteen Years on the Dark Blue Sea, Four Years with the Army of the Potomac*. Indianapolis: privately issued, 1894.

Elderkin, James D. *Biographical Sketches and Anecdotes of a Soldier of Three Wars*. Detroit: privately issued, 1899.

Finch, George M. "The Boys of '61." *G.A.R. War Papers: Papers Read before . . . Post No. 401* (1891): 237–63.

Faller, Leo W., and John I. Faller. *Dear Folks at Home: The Civil War Letters of Leo W. and John I. Faller*. Edited by Milton E. Flower. Carlisle, Pa.: Cumberland County Historical Society, 1963.

Favill, Josiah M. *The Diary of a Young Officer Serving with the Armies of the United States during the War of the Rebellion*. Chicago: R. R. Donnelley & Sons, 1909.

Franklin, William B. "The First Great Crime of the War." In *Annals of the War, Written by Leading Participants, North and South*, 72–81. Philadelphia: Times Publishing, 1879.

Fry, James B. *Military Miscellanies*. New York: Brentano's, 1889.

Gunnison, Elisha N. *Our Stars for the Army of the Potomac*. Philadelphia: Ringwalt & Brown, 1863.

Harrer, William. *With Drum and Gun in '61*. Greenville, Pa.: Beaver Printing, 1908.

Haupt, Herman. *Reminiscences of General Herman Haupt*. Milwaukee: Wright & Joys, 1901.

Hawley, Joseph R. *Major General Joseph R. Hawley . . . Civil War Military Letters*. Edited by Albert D. Putnam. Hartford: Connecticut Civil War Centennial Commission, 1964.

Haydon, Charles B. *For Country, Cause, & Leader: The Civil War Journal of Charles B. Haydon*. Edited by Stephen W. Sears. New York: Ticknor & Fields, 1993.

Hill, A. F. *Our Boys: The Personal Experiences of a Soldier in the Army of the Potomac*. Philadelphia: John E. Potter, 1864.

Hitchcock, Ethan A. *Fifty Years in Camp and Field: Diary of Major-General Ethan Allen Hitchcock, U.S.A.* Edited by W. A. Croffut. New York: G. P. Putnam's Sons, 1909.

Holzhueter, John O., ed. "William Wallace's Civil War Letters: The Virginia Campaign." *Wisconsin Magazine of History* 57 (1973): 28–59.

Howard, Oliver Otis. *Autobiography of Oliver Otis Howard, Major General, United States Army*. 2 vols. New York: Baker & Taylor, 1907.

Hunter, David. *Report of the Military Service of General David Hunter, U.S. A., during the War of the Rebellion. . . .* Edited by Moses H. Hunter. New York: D. Van Nostrand, 1892.

Janeski, Paul, comp. *A Civil War Soldier's Last Letters*. New York: Vantage, 1975.

Johnson, Richard W. *A Soldier's Reminiscences in Peace and War*. Philadelphia: J. B. Lippincott, 1886.

Keyes, Erasmus D. *Fifty Years' Observations of Men and Events, Civil and Military*. New York: Charles Scribner's Sons, 1884.

Kingsbury, Allen A. *The Hero of Medfield: Containing the Journals and Letters of Allen Alonzo Kingsbury*. Boston: John M. Hewes, 1862.

Kinkaid, Thomas H. C. *When We Were Boys in Blue, 1861–1865*. New York: privately issued, 1903.

Koempel, Phillip. *Phil Koempel's Diary, 1861–1865*. N.p.: privately issued, ca. 1925.

Livermore, Thomas L. *Days and Events, 1860–1866*. Boston: Houghton Mifflin, 1920.

Longacre, Edward G., ed. "'Indeed We Did Fight': A Soldier's Letters Describe the First Minnesota Regiment before and during the First Battle of Bull Run." *Minnesota History* 47 (1980): 63–70.

———. "An Ohio Brigadier at Bull Run: Letters of Robert C. Schenck, July 1861." *Manuscripts* 33 (1981): 21–32.

Lusk, William T. *War Letters of William Thompson Lusk*. New York: privately issued, 1911.

Lyman, Theodore. *Meade's Headquarters, 1863–1865: Letters of Colonel Theodore Lyman from the Wilderness to Appomattox*. Edited by George R. Agassiz. Boston: Atlantic Monthly, 1922.

Marshall, Jeffery D., ed. *A War of the People: Vermont Civil War Letters*. Hanover, N.H.: University Press of New England, 1999.

McAllister, Robert. *The Civil War Letters of General Robert McAllister*. Edited by James I. Robertson, Jr. New Brunswick, N.J.: Rutgers University Press, 1965.

McClellan, George B. *McClellan's Own Story: The War for the Union*. New York: Charles L. Webster, 1887.

———. *The Mexican War Diary of George B. McClellan*. Edited by William Starr Myers. Princeton, N.J.: Princeton University Press, 1917.

McCrea, Tully. *Dear Belle: Letters from a Cadet & Officer to His Sweetheart, 1858–1865*. Edited by Catherine Crary. Middletown, Conn.: Wesleyan University Press, 1965.

Merrell, W. H. *Five Months in Rebeldom; or, Notes from the Diary of a Bull Run Prisoner, at Richmond*. Rochester, N.Y.: Adams & Dabney, 1862.

Metcalf, Lewis H. "'So Eager Were We All. . . .'" *American Heritage* 16 (June 1965): 33–41.

Morse, Charles F. *Letters Written during the Civil War, 1861–1865*. Boston: T. R. Marvin & Son, 1898.

Murphy, Charles J. *Reminiscences of the War of the Rebellion*. New York: F. J. Flicker, 1882.

Peck, George B. *Reminiscences of the War of the Rebellion*. Providence, R.I.: Providence Press, 1884.

Quint, Alonzo H. *The Potomac and the Rapidan: Army Notes*. Boston: Crosby & Nichols, 1864.

Rhodes, Elisha H. *All for the Union: The Civil War Diary and Letters of Elisha Hunt Rhodes*. Edited by Robert Hunt Rhodes and Geoffrey C. Ward. New York: Orion Books, 1985.

Robinson, Charles. "My Experiences in the Civil War." *Michigan History Magazine* 24 (1940): 23–50.

Roelker, William G., ed. "Civil War Letters of William Ames, from Brown University to Bull Run." *Rhode Island Historical Society Collections* 33 (1940): 73–92; 34 (1941): 5–24.

Scott, Winfield. *Memoirs of Lieut.-General Scott. Ll. D., Written by Himself*. 2 vols. New York: Sheldon, 1864.

Shannon, James H. "A Few Incidents and Reminiscences of the Civil War." *War Papers: Read before the Commandery of the State of Maine, Military Order of the Loyal Legion of the United States* 4 (1915): 321–39.

Sherman, William Tecumseh. *Home Letters of General Sherman*. Edited by M. A. DeWolfe Howe. New York: Charles Scribner's Sons, 1909.

———. *Memoirs of Gen. W. T. Sherman, Written by Himself*. 2 vols. New York: Charles L. Webster, 1891.

Sherman, William Tecumseh, and John Sherman. *The Sherman Letters: Correspondences Between General Sherman and Senator Sherman from 1837 to 1891.* Edited by Rachel S. Thorndike. New York: Da Capo, 1969.

Small, Harold Adams, ed. *The Road to Richmond: The Civil War Memoirs of Maj. Abner R. Small of the 16th Maine Vols., with His Diary as a Prisoner of War.* Berkeley: University of California Press, 1957.

Smith, Franklin. *The Mexican War Journal of Captain Franklin Smith.* Edited by Joseph E. Chance. Jackson: University Press of Mississippi, 1991.

Stevens, John H. *John H. Stevens: Civil War Diary.* Edited by Gladys Stuart and Adelbert M. Jakeman, Jr. Acton, Me.: privately issued, 1997.

Stewart, A. M. *Camp, March, and Battle-field; or, Three Years and a Half with the Army of the Potomac.* Philadelphia: James B. Rodgers, 1865.

Stone, Charles P. "Washington in 1861." *Magazine of American History* 12 (1884): 56–61.

Strother, David H. "Personal Recollections of the War, by a Virginian: Patterson's Campaign." *Harper's New Monthly Magazine* 33 (1866): 137–60.

Swift, Lester L., ed. "'Bully for the First Connecticut': The Recollections of a Three-Month Volunteer." *Lincoln Herald* 67 (1965): 72–82.

Townsend, E. D. *Anecdotes of the Civil War in the United States.* New York: D. Appleton, 1884.

Tuttle, James Gilmore. "Recollections of the Civil War." *Michigan History* 31 (1947): 287–300.

Tyler, Daniel. *Daniel Tyler: A Memorial Volume Containing His Autobiography and War Record.* Edited by Donald G. Mitchell. New Haven, Conn.: Tuttle, Morehouse, & Taylor, 1883.

Urban, John W. *Battle Field and Prison Pen.* Lancaster, Pa.: Edgewood, 1882.

Wallace, Lew. *Lew Wallace: An Autobiography.* 2 vols. New York: Harper & Brothers, 1906.

Wallace, Robert C. *A Few Memories of a Long Life.* Helena, Mont.: privately issued, 1916.

Westervelt, William B. *Lights and Shadows of Army Life, as Seen by a Private Soldier.* Marlboro, N.Y.: C. H. Cochrane, 1886.

Whitman, George W. *Civil War Letters of George Washington Whitman.* Edited by Jerome M. Loving. Durham, N.C.: Duke University Press, 1975.

Willcox, Orlando B. *Forgotten Valor: The Memoirs, Journals, & Civil War Letters of Orlando B. Willcox.* Edited by Robert Garth Scott. Kent, Ohio: Kent State University Press, 1999.

Wilson. James Harrison. *Under the Old Flag: Recollections of Military Operations in the War for the Union. . . .* 2 vols. New York: D. Appleton, 1912.

Withington, William H. *The First Call of the Civil War: Personal Recollections of Michigan's Response.* Jackson, Mich.: privately issued, ca. 1901.

Woodruff, Thomas M. "Early War Days in the Nation's Capital." *Glimpses of the Nation's Struggle: A Series of Papers Read before the Minnesota Commandery of the Military Order of the Loyal Legion of the United States* 3 (1893): 87–105.

CIVILIANS, NORTH AND SOUTH

Akin, Warren. *Letters of Warren Akin, Confederate Congressman.* Edited by Bell I. Wiley. Athens: University of Georgia Press, 1959.

Bigelow, John. *Retrospections of an Active Life.* 4 vols. New York: Baker & Taylor, 1909.

Boyd, Isabelle. *Belle Boyd in Camp and Prison, Written by Herself.* New York: Blelock, 1865.

Chase, Salmon P. *Inside Lincoln's Cabinet: The Civil War Diaries of Salmon P. Chase.* Edited by David Donald. New York: Longmans, Green, 1954.

Chesnut, Mary Boykin. *Mary Chesnut's Civil War.* Edited by C. Vann Woodward. New Haven, Conn.: Yale University Press, 1981.

Clay-Clopton, Virginia. *A Belle of the Fifties: Memoirs of Mrs. Clay, of Alabama, Covering Social and Political Life in Washington and the South, 1853–66.* Edited by Ada Sterling. New York: Doubleday, Page, 1905.

Coffin, Charles Carleton. *Drum-beat of the Nation: The First Period of the War of the Rebellion. . . .* New York: Harper & Brothers, 1888.

———. *Four Years of Fighting: A Volume of Personal Observations with the Army and Navy.* Boston: Ticknor & Fields, 1866.

Daly, Maria Lydig. *Diary of a Union Lady, 1861–1865.* Edited by Harold Earl Hammond. New York: Funk & Wagnalls, 1962.

Davis, Jefferson. *The Rise and Fall of the Confederate Government.* 1881. Reprint, 2 vols. in 1, New York: Barnes & Noble, 2010.

Drell, Muriel Bernitt, ed. "Letters by Richard Smith of the *Cincinnati Gazette.*" *Mississippi Valley Historical Review* 26 (1940): 535–54.

Ely, Alfred. *Journal of Alfred Ely, a Prisoner of War in Richmond.* Edited by Charles Lanman. New York: D. Appleton, 1862.

Fisher, Sidney G. *A Philadelphia Perspective: The Diary of Sidney George Fisher Covering the Years 1834–1871.* Edited by Nicholas B. Wainwright. Philadelphia: Historical Society of Pennsylvania, 1967.

Greenhow, Rose. *My Imprisonment and the First Year of Abolition Rule at Washington.* London: Richard Bentley, 1863.

Hancock, Harold B., ed. "The Civil War Diaries of Anna M. Ferris." *Delaware History* 9 (1961): 221–64.

Harrison, Constance Cary. *Recollections Grave and Gay.* New York: Charles Scribner's Sons, 1912.

———. "Virginia Scenes in '61." In *Battles and Leaders of the Civil War,* edited by Robert U. Johnson and Clarence C. Buel, 4 vols., 1:160–66. New York, 1887.

Harwell, Richard B., ed. "Louisiana Burge: The Diary of a Confederate College Girl." *Georgia Historical Quarterly* 37 (1952): 144–63.

Hunt, Gaillard. *Israel, Elihu, and Cadwallader Washburne: A Chapter in American Biography.* New York: Macmillan, 1925.

Jones, John Beauchamp. *A Rebel War Clerk's Diary at the Confederate States Capital.* 2 vols. Philadelphia: J. B. Lippincott, 1866.

Livermore, Mary A. *My Story of the War: A Woman's Narrative of Four Years' Personal Experience.* Hartford, Conn.: Worthington, 1888.

Longacre, Edward G., ed. "'Come home soon and dont delay': Letters from the Home Front, July, 1861." *Pennsylvania Magazine of History and Biography* 100 (1976): 395–406.

McDonald, Cornelia. *A Diary with Reminiscences of the War and Refugee Life in the Shenandoah Valley, 1860–1865.* Nashville, Tenn.: Cullom & Ghertner, 1934.

McGuire, Judith W. *Diary of a Southern Refugee, during the War, by a Lady of Virginia.* New York: E. J. Hale & Son, 1867.

Riddle, Albert Gallatin. *Recollections of War Times: Reminiscences of Men and Events in Washington, 1860–1865.* New York: G. P. Putnam's Sons, 1895.

Ruffin, Edmund. *The Diary of Edmund Ruffin: Volume II, The Years of Hope, April 1861–June 1863.* Edited by William K. Scarborough. Baton Rouge: Louisiana State University Press, 1977.

Russell, William Howard. *My Diary North and South.* Boston: T. O. H. P. Burnham, 1863.

———. *William Howard Russell's Civil War: Private Diary and Letters, 1861–1862.* Edited by Martin Crawford. Athens: University of Georgia Press, 1992.

Strong, George Templeton. *Diary of the Civil War, 1860–1865.* Edited by Allan Nevins. New York: Macmillan, 1962.

Villard, Henry. *Memoirs of Henry Villard, Journalist and Financier, 1835–1900.* 2 vols. New York: Da Capo, 1969.

Waring, Martha Galludet, and Mary Alston Waring, eds. "Notes and Documents: Some Observations of the Years 1860 and 1861." *Georgia Historical Quarterly* 15 (1931): 272–92.

Welles, Gideon. *Diary of Gideon Welles, Secretary of the Navy under Lincoln and Johnson.* 3 vols. Boston: Houghton Mifflin, 1911.

Wilson, William B. *A Leaf from the History of the Rebellion: Sketches of Events and Persons.* Philadelphia: privately issued, 1888.

Wise, John S. *The End of an Era.* Boston: Houghton, Mifflin, 1899.

Unit Histories

CONFEDERATE

Alexander, E. Porter. "Longstreet's Brigade." *Transactions of the Southern Historical Society* 2 (1875): 53–62.

Andrus, Michael J. *The Brooke, Fauquier, Loudoun, and Alexandria Artillery.* Lynchburg, Va.: H. E. Howard, 1990.

Barclay, Alexander T. "The Liberty Hall Volunteers from Lexington to Manassas." *Washington and Lee University Historical Papers* 6 (1904): 123–36.

Bean, W. G. *The Liberty Hall Volunteers: Stonewall's College Boys.* Charlottesville: University Press of Virginia, 1964.

Bell, Robert T. *11th Virginia Infantry*. Lynchburg, Va.: H. E. Howard, 1985.

Blackburn, J. K. P. "Reminiscences of the Terry Rangers." *Southwestern Historical Quarterly* 22 (1918): 38–77.

Blackford, Charles M., Jr. *Annals of the Lynchburg Home Guard*. Lynchburg, Va.: John W. Rohr, 1891.

Brown, Maud M. *The University Greys: Company A, Eleventh Mississippi Regiment, Army of Northern Virginia, 1861–1865*. Richmond, Va.: Garrett & Massie, 1940.

Carmichael, Peter S. *The Purcell, Crenshaw and Letcher Artillery*. Lynchburg, Va.: H. E. Howard, 1990.

Chamberlayne, Edwin H. *War History and Roll of the Richmond Fayette Artillery*. Richmond, Va.: Everett Waddey, 1883.

Chapman, J. A. "The 4th Alabama Regiment." *Confederate Veteran* 30 (1922): 197.

Clark, Walter, ed. *Histories of the Several Regiments and Battalions from North Carolina in the Great War, 1861–'65*. . . . 5 vols. Goldsboro and Raleigh, N.C.: E. M. Uzzell, 1901.

Coles, Robert T. *From Huntsville to Appomattox: R. T. Coles's History of [the] 4th Regiment, Alabama Volunteer Infantry, C.S.A., Army of Northern Virginia*. Edited by Jeffrey D. Stocker. Knoxville: University of Tennessee Press, 1996.

Conrad, Daniel B. "With Stonewall Jackson before Bull Run." *Magazine of History* 9 (1909): 148–52.

Cooper, Norman V. "How They Went to War: An Alabama Brigade in 1861–62." *Alabama Review* 24 (1971): 17–50.

Daniel, Frederick S. *Richmond Howitzers in the War: Four Years Campaigning with the Army of Northern Virginia*. Richmond, Va.: privately issued, 1896.

De Laney, Richard W., and Marie E. Bowery, eds. *The Seventeenth Virginia Volunteer Infantry Regiment, C.S.A.* Washington D.C.: American Printing, ca. 1961.

Dickert, D. Augustus. *History of Kershaw's Brigade*. . . . Newberry, S. C.: E. H. Aull, 1899.

Divine, John E. *8th Virginia Infantry*. Lynchburg, Va.: H. E. Howard, 1983.

Donnelly, Ralph W. "District of Columbia Confederates." *Military Affairs* 23 (1959–60): 207–208.

Douglas, Henry Kyd. "Stonewall Jackson and His Men." In *Annals of the War, Written by Leading Participants, North and South*, 642–53. Philadelphia: Times Publishing, 1879.

Driver, Robert J., Jr. *The 1st and 2nd Rockbridge Artillery*. Lynchburg, Va.: H. E. Howard, 1987.

———. *1st Virginia Cavalry*. Lynchburg, Va.: H. E. Howard, 1991.

———. *The Staunton Artillery—McClanahan's Battery*. Lynchburg, Va.: H. E. Howard, 1988.

Driver, Robert J., Jr., and H. E. Howard. *2nd Virginia Cavalry*. Lynchburg, Va.: H. E. Howard, 1995.

Fields, Frank E. *28th Virginia Infantry*. Lynchburg, Va.: H. E. Howard, 1985.

Fishburne, Clement D. "Historical Sketch of the Rockbridge Artillery, C.S.A." *Southern Historical Society Papers* 23 (1895): 98–158.

Fonerden, C. A. *A Brief History of the Military Career of Carpenter's Battery.* New Market, Va.: Henkel, 1911.

"The Fourth Regiment of South Carolina Confederate Infantry." *Maine Bugle* 4 (1897): 111–31.

Frye, Dennis E. *2nd Virginia Infantry.* Lynchburg, Va.: H. E. Howard, 1984.

Gingles, Violet. "Saline Country, Arkansas First Infantry Volunteers, C.S.A." *Arkansas Historical Quarterly* 18 (1959): 190–98.

Goldsborough, W. W. *The Maryland Line in the Confederate States Army.* Baltimore: Kelly, Piet, 1869.

Gunn, Ralph White. *24th Virginia Infantry.* Lynchburg, Va.: H. E. Howard, 1987.

Hammock, John C. *With Honor Untarnished: The Story of the First Arkansas Infantry Regiment, Confederate States Army.* Little Rock: Pioneer, 1961.

Henderson, Lindsey P. *The Oglethorpe Light Infantry: A Military History.* Savannah, Ga.: Civil War Centennial Commission of Savannah and Chatham County, 1961.

Herbert, Arthur. *Sketches and Incidents of Movement of the Seventeenth Virginia Infantry.* Washington, D.C.: privately issued, ca. 1909.

History of the Seventeenth Virginia Infantry, C.S.A. Baltimore: Kelly, Piet, 1870.

Hoyt, James A. *The Palmetto Riflemen: Co. B, Fourth Regiment S.C. Vols., Co. C, Palmetto Sharp Shooters. . . .* Greenville, S.C.: Hoyt & Keys, 1886.

Hudson, James G. "A Story of Company D, 4th Alabama Infantry Regiment, C.S.A." *Alabama Historical Quarterly* 23 (1961): 139–79.

Iobst, Richard W. *The Bloody Sixth: The Sixth North Carolina Regiment, Confederate States of America.* Raleigh: North Carolina Confederate Centennial Commission, 1965.

Irby, Richard. *Historical Sketch of the Nottoway Grays, Afterwards Company G, Eighteenth Virginia Regiment, Army of Northern Virginia.* Richmond, Va.: J. W. Fergusson & Son, 1878.

Johnson, Bradley T. "Memoir of First Maryland Regiment." *Southern Historical Society Papers* 9 (1881): 344–53, 481–88.

Jones, Terry L. *Lee's Tigers: The Louisiana Infantry in the Army of Northern Virginia.* Baton Rouge: Louisiana State University Press, 1987.

Jordan, Ervin L. *19th Virginia Infantry.* Lynchburg, Va.: H. E. Howard, 1987.

Kleese, Richard B. *49th Virginia Infantry.* Appomattox, Va.: H. E. Howard, 2002.

Lamar Rifles: A History of Company G, Eleventh Mississippi Regiment, C.S.A. Roanoke, Va.: Stone Printing, 1903.

Loehr, Charles T. *War History of the Old First Virginia Infantry Regiment, Army of Northern Virginia.* Richmond, Va.: Wm. Ellis Jones, 1884.

Longacre, Edward G. *Lee's Cavalrymen: A History of the Mounted Forces of the Army of Northern Virginia, 1861–1865.* Mechanicsburg, Pa.: Stackpole, 2002.

Macon, T. J. *Reminiscences of the First Company of Richmond Howitzers.* Richmond, Va.: Whittet & Shepperson, n.d.

McDaniel, J. J. *Diary of Battles, Marches, and Incidents of the Seventh S.C. Regiment.* N.p.: privately issued, n.d.

McRae, James C., and Charles M. Busbee. "The 'Bloody Fifth [North Carolina Infantry].'" *Southland* 2 (1898): 180–89.

Moore, Alison. *The Louisiana Tigers; or, the Two Louisiana Brigades of the Army of Northern Virginia, 1861–1865.* Baton Rouge: Ortlieb, 1961.

Moore, Edward A. *The Story of A Cannoneer under Stonewall Jackson. . . .* New York: Neale, 1907.

Moore, Robert H., II. *Miscellaneous Disbanded Virginia Light Artillery.* Lynchburg, Va.: H. E. Howard, 1997.

———. *The Richmond Fayette, Hampden, Thomas, and Blount's Lynchburg Artillery.* Lynchburg, Va.: H. E. Howard, 1991.

Murphy, Terence V. *10th Virginia Infantry.* Lynchburg, Va.: H. E. Howard, 1989.

Owen, William Miller. *In Camp and Battle with the Washington Artillery of New Orleans.* Boston: Ticknor, 1885.

Pate, Alma H., ed. "A Story of Company D, 4th Alabama Infantry Regiment, C.S.A., by James G. Hudson." *Alabama Historical Quarterly* 23 (1961): 139–79.

Record of the Lynchburg Home Guard: Organized November 8, 1859, Mustered into the C.S. Service, April 24, 1861. Lynchburg, Va.: Bell, Browne, 1877.

Reid, Jesse Walton. *History of the Fourth Regiment of S.C. Volunteers, from the Commencement of the War until Lee's Surrender.* Greenville, S.C.: Shannon, 1892.

Reidenbaugh, Lowell. *27th Virginia Infantry.* Lynchburg, Va.: H. E. Howard, 1993.

———. *33rd Virginia Infantry.* Lynchburg, Va.: H. E. Howard, 1987.

Richmond Howitzers in the War: Four Years Campaigning with the Army of Northern Virginia, by a Member of the Company. Richmond, Va.: privately issued, 1891.

Riggs, David F. *7th Virginia Infantry.* Lynchburg, Va.: H. E. Howard, 1982.

———. *13th Virginia Infantry.* Lynchburg, Va.: H. E. Howard, 1988.

Robertson, James I., Jr. *18th Virginia Infantry.* Lynchburg, Va.: H. E. Howard, 1984.

———. "The Right Arm of Lee and Jackson." *Civil War History* 3 (1957): 423–34.

———. *The Stonewall Brigade.* Baton Rouge: Louisiana State University Press, 1963.

Scott, John. "The Black Horse Cavalry." In *Annals of the War, Written by Leading Participants, North and South,* 590–613. Philadelphia: Times Publishing, 1879.

Sketch of Page's Battery, or Morris Artillery, 2d Corps, Army [of] *Northern Virginia*. New York: Thomas Smeltzer, 1885.

Stiles, Kenneth L. *4th Virginia Cavalry*. Lynchburg, Va.: H. E. Howard, 1985.

Strickler, Givens B. "Liberty Hall Volunteers, Company I, Fourth Va. Infantry." *Washington and Lee University Historical Papers* 6 (1904): 111–22.

Stubbs, Steven H. *Duty, Honor, Valor: The Story of the Eleventh Mississippi Infantry Regiment*. Philadelphia, Miss.: privately issued, 2000.

Sturkey, O. Lee. *A History of the Hampton Legion Infantry*. Wilmington, N.C.: Broadfoot, 2009.

Thompson, J. M. *Reminiscences of Autauga Rifles [6th Alabama Infantry]*. Autaugaville, Ala.: privately issued, ca. 1880.

Varner, C. P. "Third South Carolina Regiment." *Confederate Veteran* 18 (1910): 520.

Wallace, Lee A. *1st Virginia Infantry*. Lynchburg, Va.: H. E. Howard, 1984.

———. *4th Virginia Infantry*. Lynchburg, Va.: H. E. Howard, 1986.

———. *5th Virginia Infantry*. Lynchburg, Va.: H. E. Howard, 1988.

———. *17th Virginia Infantry*. Lynchburg, Va.: H. E. Howard, 1990.

Wellman, Manly Wade. *Rebel Boast: First at Bethel—Last at Appomattox*. New York: Henry Holt, 1956.

Wilkinson, Warren, and Steven E. Woodworth. *A Scythe of Fire: A Civil War Story of the Eighth Georgia Infantry Regiment*. New York: William Morrow, 2002.

Wise, George. *History of the Seventeenth Virginia, C.S.A.* Baltimore: Kelly, Piet, 1870.

Wise, Jennings Cropper. *The Long Arm of Lee: The History of the Artillery of the Army of Northern Virginia*. New York: Oxford University Press, 1959.

Wyckoff, Mac. *A History of the 2nd South Carolina Infantry, 1861–1865*. Fredericksburg, Va.: Sergeant Kirkland's Museum and Historical Society, 1994.

———. *A History of the 3rd South Carolina Infantry Regiment: Lee's Reliables*. Wilmington, N.C.: Broadfoot, 2009.

York, Richard W. "The 'Old Third' Brigade and the Death of General Bee." *Our Living and Our Dead* 1 (1875): 561–66.

FEDERAL

Abbott, Stephen G. *The First Regiment New Hampshire Volunteers in the Great Rebellion*. Keene, N.H.: Sentinel Printing, 1890.

Aldrich, Thomas M. *The History of Battery A, First Regiment Rhode Island Light Artillery*. Providence, R.I.: Snow & Farnham, 1904.

Baquet, Camille. *History of the First Brigade, New Jersey Volunteers, from 1861 to 1865*. Trenton, N.J.: MacCrellish & Quigley, 1910.

Bates, Samuel P. *History of Pennsylvania Volunteers, 1861–5*. 5 vols. Harrisburg, Pa.: B. Singerly, 1869.

Battillo, Anthony. "The Red-Legged Devils from Brooklyn." *Civil War Times Illustrated* 10 (February 1972): 10–16.

Bicknell, George W. *History of the Fifth Regiment Maine Volunteers.* Portland, Me.: Hall L. Davis, 1871.

Bilby, Joseph G. *The Irish Brigade in the Civil War: The 69th New York and Other Irish Regiments of the Army of the Potomac.* Conshohocken, Pa.: Combined, 1998.

Bilby, Joseph G., and William C. Goble. *"Remember You Are Jerseymen": A Military History of New Jersey's Troops in the Civil War.* Hightstown, N.J.: Longstreet House, 1998.

Boyce, C. W. *A Brief History of the Twenty-Eighth Regiment New York State Volunteers.* Buffalo, N.Y.: privately issued, ca. 1896.

Bryant, Edwin E. *History of the third Regiment of Wisconsin Veteran Volunteer Infantry, 1861–1865.* Madison, Wisc.: Democrat Printing, 1891.

Caulkins, Charles A. *Camp Sketches of Life in the Old Nineteenth [New York Volunteers].* Auburn, N.Y.: privately issued, 1862.

Chase, Peter S. *Reunion Greeting, Together with an Historical Sketch . . . of the Members of Co. I, 2d Reg., Vt. Vols.* Brattleboro, Vt.: Phoenix Printing Office, 1891.

Clarke, Charles H. *History of Company F, 1st Regiment, R.I. Volunteers, during the Spring and Summer of 1861.* Newport, R.I.: B. W. Pearce, 1891.

Clowes, Walter F. *The Detroit Light Guard: A Complete Record of This Organization from Its Foundation to the Present Day.* Detroit: John F. Eby, 1900.

Conyngham, D. P. *The Irish Brigade and Its Campaigns.* New York: William McSorley, 1869.

Cowdin, Robert. *Gen. Cowdin and the First Massachusetts Regiment of Volunteers.* Boston: J. E. Farwell, 1864.

Cudworth, Warren H. *History of the First Regiment [Massachusetts Volunteers] from the 25th of May 1861, to the 25th of May 1864. . . .* Boston: Walker, Fuller, 1866.

Cummings, Harrison H. *Personal Reminiscences of Company E, New York Fire Zouaves. . . .* Malden, Mass.: J. Gould Tilden, 1886.

Curtis, Newton Martin. *From Bull Run to Chancellorsville: The Story of the Sixteenth New York Infantry.* New York: G. P. Putnam's Sons, 1906.

Damon, Herbert C. *History of the Milwaukee Light Guard.* Milwaukee: Sentinel, 1875.

Darling, Charles B., comp. *Historical Sketch of the First Regiment Infantry, Massachusetts Volunteer Militia.* Boston: Alfred Mudge & Sons, 1890.

Destler, Chester M., ed. "The Second Michigan Volunteer Infantry Joins the Army of the Potomac." *Michigan History* 41 (1957): 385–412.

Dodd, Ira Seymour. "The Making of a Regiment: What a Service of Seven Months Did for a Troop of Raw Volunteers." *McClure's Magazine* 9 (1897): 1031–44.

Dowley, M. Francis. *History and Honorary Roll of the Twelfth Regiment Infantry, N.G.S.N.Y. [National Guard, State of New York].* New York: T. Farrell & Son, 1869.

Dyer, Alexander B. "The Fourth Regiment of Artillery." In Theophilus F. Rodenbough and William L. Haskin, eds., *The Army of the United States: Historical Sketches of Staff and Line . . .*, 351–75. New York: Maynard, Merrill, 1896.

Fairchild, Charles B., comp. *History of the 27th Regiment N.Y. Vols.* Binghamton, N.Y.: Carl & Matthews, 1888.

Fitzgerald, James. "The Sixty-Ninth Regiment, New York City." *Journal of the American Irish Historical Society* 9 (1910): 161–82.

Francis, Augustus T., comp. *History of the 71st Regiment, N.G., N.Y. [National Guard, New York].* New York: Eastman, 1919.

Gaff, Alan D. *If This Is War: A History of the Campaign of Bull's Run by the Wisconsin Regiment Thereafter Known as the Ragged Ass Second.* Dayton, Ohio: Morningside Bookshop, 1991.

Gordon, George H. *Brook Farm to Cedar Mountain in the War of the Great Rebellion, 1861–62: . . . A History of the Second Massachusetts Regiment.* Boston: James R. Osgood, 1883.

———. *The Organization and Early History of the Second Mass. Regiment of Infantry.* Boston: Rockwell & Churchill, 1873.

Gould, John M. *History of the First—Tenth—Twenty-Ninth Maine Regiment[s].* Portland, Me.: Stephen Berry, 1871.

Hall, Henry, and James Hall. *Cayuga in the Field: A Record of the 19th N.Y. Volunteers, All the Batteries of the 3d New York Artillery, and 75th New York Volunteers.* Auburn, N.Y.: Truair, Smith, 1873.

Haskin, William L., comp. *The History of the First Regiment of Artillery, from Its Organization in 1821, to January 1st, 1876.* Portland, Me.: B. Thurston, 1879.

Haynes, Martin A., comp. *History of the Second Regiment New Hampshire Volunteers.* Manchester, N.H.: Charles F. Livingston, 1865.

———, comp. *Muster Out Roll of the Second New Hampshire Regiment in the War of the Rebellion.* Lakeport, N.H.: privately issued, 1917.

Hinkley, Julian W. *A Narrative of Service with the Third Wisconsin Infantry.* Madison: Wisconsin History Commission, 1912.

History of the First Regiment Minnesota Volunteer Infantry, 1861–1864. Stillwater, Minn.: Easton & Masterman, 1916.

History of the Richardson Light Guard of Wakefield, Mass., 1851–1901. Wakefield, Mass.: Citizen & Banner Office, 1901.

Holcombe, R. I. *History of the First Regiment Minnesota Volunteer Infantry, 1861–1865.* Stillwater, Minn.: Easton & Masterman, 1916.

Hopper, George C. *First Michigan Infantry: Three Months and Three Years.* Coldwater, Mich.: Courier Printing, 1891.

Hutchinson, Gustavus B., comp. *A Narrative of the Formation and Services of the Eleventh Massachusetts Volunteers, from April 15, 1861, to July 14, 1865.* Boston: Alfred Mudge & Son, 1893.

Imholte, John Quinn. *The First Volunteers: History of the First Minnesota Volunteer Regiment, 1861–1865.* Minneapolis: Ross & Haines, 1963.

Ingraham, Charles A. *Elmer E. Ellsworth and the Zouaves of '61.* Chicago: University of Chicago Press, 1925.

Jones, Paul. *The Irish Brigade.* Washington, D.C.: Robert B. Luce, 1969.

Kern, Albert, comp. *History of the First Regiment Ohio Volunteer Infantry in the Civil War, 1861–1865*. Dayton, Ohio: privately issued, 1918.

Keyes, Dwight W. "1861—The First Wisconsin Infantry, U.S.V., Its Organization and Move to the Front." *War Papers: Read before the Commandery of the State of Wisconsin, Military Order of the Loyal Legion of the United States* 3 (1903): 90–101.

Locke, William Henry. *The Story of the Regiment [11th Pennsylvania Volunteers]*. New York: James Miller, 1872.

Longacre, Edward G. *Lincoln's Cavalrymen: A History of the Mounted Forces of the Army of the Potomac, 1861–1865*. Mechanicsburg, Pa.: Stackpole, 2000.

Lucke, Jerome B. *History of the New Haven Grays*. New Haven, Conn.: Tuttle, Morehouse, & Taylor, 1876.

McAfee, Michael J. "69th Regiment, New York State Militia: The National Cadets—1861." *Military Images* 11 (March–April 1990): 26–27.

Meagher, Thomas F. *The Last Days of the 69th [New York Militia] in Virginia: A Narrative in Three Parts*. New York: Office of the Irish-American, 1861.

Moe, Richard. *The Last Full Measure: The Life and Death of the First Minnesota Volunteers*. New York: Henry Holt, 1993.

Mundy, James H. *Second to None: The Story of the 2nd Maine Volunteers, "The Bangor Regiment."* Scarborough, Me.: Harp, 1992.

Naisawald, L. Van Loan. *Grape and Canister: The Story of the Field Artillery of the Army of the Potomac, 1861–1865*. New York: Oxford University Press, 1960.

Niebaum, John H. *History of the Pittsburgh Washington Infantry, 102nd (Old 13th) Regiment, Pennsylvania Veteran Volunteers*. Pittsburgh: Burgum Printing, 1931.

Otis, George H. *The Second Wisconsin Infantry*. Edited by Alan D. Gaff. Dayton, Ohio: Morningside, 1984.

Owen, Charles W. *The First Michigan Infantry: Three Months and Three Years*. Quincy, Mich.: Quincy Herald Printing, 1903.

Petzold, Herman. *Memoirs of the Second Michigan Infantry*. N.p.: privately issued, 1897.

Quint, Alonzo H. *The Record of the Second Massachusetts Infantry, 1861–65*. Boston: James P. Walker, 1867.

Reese, Timothy J. *Sykes' Regular Infantry Division, 1861–1864: A History of Regular United States Infantry Operations in the Civil War's Eastern Theater*. Jefferson, N.C.: McFarland, 1990.

Rhodes, Elisha H. "The First Campaign of the Second Rhode Island Infantry." *Personal Narratives of the Battles of the Rebellion: Being Papers Read before the Rhode Island Soldiers' and Sailors' Historical Society*, 1st ser., no. 2. 1878.

Robinson, Frank T. *History of the Fifth Regiment, M.V.M. [Massachusetts Volunteer Militia]*. Boston: W. F. Brown, 1879.

Rodenbough, Theophilus F., and William L. Haskin, eds. *The Army of the United States: Historical Sketches of Staff and Line. . . .* New York: Maynard, Merrill, 1896.

Roe, Alfred S. *The Fifth Regiment Massachusetts Volunteer Infantry in Its Three Tours of Duty, 1861, 1862–'63, 1864.* Worcester, Mass.: Blanchard, 1911.

Roehrenbeck, William J. *The Regiment That Saved the Capital.* New York: Thomas Yoseloff, 1961.

Schaadt, James L. "The Allen Infantry in 1861." *Pennsylvania-German* 12 (1911): 149–62.

———. "Company I, First Regiment Pennsylvania Volunteers: A Memoir of Its Service for the Union in 1861." *Penn Germania* 13 (1912): 538–50.

Schneider, Frederick. *Incidental History of the Flags and Color Guard of the Second Michigan Veteran Volunteer Infantry, 1861–5.* Lansing, Mich.: M. E. Gardner, 1905.

Searles, J. N. "The First Minnesota Volunteer Infantry." *Glimpses of the Nation's Struggle: A Series of Papers Read before the Minnesota Commandery of the Military Order of the Loyal Legion of the United States* 2 (1890): 80–113.

Smith, George B. "Formation and Service of the First Regiment Rhode Island Detached Militia, April 17th–Aug. 2nd, 1861." *Bulletin of the Newport Historical Society* 58 (1926): 14–29.

Smith, James E. *A Famous Battery and Its Campaigns, 1861–'64.* Washington, D.C.: W. H. Lowdermilk, 1892.

A Souvenir History of the Charlestown City Guard, Company "H," 5th Regiment Infantry, M. V. M. [Massachusetts Volunteer Militia]. Boston: Hanover Printing, 1897.

Stone, Edwin M. *First Regiment Rhode Island Detached Militia.* Providence, R.I.: Providence, 1866.

Tevis, C. V. *The History of the Fighting Fourteenth.* New York: Brooklyn Eagle, 1911.

Thompson, William W. *Historical Sketch of the Sixteenth Regiment N.Y.S. [New York State] Volunteer Infantry, April, 1861–May, 1863.* Albany, N.Y.: Brandow, Barton, 1886.

Todd, William. *The Seventy-Ninth Highlanders New York Volunteers in the War of Rebellion, 1861–1865.* Albany, N.Y.: Brandow, Barton, 1886.

Wainwright, R. P. Page. "The First Regiment of Cavalry." In *The Army of the United States: Historical Sketches of Staff and Line . . . ,* edited by Theophilus F. Rodenbough and William L. Haskin, 153–72. New York: Maynard, Merrill, 1896.

Whittemore, Henry. *History of the Seventy-First Regiment N.G.S.N.Y. [National Guard, State of New York].* New York: Willis Mc Donald, 1886.

Williams, Isaiah T. *Address of Isaiah Thornton Williams on the Presentation of Colors to the Fifth Regiment of Maine Volunteers. . . .* New York: S. Bradford, 1862.

Williams, Newton H. *Michigan's First Regiment: Incidents, Marches, Battles, and Camp Life.* Detroit: privately issued, 1861.

Woodbury, Augustus. *A Narrative of the Campaign of the First Rhode Island Regiment, in the Spring and Summer of 1861.* Providence, R.I.: Sidney S. Rider, 1862.

———. *The Second Rhode Island Regiment: A Narrative of Military Operations. . . .* Providence, R.I.: Valpey, Angell, 1875.

Wray, William J. *History of the Twenty-Third Pennsylvania Volunteer Infantry: Birney's Zouaves. . . .* Philadelphia: privately issued, 1904.

Biographies

CONFEDERATE

Abbot, Haviland H. "General John D. Imboden." *West Virginia History* 21 (1960): 88–122.

Addey, Markinfield. *"Stonewall Jackson": The Life and Military Career of Thomas Jonathan Jackson, Lieutenant-General in the Confederate Army.* New York: Charles T. Evans, 1863.

Agnew, James B. "General Barnard Bee." *Civil War Times Illustrated* 14 (December 1975): 4–8, 44–47.

Anderson, Ellen Graham. "The Wounding and Hospital Care of William A. Anderson." *Virginia Magazine of History and Biography* 62 (1954): 205–207.

Anderson, J. H. *Notes on the Life of Stonewall Jackson and on His Campaigning in Virginia, 1861–1863.* London: Hugh Rees, 1904.

Arnold, Thomas J. *Early Life and Letters of General Thomas J. Jackson, "Stonewall" Jackson.* Chicago: Fleming H. Revell, 1916.

Basso, Hamilton. *Beauregard, the Great Creole.* New York: Charles Scribner's Sons, 1933.

Bean, W. G. *Stonewall's Man, Sandie Pendleton.* Chapel Hill: University of North Carolina Press, 1959.

Bradford, Gamaliel. *Confederate Portraits.* Boston: Houghton Mifflin, 1914.

Brown, R. Shepard. *Stringfellow of the Fourth.* New York: Crown, 1960.

Bushong, Millard K. *Old Jube: A Biography of Gen. Jubal A. Early.* Boyce, Va.: Carr, 1955.

Casdorph, Paul D. *Confederate General R. S. Ewell, Robert E. Lee's Hesitant Commander.* Lexington: University Press of Kentucky, 2004.

Castel, Albert. "Theophilus Holmes—Pallbearer of the Confederacy." *Civil War Times Illustrated* 16 (July 1977): 11–17.

Chambers, Lenoir. *Stonewall Jackson.* 2 vols. New York: William Morrow, 1959.

Collins, Darrell L. *Major General Robert E. Rodes of the Army of Northern Virginia: A Biography.* New York: Savas Beatie, 2008.

Cook, Roy Bird. *The Family and Early Life of Stonewall Jackson.* Charleston, W.Va.: Educational Foundation, 1963.

Cooke, John Esten. *Stonewall Jackson: A Military Biography.* New York: D. Appleton, 1866.

———. *Stonewall Jackson and the Old Stonewall Brigade.* Edited by Richard B. Harwell. Charlottesville: University of Virginia Press, 1954.

Coxe, John. "Wade Hampton." *Confederate Veteran* 30 (1922): 460–62.

Cullum, George W., comp. *Biographical Register of the Officers and Graduates of the U.S. Military Academy.* 2 vols. New York: D. Van Nostrand, 1868.

Dabney, R. L. *Life and Campaigns of Lieut.-Gen. Thomas J. Jackson.* New York: Blelock, 1866.

Daly, Louise H. *Alexander Cheves Haskell: The Portrait of a Man.* Norwood, Mass.: Plimpton, 1934.

Davis, Burke. *Gray Fox: Robert E. Lee and the Civil War.* New York: Rinehart, 1956.

———. *Jeb Stuart, the Last Cavalier.* New York: Rinehart, 1957.

———. *They Called Him Stonewall: A Life of Lt. General T. J. Jackson, C.S.A.* New York: Holt, Rinehart & Winston, 1954.

Dowdey, Clifford. *Lee.* Boston: Little, Brown, 1965.

Downs, Alan. "'The Responsibility Is Great': Joseph E. Johnston and the War in Virginia." In *Civil War Generals in Defeat,* edited by Steven E. Woodworth, 29–70. Lawrence: University Press of Kansas, 1999.

Dufour, Charles L. *Gentle Tiger: The Gallant Life of Roberdeau Wheat.* Baton Rouge: Louisiana State University Press, 1957.

———. *Nine Men in Grey.* Garden City, N.Y.: Doubleday, 1963.

Dwinell, Harold A. "Vermonter in Gray: The Story of Melvin Dwinell." *Vermont History* 30 (1962): 220–37.

Eckenrode, H. J., and Bryan Conrad. *James Longstreet, Lee's War Horse.* Chapel Hill: University of North Carolina Press, 1936.

Farwell, Byron. *Stonewall: A Biography of General Thomas J. Jackson.* New York: W. W. Norton, 1992.

Felt, Jeremy P. "Lucius B. Northrop and the Confederacy's Subsistence Department." *Virginia Magazine of History and Biography* 69 (1961): 181–93.

Freeman, Douglas Southall. *Lee's Lieutenants: A Study in Command.* 3 vols. New York: Charles Scribner's Sons, 1942–44.

———. *R. E. Lee: A Biography.* 4 vols. New York: Charles Scribner's Sons, 1934–35.

"General William N. Pendleton." *Southern Bivouac* 1 (1882–83): 294–301.

Govan, Gilbert E., and James W. Livingood. *A Different Valor: The Story of General Joseph E. Johnston, C.S.A.* Indianapolis: Bobbs-Merrill, 1956.

Hallock, Charles. *Sketches of "Stonewall Jackson," Giving the Leading Events of His Life and Military Career.* Montreal: privately issued, 1863.

Hamlin, Percy G. *"Old Bald Head" (General R. S. Ewell): The Portrait of a Soldier.* Strasburg, Va.: Shenandoah, 1940.

Harris, William C. *Leroy Pope Walker, Confederate Secretary of War.* Tuscaloosa, Ala.: Confederate Publishing, 1962.

Hassler, William W. *A. P. Hill, Lee's Forgotten General.* Richmond, Va.: Garrett & Massie, 1957.

———. "'Extra Billy' Smith." *Civil War Times Illustrated* 2 (December 1963): 38–41.

Hay, Thomas Robson. "Lucius B. Northrop: Commissary General of the Confederacy." *Civil War History* 9 (1963): 5–23.

Henderson, G. F. R. *Stonewall Jackson and the American Civil War.* New York: Grosset & Dunlap, n.d.

Hill, Daniel Harvey. "The Real Stonewall Jackson." *Century Illustrated Monthly Magazine* 47 (1894): 623–28.

Hughes, Robert M. *General Johnston.* New York: D. Appleton, 1893.

———, ed. "Some Letters from the Papers of General Joseph E. Johnston." *William & Mary Quarterly Historical Magazine* 11 (1931): 319–20.

James, Alfred P. "General Joseph Eggleston Johnston, Storm Center of the Confederate Army." *Mississippi Valley Historical Review* 14 (1927): 342–59.

Johnson, Bradley T. *A Memoir of the Life and Public Service of Joseph E. Johnston.* Baltimore: R. H. Woodward, 1891.

Jones, Charles T. "Five Confederates: The Sons of Bolling Hall in the Civil War." *Alabama Historical Quarterly* 25 (1963): 133–221.

Jones, Virgil Carrington. *Ranger Mosby.* Chapel Hill: University of North Carolina Press, 1944.

Kerwood, John Richard. "His Daring Was Proverbial." *Civil War Times Illustrated* 7 (August 1968): 19–23, 28–30.

Klein, Maury. *Edward Porter Alexander.* Athens: University of Georgia Press, 1971.

Krick, Robert E. L. *Staff Officers in Gray: A Biographical Register of the Staff Officers of the Army of Northern Virginia.* Chapel Hill: University of North Carolina Press, 2003.

Krick, Robert K. *Lee's Colonels: A Biographical Register of the Field Officers of the Army of Northern Virginia.* Dayton, Ohio: Morningside, 1992.

Lash, Jeffrey N. *Destroyer of the Iron Horse: General Joseph E. Johnston and Confederate Rail Transport, 1861–1865.* Kent, Ohio: Kent State University Press, 1991.

———. "Joseph E. Johnston and the Virginia Railways." *Civil War History* 35 (1989): 5–27.

The Life of Stonewall Jackson: From Official Papers, Contemporary Narratives, and Personal Acquaintance, by a Virginian. New York: Charles B. Richardson, 1866.

Long, A. L. *Memoirs of Robert E. Lee: His Military and Personal History.* . . . Philadelphia: J. M. Stoddart, 1886.

Longacre, Edward G. *Fitz Lee: A Military Biography of Major General Fitzhugh Lee, C.S.A.* New York: Da Capo, 2005.

———. *Gentleman and Soldier: A Biography of Wade Hampton III.* Nashville, Tenn.: Rutledge Hill, 2003.

———. *Worthy Opponents: General William T. Sherman, U.S.A., General Joseph E. Johnston, C.S.A.* Nashville, Tenn.: Rutledge Hill, 2006.

Lonn, Ella. *Foreigners in the Confederacy.* Chapel Hill: University of North Carolina Press, 1940.

"Major Chatham Roberdeau Wheat." *Confederate Veteran* 19 (1911): 425–28.

Maury, Dabney H. "Interesting Reminiscences of General Johnston." *Southern Historical Society Papers* 18 (1890): 171–81.

McAllister, J. Gray. *Sketch of Captain Thompson McAllister, Co. A, 27th Virginia Regiment.* Petersburg, Va.: Fenn & Owen, 1896.

McCabe, James Dabney. *The Life of Lieut. Gen. T. J. Jackson.* Richmond, Va.: James E. Goode, 1863.

McClellan, H. B. *The Life and Campaigns of Major-General J. E. B. Stuart.* Secaucus, N.J.: Blue & Grey, 1993.

McDowell, John E., and William C. Davis. "Joe Writes His Own Praise." *Civil War Times Illustrated* 8 (February 1970): 36–39.

McGuire, Hunter. "General Thomas J. Jackson." *Southern Historical Society Papers* 19 (1891): 298–318.

Mercer, Philip. *The Life of the Gallant Pelham.* Macon, Ga.: J. W. Burke, 1929.

Meynier, A. *Life and Military Services of Col. Charles D. Dreux.* New Orleans: E. A. Brandao, 1883.

Milham, Charles G. *Gallant Pelham, American Extraordinary.* Washington, D.C.: Public Affairs, 1959.

Mingos, Scott L. *Confederate General William "Extra Billy" Smith: From Virginia State House to Gettysburg Scapegoat.* El Dorado, Calif.: Savas Beatie, 2013.

Moore, Alison. *Old Bob Wheat, High Private.* Baton Rouge, La.: Ortlieb, 1957.

Osborne, Charles C. *Jubal: The Life and Times of General Jubal A. Early, C.S.A., Defender of the Lost Cause.* Chapel Hill, N.C.: Algonquin Books, 1992.

Parks, Joseph H. *General Edmund Kirby Smith, C.S.A.* Baton Rouge: Louisiana State University Press, 1954.

Paxton, John G., comp. *Memoir and Memorials: Elisha Franklin Paxton, Brigadier-General, C.S.A.* . . . New York: De Vinne, 1905.

Perry, Leslie J. "Davis and Johnston: Light Thrown on a Quarrel among Confederate Leaders. . . ." *Southern Historical Society Papers* 39 (1892): 95–108.

Pfanz, Donald C. *Richard S. Ewell: A Soldier's Life.* Chapel Hill: University of North Carolina Press, 1998.

Pierrepont, Alice V. *Reuben Vaughan Kidd, Soldier of the Confederacy.* Petersburg, Va.: privately issued, 1947.

Randolph, Sarah N. *The Life of Gen. Thomas J. Jackson ("Stonewall" Jackson).* Philadelphia: J. B. Lippincott, 1876.

Robertson, James I., Jr. *General A. P. Hill: The Story of a Confederate Warrior.* New York: Random House, 1987.

———. *Stonewall Jackson: The Man, the Soldier, the Legend.* New York: Macmillan, 1997.

Roman, Alfred. *The Military Operations of General Beauregard in the War between the States, 1861 to 1865.* 2 vols. New York: Harper & Brothers, 1884.

Sanger, Donald B., and Thomas Robson Hay. *James Longstreet.* Baton Rouge: Louisiana State University Press, 1952.

Selby, John. *Stonewall Jackson as Military Commander.* Princeton, N.J.: D. Van Nostrand, 1968.

Sharp, Arthur G. "Reynolds' Regrets." *Civil War Times Illustrated* 16 (December 1977): 22–33.

Silverman, Jason N., Samuel N. Thomas, Jr., and Beverly D. Evans IV. *Shanks: The Life and Wars of General Nathan George Evans, C.S.A.* New York: Da Capo, 2002.

"Stonewall" Jackson, Late General of the Confederate States Army: A Biographical Sketch, and an Outline of His Virginian Campaigns. London: Chapman & Hall, 1863.

Sullivan, David M., ed. "Fowler the Soldier, Fowler the Marine." *Civil War Times Illustrated* 26 (February 1988): 28–35, 44–45.

Symonds, Craig L. *Joseph E. Johnston: A Civil War Biography.* New York: W. W. Norton, 1992.

Tankersley, Allen P. *John B. Gordon: A Study in Gallantry.* Atlanta: Whitehall, 1955.

Thomas, Emory. *Bold Dragoon: The Life of J. E. B. Stuart.* New York: Harper & Row, 1986.

Thomason, John W., Jr. *Jeb Stuart.* New York: Charles Scribner's Sons, 1930.

Tucker, Spencer C. *Brigadier General John D. Imboden, Confederate Commander in the Shenandoah.* Lexington: University Press of Kentucky, 2003.

Vandiver, Frank E. *Mighty Stonewall.* New York: McGraw-Hill, 1957.

———. *Ploughshares into Swords: Josiah Gorgas and Confederate Ordnance.* Austin: University of Texas Press, 1952.

Warner, Ezra J. *Generals in Gray: Lives of the Confederate Commanders.* Baton Rouge: Louisiana State University Press, 1959.

Wellman, Manly Wade. *Giant in Gray: A Biography of Wade Hampton of South Carolina.* New York: Charles Scribner's Sons, 1949.

Wert, Jeffry D. *Cavalryman of the Lost Cause: A Biography of J. E. B. Stuart.* New York: Simon & Schuster, 2008.

———. *General James Longstreet, the Confederacy's Most Controversial Soldier: A Biography.* New York: Simon & Schuster, 1993.

Wheat, Leo. "Memoir of Gen. C. R. Wheat, Commander of the 'Louisiana Tiger Battalion.'" *Southern Historical Society Papers* 17 (1889): 47–60.

White, Henry Alexander. *Robert E. Lee and the Southern Confederacy, 1807–1870.* New York: Haskell House, 1969.

White, William Spottswood. *Sketches of the Life of Captain Hugh S. White.* Columbia: South Carolina Steam Press, 1864.

Wiley, Bell I. "A Story of 3 Southern Officers." *Civil War Times Illustrated* 3 (April 1964): 28–34.

Williams, T. Harry. *P. G. T. Beauregard, Napoleon in Gray.* Baton Rouge: Louisiana State University Press, 1954.

Winston, Robert W. *Robert E. Lee: A Biography.* New York: William Morrow, 1934.

Woodward, Harold R., Jr. *Defender of the Valley: Brigadier General John Daniel Imboden, C.S.A.* Berryville, Va.: Rockbridge, 1996.

FEDERAL

Allaben, Frank. *John Watts de Peyster.* 2 vols. New York: privately issued, 1908.

Ambrose, Stephen E. *Upton and the Army*. Baton Rouge: Louisiana State University Press, 1964.

Ballou, Daniel R. "The Military Services of Maj.-Gen. Ambrose Everett Burnside in the Civil War." *Soldiers and Sailors Historical Society of Rhode Island: Personal Narratives* 7, no. 8 (1914).

Barthel, Thomas. *Abner Doubleday: A Civil War Biography*. Jefferson, N.C.: McFarland, 2010.

Bowman, S. M., and R. B. Irwin. *Sherman and His Campaigns: A Military Biography*. New York: Charles B. Richardson, 1865.

Bradford, Gamaliel. *Union Portraits*. Freeport, N.Y.: Books for Libraries, 1968.

A Brief Statement of the Part which Brig.-General David B. Birney of Philadelphia Has Taken in the Present Rebellion. Philadelphia: privately issued, 1863.

Carpenter, John A. *Sword and Olive Branch: Oliver Otis Howard*. Pittsburgh: University of Pittsburgh Press, 1964.

Coyle, John G. "General Michael Corcoran." *Journal of the American Irish Historical Society* 13 (1913–14): 109–26.

Eisenhower, John S. D. *Agent of Destiny: The Life and Times of General Winfield Scott*. New York: Free Press, 1997.

Elliott, Charles Winslow. *Winfield Scott, the Soldier and the Man*. New York: Macmillan, 1937.

Fitzgerald, David. *In Memoriam: Gen. Henry J. Hunt, 1819–1889*. Washington, D.C.: privately issued, 1889.

Force, Manning F. *General Sherman*. New York: D. Appleton, 1899.

Gould, Edward K. *Major-General Hiram G. Berry*. Rockland, Me.: Courier-Gazette, 1899.

Greene, Jacob L. *In Memoriam: William Buel Franklin, February 27, 1823– March 8, 1903*. Hartford, Conn.: Belknap & Warfield, 1903.

Hassler, Warren W., Jr. *Commanders of the Army of the Potomac*. Baton Rouge: Louisiana State University Press, 1962.

———. *General George B. McClellan, Shield of the Union*. Baton Rouge: Louisiana State University Press, 1957.

Hay, John. "A Young Hero: Personal Reminiscences of Colonel E. E. Ellsworth." *McClure's Magazine* 6 (1896): 354–61.

Headley, Joel T. *Grant and Sherman: Their Campaigns and Generals*. New York: E. B. Treat, 1865.

Hirshon, Stanley P. *The White Tecumseh: A Biography of General William T. Sherman*. New York: John Wiley & Sons, 1997.

Hoadley, J. C., ed. *Memorial of Henry Sanford Gansevoort*. Boston: Rand, Avery, 1875.

Hubbs, Ronald M. "The Civil War and Alexander Wilkin." *Minnesota History* 39 (1965): 173–90.

Hunt, Roger D., and Jack R. Brown. *Brevet Brigadier Generals in Blue*. Gaithersburg, Md.: Olde Soldier Books, 1997.

Johnson, Richard W. *Memoir of Maj.-Gen. George H. Thomas*. Philadelphia: J. B. Lippincott, 1881.

Johnson, Timothy D. *Winfield Scott: The Quest for Military Glory*.
  Lawrence: University Press of Kansas, 1998.
Kennett, Lee. *Sherman: A Soldier's Life*. New York: HarperCollins, 2001.
Lewis, Lloyd. *Sherman, Fighting Prophet*. New York: Harcourt, Brace,
  1932.
Liddell Hart, B. H. *Sherman: Soldier—Realist—American*. New York:
  Frederick A. Praeger, 1958.
Life of David Bell Birney, Major-General United States Volunteers.
  Philadelphia: King & Baird, 1867.
Longacre, Edward G. "Charles P. Stone and the 'Crime of Unlucky
  Generals.'" *Civil War Times Illustrated* 13 (November 1974): 4–9,
  38–41.
———. "Fortune's Fool." *Civil War Times Illustrated* 18 (May 1979):
  20–31.
———. *The Man behind the Guns: A Biography of General Henry Jackson
  Hunt, Chief of Artillery, Army of the Potomac*. South Brunswick, N.J.:
  A. S. Barnes, 1977.
———. "A Profile of Major General David Hunter." *Civil War Times
  Illustrated* 16 (January 1978): 4–9, 38–43.
Lonn, Ella. *Foreigners in the Union Army and Navy*. Baton Rouge:
  Louisiana State University Press, 1951.
Lyons, W. F. *Brigadier-General Thomas Francis Meagher: His Political and
  Military Career*. New York: D. & J. Sadlier, 1870.
Macartney, Clarence E. *Grant and His Generals*. New York: McBride,
  1953.
Marszalek, John F. *Sherman: A Soldier's Passion for Order*. New York: Free
  Press, 1993.
Marvel, William. *Burnside*. Chapel Hill: University of North Carolina
  Press, 1991.
McFeely, William S. *Yankee Stepfather: General O. O. Howard and the
  Freedmen*. New Haven, Conn.: Yale University Press, 1968.
McIntyre, Philip W. *Alonzo Palmer Stinson, the First Portland Soldier
  Who Fell in Battle during the Civil War*. Portland, Me.: Lefavor-
  Tower, 1909.
McKee, Irving. *"Ben-Hur" Wallace: The Life of General Lew Wallace*.
  Berkeley: University of California Press, 1947.
Melton, Brian C. *Sherman's Forgotten General: Henry W. Slocum*.
  Columbia: University of Missouri Press, 2007.
*Memoir of William A. Jackson . . . Colonel of the 18th Regiment, N.Y.
  Volunteers*. Albany, N.Y.: Joel Munsell, 1862.
*Memorial of Colonel John Stanton Slocum, First Colonel of the Second
  Rhode Island Volunteers, Who Fell in the Battle of Bull Run, Virginia,
  July 21, 1861*. Providence, R.I.: J. A. & R. A. Reid, 1886.
Merrill, James M. *William Tecumseh Sherman*. Chicago: Rand McNally,
  1971.
Miller, Edward A. *Lincoln's Abolitionist General: The Biography of David
  Hunter*. Columbia: University of South Carolina Press, 1997.

Monaghan, Jay. *Custer: The Life of General George Armstrong Custer.* Boston: Little, Brown, 1959.

Patterson, Mrs. Lindsay. "The Old Patterson Mansion, the Master and His Guests." *Pennsylvania Magazine of History and Biography* 39 (1915): 80–97.

Pearson, Henry G. *James S. Wadsworth of Geneseo, Brevet Major General of United States Volunteers.* New York: Charles Scribner's Sons, 1913.

Peskin, Allan. *Winfield Scott and the Profession of Arms.* Kent, Ohio: Kent State University Press, 2003.

Poore, Ben:Perley. *The Life and Public Services of Ambrose E. Burnside, Soldier—Citizen–Statesman.* Providence, R.I.: J. A. & R. A. Reid, 1882.

Randall, Ruth Painter. *Colonel Elmer Ellsworth: A Biography of Lincoln's Friend and First Hero of the Civil War.* Boston: Little, Brown, 1960.

Rezneck, Samuel. "The Civil War Role, 1861–1863, of . . . Major-General John E. Wool (1784–1869)." *New York History* 44 (1963): 237–57.

Shanks, W. F. G. "Recollections of [George H.] Thomas." *Harper's New Monthly Magazine* 30 (1865): 754–59.

Slocum, Charles Elihu. *The Life and Services of Major-General Henry Warner Slocum.* Toledo, Ohio: Slocum Publishing, 1913.

Snell, Mark A. *From First to Last: The Life of Major General William B. Franklin.* New York: Fordham University Press, 2002.

Stevens, Christian D. *Meagher of the Sword.* New York: Dodd, Mead, 1967.

Thompson, Jerry. *Civil War to the Bloody End: The Life & Times of Major General Samuel P. Heintzelman.* College Station: Texas A&M University Press, 2006.

Trefousse, Hans. *Ben Butler: The South Called him Beast!* New York: Twayne, 1957.

Van De Water, Frederic F. *Glory-Hunter: A Life of General Custer.* Indianapolis: Bobbs-Merrill, 1934.

Van Horne, Thomas B. *Life of Major-General George H. Thomas.* New York: Charles Scribner's Sons, 1882.

Warner, Ezra J. *Generals in Blue: Lives of the Union Commanders.* Baton Rouge: Louisiana State University Press, 1964.

Weigley, Russell F. *Quartermaster General of the Union Army: A Biography of M. C. Meigs.* New York: Columbia University Press, 1959.

West, Richard M. *Lincoln's Scapegoat General: A Life of Benjamin F. Butler, 1818–1893.* Boston: Houghton Mifflin, 1965.

Weston, Edward P. *The Christian Soldier-Boy: An Address . . . on the Death of Joseph D. Harmon, of Company A, 5th Regiment Maine Volunteers.* Portland, Me.: Office of the Maine Teacher, 1862.

Wright, Marcus J. *General Scott.* New York: D. Appleton, 1893.

Young, Robin. *For Love & Liberty: The Untold Civil War Story of Major Sullivan Ballou & His Famous Love Letter.* New York: Thunder's Mouth, 2006.

CIVILIANS, NORTH AND SOUTH

Belden, Thomas Graham, and Marva Robins Belden. *So Fell the Angels.* Boston: Little, Brown, 1956.

Beymer, William G. "Mrs. Greenhow." *Harper's Monthly Magazine* 124 (1912): 563–76.

Boney, Francis N. *John Letcher of Virginia: The Story of Virginia's Civil War Governor.* University.: University of Alabama Press, 1966.

Bradley, Erwin Stanley. *Simon Cameron, Lincoln's Secretary of War: A Political Biography.* Philadelphia: University of Pennsylvania Press, 1966.

Cooper, William J. *Jefferson Davis, American.* New York: Alfred A. Knopf, 2000.

Craven, Avery. *Edmund Ruffin, Southerner: A Study in Secession.* New York: D. Appleton, 1932.

Davis, William C. *Jefferson Davis: The Man and His Hour.* New York: HarperCollins, 1991.

Gardner, Joseph L. "'Bull Run' Russell." *American Heritage* 13 (June 1962): 59–61, 78–83.

Goodwin, Doris Kearns. *Team of Rivals: The Political Genius of Abraham Lincoln.* New York: Simon & Schuster, 2005.

Hart, Albert Bushnell. *Salmon Portland Chase.* Boston: Houghton Mifflin, 1899.

Hassler, William W. *Colonel John Pelham, Lee's Boy Artillerist.* Richmond, Va.: Garrett & Massie, 1960.

Hattaway, Herman, and Richard E. Beringer. *Jefferson Davis, Confederate President.* Lawrence: University Press of Kansas, 2002.

Hendrick, Burton J. *Statesmen of the Lost Cause: Jefferson Davis and His Cabinet.* New York: Literary Guild of America, 1939.

Horan, James D. *Matthew Brady, Historian with a Camera.* New York: Crown, 1955.

Klein, Frederic S. *President James Buchanan: A Biography.* University Park: Pennsylvania State University Press, 1962.

McElroy, Robert. *Jefferson Davis: The Unreal and the Real.* 2 vols. New York: Harper & Brothers, 1937.

McPherson, James M. *Tried by War: Abraham Lincoln as Commander in Chief.* New York: Penguin, 2008.

Mitchell, Betty L. *Edmund Ruffin: A Biography.* Bloomington: Indiana University Press, 1981.

Nicolay, Helen. *Lincoln's Secretary: A Biography of John G. Nicolay.* New York: Longmans, Green, 1949.

Nicolay, John G., and John Hay. *Abraham Lincoln: A History.* 10 vols. New York: Century, 1917.

Niven, John. *Salmon P. Chase: A Biography.* New York: Oxford University Press, 1995.

Oates, Stephen B. *With Malice toward None: The Life of Abraham Lincoln.* New York: Harper & Row, 1977.

Quattlebaum, Isabel. "Twelve Women in the First Days of the Confederacy." *Civil War History* 7 (1961): 370–85.

Ross, Ishbel. *Rebel Rose: The Life of Rose O'Neal Greenhow, Confederate Spy*. New York: Harper & Brothers, 1954.

Scarborough, Ruth. *Belle Boyd, Siren of the South*. Macon, Ga.: Mercer University Press, 1983.

Schuckers, J. W. *The Life and Public Services of Salmon Portland Chase.* . . . New York: D. Appleton, 1874.

Sigaud, Louis A. *Belle Boyd, Confederate Spy*. Richmond, Va.: Dietz, 1944.

———. "Mrs. Greenhow and the Rebel Spy Ring." *Maryland Historical Magazine* 41 (1946): 173–98.

Strode, Hudson. *Jefferson Davis, Confederate President*. New York: Harcourt, Brace, 1959.

Thomas, Benjamin P. *Abraham Lincoln: A Biography*. New York: Alfred A. Knopf, 1952.

Thomas, Benjamin P., and Harold Hyman. *Stanton: The Life and Times of Lincoln's Secretary of War*. New York: Alfred A. Knopf, 1962.

Trefousse, Hans L. *Benjamin Franklin Wade, Radical Republican from Ohio*. New York: Twayne, 1963.

Van Deusen, Glyndon G. *William Henry Seward*. New York: Oxford University Press, 1967.

White, Ronald C., Jr. *A. Lincoln: A Biography*. New York: Random House, 2009.

General Works

Abbot, Willis J. *Battle-Fields of '61: A Narrative of the Military Operations of the War for the Union up to the End of the Peninsular Campaign*. New York: Dodd, Mead, 1889.

Adams, George Worthington. *Doctors in Blue: The Medical History of the Union Army in the Civil War*. New York: Henry Schuman, 1952.

Alger, William R. *Our Civil War, as Seen from the Pulpit*. Boston: Walker, Wise, 1861.

"American Affairs." *Littell's Living Age* 71 (October 5, 1861): 45–46.

"The American Belligerents: Rights of Neutrals." *Westminster Review* 77 (1862): 108–22.

"The American Crisis." *Quarterly Review* 111 (1862): 239–80.

Anderson, J. H. *American Civil War: The Operations in the Eastern Theatre from the Commencement of Hostilities to May 5, 1863*. London: Hugh Rees, 1910.

Andrews, J. Cutler. *The North Reports the Civil War*. Pittsburgh: University of Pittsburgh Press, 1955.

———. *The South Reports the Civil War*. Princeton, N. J.: Princeton University Press, 1970.

"April, 1861: Minnesota Goes to War." *Minnesota History* 37 (1961): 212–15.

Averell, William W. "With the Cavalry on the Peninsula." In *Battles and Leaders of the Civil War*, edited by Robert U. Johnson and Clarence C. Buel, 4 vols., 2:429–33. New York, 1887.

Bakeless, John. *Spies of the Confederacy*. Philadelphia: J. B. Lippincott, 1970.

"Baltimore and the Crisis of 1861." *Maryland Historical Magazine* 41 (1946): 257–81.

Bartol, C. A. *Our Sacrifices: A Sermon Preached . . . November 3, 1861*. Boston: Ticknor & Fields, 1861.

Barton, Michael. *Goodmen: The Character of Civil War Soldiers*. University Park: Pennsylvania State University Press, 1981.

Battle-fields of the South, from Bull Run to Fredericksburg . . . by an English Combatant. New York: John Bradburn, 1864.

Bauer, K. Jack. *The Mexican War, 1846–1848*. New York: Macmillan, 1974.

Baylies, Francis. *A Narrative of Major General Wool's Campaign in Mexico, in the Years 1846, 1847, & 1848*. Albany, N.Y.: Little, 1851.

Benedict, G. G. *Vermont in the Civil War: A History of the Part Taken by the Vermont Soldiers and Sailors in the War for the Union, 1861–65*. 2 vols. Burlington, Vt.: Free Press Association, 1886.

Beringer, Richard E., Herman Hattaway, Archer Jones, and William N. Still, Jr. *Why the South Lost the Civil War*. Athens: University of Georgia Press, 1986.

Bilby, Joseph G. *Civil War Firearms: Their Historical Background, Tactical Use, and Modern Collecting and Shooting*. Conshohocken, Pa.: Combined, 1996.

Birkhimer, William E. *Historical Sketch of the Organization, Administration, Materiel and Tactics of the Artillery, United States Army*. Washington, D.C.: James J. Chapman, 1884.

Black, Robert C., III. *The Railroads of the Confederacy*. Chapel Hill: University of North Carolina Press, 1952.

Boatner, Mark Mayo, III. *The Civil War Dictionary*. New York: David McKay, 1959.

Boehm, Robert B. "Battle of Rich Mountain." *Civil War Times Illustrated* 8 (February 1970): 4–15.

Boykin, James H. *North Carolina in 1861*. New York: Bookman Associates, 1961.

Brackett, Albert G. *History of the United States Cavalry, from the Formation of the Federal Government to the 1st of June, 1863*. New York: Harper & Brothers, 1865.

Brown, C. A. *The Buckshot War: 1838–1839*. N.p.: privately issued, 1839.

Buker, George F. *Swamp Sailors in the Second Seminole War*. Gainesville: University of Florida Press, 1997.

Bulkley, Edwin A. *Wars and Rumors of Wars: A Sermon Preached . . . on Sunday, April 21st, 1861*. Cambridge, Mass.: Miles & Dillingham, 1861.

Bunker, H. M. E. *Story of the Campaign in Eastern Virginia, April, 1861 to May, 1863*. London: Forster, Groom, 1910.

Callahan, James Morton. *The Diplomatic History of the Southern Confederacy*. Baltimore: Johns Hopkins University Press, 1901.

Canan, H. V. "Confederate Military Intelligence." *Maryland Historical Magazine* 59 (1964): 34–51.

Catton, Bruce. *The Coming Fury*. Garden City, N.Y.: Doubleday, 1961.

———. *Mr. Lincoln's Army*. Garden City, N.Y.: Doubleday, 1951.

———. *A Stillness at Appomattox*. Garden City, N.Y.: Doubleday, 1953.

"The Civil War in America." *Punch, or the London Charivari* 41 (August 17, 1861): 63–64.

Clarke, H. C. *Diary of the War for Separation: A Daily Chronicle of the Principal Events and History of the Present Revolution*. Augusta, Ga.: Chronicle & Sentinel, 1862.

Coffin, Charles Carleton. *Drum-beat of the Nation: The First Period of the War of the Rebellion from Its Outbreak to the Close of 1862*. New York: Harper & Brothers, 1888.

Connelly, Thomas L., and Archer Jones. *The Politics of Command: Factions and Ideas in Confederate Strategy*. Baton Rouge: Louisiana State University Press, 1973.

"The Convulsions of America." *Blackwood's Edinburgh Magazine* 91 (1861): 118–30.

Cooling, B. Franklin, III. "Civil War Deterrent: Defenses of Washington." *Military Affairs* 29 (1965–66): 164–78.

———. *Historical Highlights of Bull Run Regional Park*. Fairfax, Va.: Fairfax County Division of Planning, 1971.

———. *Mr. Lincoln's Forts: A Guide to the Civil War Defenses of Washington*. Lanham, Md.: Scarecrow, 2010.

———. *Symbol, Sword, and Shield: Defending Washington during the Civil War*. Hamden, Conn.: Archon, 1975.

Coski, John M. *The Confederate Battle Flag: America's Most Embattled Emblem*. Cambridge, Mass.: Harvard University Press, 2005.

Costello, Augustine E. *Our Firemen: A History of the New York Fire Department*. New York: Knickerbocker, 1997.

Coulter, E. Merton. *The Confederate States of America, 1861–1865*. Baton Rouge: Louisiana State University Press, 1950.

Couper, William. *One Hundred Years at V.M.I.* 4 vols. Richmond, Va.: Garrett & Massie, 1939–40.

Crackel, Theodore J. *West Point: A Bicentennial History*. Lawrence: University Press of Kansas, 2002.

Croffutt, W. A., and John M. Morris. *The Military and Civil History of Connecticut during the War of 1861–1865.* . . . New York: Ledyard Bill, 1869.

Crook, D. P. *The North, the South, and the Powers, 1861–1865*. New York, Wiley, 1974.

Crozier, Emmet. *Yankee Reporters, 1861–65*. New York: Oxford University Press, 1956.

Cummins, Edmund H. "The Signal Corps in the Confederate States Army." *Southern Historical Society Papers* 16 (1888): 93–107.

Cunliffe, Marcus. *Soldiers & Civilians: The Martial Spirit in America, 1775–1865*. Boston: Little, Brown, 1968.

Cunningham, H. H. "Confederate General Hospitals: Establishment and Organization." *Journal of Southern History* 20 (1954): 376–94.

———. *Doctors in Gray: The Confederate Medical Service*. Baton Rouge: Louisiana State University Press, 1958.

Dabney, Virginius. *Virginia: The New Dominion*. Garden City, N.Y.: Doubleday, 1971.

Daniel, Edward M., comp. *Speeches and Orations of John Warwick Daniel*. Lynchburg, Va.: J. P. Bell, 1911.

Davis, Julia. *The Shenandoah*. New York: Farrar & Rinehart, 1945.

Deaderick, Barron. *Strategy in the Civil War*. Harrisburg, Pa.: Military Service, 1946.

"Democracy on Its Trial." *Quarterly Review* 110 (1861): 247–88.

Detzer, David. *Allegiance: Fort Sumter, Charleston, and the Beginning of the Civil War*. New York: Harcourt, 2001.

"The Disruption of the Union." *Blackwood's Edinburgh Magazine* 90 (1861): 125–34.

"The Dissolution of the Union." *Cornhill Magazine* 4 (1861): 153–66.

"The Disunion of America." *Edinburgh Review* 114 (1861): 556–87.

Donald, David. *Lincoln Reconsidered: Essays on the Civil War Era*. New York: Knopf, 1956.

Dornbusch, C. E., comp. *Military Bibliography of the Civil War*. 3 vols. New York: New York Public Library, 1971.

———, comp. *Military Bibliography of the Civil War, Volume Four*. Dayton, Ohio: Morningside, 1987.

Dowdey, Clifford. *Experiment in Rebellion*. Garden City, N.Y.: Doubleday, 1946.

———. "In the Valley of Virginia." *Civil War History* 3 (1957): 401–22.

———. *The Land They Fought For: The Story of the South as the Confederacy, 1832–1865*. Garden City, N.Y.: Doubleday, 1955.

Dupuy, R. Ernest, and Trevor N. Dupuy. *Encyclopedia of Military History, 3500 B.C. to the Present*. New York: Harper & Row, 1970.

———. *Military Heritage of America*. New York: McGraw-Hill, 1956.

Dyer, Fredrick H., comp. *A Compendium of the War of the Rebellion, Compiled and Arranged from Official Records of the Federal and Confederate Armies. . . .* Des Moines, Iowa: privately issued, 1908.

Edwards, Frank S. *A Campaign in New Mexico with Colonel Doniphan*. Philadelphia: Carey & Hart, 1847.

Edwards, William B. *Civil War Guns: The Complete Story of Federal and Confederate Small Arms. . . .* Harrisburg, Pa.: Stackpole, 1962.

Eisenhower, John S. D. *So Far from God: The U.S. War with Mexico, 1846–1848*. New York: Random House, 1989.

Eisenschiml, Otto. *The Hidden Face of the Civil War*. Indianapolis: Bobbs-Merrill, 1961.

Eisenschiml, Otto, and Ralph Newman, comps. *Eyewitness: The Civil War as We Lived It*. Indianapolis: Bobbs-Merrill, 1956.

"English and French View of the American Rebellion." *North American Review* 94 (1862): 408–35.

Estvàn, B. *War Pictures from the South*. 2 vols. London: Routledge, Warne, & Routledge, 1863.

Everett, Edward G. "The Baltimore Riots, April, 1861." *Pennsylvania History* 24 (1957): 331–42.

———. "Pennsylvania Raises an Army, 1861." *Western Pennsylvania Historical Magazine* 39 (1956): 83–108.

"Famous Cavalry Mounts: Baldy." *Cavalry Journal* 36 (March 2011): 16–17.

Faust, Patricia L., ed. *Historical Times Illustrated Encyclopedia of the Civil War*. New York: Harper & Row, 1986.

Feldberg, Michael. *The Philadelphia Riots of 1844: A Study of Ethnic Conflict*. Westport, Conn.: Greenwood, 1975.

Fieberger, G. J. *Campaigns of the American Civil War*. West Point, N.Y.: U.S. Military Academy Printing, 1914.

Fishel, Edwin C. "The Mythology of Civil War Intelligence." *Civil War History* 10 (1964): 344–67.

Fleming, Thomas J. *West Point: The Men and Times of the United States Military Academy*. New York: William Morrow, 1969.

Fleming, V. M. *Campaigns of the Army of Northern Virginia, including the Jackson Valley Campaign, 1861–1865*. Richmond, Va.: William Byrd, 1928.

Fletcher, Henry C. *History of the American War, Vol. 1: First Year of the War (1861–62)*. London: Richard Bentley, 1865.

Franklin, William B. "The First Great Crime of the War." In *Annals of the War, Written by Leading Participants, North and South*, 72–81. Philadelphia: Times Publishing, 1879.

Frassanito, William. *Antietam: The Photographic Legacy of America's Bloodiest Day*. New York: Charles Scribner's Sons 1978.

Fredrickson, George M. *The Inner Civil War: Northern Intellectuals and the Crisis of the Union*. New York: Harper & Row, 1965.

French, Samuel L. *The Army of the Potomac from 1861 to 1863*. New York: Publishing Society of New York, 1906.

Frost, James A. "The Home Front in New York during the Civil War." *New York History* 42 (1961): 273–97.

Furniss, Norman E. *The Mormon Conflict, 1850–1859*. New Haven, Conn.: Yale University Press, 1960.

Garraty, John A., and Mark C. Carnes, eds., *American National Biography*. 24 vols. and supplements. New York: Oxford University Press, 1999–.

Gavronsky, Serge. *The French Liberal Opposition and the American Civil War*. New York: Humanities, 1968.

Geddes, Jean. *Fairfax County: Historical Highlights from 1607*. Middleburg, Va.: Denlinger's, 1967.

Geer, Walter. *Campaigns of the Civil War*. New York: Brentano's, 1926.

Geffen, Elizabeth M. "Violence in Philadelphia in the 1840s and 1850s." *Pennsylvania History* 36 (1969): 381–410.

Gillette, William. *Jersey Blue: Civil War Politics in New Jersey, 1854–1865*. New Brunswick, N.J.: Rutgers University Press, 1995.

Glazer, Walter S. "Wisconsin Goes to War, April, 1861." *Wisconsin Magazine of History* 50 (1967): 147–64.

Glazier, Willard. *Heroes of Three Wars*. Philadelphia: Hubbard Brothers, 1882.

Goff, Richard D. *Confederate Supply*. Durham, N.C.: Duke University Press, 1969.

Gregg, Josiah. *Diary and Letters of Josiah Gregg: Southwestern Enterprises, 1840–1847*. Edited by Maurice Garland Fulton. Norman: University of Oklahoma Press, 1941.

Guillemin, A. V. *The World of Comets*. Translated by James Glaisher. London: Sampson, Low, Marston, Searle, & Rivington, 1877.

Hagerman, Edward. "From Jomini to Dennis Hart Mahan: The Evolution of Trench Warfare and the American Civil War." *Civil War History* 13 (1967): 197–220.

Harrison, Royden. "British Labour and the Confederacy." *International Review of Social History* 2 (1957): 78–105.

Harwell, Richard B., comp. *The Land They Fought For*. New York: Longmans, Green, 1960.

Hattaway, Herman, and Archer Jones. "Lincoln as Military Strategist." *Civil War History* 26 (1980): 293–303.

Headley, Joel T. *The Great Rebellion: A History of the Civil War in the United States*. 3 vols. Hartford, Conn.: American Publishing, 1866.

Heitman, Francis B., comp. *Historical Register and Dictionary of the United States Army*. 2 vols. Washington, D.C.: Government Printing Office, 1903.

Henderson, G. F. R. *The Civil War—A Soldier's View: A Collection of Civil War Writings by Col. G. F. R. Henderson*. Edited by Jay Luvaas. Chicago: University of Chicago Press, 1958.

Hess, Earl J. *The Union Soldier in Battle: Enduring the Ordeal of Combat*. Lawrence: University Press of Kansas, 1997.

Hewett, Janet, et al., eds. *Supplement to the Official Records of the Union and Confederate Armies*. 3 series, 99 vols. Wilmington, N.C.: Broadfoot, 1994–2001.

Hicks, John D. "The Organization of the Volunteer Army in 1861 with Special Reference to Minnesota." *Minnesota History Bulletin* 2 (1918): 324–68.

Hill, Daniel H. *Bethel to Sharpsburg: A History of North Carolina in the War between the States*. 2 vols. Raleigh, N.C.: Edwards & Broughton, 1926.

Hill, Jim Dan. *The Minute Man in Peace and War: A History of the National Guard*. Harrisburg, Pa.: Stackpole, 1964.

"Home Duties during the War." *New Englander* 19 (1861): 674–84.

Johnson, Allen, and Dumas Malone, eds. *Dictionary of American Biography*. 20 vols. plus supplements. New York: Charles Scribner's Sons, 1928–.

Johnston, Angus James, II. "Virginia Railroads in April 1861." *Journal of Southern History* 23 (1957): 307–30.

———. *Virginia Railroads in the Civil War*. Chapel Hill: University of North Carolina Press, 1961.

Jones, Katherine M. *Heroines of Dixie: Confederate Women Tell Their Story of the War*. Indianapolis: Bobbs-Merrill, 1955.

Journal of the Congress of the Confederate States of America, 1861–1865.
    7 vols. Washington, D.C.: Government Printing Office, 1904–1905.
Kane, Harnett T. *Spies for the Blue and Gray.* Garden City, N.Y.: Hanover
    House, 1954.
Kean, J. Randolph. "The Development of the 'Valley Line' of the Baltimore
    and Ohio Railroad." *Virginia Magazine of History and Biography* 60
    (1952): 537–50.
Kellogg, Sanford C. *The Shenandoah Valley and Virginia, 1861 to 1865.*
    New York: Neale, 1903.
Laugel, Auguste. *The United States during the Civil War.* Edited by Allan
    Nevins. Bloomington: Indiana University Press, 1961.
Lavender, David. *Climax at Buena Vista: The American Campaigns in
    Northeastern Mexico, 1846–47.* Philadelphia: J. B. Lippincott, 1966.
Lee, Richard M. *General Lee's City: An Illustrated Guide to the Historic
    Sites of Confederate Richmond.* McLean, Va.: EPM, 1987.
Leech, Margaret. *Reveille in Washington, 1860–1865.* New York: Harper &
    Brothers, 1941.
"The Lessons of Our National Conflict." *New Englander* 19 (1861):
    894–912.
Lewis, Berkeley R. *Notes on Ammunition of the American Civil War,
    1861–1865.* Washington, D.C.: American Ordnance Association, 1959.
Livermore, Thomas L. *Numbers and Losses in the Civil War in America,
    1861–65.* Boston: Houghton, Mifflin, 1900.
Lockwood, John, and Charles Lockwood. *The Siege of Washington: The
    Untold Story of the Twelve Days That Shook the Union.* New York:
    Oxford University Press, 2011.
Long, E. B. *The Civil War Day by Day: An Almanac, 1861–1865.* Garden
    City, N.Y.: Doubleday, 1971.
Lord, Francis A. "Flags, Torches, Rockets, and Flares Used by Both Sides
    for Signaling." *Civil War Times Illustrated* 2 (February 1964): 30–31.
Luvaas, Jay. *The Military Legacy of the Civil War: The European
    Inheritance.* Chicago: University of Chicago Press, 1959.
Maddox, Robert. "The Grog Mutiny: One Merry Christmas at West
    Point." *American History Illustrated* 16 (December 1981): 32–37.
Maguire, Thomas Miller. *The Campaigns in Virginia, 1861–62.* London: W.
    H. Allen, 1891.
Mahan, Asa. *A Critical History of the Late American War.* New York: A.
    S. Barnes, 1877.
Mahon, John K. "Civil War Infantry Assault Tactics." *Military Affairs* 25
    (1961): 57–68.
May, George S. "Ann Arbor and the Coming of the Civil War." *Michigan
    History* 36 (1952): 241–59.
McCarthy, Carlton. *Detailed Minutiae of Soldier Life in the Army of
    Northern Virginia, 1861–1865.* Richmond, Va.: privately issued, 1882.
McMaster, John Bach. *A History of the People of the United States during
    Lincoln's Administration.* New York: D. Appleton, 1927.
McPherson, James M. *For Cause and Comrades: Why Men Fought in the
    Civil War.* New York: Oxford University Press, 1997.

McWhiney, Grady, and Perry D. Jamieson. *Attack and Die: Civil War Military Tactics and the Southern Heritage*. University: University of Alabama Press, 1982.

The Medal of Honor of the United States Army. Washington D.C.: Government Printing Office, 1948.

"Message to Congress, by Jefferson Davis [July 10, 1861]." *Civil War History* 3 (1957): 16.

The Mexican War and Its Heroes: Being a Complete History of the Mexican War. 2 vols. Philadelphia: J. B. Lippincott, 1857.

Milton, George F. *Conflict: The American Civil War*. New York: Coward-McCann, 1941.

Minnesota in the Civil and Indian Wars, 1861–1865. . . 2 vols. Saint Paul: Pioneer, 1890–93.

Mitchell, Joseph B. *The Badge of Gallantry: Recollections of Civil War Congressional Medal of Honor Winners*. New York: Macmillan, 1968.

———. *Decisive Battles of the Civil War*. New York: G. P. Putnam's Sons, 1955.

Mitchell, Reid. *Civil War Soldiers*. New York: Viking, 1988.

"Monthly Record of Current Events [for July, 1861]." *Harper's New Monthly Magazine* 23 (1861): 543–47.

Moore, Frank, ed. *The Rebellion Record: A Diary of American Events*. 11 vols. New York: G. P. Putnam and Henry Holt, 1862–68.

Morrison, James L., Jr. *"The Best School in the World": West Point, the Pre–Civil War Years, 1833–1866*. Kent, Ohio: Kent State University Press, 1986.

Morton, Frederic. *The Story of Winchester in Virginia: The Oldest Town in the Shenandoah Valley*. Strasburg, Va.: Shenandoah, 1925.

Nevins, Allan. *The War for the Union, Volume I: The Improvised War, 1861–1862*. New York: Charles Scribner's Sons, 1959.

Nicolay, John G. *The Outbreak of Rebellion*. New York: Charles Scribner's Sons, 1882.

Niven, John. *Connecticut for the Union: The Role of the State in the Civil War*. New Haven, Conn.: Yale University Press, 1965.

Nosworthy, Brent. *Roll Call of Destiny: The Soldier's Eye View of Civil War Battles*. New York: Carroll & Graf, 2008.

Owsley, Frank L. *King Cotton Diplomacy: Foreign Relations of the Confederate States of America*. Chicago: University of Chicago Press, 1959.

Paris, Comte de. *History of the Civil War in America*. 3 vols. Philadelphia: Porter & Coates, 1875.

Parish, Peter J. *The American Civil War*. New York: Holmes & Meier, 1975.

Parker, Kathleen A., et al. *Portici: Portrait of a Middling Plantation in Piedmont Virginia*. Washington, D.C.: National Park Service, 1990.

Paullin, Charles O. "Wisconsin Troops at the Defense of Washington in 1861." *Wisconsin Magazine of History* 8 (1924): 181–85.

Petersen, Eugene T. "The Civil War Comes to Detroit." *Detroit Historical Society Bulletin* 17 (Summer 1961): 4–11.

Plum, William R. *The Military Telegraph during the Civil War.* 2 vols. Chicago: Jansen, McClurg, 1882.

Pollard, Edward A. *The First Year of the War.* Freeport, N.Y.: Books for Libraries, 1969.

Rafuse, Ethan S. *McClellan's War: The Failure of Moderation in the Struggle for the Union.* Bloomington: Indiana University Press, 2005.

Ramsey, T. N. *Sketches of the Great Battles in 1861 in the C.S.A.* Salisbury, N.C.: J. J. Bruner, 1861.

Reardon, Carol. *With a Sword in One Hand and Jomini in the Other: The Problem of Military Thought in the Civil War North.* Chapel Hill: University of North Carolina Press, 2012.

Record of Service of Michigan Volunteers in the Civil War, 1861–1865. Kalamazoo, Mich.: Ihling Brothers & Everard, 1905.

Register of the Officers and Cadets of the U.S. Military Academy. West Point, N.Y.: privately issued, 1826–29, 1835–38.

Reid, Whitelaw. *Ohio in the War: Her Statesmen, Her Generals, and Soldiers.* 2 vols. Cincinnati: Moore, Wilstach & Baldwin, 1868.

Reilly, Tom. *War with Mexico! America's Reporters Cover the Battlefront.* Edited by Manley Witten. Lawrence: University Press of Kansas, 2010.

Report of the Congressional Committee on the Operations of the Army of the Potomac: Causes of Its Inaction and Ill Success. New York: Tribune Association, 1863.

Rhodes, James Ford. *History of the Civil War, 1861–1865.* Edited by E. B. Long. New York: Frederick Ungar, 1961.

Richardson, James D., comp. *A Compilation of the Messages and Papers of the Confederacy, Including the Diplomatic Correspondence, 1861–1865.* 2 vols. Nashville, Tenn.: United States Publishing, 1905.

"The Right of Secession." *North American Review* 93 (1861): 212–44.

Ripley, Warren. *Artillery and Ammunition of the Civil War.* New York: Van Nostrand-Reinhold, 1970.

Roll of the Cadets Arranged According to Merit in Conduct. . . . West Point, N.Y.: privately issued, 1826–29, 1835–38.

Ropes, John Codman. *The Story of the Civil War: A Concise Account of the War in the United States of America between 1861 and 1865, Part I: To the Opening of the Campaigns of 1862.* New York: G. P. Putnam's Sons, 1894.

Russell, William Howard. *The Civil War in America.* Boston: Gardner A. Fuller, 1861.

Sanger, George P., ed. *The Statutes at Large, Treaties, and Proclamations, of the United States of America, from December 5, 1859, to March 3, 1863. . . .* 12 vols. Boston: Little, Brown, 1863.

Scheips, Paul J. "Union Signal Communications: Innovation and Conflict." *Civil War History* 9 (1963): 399–421.

Scott, H. L. *Military Dictionary: Comprising Technical Definitions; Information on Raising and Keeping Troops; Actual Service . . .* New York: D. Van Nostrand, 1861.

Shieh, Wayne W. *West Pointers and the Civil War: The Old Army in War and Peace.* Chapel Hill: University of North Carolina Press, 2009.

Shotwell, Walter G. *The Civil War in America*. 3 vols. New York: Longmans, Green, 1923.

Sixteenth Annual Reunion of the Association of Graduates of the United States Military Academy at West Point, New York, June 12th, 1885. East Saginaw, Mich.: Evening News, 1885.

"The Skirmish Line." *Southern Bivouac* 2 (1883–84): 523–24.

Smith, George Winston, and Charles Judah, eds. *Chronicles of the Gringos: The U.S. Army in the Mexican War, 1846–1848—Accounts of Eyewitnesses & Combatants*. Albuquerque: University of New Mexico Press, 1968.

Smith, Robin. *American Civil War Zouaves*. Westminster, Md.: Osprey, 1996.

"Soldiers of '61 and '65." *Southern Bivouac* 1 (1882–873): 308–10.

Starr, Louis M. *Bohemian Brigade: Civil War Newsmen in Action*. New York: Alfred A. Knopf, 1954.

Stern, Philip Van Doren, comp. *Secret Missions of the Civil War*. Chicago: Rand McNally, 1959.

Stutler, Boyd B. *West Virginia in the Civil War*. Charleston, W.Va.: Education Foundation, 1966.

Sullivan, David M. *The United States Marine Corps in the Civil War: The First Year*. Shippensburg, Pa.: White Mane, 1997.

Swanberg, W. A. *First Blood: The Story of Fort Sumter*. New York: Charles Scribner's Sons, 1957.

Tarbell, Ida M. "Lincoln Gathering an Army." *McClure's Magazine* 12 (1899): 323–31.

Thian, Raphael P., comp. *Notes Illustrating the Military Geography of the United States, 1813–1880*. Washington, D.C.: Adjutant General's Office, 1881.

Thomas, Emory M. *The Confederate State of Richmond: A Biography of the Capital*. Austin: University of Texas Press, 1971.

Tomes, Robert, and Benjamin G. Smith. *The War with the South: A History of the Late Rebellion*. 3 vols. New York: Virtue & Yorston, 1862–66.

Turner, Charles W. "Virginia Ante-bellum Railroad Disputes and Problems." *North Carolina Historical Review* 27 (1950): 314–35.

U.S. Congress. House. *Message from the President. . . .* 30th Cong., 1st sess., 1847, H. Exec. Doc 8.

———. House. *Mexican War Correspondence*. 30th Cong., 1st sess., 1847, H. Exec. Doc. 60.

———. Senate. *Message from the President. . . .* 30th Cong., 1st sess., 1847, S. Exec. Doc. 1.

U.S. Infantry Tactics, for the Instruction, Exercise, and Maneuvres of the United States Infantry . . . Authorized and Adopted by the Secretary of War, May 1, 1861. Philadelphia: J. B. Lippincott, 1861.

Vandiver, Frank E. *Their Tattered Flags: The Epic of the Confederacy*. New York: Harper's Magazine, 1970.

Van Fleet, James A. *Rail Transport and the Winning of Wars*. Washington, D.C.: Association of American Railroads, 1956.

The War of the Rebellion: A Compilation of the Official Records of the Union and Confederate Armies. 4 series, 128 vols. Washington, D.C.: Government Printing Office, 1880–1901.

Wayland, John W. *Twenty-Five Chapters on the Shenandoah Valley.* Strasburg, Va.: Shenandoah, 1957.

Weigley, Russell F. *A Great Civil War: A Military and Political History, 1861–1865.* Bloomington: Indiana University Press, 2000.

———. *History of the United States Army.* New York: Macmillan, 1967.

Weisberger, Bernard A. *Reporters for the Union.* Boston: Little, Brown, 1953.

Wellman, Manly Wade. *Harpers Ferry, Prize of War.* Charlotte, N.C.: McNally, 1960.

Wells, Robert W. *Wisconsin in the Civil War.* Milwaukee: Journal, 1962.

Wheeler, Kenneth W., ed. *For the Union: Ohio Leaders in the Civil War.* Columbus: Ohio State University Press, 1968.

Whitman, Walt. *Prose Works 1892: Volume I, Specimen Days.* Edited by Floyd Stovall. New York: New York University Press, 1963.

Wiley, Bell I. *The Life of Billy Yank: The Common Soldier of the Union.* Garden City, N.Y.: Doubleday, 1971.

———. *The Life of Johnny Reb: The Common Soldier of the Confederacy.* Garden City, N.Y.: Doubleday, 1971.

Williams, David A. *The Manassas Place Name.* Charlottesville: University of Virginia Press, 1963.

Williams, Frederick D. "Michigan Soldiers in the Civil War." *Michigan History* 44 (1960): 1–35.

Williams, Kenneth P. *Lincoln Finds a General: A Military Study of the Civil War.* 5 vols. New York: Macmillan, 1949–59.

Williams, T. Harry. *Lincoln and His Generals.* New York: Alfred A Knopf, 1952.

Wilshin, Francis F. *Manassas (Bull Run) National Battlefield Park, Virginia.* Washington, D.C.: National Park Service, 1957.

Wilson, James Grant, and John Fiske, eds. *Appleton's Cyclopaedia of American Biography.* 7 vols. New York: D. Appleton, 1887–1900.

Wilson, John M. "The Defenses of Washington, 1861–1865." *Military Order of the Loyal Legion of the United States, Commandery of the District of Columbia, War Paper 38.* N.p., 1901.

Wolseley, G. J. *The American Civil War: An English View by Field Marshal Viscount Wolseley.* Edited by James A. Rawley. Charlottesville: University Press of Virginia, 1964.

Woodworth, Steven. *Davis and Lee at War.* Lawrence: University Press of Kansas, 1995.

Yearns, Wilfred Buck. *The Confederate Congress.* Athens: University of Georgia Press, 1960.

Zenzen, Joan M. *Battling for Manassas: The Fifty-Year Preservation Struggle at Manassas National Battlefield Park.* University Park, Pa.: Pennsylvania State University Press, 1998.

Manuscripts, Theses, Typescripts, etc.

Beane, Thomas O. "Thomas Lafayette Rosser, Soldier, Railroad Builder, Politician, Businessman (1836–1910)." M.A. thesis, University of Virginia, 1957.

Benson, Harry King. "The Public Career of Adelbert Ames, 1861–1876." Ph.D. dissertation, University of Virginia, 1975.

Buffington, A. P. "The First Battle of Bull Run: Notes for a Discussion of the Movement on the Grounds." Army War College Study, 1913. Typescript at U.S. Army Heritage and Education Center, Carlisle Barracks, Pa.

Burgess, James, Jr. "Stonewall Jackson's Line at First Manassas: An Analysis of the Current Park Interpretation Concerning the Position of Jackson's Brigade on Henry Hill and the Historical Documentation of Jackson's Position." Typescript at Manassas National Battlefield Park Library, Manassas, Va.

Cauble, Frank P. "A Biography of Wilmer McLean (May 3, 1814–June 5, 1882)." Typescript at Appomattox Court House National Historical Park, Appomattox, Va.

Hasbrouck, Alfred. "The First Battle of Bull Run." Army War College Study, 1912. Typescript at U.S. Army Heritage and Education Center, Carlisle Barracks, Pa.

Hennessy, John J. "The First Hour's Fight on Henry Hill." Typescript at Manassas National Battlefield Park Library, Manassas, Va.

———. "Jackson's Stone Wall: Fact or Fable?" Typescript at Manassas National Battlefield Park Library, Manassas, Va.

Henry, Elena H. "Some Events Connected with the Life of Judith (Carter) Henry and the Circumstances Surrounding Her Death in the 1st Battle of Bull Run, July 21, 1861." Manuscript at Virginia Historical Society, Richmond.

Kelly, Dennis P. "Plan to [Re]locate Artillery, Manassas National Battlefield Park." Typescript at Manassas National Battlefield Park Library, Manassas, Va.

Lucas, L. C. "The First Battle of Bull Run." Army War College Study, 1910. Typescript at U.S. Army Heritage and Education Center, Carlisle Barracks, Pa.

Naisawald, L. Van Loan. "The Location and Fate of Griffin's and Ricketts's Batteries atop Henry Hill—21 July 1861." Typescript at Manassas National Battlefield Park Library, Manassas, Va.

Patterson, William Houston. "Patterson's Shenandoah Campaign: A Reply to Colonel Thomas L. Livermore, Massachusetts Military Historical Society." Typescript at Historical Society of Pennsylvania, Philadelphia.

"The Patterson Mansion." Typescript at Historical Society of Pennsylvania, Philadelphia.

"Patterson's Shenandoah Campaign." Typescript at Historical Society of Pennsylvania, Philadelphia.

Sivertsen, Bruce O. "General Irvin McDowell and the Campaign of First Manassas, July 1861." M.A. thesis, University of Maryland, 1959.

Webb, Willard. "Barnard Elliot Bee (Who First Called Jackson 'Stonewall')." Typescript at Manassas National Battlefield Park Library, Manassas, Va.

Williams, H. O. "The First Battle of Bull Run: Notes for a Discussion of the Battle on the Ground." Army War College Study, 1911. Typescript at U.S. Army Heritage and Education Center, Carlisle Barracks, Pa.

Wyllie, Robert E. "Sketch of the Operations of 1861." Army War College Study, 1915–16. Typescript at U.S. Army Heritage and Education Center, Carlisle Barracks, Pa.

Maps

Alexander, E. Porter. *Battle of Bull Run (Fought July 18, 1861)*. Manassas National Battlefield Park Library, Manassas, Va.

Bearss, Ed. *First Manassas Battlefield Map Study*. Lynchburg, Va.: H. E. Howard, 1991.

Esposito, Vincent J., ed. *The West Point Atlas of American Wars*. 2 vols. New York: Frederick Praeger, 1959.

Gottfried, Bradley M. *The Maps of First Bull Run: An Atlas of the First Bull Run (Manassas) Campaign. . . .* New York: Savas Beatie, 2009.

The Official Atlas of the Civil War. New York: Thomas Yoseloff, 1958.

Seat of War: Manassas and Its Vicinity. Richmond, Va.: Enquirer Book & Job, 1861.

Web Sites

Smeltzer, Harry. *Bull Runnings: A Journal of the Digitalization of a Civil War Battle* (blog). http://bullrunnings.wordpress.com.

Find a Grave. http://findagrave.com.

Index

Page numbers in *italics* indicate an illustration.

as scapegoat for defeat at Bull
Run, 247–48, 496, 539n41,
539n44; in Shenandoah Valley
operations, 30; on Shenandoah
Valley strategy, 245–46;
unwillingness to engage Army
of the Shenandoah, 168, 169,
170–71, 175–77, 182–83, 243–
44; on volunteers' terms of
service, 185
Patterson, Robert Emmet, 42
Patterson, Sarah, 42
Patterson & Company, Wholesale
Grocers, 42
Paxton, Elisha, 405, 483
Paxton, William, 382
Payne, William Henry Fitzhugh, 457
Peck, Harry, 359, 412
Pelham, John, 132, 324, 356, 375,
404
Pendleton, William N., 67, 132,
133, 167, 178, 238, 357, 552n34
Perkins, D. D., 134
Peters, Winfield, 433
Philadelphia Press, 496
Phillips, Wendell, 501
Pickens, Francis W., 22, 23, 86, 179,
211
Pierce, Franklin, 13, 17
Pillow, Gideon, 52
Pittenger, Garret, 189
Pitts, Thomas Henry, 207–208, 477
Platt, Edward R., 303
poisoned wells, 534n17
Polk, James K., 14, 16, 46, 48, 50–51
Porter, Andrew, 104, 157, 183, 327,
330, 349, 352, 386
Porter, Fitz John, 61, 64, 70, 175–
176, 182
Porterfield, William R., 165
"Portici," 297, 334, 369, 381, 392,
421, 423, 429, 430–31, 448,
474–75
Potomac Department, 73, 74
Pratt, Calvin E., 304
Preston, James F., 356
Preston, John S., 147
Preston, Robert T., 421, 423, 424
Preston, Thomas L., 371

Prime, Frederick E., 301, 305, 307
prisoners of war, 449, 452, 453, 455,
457, 462, 464, 471, 473, 482,
568n14; congressman as, 468–
69; Corcoran as, 564n19
privateers, 564n19
Providence Journal, 500
public opinion. *See* home-front and
public opinion
Purcell Artillery, 201
Putnam, Haldimand S., 95

Quinby, Isaac, 359, 412, 413, 414
Quitman, John A., 14

Radford, E. Winston, 455, 464
Radford, R. C. W., 83, 383, 392,
453–56, 474
Radical Republicans, 282
Rafuse, Ethan, 367, 555n6
railroads and railroad lines: in
Army of the Shenandoah
transport, 235–41, 266–69;
Confederate destruction of,
130, 169; at Harpers Ferry,
123; at Manassas, 72–73, 76;
reconnaissance of lines to
Vienna, 110–11; routes to
Washington, 62; as strategic
objective, 30; strategic use of,
514n36; in Union strategic
planning, 152; in Union supply
system, 278–79
Ramsay, Douglas, 410
Rebel yell, 256–257, 540n64
"Red-Legged Devils of Brooklyn," 405
Reed, Horatio B., 396
regimental colors, 346
retreat routes, *450*
Reynolds, John G., 330, 391, 418
Reynolds, William, 326, 454
Rhett, Thomas G., 375, 464
Rhodes, Elisha Hunt, 328, 465, 500
Richardson, Israel Bush, 156–57,
214, 224, 301, 303–304, 304,
305, 306, 309, 444, 445, 446,
447, 540n61, 541n74; skirmish
of Blackburn's Ford and, 249,
252, 253, 255–56, 259–60